CW00501685

Battledress, Bedblocks, and Bashas

Battledress, Bedblocks, and Bashas

The Random Jottings
of a
Royal Electrical and Mechanical Engineer
National Service Subaltern
1958 –1960

Anthony Caffyn

OWLERS
BOOKS

Hardback edition
ISBN 0-9553838-0-3
ISBN 978-0-9553838-0-9

Paperback edition
ISBN 0-9553838-1-1
ISBN 978-0-9553838-1-6

Printed and bound in the UK by
William Clowes Ltd., Beccles, Suffolk

First published in the UK in 2006 by

OWLERS BOOKS
Owlers Farm House, Pick Hill, Horam, East Sussex TN21 0JR
email: sales@owlersbooks.co.uk
website: www.owlersbooks.co.uk

For the over two million young men, and I count myself
fortunate in having been one of that number, who
between 1947 and 1963, were compulsorily called-up
for National Service, and who saw service in the UK,
Germany, Cyprus, Kenya, Aden, Korea, Egypt, Malaya,
and other countries where Britain had world wide
obligations and commitments.

Also especially in memory of the three hundred and

ninety-five National Servicemen who lost their lives

on post-World War II active service.

"They died for all free men"

Foreword

by

Brigadier D. V. Henchley, OBE, MA, CEng

I have known Anthony since he came out to the Far East in 1959. I was then Director of REME in the Far East Land Forces. I knew Anthony's father Brigadier Sir Edward Caffyn very well, as he was the Director of REME in 21st Army Group for the invasion of Normandy in 1944 and I was his deputy.

Inevitably as we got to know each other we swapped stories about our families and so I heard about Anthony who was then a small boy. His father and I kept in touch after the war, and the next I heard about him was when his father wrote to me to say that Anthony was doing his National Service in REME, was now a subaltern in the Corps and had been posted to the Far East. In view of the friendship between Anthony's father and myself, I decided that I would endeavour to ensure that Anthony made the most of his time in the Corps.

The best possible experience for a young subaltern was to be gained in Malaya, where the 'Emergency' was still ongoing. So, initially I had Anthony posted to the 10th Infantry Workshop in South Malaya, which gave him valuable experience in how a REME workshop maintained and repaired those vehicles of an infantry brigade.

In those days, REME Light Aid Detachments attached to Armoured Regiments warranted two officers, a fairly senior captain and a 2nd Lieutenant. Due to a vacancy, I was then able to post him as the second officer to a regiment I had known in the BEF in the early years of the Second World War – the 13th/18th Royal Hussars, then operating up country in Malaya. I went to visit the regiment, then stationed at Ipoh. Anthony had obviously settled in well both with the LAD and the Hussars, a famous cavalry regiment with an impressive history. I think this posting did him a lot of good, as he learnt a fair amount about armoured cars and other army transport, and in particular what made them 'tick', which no doubt was of use to him in later life when he returned to the UK and joined the family business – Caffyns Limited – where his father was then Vice-Chairman and Joint Managing Director.

Anthony then passed out of my life.

When I retired from the Army, I took a position as the Bursar at the Henley Management College. One day, to my surprise, Anthony came to see me when he was on a management course at the College. So for a few years we kept in touch, until I retired as the Bursar, for Anthony who travelled on business to Oxford fairly regularly, would call in and see me on his way back to Sussex.

Anthony again then passed out of my life.

When I came to live in Oxford I found that an ex-REME officer working in the Dept of Engineering at the University had established a retired REME officers' luncheon club, which met twice a year – once in the summer and once on a date as near as possible to St Eligius Day (REME's Patron Saint) on December 1st. So I invited Anthony to come up to one of the lunches and we re-established the association, which began with Anthony's father in 1944 and has lasted over 60 years and is still continuing.

I was very glad when Anthony told me he had written his memories about his National Service, and he has asked me to write the Foreword. I am sure Anthony's book will bring back many memories to all those who did their National Service and who will no doubt enjoy reading it.

Acknowledgements

My thanks go to my DEME (Director of Electrical and Mechanical Engineering) from the FARELF (Far East Land Forces), Brigadier (Retd) Douglas Henchley for not only graciously consenting to write the Foreword, but also for his encouragement in emphasising the importance, from a military historical aspect, of writing about my National Service.

I must also thank both the REME and the National Army Museums for their interest and encouragement for me to complete the project.

My thanks go to the Regimental Headquarters of the Corps of REME for giving permission for me to quote from Volume I of the 'Craftsmen of the Army'; from 'The Craftsman' Magazine of May 1960; and also to use photographs of Nos 1 & 2 Trg Bns, Nos 4 (Armt) & 6 (Veh) Trg Bns and the Training Centre, Arborfield. These were not taken when I was passing through these establishments, but do I hope, give an indication of these Training Battalions at the time of National Service in the 1950s.

Also my thanks to the National Army Museum (NAM) for permission to quote from their publication '730 Days until Demob.'

Although I have a full photographic record of my year in the Far East, I must thank Mrs Sylvia Wright, for allowing me to use photographs taken on her late husband's camera, of the recovery job the LAD 13/18H were involved in between Grik and Kroh in North Malaya.

I must also thank Lt Col (Retd) Ronnie Rust (Late REME & RAEME) for his permission to use his photographs of the Inspection of 'D' Coy, 2 Trg Bn, Honiton by the DEME (photo no 4), and of Ron in conversation with Brig Douglas Henchley (photo no 18).

My thanks also go to Lt Frank Chitty of the Sussex Army Cadet Force, for making up and photographing a 'bedblock'. For all those who did National Service, this will probably bring back mixed memories. For those who were not called-up, they can see what they were missing!

Finally, my most sincere thanks go to Col (Retd) Chris Blessington, (late Royal Signals) who is a very talented artist, and it is his superb sketches that have so enhanced this book. I feel that I am unable to sufficiently express my gratitude to Chris for the artistic imagination and skill he has displayed in producing these drawings.

Contents

Illustrations

Plate section between pages 256 & 257

1. The REME War Office Team 1942
2. The Infamous Bedblock
3. Passing-Out Parade. No 1 Trg Bn REME, Blandford
4. Maj-Gen Tyler Inspecting 'D' Coy, No 2 Trg Bn REME
5. Annual Admin Inspection. No 6 (Veh) Trg Bn REME
6. Early Morning Recovery Training
7. Austin K9 Gantry Recovery Vehicle
8. World War II Gun Testing Equipment
9. World War II Gun Testing Equipment
10. 5.5-inch Gun-Howitzer
11. 5.5-inch Gun-Howitzer Breech Block
12. 5.5-inch Gun-Howitzer Elevation Quadrant
13. Entrance and Guard Room, No 2 Trg Bn REME, Honiton
14. The Poperinghe Barracks Guard Room, Arborfield
15. The DME, Brig E.R.Caffyn & the DDME, Col D.V.Henchley. Hamburg 1945
16. The DEME, Brig D.V.Henchley OBE, MA, CEng. Far East Land Forces (FARELF) 1958-61
17. The 'Baby' EME (EMELET), 2 Lt Anthony Caffyn. Malaya 1959-60
18. Brig D.V.Henchley and Maj Ronnie Rust
19. Entrance to Johore Bahru, Malaya 1959
20. Evening, Fishing Kampong, Officers' Mess 10 Inf Wksp
21. Open Day. 10 Inf Wksp. OC's Office first floor on right
22. The Ferry at Temerloh
23. 'Where the Hell's the Echelon?'
24. Beserah Beach
25. My camouflaged Land Rover, Beserah Beach
26. Setting up Ground Wireless Station, Beserah Beach
27. The latest beach wear modelled by the Officers of 10 Inf Wksp, Beserah Beach
28. S/Sgt Davis with supporters, Land Rover Flotation Exercise
29. Return Journey from Beserah to 10 Inf Wksp, Pandan. Laterite Track Temerloh to Bahau
30. Annual SMG Classification, Majedee Barracks, Johore Bahru

Sketches

Map

Introduction

Some three years after I had completed my National Service in 1960, I thought that, when I reached retirement age, I would like to try my hand at writing about my two years with the Colours. So whilst everything was still fresh in my mind, I wrote copious notes. I also ensured that the three hundred colour slides and black and white photographs that I took in the Far East were kept in good order. Unfortunately some slides have succumbed to fungus growth, which I was warned was a danger in the hot and humid climate of Singapore and Malaya.

There have been many books written about National Service, notably 'Virgin Soldiers' by Leslie Thomas; 'Jungle Campaign' by John Scurr and 'Brasso, Blanco and Bull' by Tony Thorne. These three authors have done a far better job than I can expect to do in recording their National Service experiences. But I hope that although conscription finished over forty years ago, I can add something not only to the memories of those who did, however unwillingly, their two years, - some were fortunate and only did eighteen months, but as a record of those times, which is now part of this country's military history.

Although I have written about the many people that I served with and whose company and comradeship I enjoyed during the two years of my National Service, I must apologise if, however inadvertently, I have caused any offence, which has never been my intention.

However, due to the passage of time coupled with the confusion and pressures of the early part of my National Service, has resulted in that there are very few names I can recall from those days. For National Servicemen to be turned into effective soldiers, meant that regimental training officers, senior and junior NCOs were themselves under pressure to achieve this in the few weeks of basic training. Therefore, the training methods that were employed might not, in today's politically correct society, be looked on as being really acceptable. However, I must emphasise that although the training up to my being commissioned was rigorous, there was never any bullying from the NCOs. Nevertheless, it would be most unfair of me to name our instructors, even if I could recall their names, for doing no more than their duty. So, I have resorted to exercising artistic licence by introducing some fictitious characters.

There have been reports in the National Press that there has been concern in the MoD that the reduction of the Officer Cadet Course at the RMA Sandhurst from two years down to one, may have resulted in insufficient training being given to newly commissioned subalterns, in the care of the troops under their command, especially in a combat situation. When I think back to my National Service days, and realise that after only sixteen weeks of officer cadet training, we were deemed to be competent subalterns, capable of caring for the men under our command in combat postings such as Korea, Malaya, Cyprus or Kenya; then there would appear to be other reasons why junior officers now appear to be insufficiently trained in 'man management' techniques. Such training can only come from the experience gained by more senior officers, who have made the Army their career. However, I do wonder whether many officers nowadays only make the Army a stepping-stone before embarking on successful and profitable civilian careers, and consequently the experience gained and commitment to a service life by middle ranking officers is lacking, which is essential in the training and guidance of young officers. This argument also applies to warrant officers and senior NCOs, who have been called 'the backbone of the British Army'.

I believe that in trying to write about my National Service, it is important to record everything, warts and all. I hope I have achieved what I set out to do; namely from starting out by being total anti-conscription to being, after two years, very supportive of our armed forces, and what they have achieved and still are under constant political and financial pressures. My only regret has always been that I did not sign on for further service.

Anthony Caffyn
July 2006

Chapter One

The Buff Coloured Envelope

I was twenty-two years old, when on the 24th July 1958, a buff coloured envelope dropped through our letterbox, officially notifying me that on the 7th August 1958, I was to report to No 1 Training Battalion REME at Blandford, Dorset to start my two years National Service in the Army. Also enclosed was my rail travel warrant.

'Beware of women who hang around Army Camps'.

I had left home on the morning of 7th August 1958 and those were the final words my father had spoken to me, as he dropped me off at the railway station at Haywards Heath in Sussex. I pondered over his advice, which conjured up in my mind an image of serried ranks of 'women of the night' on their day shift, lined up with military precision to be inspected by their 'Madam' on the road outside the Guard Room of an Army Camp, waiting for the licentious soldiery, having also been inspected by the Guard Commander, to disgorge through the camp gates.

I did, however wonder what experience my father had had of *'…women who hang round Army Camps'*. He was a Territorial Army (TA) Major when the Second World War started in September 1939, and finished the war as the Brigadier (Director of Mechanical Engineering) responsible for all Royal Electrical and Mechanical Engineers (REME) units in 21st Army Group in the North West Europe campaign from 1944 to 1945; and I couldn't believe that from his exalted rank in the middle of such a tough campaign knowing of such affairs. Also I found it difficult to visualize Territorial Army personnel with their limited training commitments, having much opportunity to befriend *'…women who hang around Army Camps'*. Perhaps the TA had more experience than I imagined, and maybe the old name for the 'Terriers' of 'The Saturday Night Soldiers' had another connotation.

~

Although it was meant to be high summer, my mood matched the greyness of the overcast day as I sat alone in the station waiting room for my train to arrive; enjoying, if that was the right expression, my last few hours of freedom before I arrived at Blandford Forum, and where I would enter the closed world of the military for the following two years. In my mind's eye, I imagined that regular army NCOs were no doubt licking their lips in anticipation at the thought of turning me, by whatever means, into some semblance of a soldier. The prospect filled me with such fear, which almost bordered on sheer panic.

I sat, staring out of the grubby compartment window, feeling thoroughly miserable, unable to appreciate the countryside as the train trundled on its way along the South Coast from Brighton to Bournemouth, via Portsmouth and Southampton. It would have been of some comfort if I had had someone else in the compartment who was also starting his National Service. We could have shared our fears, calmed our nerves, and tried to take our minds off what the two years were going to bring. However, for far too many years I had become accustomed to being on my own, and as I stared at my reflection in the carriage window, memories of my life to that point came flooding back.

It was not my father's fault that at the outbreak of the Second World War in September 1939, when I was just three and a half years old that he went off to war.

Due to the threat of a German invasion, we had left Eastbourne in June 1940, and except for short stays in Oxford, Stirling and Malvern, as a result of my father's appointment as Assistant Director of Ordnance (ADOS) Northern Command, we had moved into a rented house on the outskirts of York shortly before Christmas 1940, where we stayed for some eighteen months. Due to the demands of his job, and although very young at the time, I cannot remember seeing him at our home during those two years.

As a result of the mechanisation of the Army, the government had decided that the Army needed a specialised Corps to be responsible for the maintenance of its equipment. It was early in 1942, that my father was posted to the War Office, as a member of the team under Major General Bertie Rowcroft, responsible for the formation of the Corps of the Royal Electrical and Mechanical Engineers (REME) in October 1942.

We moved south and instead of returning to our own house in Eastbourne, we rented a semi-detached house at Wannock, a residential area nestling at the foot of the South Downs some three miles out of the town. Eastbourne had been very much 'in the front line' and had been subject to German 'Hit and Run' bombing raids, which had lasted for some four years. The town was officially designated by the Home Office as 'the most raided town in South-East England during the Second World War'.

There was no strategic reason for Eastbourne to have been so heavily bombed. But apparently the German Luftwaffe sent newly trained bomber pilots on their first operational flight across the Channel, flying under the radar station on the top of Beachy Head, up the Birling Gap valley to the west of Eastbourne, and then they would drop their bombs indiscriminately on the town as they flew back out across the Channel again. They were obviously not cricket fans, as on one raid, a plane planted a stick of bombs right across the cricket square at 'The Saffrons' – a ground of county standard. In June 1944 the V1 Flying Bomb campaign started, many of which came down in the Eastbourne area and my mother told me after the war, that the house in which I was born in Hampden Park on the outskirts of the town had been totally destroyed by a flying bomb.

~

However, it was in 1944 after D-Day that my mother, elder brother and I returned to our house in Eastbourne, and it was that September, at the tender age of eight I was packed off, as a boarder to St Bede's Preparatory School. All the Eastbourne schools had been evacuated from the town in 1940, and as Ken Harding, the St Bede's Headmaster was an old boy of St Edward's School, Oxford, the school had been evacuated to 'Teddies'. I can remember to this day, the misery, the tears and homesickness I felt for the first week or two being so far away from home. It wasn't until May 1945 that St Bede's returned to Eastbourne. When my father was 'demobbed' in August, I hoped that after several years apart we would be together as a family once again, and even though at boarding school, I would really be able to get to know him. But, for reasons, which at the time I did not understand, my parents divorced later that year. A short time later my father remarried and lived in the house my grandfather had owned, some fifteen miles north of Eastbourne. My brother, nearly four years my senior, lived with my father and stepmother, whilst I lived with my mother in Eastbourne, who never remarried and died of cancer many years ago.

It was probably an unworthy thought on my part, but I felt that I had been packed off to boarding school, as it was possibly convenient to have me out of way as the divorce went through.

I have never regretted that I 'boarded' at both my preparatory and public schools, as I believe that the experience helped mould my character, taught me to stand on my two feet and accept discipline. The downside being that I became fairly independent and developed into rather a 'loner', which I believe was initially as a result of the number of moves we had made during the war. Also being away from home at boarding school and subsequently on a four-year residential course at what was then Loughborough College of Technology, resulted in my feeling of being an 'outsider' during the school and college holidays, as many boys of my age were educated locally and had developed their own friendships.

Before I moved to live with my father and stepmother, I would visit my father from time to time, but having had little contact with him since September 1939, I always felt I was not close to him. In fact, I was somewhat in awe of him, especially when he went into his 'brigadier' mode.

There were many occasions during school and college holidays when I would be on my own; my brother having started his farming career, and I would spend hours either coarse fishing in our small lake (a large pond really) for carp, tench and rudd; or shooting, initially with my air rifle, before subsequently moving onto a .410 shot gun – rabbits, grey squirrels and wood pigeons.

As the train trundled on to Bournemouth, I reflected that, although I had had many advantages in my life, and I was certainly not ungrateful for these; circumstances dictated that outside of school and college, home life was somewhat isolated and lonely, for living in the country with the nearest public transport being some two miles away and with, in the 1950s a smaller car owning population, arranging what local friends I had to come and visit had to be planned well in advance.

As a result of being at boarding schools and at a residential college, where fellow students came not only from all the UK, but also from overseas, I did not find it easy to make and keep lasting friendships. However, I hoped that my two years in the army would change that. Time would tell whether my hopes would be realised.

~

Staring out of the carriage window, for some reason, memories of wartime incidents came flooding back, which have always stayed with me. I must have been about five or six years old, when in the middle of one night, my mother woke my brother and myself and told us to get dressed, as York was being blitzed, and we had to go up to a friend's house, who had a reinforced cellar. We left our house and I can distinctly remember looking across open fields and clearly seeing York Minster totally silhouetted against a backcloth of flames.

Later that night, huddled together and wide awake in the cellar, where being so young and naïve I was enjoying the excitement, whereas my elder brother was more aware of what was going on and showed his concern over the raid, we were shaken by the noise of an aircraft flying very low over the house, followed almost immediately by the sound of a second aircraft. The next day we walked back to our friend's house to thank her for looking after us during the raid. She took us into her garden, and we were amazed to see that the tops of a row of poplar trees had been completely taken off by a German bomber and one of our night fighters.

Some weeks later RAF fighters could be seen carrying out mock attacks on repaired German bombers shot down in the York blitz.

When I was older, I had a better understanding about the war. In 1942, when we had moved back to Sussex, on one summer evening there was the noise of aircraft engines approaching, I looked up and a flight of German JU 88s were flying low overhead. I cried out in fear, ran indoors and took cover under our Morrison shelter, - a sturdy steel cage, named after Herbert Morrison, the Home Secretary who had introduced this indoor shelter, which could be used as a table and was designed to give some protection from bombs. For those who could afford it the shelter cost £7, but was issued free to those who could not.

A few weeks later the engine of a V1 'doodlebug' died when the flying bomb was overhead, and after a few moments of silence there was a tremendous explosion as it came down nearly a quarter of a mile away. A neighbour's wife was in a dreadful state as her husband was out walking their dog in the direction where the V1 came down. Fortunately, he was not hurt.

The village of Wannock nestled at the foot of the landward side of the South Downs. One very dark night with the Downs hidden in a sea fret, a Spitfire crashed into the hillside behind us. The next morning we all climbed up to the crash site. The wreckage was spread over a wide area; with cannon shells and machine gun bullets littered everywhere, and the pilot's flying boots lying on the grass, but there was no sign of the body. There was no sentry guarding the site and we could have walked away with anything.

Shortly before we moved back to our house in Eastbourne, we were woken up one night, with the thundering roar of aircraft flying overhead. The noise seemed to go on for hours. My mother felt the invasion of France had started. Sure enough, it was the morning of 6th June 1944, - D-Day.

Some weeks later my mother, my brother Mic and myself, on a lovely summers afternoon climbed up to the top of the Downs behind Eastbourne for a picnic. From there we had uninterrupted views across the town to the Channel, the sea being a deep sparkling blue in the bright sunlight. Suddenly, about a mile or so offshore, the sea erupted into great plumes of water from enormous explosions. At the same time, we became aware of the noise of high-flying aircraft. They were American B-17s bombers returning from their bombing mission and offloading unused bombs.

It has always puzzled me as to why I have such clear wartime memories, which my brother cannot remember, and yet I have no recollection whatsoever of what must have been a fairly traumatic part of my life, being packed off to boarding school with my parents going through a divorce.

I must have been born with a natural military instinct. For in 1940 on our way from Eastbourne up to Stirling we stayed, for a few days in Oxford at the Mitre Hotel. Our room was over the main entrance to the Hotel, and one morning my mother was talking to the manager, when they heard a commotion from outside in The High. Apparently, I was having great fun bombing unsuspecting pedestrians with the potted geranium plants from our small balcony. I subsequently learnt that due to my hostile action, children under the age of fourteen were barred from the Mitre Hotel. A ban that was still in force when I started at St Edward's School in 1950. My one claim to fame!!

~

After I had left St Edward's School, Oxford in 1954, I had followed in my father's footstep and went onto Loughborough College of Advanced Technology (now Loughborough University) to study Automobile Engineering for two years, followed by a further two years taking the Distribution and Maintenance Course sponsored by The Institute of the Motor Industry. As a result, I had been deferred for four years from National Service, and for most of that time, I had given little thought to the inevitability that I would be called-up.

The majority of students went to Loughborough straight from school. However, there were a few students, who had done their National Service first. At the time, I could not understand the reason, but there was definitely a gulf between them and the rest of us. Every month these students would spend an evening together, and I knew that there was a bond which had been forged through their time in the Services, and from which we were excluded. A number had seen active service in Korea, where one of my friends had won the Military Cross. Although they were only some two years older than the rest of us, they had a discipline, maturity and a bearing, which at the time I found difficult to understand.

As the train sped towards Bournemouth, I became more and more depressed, nervous and feeling very much alone in my empty compartment. I even began to wish that I had been born a girl!!

I had hoped that my father, being ex-REME would have driven me down to Blandford, but he followed his normal procedure, which had started shortly after I started at St Edward's School, of seeing me onto the London train at Haywards Heath station and letting me make my own way from Victoria Station to Paddington to catch the school train to Oxford. Upon reflection, arriving at the Guard Room of No 1 Trg Bn REME in a Bentley would probably not have been a very good idea.

Trying to cheer myself up, I thought back to some of the more light-hearted moments at College. Students always have had a reputation of being somewhat wild, and certainly we were no exception. Being at monastic boarding schools from the age of eight to eighteen, the freedom I found at Loughborough probably went to my head. Most of the pranks we got up to were harmless, but no doubt caused irritation and inconvenience to the college authorities and to the local constabulary.

Early on during my first term, word went round that despite many representations to the authorities over the poor quality of the college food, there would be a lunchtime boycott of the College Dining Hall. This was a great success. Some fourteen hundred lunches went to waste.

Although we had tried to get national press coverage, it was disappointing that the media showed no interest whatsoever. No doubt, if we had carried out a similar boycott in the 1970s or later, there would have been press and TV interest with headlines such as: 'Students at a Loughborough College riot over food and trash 1,500 meals.'

Through the efforts of a Brigadier (Retd) Armstrong, who was appointed by the authorities as the link between the College hierarchy and the Students Representative Council (SRC), catering improvements were gradually put in hand, but not quickly enough to satisfy the students. Therefore, to warn the college authorities to implement the improvements without any further delay, a group of students, took it upon themselves in the middle of one night, to wheel one of the College 1st XI large cricket sight screens some 400 yards down Ashby Road (a major road into the town) and park this on the immaculately tended lawn of the Brigadier's front garden.

There was another occasion when, and I cannot remember what the reason was, but the local constabulary had upset the students. Again, one lunchtime, we all took ourselves into the centre of Loughborough, and for an hour we continuously crossed and re-crossed all the zebra crossings without a break. The town being a hub with roads coming from and leading to Derby, Nottingham, Leicester and Ashby was grid locked. Rumour had it that there were at least five-mile tailbacks into Loughborough on every approach road. The police were seriously 'pissed off' with us!

How times have changed! What we students regarded as innocent fun in the 1950s would probably, in the 21st Century be regarded as malicious. The College had a contract with the Pakistan Army to give practical automobile training to young officers from the Pakistan Corps of Electrical and Mechanical Engineers. The Aeronautical and Automobile Faculties occupied hangers on the College aerodrome on the Derby Road out of Loughborough. We did our practical work in a hanger, where engines were mounted on test beds connected to dynamometers and cars were stripped down to their chassis; one of these being an old Ford Prefect with its side valve four-cylinder engine. Mr Draper, our Workshop Superintendent gave the Pakistani Army Officers, whom we got on well with and were our friends, the task of stripping the Ford engine down, prior to 'decoking' it. They soon had the cylinder head off, but they were stuck on how to remove the valves, and seeing a slot in the head of each valve, they came to the conclusion that a screwdriver was needed to unscrew and remove the valves. I am ashamed that we watched them doing this for about an hour before Mr Draper returned from an errand, and quickly put them out of their misery, by showing them how the valves were removed from the valve chest in the side of the engine. Mr Draper was not best pleased with us, but which we regarded as just a bit of harmless fun, for we had had the same trick played on us the previous year. The Pakistani Army Officers fortunately had a good sense of humour.

Not all ex-National Service students were 'angels'. The curriculum at Loughborough was such that most Faculties alternated weekly, between lectures and practical work in one of the many workshops, whether it was the foundry, machine, grinding, welding or other shops.

Rumour had it that it was a group of 'more mature' students, probably from the Mechanical Engineering Department, who were responsible for the design and manufacture of steel clamps, which were fixed to the main gates to the college grounds and locked together the night before the annual Graduation Ceremony. Panic was rife amongst the authorities as the workshop supervisors desperately tried to free off the clamps and get the gates open before the arrival of several hundred VIPs, other dignitaries and parents for the most important day in the academic year. It was a great spectator event watching the struggle to unclamp the gates in time, and bets were laid that the Ceremony would have to be delayed. Eventually, the workshop supervisors having brought in mobile cutting equipment were successful; but it was a close run thing, and there was a large build up of traffic down the Ashby Road waiting to drive into the College grounds, which involved the hard put-upon local constabulary having to provide officers for traffic control duties!

We were inward looking at College, and were not fully aware of what was happening in the outside world. We attached more importance to whether the BRM would actually finish at the British Grand Prix, or whether Stirling Moss would beat Juan Fangio.

One of the subjects we studied was the 'Law affecting the Motor Trade'. Our lecturer was a Greek Cypriot lawyer with a poor command of the English Language, and who always lectured us in a loud and hectoring manner.

So it was a considerable shock to us at the beginning of the Spring Term 1958, when he announced that he had to return to Cyprus and that our final examination in Motor Trade Law would be in three weeks time. I subsequently heard that the reason for his sudden return to Cyprus were the EOKA troubles, and for many years I wondered whether he was on our side or that of General Grivas. Very unkindly, I imagined that it could have been the latter.

Our lecturer had warned us at the start of our Course two years previously that, unless we seriously studied the subject from the beginning, we did not stand a chance of passing our 'finals'. Most of us had not taken his advice and there were those amongst us, who had not even, in our penultimate term bothered to acquire the mandatory textbook 'The Law affecting the Motor Trade'. Absolute panic set in. I personally skipped all lectures and workshops for those three weeks, shutting myself away in the college library, and trying to cram two years work into those twenty-one days. Fortunately, my concentrated swotting worked and I passed my 'finals' exam, but without any long-term retention of the subject.

~

It was early in May 1958 that I was made aware of the threat of National Service. I together with others, had received official notification under the National Service Acts, that we had to present ourselves to the Medical Centre at Leicester for the Army Medics, who were no doubt given the widest latitude in pronouncing that we were all fit to serve Queen and Country. The only exception being those with flat feet. I have never been able to work out why fallen arches could exempt one from National Service, especially when, for the first eight months of my service life; I did enough marching around parade grounds to have developed flat feet for life.

We were an unhappy, silent bunch of young men seated around the waiting room at the Centre, and no doubt, we all had the same thought of wishing we were elsewhere. We sat there clutching our specimen bottles, which were no doubt of interest to the medics, especially as the colour of the urine samples seemed to cover the whole spectrum!

I was prodded, tapped and inspected to ensure that I did not suffer from waxed ears, hair nits, foot rot, DTs, VD, housemaid's knee (with the number of fatigues and barrack room cleaning that no doubt we were going to have to carry out, this complaint was definitely 'a bad thing'), and tennis elbow (also 'a bad thing' with the amount of elbow grease which was going to be needed for blancoing webbing and polishing both brasses and boots). In addition, having dropped my trousers, I was invited to cough to check that my private parts moved as nature had intended. Finally, I was asked to look at pages of circles made up of coloured dots and asked to sing out what number I saw in each coloured circle. This I decided was an easy test, but I did not know what this was going to prove. So, somewhat nonchalantly, and to show that I could recognise numbers, I reeled off '8, 12, 87 and 9.'

'Ah! Ah!' the medical boffin exclaimed enigmatically, leaving me no wiser.

Although the medical was a stiff examination, at least I did not suffer some of the indignities that the medics imposed on those who they felt were malingerers and trying 'it' on; like for instance eating soap and hoping to be declared unfit for National Service.

Eventually, the medics had either worn themselves out or, unless they consulted the Readers Digest Family Medical Advisor, had run out of tests; so the time had arrived for the interview by the Review Board.

'Now,' said a captain from a Regiment or Corps whose cap badge and shoulder flashes meant very little to me, but was probably something Medical or Veterinary. 'What regiment do you want to join in the Army?'

I thought I would try a different tack.

'I want to go into the Navy.'

'You can't. With National Service coming to an end, the Navy isn't taking any more National Servicemen. 'It's the Army. So I'll ask you again, what do you want to go into?'

'The Royal Electrical and Mechanical Engineers,' I replied.

At which point he rather lost interest.

'Why?' He demanded

'Well, I've been on an automobile engineering course, and my father was one of the founder members of REME, and was DME 21st Army Group in 1944-45.'

That did not seem to impress him.

'You've got to make a second and third choice.'

That stumped me. I hadn't the foggiest idea. Eventually, having decided I was not very keen on marching and preferred motorised transport, I came up with the bright suggestion of; 'Tanks.'

'No, I'm afraid that's not on. You have a colour blindness condition', ('Great', I thought; 'this will exempt me from National Service') 'and tank shells have different coloured nose cones to denote whether they are H.E., H.E.S.H. or whatever else the tank people shoot, and the Army can't take the risk that on active service, you would not be able to recognise what type of shell you should be firing.'

Eventually, after some bargaining we compromised on the Royal Army Ordnance Corps (the Donkey Wallahs).

The afternoon's tests resulted in my Grade Card N.S. 55 recording that I was a 'Man. Height 5ft 9ins. Colour of eyes...Brown. Colour of hair...Brown'. The Card also recorded that I had been '... medically examined at Leicester on the 19th May 1958 and placed in GRADE One (I)'. So there I was, in spite of being colour blind being graded fit for anything (except firing shells). I am only colour blind on pastel shades and I do have difficulty in picking out subtle pink shades, which to identify, I have to compare against something white. However, not in my wildest imagination could I have believed that tank or even artillery shells are colour coded in delicate shades of pink...'I say Luvvy corporal, do pass up that shell with the delicate rose pink nose cone, I want to 'stonk' those poofs around that '88' over there.'

It seemed strange that due to partial colour blindness, I could not join the Royal Tank Regiment or the Royal Artillery; yet I could join REME, even though vehicle electrical wiring was colour coded, and there could have been a risk that I would have incorrectly connected up wires with unfortunate results.

~

My hopes were raised at one stage when the Government of the Day announced that National Service would end in 1961. However, even with my limited mathematical ability (I had initially failed my Common Entrance Maths exam to St Edward's School in 1949), I quickly realized that there was an unbridgeable gap between 1958 and 1961. However, I did hope that the Government, in view of the imminent demise of National Service might take pity on us poor souls who were still due to be called-up, and reduce the sentence to a more acceptable twelve or even fifteen months. I even fantasized that the Government would introduce, especially for automobile engineers, the same policy they had had in the early 1950s, whereby prospective farmers, so long as they spent two years working on the land, were exempt from National Service. My elder brother fell into this category. That policy was subsequently changed and even prospective farmers had to do National Service.

After the medical, the threat of National Service was pushed firmly to the back of my mind as I, and many others, were faced with the imminent approach of our 'finals', and desperately wishing that we had been more conscientious in studying during the previous four years.

Four of us had gone winter sporting at Mayrhofen in Austria immediately after Christmas 1957, and we had arrived back to college three days after the term had started. We were immediately 'rusticated' for a week. My father ensured that I stayed at home studying for my 'finals', but the other three, two of whom - Roly Hutchings and Hugh Caustin, came from Southern Rhodesia, immediately headed back to Mayrhofen and enjoyed a few extra days skiing. The college hierarchy was not amused at being made to look such asses, but to us students they were heroes.

The train drew out of Southampton station, and I found that my efforts in trying to cheer myself up had failed miserably and my depression deepened as the train drew closer and closer to Bournemouth, where I would have to change onto a local train for Blandford Forum.

~

Having, which was a surprise to me, successfully passed my 'finals' and graduated from Loughborough; for had I failed, I imagined I could re-sit my final year and may have possibly avoided National Service. A pipe dream! I returned back home to Sussex and waited for what I regarded at the time, as the dreaded call-up. Unfortunately, I did not have to wait too long, for on that fateful 24th July 1958 the postman delivered that ominous looking buff coloured envelope headed 'On Her Majesty's Service'; and even before I had opened this, I knew that my last few days of freedom had arrived. A fortnight was spent frantically trying to cram enough enjoyment into life to last me, for what I regarded was going to be the virtual equivalent of two years being detained 'at Her Majesty's Pleasure'. Visiting and saying 'goodbye' to friends and relations took up a good part of the time, and a week before my departure my father and step-mother took me to a Promenade Concert at the Royal Albert Hall, where Vaughn Williams' Ninth Symphony was performed for the first time at a 'Prom'. At the end of the performance, the conductor led the Composer onto the stage to an enthusiastic reception. Vaughn Williams, was eighty-six years old, very frail and it was obviously a tremendous effort for him to appear on the podium. I believe that this was his last public appearance. Sadly, he died a few weeks later.

The fortnight between receiving my call-up papers and reporting for duty passed all too quickly and the dreaded 7th August duly dawned. Those who had done National Service, seemed to take a perverse pleasure in telling stories of how dreadful it was, and that I did not know what was going to hit me; - the discipline, the abuse, the discomfort, the boredom and the harshness of service life, which would make boarding school seem like a picnic.

Even though some of the stories of military life were probably exaggerated, I was convinced that 'There is no smoke without fire'; and as far as I was concerned there was probably little smoke, just a hell of a lot of fire. Many of those I knew who had done their National Service had not enjoyed the experience and took the view, even prior to being called-up, that National Service was going to be a complete waste of time, unnecessary and was a hindrance to their chosen careers.

As 7th August approached, I found that getting off to sleep at night had become increasingly difficult, as my mind was actively thinking about and dreading the following two years of my life. It has often been said that one is at one's lowest ebb an hour before dawn, and even when I eventually drifted off to sleep, I would wake early and work myself-up into a fine old state of nerves and worry in that pre-dawn period. There was no doubt that I was dreading military service. My trouble was fear, - fear of the unknown. This can be very unnerving, especially at 5 o'clock in the morning. I was surprised at myself, for even though I had started at boarding school at the age of eight and then spent at least two-thirds of the next fourteen year s away from home, I had never experienced 'fear'; - homesickness and loneliness yes, but not fear. Perhaps being older and hopefully somewhat more mature, I had lost any naivety I had and was more worldly wise.

How I wished, alone in my compartment that I had paid more attention to those who had devised weird and wonderful methods of failing their Medical (all unsuccessful), such as eating a bar of soap or feigning flat feet. As the train neared Bournemouth I was wishing that I had tried the same tactics. Perhaps it was pride and self-respect, which prevented me from taking such a cowardly step.

As the train slowed on its approach to Bournemouth Station, I was also regretting that I had not gone straight into the Army from school, for I would have been out by 1956. However, I was certainly determined not to indulge in any heroics for Queen or Country, and to follow two pieces of advice I had been given of 'never volunteer' and 'never raise ones head above the parapet'.

The train drew into Bournemouth Station, where I was supposed to change trains for Blandford Forum. However, for some reason, known only to British Rail, no trains were running between Bournemouth and Blandford Forum on that day, but British Rail had laid on buses to take passengers to their destination. Standing around, whilst waiting for the transport, were a number of young men, all white faced, looking worried and nervous. We eyed each other, wondering if we were all in the same boat and yet strangely shy about striking up a conversation. Eventually, in the early afternoon the buses left Bournemouth and in true British style, we sat in complete silence, making no attempt to talk to the person in the next seat. We were all no doubt wrapped up in our own thoughts.

After about an hour, the buses drew into the forecourt of Blandford Station, and some twenty unhappy looking young men debussed.

I did not know what sort of reception we expected, but there were no Army lorries or personnel around. We had no idea what to do, nor where the REME Camp was. We hung around for some time in the station booking-hall with the air becoming increasingly thick with cigarette smoke, as most of us chain-smoked trying to calm our nerves. I hoped to try for a commission and consequently, I felt that as one of the requirements of an officer was to show initiative, I decided to show my officer potential and taking my courage in both hands, I telephoned the camp to announce our arrival at Blandford Station.

A gruff and rather cross voice answered, ' Guard Room. No. 1 Training Battalion REME.'

Nervously I replied, 'There's a crowd of us at the Station who have been told to report to the REME Camp for our National Service.'

'Where've you been? We expected you hours ago.'

I explained that there were no trains running between Bournemouth and Blandford and British Rail had laid on buses.

'What's your name?' the gruff and cross voice snapped.

In my ignorance of army procedure, I imagined at least the Regimental Sergeant-Major on the other end of the telephone. What did I call myself: Mister, Private, Recruit, or what?

'Er! ... Private Caffyn.' I stammered.

'Right! Stay where you are. Transport will be down in twenty minutes.'

I put the telephone down and mentally visualised a conversation between two long serving leathery old Sergeants, which was possibly going on up at the other end: 'We've got a right ferkin' plonker down there - name of Caffyn. Phoning from the station to say there's no transport. What the ferkin' hell does he think this is? A ferkin' taxi service? Next thing he'll be imagining himself a ferkin' Orficer and we'll have to ferkin' salute the bugger. We'll ferkin' show him.'

I cursed myself for taking the initiative. Why couldn't somebody else have done it? I returned to the yard.

'Transport will be here in twenty minutes.' I said. Stony silence greeted this remark.

I could imagine each of them thinking; 'I don't trust him - wants to get on the right side of authority at the Camp. End up by being a bloody officer.'

Chapter Two

National Service Starts with a 'Bang'

Promptly to the minute, two three ton Bedford trucks turned in to the station yard, stopped, and the drivers jumped down. They let down the tailgates and ordered us to climb aboard. At least our luggage was fairly minimal, so fortunately we were not too squashed together. The tailgates were shut with a resounding 'clang', which to our ears sounded like prison gates being closed. There was little effort to make conversation and although one or two people came up with some forced light hearted remarks, these fell 'upon stony ground' and were greeted with absolute silence. There was a palpable feeling of fear in the back of our truck.

The lorries soon left the town behind and started climbing up a long steep hill. The hedgerows became less frequent and the countryside more open, and as the road levelled out along the top of the Downs tall water tanks came into view, which gave us our first sight of an Army Camp. We turned left and stopped by the Guard Room, waiting for the barrier to be lifted. A sergeant with a red sash emerged, looked at the driver's papers, walked round to the back of our truck, peered in, smirked and shook his head, waved us through, before moving onto the next truck. In front of us was the parade ground, which was surrounded on three sides by wooden huts, all laid out with geometric precision and which probably dated from the First World War, or maybe even the Boer War. We were driven round the perimeter of the parade ground to a vehicle park, passing on the way those water towers, which appeared to dominate the whole Camp. It was a dull afternoon with a low cloud base and the Camp looked as drab and grey as the weather. I was thankful that it was summer; in winter life in the Camp, set on top of the Downs and open to the elements from all quarters of the compass must have been hard and very depressing.

Smoke and the smell of cooking from the cookhouses hung in the air.

Even though I had not eaten since breakfast, and then only a little, my nerves were such that even the smell of food nearly made me gag. Everywhere, were signs of frantic activity, with khaki clad individuals moving at the double, seemingly in ever-decreasing circles and being screamed at by either one or two stripe corporals. Behind them sergeants were vocally adding to the general hubbub. We watched in trepidation, as a sergeant-major, as befits his rank and status, with his chest stuck out, preening himself like a puffed-up peacock and waving his pace-stick like the baton of an orchestral conductor, drilled a group of recruits on the 'Square'. His voice could no doubt be heard in the next county. There was so much shouting and stamping of boots, that it was a wonder how each group of recruits knew which drill orders applied to them. Disobeyed or ignored orders were rapidly dealt with, as corporals were sent scurrying round at the double, to threaten the offending soldier or soldiers with a 'fate worse than death'. In our ignorance, it appeared that the groups were continuously marching around in different directions in ever decreasing circles. However, we had very little opportunity to watch the action, as we were 'invited' to debus in double quick time, and to 'fall-in' in a straight line but which, despite our best efforts made the proverbial 'donkey's hind leg' look very straight, and prompted a ferocious looking sergeant to remind us in no uncertain way that: 'You're in the Army now.'

We must have looked a motley bunch. We were from all walks of life and different backgrounds; some, as I was, being reasonably smartly dressed in blazers and slacks, whilst others wearing 'Teddy Boy' long fur collared jackets, drain pipe trousers, 'bovver' boots and with what appeared to be carefully coiffured hair styles with lacquered quiffs. As we didn't know what to expect, our collective baggage varied from small cases with washing and shaving kit and other personal belongings, to two or three large suitcases, big enough for their owners to embark upon a world cruise. Little did we know what was in store for us!! We were 'thrown into the deep end' from the word 'go'.

~

Those first few days of Army life were very confusing and quite frightening. The days were full of inexplicable and incomprehensible alien activities, which all had to be carried out at the double. All orders were delivered at such a volume that, in the 21st century's politically correct and 'nanny' state, the Health and Safety Executive would probably have issued an Enforcement Order, banning all vocal communication above twenty-five decibels with the compulsory use of ear defenders on the Parade Ground.

However, our first experience of National Service was the 'Army Haircut'. As, thanks to British Rail our induction into National Service had been put back by a couple of hours or so, and as a consequence we were late for the camp barbers; who had been kept waiting for our arrival, and were not in the best of humours and wanted nothing more than to get off duty. The only training they had received in the art of hair styling, was the 'pudding basin' short back and sides cut. Some of those carefully nurtured 'Teddy Boy' styles and quiffs, which no doubt had taken months to perfect were, with the electric cutters wielded like sheep shears, dispatched to the floor in seconds. There was no doubt that the barbers made up for lost time. With our prison style short haircuts, we must have looked a pathetic bunch as we lined up, still in 'civvies', with those who had 'lost' their carefully styled hairstyles looking very miserable and in a state of considerable shock.

The lance-corporals, some of whom we quickly came to despise, hustled around us shouting the whole time at the top of their voices, like a pack of Jack Russell terriers snapping at the heels of their prey, and demonstrating their supposed superiority, by demanding instant obedience, whilst ordering us to stand rigidly to attention when confronted by all NCOs.

Before we could get over the shock of the camp barbers, we were formed up into three ranks, and with the lance-corporals ('lance-jacks') still snapping at our heels, we were doubled over to the Quartermaster Stores, where we queued up to be kitted out from head to toe in army kit. I must admit that the organisation in the QM's Stores could not be faulted, as each member of the Quartermaster's staff was responsible for issuing a particular range of kit. We were processed rapidly down the line, collecting an astonishing amount of gear. Battledress-khaki (two), denims (two), boots (pair two), laces-black (pairs two), shirts-khaki (two), beret-black (one), drawers-cellular-green (two), vests-cellular-green (two), socks (grey-woollen two pairs), gloves-green-woollen (one pair), greatcoat (one), vests PT-white (two), shorts PT-blue (two), jersey (one) and shoes canvas-black (one pair). The list seemed endless. My arms ached and there was a danger that due to the weight, my kit would end up on the floor as gravity took over and my outstretched arms left the horizontal and moved downwards to face the floor. Bedding, kit-bag, helmet-steel (was there any other?), and the 'housewife'. Housewife! This sounded promising, but our hopes were dashed as we were given a small white cloth bag in which there was a thimble, needle and a reel of khaki cotton. Mess tins (two), knife (one), fork (one) and spoon (one) - commonly known as 'eating irons', brushes-black-boot (two), polish-boot-black-tin (one). Still we had not finished, cap badge-REME-staybright (one), belts-webbing, gaiters, pack-large, pack-small, pouches-ammunition, webbing-cross straps, scabbard-bayonet, rifle sling, water bottle, polish-Brasso-tin (one), and blanco-tin (one). The Army, with many centuries of experience, obviously left nothing to chance and had an item of kit to cover every eventuality.

Finally, we had finished, and by stuffing most of our kit in our kitbags, we managed, in a decidedly unmilitary manner, with the baying pack of lance-jacks still snapping at our heels, to make our way to the barrack block. This must have been the 'bog' standard wooden open plan First World War vintage design, with the hut corporal having his own room at one end. The iron beds were situated with military precision opposite each other in two serried rows, each bed being precisely separated from its neighbour, measured to the inch. The floor was highly polished brown linoleum. Alongside each bed, there stood a tall, green metal cabinet. Each bed space was to be our 'home' for the eight weeks of basic training. Each individual (sorry - 'recruit'. We did not have any individuality) was responsible for the condition and cleanliness of his own bed space, and we were collectively responsible for the cleanliness of our barrack block. At one end of the room, all the brooms, polishes, cleaning clothes and dusters were neatly laid out as if ready for inspection. In spite of tentative friendships, beds were allocated in strictly alphabetical order. We had only just dumped our kit on our beds, when a Lance-Jack stormed into the room:

'Right! Listen in you manky lot of recruits. For my sins, I am your Hut NCO. There's brown paper and string here. Get your 'orrible civvies off, wrap them all up into a parcel, and fill in the card with your name, rank, number and the battalion address so your loving mums know where you are and you're still alive; at least until I get my hands on you miserable furkin' bunch of gits.'

'Please,' a voice spoke up, 'What's our rank?'

'Rank ! You want to know what your rank is? You have no rank, you're all just furkin' recruits. I have rank. See this stripe, I am a Lance-Corporal and you will always address me as 'Corporal', and you will carry out my orders immediately and without furkin' question. Do I make myself furkin' clear?'

'Yes, Corporal.'

'Yes what! I don't furkin' hear you.'

'YES, CORPORAL.'

'I still can't furkin' hear you.'

'YES, CORPORAL.'

'That's better. Now get on and get your furkin' kit packed.'

It was changing out of our civilian clothes, putting on the shapeless and badly fitting denims and packing up and posting off our 'civvies', that really brought home to us the Army owned us for the following twenty four months, and that we had lost our individuality, freedom and independence.

We had barely time to finish this job, when our 'user friendly' Lance-Corporal screamed at us:

'Come on, you lazy lot of furkers. Grab your plates and eating irons if you want to eat and fall in outside in three ranks'.

We formed up as ordered outside our hut, and now that we were getting the hang of it, in some semblance of three ranks, and were doubled over to the cookhouse at the far side of the camp. Here there was a long queue. Nervously we joined this. We must have looked a strange bunch quietly standing in the queue in our badly fitting denims, berets, which had not as yet been shaped and were perched on our heads like inverted birds nests or pork pies. Recruits, from previous intakes either warned us what to expect, or tried to reassure us that life was not too bad, so long as one kept a low profile and kept one's head below the parapet. How we envied them. Even the previous intake, only a fortnight ahead of us seemed to have so much more service. Still I thought, in another fortnight we should appear in the eyes of the next intake 'to have got some in'. An experience I was not to enjoy, as I was posted-out after only ten days.

I was impressed by the quality of the food. There was plenty of it with a wide choice of dishes, and was a great improvement on school food, and although by the time I left, I fondly regarded my old school as my alma mater; nevertheless, I was at times, and with some justification critical of the school, having to put up with, in the early 1950s fagging, caning and indifferent food. I really could never fault the standard of Army food, whether it was prepared by unit cooks, or by Army Catering Corps (ACC) chefs. However, we never did confirm whether the rumour was right and that bulk bromide was added to the tea urns. Certainly celibacy ruled, but I never found out whether this was due to the bromide or to exhaustion from the physical pressures of basic training. Many years later, I was to spend three days in Kosovo with HQ 3 Commando Brigade, and the quality and quantity of the food produced in the Messes would not have disgraced a four star hotel.

During the meal we had our first sighting of an officer, when the Orderly Officer and Duty Sergeant for the day passed round asking if there were any complaints. It would have taken a brave, or foolish man from our intake with only four hours service to complain.

Once we had finished, we queued again outside to wash our plates, mugs and eating irons. Many recruits from No 1 Trg Bn REME must have memories of the washing up facilities. The first tank was meant to contain hot water with bulk washing–up liquid added, but with use the water got progressively colder and the washing-up liquid less effective, whilst the scum from dirty plates became progressively thicker. The second tank was for rinsing, but the water was invariably cold and the scum was only marginally less thick than the washing-up tank. The third tank, which possibly contained disinfectant, was invariably stone cold. It was therefore difficult to ensure that our plates, mugs and eating irons were spotlessly clean after each meal to pass kit inspection. Dirty eating irons, plates and mess tins were regarded as a chargeable offence. I never knew whether other basic training camps used the same method for washing-up, but in view of the Army's paranoia about cleanliness, I was surprised that it tolerated such an unhygienic procedure.

Our evening meal over, we returned at the double, back to our barrack hut, where our little 'Führer' of a Lance-Corporal (L/Cpl) issued a shouted order to get out our 'housewives' and start either sewing labels, or mark with an indelible pencil, all our clothing and equipment with our number, rank and name – '23578036–Private-Caffyn'.

'Come on get a furkin' move on you idle lot,' shouted the 'Führer', 'you've got to store all your furkin' gear in your lockers. You see that furkin' picture on the wall there, that's how you do it. Okay?'

We very quickly realised that the Army demanded order in everything. As someone wiser than I once said, 'There are two ways of doing things – the Army way and the other way. Heaven help anyone who doesn't do things the Army way!' After a great deal of effort and concentration, we eventually had our kit stored away as per the photograph, with large packs, pouches and helmets correctly positioned with military precision on the top of our metal lockers.

We thought we had finished. But, oh no! We were next introduced to the mystery of making bedblocks. We had naively presumed that each morning we would neatly make our beds and leave our bed space in 'good order'. Not so! The army demanded that we would strip our beds and very precisely fold each sheet and blanket

'I don't care oo you say your Dad was - Sunshine. Y'er in the proper Army now.'

into an exact geometric rectangle. These were placed alternatively one on top of each other, and with the top blanket being used to 'wrap' around the other sheets and blankets. This, surely, has caused recruits more trouble than anything else during basic training. I certainly had considerable difficulty in producing properly squared bedblocks, with no open edges or corners showing, so that one could lay a spirit level both vertically and horizontally to the bedblock to show that it was in perfect alignment. I was by no means alone in struggling to produce a perfect bedblock day after day.

The Training Battalions certainly had a fetish with bedblocks. I could never see what was to be gained by leaving your bed each morning with a supposedly immaculate bedblock, only to find on returning later during the day, that a room inspection had been carried out and your kit, blankets and sheets had been dispatched to the four corners of the barrack room. Not only did the bedblock have to be remade, but also all one's kit had to be correctly replaced in the locker. As a gesture of goodwill, we were given

'Caffyn. Who said you could bring your bear with you?'

two days to reach the required standard, but thereafter failure to reach this standard resulted in either punishment drill or extra fatigue duties. I have always felt that the barrack room and individual bed space inspection was very subjective. An acceptable standard depended upon the mood and disposition of the inspecting officer or senior NCO at the time. Sometimes I felt that fairness was not part of the equation, for whether one's kit passed inspection could depend upon the likes or dislikes of the NCOs, or whether one had rubbed a NCO up the wrong way. Finally, Lance-Jack 'Führer' drew our attention to a second photograph on the end wall of the barrack room showing how to lay one's kit out for inspection. This had to be followed in every detail, even to the proper display of the contents of the 'housewife'.

By this time of the evening, we were all absolutely exhausted, both physically and mentally, confused, unhappy and thoroughly demoralised.

'Lights out at 2130 hours. Reveille 0500 hours.'

'Why so early, Corporal?'

'When you see what you've got to do in the furkin' morning, you'll want all the furkin' time you can get, and that won't be furkin' long enough.'

~

Our first day in the Army had come to an end and although exhausted as I lay, waiting for sleep to come in the uncomfortable bed, lying on what could possibly have been either a straw mattress or a thin and lumpy over-used one, I felt somewhat calmer now that I had actually started my National Service, and whatever the two years were to hold, the fear of the unknown was over. But I was still apprehensive as to what the future was to hold and how I was going to face and handle the deprivation, the loss of individuality and freedom, and the necessity to conform to the rigid discipline and regime that the Army demanded.

But it was the shock and suddenness, within just a few hours, of the totality from being a private individual where one could behave and act, within acceptable standards, as one wanted to with freedom and impunity, to a life where there was little individual freedom and one was subjected to strict military discipline and obeying orders without question. REME, being a technical Corps, recruited National Servicemen with technical qualifications, and in our intake there were trained vehicle and electrical mechanics, panel beaters and paint sprayers who had served an apprenticeship, as well as others who had, like me attended college after leaving school.

From Volume One of the 'Craftsmen of the Army', the story of REME: '*It was noticeable that the Regular soldier recruit was, generally speaking, less mature than his National Service counterpart. Many had received no further education since leaving school two or three years earlier, by contrast with the National Serviceman who, in many cases, was a Deferred Apprentice, that is to say, his call-up had been deferred pending completion of civilian apprenticeship training.*'

That first day was certainly a shock to one's system, but over the next few days as one gradually became accustomed to the Army, one hoped that life must surely improve. Being at boarding school was certainly a good preparation for Army life. I was used to dormitory life, to cold showers and to having a bath twice a week in a round tin bath. For my first two years I was used to 'fagging' for the prefects. I was prepared, although it only happened to me once, of being canned for some petty reason by the Head of House, or for a more serious offence by either the Head of School, one's Housemaster, or in extreme cases by the Warden (Headmaster) himself. I was used to the discipline, and the ordered life style and security that a boarding school imposed on its pupils.

I had shed tears when I first left home and was sent away to boarding school at the tender age of eight, and as a consequence I was perhaps in a better position to handle those first few nights in the Army, and I felt so sorry for those of my newfound friends in our barrack room, for whom this was their first time away from their home environment. Although they must have felt dreadfully lost and alone, most did not openly show their feelings of the despair and helplessness that we all felt. There were a few however, who from the noise of muffled sobs from under the blankets took the change very badly, and I felt desperately sorry for them.

~

'Right, let's have you! Rise and shine! Out of your furkin' pits.'

The bright hut lights and the raucous voice cut through our sleep drugged minds as we struggled into consciousness. Suddenly, with a feeling of dread and apprehension, we all realised where we were. We leapt out of our beds, our eyes adjusting to the bright lights, grabbed our washing kit, and in our army issue pyjamas we raced to the communal washroom to carry out our ablutions.

At school we always had to take a cold shower first thing in the morning, whether it was summer or winter, and pyjamas were discarded as we leapt out of bed, fixing towels around our waists, as some thirty boys sprinted down the length of the dormitory to the bathroom. This was a problem with one boy who invariably woke with a very large erection, and would race down the 'dorm', unsuccessfully trying to tie his towel around his waist. We suggested that he should give up and hang his towel from the offending member!! The cold shower certainly had the desired effect.

In the ablutions complete chaos reigned. There were not enough basins for everybody and we very quickly learnt that, unless we got there first, not only had the hot water run out, and shaving in cold water was not funny, but one ended up in dire trouble, because it was almost impossible to complete all the essential housekeeping chores before breakfast. We raced back to our barrack rooms, hurriedly dressed in our shapeless denims, checked that our kit was correctly folded, and then began the dreadful business of turning sheets and blankets into bedblocks. All the while, L/Cpl 'Führer' was shouting and swearing at us to get a move on. Corridors had to be swept, barrack rooms, ablutions and latrines cleaned. Everything had to spotless.

'I don't expect to get my gloves dirty.'

It was just bad luck if we had not finished in time. It was most depressing to return from breakfast, or later during the day, to find that in our absence the hut had been inspected, and that ones bedding and kit had failed to reach the required standard and had been 'trashed' all over the room. Valuable time was lost trying to find everything, to remake bedblocks, and to replace kit correctly in lockers. No extra time was given for tidying up, and if the following session was physical training, as there was only five minutes allowed to change into PT kit, one was under tremendous pressure to complete everything, before parading outside the 'hut' and being doubled down to the gym. If a barrack room was in 'bad order', there would invariably be a second inspection, whether this was carried out by the Platoon Sergeant, Platoon Commander accompanied by the Company Sergeant-Major (CSM), or the Orderly Officer with the Duty Sergeant. Failure in their eyes to reach their standards resulted in everything being thrown out once again.

Being late 'on parade' for any activity also resulted in, at the very least, a major 'bollocking' in front of ones mates, to being given fatigues. At PT, the Physical Training Instructors (PTIs) seemed to delight in awarding extra press or sit-ups at the slightest misdemeanour, whether genuine or imagined.

One had the impression, in those first few days of a complete rat race in which one either swam and survived, or sank without trace; and although there was a certain amount of helping one another, it was very much a question of self-preservation and the survival of the fittest.

~

Those first few days passed in a confused blur. Everything was so strange. We doubled to the MRS to be medically processed, where we joined a long queue in a large hall to be inoculated against every real or imaginary disease that the medics could think of. We were jabbed so many times, that in the end one felt that every new injection was simply passing across the body and coming out again through a previous puncture. The orderlies seemed to change faster than the needles of the syringes, which gradually became blunter and blunter with every injection. All these were administered in full view of everyone, so it was inevitable with such a queue, that there was the occasional 'crash' as a recruit passed out and collapsed in a heap on the floor, to be unceremoniously removed by one of the orderlies. After the inoculations we were individually shepherded into small wood framed hessian cubicles, prodded, poked and told to 'Drop 'em and then cough'. Finally we were pronounced 'FFI' – 'Free from Infection', or was it 'Fit for Infantry'.

We were issued with our AB 64 Service and Pay Book and warned that it was either a chargeable or even a court-martial offence to lose this and that it had to be treated with as much reverence as the Bible. When I looked in the back of the Pay Book and saw the 'Form of Will' for completion on active service, I could understand one reason for the importance placed on the AB 64.

Surprisingly, the Army tried to ensure that recruits were placed in units, which matched their skills and to ensure that square pegs were not put into round holes, so we undertook aptitude and intelligence tests from Personnel Selection Officers (PSOs).

We were ordered to do fatigues; we were drilled; we bulled our kit; we buffed the barrack room endlessly and we were given any other activity that the junior NCOs could dream up. These we would have to carry out at the double and were invariably accompanied by continuously shouted abuse. We were worked very hard by burly Physical Training Instructors with bulging biceps and triceps, straining to burst out of their far too tight body hugging dark blue sweat shirts, with the words 'Army Physical Training Instructor' (APTI) boldly emblazoned in red on their fronts. The gym was their domain and there they would not tolerate being messed about by anyone, least of all by recruits, and the slightest mistake or sign of idleness resulted in instant punishment.

The sheer speed, at which the junior NCOs doubled us everywhere, together with the incessant shouting was very stressful, and if the intention was to cower us into dumb compliance with the system, then it was in danger of being counter productive, as we were getting so fed up with the attitude of a few of the junior NCOs that physical violence may well have been perpetrated. It was probably the fear of reprisals that saved the skins of those junior NCOs who were, in our eyes, particularly obnoxious. We would be doubled to a classroom for a lecture on, for instance the Light Machine Gun (LMG), then doubled back to our Barrack Room, given two minutes to change into our PT kit, - and heaven help anyone who did not make it in time, and then doubled round to the Gym, and left to the tender care of the PTIs.

Afterwards, exhausted, we would be doubled back to the barrack room to change back into denims and then straight out on to the Square for an hour of drill.

'Stand up straight - stomachs in, heads up. You in the second rank, yes - you next to the comedian whose beret looks like a squashed pork pie, you are standing like a pregnant fairy. By the left, quick march, 'eft, 'igh, 'eft, 'igh. Squad - Squad 'alt. The Squad will advance in threes. Left - wait for it - Turn. You, you prize nit, the Army left. You there– Coffin, Chaffin or whatever your name is you're meant to swing your right arm with your left foot, not both left arm and left leg together. You 'orrible little man! You, there in the rear rank, you are a furkin' dummy. What do you think you've furkin' got – two left feet? Get in step.'

And so, it went on. At times, the platoon sergeant took drill, ably assisted by corporals and lance- corporals. On other occasions, it was left to the corporals and the lance-jacks. This was worse. At least the sergeants knew what they wanted and the best way to get it from us, but the corporals (and there was one in particular, who was incredibly coarse) were under the illusion that by swearing, shouting and abusing us they could get us to follow their every order. However, in reality they only succeeded in putting our backs up. But we were too intimidated by authority, and the threat of fatigues, not to obey their every order.

Fatigues were a pain. We were given these for even the most insignificant offence, such as incorrectly laid out kit, dirty eating irons, mess tins, or a badly made bedblock. The fatigue, and if it was given by a corporal or a lance-jack, was the nastiest he could come up with, which was invariably cleaning out the latrines or ablutions, using cast-off tooth brushes to scrub round the corners which other brushes could not reach. The sergeants generally favoured cookhouse fatigues as a punishment and being made to peel potatoes for an hour or two. So, we learnt very quickly to ensure that our kit, bedblocks and bed spaces were up to and beyond the required standard.

Punishment fatigues had to be carried out at the most inconvenient times, which meant that if one fell behind with other tasks, it became increasingly difficult to catch up, which then resulted in more punishment fatigues. It could become a vicious circle. When, and there were such moments, there were 'holes' in our training programme, these gaps were filled with the easy options of giving us extra fatigues, thus ensuring that we were never idle.

One of our fellow recruits was brave, or foolish enough to ask, 'Sergeant, why do we have to do so many fatigues?'

We held our breath, waiting for the inevitable explosion to erupt. Surprisingly, the sergeant in a very quiet and calm voice replied:

'Fatigues are good, for they instil obedience and stop you getting bored. Now, you get your miserable little body out of here, and get over to No 1 cookhouse, and tell the duty cook sergeant that I've sent you to do two hours of fatigues there. Do I make myself clear?'

'Yes, Sergeant.'

That was the first and last time we raised any queries about our treatment.

'Corporal Bloggs.'

'Yes, Sgnt.'

'No 2 Platoon look fuckin' idle. Double them over to the Cookhouse. They can peel fuckin' spuds and clean all the fuckin' cooking utensils. Tell the Cook Sergeant, I want that dozey and manky lot back on the Square by 1100hrs. Now! Get them fuckin' moving.'

'Yes, Sgnt.'

At least these fatigues did not come out of what little spare time we had.

One day merged into another. The only time we were left alone was at night when we were asleep, and no doubt the NCOs would have thought of some reason to wake us up, if they also hadn't needed their kip. I was surprised though that we never had a fire practice in the middle of the night.

~

In the 1950s REME had 11 training battalions, with Nos 1 and 2 Battalions being responsible for the basic regimental training of both Regular and National Service recruits. No 1 Trg Battalion at Blandford was originally designed to handle 800 recruits, but in the late 1950s, peaked at over 2,000 passing through the Camp at any one time, which meant that there was an awful lot of 'square bashing' going on all the time. With a fortnightly intake, some 8,000 recruits annually passed through Blandford. No wonder the place was crowded!

REME only had eight weeks of basic training to turn us civilians into something vaguely representing soldiers. This obviously resulted in there being non-stop and constant pressure on us to 'acclimatise' to Army life and to lose any 'civvy' tendencies in the shortest possible time, and to accept discipline and obey orders without question. With hindsight, this policy, which at the time seemed designed to wear down our resistance and turn us into faceless, green clad automatons, was probably the only effective method, within the limited time scale, of making soldiers out of a bunch of unenthusiastic, 'bolshie' and anti-National Service conscripts.

~

I cannot remember seeing many officers, which was probably just as well, for we had not been taught how to salute correctly. If we had been unfortunate enough to meet one, our salute would probably have been halfway between a regal wave and a reversed Churchillian two finger one; which may have earned us either an acknowledgement with a touch of the swagger stick to the peak of the officer's hat, or extra fatigues for not saluting in the proper military manner.

We had a platoon commander, who generally only seemed to put in an appearance when our backs were turned, judging by the number of times we found our bedblocks and kit thrown around the hut when we returned to the barracks after duties.

But there were rare occasions when the platoon subaltern did put in an appearance, accompanied by his entourage of the company sergeant-major, the platoon sergeant and corporals. We came to fear and hate the shouted order given by the room corporal to, 'Stand by your beds,' and we would leap to our feet and stand rigidly to attention, whilst, the officer and his retinue, would slowly parade down the length of the hut. The officer, using his swagger stick as a fly swat would flick items of kit that offended him to the floor. The CSM would complete the devastation by using his pace stick, which being longer and sturdier and with complete disregard to any safety regulations, would dispatch further items of kit to all four corners of the hut. The sergeant with notebook and pencil in hand, and trying to keep up, would despairingly be taking down names.

Through fear, and standing rigidly to attention, with eyes firmly fixed to the front, one could hear the progress of the inspection as items of kit, mess tins, eating irons and bedding were dispatched with force and speed to the four points of the compass. You knew your turn had come when your kit would fly past your head, under the twin assault of both the swagger and pace sticks.

'Take his name, Sergeant. His fork is filthy.'

'That housewife, it's not straight.'

Wham! The offending item with the full force of the pace stick behind it, took off into space, colliding with and shattering an overhead light bulb on its way into orbit. From the corner of my eye, I thought I caught the officer mouthing 'Good shot' to the CSM. No doubt we would all be on a charge for damaging Government property and have the cost of the light bulb deducted from our meagre pay as 'barrack room damages'.

'That bedblock is disgusting.' The CSM dumped it onto the floor.

'Your boots are filthy. When did you last polish them?' They disappeared through a window, which fortunately was open, otherwise 'barrack room damages' would be getting out of hand for, as recruits our pay was only 36 shillings (£1.80) a week.

'Those straps there,' the officer, who must have had telescopic eyesight, pointed his swagger stick to the top of my locker, where the large and small packs were stored. 'They haven't been folded properly.'

The webbing straps to both the large and small packs had to be neatly coiled in a circle alongside the packs. Unfortunately, they were not beyond the reach of the CSM's pace stick, and were dispatched together with the two packs, in a northerly direction towards the ablutions. And so it went on. None of us were exempt. By the time the inspection had finished, our hut looked as though a hurricane had hit it.

Our Hut Corporal returned, his face like thunder, as no doubt he had been bawled out for the state of the hut.

'You furkin' miserable lot of horse shit,' he screamed. 'The orrifer said that this is the worst 'ut he's ever seen. You've got an 'our to get it right, before they come back for another inspection. Now pull you furkin' fingers out and furkin' MOVE.'

We pulled our 'furkin' fingers out, and 'furkin' MOVED.

An hour later, the end door was thrown open and we stood trembling by our beds, as the 'General Staff' marched in, went through the hut like light infantry, hardly bothering to glance either to the left or the right and departed through the far door. We could not believe it. I suppose it must have been part of the softening up process to instil discipline and obedience, and to which could be added 'fear'. If I was right, the policy was certainly working.

~

The only time we had contact with officers were those from the Royal Army Educational Corps, who carried out intelligence and psychometric tests on us and tried to establish IQ levels. I was worried that although I could probably produce a detailed engineering drawing of a gearbox, or talk about industrial psychology, I would have little idea of how to match up shapes, work out simple arithmetical progression or complete other psychometric tests, which could result in my failure in being considered suitable for a commission.

However. 'Now, tell me Caffyn, why do you want to be an officer?'

Saying that one wanted a 'cushy' life; that one had had a private education and one did not want to be chased around by NCOs for two years, would not have earned one any 'brownie' points and would have probably condemned one to spending the two years as a batman to a number of 'browned off' National Service subalterns at Blandford.

'Well, Sir. Although I have had some technical training, the management course I went through at Loughborough; together with being a prefect at school, and also being captain of successful cricket and hockey teams both at school and college, has given me experience in leadership and man management. I believe that the Army can further enhance these skills, which I hope I can repay, as an officer, in leading and looking after the men under my command.'

What a load of 'cod's wallop!'

~

We were somewhat surprised that our indoctrination into the British Army appeared to rest solely in the hands of the NCOs. This was possibly deliberate policy as only they could achieve the desired result in the shortest possible time, using psychological and even physical tactics to condition us to army life.

To our civilian ears the abusive and coarse language, which was directed in our direction was, initially a shock, but very soon one got used to it and realised that this was army 'speak'. The most common word was the 'f' one, which with a little imagination could encompass most of the demands of English Grammar, whether as a noun, adjective, verb, adverb or pronoun.

To soldiers, the 'f' word is really one of the most useful words in the English Language and can cover a whole range of sentiments and feelings. The written word cannot really express the full value of the 'f' word, but the spoken word can be pronounced and used in many effective ways. The Army NCOs had developed the verbal use of the word to a fine and effective art form, but the excessive use of it, devalued and reduced its impact.

However, it was not just the use of the 'f' word, there were other words and probably the worst we came across was from our hut lance-corporal, a

47

small man, who appeared to suffer both from a chip on his shoulder and an inferiority complex. A fairly lethal combination, and his method of man management was to shout and scream at us in a bullying and hectoring manner. Unfortunately, we were not in a position to answer back. His favourite abusive phrase directed to whosoever crossed his path, was to call that person a 'Furkin' Melk'. After a few days, we plucked up sufficient courage to ask him what the word 'Melk' meant. 'A furkin' pervert who goes round smelling ladies bicycle saddles' was the answer. This shocked even the most broad-minded of us.

~

After some ten days of this undignified and degrading life, I was informed by those who had the power of life or death over us, that as they were unable to fit me into any useful and productive trade, I with fifteen others from our Company had been selected as potential officer material and we were being transferred to No. 2 Training Battalion at Honiton in Devon. A feeling of relief went through us; although we did incur a little jealousy from some of our fellow recruits. A few junior NCOs who had failed the War Office Selection Board (WOSB) for potential officers and had been RTUd (Returned-to-Unit), warned us that life at Honiton was not going to be easy and advised us that the fear of failure was the incentive to keep us going when the going got tough. Most of our Company however, took our posting out with good grace and humour, and we left our platoon with calls of 'Good Luck', coupled with jokes about leaving a 'cushy' life behind us. Of course, true to type, Lance-Jack 'Führer' showed the chip on his shoulder and his inferiority complex by making life as unpleasant as he could for those of us in his hut who were moving on to Honiton. The abuse and coarse language we had suffered for the previous ten days paled into insignificance, as he let rip with a string of obscenities expressing what he thought of National Service subalterns.

We could not get away from Blandford fast enough. Anything was going to be better than what we had experienced over the previous ten days. However, looking back, I wonder if I have not been too critical about No.1 Training Battalion. Later on during my two years service, I met fellow soldiers, who had completed their basic training at Blandford, and who said that once the first fortnight was over, the pressure lifted and life seemed to improve, and by the time the eight weeks of basic training were over, they were really settling into army life and routine. The Army only had one objective. They had eight weeks in which to turn a group of undisciplined and resentful young men into something like soldiers. Hence the constant pressures, the shouting, the swearing, the frequently administered punishments, either through extra fatigues or through extra drill and PT. The system worked; discipline and obedience was instilled into all of us, mainly I felt through fear, but I must admit I cannot see how, in the limited time available, any other method could have succeeded so well. Basic training probably seemed harder than it actually was. We were unused to the discipline and the rigours of Army life. Everything was alien after the security and comfort of our home environment.

Having been used to our independence in civilian life, we were now faced with the loss of that independence and having to accept that the Army now controlled our lives. Where the system appeared to have a weakness was in the attitude and ability of a few of the junior NCOs. The vast majority I came across in my two years were very competent and professional, but at Blandford there was a very small number of lance-corporals, who seemed to suffer from delusions of self-importance, and who could only assert their authority over the recruits through verbal abuse and a hectoring behaviour. Of course they had a job to do, and they were no doubt jumped on by the chain of command if they did not do it well. I suspect their ability to do the job was measured by the standard reached by the recruits at the Passing-Out Parade at the end of their basic training. With the number of recruits, both regular and National Service passing through No 1 Trg Bn, and with the number of NCOs needed to train and instruct them; it was not surprising that there was this very small minority of junior NCOs promoted, I believe beyond the level of their competence. The vast majority who had been promoted, had shown ability and leadership qualities; had been properly trained, and achieved better results in a shorter time span, mainly due to recruits responding positively to a more enlightened approach, rather than to the traditional hectoring and abusive method.

So, it was with no small measure of relief that the fifteen of us packed our gear into kit-bags, piled into the transport and turned our backs on No. 1 Training Battalion and looked forward, but with a certain amount of trepidation to what was going to hit us at No 2 Training Battalion. However, we felt it could be no worse than those first ten days in the Army.

Chapter Three

Early Days. 'D' Coy 2 Trg Bn REME

The drive from Blandford to Honiton took some three hours, so we consumed our haversack rations 'on the hoof'. Although nervous, I found that I could still appreciate the scenery; at least what it was possible to see from the back of a Bedford RL 3 ton truck. Our route took us through Dorchester, Bridport, Lyme Regis and up the A35 to Honiton, which we drove through towards Exeter and as we left the town, on the left hand side of the road just beyond the turning off to Sidmouth, lay No 2 Training Battalion REME. My first impression as the truck turned into the camp, was how compact it looked compared to the sprawling layout of No 1 Training Battalion and not dominated by giant water towers.

It was a bright sunny afternoon when we reached Honiton, in contrast to the murky, depressingly grey and miserable day when we had arrived at Blandford. We stopped by the Guard Room, and were ordered to debus. As we lined up, we had our first good look at the camp. The Guard Room was to our left, whilst Battalion Headquarters was to our right. Ahead was the Parade Ground, which sloped from left to right. Beyond this to the left and to the front were the Company Lines. To the right were the Cookhouse, N.A.A.F.I. and the Medical Centre (MRS). The Camp was built on the same lines as at Blandford with wooden barrack huts and company offices, which probably dated from the First World War. Honiton, prior to REME acquiring it in 1942, was an Army Training School under the direction of the Director-General of Military Training.

The camp nestled at the foot of a steeply wooded hill, with the different shades of green foliage from the ash, elm, oak and other trees shimmering in the sunlight and whispering in the breeze of a summer's afternoon. I had a feeling, as we stood waiting to be marched off, that No 2 Trg Bn was going to be, as far as was possible for us raw recruits, less of a cultural shock compared to No 1 Trg Bn and as we got used to the army, possibly more enjoyable, if army life could be enjoyable.

~

After a short wait, a sergeant and corporal hove into view from buildings on our left.

'Right. Listen in you lot. I am Sergeant (Sgt) Henderson and this is Corporal (Cpl) Jones. I shall be your Platoon Sergeant and Corporal Jones is my deputy. The Corporal will show you where your huts are.' At 1600hrs you will parade outside the Company Office, where you will be addressed by the Company Commander, Major Rust. Do I make myself clear?'

'Yes, Sarnt,' we all mumbled.

'Yes what? I don't hear you, and don't call me Sarnt. I am a Sergeant.'

'Yes, Sergeant.' We all shouted.

Cpl Jones split us into two squads and marched us off to 'D' Company lines, situated on the left hand side of the camp, and up to a row of wooden barrack huts set at the back of the camp and nestling at the foot of the hill.

'Right. These are your huts, D8 and 9. Don't forget where they are. Now find yourselves a bed and get your kit squared away in the proper manner. You lot,' pointing at the squad I was in, 'you're D8. Parade outside at 1500hrs, when I will march you to the QM stores for your bedding. When you get back, you will make up your bedblocks, which I shall inspect later on. Okay?'

'Yes, Corporal.'

As there were only fifteen of us, the hut was a considerable improvement on our Blandford barrack block. From what we could see, all the accommodation huts were individually sited, but as the Army's budget did not run to central heating, we were, nevertheless pleased to see that we had two coke burning stoves in the hut, which together with the bases, surrounds and fire irons were immaculately blacked and highly burnished. Even the small stocks of coke had been washed and dried, so that there was no coke dust to mess up the cleanliness of the hut. We all agreed that the stoves were probably only there for decorative purposes. I would have hated to clean them out and polish them ready for a hut inspection. I was thankful that our course would only last until mid-November, and that hopefully we should not need to light them. As we unpacked our kit and laid it out correctly in our lockers, we chatted amongst ourselves, and we all believed, that although we were no doubt going to be put through the wringer, we nevertheless felt reasonably confident from our first impressions that we possibly might enjoy No 2 Trg Bn.

As we waited outside for Cpl Jones to march us down to the QM's Store, we noted how immaculate the Company Lines were. The grass was cut, the flowerbeds with not a weed in sight, the white painted stone path edges 'squared off', as were the risers of all the steps leading to the Company Offices and barrack huts. The old saying came to mind: 'If it moves, salute it. If it doesn't, paint it.'

~

After we had collected our bedding and made up our bedblocks to the satisfaction of Cpl Jones, the platoon paraded outside the Orderly Room, standing easy, waiting for the OC to appear.

'No 3 Platoon'. We assumed our version of the 'at ease' position. 'ATTEN…wait for it….SHUN'. We shuffled to attention; a drill movement, which was about as far removed from those of the Brigade of Guards as one could imagine. Sgt Henderson turned a whiter shade of pale, and looked as though he was about to throw up. Even Major Rust as he appeared on the veranda of the Company Offices winced.

'Sergeant, stand the Platoon at ease.'

'Yes, sir. Platoon. Platoon. STAND AT EASE.'

'Stand them easy'. Sergeant Henderson gave the order.

'Right. I believe it is important that you are fully aware of what you are embarking on as potential National Service subalterns. Becoming an officer is not a sinecure for a comfortable life. It is a responsible position and you can only earn the honour of holding the Queen's commission through dedication, hard work and ability.

'It is my job and that of the Platoon Commander, Warrant Officers and NCOs to ensure over the next ten weeks that you have what it takes to become an officer. At the end of this period, you will attend the War Office Selection Board, known as WOSB' (The Company Commander pronounced it as 'WASBEE'). 'Those who pass will be posted to Mons Officer Cadet School at Aldershot for four months of infantry training. Only then, if you successfully complete the course at Mons will you be commissioned.

'For those who fail 'WASBEE', or subsequently during the course at Mons OCS, will be returned to this battalion and remain in the ranks before being posted elsewhere.

'D' Company has been specifically set up to prepare you, as potential officers, for 'WASBEE'. I demand the highest standards, commitment and hard work. Failure to keep up will result in being 'back squadded' to week one of the course, but any signs of slackness and lack of commitment will result in instant Return-to-Unit (RTU). Do I make myself clear?'

'Yes, Sir'

'Right. Dismiss the men, Sergeant.'

'Platoon. Platoon. ATTEN…..SHUN.'

We must have been getting better, as the echo bouncing back from the 'D' Company's buildings was considerable shorter as we came to attention.

'OFFICER ON PARADE. DISMISS.'

That really threw us. We had no idea what Sgt Henderson was ordering us to do. What does 'Officer on Parade' mean? We hadn't covered that at Blandford. Instinctively most of the Platoon decided to see the OC off, with a sort of half wave salute, before we started to amble away.

The reaction was instantaneous. Major Rust decided discretion was the best course of action, and disappeared into the Company Office. Sgt Henderson almost had apoplexy, but the very tall 'gentleman', who had stood behind, and almost out of sight behind the OC, went ballistic. He turned out to be the Company Sergeant-Major.

'Stand fast you 'orrible shower. Sergeant Henderson,' he screamed. 'I have never seen anything so disgusting in my whole life as this horrible, idle bunch in front of me. Potential Officers! I'll give them Potential Officers. They aren't even fit to muck out the latrines. Double them to the Square for an hours drill, and for fucks sake teach them how to salute properly.'

'Yes, Sarnt-Major. Right! You dosey lot of time wasters. Stand still there. ATTEN…SHUN. The Platoon will move to the left in threes. LEFT…wait for it….TURN. By the left. QUICK MARCH.'

Off we shuffled, trying to keep in step. Cpl Jones let rip at the top of his voice. 'EP, IGH, EP, IGH'.

'DOUBLE MARCH'. This order from Sgt Henderson.

What with trying to keep in step, swing our arms, and then march at the double proved beyond our capability. However, we contrived to reach the Square at roughly the same time, even if the order in which we finished was nowhere near the same as it was when we set off. Sgt Henderson trying to maintain a semblance of dignity, was no doubt calling on the Almighty to ensure that the Battalion Regimental Sergeant-Major was engaged elsewhere and not observing us rabble.

'You lot are an unmitigated disaster. You are a disgrace to the Cap Badge. I don't know who the bright spark it was who thought you are bleedin' bright enough to become officers. He must have been a fuckin' head case. All I can say is, God help the Army.'

Sgt Henderson was getting really steamed up.

'That drill back there was bloody pathetic. I don't know what I've done to deserve you lot, but I'm going to make your lives so fuckin' miserable over the next few weeks, that you had wished that you had never been born. You there in the middle of the front rank, what's your name?'

'Carruthers, Sergeant.'

'Corporal Jones, take the right hand lot of misfits from la-de-da fuckin' Carruthers over to the other side of the Square, and teach them how to come to attention, how to stand at ease, and how to salute properly. I don't want to see those idle sods again, until they can drill properly and begin to act like soldiers.'

I was with the half of the platoon that stayed with Sgt Henderson.

'Right! For the next hour you are going to work, as you've never worked before. When I've finished you're only going to be fit enough to crawl into your fuckin' pits.

'Middle rank stand fast. Front rank. Two paces forward MARCH. Rear rank. Two paces backward MARCH, One, Two. Now that manoeuvre is known as 'open order' and the reverse is 'close order'. Now, let's try it.'

We practised it several times, until Sgt Henderson was reasonably satisfied.

We were in open order and standing easy.

'Now let's try coming to attention and standing at ease. When you are standing at ease, your feet must be at the 10 to 2 o'clock position, your heels will be no more than 12 inches apart, and your arms will be stretched straight down your back with your right hand and right thumb over your left hand and thumb. Your shoulders will be straight and pulled back, with your tummy held in, - not like a pregnant fairy. Head up, eyes straight to your front. You do not move. Like this.'

The sergeant demonstrated the 'at ease' position from the front, the side and the back. Then, he made us to do the same. He stalked along and between the ranks correcting each of us, until we were all able to give a fair representation of the 'at ease' position.

'Now. When you are given the order to 'stand easy', you don't move, you just relax the shoulders and stand comfortably. But, you do not talk. Okay?'

'Yes, Sergeant.'

'Right. Stand easy. We are now going to practice coming to 'Attention' from the 'Stand Easy' position. When you hear the warning word, whether it is 'Company', 'Platoon' or 'Squad' you immediately straighten up and come to the 'At Ease' position. The warning word is given again, followed by the order. Like this 'Squad. Squad. Attention'.

'Now, when you come to attention, you immediately bring your arms to your sides, with your arms straight, ball your hands into fists with your thumbs to the front and 'pointing' straight down the seams of your trousers. At the same time you bring your left leg over towards your right and raising it, so that your upper left leg is parallel to the ground. Then you force your left leg down trying to drive your boot into the ground, finishing up with your arms to your sides and your heels together with your boots at the ten to two position. Now let's try it.'

'SQUAD.' We came to 'At Ease' and braced ourselves. 'SQUAD. ATTENSHUN!!'

Our boots gently kissed the tarmac, as if we were standing on a bed of eggs.

Sgt Henderson gave a deep sigh. 'Right. Let's do it again, and this time I want to hear your boots stamp into the ground.'

We were more successful the second time, but the sound of our boots driving into the tarmac must have appeared to a passer-by that he was under sustained machine gun fire.

'Right. And this time when you come to attention, do not bend the upper half of your body forward like a sagging sack of potatoes. You stand straight with your eyes firmly fixed to your front. Now, let's try it again.'

Again and again we practised the movement, and very gradually we started to get it together, until our boots driving into the tarmac of the Square sounded less like the 'Clog Dance' from the ballet 'La Fille Mal Gardée' and more like a single rifle shot.

At one stage in the sudden stillness of the summers' afternoon, we heard a door bang behind us. Sgt Henderson glanced to his left, blanched, stiffened, and said to us in a low voice: 'The RSM is watching us. Show him what you can do.' Eventually, he must have moved on, as Sgt Henderson relaxed and complimented us on our progress.

'Right. Before we finish, I'm going to show you how to salute properly. So you don't balls it up next time. Now, when you hear the order, 'Officer on Parade. Dismiss', you turn smartly to your right, salute, take two or three paces and then break off in an orderly manner. When you are ordered to 'dismiss' without an officer on parade, you just 'right turn' without saluting.

'Now. Remember. You always salute with your right hand. You bring your right arm up in an arc from your side, with your hand open and facing to the front. Your forefinger must be no more and no less than once inch above your eyebrow. There must be a straight line from your hand to your elbow. I do not want to see a cocked wrist like this. You hold the salute to the count of three….'Up, two, three. Down, two, three.' Then you smartly bring your arm round to the front, and cut your hand away to the side of your body. The easiest way to remember this is 'the longest way up; the shortest way down.' Right, let's practice this.'

Needless to say, we all came to the salute with cocked wrists and our elbows sticking out in front of our bodies. Sgt Henderson, in order to save time, made each of us, grinning like Cheshire cats practice saluting each other.

'Now a final point. When you salute, unless you are ordered otherwise, you always turn your head in the direction of the officer you are saluting. If you are marching or walking, as you salute, you keep your left arm still against your left side until you have finished saluting.'

We had drilled for the hour, when Cpl Jones marched the other squad over and as a platoon we were marched back to 'D' Company Lines. Before dismissing us, Sgt Henderson had one more word to say:

'At 1600 hrs every afternoon, Company Orders, giving details of the next days duties, are posted outside the Orderly Room. You must read these. You will be in serious shit if you fail to turn up for guard or some other duty. Ignorance is no excuse in the Army's eyes.'

We were dismissed and we all rushed, pushing and shoving to the notice board outside the Company Office, to read what Parts I and II Orders had in store for us the next day.

We staggered back to our hut, absolutely drained, both physically and mentally. The extra drill had really taken it out of us. Yet we had not finished for the day, for after our evening meal, we had to start cleaning, blancoing and polishing our kit.

~

At Blandford, we had not been instructed in the mysteries of 'bull. We had of course been expected to polish both pairs of boots and clean all brasses, but applying blanco to our webbing had not been a major priority; although I suspected the NCOs there knew what was in store for us when we got to No 2 Trg Bn.

Blanco came in a tin, and was mixed with a little water to make a somewhat runny paste. The webbing was dampened to make it easier to apply the 'goo', which was then brushed onto the webbing. A toothbrush was particularly useful for applying it into very small out of the way corners of the webbing. Blanco came in various shades of khaki, depending upon the Army unit to which one was posted. It should not have been too difficult to apply, one just had to mix it to the right consistency and ensure, like custard there were no lumps in the mixture. However, the skill lay in applying it over each piece of webbing in a smooth and even layer. Too thin, and the basic material of the webbing could be seen through the blanco. Too thick, and the blanco started to crack when the belt, gaiters or other webbing equipment was flexed and moved with use.

Due to their size, the 'large' and 'small' packs were the most difficult to blanco evenly. Both packs had to be stored 'squared off' on the top of ones locker. The helmet was then placed on top of them. However, the weight of this was sufficient to flatten the packs like deflated soufflés. The trick was to cut strips of cardboard to the internal dimensions of the large and small packs and place these inside down the sides and across the ends. This made the packs perfectly 'squared off'. The only problem was that, if during a hut and kit inspection, it was found that you had used cardboard in the packs, you could end up on a 'charge'. However, this generally only happened if the officer or warrant officer was in a bad mood; had a hangover; or had not, as we suspected, fulfilled his monthly quota of 'charged' recruits. Although it was a well-known and accepted practice, we could not win. If we did not use cardboard to square up the packs, we would be charged with having a 'shitty' layout. If we did use cardboard, and had perfectly squared packs, we would also be in the mire.

When we went on exercises, we were expected to fill, whichever of the packs we were ordered to take, with all the necessary spare gear such as 'underpants green-cellular', socks-grey, washing kit, mess tins and eating irons etc, to last for the duration of the exercise. The only problem on return to Camp was that we had to start all over again getting the pack, which would invariably have ended up very dirty and muddy into 'good order' again.

I was to find out later, having got my blancoing technique up to scratch at Honiton, that at Mons OCS, a different colour and type of blanco was used, which meant that all my webbing had to be scrubbed completely clean of the REME blanco before applying the Mons OCS type.

The big problem was that the various pieces of webbing had brass bits fitted to them. All these had to be highly polished using Brasso or Duraglit. There was no problem in cleaning them. The problems began when blanco either got onto the brasses or conversely, the Brasso or Duraglit got onto a newly blancoed piece of webbing. The former was a fairly easily solved problem, but the latter - that was trouble. The offending spots of Brasso, or Duraglit dried white on the blanco, with the result that as it was not possible to remove the white stain by scrapping it with a knife without leaving a mark. Re-blancoing the spot did not work, as a 'join' could be seen where the extra coat of blanco had been applied. The only answer was to blanco the whole piece of webbing again. This, in turn took time to dry, before the brasses could be buffed up, and would result in panic as the time fast approached for a parade or a hut inspection. It was always a dilemma whether to blanco or Brasso first. I preferred the latter method, as it was easier to clean blanco off brasses than the other way round.

Fortunately, by the late 1950s the Army was using 'Staybright' cap badges and buttons, which helped to reduce the amount of polishing to a certain degree. For daily duties, we mainly used the belt, rifle sling and gaiters (also known as 'anklets'). The belt was of fairly substantial construction, with two brass clips in the centre at the back to which the ends of the cross straps were fixed. At the front were brass buckles, with the 'male' clasp clipping into the 'female' one. The belt at each end had brass plates with two 'hooks'. These were clipped into tiny slots at the top and bottom of the reverse side of the belt and provided adjustment to fit the girth of its owner. The webbing was not a soft or pliable material, and it was quite a struggle to locate the 'hooks' in the right slots without cracking the blanco. Finally, there were two brass 'clips' which were moved to 'secure' the two buckles tightly where the belt folded back on itself. Needless to say the two brass end pieces had to be polished, and it was not unknown on parade, for a recruit to be 'invited' to undo his belt to check the inside brasses. The anklets-web (2), had to be blancoed, brass straps cleaned and the leather fixing straps polished with black boot polish, without leaving any polish on the blancoed webbing.

The rifle sling was straightforward. A longish length of webbing, with two hooked brass end pieces, which were passed through the upper and lower sling swivels of the rifle, with the hooks being clipped to the rifle sling, so that this was taut. The only problem here being that as one fastened the hooks to the sling, the perfectly blancoed rifle sling was scored by the hooks when they were being pressed into position.

Every piece of webbing seemed to have been designed in such a way that it was virtually impossible to successfully assemble the blancoed kit for an inspection without marking it, and ending up having one's name taken.

Lance-Corporal (L/Cpl) Garner was the junior NCO in charge of our hut. Unlike those we had come across at Blandford, Jack Garner, although his language could be as bad as any other NCO, did explain things to us, and helped us to stay on the right track. Although, quite rightly, he took it as a personal insult if our hut failed an inspection. It was the 'Corp' who showed us the best way to clean our kit, how to shape our berets and how to start 'bulling' our boots.

I found it amazing how many different shapes a beret could be 'teased' into. The shape of a new beret when issued, sat on one's head like a pork pie. The aim was to style the beret so that it properly fitted the head, with the leather rim precisely one inch above and parallel with the eyebrows. The beret, through many hours of steaming, ironing, pulling and pushing would eventually be so styled, with the REME cap badge correctly positioned over the left eye and the beret pulled down towards the right ear. It was always possible to spot a new recruit by the shape of his beret, and one felt a certain feeling of superiority with a properly shaped one.

We had been issued with two sets of battledress (BD for short). One of which we had to nominate as 'best', and which was only worn for formal parades and 'walking out'.

The design for the battledress went back to 1937, and was initially issued to conscripted militia in October 1938. The BD went through several pattern changes during its life, before being progressively withdrawn from service during the 1960s. The BDs with which we were issued were of the 1949 Pattern, allowing all ranks, not just officers to wear collars and ties. Bar from a small modification in 1954, the 1949 version known as the 'No 5 Dress' was the pattern which remained as standard until the BD was withdrawn from service.

Battledresses were made up from serge material and described as 'Serge

Service Dress No.4 56" '. The material was rough, and we hoped that we might have been issued with BDs manufactured in Canada or Australia as they were made from a softer cloth. But, we were not so lucky. Presumably, rank counted, and no doubt, the higher one was in the Army's chain of command, the better the chance there was of getting the best kit. National Servicemen were no doubt, at the bottom of the chain.

However, the Army went to quite a lot of trouble to ensure that best battledresses were a good fit, and would not be a disgrace to the Regimental or Corps cap badge. BDs blouses and trousers could, and did vary in weight and colour, depending on the batch material and the date of manufacture. So, the first time we paraded in our BDs, we were inspected to check that the colour of the blouse matched that of the trousers, which in many cases they did not. The Camp tailor was kept very busy, not only in making alterations to ensure that our BDs were a good fit, but also having to put up with a certain amount of 'buttering up' by those who were in the know, to have their best BD 'personalised'. This usually consisted of having two of the pleats at the back of the blouse where they joined the waistband removed, and having the remaining pleats pressed into a fan shape. If one was particularly good at the 'buttering up' line, the ultimate sign of sartorial elegance was to have a well tailored blouse with 'box' pleats, rather than the fan shape put in at the back. However, there was a danger with such pleats, as certain commanding officers did not approve of them, although senior NCOs seemed to get away with them.

We wore our second battledresses more often, mainly for everyday duties and parades, such as the morning muster parade or guard duty.

At this early stage of our basic training, on most days we wore the shapeless and ubiquitous denims, which I supposed could best be described as the equivalent to the civilian everyday working overalls. In no way could they be described at being at the cutting edge of sartorial fashion. 'Overalls, Denim', were based on the 1937 pattern BD, and made from a greyish-brown jean like material, and were apparently designed to be worn over BDs, which would not have been a good idea in hot weather. Although, I would wear them over my battledress on exercise during the winter months at Mons OCS, to keep warm and to protect my BD. Denims being our every day order of dress needed to be laundered weekly. The plastic buttons on the overall were secured by spiral clips, which we had to remove before they were washed. As the denims were sent off 'en masse', we never got the same ones back, and a serious mêlée would take place each week, as we all fought to find a pair of denims that were a passable fit. I would usually end up with a jacket, which was too small and a pair of trousers that were too large, and made me look like an animated sack of potatoes. The army issue braces were therefore a very necessary piece of kit to keep the trousers up.

The army denim outfits were so shapeless, that a committee must have designed them. However, I liked to day dream that some high ranking officer in the War Office, who probably wanted to make a name for himself, brought vast quantities of these demeaning and demoralising clothes at a very knock down price from a 'Dell Boy' trader in the East End. I would also imagine that the procurement staff in the 'War House' had not thought through how they were to be used. One could not blame the Prison Service, if they had been offered the denims, and turned them down as not being of the right quality for prisoners. I could also visualise some little known Brigadier from the 'Donkey Wallahs', who over his second G & T in the 'In and Out' Club, suddenly exclaiming: 'Eureka. I've got it! Let those National Service squaddies have the bloody denims.' The Brigadier, being only a one star general was probably immediately shown 'Out' for disturbing the post-prandial siesta of several senior admirals and generals, but was possibly made a MBE (My Bloody Effort) for helping to resolve the Army's excess denim stock situation.

~

I was for many years intrigued as to why in the American and other nations' military forces a one star generals' rank was and is known as a 'Brigadier-General', whilst in the British Army it is simply 'Brigadier'. We had Brigadier-Generals in the First World War. I subsequently learnt that at the end of the Great War, when demobilisation was in full swing, the Government of the Day told the Top Brass there were too many Generals in the Army. The Top Brass acted immediately, and overnight, removed the word 'General' from Brigadier-General. They then went back and said to the Government; 'We've carried out your wishes. We've halved the number of serving generals in the Army. Aren't we clever?'

~

The one bit of kit that demanded the greatest attention and constant 'tender loving care' was one's best pair of boots. When we had joined up, we had been issued with two pairs. One pair was for every day working purposes, but the other pair had to be highly 'bulled'. The Army boot was officially designated as 'Boot-Ammunition'. It was a heavy, black, ankle lace-up boot with a leather hob-nailed sole and steel toecap and heel supports.

L/Cpl Garner instructed us in the gentle, but skilled art of 'bulling' one's boots. Except for the toecaps and the heels, the boots were covered in a myriad of tiny pimples. These were of no concern on one's No 2 boots. However, heaven help one if there were pimples spotted on the No 1 boots.

'Right gather round you lot.' The Lance-Corporal had us stand round the communal hut table.

'I'm only going to show you this once, and if you get it wrong and you're nicked on parade for gungy boots, then it's your fuckin' fault. This 'ere is one of my No 1 boots. As you can see, you can see your 'orrible greats mugs in it. It's going to take you idle lot 'ours and 'ours of your fuckin' spare time to get your boots like this 'ere one of mine. Okay so far?'

'Yes, Corporal.'

'Right, you start with a candle and a spoon. You 'eat the back of the spoon in the candle flame, and then you bit by bit burn off the pimples. For Christ's sake don't fuckin' over 'eat the spoon, else you'll get fuckin' burn marks on the boot, which won't polish out, and you'll be on a charge causing wilful damage to WD property. When you've got the surface of your boots completely smooth, you've got the long fuckin' job of 'bulling' them up. When you've finished, I want to be able to see my face in each of your boots. Also you've got to get your boot studs highly 'bulled' as well. Do I make myself fuckin' clear.'

'Yes, Corporal.'

The long, slow process of polishing started. Masses of spit and polish were required. The form was to spit into the open lid of the boot polish tin and then, using a cloth and one finger, to gather a little black boot polish on the cloth, and 'dunk' this into the spittle. Then, with the finger one rubbed and rubbed the spit and black polish mixture in very small circles over the surface of the boot. However, in the initial stages of building up the shine, one used the back of a hot spoon to 'feed' the boot polish into the surface of the boot. It could take weeks of spit and polish before one reached an acceptable shine on the boots. There were times, during a 'bulling' session that one's mouth became so dry, it was impossible to produce any more spit. A natural break! I never learnt why spittle worked, water was never so effective. Having spent so many hours in building up a deep shine, with the cloth having to be constantly washed out, the final touch was to run over the boot with a cloth dampened with methylated spirits. We were given one word of warning though. There was a danger, if one tried to take a short cut by applying too much boot polish at one time, that the polish could peel away from the boot. There were stories of recruits and cadets with gleaming best boots, but when they carried out the first drill movements on parade, the polish cracked and flaked off. It has been known after a parade for a line of flakes of black polish to be left on the parade ground.

~

Our first full day at Honiton, started with a head count parade outside the Company Offices before being marched over to the Armoury, to be issued with our rifles; or to use a more modern expression our 'personal weapon', which I felt had an unfortunate connotation. We had heard rumours that the Army was introducing a new self-loading rifle, but National Servicemen not in a 'teeth' (frontline) unit, would still be issued with the venerable .303 Lee Enfield bolt-action rifles. I was delighted. I had first come across the weapon in the Combined Cadet Force at school, and had had live firing experience at CCF camp at Brandon in Norfolk. I loved firing the rifle and found that once the sights had been 'zeroed' I could achieve good results up to six hundred yards. It had a kick like a mule though, and it was normal practise to stuff a handkerchief under ones BD or denims to protect ones shoulder from bruising. There was also a risk that the raised rear sight, on kick back could bruise or cut one's face. I was fortunate in having some shooting ability, although my only achievement was at my prep school, where I gained a Class 'A' Junior NSRA (National Small Bore Rifle Association) Marksman Badge.

I suppose in 1958, it must have appeared an anachronism for the British Army still to be equipped with a rifle that was originally introduced in 1895, and first saw action in the Second Boer War (1899-1902).

Apparently, bolt-action rifles used by the belligerents in the Great War, were expensive to make, as they were manufactured from the best materials and were virtually hand built. At the end of the First World War, there were so many rifles left over, that Governments were loath to scrap such expensive weapons, and so they were put into store. Consequently, when the Second World War started, it was logical for Governments to re-issue the stored bolt-action rifles, instead of developing self-loading rifles, which would have been more appropriate for mobile warfare, rather than the static trench warfare of World War I.

The rifle with which we were issued was known as the SMLE (Short Magazine Lee Enfield) No.4 Mk I, and although the design for this model went back to 1933, the No.4 was not put into production until late 1940. It always intrigued me to see stencilled on ammunition boxes the words '.303 Ball ammunition'. I failed to see why the word 'ball' was used, when the bullet was pointed. The brass cartridge case was rimmed at the base and cordite sticks made up the propellant.

At my prep school David, the headmaster's son and I were good friends. One summer holiday when he and I were exploring the school carpentry shop, which also doubled up as the small bore twenty-five yard shooting range armoury, we came across some .303 ammunition. I have no idea how we found it. All ammo should have been securely locked away. Being ignorant and incredibly foolish, and wanting to find out what was inside the round, we fixed a cartridge case in a vice, and then with great care, we removed the bullet and extracted the cordite sticks. We did the same with two or three other rounds. Not knowing what to do with the cordite, we tentatively stuffed the sticks into a hole in the back flint wall of the carpentry shop, applied a match, and swiftly retired to a safe distance. We were very disappointed when the cordite just fizzled and burnt away. Having removed the cordite, we replaced the bullets back into the cartridges. As the percussion caps in the base of the cartridges had not been struck, the rounds looked as if they had not been fired.

Some time later, my father discovered one of these rounds in my bedroom, and went absolutely ballistic. I assured him the round was perfectly safe, and had no cordite in the cartridge. He did not believe me, and as I was not going to drop David 'in the proverbial', by telling him what he and I had been up to, I decided to take the flak myself, and keep David, as the son of the headmaster out of it. This was my first experience of showing loyalty to a friend. The carpentry shop has long gone and is now a sports hall.

The only disadvantage I found with the Lee-Enfield, was the business of loading the magazine with the two clips of five rounds each, ensuring the rimmed bases were properly aligned in the clips, before pushing down into the magazine, otherwise a round could become jammed at a crucial moment. Many years later, I was interested to learn that a variation of the original No.4 Mk I, which had been modified to take the standard 7.62mm NATO cartridge, was only withdrawn from the Army as a sniper's rifle in 1992, nearly one hundred years after the Lee-Enfield had first been introduced into service.

Having been issued with our 'personal weapon', we were marched over to a lecture hut, and instructed on the rifle by the Platoon Sergeant.

'Right. Listen in. This rifle, which you will guard with your life, is the Short Lee-Enfield Mark 4. It is without doubt, the finest rifle that the Army has ever had. It fires point three-oh–three ammunition, and the magazine holds ten rounds.'

The lecture proceeded, and the Sergeant showed us how to load the rifle, how to set the sights, how to fix the bayonet, how to remove the bolt and finally:

'Now in the base plate of the rifle, you will see a hinged trap door. Open this and inside you will find a cord with a weight on one end. This is known as the 'pull through'. You will also find a small piece of cloth, known as the 'four-by-two' and you will also find a small tube of gun oil. These are there so that you can keep your rifle in pristine condition. The Army takes a very poor view of anyone who is found with a dirty rifle, and any of you who have one, will be on a charge straightaway. Your rifle is your best friend. Treat it as such and look after it. In a shooting war, your life may depend on your rifle, and as I've already said guard it with your life. The ultimate sin is to lose your rifle. This is a court-martial offence, and you could end up in the 'Glass House' at Colchester'. This was the Army's infamous prison, which apparently had an unenviable reputation. We returned to our hut suitable subdued, with the sergeant's warning ringing in our ears.

~

We were broken in fairly gently for the first few days, which enabled us to get used to the Camp, and especially 'D' Company routine. We were able to start bulling our kit. Blanco was being freely applied to our webbing to such an extent that it took us hours to scrub the blancoing room clean enough to pass inspection. The pimples on our best boots were being burnt off, and a start was made on the laborious process of applying and building up the polish. The elbow grease that was being put into boot bulling was such that dusters had to be constantly washed and hung out to dry.

We met our Platoon Commander, 2Lt John Stevens, a National Service Subaltern, who only had a few months of service left, and could not wait for his 'demob' day to come, so that he could return to his interrupted career as a trainee engineer with the British Motor Corporation (BMC). He had spent National Service on Regimental Duties at REME Training Battalions and disliked every minute.

One afternoon, after we had been at Honiton for a few days, John Smith, a fellow recruit, burst into the hut and announced:

'Hey! Listen everybody. Part I Orders are up and we're on Muster Parade at 8 o'clock tomorrow morning.' (We still had not got used to the Army's use of the 24-hour clock).

We had been warned about our first Muster Parade, and that we would be put 'through it'. We had to parade in our second best BDs, with our webbing, brasses, boots and rifle in spotless condition. That evening our hut was a hive of industry, as we blancoed our webbing, polished our brasses and boots and ironed our battle dresses, so that we had razor sharp creases on both the sleeves of the blouses and the trousers. Our berets had started to take on a decent shape. Overall, we reckoned we were in pretty good order, and without doubt, our mothers would have been proud of us.

The recruit

Promptly at 0745 hours, we tipped toed out of our hut, so as not to damage the highly polished linoleum floor, nor scratch the surface of our best boots, and paraded outside the Company Office.

'Right, you idle lot. GET FELL IN!' Cpl Jones was in fine voice.

'MOVE THOSE FAT ARSES AND GET YOUR DRESSING. FROM THE RIGHT YOU IDIOT.'

We shuffled our feet about to give the impression that we were 'on the ball', as each of us extended our left arm to touch the right shoulder of the man on our immediate left, as we turned our heads to the right and shuffled our feet to line up with the right hand man in the front rank, who was the right marker. L/Cpl Garner, officiously marched round to the left of the platoon, and marshalled each rank in turn:

'You, No 3 in the front rank, dress forward – NOT THAT MUCH. WHAT DO YOU THINK I AM, AN IDIOT? You in the middle – PULL YOUR ARSE IN, and the man next to you, YES, YOU with the bird nest of a beret – PULL YOUR FUCKIN' STOMACH IN. WHAT DO YOU THINK YOU ARE? A FUCKIN' PREGANT FAIRY?'

'No, Corporal.'

'WELL STOP FUCKIN' ACTING LIKE ONE!'

'Yes, Corporal.'

Sotto voce 'I suppose his mother loves him.'

'WHAT DID YOU SAY?'

'Nothing, Corporal. Just clearing my throat.'

'HUH!!'

Eventually, the corporals were satisfied that we looked reasonably like soldiers, and we were stood easy waiting for the Platoon Commander and Sergeant to appear on the scene and put us through our first inspection.

We were all nervous. After all our hard work, we felt that we were in good order. Before we had left our hut, we had inspected each other, looking for any faults, and we certainly took pride in our appearance.

We did not have too long to wait before 2Lt Stevens and Sgt Henderson hove into view. From the expressions on their faces, breakfast in their Messes could not have been much to their liking, as they both looked as if they could do with a good dose of Andrews Liver Salts.

'PLATOON. WAIT FOR IT. PLATOON 'SHUN'. We came smartly to attention. Cpl Jones smartly pivoted through 180 degrees and saluted.

'No 3 Platoon ready for your inspection, SIR'.

'Very good. Corporal Jones, carry on.'

Cpl Jones saluted and pirouetted through 180 degrees again.

'No 3 Platoon. OPEN ORDER MARCH!'

The front rank took two paces forward, whilst the back rank took two paces backwards. The Platoon Commander and Platoon Sergeant split up. The former took the front rank, and the latter the middle rank. I was in the rear rank.

There was no doubt that 2Lt Stevens and Sgt Henderson, were suffering from a combination of hangovers, lack of sleep, indifferent breakfasts and dyspepsia.

The Platoon Commander

The confidence I had felt, evaporated, when we saw the demonic expressions on their faces, and it became obvious we were going to be 'shafted' in a major way. It was as if they had both taken a dose of Syrup of

Figs to rid themselves of their gastric problems. They went through us in the same way.

Having grounded their rifles, and armed themselves with pencil and paper, Cpl Jones attached himself to the officer and L/Cpl Garner to the Sergeant.

'Take that man's name, Corporal. His rifle sling isn't tight enough.'

'You! You 'orrible example of humanity, Am I 'urtin' you?'

'No, Sergeant.'

'Well. You fuckin' should be 'urtin'. I'm standing on your hair. GET IT CUT.'

'That belt has got Brasso on it. Take his name.'

'Your rifle is fuckin' filthy. What have you been doing with it? Fuckin' gardening?'

And so it went on, more and more members of the platoon were having their names taken for the most insignificant faults. I was really quaking in my boots, and was hoping against hope, that 2Lt Stevens and Sgt Henderson would have 'gone off the boil' by the time they had reached the rear rank. But no chance! They joined up together, and then split their forces, with the officer doing a right flanking movement to take our front and the Sergeant a left flanking movement to cover our rear. Not only were our webbing, brasses and boots minutely inspected, but we were also pushed and pulled to check that we had properly assembled and tightened our kit. I figuratively breathed a sigh of relief as the officer moved on from me, only to smell onions, as Sgt Henderson's head appeared from behind my right shoulder, and he whispered into my ear:

'You, Caffyn. Your beret is a disgrace. TIDY IT UP.'

My name was added to the ever-growing list. I could not begin to imagine what was wrong with my beret. I had been carefully heating it and shaping it. In fact, I was proud of my beret. So why had Sgt Henderson taken my name? I was soon to find out. At the back of the leather headband of the beret was a small gap where the ribbon, which passed through the band, ended in a tiny, neat bow. Nobody had warned us that the bow should have been undone and the two ends tucked neatly into either side of the gap in the headband.

So ended our first Muster Parade. The whole platoon had had their names taken. We were devastated and our morale plummeted. I presumed it was all part of the softening up process to de-civilianise us, to knock us down figuratively speaking to ground level, before starting to re-build us mentally as soldiers able to accept discipline and carry out orders without question. I also suspected there was a hidden agenda to see whether any of us would break under the pressure, and exhibit behaviour unbecoming for an officer and which would have resulted in instant 'Return-to-Unit'.

We found out subsequently that what we had endured at our first Muster Parade was standard procedure, and every new 'D' Company platoon went through the same experience.

However, it did not end there. Having our names taken meant that we had to parade outside the Company Office at 1900 hours in battle dress order, which included ammunition pouches and small packs. So after we had finished work for the day, we had to re-clean our kit ready for the inspection, which was carried out by the duty corporal. The length of the punishment parade depended upon which corporal was on duty and the mood he was in. The corporals regarded this parade as a sport, for once we had been inspected, we would be ordered to report back within three minutes in our PT kit. Webbing would be unfastened as we dashed back to our barracks, our bed spaces would be strewn with boots, BDs and webbing as we pulled our PT kit from our neatly stowed lockers, with other items spilling out onto the floor. Frantically tying the laces to our gym shoes, we would race back down the hill to the Company Office, where the corporal would be timing us with a stopwatch. We would be inspected to ensure that we had the right gear on. Then yet again, we would be given three minutes to change into denims. Depending upon the sporting nature of the duty corporal, this 'game' could go on for some time. There was one corporal, who obviously hadn't got a home to go to and would prolong the torture by making us change five or six times before calling it a day. Most corporals were satisfied after we had carried out two or three quick changes. However, those of us who failed to make the three-minute deadline, or were incorrectly dressed, would be made to stay on after the rest had been dismissed and continue to indulge the corporal in his little 'game'. Eventually, the corporal would become bored and as this was his last duty of the day, was no doubt itching to get to the Corporals' Club to join his mates and get some ale or 'scrumpy' cider inside him.

For those of us who had been on punishment parade, we then had the task of clearing up all our gear, re-packing our lockers and preparing our kit for the following day. This would probably also include re-blancoing and polishing the brasses of those items of webbing which we did not normally use on a day-to-day basis, but which had got scuffed during the punishment parade. On such an evening, a visit to the NAAFI was generally not on.

The problem with which we were faced, was that although there was an official hut inspection every Saturday morning, there were also snap locker and hut inspections carried out during the day in our absence. The only sign that there had been one was when we returned and found our bedblocks or kit from our lockers had been strewn all over our own and other bed spaces. A very bad locker and kit layout or a badly made bedblock could result for the unfortunate recruit, returning to the hut, finding all his gear had been thrown out of the window and was strewn across the grass, irrespective of whether it was dry or wet. Then it was a question of tidying everything up and being 'named' for punishment parade again. It was difficult, once in the defaulter's cycle, ever to get clear from it. The pressure just to satisfactorily complete the daily tasks was bad enough, without having the added stress of having to remake ones bedblock and replace ones kit correctly in the locker after a hut inspection, and then re-blanco webbing, polish brasses and boots after being on punishment parade.

~

What we dreaded most was the Saturday morning hut inspection, which was carried out by the Company Commander and the Company Sergeant-Major. We had learnt from his opening remarks on our arrival, that the OC, Major Rust set very high standards, but since then we had not seen a great deal of him. Our first contact with the CSM had not been auspicious, but he had a reputation of being a martinet. It would only take one hut inspection to find out what we were up against.

A Friday evening was a scene of frenetic activity. The hut, ablutions, latrines and the immediate surrounding area had to be spotless. Simultaneously, as well as preparing for the hut inspection, we had to get our kit ready for the normal morning muster parade.

In our hut we decided to divide the tasks up, to ensure that every area and item was covered; that we did not double up and miss places by not being properly organised. One of the main problems was getting the beams dusted and cleaned. We did not have anyone as tall as the CSM who was well over six feet and could reach places a shorter man could not. Poor old Mike Smith, who was the tallest person in the hut, was always detailed to clean the beams. The poor chap spent Friday evenings standing on a chair, duster and brush in hand, working from one end of the hut to the other. It was to his everlasting credit that we were never pulled up for dusty and dirty beams. Mike was a great guy, but had this unnerving habit of sleeping with his eyes open, and the first time we came across him asleep on his bed, we thought he had died on us!

My responsibility was the two coke stoves at each end of the hut. Fortunately, cleaning in the summer months was easier than in the winter. However, it was still surprising how much dust collected around these each week, especially in the joints of the various parts of the stoves. I virtually had to dismantle each one to ensure that there was no dust and dirt anywhere, and then re-assemble them before blackening the stoves. I also had to clean and polish the base surrounds and ensure that the fire irons were aligned with military precision. By each stove was a small pile of coke and we quickly found out that each piece had to be washed, dried and neatly stacked. The CSM had this delightful habit of donning white gloves and running his hands over the blackened stoves and picking up each lump of coke. He did not expect to get his gloves dirty. He also used the same technique on the beams, which he could reach without standing on a chair.

The floor was always a problem. We swept it first. Then, on our hands and knees the first echelon, which included me, applied polish. Following us, also on their knees was the second echelon furiously polishing, and finally we used the 'buffer', a heavily weighted polisher to produce a real shine to the floor.

Being August the grass outside the hut had to be cut, and this without a mower! Weeds had to be dug up and the steps to the hut and the stones lining the path to our 'front door' had to be re-painted white. By the time that 2 Trg Bn was closed down, the steps and stones, over the years must have had at least an inch thickness of paint. Finally, the waste bin had to be emptied and scrubbed out, so that this too was in good order.

It was important that all cleaning and polishing of our kit was done before we

The weekly hut inspection

started on the hut, as blancoing, in particular was a messy job. All this had to be done before lights-out at 2200hrs. The NAAFI was definitely out on a Friday evening, which no doubt reduced their profit levels. Several decades later, when the name of the game was cost cutting, budgeting and profit margins; the loss of an evening's sales and profit would no doubt have been regarded as a serious matter. The 'bean counters' in what became the Ministry of Defence, would probably have regarded hut and individual kit inspections as not being cost effective, balanced against the loss of NAAFI sales and profit.

Saturday morning could best be described as total and unmitigated chaos. We were out of our 'pits' early. We washed and shaved quickly; dressed and downed breakfast in the shortest possible time, and then it was back to the hut. Especial care was taken with bedblocks, with exact right angles to the folded sheets and blankets; beds and lockers were as correctly aligned as Guardsmen on parade. Our kit was properly laid out on our beds, with the contents of the 'housewife' fully displayed and spare bootlaces laid out as straight as if they were mathematical rulers. Our eating irons and especially our mugs were spotless and were positioned in their correct places on beds. Indeed, whoever had thought up the kit layout must have suffered from deep psychological problems (his mummy may have paid him insufficient attention when he was a child), for no sane person could surely have dreamt up such a diabolical layout.

Time was never on our side, and as well as ensuring that the hut was spotless, we had to make sure that the ablutions and latrines were thoroughly clean with no nasty stains in and around basins, baths, urinals and 'bogs'. We were usually in a 'blue funk' by this time, and it was never wise to ask those who were responsible for the washrooms and 'bogs' what implements they had used to clean them. A final dust around the hut, before the stentorian tones of the Lance-Corporal ordered us out on parade. Having polished the floor to produce a very deep shine, we tied dusters around our hob nailed boots so as not to mark the surface as we left the hut for the muster parade.

One member of the platoon was left behind and was in charge of the hut. The official reason for this was security, as it would have been all too easy for someone to sneak into the hut, and nick any amount of kit which had been so conveniently laid out for the inspection. We never found that stealing was a problem in the camp. However, we believed the real reason was that the poor sod who was left on hut duty, would receive the full verbal onslaught from the OC and the CSM for an unsatisfactory hut and kit inspection.

It was an unnerving experience being the hut orderly, waiting for the Company Commander and Company Sergeant-Major to hove into view. As our hut was at the back of 'D' Company lines beyond Hut 7, we were usually the last one to be inspected. This did have one advantage in that the person on duty had time to check on the condition of the hut and everybody's kit layout and correct anything that was wrong.

My turn as hut orderly, 'Caffyn' being near the beginning of the alphabet, came early in the Course. After our section had left for Muster Parade, I imagined I was the inspecting officer, and slowly went round the hut, straightening a bed here and a bedblock there. The stoves and the beams seemed okay. The floor shone and I could not see any scuff marks. The windows were clean, and everything appeared to be correctly lined up with military precision. I reckoned we were in pretty 'good order'. However, I thought back to our first muster parade when we all thought we were in 'good order', yet the whole platoon had ended up having their names taken. I could see through a window that the OC and CSM were entering the next hut down the slope from ours, so I went to the door to await their arrival. I did a final visual check from the doorway, and I do not know what made me look up, but horror upon horror, I suddenly realised that we had not dusted the overhead light bulbs and shades. 'Oh shit!' I said to myself.

'Have I've got time to dust them?' I grabbed the communal chair, placed it under the first light and not daring to use one of the dusters which had all been washed, ironed and neatly laid out, together with the brushes, the 'buffer' and the other cleaning equipment for inspection, so I pulled my handkerchief from my pocket and I dusted the light shade, bulb and flex. Perspiring freely I did the same to the other three lights, but as I stepped down from the last light, the chair slipped and the chair legs and my boots scuffed our highly buffed floor.

'Oh fucking hell!! Now I was in the shit.' A quick glance out of a window. 'Good, they haven't left No 7 Hut yet.'

At the risk of ruining the creases in my BD trousers, I once again pulled the handkerchief out of my trouser pocket, and sinking to the floor managed to polish out the scuffmarks at the expense of the handkerchief. I stuffed this back in my pocket, hoping I would not have to empty my pockets and be charged with having a dirty handkerchief. I replaced the chair and gingerly tiptoed back to the door, just as the OC and CSM left Hut 7. I straightened my beret, pulled down my battledress blouse and checked that my BD trouser bottoms were still tucked into my socks and had not ridden up from the anklets.

I hoped I wasn't sweating too much. However, I felt it more important not to let my mates down over the state of the hut, rather than ensuring that I was in good order. It was a risk I had to take. The two strode purposely up the hill towards me. The CSM's eyes darted to the left and to the right, not missing anything.

I came smartly to attention (at least I hoped it was smartly), saluted ('Up, two, three. Down, two, three.') 'Good morning, Sir. Hut No 8 ready for your inspection, Sir.'

The OC returned my salute. 'Morning, Caffyn'. The CSM, in the meantime was visually giving me the once over.

They entered the hut. The OC and the CSM obviously had a plan. The former took low level and the latter high level. They were thorough in their inspection. The CSM, donned his white gloves and ran his hands along the beams, the lights and over the stoves and lumps of coal. I was so relieved that when he had finished, his gloves were still white. The OC concentrated on our beds, bedblocks, the layout of our kit, and the cleanliness of our eating irons, especially the state of our mugs.

Finally, after what seemed an age.

'Not bad, Caffyn. The beds could do with more straightening though, and the floor there,' he pointed to where I had tried to erase the scuff marks caused by the chair and my boots, 'Needs more work on it. But an improvement on last week. I think you need to tidy yourself up a bit more though. What do you think, Sergeant-Major?'

I quaked in my boots. Once the CSM got going on me, it would be a miracle if I didn't have my name taken.

'SIR.' The Sergeant-Major looked me up and down, as I stood rigidly to attention, and then walked round me. 'Show me hour hands.'

'Here we go,' I thought, as I held out my hands. The CSM looked closely at them, and then checked that my nails were clean.

'You'll just pass, Caffyn. But if you are going to carry a handkerchief, don't stuff it in your pocket with the end sticking out so the whole world knows you've got one. I DON'T WANT TO SEE IT. You had better get a grip on yourself otherwise next time your name will be taken. UNDERSTAND'

'Yes, Sergeant-Major.'

'Right. Carry on, Caffyn.'

I saluted and breathed a very deep sigh of relief as the two of them walked away down the hill to the Company Offices. I felt as if I had aged ten years in fifteen minutes. The weekly hut and kit inspection was stressful enough to give one ulcers. Still, I thought I had detected the slightest twinkle in the CSM's eyes when he ticked me off about the handkerchief. He probably knew full well that I had used it for a panic bit of last minute cleaning.

Fifteen minutes later the others came hurrying back, with worried looks on their faces. However, when they saw the broad grin on my face, they all visibly relaxed.

The Saturday morning inspection assumed even greater importance, for after a month, the Army reckoned that we were sufficiently militarised to be allowed out of Camp on thirty-six hour passes; so long as the hut successfully passed the Saturday morning inspection, otherwise a failed one would result, at the very least, in the members of the hut having to go through the whole procedure once again before getting their passes, or at worst, the whole hut having their weekend passes cancelled.

~

One of the things we missed most was, for the first few weeks, being completely cut off from the outside world. We saw no newspapers, had no radios and were not allowed out of Camp. The Third World War could have started, and we would have been none the wiser. Letters from home were our only source of news.

Late one Saturday afternoon as we were relaxing in our hut, Peter Sykes who hailed from Yorkshire, was glancing through some back copies of the Daily Telegraph, which he had picked up after doing some fatigues in the Officers' Mess, when he looked up and said to me:

'Anthony, you come from Eastbourne, don't you?'

'Yes, well a few miles north though. Why?'

'Well, according to this newspaper, there was a major train crash at

Eastbourne Station, where the report says several passengers were killed, but one of the survivors was a Robert Caffyn. Any relation?' He handed me the Daily Telegraph.

'Yes, he's my cousin.' I quickly read the article. Apparently, one Monday after I was called up, Robert, who was returning to London to continue his accountancy course after spending the weekend at home, was sitting in the front part of the first carriage of the London bound train. In the late 1950s there was an overnight train from Stirling to Eastbourne, and as the train approached the station, it was routed onto the wrong line and the steam locomotive ploughed into the waiting London train. Apparently, several of the passengers in the front of the London train were killed, but Robert, was one of the very few lucky ones, and after major surgery, recovered to lead a normal life.

'Bloody marvellous!' I thought. 'It's typical of our family not to pass on the news.'

If it hadn't been for Pete Sykes happening to spot the article, I would have gone home on our very first thirty-six hour weekend pass since joining the Army, without knowing about the train crash, and I wondered when I would have been told about the accident. In fact, I felt so pissed off with the family about not being told the news about Robert, that I did not bother to take the weekend pass and stayed in Camp.

~

We quickly settled into Camp life, and soon learnt not only the correct routines, but also what to avoid. This also applied to which officers, sergeant-majors and sergeants should be given a wide berth. There was one subaltern, who when he was orderly officer, and was carrying out the duty of inspecting the cookhouse and asking if there were any complaints, had a very nasty habit of making a beeline for 'D' Company personnel, recognisable by our white shoulder flashes, and minutely inspecting our mugs. When we knew he was orderly officer, we made a special point of ensuring our mugs were spotless. Duraglit was especially good at removing dirty marks and stains. I never found out why this subaltern had a 'down' on us potential officers. I can only imagine that, as a regular he was suffering from a chip on his shoulder and felt it was beneath his dignity serving in a training battalion, and possibly suspected that after we had been commissioned, we were probably going to be posted to more exciting overseas units. Such deployments he possibly felt, should be the exclusive prerogative of regular subalterns, and National Service subalterns should only be posted to training battalions.

I often wondered whether the other recruits in the Battalion resented us in 'D' Company. Not a bit of it. The ones we met in the NAAFI were not at all envious, rather the reverse, they pitied us, as one other recruit said to me:

'We feel sorry for you lot in 'D' Company. Life is much tougher for you. We've only got eight weeks of basic training and then we should end up in a cushy unit.'

He certainly had a point. A business colleague of mine did his National Service in REME as a vehicle mechanic some two years before me, and was posted to Cyprus. Bar from living under canvas in a lovely Mediterranean climate for the two years, where life was decidedly unmilitary, and although the EOKA troubles had started, the REME Base Workshop was not in the direct 'line of fire'.

~

During basic training, the Army did not believe in 'idle hands'. We were kept fully occupied, but our training became more interesting as we progressed further into the Course. We were still subjected, although in a more gentle way, to the process of having all our civilian traits knocked out of us, and turning us into what could best be described as military automatons, conditioned to accept discipline and to obey orders without question. As one senior NCO put it to us:

'If in the heat of battle you were ordered to charge the enemy, or carry out some dangerous task and you questioned the order, not only could you end up dead, but you could also jeopardise the lives of your mates. So, when you are told to jump, you don't ask how high. You just jump as high as you can.'

For the first two weeks of basic training, we concentrated on drill and fitness, the 'bulling' of our gear, the standards that we were expected to reach and maintain with our kit and hut cleanliness.

After ablutions, breakfast, kit and hut cleaning, we assembled for muster parade, dressed accordingly to the days' timetable. We might have started in PT kit for an hour of physical exercise in the gym, with the Physical Training Instructors really making us work hard. We became very proficient in press-ups and sit-ups, which seemed to be the standard punishment drill. However, the muscles we developed did help on the Assault Course. The PTIs had this delightful habit of keeping us to the very end of the hour, which left us very little time to double back to our hut and change into, probably denims for our next activity without being late and having our names taken. This could have been weapon training, where in a lecture room we would be instructed in the workings of the Lee Enfield rifle, the Bren LMG or the Sterling sub-machine gun. We learnt how to strip, clean and reassemble each weapon and how to overcome blockages, which mainly applied to the Bren, as any problems with the rifle and Sterling were mainly caused through incorrectly loaded magazines.

I liked the Bren Mk 2, which had originally come into service in 1937. The gun was originally of Czech design; the name an amalgam of <u>Br</u>no, the factory in Czechoslovakia where the gun was initially produced and Enfield, the British Company who manufactured it. I had first come across the Bren in the CCF at school, where in order to pass Cert 'A' Parts I and II, we had to be able to strip and reassemble the light machine gun within a set time. Desmond Hill, my form master at 'Teddies' who was also a captain in the CCF, used to blindfold us, so that we were able to strip and reassemble a Bren with our eyes closed in well under a minute. This entailed removing the barrel, the bipod, the butt, the magazine, the piston, the breechblock and the gas chamber. The magazine held twenty-nine rounds, which were rapidly shot off if we were firing on the 'automatic' setting and not the 'single' round one. If one had sufficient loaded magazines and the No2 on the Bren was mustard on changing these, the LMG was capable of a cyclic rate of fire of 500 rounds per minute. The Bren had a reputation, due to its accuracy, reliability and ease of maintenance of being one of the best LMGs ever made, and it continued in service with the Army well into the 1990s, although it had been modified to fire the standard NATO 7.62mm ammunition.

As one of our instructors told us; 'The only disadvantage of the Bren is that it is too accurate, and if firing the gun on automatic and using the bipod, it is difficult to get a wide spread of shot.

If the gun stopped firing; there were two actions that had to be carried out, the first IA (immediate action), 'Cock the gun. Mag off. New mag on. Carry on firing.' The second IA, similar to the first, had to be carried out if a round had become jammed and had not ejected properly.

There was a small range at Honiton, and one afternoon a few weeks into our training, we paraded in battle order and were marched down to the range to live fire the LMG.

'Right, listen in and pay intention,' said Sgt Henderson. 'Remember when you get down, you lie with your legs straight out behind the gun. It's not like firing the rifle when you have your legs splayed out at an angle from the gun. Also when you fire, especially on 'rapid' fire the Bren has a tendency to run away from you. So firmly hold the pistol grip with your left hand keeping the butt pressed into your shoulder. Okay?'

'Yes, Sergeant.'

'Right. To start with, you will be firing single rounds, and then you will move onto rapid fire. This should be a short burst of three to four rounds. I do not want one of you jokers to fire off your magazine in one long sustained burst. If anybody does that, he will be cleaning all the Brens by himself at the end of the shoot. Also, when you have finished firing, DO NOT touch the barrel. It will be very hot. Do I make myself clear?'

'Yes, Sergeant.'

'If there is a problem with a gun, lie the butt down and raise your right arm, and wait for me or one of the corporals to come to you. Don't move the gun, and NEVER point it towards anybody. Okay. Now, No 1 Section line up behind the firing point, No 2 Section behind No 1, and then No 3 Section. Move.'

We swiftly got into position. The corporals came round with .303 ammunition, and taking the Bren magazine we had been given from one of our webbing ammunition pouches, we nervously loaded the magazine; for many of the platoon this was the first time they had handled live ammo.

The first detail was called forward. Soon the sound of the LMGs firing assailed our ears and reverberated around the camp and probably the town as well. Although safety was of paramount importance, the 'health' part of Health and Safety had not at the time been thought of, so ear defenders had not become standard issue. Was this, I wondered why sergeant-majors and drill sergeants always screamed and shouted whilst taking drill. They had no doubt been firing infantry weapons for so many years, that their hearing was possibly impaired and they could only hear themselves by shouting.

Eventually my turn came. I lay down behind the Bren, legs stretched out straight behind me. I checked the leaf back sight and snapped the magazine into place. I firmly grasped the pistol grip, cocked the gun, set the safety catch to 'on' and waited the order to fire.

'Right. Range 50 yards. Target to your front. Five single aimed shots. Shoot!'

Adjust sights; set to 'single' rounds; safety catch off; line up the foresight on the centre of the static target and squeeze the trigger. My ears rang with the noise of the gun firing, as I pressed the trigger five times. As this was our first live firing practice, our shots were not being spotted. The LMGs fell silent as our detail completed the single rounds shoot.

'Okay. Same range, same target. Rapid fire. Shoot.'

I set the Bren to 'automatic' and squeezed the trigger. The gun seemed to explode in my grasp, and I had great difficulty in preventing it running away from me. On 'automatic' the gun fired so fast that it was difficult to only shoot off four or five rounds. The hot spent cartridges, which were ejected from the bottom of the gun hit the matting on the concrete firing point and spun away in various directions. The noise was deafening as six Brens in a somewhat enclosed firing point let rip simultaneously. I found it exhilarating. Suddenly I felt a sharp pain on my left cheek. I ignored it and went on firing. The pain got worse. I stopped firing and put my hand up to my cheek and withdrew it immediately as my fingers touched a very hot metal object.

'What's wrong with you, Caffyn?' snarled the sergeant.

'There's something burning my cheek, Sergeant.'

'Detail. Stop firing. Apply safety catches and rest your guns. Corporal Jones. Go and see what Caffyn is whinging about.'

The Corporal came over, bent down and removed an object from the chinstrap of my helmet.

'It's a spent cartridge case, Sergeant,' explained the Corporal.

'Right, Caffyn. Get down to the MRS and have your face checked.'

When a round was fired, the exploding cordite in the cartridge generated great heat, with the result that the brass cartridge was extremely hot as it was ejected from the gun. One of these had bounced off the concrete and lodged between my cheek and the chinstrap of my helmet.

The wound, if that is how it could be called, was treated and covered with a burn dressing, which I had to keep on for a few days to prevent infection. I was left with a scar, which over several years gradually disappeared, although it was more noticeable when I had a suntan. However, I did have some puerile fun, trying to impress girl friends who would ask me how I got the scar.

'Well,' I explained, 'I was once shot at by a Communist Terrorist in Malaya, and that is where the bullet creased me.'

'Yes, but why didn't it take your ear off?'

'Oh, I moved my head away just in time.'

Ouch! That was pathetic! That must have been one of the worst ever jokes. It certainly did not impress girls and was probably a 'turn off' for them.

~

For the first few weeks, 'Square Bashing' was a real pain. Not only did we find many of the drill orders confusing, but also constantly being shouted and sworn at by the NCOs generally had a negative effect on us.

Drill movements such as: 'Quick March'. 'Halt.' 'Left or Right Wheel.' 'Left or Right Turn.' 'About Turn.' 'Mark Time.' We could understand and comply with. But, such orders as 'The Platoon will advance in column of threes', or ' Move to the Left (or Right) in Threes' were initially quite bewildering. Initially I wondered, after we had 'fallen in' on parade and carried out the order: 'Right Dress' (to get into three equally spaced straight lines) on our Right Marker, why we were then ordered 'By the Left – Quick March.' Why not –'By the Right – Quick March.'

Obviously, the more drill we did, the better we became as we began to understand such phrases as: 'advance', 'retire', 'column' and 'line'. There were many others. We also became quite inured to the insults thrown at us: 'Swing those fuckin' arms.' 'Can't you count? You useless piece of shit.' 'You there, stand up straight! You look like a fuckin' sack of fuckin' potatoes.' 'What are you, nine bleedin' months pregnant?' 'Come on move yourself like a bleedin' politician caught coming out of a brothel.'

'You there in the second rank, yes you in the middle. Why are you grinning like a demented baboon? Come here. What is so fuckin' funny?'

'Nothing, Corporal.'

'Right. Take that fuckin' grin off your face then, and double round the Square until I tell you to stop.'

There were many others, with references to parenthood, manhood, and virility being the most common, all accompanied by the Army's favourite 'f' word adjective. 'Being fuckin' idle on Parade' and 'Failing to get a fuckin' grip' resulted in names being taken, thus giving the duty corporal his evening entertainment as the defaulters paraded outside the 'D' Coy Office.

Drill was bad enough, but when this included the rifle, we started to panic as this gave an added dimension to the NCOs ability to shout, discipline and punish us. 'Slope Arms.' 'Present Arms.' 'Order Arms.' 'For Inspection - Port Arms.' 'Examine Arms.' became so second nature to us, that we could have probably executed these in our sleep. The order 'For Inspection – Port Arms' was given after we had been either firing live or blank rounds. This entailed canting the rifle across the body and opening the bolt to the time of 'One, two, three. One, two, three. One.' On the order 'Examine Arms', one took one pace forward with the left foot only and swung the rifle to the front at an upward angle, trying to avoid gauging out an eye or removing a tooth from the inspecting officer or senior NCO with the rifle's foresight. The right thumb was placed over the firing pin with the nail facing towards the barrel. This enabled the officer or NCO to peer down the barrel from the sharp end, where he was supposed to see, from the reflection of the thumbnail if there were any 'grotty' bits in the rifling of the barrel. This did depend to a large extend on the cleanliness of the thumb. After the rifle had been inspected and hopefully passed as 'clean', the rifle was returned to the 'port' position. At the end, we would be ordered to 'Ease Springs', which was not an invitation to go to the loo, but for working the bolt up and down several times of one's personal weapon, before pulling the trigger and applying the safety catch. This action was designed to ensure that there were no live or blank rounds left in the magazine.

As well as being able to carry out drill movements correctly, we had to carry them out in the right time. Many a visitor to a training camp with 'squaddies' on the Parade Ground, would no doubt have been somewhat bemused by the repeated shouts of, 'One, two, three. One, two, three.' All drill movements, with, or without rifles were carried out in 'one, two, three' time. This enabled those of us who were not very proficient in mathematics and had trouble counting, to get the right timing for drill movements. On the other hand, for all I knew, the 'one, two, three' timings may have been introduced to help junior NCOs who perhaps themselves suffered from mathematical learning difficulties. I even imagined giant metronomes with inbuilt amplification, placed to one side of the Parade Ground, which could have been beneficial in teaching us all to carry out the 'one, two, three' drill timings in unison. My imagination would sometimes get the better of me, and I would dream up rather ridiculous situations where the 'one, two, three' timings could be used.

My most tasteless one involved a lance-corporal from the Pioneer Corps who would demonstrate to the time of 'one…two…three' the correct procedure for 'bogging' down in the bushes or elsewhere. My imagination could get out of hand and almost proved counter productive during 'WASBEE'.

The poor old Pioneer Corps, which did such important work, was rather a butt for jokes during my National Service. Alas, the Corps is no longer, having been absorbed into the RLC, officially the 'Royal Logistic Corps', but more commonly known as the 'Rather Large Corps'.

Eventually, we became fairly good at drill. However, we never overcame the fear of Drill Parades. It was the easiest way of ending up on a charge for even the tiniest of mistakes. When we had the CSM, the Platoon Sergeant, and the Corporals on parade together, all shouting at us at the same time, it was a wonder that we remained on the same planet, as it was so difficult sometimes amongst all the noise of screaming voices and the stamping of boots – ammunition, to hear an order.

It became even more difficult to carry out drill movements correctly, when the platoon was divided up into two or three squads. Three NCOs bawling out orders at the top of their voices, trying to control the squads as we marched and counter marched across the Square, in competition with other platoons who were also going through the same drill exercises.

'No 1 Squad, RIGHT…. (We heard '…TURN.') …WHEEL.'

Inevitably, the rear half of the squad would turn right, whilst the front half right wheeled. The result being that the two halves of the squad marched across the Square in the direction of the Battalion Offices as two independent sub-units, one in-line ahead and the other in-line abreast formation.

'Halt! You miserable scumbags.' The Corporal would scream. However, which Corporal and which miserable scumbags was he addressing? We had to make a decision, and fairly quickly, as the Camp entrance and the Guard Room were getting dangerously close, and before too long we would be crossing the A30, no doubt much to the alarm of passing traffic.

Fortunately, the decision was taken out of our hands, as our Corporal abandoning any semblance of dignity and authority, broke the Army fifty-yard hob nailed boot sprint record, by reaching us before we went AWOL. At the same time another Army record was broken as his voice, normally a baritone went up several octaves, and he was in danger of permanently becoming a counter-tenor. His complexion described the colours of the rainbow, and ended up as a deep and mottled puce. He was so apoplectic, that it took a minute or two before his voice returned to normal and he became coherent. By this time, we felt sorry for him and expressed our hope that none of his symptoms were permanent.

Although, in the majority of cases, genuine mistakes were made on drill parade; there were times when we were being drilled by an unpopular junior NCO, and we would collectively become hard of hearing and end up, either marching off the Square, or having a face-to-face confrontation with another squad, approaching us from the opposite direction.

'Sorry, Corporal, with all the shouting going on, we really didn't hear you.' We could get away with this excuse two or three times with the same NCO, but even the thickest lance-corporal would smell a rat if we played the trick too often.

'Square bashing' appeared fairly straightforward when an NCO was drilling us. But, when each of us individually had to drill the Squad, the fun really started and drill suddenly became difficult and complicated. The poor recruit initially selected to drill the Squad, would smartly march out to the front, with the rest of us grinning and sniggering. The NCO quickly stamped out the noise, and threatened us with the evening defaulters' parade. We very soon learnt that we needed the co-operation of the whole Squad if we were to be successful as drill instructors.

'No! Caffyn. You're a stupid lump of lard,' screamed the Corporal. 'You give the order to 'ABOUT TURN' as the other foot reaches the ground, and 'HALT' on the right foot. Now get them to swing their fuckin' arms properly. You are in charge. Act like a man and not a fuckin' mouse.'

'Yes, Corporal.' A deep breath. 'Squad. By the right. QUICK MARCH. LEFT, RIGHT, LEFT, RIGHT. SWING THOSE ARMS PLEASE'.

'SQUAD. HALT.' This from the corporal, as the Squad continued to march away from me and out of my vocal range.

'Caffyn. I'll give you LEFT, la–de–da, bloody RIGHT. You are not drilling a load of poncing ballerinas. It's 'EPP EIE, EPP EIE'. You really are a useless piece of shit. And 'ow the fuckin' 'ell do you expect the Squad to 'ear your commands, if you say them as if you're whispering into the ears of the local fuckin whore.'

'Yes, Corporal.'

'Louder.'

'Yes, Corporal.'

'Louder.'

'YES, CORPORAL.'

'That's better.'

The Corporal turned to the Squad.

'As for you lot. You're a load of fuckin' scumbags. You're all fuckin' idle, and you're all fuckin' dosey. You're spending too much time in your fucking wankin' pits. If you don't start getting a fuckin' grip of yourselves, I'll 'ave you out here for a fuckin' 'ours drill before breakfast for the next fuckin' week.'

''iggins. You fuckin' should know how to march properly by now. You swing one bleedin' arm straight out to the front, reaching shoulder height, with your balled fist tightly closed and the thumb on top pressing down on it, and you force your other fuckin' arm straight back behind you as far as possible. YOU,' as the Corporal went eyeball to eyeball with 'iggins, 'DO NOT FUCKIN' BEND YOUR ARMS LIKE A FUCKIN' WINDMILL. SO STOP TAKING THE PISS AND DOUBLE ROUND THE SQUARE UNTIL I TELLS YOU TO STOP.

'Now the rest of you fuckin' scum bags. Stop taking the fuckin' mickey out of your Squad leader and drill properly. Do I make myself fuckin' clear?'

'Yes, Corporal.'

'Louder.'

'YES, CORPORAL.'

'Okay. Let's try it again Caffyn, and get it right this time.'

~

And so it went on. The same routine day after day. We had at least one daily period of 'square bashing'. This was usually taken by one of the corporals. Sgt Henderson would often take over, and very occasionally, if he was feeling in a bad mood, the Company Sergeant-Major would take the drill period. We dreaded this, for not only did the CSM have eyes in the back of his head, but also with the Platoon Sergeant and Corporals in attendance, the shouted commands and admonishments, in conjunction with the alarmed shrieks from crows, rooks and magpies in the woods must have been heard miles away in Budleigh Salterton. Birds resting in their nests would decamp rapidly and set out on an early migration when the CSM let loose. He was also a dab hand with his pace stick, not only using it as it should be, but also as an offensive weapon jabbing us in the chest when one of us incurred his displeasure, which was frequently, and the evening defaulters parade usually included most members of the Platoon.

~

After we had been at 2 Trg Bn for a fortnight, we were told that we were going to be let loose the following evening on the unsuspecting burghers of Honiton.

This was going to be the first contact we had had with the outside world since we reported for duty. We had no wireless, no television (rare anyway) and no newspapers. I doubt we would even have been told if England had won 'The World Cup'. Although we did have a weekly lecture on 'current affairs' given by the platoon commander, who was more interested in updating us on relations between the USSR and the West, the state of play in Cyprus and our African Colonies, rather than discussing cricket, football and other interesting bits of 'home' news.

We pressed our best BDs, blancoed our belts and gaiters, polished our brasses and 'bulled' our best boots until we could see our faces in the gleaming toecaps. There was nothing more demoralising than to be inspected by the duty sergeant at the Guard Room, and sent back to our billets because he felt that we were 'in shit order' and not fit to be unleashed on the sophisticated citizens of Honiton. There was a large mirror fixed to the wall outside the Guard Room, which was meant to help us ensure that we were in 'good order' before being subjected to the eagle eyes of the guard sergeant.

Anyway, that first evening we all passed 'muster' and turning right out of the Camp, on to the main A30 we walked in what we took to be a smart military fashion along the town's long and straight High Street, passing tourist cafés, lace shops and a couple of down-market looking pubs, before we 'invaded' one which took our fancy.

We were still very naïve at this early stage of our military life, and we did not appreciate that a too smart a pub would attract officers or warrant officers, which from our very low position in the military chain was not a good idea. Similarly, with our white shoulder 'D' Company flashes, denoting we were potential officers material, frequenting a pub mainly used by recruits from other companies could possibly result, especially after a few pints, in aggravation with derogatory remarks about 'fuckin' 'erberts' being banded about. This also was not a good idea, for we soon learnt that our company commander, other officers, warrant officers and sergeants took an extremely dim view of 'D' Coy recruits brawling with those from other companies.

As we waited at the bar to be served, we looked round taking in the warmth and comfort of the pub with the quiet murmur of voices coming from the saloon bar. We looked at each other and realised that there was still a sane and normal world going on outside our monastic Camp life.

Not liking the taste of beer, preferring scotch, I perversely ordered a pint of 'Scrumpy' cider.

'Have you had it before?' The barman asked.

'No,' I replied.

Obviously, he was used to 'sprogs' from the Camp, pouring rough cider down alcohol-deprived throats as if 'bingeing' was going out of fashion. The cider tasted like nectar to us, and it did not take many seconds before second pints were on the way. We were well into these when one of our corporals in mufti came into the pub. Seeing us he came over, and turned down our offer to join us.

'Look,' he said, 'This may be your first time out, but I warn you, just as your behaviour in Camp is watched, so is it watched out of Camp as well. Brawling and staggering drunk back to Camp will result in being thrown into the cells in the Guard Room and being charged to appear before the Company Commander. You could even be RTUd. So, watch it! Okay?'

'Yes, Corporal. Thank you.'

There it was; if we were hoping to be commissioned, then we were expected to conduct ourselves in a manner befitting officers, but without actually being one; neither could we 'mix-it' with the recruits from the other companies. All in all, we were rather 'in-limbo', until such time as we had passed the War Office Selection Board (WOSB), and passed into Mons Officer Cadet School at Aldershot. The threat of being Returned-to-Unit always hung over us like the Sword of Damocles.

The corporal's words had a sobering effect on us, so as 2200 hours approached we were a rather staid, but slightly merry bunch as we reported to the Guard Room. The duty sergeant watched us like a hawk, just waiting to pounce if one or more of us showed any sign of drunkenness. He would have had us on 'a fizzer' so fast, that out feet would not have touched the ground, and we would no doubt have been charged with 'behaviour prejudicial to military good order and discipline' or something like it.

Still it was good to be let out into civilisation; it did wonders for our morale and surprisingly we had even begun to feel like soldiers. Although we did not appreciate it at the time, those in authority must have had some faith in us with the training we had received to that date and had confidence that we were not likely to disgrace the Battalion or the Cap Badge.

Reality returned once we were back in our hut, and it was all 'stops out' to blanco our webbing, shine our brasses and polish our boots ready for the next days' activities.

Chapter Four

Later Days. 'D' Coy 2 Trg Bn REME

As our training progressed, we spent an increasingly amount of time out of camp. In the centre of Honiton was the turning off to Sidmouth. The road climbed steeply up Gittisham Hill, zigzagging through woods of oak, elm, and birch trees. At the top of the hill just before the turning off to the village of Gittisham was the popular 'Hare and Hounds' Inn. Opposite the pub was Gittisham Heath, a large area of common land.

In a car it was a very pleasant drive from Honiton up Gittisham Hill. However, we were not in the fortunate position of having transport to take us up the hill to the training area. It was our sad lot that we had to use 'shanks's pony', and our NCOs liked nothing better than to route march us up the hill in full battle order. Although autumn had set in, there were days when the weather was very warm, and it was on those days that we were invariably made to march up to the Heath. In full battledress with cross straps, weapon pouches, small packs, water bottles and bayonets in their scabbards attached to our web belts, with helmets perched precariously on our heads and our rifles at the 'short trail', we stomped up the hill, sweating profusely, whilst the corporals, not in battle order circled around us like a pack of hounds snapping at our heels.

At least we marched mainly in the shelter of the trees, which made the conditions slightly more bearable. It was always a relief when we reached the top and turned off onto the Heath. There we were allowed to rest and drink from our water bottles. We eyed the 'Hare and Hounds' with great longing. It was usually at this moment that the platoon sergeant and corporals, on the pretext that they either needed to hold an Orders ('O') group to organise our activities, or to take a 'leak', would take off to 'ease springs' in the pub; which seemed to take for ages, and there would be a strong smell of beer when they returned. However, when we asked if we could go to the Gents, the answer came back 'to use the ferkin' bushes'.

Eventually, after we had passed 'WASBEE', we would also be allowed into the public bar, where on the walls were displayed the cap badges of every regiment and corps in the British Army. When we had been allowed to take refreshment at the pub, the return journey down the hill was usually carried out with a certain light heartedness and at the cracking light infantry rate of 140 paces to the minute, as opposed to the normal infantry plod of 120 paces to the minute!

The open area at the top of Gittisham Hill was common land, so there was a limit to the training we could carry out. The locals would not have been very happy, if whilst walking their dogs a bunch of warlike - at least to the dogs and their owners - soldiers, suddenly emerged from the trees and bushes firing blank rounds and letting off thunder flashes as if the Third World War had started. No doubt there would have been a lot of stressed and neurotic dogs together with their owners requiring psychiatric treatment.

The training was low key, and generally centred around the use of the Army's prismatic marching compass, a splendid piece of kit; its solid brass case was painted black for service use, which protected the high quality liquid dampened movement, with the degrees and minutes being read through a Tritium illuminated 24 magnification prism. We learnt to march on a fixed bearing, to take back bearings, how to find 'South' using one's watch and how to judge distances.

'Field craft' was fun. Learning how to make the best use ground and how to make the best use of cover:

'Never look over cover, either look round it or through it, otherwise you're liable to have your head blown off.'

When moving across open ground:

'Never cross the skyline of a hill, you'll stick out like a bunch of pregnant fairies.'

How to describe objects using the clock face method:

'To your front. Four hundred yards at ten o'clock bushy topped tree, enemy in hedge at base. Five rounds rapid – FIRE.'

We became proficient in the various crawls, the 'leopard' being the most used.

'Keep your ferkin' arse down Caffyn, it's sticking up like a blue arsed baboon.'

Even though we were REME cap badged and members of a technical corps, we nevertheless had also to be trained as fighting soldiers. So, we were instructed in the use of infantry weapons.

From an obviously long-serving Staff Sergeant: 'This 'ere is the two-inch mortar. A 'andy and effective two man platoon weapon. Jones, come 'ere! You are Number One on the mortar. You either lies down, with your feet straight behind you on the ground, or you kneel on your right knee, with your bent left leg pointing to the left. You 'olds the mortar tube low down in your left 'and, firmly bed the base plate in the ground in front of you and point the mortar towards the enemy. There ain't no sights, you 'ave to guess the distance and angle, and you 'old the firing lever lanyard in your right 'and. Now Smith 528, come over 'ere and squat down to the left of Jones. You takes the mortar bomb in your right 'and and you guides it down the tube, at the same time you continues to slide your 'and down the mortar, else your 'mucker' could pull the fuckin' lever with your 'and waving about over the barrel like a fuckin' windmill. If you 'ain't taken your fuckin' 'and away, you ain't going to 'ave one; the same with your bleeding 'ead if you get it in the way. If you 'ain't firmly bedded down the base plate, it will shoot backwards or sideways when the mortar fires, and you ain't going to be able to fuck anything. Don't point the mortar straight up, otherwise you'll and end up mortaring yourself.' Right! Let's try it. Jones, point the mortar to your front, up a bit, and grab the lever in your right 'and. Smith 'ere's the bomb. 'Old it in your 'and and guide it into the barrel with your 'and sliding down the tube. Where are you lot going? It's all right. It's a DP mortar and bomb. You're a load of sissy, mambee pambee mummies boys!' Whilst I waited my turn, I felt that in the wrong hands this weapon could pose more of a danger to our side than to that of the enemy.

~

It was a balmy September day, warm, very little breeze with white fluffy clouds chasing each other across the sky in a rather leisurely fashion. We lay relaxing on the soft and dry grass after our march up Gittisham Hill. Our NCOs were one again enjoying the facilities of the 'Hare and Hounds'.

'I wonder what delights they're planning for us,' mused John Howard. 'Whatever it is, it's no doubt going to cause us grief.'

'Watch out, here come the heavy mob.'

'Right! On your feet you dozy lot. Come on! MOVE your fat arses.' L/Cpl Garner had so much charm.

'Now,' said our rather venerable Staff Sergeant Instructor, 'this 'ere is the rifle grenade launcher.' We were becoming accustomed to the silent 'h', as 'e 'eld (it's catching) it up for us to inspect, what looked like a metal tea mug with no handle but with an attachment at one end.

'It 'ain't fired much as it buggers up the rifle if used too much. It fires a grenade about eighty yards, further than a grenade can be thrown. Now, you fixes this end 'ere to the front of your rifle. You loads this special cartridge into the magazine. You kneel as you do with the two inch mortar, but you jam the base of the rifle firmly against your 'ip and you 'old it inverted with the trigger on top. With your left 'and you places the grenade into the cup, 'aving removed the safety pin, BUT NOT the spring lever. Facing your front you point up the end of the rifle, then you squeezes the trigger and out pops the grenade. If you don't 'old the rifle firmly against your 'ip, the 'kick' will smash your 'ip bone. Also don't lower the end of the rifle, otherwise the grenade will slip out, the spring lever will fly off, and you've got about five seconds before you become strawberry jam. Also 'olding the rifle at too 'igh an angle will mean the grenade only goes a few yards, and if it lands and explodes on 'ard ground could wound or kill you, as the grenade base plate can be lethal up to two 'undred yards.'

I could imagine the enemy reacting aggressively to seeing one of us kneeling, exposed above cover and trying to fire off a grenade in their direction. I was glad I was not in the infantry, as I felt that this was a dodgy weapon and to be avoided at all times.

Another weapons lecture.

'This 'ere is the Sterling Sub Machine Gun or SMG. It is a close range weapon, most effective at about a 'undred yards; it is not particularly accurate for aimed single shots, but on rapid fire it 'oses out bullets in a wide arc. The original Sten SMG was made in great quantities during the Second World War. It was cheap to produce, but it 'ad one big disadvantage. It did not 'ave a safety catch, and if you dropped it, it was liable to go off with unfortunate results. The Sterling is a better weapon and it 'as a safety catch. The magazine slots into the left of the gun and 'olds thirty-two rounds of 9mm ammunition.'

Most of these weapon instruction lectures took place on Gittisham Heath, which was a very pleasant change from being in Camp, where one felt under the constant scrutiny of officers, WOs and NCOs waiting to pounce for some real or imaginary misdemeanour.

'You there. What's your name?'

'C....C....C....Caffyn, Sir.' This to an unknown major.

'Who taught you to salute like that? Your arm is like a donkey's hind leg, and your wrist is cocked. You're 'D' Company aren't you? Well if you expect to become an officer you must set an example, and returning a salute in a sloppy way will not earn you any respect from the other ranks. Remember, as an officer, it is not you that is being saluted; it is the Queen's commission that you hold. You will report to the Company Office, Caffyn.'

'Yes, Sir.' In the shit again.

~

September gave way to October. The mornings and evenings were drawing in, and there was a definite increase in the number of grey, overcast and damp days. It was on such a day that we were going out to the ranges between Honiton and Exeter to take part in live grenade practice.

The previous intake to us, prior to their departure to MONS OCS had tried to put the fear of God into us over the throwing of fully primed grenades.

'It's quite straightforward really, so long as you throw the grenade as far as you can in the right direction. It has been known for a recruit to be so terrified about throwing the grenade that he drops it at his feet, or he suddenly goes all weak and throws it straight up in the air, or it fails to clear the parapet and it rolls right back into the firing point bunker. Don't worry too much if that happens, you won't know much about it. The worst thing is if your grenade doesn't go off, you've got to go and retrieve it. Now, that is definitely a dodgy operation.'

Needless to say, when we were waiting to go on to Officer Cadet School, we also put the fear of God into the intake behind us.

Mid-morning the platoon embussed onto the ubiquitous 3-ton Bedford RL trucks, in a somewhat thoughtful and silent mood. After some thirty minutes, the trucks left the main road and bumped down an unmade rough track and at such a speed, that for most of us, it was a toss up which would come first, the range or losing our breakfast. Fortunately the range won. We debussed, whilst the trucks drove off and parked some distance away from the firing point. The drivers had obviously been to the range before. This really filled us with confidence, just as did the sight of an army blood wagon (ambulance) parked nearby. Those of us who had adopted a nonchalant air, 'Oh I say, I'm jolly well not worried about throwing a silly old grenade. I won the 'throwing the cricket ball' competition at my prep school's sports day,' suddenly became very quiet and turned a whiter shade of pale

Sgt Henderson marshalled us together and led us to the firing point; there laid out on a trestle table were three rows of dark green menacing looking grenades. Behind the table sat an armament sergeant, wielding what looked like a piece of surgical kit and doing unmentionable things to the grenades.

'Don't looked so goddamned worried,' laughed Sgt Henderson, 'Sergeant Graham is just putting the detonators and fuses into the grenades you will be throwing. You nearly finished, John?'

Sgt Graham, without looking up, 'I'm on the last one Bill.'

'Right, you lot. Over here, and I want you to listen very carefully to what Sgt Graham is going to tell you. Okay?'

'Yes, Sergeant,' we all mumbled, as Sgt Graham wandered over to where we were standing, nonchalantly tossing a grenade up and down in his hand.

'Right, listen in,' Sgt Graham started off. 'First off, don't ever do what I've just been doing with a grenade, tossing it up and down. This one has not had its detonator or fuse fitted. The grenade is a lethal weapon and needs to be treated with respect, and as long as you follow the ground rules, it is perfectly safe to handle. Do I make myself clear?'

'Yes, Sergeant.'

'Okay, this is the Mills 36M hand grenade, used by the British Army for many years. There are two types of grenade, defensive and offensive. The defensive grenade is designed, when it explodes to kill and maim the enemy with steel fragments. The offensive grenade mainly made of bakelite is designed to explode with the maximum amount of noise, flash and blast to the enemy, but with few lethal fragments, so there is little danger that attacking troops will be hurt. The Mills 36 grenade is a defensive one. As you can see, the body of the grenade is made of steel and is serrated. This makes the grenade fragment when it explodes. This,' pointing to a large cap near the top of the grenade, 'is where the explosive is packed. Here at the top there is the striker, the safety pin and the lever. When the safety pin is pulled out, the striker is only kept in place by the lever, which itself is held in the hand or a grenade launcher. Letting go of the spring–loaded, fly off lever, releases the striker, which strikes the percussion cap in the base of the grenade, which sets off the fuse, which in turn sets off the detonator, which then sets off the explosive and 'bang'- the grenade detonates, about five to seven seconds after the lever has been released. Do you all understand how the grenade works? Any questions?'

'Sergeant. If you let go of the lever by mistake, and you're still holding it; if you've got time, can you put the lever back in place?'

'You must be joking, Son. Once the lever has sprung off, the firing sequence has started, you've got about five seconds, to get the hell out of the way. On very hard ground the base plate can travel up to two hundred yards. Any other questions?'

He was answered by silence. 'Right, let's get on with it.' He looked to his right where 2Lt Stevens, our platoon commander was standing. 'Do you want to take over, Sir?'

'Right. Thank you, Sergeant. Now before we start, a few safety rules. We will all go down into the firing point bunker. You will all stay in the enclosed part of the bunker, and Sergeant Henderson will call you out one at a time to the actual throwing point. Once you have thrown your grenade, you will return to the bunker. If anything goes wrong outside, you are not to move, until ordered to do so. Do I make myself clear?'

'Yes, Sir.'

'Now, when it is your turn, Cpl Jones will hand you a grenade and you will join me on the firing point. You will stand sideways to the direction you are throwing, with your feet apart and firmly planted on the ground. Hold the grenade in your right hand, or left if you are left handed, with your fingers firmly holding the spring lever in place. With the grenade in front of you, pull out the safety pin, but at the same time ensuring that the spring lever doesn't fly off. On the order 'throw' extend your left arm straight out in the direction you are throwing. This will help keep your balance.

Now, fully extend your right arm, still holding the grenade and spring behind you. Count to 'two' and throw the grenade over the wall as far as you can. The spring will fly off and there will be about five seconds before the grenade detonates. Watch me.' 2Lt Stevens picked up a practice grenade and demonstrated the drill for throwing it.

'Now, I don't want any of you playing silly buggers, and trying to throw the grenade under arm, or just chuck it without taking your arm back. The grenade weighs about 2 lbs and you will only be able to throw it between twenty-five to thirty yards. Now, **and this is most important**, after you have thrown your grenade, watch and note where it lands before you duck down and take cover behind the parapet. The reason being, that if the grenade fails to explode; after waiting three minutes, I have to go out and defuse it. So, I need to know where it lands. If you drop the grenade before you throw it, or for some reason you let go of it too soon and it just goes up in the air and comes straight down, don't try any heroics like trying to pick it up or to catch it; throw yourself over the wall on your left, and I shall go over the wall on the right. Also, don't forget to take cover once you have marked its fall. I've known some recruits, who are so relieved at having thrown the grenade, they stand transfixed staring at the spot where it landed, and I've had to pull them down behind the parapet.

'I know you are all feeling apprehensive, I did when I did my basic training, but so long as you follow the correct drill, it's very straight forward. I've not had to defuse a grenade and I've not had a disaster here on the firing point, although there have been some close shaves; mainly caused by arms suddenly turning to jelly and the grenade only being thrown a few yards.

'Right. Any questions? No? Good, let's get started. Who's going first?' Dead silence.

'Okay, we'll do it in alphabetical order. Adams, you're first.'

Adams turned a whiter shade of pale, as he went to collect his grenade. We beat an undignified retreat into the shelter of the bunker and waited, with baited breath for the explosion.

From the other side of the bunker wall, we heard the muffled voice of 2Lt Stevens: 'Throw.'

A squeaky 'One, Two' from Adams. Shortly to be followed by a bellow from the Officer: 'Get down!' and almost immediately the muffled explosion of the grenade detonating.

'Well done, Adams. That wasn't as bad as you thought it was going to be, was it? Right next. Baxter.'

A few moments later Adams came into the bunker grinning from ear to ear and looking very pleased with himself, 'Piece of cake,' he bragged.

Being near the beginning of the alphabet, it was soon my turn. Cpl Jones handed me a grenade, and I checked, as we were instructed, to ensure that the safety pin and release lever were in place. I stepped forward and onto the firing point. I looked over the parapet wall, the ground to my front was pocked marked with small craters from the multitude of grenades, which had been thrown over many years. 2Lt Stevens checked that I had adopted the correct position; sideways on, holding the grenade in front of me in my right hand, with my left hand ready to pull out the ring of the firing pin.

'Ready?' He asked. I nodded, not trusting my voice, and with my legs feeling as if they were going to turn to jelly.

The order was given. 'Throw!'

I pulled out the ring, ensuring that I tightly held onto the spring loaded release lever. I raised my left arm and pointed it down range, my other arm straight out behind me. I took a deep breath, and shouted 'One, Two.' Actually, the words came out more like a strangulated squeak. With my arms gyrating like a whirling dervish, the grenade and I parted company, with the former, fortunately describing a graceful arc, if a grenade in flight can be described as 'graceful' before coming to land some twenty-five yards away. I mentally marked the spot and was down behind the parapet wall before 2Lt Stevens had shouted: 'Duck,' an order which was probably only acted upon by any of our feathered friends who happened to be in the vicinity at the time. I prayed that the grenade would detonate, and I was filled with relief, as no doubt was our Subaltern, when there was the most satisfying ear shattering crack of it exploding.

I also returned to the bunker grinning like the proverbial Cheshire Cat.

The rest of the platoon successfully threw their grenades, without dropping one or having a 'dud'. We chatted away happily as we travelled back to Honiton.

We really had got ourselves worked up over the grenade throwing exercise. What with probably watching too many war films; having the previous intake putting the fear of God into us; coupled with the thought of what would happen if something had gone badly wrong, was enough to make us feel very nervous.

~

These sudden bursts of interesting activities were interspersed with the mundane tasks of drills, PT and the constant cleaning of ones kit and the hut. We seemed to spend endless hours marching in a smart military manner to and fro; from the company lines to the Square, to lecture rooms, to the cookhouse, to the assault course, and at the end of the day, if time allowed to the NAAFI. We learnt to have eyes in the back of our heads. Officers would appear from any direction, and woe betide any of us, who failed to spot and salute them. The Battalion RSM had a nasty habit of hanging around outside battalion HQ, as if he was pacing the bridge of some navel vessel. As Battalion HQ was at ground level, it was probably more akin to pacing in his dinghy. At times he appeared to have nothing better to do than to play 'let's be nasty to 'D' Company recruits.' No doubt, this was his equivalent of a days game shooting, seeing how many 'D' Company personnel he could 'bag'. When he had his prey in his sights, he would vocally let fly. I do not know how the enemy would have reacted to his stentorian tones, but he certainly put the fear of God not only into us, but also into the sheep, cattle and horses on the neighbouring farm, which could be seen, at full gallop seeking shelter in the corners of the field furthest from the Camp. We were in such trepidation that, if we had to cross the camp to the NAAFI, we would detour round the Square and try to remain out of sight by sneaking between various huts.

~

However, there came the time when the RSM was going to exercise his professional skills, when No 2 Training Battalion REME was due to undergo its Annual Administration and Technical Inspections. All hell was let loose for weeks before the actual inspection day. We did not really appreciate what all the fuss was about. All we knew that whatever was the purpose of these inspections, it involved us in further aggro and grief; as if we hadn't enough on our plates already just to survive and get through 'WASBEE'. Obviously the promotional prospects of the Battalion's Commanding Officer and his 'fitness to command' were at stake, and he was jolly well not going to allow his command to receive a less than 'excellent' grade.

The NCOs, with ruthless efficiency applied the First Law of Basic Training: 'You can't go wrong if you paint everything that doesn't move.' For many days prior to the inspections we virtually lived and slept in our denims. The amount of paint of various colours applied around the camp, must have depleted the Army's Quartermaster's stock to a very significant amount. Obviously the cost in monetary terms of preparing for the inspections was not a consideration, neither was the use of 'cheap' labour, – us poor long-suffering recruits.

We were very quickly disabused if we thought that the standard we had achieved for the Saturday morning hut inspection was good enough for the Annual Admin Inspection. Not only was it a case of all the internal fittings being taken outside and cleaned, but also the hut was virtually dismantled plank by plank, cleaned, painted, polished and put back together again. When completed to the satisfaction of the Company Commander and the CSM., we hardly dared step back into the hut again. There was more than one semi-serious suggestion that we ought to bed down outside. This was quickly turned down, as it was felt that we would spoil the immaculately mown grassed areas, the flowerbeds, and the tarmac paths with their neat white painted edges. All this extra 'bull' was carried out on top of our normal duties. However, the worst aggro was the amount of drill to which we were subjected. Drill parade after drill parade. Not just for 'D' Company, but also for all the other companies. We even had a dress rehearsal for 'The Dress Rehearsal'!!

On the morning of the inspection, the whole Battalion was to be paraded on the Square; inspected by a bevy of high ranking officers and then marched around the parade ground by platoons and companies in both slow and quick time, to show off, hopefully, the high standard of our drill, before marching past the saluting base and disappearing in an orderly fashion to the various Company Lines.

The RSM had a field day. Actually, several such days. Although by October, the hours of daylight were drawing in; we were paraded at first light, midday and at dusk. Without decrying the standard of drill of the other companies, 'D' Company, as part of our pre-WOSB training had spent more time drilling, and we did pride ourselves on the standard we had reached. Consequently, for the parade, 'D' Company was placed in the forefront of the Battalion. We felt sorry for the recruits in the other companies. Their basic training course was shorter than ours, and when they had completed this, they were expecting to be posted, depending upon their skills as electricians, armourers or vehicle mechanics to either Front Line or Base Units either in the UK or abroad. So it must have come as a rude shock to them when they were launched into a period of sustained and intensive drill.

The WOs and Sergeants were in their element. Initially, drill rehearsals were at a platoon level with several platoons being drilled on the Square at the same time. The noise was deafening. There would be the four Company Sergeant-Majors with pace sticks wielded as offensive weapons; at least twelve Sergeants and a clutch of Corporals all screaming out orders simultaneously.

'Swing those fuckin' arms No 2 platoon.'

'Keep in step, that fuckin' idle man in the middle rank.'

'No 3 platoon, what do you look like? Stand up straight and stop ferkin' slouching along like sacks of ferkin' potatoes.'

'Sergeant Green! That man there in the rear rank of No 6 platoon he's talking. Take his name.'

'Who dropped his rifle? Right YOU! Fall out and march yourself to the Guardroom. You're under arrest.'

So it went on, day after day. We worked up from platoon drills to company drills and finally the whole Battalion was drilled as one unit, under the tender care of the RSM. Eventually, after the Company Sergeant-Majors, through excessive use had worn down their pace sticks, and the

Sergeants and Corporals had used the 'f' word enough times to fill the complete Encyclopaedia Britannica; the Commanding Officer and the RSM professed themselves satisfied that the Battalion was marching and drilling, with a certain amount of cohesion and unity.

There was one evening, which gave us much amusement. We had been warned that although we were hoping to be commissioned, a National Service subaltern was 'the lowest of the low'. It was a few days before the great day of the Inspection, and we were returning to our hut from the cookhouse, when we could hear the dulcet tones of the RSM, behind 'D' Coy HQ, carrying out what was obviously a drill parade. We wondered which poor sods had upset the RSM enough to warrant such a punishment, so we surreptitiously peered round the corner of the Company Offices, and to our great surprise and delight, all the Battalion's subalterns were going through intensive drill. We would dearly liked to have stayed and watched, but we knew if we had been spotted, we would have been in the shit right up to our necks from both the RSM and the subalterns. So, discretion being the better part of valour we beat a hasty retreat.

However, we did feel better knowing that even officers were not exempt from drill parades; although the sight of the subalterns being drilled was rather sobering, as we had been hoping, that once commissioned we would have left all that behind us.

The last few days before the Admin Inspection passed in a blur as we were chased from morning to night and from pillar to post, cleaning this, polishing that, painting the flagpole and the stones arranged around its base. Grass was mowed, and where a mower could not be used, scissors and even razor blades were used to ensure that the grass was as short as our army hair cuts. The Company Commander was much attached to the small flowerbeds dotted around the company lines, and these were subjected to regular inspections, to ensure that nature, with the help of fertilizers was preparing for the Day with flowers bursting into bloom at the right time. Aphids were dealt with just as severely as were us recruits, and weeds were instantly banished.

However, there was one problem though; the Company Commander was himself under pressure to ensure that 'D' Coy did not let him down, and as he could not do everything himself, he therefore delegated to us recruits, the responsibility for the garden. But, we soon discovered there was not one amongst us who had any horticultural knowledge whatsoever. We recognised roses, so we worked on the principle that if a plant was big enough it was probably wise not to touch it. However, the problems started when we came across small and rather insignificant flowers, as we could not decide whether they were flowers or weeds. So working on the principle that weeds left in the ground on Inspection Day would earn the Company and especially the OC some demerits, which was not a good thing, we decided to pull up everything we were not certain about.

When we had finished, there were many gaps in the flowerbeds. These we hoed, raked and removed any stones that we came across. We stood back and admired our handiwork. The grass and the beds looked very neat and well cared for.

Peace reigned for about two hours, and then the shit really hit the fan. The Company Commander decided, in the late afternoon, to inspect the results of our labours. Horror upon horror!! Many of his priceless annuals and perennials, which he had been nurturing so carefully, had vanished. We were ordered out of our huts in double quick time, and quaking in our boots we fell in outside the Company Office. We really felt we were for the high jump, as we were taken to task over our irresponsibility; and we had visions that at best we were either going to be doing fatigues for many weeks, or at worst RTUd, on the grounds that we had wilfully destroyed War Office property, which was prejudicial to good order and discipline, - namely decimating the OC's garden. Fortunately, he was wise enough to realise that we had not ruined his garden maliciously, but through ignorance had acted with the best of intentions. After a tongue lashing, we were dismissed without being charged. However, the looks that both the CSM and Sgt Henderson gave us did not bode well, and we felt that they would extract retribution from us at a later date on behalf of the Company Commander.

Eventually, the day for both the Admin and Tech Inspections arrived. Fortunately, we had not been involved in the preparation work for the Technical Inspection. However, we could see that there was a tremendous amount of 'bulling' on all the Battalion's vehicles and equipment.

In 1948, a Central Inspectorate had been set up with a Chief Inspector reporting directly to the Director of Mechanical Engineering (DME). The Inspectorate was responsible for setting the repair and maintenance standards of equipment throughout the Army. Inspection teams were sent out to carry annual inspections of a unit's vehicles and equipment to check that these standards were being maintained and to ensure that all equipment was fit for combat use.

There was no doubt that the amount of 'bull' applied to the Battalion's vehicles and equipment was impressive. Bodywork was polished; wheel nuts painted white; trailer connections painted red and tyres were blacked. The canvas canopies of the one-ton Austins and the three-ton Bedford RLs trucks were scrubbed clean and carefully fitted to their vehicles without a crease in sight. The sign writer repainted the unit and REME signs. I wondered what the reaction would have been from Battalion HQ if a sudden international crisis had arisen and the camp's vehicles had had to be deployed just prior to the Inspection. The CO, Adjutant and RSM would probably have had apoplexy. We did however, manage to sneak a look at the MT (Motor Transport) Lines the day before the Inspection. We thought we had problems preparing for the Admin Inspection, but the poor VMs (vehicle mechanics) and other craftsmen not only had the vehicles and ancillary equipment to prepare, but they also had to 'bull' the MT Lines, as well as their huts and own personal kit. The immaculately lined up vehicles and equipment certainly looked impressive, and it seemed to us 'rookies' that standards were very high; but it was debatable whether any of the vehicles and other equipment were in a battle worthy condition with all the paint and polish that had been applied. I did wonder whether there were certain 'tricks' used, such as draining all the oils out of engine sumps, gearboxes and back axles, and water from radiators to ensure there were no oil or water seepages seen during the Inspection. Probably not, as no doubt oil and water levels were checked by the inspecting officers.

The day itself was dull, dampish and rather cool. The junior NCOs rousted us out of our 'wanking' pits at a positively indecent hour. We washed and shaved as best we could in cold water, taking especial care to ensure that we did not nick our skins whilst shaving, but nevertheless ensuring that we were clean shaved. It was a chargeable offence to be unshaven on parade, which was particularly hard for those, who however well they shaved, permanently suffered from a seven o'clock shadow.

Most of us skipped breakfast, as our eating irons, mess tins and mugs had been thoroughly cleaned and polished the evening before. Our best BDs were pressed with razor sharp creases in the trousers. Although ironing through brown paper helped prevent scorching; nevertheless, there were still calls at times for a half-crown coin, which would remove a minor scorch mark when rubbed over it, unless of course, the scorch mark was too bad, and then blind panic set in. To line up on parade with the imprint of an iron on one's battle dress was not to be recommended. We folded back our BD trouser bottoms at the sides before tucking them into the tops of our socks. This kept the creases to the front. The gaiters were fitted over the tucked-in trousers, and then a bicycle chain or leads weights were dropped down the inside of trousers, and after stamping our boots on a hard surface the chain or weights ended up in the right position to give a smart overhang to the gaiters. But, woe betide anyone stamping on the highly polished, gleaming hut floor. We could have shaved in the mirror finish of the toecaps of our boots, which had been spit polished to the nth degree. Brasses and the blanco on our webbing was given a final going over, to ensure there were no white residue Brasso left on the undersides of our brasses or on our webbing. The platoon had bonded as a team and we helped each other as much as possible. On a parade day, we inspected each other and tried to ensure that we were all in 'good order'. But, however thorough we were, an officer or NCO if so minded, could always find fault. A favourite one, which I found out to my cost some months later, was when it was very cold and greatcoats were worn, one of the small buttons on the slit at the back of the coat invariably would come undone. However carefully one checked that these back buttons were correctly fastened, by the time that webbing, with perhaps pouches and small pack attached, had been fastened over the greatcoat, a back button had invariably come undone and it was impossible to see it, or do it up encumbered with so much webbing. Result: Name taken.

The greatest care was taken with our boots. We would gingerly, almost tiptoe, down to the 'falling in' point outside the Company Office. Rifle butts were held away from the boots, and the 'buddy, buddy' concept was somewhat strained at times, as there was nothing more likely to ruin a friendship than somebody else's boot landing on one's own highly 'bulled' one. The greatest risk was when the platoon had fallen-in and were being marched onto the Square. Drill had to be carried out correctly at all times, and NCOs would not tolerate anything less than total effort, even though we were trying to preserve the mirror finish of our boots before an inspection. An incorrect 'order arms' from the slope position could result in the rifle butt landing on the boot and not the ground, with unfortunate results.

At a positively indecent hour, 'D' Company, having 'fallen-in' by platoons was marched onto the Square, where other Companies were forming up. The noise was deafening, what with the Sergeant-Majors, the Sergeants and Corporals all shouting out orders, interspersed with the clump of marching boots, followed by the crash of boots as platoons and companies came to a halt. The long-suffering residents of Honiton must have thought that the Third World War had started.

'D' Company was marched to its allotted position at the centre of the Parade with the other Companies to the left and right of us. Having got our dressing, the Sergeant-Majors from the right of the parade, checked to ensure that each rank of each company was in a dead straight line. Then we were subjected to the most rigorous inspection by every warrant officer, senior and junior NCO. Berets were adjusted, BD blouses straightened, trousers creases properly aligned, and even corporals produced dusters and bent down to give boots where necessary a final polish. We were ordered to: 'Open Order. March!' Followed by: 'For inspection – Port Arms,' and then: 'Examine Arms.' The pre-inspection seemed endless. We were right dressed; dressed by the centre; we opened and closed ranks; we sloped and ordered arms and finally we practised 'Present Arms.' Eventually, the RSM and CSMs appeared satisfied with the standard of the Parade, and after the corporals and lance-corporals took up their positions with their platoons, and the sergeants had fallen-in behind their platoons, we were stood at ease, and then the order was given: 'Stand Easy.' And there we stayed, motionless for over an hour, with nothing apparently happening. Bladders were beginning to feel uncomfortable, and at one time there was a crash to my right as a rifle fell to the ground followed by its owner as he collapsed to the ground in a dead faint. He was hurriedly removed from the Square and deposited in the Medical Reception Centre and his platoon 'closed up'. The weather had not improved, it was still cool and damp, but fortunately there was no wind. However, hands and feet were beginning to become numb, and as far as one could in the 'stand easy' position, toes were wriggled and fingers stretched as surreptitiously as possible. Eventually, after what seemed like an age, officers started to appear from various parts of the Square and lined up in front of RHQ. The order: 'Fall in the Officers' was given, and they smartly marched across the Parade Ground and took post in front of their companies and platoons.

Then there was a further wait. The Guard of Honour had lined up outside the Guard Room. The REME flag fluttered lazily in whatever breeze there was from the flag-pole, just in from the main entrance. Bladders were definitely stretched; the desire to scratch grew as irritating itches suddenly started up. Throats inexplicably became ticklish and it became increasingly difficult to suppress coughs.

After what seemed like an eternity, there was a flurry of activity at the Main Gate. The Guard came to attention and sloped arms, as staff cars at speed swept in from the main road and just managed to stop before the Guard of Honour would have been forced to take evasive action. The Battalion second-in-command with his back to us, which made carrying out his orders a bit tricky, as he did not have the strongest of voices, shouted:

'PARADE!' We came from easy to at ease.

'PARADE!' By now, we had definitely got the message, and could reasonably guess with a fair degree of accuracy what was coming next.

'ATTENSHUN.' The sound of boots crashing down on the tarmac echoed and re-echoed around the Square. We still had not achieved the Brigade of Guards single thundering 'crack'. Still it probably was not too bad for a Training Battalion, and no longer sounded like 'The Clog Dance'

From the corner of my eye, I could see a bevy of 'brass' debussing from their staff cars as the Guard of Honour 'Presented Arms.' The Battalion's Commanding Officer saluted, and after a brief conversation, the CO led a Brigadier and his entourage in our direction.

'PARADE! PARADE!' This from the 2i/c. 'SLOPE ARMS!' Up–Two–Three. Across-Two-Three. Cut away-Two-Three.

As the Brigadier and his entourage approached.

'PARADE!' Here we go again. 'PARADE! PREEE – SENT ARMS!' Right arms shot across our bodies and right hands grabbed the small of the butt of our rifles and carried them across in front of our faces, with left hands 'smacking' the underside of the rifles near the upper swing swivels, causing blanco to fly off rifle slings, whilst at the same time the inside of our left wrists slapped hard against magazines, which if not fully pushed 'home', became locked in place with a most satisfactory 'crack'. Finally, rifles were turned to the front, smartly lowered to the full length of our arms; simultaneously right legs were raised and then driven hard down so that the insteps of the angled right feet ended up against the heels of the left boots. When carried out correctly the sight and sound of a unit 'presenting arms' was impressive. However, it was a drill movement, not without its dangers, for there was a risk that, in the second phase of grabbing the small of the butt and bringing the

The annual administration inspection

rifle smartly in front of one's face, of missing the butt with the rifle falling to the ground, with dire consequences to its owner. Another hazard, prior to being inspected, was ruining the polish on one's boots, if the right one came down onto the left one on the final drill movement of 'present arms'.

After the 'present', we 'sloped and ordered arms'; were then stood at ease, waiting our turn to be inspected, when we were brought to attention. The inspection proceeded at great pace, as if the Brigadier could not wait to get to the Mess for his first(?) G & T of the day. He was no doubt used to carrying out inspections, as he had obviously developed a set procedure of stopping in front of two soldiers per section.

'Oh no! He's going to stop in front of me.' Definitely a bad thing, as this gave the CO, the OC, the Adjutant, the RSM and the Platoon Commander the opportunity of inspecting me whilst the Brigadier addressed me. Five pairs of eyes must find something amiss with one's turnout.

'What's your name?'

'Caffyn, Sir.'

'How long have you been in the Army?'

'Eight weeks, Sir.'

'Enjoying Army life?'

Bloody silly question. 'Yes Sir.'

'Jolly good. Carry on.' I wasn't certain, standing rigidly to attention, how I was meant to 'carry on.'

Off he would set again, at a fair old pace. To pass the time, I mentally worked out that with three sections per platoon, three platoons per company and four companies in the Battalion, the Brigadier would stop to talk to seventy-two recruits. Add on the time for each Company and Platoon Commander to do his 'stuff' greeting the Brigadier and saluting his backside as he marched off to the next platoon, then the 'Brig' could get through each platoon in about five minutes. These meant that the inspection would

'Enjoying army life?'

take about an hour; but then add on another thirty minutes for the march past, giving a total of at least another ninety minutes to add onto the time we had been waiting on the Square, before fully distended and painful bladders could be relieved; which could result in serious internal injury to an individual and which the Army would probably consider as a self inflicted one, which was a chargeable offence.

At the start of the inspection, the Brigadier and his entourage were nicely bunched, but towards the end, the 'Brig' followed by his Staff Officer, the Commanding Officer, and the Adjutant, were starting on another platoon before the RSM, Company Commander and Platoon Commander had finished the previous one.

However, having finished the inspection, the Brigadier was led to the saluting base and prepared to enthusiastically admire the Battalion marching past in both quick and slow time; wheeling to the left and to the right; advancing and retiring in columns (or was it in line?) and generally showing off our drill skills. Eventually, we carried out the final march past, executing the 'eyes right' order as we approached the saluting base, with the exception of the right marker who marched facing 'forrard' to keep the platoon on the straight and narrow.

This proved to be a wise precaution as only he could see whether there was trouble ahead, which was just as well as we were about to ram the platoon ahead of us and which, for some inexplicable reason had decided to 'mark time'. As the whole platoon including the Platoon Commander, the Sergeant and the Corporals were at 'eyes right', our right marker, as he told me later, was about to execute a right wheel to avoid a collision, which would have resulted in the platoon disappearing down the bank at the end of the Square. Fortunately the CSM spotted the impending disaster and just in time ordered us to 'mark time' as well. There was such a back-up of platoons, that the one behind us was at 'eyes right' marking time in front of the saluting base for some considerable time. This no doubt gave the Brigadier cramp in his saluting arm before the RSM managed to unscramble the traffic jam.

Whilst the Brigadier and his retinue disappeared to the Officers' Mess, no doubt to down a well earned G & T we were marched off, and were finally dismissed outside the Company Office. We staggered up the slope to our hut, and once there we threw our webbing, berets and rifles onto our beds, before racing to the latrines or to the trees at the back of the camp. What relief!! We couldn't care less whether the hut had been inspected or not as we collapsed onto our beds, absolutely exhausted. Thank goodness, the Administrative and Technical Inspections were only an annual event. We felt better when the Company Sergeant-Major strode in and, as we struggled to our feet, congratulated us on a smart turnout and good drill. This made up to a certain extent for all the 'aggro' we had had to endure before inspection day.

~

Although most of our training took place out doors, we did have a weekly lecture given to us by John Stevens, our Platoon Commander. As we had neither access to television, which the War Office in 1958 possibly had not heard about, nor radio or newspapers, the lecture was invariably on the subject of 'Current Affairs'.

'Right settle down.' 2Lt Stevens sounded just like a schoolmaster, as we tried to make ourselves comfortable in the most uncomfortable metal chairs imaginable, which were so hard, that even the most upholstered backside would be guaranteed to be 'saddle sore' within ten minutes. 'Dozing off' was not an option.

'This period is given over to current affairs, and to keep you abreast of what is happening in the world. Now, this last week has seen the appointment of a new Prime Minister in South Africa, Dr Hendrik Verwoerd, following the death of his predecessor Johannes Strijdom. Dr Verwoerd was born in Holland and, according to the newspapers has a reputation as a hard-line race segregationist. If this is true then we may see apartheid enforced even more strongly.

'You may have heard, that Iceland has imposed a twelve mile fishing ban around its coasts, which will cause our trawler men hardship, as most of their catches come from there. An Icelandic gunboat seized one of our trawlers, the 'Northern Foam'. However a boarding party from a Royal

Navy frigate boarded the trawler and 'captured' the Icelandic seamen. Apparently, this caused quite a stir in Reykjavik and there was a demonstration of over a thousand people outside the British Embassy. This incident could lead to further confrontation between the Royal Navy and Icelandic gunboats, as the government is refusing to accept the twelve-mile fishing limit, and the Navy has been ordered to send in frigates to patrol the fishing grounds and protect our trawlers. We will have to wait and see what develops.

'What is worrying though, is that race riots have taken place in the country. White youths apparently started taunting black immigrants with racist slogans in the Notting Hill area, and when the police arrived, they had petrol bombs and milk bottles thrown at them. I hope this is not the start of race riots in this country.

'The security forces in Cyprus have started a new drive against EOKA and arrested some 2,000 Greek Cypriots. In retaliation EOKA terrorists tried to assassinate General Kendrew, the Army C-in-C.

'Finally, there is trouble brewing in Cuba. Fidel Castro, the rebel leader, who has sworn to overthrow the Batista Government, has apparently, according to the rebel's radio, started his offensive from the mountains. If Castro is successful, this could be a good thing for Cuba, as the present government is reputed to be fairly corrupt. Right, that really brings you up to date with current world affairs. Any questions?'

'Sir. Who's won the County Cricket Championship?'

'Oh, come on! Can't you do better than to worry about a bloody cricket competition? Well, if it's going to stop you asking bloody silly questions, I believe Surrey has won the Championship. Any sensible questions?'

'Sir.' This sounded just like school. 'What is meant by the word apartheid?'

'It is the policy rigidly enforced by the South African Government of racial segregation in order to maintain white supremacy.'

'You've just told us about race riots in this country. Won't the policy of apartheid cause similar but worse riots in South Africa?'

'Possibly. I believe that a minority cannot subjugate the majority forever. At some time that majority will rise up against the white minority. I certainly wouldn't want to be around when that happens. Okay. That's it. You better get off to whatever's next on your programme.'

Towards the end of our course at Honiton, we got to know John Stevens better, and he opened up to us how he much he disliked National Service and couldn't wait for his demob. He was training to become an engineer and was waiting to go up to university before rejoining the British Motor Corporation (BMC). He felt the two years of National Service had not only put back his education, but that it was going to take time for him to regain the academic standard that he had achieved when he left school at eighteen. As far as he was concerned, National Service was a complete waste of time, not helped after being commissioned, by being posted to a Training Battalion, and having to spend the best part of his two years on Regimental duties. He believed that he would have enjoyed his National Service more if he had he been posted to a REME workshop unit, preferably abroad, where he could have made use of his engineering skills. We hoped, if we passed WOSB that we wouldn't end up as subalterns in one of the REME Training Battalions. From my point of view, being posted to Blandford would have been a fate worse than death.

~

A few days after we had arrived at Honiton, I was called to the Company office, where I found that the CSM wanted to speak to me.

I came as smartly to attention as I could in my ill-fitting denims and shapeless beret, wondering what crime I had committed. One was not normally called to the Company Office, unless one had committed some heinous offence, such as not reading Company Orders, and failing to be where one should be, at a certain time to indulge in some strenuous activity.

'You wanted to see me, Sir.'

'Yes, Caffyn.' The CSM eyed me up and down, seeing if he could bawl me out for being in scruff order or something. Fortunately, as I couldn't be any scruffier than being in denims, he did not appear to find anything he could have a go at me for.

'When you completed this form at Blandford,' said the CSM, waving a buff coloured piece of paper under my nose, which probably rejoiced in being given a nomenclature of AF 2563 or something (the piece of paper that is, not my nose). 'You wrote down that you played hockey for Loughborough Colleges. Is that right?'

'Yes, Sir.'

'Okay. We've got a trials game on Saturday afternoon. You will play in the Battalion 'A' team. What position do you play?'

'Left back, Sergeant-Major'

'Oh no you don't! That's the RSM's position. You will be centre forward. Okay?'

'Yes, Sir.'

'Report to the QM stores at 1600hrs on Saturday to draw your kit and hockey stick. The match will be played on the Square at 1700hrs. Now bugger off.'

'Yes, Sergeant-Major.' 'Thank you, Sergeant-Major.' 'Up yours and bugger off yourself,' I felt like adding. I have never played as a forward in my life. What limited success I had achieved on the hockey field, had been as either at left or right back, preferably the former. Playing for the

Loughborough Colleges 1st Hockey XI in the UAU (Universities Athletics Union) Championships, my position was left back, and the team had had a very successful 1957/8 season under the captaincy of John Cadman, an England International. Still, I was out ranked, and within any Battalion or Regiment the RSM was and still is regarded as God.

Saturday came and I drew my kit from the QM stores, changed and reported to the Square at half past four. Both teams were warming up. Looking round at the other players, I realised that I was the total outsider. I recognised several officers, sergeant-majors and sergeants and of course the RSM. I appeared to be the only recruit. I felt totally overawed.

Hockey can be a dangerous game, especially if hockey sticks are raised above shoulder height (illegal), or sticks are used, not to play the ball, but to scythe at an opponent's ankles. A hockey ball hit hard and travelling at speed in the air can cause injury and is rightfully regarded as unsporting. One of my most frightening moments occurred when Loughborough Colleges 1st XI was playing an away semi-final UAU match against Nottingham University. During the match, our goal came under attack, and at one moment, with the keeper out of position, I was the only player in our goalmouth. Fortunately, I managed to block the shot, and all I could do to clear the danger was to hit the ball as hard as I could. The ball, at great speed and at knee height, departed from our pitch and shot onto the adjacent Nottingham University Ladies Lacrosse ground, where a match was in progress. I have never seen a group of players scatter so quickly, as our hockey ball, travelling like a ballistic missile, finished up against a wall at the far end of the lacrosse pitch. There was no move by the girls to give the ball back to us. It was left to me to cross their pitch to retrieve it.

The girls, many of whom would not have disgraced a women's wrestling team just stood there, with their lacrosse sticks raised in a most threatening manner in the Army 'high port' position across their well developed bosoms. If I hadn't got back-up from the rest of our team, I felt I would not have returned from the lacrosse field unscathed.

The Parade Ground where the game was to be played was not level but had a distinct slope from Honiton in the direction of Exeter, which would no doubt give an added dimension to the game.

Only ever having played hockey on grass, a tarmac surface certainly added speed to the game, even though the life expectancy of the hockey sticks would appear to be somewhat limited, as wood chips flew in all directions from the bottom of the sticks as they were scraped along the tarmac. The 'A' team won, but what was even more astonishing was that I scored my first ever goal and as a consequence I was confirmed as the Battalion's centre forward for the rest of my time at Honiton. The RSM 's position as left back was secure, which no doubt came as a great relief to the RSM.

Being in a representative team had its advantages, for when there was a match, I would miss other activities. There was one such occasion when I was very glad I was playing an away match. The Army took the subject of venereal disease very seriously and any soldier who contracted the disease would be in serious trouble. During WWII, the Army issued the troops 'Waterproofs – FLs' (French Letters). Apparently, prior to the Rhine Crossing in 1945, all Sherman Tanks needed their spark plugs waterproofed and 'Waterproofs – FLs' was found to be a most effective modification! We had been warned that during our training we would be shown the Army's film on VD. This pulled no punches and showed in vivid colour and graphic detail the dreadful effects in close up of syphilis and gonorrhoea. It was fairly normal apparently, for quite a few of the audience either to faint or be physically sick during and after the screening of the film. Whether showing it in such explicit and graphic detail actually worked as a deterrent, was debatable (probably the bromide was more effective). But from what my mates in the platoon told me after they had seen the film, I was very glad that I was in Taunton playing a match against No 8 Training Battalion, and I was thankful that I never did get to see the VD film.

I only played some half dozen games during my time at 2 Trg Bn, but one of the most memorable but tough matches was against the Royal Marines at Lympstone Camp. Their sports ground overlooked the Exe Estuary, and everywhere we looked there were small groups of marines involved in some strenuous form of physical exercise. Certainly, their hockey players were a darn sight fitter than we were, although we had better skills. It was a close fought game and we did not disgrace ourselves.

~

One activity, which I did not escape, and which none of us were looking forward to, was the gas chamber, where we were to experience the effects of tear gas. Earlier in our training, we had been given instruction on the use of our gas masks. We were taught how to quickly put them on if we heard the dreaded word 'gas'. We were told how to maintain the masks, how to check the filter and how to keep the lenses spotlessly clean.

The tear gas day arrived and we were marched over to a brick and concrete structure at the far corner of the Camp. Sgt Henderson stood us at ease and explained the procedure.

'Right.' He started. (All instructions seemed to be prefaced with the word 'Right'. It was probably the second most used word after the 'f' word.) 'Now listen carefully. There is nothing to be frightened about. We are not using full strength tear gas, but sufficient for you to experience what the effects are like.

You will, in pairs enter the chamber wearing your gas marks. You will run round the chamber, and I will set off a canister of tear gas. On a signal from me, you will take off your masks. You will continue to run round the chamber for precisely one minute, before you leave the chamber. Your throats will feel tight, your skin will tingle and your eyes will water. BUT, do not rub your faces or eyes. If any of you try to put your mask on or leave before the minute is up, you will do it all over again. Do I make myself clear?' (Another favourite NCO expression.) 'Any questions?'

'Yes, Sergeant. No, Sergeant.' We mumbled.

'Right. Let's start with No 1 Section. Corporal Jones send in the first pair in two minutes.'

Sgt Henderson, put on his gas mask, and entered the gas chamber carrying a quantity of small gas canisters. Cpl Jones ordered the first two to don masks, and having checked they were properly fitted, sent them into the chamber. A couple of minutes later, they emerged into the open air, and sank down onto the ground choking and retching, with tears running down their faces. After some two minutes the effects appeared to wear off. Being in the rear section it was eventually my turn, and in spite of the Sergeant's words I felt distinctly nervous, as Bob Howard and I stepped over prostrate bodies still coughing and spluttering.

Inside the chamber, from the light of the one small window set fairly high up in one wall, I could see Sergeant Henderson, with his mask on, standing in one corner. With the door firmly closed, he made us run round the chamber with our masks on and by the time he motioned us too remove them, we were already panting; so when he set off the canister, our lungs were very quickly filled with the gas. As we ran round the room, breathing became more difficult and eyes were streaming to such an extent that it became difficult to see where we were going. Both Bob and I were also choking and retching, our chests felt tight, our heads were spinning and we really were not feeling at all well. Eventually, after what seemed an age, Sergeant Henderson threw open the door and we staggered out into the sunlight, collapsing onto the ground, and drawing into our lungs, quantities of beautiful fresh air. As the others had found, the effects soon began to wear off.

Although we had all been apprehensive, the experience, which was bad enough, had not been quite as dreadful as we had feared; but nevertheless I would have hated to experience full strength tear gas. Upon reflection, perhaps we had; and Sgt Henderson had only said it was not full strength so as not to scare us too much.

~

Honiton could not have been regarded as the centre of the universe, and was a most law abiding town, however the Camp nevertheless, as per

Army Standing Orders, had to be properly guarded at night. To this end, a Guard was mounted at 1800 hrs every evening and dismissed at 0600 hrs the following morning. The Guard consisted of twelve soldiers, who stood turns of duty of two hours 'on' and four hours 'off'. A Duty Sergeant and Corporal were on duty at all times in the Guard Room. The Orderly Officer's tour of duty was for twenty-four hours.

We knew that we would have to stand guard at least once, or for the unlucky ones, twice whilst at 2 Trg Bn, and it was a duty that nobody looked forward to. At the end of the days' normal training, you had to clean and press your battledress, and polish and shine your kit. The Guard, at least for the Mounting Parade, had to be smartly turned out. After a quick meal, it was a rush to be ready to parade outside the Company Office to be inspected and then marched round to the Guard Room. The Orderly Officer and Duty Sergeant carried out the Guard Mounting inspection. Again, names would be taken if either of them were not satisfied with the standard of turnout. Lots were then drawn for the two hours 'on' and four hours 'off' duty roster. Three members of the Guard spent two hours patrolling around the Camp, whilst the fourth one stood sentry duty outside the Guard Room. At the end of the two hours, fully dressed with boots on, you tried to get some sleep on one of the bunk beds in the Guard Room, lying on what felt like a straw palliasse. Invariably, you would just be getting off to sleep, when the next change over would take place, and you would be awoken by the clattering noise of the new guard leaving the Guard Room and the old guard clambering up onto the bunk beds.

You would just be nodding off again, when the Orderly Officer would probably arrive to 'call out' the Guard. The person on sentry duty would turn and yell out at the top of his voice: 'CALL OUT THE GUARD!' This order would be repeated, suitably embellished by the Duty Sergeant or Corporal. Pandemonium would ensue with members of the Guard leaping and tumbling out of the bunks, falling over each other, grabbing rifles and ramming berets onto heads at any angle. We would form up in single file, whilst the Orderly Officer would give us the once over. If he felt that we had taken too long to line up, we would be subjected to a tongue lashing, and if the officer, a subaltern was in a sadistic frame of mind and suffered from insomnia, he might, an hour or so later call us out again. If this happened, the wrath of the Duty Sergeant was dreadful to behold. The range of the invective vocabulary of the NCOs never failed to amaze me. They must have had their own dedicated NCO's dictionary and phrase book. Getting on the wrong side of an irate NCO was without doubt, equivalent to being faced by an angry rhinoceros. Anyway, after the Guard 'call-out', it was back to the bunk bed and trying to get some sleep again and having just dropped off, you would be rudely disturbed by your shoulder being violently shaken to wake you up to go on duty again. Depending on which stints you had, it was probably not worth trying to get any further sleep at the end of the second tour of duty.

At 0600hrs the Guard was paraded for the last time in front of the Orderly Officer and dismissed. We would turn smartly to our right, give a rifle butt salute; march off for four paces and then break off. Back to our hut, change, wash, shave, have breakfast, and then fall in for the morning muster parade before starting on the days' activities. No wonder we were knackered for the rest of the day.

So, it was with a sinking feeling in the pit of my stomach, when one afternoon reading Company Orders, I saw my name down for the following days guard duty.

The usual mad rush to get ready and parade on time outside the Company Office. The Guard Mounting went without a hitch, and then we drew lots for the roster. As luck would have it, I drew the short straw for the 2200hrs to 2400hrs stint outside the Guardroom, and the camp patrol stint from 0400hrs to 0600hrs in the morning; which were the worst possible times, as it was far too early to get to sleep before ten o'clock, and sometime after midnight the Orderly Officer was bound to 'call out' the Guard.

Sure enough, I was still awake when I was ordered; 'to stop being so ferkin' idle, move my arse and get outside!'

I literally tumbled off the top bunk bed, with my legs thrashing dangerously around as my feet tried to make contact with the floor, but only succeeded in nearly permanently rearranging 'Nobby' Clarke's features, as my hob nailed boots swung within a few inches of his face, as I lost my balance and landed in an untidy heap on the floor with an almighty crash. This resulted in a considerable amount of ribald comments from the rest of the Guard, but a great deal of highly descriptive abuse from the Guard Sergeant and Corporal, who suddenly took an unhealthy interest in my ancestry.

The 2200hrs to 2400hrs sentry duty outside the Guardroom was not too bad a stint. There was a fair bit of coming and going, especially the former, as the permanent staff returned from an evening out in the town, or elsewhere, and no doubt doing what soldiers do when they are off duty and out of Camp. The big problem was watching out for officers, especially those who were in mufti. The Army, being status conscious, made a distinction between captains and majors. The former were only accorded a rifle 'butt salute', but the latter, being of field rank were honoured with a 'present arms'. So there I was on sentry duty, standing 'at ease' and blissfully daydreaming, when a figure, dressed in civvies, whom I vaguely recognised hove into view from the direction of the town. As he entered the floodlit area, I quickly realised that he was an officer. But was he a captain or a major? I was suddenly seized with panic as he approached. For a moment I suffered a complete mental blank as to whether a captain got a 'butt salute' or a 'present arms'. I decided it was safer to give him a 'present arms'. If he was a major I would be right; if a captain, I might have been ticked off for giving him the 'present arms' instead of a 'butt salute'. But as a captain, he hopefully would be 'chuffed' that I had 'promoted' him; whereas I would be in worse trouble if I 'butt saluted' and 'demoted' a major. As he came closer, I recognised that he was the major who had bawled me out on the Square for his subjective opinion on the standard of my saluting. He was unpopular with the lads of 'D' Company, as he seemed to go out of his way to jump on us from a great height. I never knew why he had this attitude problem; we had never done him any harm. Perhaps being a single officer was the problem, and what he needed was a good woman (or perhaps not).

I decided to give him my best 'present arms'. But before that, with my rifle in the 'on guard' position and in, what I hoped was a threatening manner:

'Halt! Who goes there?'

'Friend.'

'Advance friend and be recognised.'

Then, in my book I smartly gave him a 'present arms', with my eyes staring straight ahead, and not trying to see what he was up to. (At Mons OCS I twice got into trouble for moving my eyes on the Adjutant's parades. The RSM referred to the offences as 'moving my head'). Fortunately, the major must have either decided that he could not find anything wrong with me, or that he had his mind on other things, such as contemplating a pleasant and successful evening, or perhaps on opportunities missed. Anyway after a gruff 'Goodnight', he disappeared from view, and left me to retire back into my own tiny little world. To vary the monotony of standing at ease or at attention for two hours, we were permitted to march ten paces one way and ten paces in the opposite direction, which helped one to keep warm and keep the circulation going in one's extremities.

It was approaching midnight and nearing the end of my first stint, and as everyone was back in Camp it was very quiet. I was parading up and down looking forward to lying down on my bunk and trying to get some 'kip', when from my left I heard footsteps approaching. Who could it be at this time of night? I adopted the 'on guard' position and nervously shouted out:

'Halt! Who goes there?'

'Friend.' Came the answer.

'Advance friend and be recognised.'

The Orderly Officer, a subaltern, walked into the floodlit area, and I gave him a butt salute.

'Call out the Guard, Sentry.'

I screamed at the top of my voice. 'Call out the Guard!'

Immediately, the peace of the night was shattered, with the Sergeant and Corporal shouting, and referring to an idle lot of "piss artists", as bodies tumbled out of bunks, colliding with others, before disgorging through the Guard Room door in an unholy mass of humanity. In very short order, the Guard was lined up, inspected, dismissed and the Orderly Officer disappeared into the darkness. 'Thank goodness,' I thought, 'he shouldn't be coming around again tonight.' There is nothing worse than, having just come off guard duty, and got one's head down for some shuteye, to be rudely awoken by those fearful words; 'Call out the Guard'. Very soon after I was relieved, I settled down on a top bunk bed, still fully clothed and tried to get some sleep on a thin and well-worn straw palliasse, before I went on duty again at 0400hrs.

Although very uncomfortable, I must have fallen asleep, as I was only vaguely aware of the Guard changing at 0200hrs. But all too soon I was being rudely shaken, and once again being invited to 'move my ferkin' arse.' This time I managed to reach the floor in one piece without disfiguring George in passing, who was asleep in the bottom bunk.

In full kit and with my rifle shouldered, I set off towards the right where I was to patrol the Cookhouse, the NAAFI, The Medical Reception Centre, as well as 'B' Company lines. It took me about 15 minutes to patrol the circuit. Except for a few security lights at strategic points most of my beat was in darkness. I carried a torch to light me round the darkest areas. The two hours seemed interminable, but at least for the last half an hour I completed my stint in the grey light of dawn.

Although patrolling part of the Camp might not have seemed too arduous, it was a very lonely two hours, especially in the middle of the night, when the whole camp was asleep. In spite of the hazards of not recognising and saluting officers correctly as befitted their rank, I did in fact prefer the sentry duty outside the Guard Room. There was always something going on, especially before midnight.

But, as I patrolled around 'B' Company lines, thoughts kept coming into my mind, mainly in the form of questions; 'What am I doing here? I know I have to do National Service, but why am I subjecting myself to greater pressure trying for a commission, when I could opt for a quiet life by just being a private for two years?' I was beginning to envy that business colleague, who in the mid 1950s had that cushy posting as a vehicle mechanic to Cyprus for his two years in REME, and although living in tented accommodation, had an enjoyable time in a rather unmilitary atmosphere, although there was plenty of work to be done during the time of the EOKA emergency.

We had already been warned that, at the War Office Selection Board, we would be asked the question; 'Why do you want to become an officer?' To amuse myself on my guard duty round, I dreamt up stupid answers, which would definitely guarantee failure and instant Return-to-Unit; 'Because, I want a more comfortable life with a batman looking after me,' and; 'as an ex-public school boy, it is my right and fits in with my social status to be commissioned,' would not have earned me any 'brownie' points. However, especially if the Directing Staff (DS) at 'WASBEE' were cavalry officers, then the answer; 'I ride, hunt, enter steeplechases and play polo and have my own ponies and horses' may well have been a successful ploy.

I must admit, that this question did exercise my mind for a fair part of my sentry duty, and in trying to work out a reasonable and sensible answer, which did not sound patronising. I felt mentioning that my father as a TA officer had had a distinguished Second World War record; had been one of the founder members of REME and was, as a Brigadier, the Director of Mechanical Engineering (DME) of 21ˢᵗ Army Group (21AG) in North West Europe, may have been counter productive; as apparently, there had been a certain amount of resentment in a few quarters of the Army, that TA officers during the Second World War were blocking promotion opportunities for regular officers.

Eventually, I decided to base my answer on the fact that the family business was in the Retail Motor Trade, (although I was somewhat worried by using the word 'Trade' – 'You know My Dear, the man's going nowhere, he's in TRADE') and that I had attended a four year residential automobile engineering and management course, sponsored by the Institute of the Motor Industry (IMI) at Loughborough College of Advanced Technology. I also felt that whatever management skills I might have had, could possibly be built on and put to better use by the Army if I was commissioned, as I certainly was not really mechanically competent.

Pondering these questions did help the two hours of patrolling pass fairly quickly and the last thirty minutes prior to the Guard being dismounted, provided some interest as the camp came to life. The cooks making their way to the cookhouse to prepare breakfast, the raucous sounds of junior NCOs rousing everybody out of their pits. 'Come on, let's be having you. Hands off cocks, on with socks.' The sight, which amused me in the grey light of dawn, of semi-naked recruits, with towels fixed around their waists, which were prone to part-company with their owners, especially in a high wind, army plimsolls on their feet and gripping their washing kits, rushing to the ablutions to get there before the hot water ran out.

At last it was 0600 hrs. Our first guard duty was over. We paraded outside the Guard Room, were inspected by the Orderly Officer, and to the order: 'Officer on parade. Dismiss!' We smartly (well as best we could, after a nights guard duty with very little sleep and in rather smelly and crumpled

BDs,) turned right, executed a 'butt salute', took four paces, broke off and hurried back to our hut, to wash, shave, prepare and lay out our kit, ensure our bedblocks were correctly squared off and have breakfast, all before muster parade at 0800hrs. It was just our luck, that the days' programme included PT, drill, the assault course and a couple of lectures and a training film. After a near sleepless night, it was very difficult to stay awake in the lectures and the film show. By the end of that day, we were totally knackered.

Fortunately, with four companies at 2 Trg Bn, guard duty did not come around very often. The second and last time I had to do it did not seem so bad.

~

The early autumn of 1959 was fairly dry and warm in our part of Devon, which was fortunate when we were involved in a night exercise. In reality, it was more like a 'jolly' with one half of the platoon being nominated as 'defenders' and the other half as 'attackers'. The exercise was held on the open heath land at the top of Gittisham Hill. The defenders were allocated what was supposed to be a Forward Defence Locality (FDL), with an HQ marked with a red lantern, set up within its perimeter. It was the task of the attacking force to penetrate the FDL at night, without being challenged and capture their HQ and lantern.

The exercise actually started early afternoon, when the platoon assembled in a lecture hut and was briefed by 2Lt Stevens. On a blackboard was chalked a rough sketch of the exercise area with the FDL and the Start Line for the attacking force marked. In true army democratic style, Mark Hughes, was 'volunteered' to the exalted position of 'OC Blue Defending Force'. Mark was quiet, rather studious, a bit of a boffin as he wanted to be an auto engine designer, but was not one to push himself forward. We felt that the Directing Staff (DS) comprising the platoon commander and sergeant had decided to appoint Mark to this position, as a test of his leadership qualities and tactical skills. The DS 'volunteered' Bob Clarke to be 'OC Red Attacking Force'. Bob was the opposite of Mark, ebullient, cocky, and very sure of himself. He would no doubt make a very good car salesman, which was his ambition, but not just a car salesman, but THE CAR SALESMAN for the most prestigious British car manufacturer at the time – Rolls Royce. An interesting choice by the DS. It was obvious that 'Red Force', once it had crossed the 'Start Line' was going to have to exercise the most silent approach to the 'Blue Force' FDL; but Bob was never one to be quiet.

After the appointments had been made, and we had been given the outline briefing, we were left to 'kick our heels' as Mark and Bob were separately taken up Gittisham Hill to the exercise area to reconnoitre their respective positions. In Mark's case, working out his two man defence posts to cover all likely approaches and deciding whether to 'push' his troops forward as a single line of defence, or whether to organise what was known as 'defence in depth', as far as he could with fourteen men (by the middle of October we were getting fairly good at using army phraseology). Bob was shown his 'Lining-up-Point', and the direction of his approach march to the 'Start Line'. He had to plan how he was going to organise and divide his half-platoon into small sub-units, the route each one was to take to penetrate the defence posts without being discovered, and trying to determine, from a distance, where Mark would be siting his two man defence posts. The reconnaissance and planning was carried out in daylight.

On their return to Camp Mark and Bob, still separated, prepared their plans and then briefed their own squad. The complication was that the exercise was to be at night, and it was one thing to spy out the lie of the land in daylight, but it added another interesting dimension when the action was to be carried out in darkness, when only the squad leaders had seen the ground.

I was part of 'Red Force'. So after our evening meal, we prepared for the fun and games, which we were all looking forward to, as the exercise was going to make a refreshing change from the normal 'in-Camp' training.

As it was cold, most of us wore pyjamas under our denims, and for those who had them – 'cap comforters' (a woollen khaki sort of hat, which had the advantage when pulled down of keeping ones ears warm, and for those who were bald provided suitable camouflage on moonlit nights, especially from the air).

We had not been issued with any camouflage cream, so using anything which came to hand, such as black boot polish or burnt cork (scrounged from the cookhouse), we did our best to cover up faces, hands and the 'shiny' bits of our webbing. We also had to ensure that we did not carry anything that would make a noise as we made our 'approach march to contact'.

At 2030hrs the Blue Force departed by truck, and we were to follow half an hour later at 2100hrs. At the appointed time, we piled into the back of the Bedford 3 ton truck for the short drive up Gittisham Hill and onto the Common.

The DS had chosen the night well. No moon, no wind and 10/10th cloud cover. As we debussed from the truck and waited for Bob to issue his orders, the only sounds were those of an owl hooting close-by (was this the enemy?) and of distant traffic on the A30. We would have to move very slowly if we were not to be heard, and we would have to adopt the 'leopard' crawl as we neared the 'enemy' FDL. Yet the exercise had to finish by midnight, so we could not afford to dawdle. Failure to reach the 'target' would not have earned us, and especially Bob, any 'Brownie' bonus points and would not have been regarded by the DS as a positive career achievement.

Bob, lined us up and we split into pairs as previously arranged. I was teamed with John Hutchings, who was always cheerful, capable with a great sense of humour, and who never let anything faze him, (I believe he later may have entered the Church). I felt that we would successfully make it into the 'enemy' camp.

'Right,' said Bob, 'we have a quarter of a mile approach march before we reach the 'Start Line'. I want absolute silence.' This was a bit rich coming from the noisiest member of the platoon. 'The 'enemy' may have listening patrols out. We shall proceed in single file. I shall lead and use hand signals to communicate.'

'Bloody hell,' swore John. 'How are we going to see hand signals in the dark and how are we going to keep the right distance from the man in front?'

'If I was the 'enemy',' I added, 'I would definitely have an advance listening patrol out and given the chance I would capture the lead man of the Red Force.'

'Shut up, you two,' whispered Bob, which in the quietness of the night must have been heard a good 200 yards away.

The DS in the form of Sgt Henderson, quietly pointed out that the time was fast approaching 2130hrs and we really needed to get a move on. As if an afterthought he added, 'If you are not back here by 0030hrs, the transport will leave without you and you will have to make your own way back to Camp. Oh, the Guard Room has not been warned about this, and you will probably be locked up for the night. I think the Company Commander and the CSM will be thoroughly 'pissed off' if this happens, and I can't see forty-eight hour passes being handed out. So, you better get your fingers out and move out.'

'Okay,' whispered Bob, 'let's go.' He turned left away from the truck, and set off at a smart pace. Fortunately, John and I brought up the rear, for after about 50 yards there was a loud crash followed by someone splashing about in water. 'Bloody hell!' shouted Bob, 'who was the fucking idiot who put that ditch there? It wasn't there this afternoon.' Unfortunately, Bob had been setting such a pace, and so as not to get lost, those immediately behind him had bunched up, with the result that half the Red Force also joined him in a very wet and smelly ditch.

After much noisy cursing and swearing, which not only must have been heard on such a still night back in Honiton; but also from the calls of alarm from nearby trees, woken the whole of the bird population of Gittisham Common, we managed to shake ourselves out into some sort of order. Bob decided, that those of us who were dry should lead, and the wet ones would 'squelch' at the back. I suggested that Bob should take those with him and create a noisy diversion from a flank, hopefully drawing the 'enemy' away from their positions and leaving the rest of us to have a clear run into their camp. Bob declined my suggestion, but instead decided I should lead, with the result that I probably end up by being the first to be captured. So much for opening my big mouth!!

'Okay,' I hissed, 'what our heading?'

'What do you mean heading?' hissed Bob back.

'What's our compass bearing to the 'Start Line', and how many paces do we have to take to reach it?' I returned the compliment by hissing back at him.

There was what is known as a 'very pregnant pause', and I was sure that if it had been daylight Bob's face would have been as red as a beetroot.

'Oh Bob!' I exclaimed, giving up hissing. 'Don't say you didn't take a compass bearing and pace out the distance. How do you expect us to get to the 'Start Line'?'

'I didn't think about it,' mumbled Bob, 'I just turned left from the lorry and followed the path.'

'Yes, but what about the ditch?' chipped in John.

'I swear it wasn't there this afternoon.' Silence. 'What are we going to do now?' asked Bob plaintively.

We were silent as we pondered our next step. Then, and it must have been divine intervention, John spoke up; 'Bob, when you came up this afternoon, did the truck drive straight into the parking area, or did it reverse in?'

After some thought. 'It drove straight in,' answered Bob.

'It didn't this evening,' said John, 'the driver reversed in. So, when we debussed you were facing in the opposite direction from this afternoon. You should have turned right and not left from the truck.'

Bob remained silent.

We trooped back to the Bedford RL. John and I had decided that he would follow immediately behind me, counting our paces, and hopefully when we had reached 440 we would be at, or near our 'Start Line'.

'Bob, what is the 'Start Line'?'

'A row of bushy topped trees either side of the path.'

We hadn't the heart to ask him how we were going to see trees in the dark. We also got everybody to hold onto the webbing belt of the man in front of him. It was after 2200hrs when we eventually set off in the right direction. Trying in the dark to follow a narrow track without the use of a compass was not easy, and I only knew I had strayed off the path when I collided with spiky gorse bushes. By the time we had finished I felt, and probably looked from the front like a pincushion, whilst the middle of my back was black and blue from the number of times John's fist drove into my back when I stopped unexpectedly. Our progress must have been heard miles away, 'shuffle, shuffle' from the front, answered by 'squelch, squelch' from the back. Even if the 'enemy' didn't hear us, then the smell of rancid water from those who fallen into the ditch must have warned them of our approach.

Needless to say our efforts to penetrate the 'enemy' HQ and capture the lantern was an unmitigated disaster. For, when John whispered to me to stop as we had covered the 440 paces, there was rustles from all around us as Blue Force appeared from nowhere, surrounded and captured us. The only good thing that came out of the evening was that we were in time to be transported back to Camp, cold, wet (some of us), hungry and thoroughly depressed. We knew that we would be in for a 'roasting' at the post-mortem in the morning. Poor old Bob was no doubt going to be 'hung out to dry'. The Company's Officers, WOs and NCOs would be seriously 'pissed off' and in no mood to take prisoners.

Our mood did not lighten, even though there was hot soup waiting for us back at Camp, but for those who had worn pyjamas and denims and fallen into the ditch, sleeping either in cold, wet and smelly pyjama trousers or in 'drawers cellular' was not going to be funny, as it was a chilly night and stoves were not allowed to be lit before November. Although we had been issued with two sets of pyjamas, one set was invariably at the laundry. Fortunately, due to the exercise, the hut was not being inspected in the morning, which gave those who had wet and smelly pyjamas trousers a chance to wash and dry them for the following night. However, with only one pair to hand, those with wet and smelly denims were not going to be able to wash and dry them for the next days' activities. I hoped for their sakes, that the RSM wasn't around when we were drilling on the Square.

The post-mortem was as we expected. It transpired that Sgt Henderson had noticed that Bob, on the 'recce' the previous day, had neither used a compass nor paced out the distance from the 'Lining-up-Point' to the 'Start Line'. So he ordered the driver of our truck to reverse into the 'Drop-off-Point', hoping that Bob would not notice the difference. It worked. Also it was only 300 yards from the 'Lining-up-Point' to the 'Start Line'. So the 440 paces took us right up to the 'enemy' HQ. Lessons harshly learnt.

~

We had been issued with bayonets at the same time as we had been issued with our rifles. These were long, decidedly sharp and were a definite hazard, for on the order to; 'Fix bayonets,' there was a risk of incurring a self-inflicted injury in the vicinity of one's left buttock, when withdrawing and especially returning said weapon from and to its scabbard.

Came the day when we were to go to the training ground near Lympstone and be instructed in the delicate art of bayonet drill.

We debussed to find the platoon NCOs, headed by Sgt Henderson waiting for us.

'Right. Gather round and listen in. This is the nine inch Mark VI bayonet, and is a highly effective close combat weapon when used correctly and aggressively. Obviously, it is only used in hand-to-hand combat, but when used, it puts the fear of God into the enemy.

'You will first practice the drill, and then you will carry out live practice on those dummies over there.' Sgt Henderson pointed behind us. We turned and looked to what appeared to be a row of gallows with straw filled dummies suspended from them and beyond, there was a line of similar shapes lying on the ground.

'Right. Pay attention.' Sgt Henderson took the rifle from Cpl Jones and fixed the bayonet onto the rifle. 'The bayonet is a lethal weapon, and you only 'fix bayonets' when you are ordered to do so. Having done so you hold the rifle in the 'High Port' position, like this.' He demonstrated by holding the rifle diagonally across his chest, with the bayonet pointing across his left shoulder towards the sky.

'The next order is; 'On Guard', where you place your left foot forward, and hold the rifle with bayonet attached to your front pointing towards the enemy. Like this.' The Sergeant demonstrated the movement.

'Right. Let's practice this.' We did so several times without bayonets until Sgt Henderson was satisfied.

'Now, the next stage is, on the order; 'Charge', you double with the rifle and bayonet held in front of you to those stuffed dummies in front of you, plunge the bayonet in, turn and twist it; then withdraw the bayonet, assume the 'On Guard' position, move to the left and attack those dummies on the ground. Okay?'

'Yes, Sergeant.'

'Right, you six, you will be the first detail. Line up there and fix bayonets. Corporal Jones sort the rest of the platoon into details of six.'

Fixing bayonets was a rather undignified manoeuvre as one had to grip the rifle between ones knees, whilst withdrawing the bayonet from its scabbard from the vicinity of the left buttock and fixing and locking it in place on the bayonet boss of the rifle.

The first detail lined up on the 'Start Line'.

'Okay. Three further points. When you charge I want you all to scream as loudly as you can, which is what you would actually do in action to frighten and put off the enemy. Secondly keep your finger on the trigger of your rifle. In action you might need to fire the rifle as you are charging, and lastly when you reach the dummies, I want you to shout 'In–Twist–Withdraw.' Okay?'

'Yes, Sergeant.'

'Right. Here we go. Assume the 'High Port position'. Okay. 'On Guard'. Ready? 'Charge'.'

The first detail set off at a fast trot, sotto voce, and on reaching the dummies gently pushed their bayonets into them.

'Stop!' shouted Sgt Henderson. 'That was pathetic. Who do you think you are, a load of ponces? If that had been the real thing, the enemy would probably have died of laughter instead of shooting you first. Now come on, get a grip and let's do it properly. Corporal Jones show them.'

The Corporal obliged, screaming at full volume and at a full gallop plunged, twisted and withdrew his bayonet from the dummy before moving to the ones on the ground.

'Right, that's how it should be done, and when you plunge your bayonet into a dummy, I want to see the blade come out the other side. Just as you would have to do with a real body, you will have to put a foot on your dummy on the ground to withdraw the bayonet, as it will have penetrated into the earth. Okay. Let's try it again.'

The first detail set off again, this time louder and with more determination. But it wasn't until the fourth time, that Sergeant Henderson was satisfied. By then we had all got the idea, and the rest of us managed to achieve the required standard on the second run.

Initially, it was a strange feeling, even on a straw filled dummy, sticking a bayonet into what could have been someone's guts, and the order to 'Twist and Withdraw' added to a feeling of squeamishness. However, under the 'gentle' guidance of Sgt Henderson and Cpl Jones, our inhibitions began to evaporate, and by the end, with adrenaline flowing, we were performing as effectively and as noisily as any 'crack' infantry regiment.

~

Before taking WOSB, we had one further exercise to undergo, which was a forty-eight hour initiative test in the general area of Ottery St Mary, Newton Poppleford and Sidford in East Devon.

Late one Tuesday morning, the whole platoon piled into the Bedford trucks; each of us loaded down with our large pack, filled with groundsheet, poncho, mess tins, washing kit, spare underwear, stamped 'W↑D' loo paper (on each sheet) and entrenching tool (folding, shovel), but so as not to frighten the local populace we left our rifles behind. After about an hour, we drove into an opening set deep in woods, and were ordered to de-buss in double quick time and fall-in as a platoon.

'Right. Listen in,' said Sgt Henderson, 'we're going to march into this wood for a couple of miles, and then we shall set up camp. You will be split up into teams of two and each team will set up a two-man 'bivi' (bivouac) using your groundsheets and ponchos. As we are out of camp for only one night, we don't have the luxury of 'thunder boxes' (temporary hessian enclosed loos), nor are we going to dig a pit with a log suspended over it for you idle lot to squat over. If you've got to have a shit, you've got your entrenching tool and you've got bog paper, so you take yourself off further into the woods downwind from the camp and you dig yourself a hole to bog down in. But make sure you fill in the hole properly afterwards. Now when we break camp tomorrow morning, I do not want to see any rubbish left. I want the site left as if we hadn't been there. Understand? Talk to me. DO YOU UNDERSTAND?'

'Yes, Sarn't.'

'Right. Tomorrow morning each team will be given a sheet of paper and you have to fulfil the tasks listed on that sheet. So that you idle lot don't fucking follow each other round like a load of dozy sheep, each team will set off from different drop-off points. You will have no money on you. This is an initiative test. You will be issued with maps in the morning, and if you want transport back to camp you must be at the final map reference point, no later than 1700hours. If you're late – you walk. Do I make myself clear?'

'Yes, Sarn't.'

'Right. Left turn. No 1 Section leading followed by No 2 and No 3. At ease, quick march.'

After about 30 minutes, we halted and were told that this was our campsite. We quickly paired off. Once again John and I joined up, and quickly found ourselves a suitable spot for our 'bivi', where we could suspend our ponchos from the low branches of a tree and we found enough moss, pine needles and leaves to make a soft mattress for our groundsheets and we could use our packs as pillows.

I had never been a Boy Scout, but that evening I realised the attraction of scouting. It was a warm autumn evening, hot food had been bought out from the Camp, and as we sat round a blazing fire, chatting, laughing and breaking into bawdy rugby songs, with 'Eskimo Nell' being the favourite, I really felt the bonding and companionship with the members of the platoon. We had come from many diverse backgrounds, but after putting up with everything that had been thrown at us, we had become an effective and cohesive unit. I have always believed that one of the Army's strengths has been, and still is, the ability in a very short space of time to weld a group of individuals into an effective and bonded unit. Eventually, as the fire died down we each crawled into our 'bivis' to get what sleep we could.

Dawn broke all too soon and the platoon sergeant and corporals showed no compassion in roughly booting us out of our temporary 'pits'. We washed and shaved in cold water, and whilst waiting for the transport to arrive from Camp with our breakfast and haversack rations, various members of the platoon, myself included, disappeared further into the woods, with their entrenching tools and loo paper rolls in hand. It was neither comfortable nor easy 'bogging' down in the bushes, and the 'W↑D' loo paper was just as rough as I remembered from CCF camp at school. After a quick breakfast, we picked up our haversack rations, broke camp and cleaned up the site to the satisfaction of the NCOs. Then it was time for Sgt Henderson to hand out our task lists and maps.

One final admonishment. 'Don't forget you have to be at map reference 43837156 by 1700hrs or you walk back to camp. And I don't want to hear from any locals that a group of rude and unkempt soldiers have been nicking things. Okay?'

'Yes, Sarn't.'

We boarded the trucks and were driven down narrow and winding Devon lanes. Every few minutes our truck would stop and another team would de-bus. Eventually, it was our turn and John and I jumped down to find ourselves in a lane with high hedgerows in either direction with the lane disappearing round a bend some 200 yards away. We moved away, and found a log to sit on whilst trying to make sense of our tasks and plan how we were going to achieve them. Where do we find a peacock's tail feather? If there is only one such bird in the area, with fifteen teams out, he will certainly end up with a cold bum and no doubt, a very irate owner. A goose egg shouldn't be too difficult. What does one find at grid reference 43546986? The list seemed endless. John and I decided to split up wherever possible in order to complete as many tasks as we could in the available time.

The biggest problem we had was that we had no idea where we were. This had to be our first priority. Fortunately, being a sunny morning, we could work out north, south, east and west. We couldn't see over the hedge, but there seemed to be the noise of traffic from the south, so we set off in that direction. Luckily, we soon came to a sign posted crossroads, got our bearings and started to carry out our tasks. The locals were fantastic, and when we explained what we were up to, gave us a tremendous amount of help. We even managed to acquire a rather tired and moth eaten peacock tail feather.

We must have been one of the last teams to reach Ottery St Mary, where our task was to find out what was the vicar's favourite meal. When we eventually found the vicarage, there was a note headed **'Text For The Day'** pinned to the front door. *'Roast beef. Roast potatoes. Yorkshire pudding. Runner beans.'* **'DO NOT DISTURB!!'**

'Do you think we could ask what his favourite pudding is and then ask for his blessing?' John wondered. 'Come on,' I replied, 'let's not push our luck. We've still six more tasks to complete and we're running out of time.'

We did not complete all these tasks, and having spent some eight hours on our feet, we had no intention of missing the transport back to camp. We made it by the skin of our teeth.

It was absolute bliss to get boots off, and to collapse onto our beds. But, there was to be no rest. The door to the hut swung open and: 'Right, foot inspection,' as Sgt Henderson entered. 'Get those socks off.' I rarely felt any sympathy for the NCOs, but inspecting a load of smelly feet, which had not been out of their socks and boots for nearly forty-eight hours, must have been one of their more unpleasant duties.

Personal cleanliness, or lack of it, was a chargeable offence. Baths and showers were limited, and the use of deodorants unheard of. So smelling to high heaven and, or failing to shave would result in being paraded before the Company Commander.

We had all enjoyed being out of Camp on the initiative test, which was really no more than a glorified treasure hunt; but it was certainly a welcome break from the normal routine of inspections, drill, assault course, PT and other such boring military activities. Still, we had learnt a lot. Our map reading skills improved considerably; physically we had walked miles and the methods we used and the stories we told in order to complete our tasks, certainly exercised our imagination, our veracity and our acting ability. But, I suppose that was what it was all about. We were stretched both physically and mentally, and the DS found out how well we reacted and performed to the set tasks, even in such an innocuous training situation as an initiative test.

~

We were nearing the end of our training and to give credit to the officers, warrant officers, sergeants and junior NCOS in 'D' Company, they were doing their best, not only to instil a military ethos into a bunch of, initially unwilling recruits in the shortest possible time, but also to prepare us to pass the War Office Selection Board, and to be fit to hold the Queen's Commission.

But to achieve this, we had to endure a more rigorous training regimen and reach a higher standard than the ordinary 'squaddies'. We certainly spent more time on the Square than the other companies, and our platoon was rapidly becoming proficient in the 'art' of drilling and, although we were all heartily sick of being shouted at to 'keep in fucking step,' or 'swing those fucking arms,' and all the other 'fucking' drill movements that we could be picked up on; there was a marked decrease in the amount of shouting and abuse that was directed at us as our drill improved.

But, in the middle of our course a new company sergeant-major arrived. CSM Derek Colquhoun was not, to my mind in the mould of the traditional company sergeant-major, who mainly stamped his authority and achieved discipline through fear. Sergeant-Major Colquhoun was softly spoken, and I cannot recall that he ever shouted at us. He loathed the term 'man management', and believed one only managed logistics, men one had to lead by example. He was a great believer in communication and, on the Square would explain what drill movements we were going to do, and how he wanted us to perform them. He would demonstrate each one; then get us to practice them individually, before we tried them out as a platoon. When we went wrong, which happened fairly frequently, he would halt us, explain and demonstrate the mistake, before we had another go. We must, at times have tried his patience. But, although he could be a stern disciplinarian when necessary, he did not believe in issuing threats or resorting to abusive language, as we were accustomed to. The result was the standard of, and confidence in our drill improved dramatically in a very short time.

After WOSB and before our posting came through to Mons Officer Cadet School, there were two to three weeks, where we rather 'kicked our heels', and it was during this period that Derek Colquhoun taught us intricate drill movements, over and above what was expected of us at our stage of training. As he said to us at the time:

'What I am going to show and teach you, are some of the drill movements that are carried out at the 'Trooping of the Colour' Ceremony on Horse Guards Parade. These are not written down, but are passed on from one Guards Sergeant-Major to another by word of mouth, and are perfected by countless practice and rehearsals.'

We asked CSM Colquhoun how he came to know these drill movements. He replied that he had attended Brigade of Guards Training Courses, where he had been taught sixty-four Guards drill movements, and he proceeded to show us one, with the Squad acting the part of a Guards Company.

'Company'. (The Squad braced up and stood properly at ease) 'Pay attention to the Company Commander's word of command and the detail for a company at the halt in line, required to form close column of platoons facing a flank and halted.'

'Company stand easy.'

'The Company Commander's word of command will be:'

'Company – Company 'Shun.'

'Slope Arms.'

'Close order - March.'

'Right Dress.' (Followed by the CSM giving 'Eyes Front')

'Move to the right in Column of Threes.'

'Right Turn.'

'Company will March Past in Column of Route – By the left Quick March.'

If that was only one of the sixty-four drill movements Derek had been taught, I shuddered to think what the other sixty-three must have been like; all of which had to be memorised.

With endless patience he led us through a series of movements, which we initially found very confusing. We practised marching and counter marching in column and in line. We marched in open and in close order, and in quick and slow time. Fortunately, the Brigade of Guards and the majority of Regiments and Corps (including REME) march at 120 paces a minute, unlike the Light Infantry who march at a fast pace of 140. Derek Colquhoun also explained that the Light Infantry double at a fast 'trot' of 180 paces a minute with their rifles at the trail. If any of us were posted to a Light Infantry Regiment LAD, Derek showed us how these two paces could be maintained carrying the rifle at both the trail and the short trail. We did not have sufficient time to practice these movements, but we knew what to expect.

It was during this period in our training that I sprained my ankle on the assault course, and the Medical Officer put me on light duties. I was returning from the Medical Centre one day, whilst my platoon was being drilled on the Square by the CSM. As some of the original platoon had by now failed WOSB, and as a consequence had been RTUd (Returned- to-Unit), the platoon was really no more than a large squad. As I stopped and watched the platoon completing in an exemplary fashion, with precision and snap the intricate drill movements that were being ordered by Sgt-Maj Colquhoun, I felt a sense of pride that I was a member of the platoon - but was very annoyed with myself that I was excused drill, as I so wanted to be on the Square with the rest of my mates. It was the only time during my National Service that I, and the others enjoyed drill and took pride in what we were doing. We knew we were good, and we also knew we could go off to Mons OCS for the next phase of our training with confidence.

~

The War Office Selection Board was a balance of mental and physical tasks, and to prepare us Army Physical Training Instructors, with a certain amount of sadistic pleasure, would make our lives hell by chasing us around and around the Assault Course until with lungs busting, hands sore and red from clambering up walls and scrambling nets, with legs that felt like jelly, we would collapse in an unmilitary heap, beyond caring whether we would be put on a charge for insubordination and unmilitary behaviour.

'Right, you ferkin' idle bunch of couch potatoes.' At least, I think that is how the APT corporal started, but as a Southerner, I found it somewhat difficult to decipher a broad Scouse accent. 'You think I'm trying to kill you lot off. I'm not, I'm trying to 'elp you. You think this 'ere assault course is difficult, but you ain't seen nothing yet. You wait to you get to Barton

Stacey, the assault course there makes this one look like a ferkin' kiddies playground. So get off your ferkin' arses, you ferkin' idle shower of worthless layabouts. I suppose your mums love you, 'cause I certainly don't. So let's do it again, and this time look as if you're bleedin' trying.'

By the time the APT corporal had finished with us, we were black and blue, hands red and bloody from cuts and burst blisters. We ached from every part of our body, even from places where we didn't think it was possible to be sore. Although I had played team sports at school and college, I did not find assault courses easy, and came to the conclusion that I was not built to scale walls, crawl through muddy drain pipes, clamber up and down scrambling nets, and other assorted 'nasties'. But the worst one as far as I was concerned, was crossing a water hazard by rope, strung at high level between two 'A' frames. One tried very hard to inch along it, with one leg hooked over the rope, which gave a certain degree of stability and propulsion without losing balance. But it was inevitable that balance would be lost and one would slide over, ending up suspended upside down on the rope, with legs entwined around it, and desperately trying to swing oneself back on top again. However, gravity would win, and with arms and legs flaying about wildly, one was unceremoniously dumped into the water hazard.

As one surfaced with water flowing from every part of the body and giving a passable imitation of a whale; 'Right, you idle so and so, get your ferkin' self out of there, and do it again.' It was bad enough trying to cross this hazard dry, but it was virtually impossible with soaking wet denims, boots and a sopping beret jammed on ones head, and another involuntary and fully clothed 'dunk' was the inevitable outcome. Even the APTIs realised they were on a hiding to nothing, and obviously loathe to miss out on their drinking time, would give up the 'game', dismiss us and we would troop back to our huts, a wet bedraggled and thoroughly knackered lot. We would avoid crossing the Square, dodging between other huts and buildings, otherwise we stood the risk of being spotted by an officer, the RSM or the CSM, who would no doubt place us on a charge for being in 'bad order prejudicial to good order and discipline'.

Although we initially tackled the assault course individually and in our own time, as our course progressed, the APTIs starting timing us, and finally we were split up into teams, where we had to compete not only against each other but also against the clock. I did not enjoy assault courses.

~

One morning, towards the end of October we had assembled outside the Company Office for the daily muster parade, when, before we expected it, we were called to attention as 2Lt Stevens emerged from the Company Office. With the exception of our first muster parade, our Platoon

Commander had never put in an appearance at our subsequent morning parades, so we wondered what had got him out of his bed so early. We couldn't think of any misdemeanours we had committed, so thoughts revolved round the possibility that the Government had declared war on some poor unsuspecting third world country, or that the Army had decided that it needed reinforcements deployed to Cyprus to contain EOKA and that, as National Servicemen it would be a cheap option to send us, as 'bleeding infantry' to that island.

'RIGHT. PLATOON. PLATOON, WAIT FOR IT... SHUN,' bellowed Cpl Jones. We smartly came to attention with our boots driving into the ground like a single rifle shot.

'THAT WAS 'ORRIBLE,' screamed the Corporal, 'STAND AT EASE. STAND EASY.' We knew it wasn't, but no doubt he wanted to prove a point in front of the Officer.

'NOW, BLEEDIN' WAKE YOU IDLE LOT OF SCUM BAGS AND LET'S DO IT AGAIN AND THIS TIME PUT SOME SNAP INTO IT. PLATOON. PLATOON.' We casually straightened from the 'Stand Easy' position to 'At Ease'. 'WAIT FOR IT. ATTENSHUN.' This time our 'attenshun' sounded more like a burst of machine-gun fire.

'THAT'S BETTER. WHY COULDN'T YOU FRIGGING DO THAT THE FIRST TIME?' We could barely stop ourselves grinning. Even 2Lt Stevens looked somewhat bemused, whilst Sgt Henderson looked as if he was going to explode with apoplexy, but instead decided to take charge.

'Thank you, Corporal, now get fell in'. Cpl Jones, executed as far as he was concerned, a smart 'about turn' and took up position at the right hand end of the platoon.

'Now, listen in,' this from Sgt Henderson, 'Mr Stevens has something to say.'

'Thank you, Sgt Henderson. Please stand the men at ease.' The movement was carried out with snap and precision.

'Right, your orders have come through. You will be going to 'WASBEE' in three weeks on the sixth of November. So you've got a lot of work to do before then. Any questions?'

Although the news was not unexpected, we were too surprised to have any questions.

'Okay. Dismiss the platoon, Sergeant.'

'Officer on parade. Dismiss.'

A smart right turn. Salute. March for four paces then break off.

We wandered back to our huts, each with our own thoughts. Crunch time was fast approaching. For those who passed WOSB, there was going to be four months of infantry training at Mons OCS before being commissioned. But for those who failed there was the ignominy of being

RTUd and having to face others, who would know pretty quickly that one had failed WOSB. But we were left to wonder what our Officer meant by '…. you've got a lot of work to do…'

We weren't left in doubt for too long. A few mornings later we were marched down to one of the lecture rooms, where a strange staff sergeant was waiting for us.

'Right, pleased be seated everybody. I am Staff Sergeant Peters, and I am here to prepare you for one of the tests you will be undertaking at 'WASBEE'. As you probably know by now the tests are not all physical. You will be expected to give a five-minute talk, without faltering and without notes on a subject of your own choice. You may think that five-minutes doesn't sound very long, but you will be surprised, when you're on your feet how long it actually is. Now, just to prove this, will one of you give me a subject and I will try and talk for five-minutes, and you can time me. Right, let's have a subject.'

We all shouted out our choices, and somehow from the babble of noise, Staff Sergeant Peters chose 'Tomatoes'. I didn't actually hear anybody shout the word, and I've long suspected that was what he was going to talk about anyway, and he just pretended amongst the general hubbub that someone had shouted out the word 'Tomatoes'.

'Tomatoes,' he began, 'originally came from South America and are round, soft vegetables, or are they fruit? There are two opinions on this. However, tomatoes are about the size of a golf ball, although in hot climates like the Mediterranean they grow green ones and very small ones, called 'cherry' tomatoes. However, in this country they are either grown in greenhouses or out of doors. Generally, tomato seedlings are started off under glass, and then, when the danger of frosts are over, the young plants are transferred outside. They like a sunny spot, so that the fruit can ripen, but if there is little to no rain the roots must not be allowed to dry out. The size and the number of tomatoes that can be picked over a period of weeks depends on the type of soil and how well the plants are fed with tomato fertilizer, or good old fashioned manure.

'Tomatoes can be eaten raw, fried or grilled. They are also used in many culinary dishes such as spaghetti bolognaise. The Italians are great tomato eaters and put them into nearly every pasta dish. They are meant to be very good for one, and everybody should eat at least one every day.'

I was not enjoying this subject. For some inexplicable reason in the dim and distant past, I was probably forced to eat tomatoes, and even today, if I try to eat one I nearly gag on it and throw up. There is something about the texture I cannot stand. I don't mind tomatoes being used in cooking and I definitely like tomato soup and Ketchup. But real live tomatoes. Ugh!!

Staff Peters continued: 'Tomatoes have one further use, and over-ripe ones make very good ammunition to throw at unpopular politicians, or whoever. Although, as future officers and gentlemen, you would not dream of chucking them at anybody. Would you?'

'No, Staff,' we chorused.

'Tomato growers, who enter for flower and vegetable shows will go to extraordinary lengths to ensure that theirs are perfect. Even amongst neighbours there can be fierce competition and it is not unheard of for underhand methods to be used. In the village I was brought up in before I joined the Army, there was fierce competition between the vicar and his neighbour, who were both keen tomato growers. This is a true story, because I heard the vicar tell my mum and dad it. One year, in his greenhouse the vicar's tomatoes had no fruit on them. As his neighbour was due to come round for tea one afternoon, and the vicar not being able to face him and admit that his tomatoes were a failure, went out to the local shops and bought bags of tomatoes, which he proceeded with fine twine to tie onto his plants. His neighbour could not believe his eyes when he saw the vicar's heavily laden tomato plants. 'George,' or whatever the vicar's name was, 'however have you managed to grow so many tomatoes? I haven't any. What's your secret?' The vicar, not wishing to upset his friend and as far as I know, never did let on what he had done. But it goes to show the lengths tomato growers will go to protect their reputation.'

The Staff Sergeant continued, and easily filled the five minutes. It was a too professional talk to have been 'ad-libbed', and must have been his standard 'spiel' to every platoon, prior to their taking 'WASBEE'. I had to decide what subject I was going to give in my presentation.

As part of my Finals at Loughborough, we had to research and write a thesis on an industrial subject, and for some unknown reason I chose to write on the history of 'The Trade Union Movement'. Being basically idle, rather than starting from scratch on another subject, I decided to modify and shorten my thesis, and give the Directing Staff at the Selection Board my talk on that subject, which no doubt would be of great interest to military minds.

We had to rehearse our presentations and from the reaction I got from the rest of the platoon, I did wonder whether I should have chosen a less serious subject to talk about. However, I decided to stick to my guns with 'The Trade Union Movement'.

Although we had been given our WOSB date by 2Lt Stevens, we knew that the time was fast approaching, when the platoon senior to us returned from their Selection Board and those who had passed inserted white discs behind the REME cap badge. Those who failed were quickly posted out to other units. We, of course, tried to find out as much as we could from the previous platoon, but they were not very forthcoming, taking the attitude,

'Sod off. We've had to go through 'WASBEE'. Why should we tell you all about it and make it easier for you. You find out for yourselves.' I must admit we took the same attitude to the platoon behind us.

'D' Company's Officers, WOs and NCOs had done their utmost in a most professional way to prepare us for the War Office Selection Board, which they had more than a vested interest in wanting us to pass. A high success rate would reflect upon their training and teaching methods, and must have been regarded as a positive career achievement for the Company Commander.

At last, after some ten weeks of fairly intensive training the day had arrived for us to set off for the next stage of our National Service career – 'WASBEE'

Chapter Five

The War Office Selection Board (WOSB)

On 6th November 1958, with our travel warrants in hand, and large packs on our backs, containing everything we were likely to need for the three days of the WOSB examination, we entrained for our journey to Andover. At the station, a Sergeant from an infantry regiment, the first time we had seen a different cap badge from the REME one, was waiting for us. We embussed in a Bedford RL 3 ton truck, for the five mile drive to the Barton Stacey camp, which was a short distance from the village itself, and lay alongside the A303.

We drove in through the open gates by the unmanned Guard House into what looked like a very deserted camp, as the truck stopped alongside a row of rather dilapidated Nissen huts; so named after an Army Engineer, Lt Col Peter Nissen who lived from 1871 to 1930. The huts were of half cylindrical shape, prefabricated from corrugated iron. The one which was detailed for us, looked as though it was of Mark 1 vintage. We were thankful that we only had to spend three nights there, as the windows were badly fitting; paint was peeling off walls; lighting was from an inadequate number of 40watt bulbs and if there was any insulation, it was probably asbestos cladding. We were pleased to see that there was a coke stove, although we could not see any coke, coal or firewood. These, we thought were probably stored outside somewhere.

The Sergeant briefed us on the administrative arrangements for the three days we would be in Camp. He showed us where the cookhouse, ablutions and latrines were and where we had to report the following morning at 0800hrs. He told us eating times were fixed, and if we did not want to miss our 'scoff' we should be at the cookhouse on time. He also explained that after the daily 'WASBEE' tests, the time was our own, but we were not to leave Camp.

He then left us to our own devices. Although we were all dreading what lay ahead of us over the following three days; we were that first evening, in a certain state of false euphoria as we realised that for the first time in the ten weeks we had been in the Army, we did not have to blanco and shine our kit, nor 'bull' our boots, neither did we have to make bedblocks, or clean our hut. Although on our last morning we did receive a 'right royal' bollocking from an officer for, in his opinion, the disgusting condition of our hut. Fortunately, he was not able to do any more than bawl us out.

The autumn had been warm and relatively dry; but our arrival at Barton Stacey, appeared to signal the start of winter, for on that very day there had been a heavy frost, and as our hut seemed to have been uninhabited for some time, it felt decidedly on the chilly side. So, before we settled down for a quiet evening and prepared ourselves for what lay ahead, we, by common agreement (all twelve of us), decided that it would make life more comfortable if we lit the stove, and kept it in all night as it was obviously going to be a cold one. We were somewhat bemused by the number of cobwebs that were festooned on and around the stove; but were of the opinion that the stove had probably not been used since the previous winter. We had no idea how busy the camp was, but we felt from the rather dilapidated state of the accommodation huts that it was only used for WOSB candidates. In passing, the food was not great either, and we were pleased to return to Honiton catering which was undoubtedly superior.

Anyway, back to our stove. We searched high and low but there was no fuel or firewood to be seen. So, splitting up into pairs we dispersed to various parts of the Camp on a coal, coke and firewood scrounge. The wooden directional and unit signboards were a temptation, but we decided that the Directing Staff would not be best pleased if we removed them, as they probably would get lost without them, and they would possibly be so thoroughly pissed off with us, that we would be RTUd. Although we were prepared to argue our corner that we had been displaying 'initiative', one of the qualities looked for in an officer.

However, we eventually found a source of dubious quality coke and firewood outside the cookhouse, which we 'humped' back to our hut. Then the fun really started. We cleared away the cobwebs and de-coked the stove, prior to laying a new fire. The newspapers and wood we used we realised were somewhat damp, but we were not prepared for the sheer volume of vile smelling smoke that emanated not only from the stove itself but from numerous gaps in the chimney, which seemed to have more holes than metal, and we began to understand why the stove had not been lit, apparently for a very long time. Also, there were probably several years of compacted birds nests on top of the chimney. The acrid smell from the brown coloured coke coupled with that from the several years of fermenting bird shit, was enough for us to beat a tactical withdrawal from the hut, wait for the smoke and acrid fumes to disperse. We then reached the decision that however cold the hut was we would have to make do without a stove. With only a sheet and two blankets we had to pile our battledresses and greatcoats on top of us in order to keep warm.

~

Whether or not it was deliberate policy to let us alone that first evening, so that we would be 'bright eyed and bushy tailed' and not be stressed out in the morning; we certainly appreciated the time to mentally prepare ourselves for the tests we would have to undergo.

I lay on my bed and took stock of where I now found myself in my National Service career, to search my inner self and to be completely honest with myself for the true reason why I wanted to become an officer. The obvious reasons of life being more comfortable, with status and privileges as an officer rather than remaining in the ranks were glib, shallow and trite. As I was to find out much later, you cannot be much lower in the Army's chain of command than as a National Service subaltern, especially in the eyes of an adjutant, senior subaltern or a regimental sergeant-major.

There had been a few occasions early on, when the pressure got so bad that I had contemplated asking to be returned to the ranks, which some from our platoon had done so for various reasons. Our basic training in 'D' Coy was longer and more concentrated than those for other ranks, and it was a temptation to stay in the ranks with only eight weeks of basic training before being posted either for technical training or, depending upon civilian qualifications and skills, to either Base or First Line REME units. I believed the worst scenario was to spend ones National Service, not as a Craftsman (Cfn) but as a Private carrying out regimental duties in a training battalion, with the possibility of promotion to Lance-Corporal.

'No', I thought. 'Why do I want to become an officer? Was it pride, ambition, family pressure, bloody mindedness, or 'Ne te confundant illegitimi', which very loosely translates as: 'Don't let the bastards get you down'?'

'Pride'? I did not think so. Although years later, I developed pride in the fact that I had been a National Serviceman, but at the time pride did not come into the equation as a reason why I wanted to become an officer.

'Ambition'? At that time in my life, I had not developed any ambition for anything in particular. As my father had organised my life through school and technical college and as he expected me, as a matter of duty to join the family's car business, a decision that did not require me to show any ambition. Neither did I have, at the time any interest in staying on in the Army beyond the two years. So, ambition was also not part of the equation, except for a mild feeling that I wanted to be an officer.

'Bloody Mindedness'? This could certainly have been one of the reasons for becoming an officer. Although there had been times when the pressure almost became too much, that I weakened and thought that the buggers would win; but I quickly came to my senses and was determined, after all that I had been through, was still going through and if I passed WOSB, would continue to go through at Mons OCS, that I was not giving up on going for a commission. In the words of a popular business adage: 'When the going gets tough, the tough get going.' I hoped that I could prove to myself that I was in that category and I didn't want to be accused of lacking in moral fibre. So stubbornness was part of the equation.

'Family Pressure'? My father had finished the Second World War as an Honorary Brigadier, and was subsequently Chairman of the Sussex Territorial Army Association and Vice-Chairman of the National Territorial Army Association. He obviously expected me to take a commission, especially as three of my cousins had gained National Service commissions (two in the RAF), although my brother had missed National Service by becoming a farmer instead. I did not realise until many years later the importance, in the eyes of many people, of achieving what is expected of one, and the family would probably have felt I had let the side down if I had failed WOSB or, even worse chosen to be RTUd. Nine years of boarding school had instilled in me discipline, obedience and that parents must be respected and also obeyed. The culture, which existed at the time, was best expressed by ex-RSM Ken de Torre, the Games Master at my Preparatory School, who believed that a boys' moral and mental character was developed through boxing. 'However well boys may be taught the Noble Art,' quoted Ken de Torre, 'it is the determination and courage of the individual which count for so much….'. So, although boxing may have been character forming ('…Caffyn ii, a real boxer in the making...'), I believed that were I to fail WOSB, or voluntarily return to the ranks, the family would have felt that I had failed to achieve what was expected of me.

Therefore, I came to what I believed was an honest conclusion that my main reason for becoming an officer was 'bloody mindedness' and I was determined that 'Ne te confundant illegitimi' would not apply, and also to a lesser reason it was what the family expected of me, and I did not want them to accuse me of lacking in moral fibre.

Subconsciously, I possibly feared my father rather more than a drill sergeant. A very minor reason was that if during our training at Honiton I had decided to give up and asked to be RTUd, I may well have been posted back to No1 Trg Bn at Blandford. That possibility was enough to deter me from harbouring any such thoughts.

Our platoon officer and NCOs had done their best in a very professional way to prepare us for WOSB; but at the end of the day it all came down to the individual. Even with team tasks, the team leader must have the rest of his group working with him; otherwise lack of bonding and co-operation could spell disaster for him and would highlight a failure in his leadership qualities.

We lay on our beds and mused amongst ourselves as to what characteristics the Examining Officers would be looking from us. The obvious one being 'potential officer material' and from which would spring enthusiasm, determination, leadership, initiative, stamina, physical ability, discussion and presentational skills. Quite a daunting list and we were certain that we were going to be well stretched over the three days. With such thoughts in mind, and in spite of the cold, we settled down to get what sleep we could.

~

The next morning, after little sleep what with nerves and the cold, we set off and crossed the road to the Camp HQ where the WOSB briefing was to be held. With butterflies in our stomachs we were unable to appreciate the beautiful autumn morning, with trees, bushes and grass heavy with hoar frost glistening in the early morning sun.

A Sergeant greeted us and showed us into a lecture room with chairs laid out facing what could best be described as the 'top table'. The room was already full of other hopefuls drawn from all regiments and other corps. We all looked somewhat pale and there was a perceptible feeling of nervousness in the room, and any conversation, which was mainly between friends, was very muted.

'Right', bawled out the Sergeant, 'let's have some 'ush. Find yourselves chairs and no talking. You will stand to 'attenshun' when the Colonel and the other 'Orrficers' enter. You will only sit when invited to by the Colonel, whereupon you will sit at 'attenshun', unless the Colonel tells you to sit 'at ease'. You may then relax, but there will be no lounging in your chairs. Remember, and although you are only National Servicemen, if you want to become 'orrficers', you better behave as 'young gentlemen'. You will be watched the whole time. Do I make myself clear?'

'Yes, Sergeant', we murmured in reply, and were given a very frosty look, as the Sergeant was about to enter into his 'parade ground' mode and bawl us out for insubordination, by not shouting out our answer. Fortunately for him, with so many 'orrficers' in the near vicinity, he thought better of it, and contented himself with giving us, what he presumed to be a withering look, which brought grins to our faces, and he stalked out of the room with as much dignity as he could muster.

After a few minutes, the Sergeant marched smartly back into the room. 'Attenshun', he bellowed, and bearing in mind his words about our behaviour being constantly monitored, we leapt to our feet with the greatest

135

alacrity. It was unfortunate, that the rows of chairs had been placed rather too close together; it was also rather unfortunate that some of the candidates were no doubt second row forwards in their rugby teams, with the result that in their haste to get to their feet, they managed to collide with and knock over the chairs in front of them. It was also unfortunate that the chairs were the metal collapsible type, and which they did most effectively as they hit the floor. The ensuing noise and chaos were sufficient to sound and look as though another World War had started. The red tabbed Colonel with his assorted band of Lieutenant-Colonels and Majors looked distinctly put out and not amused; and we had the feeling that they were considering failing the lot of us on the grounds of 'behaviour unbecoming of officers' and throwing in 'behaviour prejudicial to good order and discipline' for good measure.

Eventually, order was restored, and the Colonel Boss Man invited us to sit, but not 'at ease'. So we sat at 'attention' for the whole briefing, a most uncomfortable position, especially as the seats of the chairs were not level but sloped downwards, and had a tendency to dump those who were perhaps nodding off unceremoniously on the floor. However, this was not likely to happen, as the stakes were too high; even though sitting bolt upright with arms straight down to our sides was damned uncomfortable, and not being able to move to ease 'bums' as saddle soreness set in. I had a suspicion that Colonel Boss Man, to prolong our discomfort, had decided, as punishment to draw out the briefing for as long as he decently could.

This was obviously not a good start to our 'WASBEE', for no doubt as a result of the chairs incident, Colonel Boss Man and the rest of the Directing Staff (DS) looked as though there were attending a court-martial rather than a Selection Board. Perhaps as this was being held on a Friday, Saturday and Sunday had something to do with their unsmiling and grim expressions. Golf and polo, interspersed with G & Ts were obviously not on their weekend agenda.

Colonel Boss Man started his briefing in slow and measured tones.

'Right, you all know what you are here for. Over the next three days you will be tested to your limits, so that we can judge whether you have it in you to become officers.

'If we believe so, you will attend the Officer Cadet School at Mons OCS for sixteen weeks of infantry training before being commissioned. At any stage, if it is felt that you are not suitable, you will be failed and returned to your unit. You needn't think that by becoming an officer you are in for a cushy life. Far from it, the path you have chosen is not an easy one, and it will take hard work, dedication and commitment to prove that you have what it takes to hold the Queen's Commission.

'Whilst you are here, each of you will be monitored at all times on your performance and your behaviour. The tasks you will be set will test ability, intelligence, initiative, leadership and command, communication, stamina, confidence, enthusiasm and physical fitness. You will also have to undergo an interview, take part in a discussion group and give a five-minute presentation.

'You will be divided up into teams of eight, and there will be a captain and senior NCO with you at all times, not only to observe and mark your performance, but also to ensure that you don't do something bloody silly and injure yourself or one of your team. Are there any questions?'

We were too 'bum' numbed and uncomfortable from sitting at 'attention' to prolong the agony by asking questions.

'Right. Let's get started. Sergeant, carry on'.

'Room. Attenshun', roared the Sergeant. We rose, with considerably more care, and stood as the Colonel Boss Man and the rest of the 'top table' left the room.

I have often felt it somewhat strange, that although I have many very clear memories of my two years of National Service; the one part of my service, which I only have hazy memories is that of my WOSB, although I can recall the content of some of the major tasks. Psychologists would possibly have analysed me as having been in a state of deep WOSB trauma as a result of the experience, and in order to come to terms with this, I had buried the three days deep into my subconscious. However, to throw cold water on their prognosis, the memory lapse was probably as a result of the very hectic and stressful three days, involving many varied and complex tasks usually against the clock, so that there was little time to fully assimilate what one was doing. It was a question of completing each task with a degree of urgency, under pressure and then moving on to the next one.

Our eight-man team was made up with candidates from infantry and cavalry regiments as well as from various Corps, but I was the only REME candidate. The DS had sensibly mixed us all up, so that no team had more than one person from the same regiment or corps. We therefore started the tests as complete strangers, with the result that if we were going to function as a cohesive unit, we would have to get to know each other and bond pretty damned quickly, so that we could support each other with the team tasks. I presumed the objective was for the DS to discover each candidate's leadership, command and communication ability working with seven strangers.

Our group had been allocated a Captain from the East Anglian Regiment, with back up from a RAOC Sergeant, whose prime function it appeared, and he had the right cap badge for this, was to keep the Captain supplied with sufficient paper, pencils and rubbers for his clipboard; to ensure that the Captain did not run out of cigarettes, and to move us on from one task stand to another in the shortest possible time.

~

If there was one WOSB task, which was infamous, and which fully deserved its reputation, it was the one designed to test initiative, ingenuity, leadership skills and team spirit. It took the whole of one day for this one task to be completed, as it had to be done eight times, with a change of scenario for each new team leader, and it is one of the tasks which I can remember in some detail.

The DS appeared to have a dangerous fascination with water, both real and imaginary; for basically, with very few aids, each of us had to transport his team, or if our DS was out of fags and in a bad mood, the whole of the 8th Army across an imaginary river, with the enemy, in the form of a whole Panzer Division coming up fast at the speed of an old BRM racing car. The complexity of the task was governed by the mental ability and imagination of the DS officer. In reality, the options were somewhat limited, but to make it more interesting, at least one member of the team was a wounded stretcher case. The aids normally consisted of a few planks, poles, rope and an empty forty-gallon oil barrel. Each member of our team tried different methods of crossing the water hazard, for although the task was varied for each team leader, the basic concept remained the same.

One very practical, and simple solution was for the best swimmer in the team to swim with one end of the rope across the river.

Captain East Anglian woke up. 'You can't do that, the river is in flood', and he lit another fag.

'That's okay', I said, 'you see that spit of sand over there jutting out from the bank opposite us. If we go upstream, and then tie one end of the rope around the barrel and also round John (our strongest swimmer), he could swim across pushing the barrel ahead of him, which would give him buoyancy, and the river's flow would carry him downstream towards the opposite bank.'

Captain East Anglian vetoed my suggestion, on the grounds that it would be too dangerous. I commented that with a Panzer Division coming up behind us, nothing would be too dangerous. The Captain was not amused and furiously tried to write something down on his clipboard, but only succeeded in breaking the lead in his pencil. By the time the Ordnance Sergeant had visited the local RAOC BSD (Base Supplies Depot) to indent for a further supply of pencils and the NAAFI for more packets of full strength Capstan cigarettes, the team was having another go at trying to reach the opposite bank, and Capt East Anglian's attention was fortunately diverted from his clipboard, as I feared he would be writing down that I was being facetious by coming up with ridiculous ideas.

This time, the idea was, and it certainly wasn't mine, that we would build from our equipment the tallest wooden tripod we could. I being the lightest member of our team would have one end of the rope tied to me, and using the tripod for height, I would be swung like a playground swing higher and higher, until the others decided I had enough momentum and height, and would release me, so that with the rope paying out through the top of the tripod, I would fly gracefully through the air, and land on the opposite bank. I was however seriously worried; it was one thing to swing between two uprights, but with a third one to give stability and rigidity to the structure, this could have been a recipe for disaster, and I wondered how the rest of the team were going to 'aim' me between the three wooden uprights without me crashing into one. I had a sinking feeling that my manhood was in serious jeopardy before it had been properly tested. From the gleam in his eye, Capt East Anglian obviously thought that this was a splendid idea. Fortunately for me, he realised that a damaged candidate would not look good on his Annual Fitness Report. So, and I could see it was with some reluctance; he vetoed this idea as well.

Tying the planks and poles together and fixing the barrel at one end, and pushing the whole contraption out across the river like a cantilever with John sitting astride the barrel seemed a possibility, but it was some three yards short of the other bank, and as the Captain reminded us, the river was in flood.

Eventually each of us, taking turns as team leader, did successfully complete our given task. Although, one leader directing operations, got the team and our equipment safely across the 'river', before the realisation set in that he had not planned how he was going to get himself across, and he was left stranded on the near bank, and from the simulated 'booming' noises Captain East Anglian was making, the Panzers were getting dangerously close. We did suggest to the candidate in question, being from a cavalry regiment that he should ride his horse across the 'river'. A suggestion that was not appreciated. Robert, a Royal Engineer, designed a most ingenious system, based on using two tripods, one on either bank, and adopting the principle behind the Navy's bosun's chair, got the team across the river, in what most have been near record time. Although not a race the DS noted down times and we were all congratulating Robert, when Capt East Anglian stubbed out his cigarette, and by 'walking on water' crossed over to our 'bank' to point out that the objective was not only to get the team over the river, but also to bring the equipment over with us, as it mustn't be allowed to fall into enemy hands.

I felt the equipment wouldn't be much use in getting a Tiger tank across a river in flood. If we left the equipment behind and if, hopefully the enemy tried to use it to get their tank across, this would undoubtedly have sunk, and we could have chalked up 'one enemy tank destroyed'. However, having pushed my luck once with Captain East Anglian, I wasn't about to enter into a debate with him on the viability of getting a 50 ton tank across a raging torrent with a forty-gallon barrel, some planks, poles and a rope.

~

As I feared the assault course was particularly tough, and it was no mean feat, both individually and as a team to successfully complete it in the shortest possible time in competition with the other teams. I had no idea who devised and built the assault course, probably some sadistic and 'gung-ho' physical training instructor; suffice it to say, that after I had completed the course, not only was I mentally throwing doubts on his ancestry, but also imagining what I would like to do to him with a hockey stick, which would have been outside 'The Queensberry Rules' for hockey.

The Colonel Boss Man had warned us that WOSB was about physical fitness and stamina, and he was not joking. There were walls to scale; ropes and netting to climb; water hazards to be either crossed or jumped over; loads to be lifted over obstacles; underground pipes to be crawled through and barbed wire to be crossed.

'Don't worry. One of you has to throw yourself on the wire with your arms stretched out in front of you, whilst the others climb over you, and then they pull you over.' Ha! Ha! Funny man!!

Although it sounded simple, crawling under pegged down camouflage nets was not so easy, with the heels of our boots, buckles on our webbing belts and berets constantly snagging on the netting, with time lost untangling these. Time was of the essence, as each team was racing against the clock, and although there were obstacles that were taken individually; there were others, such as scaling a high wall set at the top of a steep ramp, which could only be tackled as a team, who had to work out very quickly the best way to get everybody over the wall. This usually resulted in the lightest member of the team climbing on the shoulders of the tallest man, who then 'launched' him to reach out for the top. This was fine, if the top was in reach, but there were assault courses and Barton Stacey was one, where the height of the wall was too high for this method. However, by forming a pyramid, two team members could climb up the pyramid and scramble onto the top of the wall, and with one reaching down with outstretched arms and with the other sitting on his bottom, the others could be hoisted up the wall, until there were only two left, when the strongest member of the team, with his back to the wall and cupped hands would 'throw' what should be the lightest man up to the outstretched arms of the man on top. This usually worked well, but there was always a risk that the strong man of the team not knowing his own strength, might inadvertently 'throw' the lightest member right over the wall, which whilst certainly saving time, was a rather dangerous practice, and not to be recommended.

For the last man, the lightest man, presuming he hadn't been 'thrown' right over the wall, was held by his ankles by two of the team, and with outstretched arms reached down and grabbed the hands of the last man, who had to 'walk' up the wall with the rest of the team 'reeling' them both in, until someone could reach down and grab hold of the last man's belt and pull him up. Again there was a risk; too hard a 'yank' could result in loss of balance by he who was 'yanking', with the result that several members of the team would make a sudden, unexpected and rather painful descent on the other side of the wall. However, this procedure did save a few precious seconds for the next obstacle.

As the assault course was a timed event, we doubled between obstacles and then tried to take these 'on the run' as well. All this activity was accompanied by vocal encouragement from the other members of the team in the most positive and helpful manner: 'Get your fucking boot out of my face,' or 'Go for it and move your bloody arse', or 'Go on, jump for it, you can make it', followed by, 'Sorry, thought you could jump that far. Never mind, keep running, the water will soon drain off you.'

The assault course was the worst physical activity that I had ever undertaken. At the end I was shaking like a leaf, gasping for breath, and with an overwhelming desire to throw up. 'Don't worry, Mate.' This from an RAOC candidate. 'You should see the assault course at Pirbright, it's a mile long and has twenty seven obstacles.' I didn't wish him any harm, but, at that moment I had no intention of wanting to be his 'Mate' and if he was so proud of the Pirbright assault course, I wished he would bloody well take himself there.

Although, I had finished the course, there were a few obstacles that were beyond me and which I had not completed. I observed Captain East Anglian had duly recorded these on his clipboard.

I was convinced that I had failed the assault course, and I could only hope that I had faired better in the other tasks. It was some consolation that I found others who had fared no better than I had on the assault course.

~

The five-minute lecture did not worry me too greatly. Fortunately, I had brought my thesis on the 'History of the Trade Union Movement' home with me when I came down from Loughborough, and which I had brought back to camp at the end of a forty-eight hour weekend pass. The main problem was deciding what to leave out in order to keep to the time limit. This, I eventually managed to do, and as I had spent a considerable time at Loughborough preparing my thesis a great deal of the content was still fresh in my mind.

With the other team members, we waited in one of the lecture rooms, to be called individually into the next room where Colonel Boss Man and his cohorts were listening to and judging the presentations. Whilst awaiting my turn I mentally rehearsed what I was going to say, concentrating on dates and the several Employment Laws that had been promulgated over the years. If, during my presentation I forgot the odd date or two, I decided to quote any old one instead, as I felt fairly certain that none of the Directing Staff knew anything about the Trade Union Movement, and probably did not want to.

The candidate ahead of me, from an Irish Regiment was obviously giving a good presentation, from the laughter that we could hear coming from the next room.

Then, the door opened and Captain East Anglian stuck his head through. 'Caffyn, you're next.' Although, confident in knowing my subject, I nevertheless, suddenly succumbed to what can only be described as stage fright; my legs turned to jelly and butterflies were churning up my stomach 'something terrible'. At the same time I had a panic attack thinking, that in my laziness I had chosen a most inappropriate subject to give to a Military Examination Board. However, I had no time to change my mind, as I smartly, I hoped, came to attention and saluted the Board, comprising Colonel Boss Man, the odd Lieutenant-Colonel, and an assortment of Majors; with Captains at the back of the room as Team Observers. I took my place at the lectern, as the Members of the Board looked at me expectantly and with interest in their eyes, as they seemed to be on a 'high' from the previous candidate's amusing presentation.

'The subject I am going to talk about today, is the history of the Trade Union Movement.' Wham! The faces before me suddenly went blank, and glazed expressions replaced the keenly expectant ones that were there only a few moments ago. It was too late to stop. I was committed.

'Trade unionism in Britain dates back to the beginning of the 18th century, and pre-dates the Industrial Revolution; but it may go back even further than that date, for certain skilled trades such as printing has always had and still has strong 'closed shop' union membership. Our Trade Union Movement is the oldest in Europe and until the end of the 19th century was much larger than in other countries, when German trade unionism caught up with us in size…'

As I ploughed on, I could see several heads beginning to droop, and hands were raised to cover mouths to stifle yawns. My heart was metaphorically sinking downwards towards my boots, and I thought, that after my indifferent performance on the assault course, I had really 'blown' my chances of getting a commission. If I did pass WOSB, I would probably be the only candidate to have ever done so by boring 'the pants off' the Selection Board.

Eventually, and it seemed like an eternity, I finished my presentation, and asked for questions. There was a general stir from the Board as attention was re-focused on me, and brains were put into gear. Fortunately there were none.

'Thank you, Caffyn. That was most interesting.' At least the Colonel knew his manners, so I presumed that he was an ex-cavalry man. 'Would you mind leaving by that door,' he continued, pointing to one of the doors at the far end of the room.

I saluted, turned and moved to the designated door, thinking, 'There are two doors at this end of the room. Is one for successful candidates and the other for unsuccessful ones?' Happily, when I walked through to the other room, I found to my relief that all those who had given their talk before me were gathered there.

One of the least onerous tasks was when each team, (re-defined as a syndicate for indoor tasks and which certainly sounded more up-market) was given a subject to debate, whilst the DS would listen in and take notes of how we participated in a group discussion, and whether our contributions were constructive, intelligent and enthusiastic, and also how we would react if the debate became heated.

Our syndicate's subject was; whether it was right in the 1930s for the Oxford University Union to debate the motion: 'This House will not fight for King and Country.' The subject, on the face of it appeared to be a fairly straightforward one, but upon reflection, I realised that the DS, as well as judging our debating skills, were also attempting to determine, as National Service conscripts, whether any of us had 'bolshie' tendencies and were in sympathy with that Oxford Union motion. Our discussion was fairly robust, for even the most introverted members of our syndicate realised that it was vital to actively participate and contribute to the debate. We were, fortunately all of the same mind, believing as a democracy, it was vital that the right of 'free speech' must never be stifled, and the Oxford Union had the right to debate the motion, even though we as a syndicate did not agree with it. So at the end of our debating session, we left the DS in no doubt that if the situation arose we would fight for Queen and Country. This no doubt pleased them and hopefully would have earned us some 'brownie' points.

~

After nearly three days of endeavour, we faced the final test, - the interview. Our syndicate was corralled together in one of the lecture rooms, and for some inexplicable reason the door to the interview room was guarded by our inscrutable RAOC Sergeant, presumably with the intention of preventing us indulging in some keyhole eavesdropping in an attempt to find out what questions were being asked.

143

'Sergeant, can I go for a pee?' This from John, a cheerful, and somewhat cheeky character from the Oxs and Bucks Regiment.

'Tough,' responded the Sergeant, without any trace of sympathy. 'Tie a knot in the bleedin' thing.'

'But Sergeant, I'm getting desperate.' John, whom I had got to know and like over the previous three days, had mentioned to me that he had enjoyed appearing in school plays, was certainly putting on a good act, but I was certain it was an act to test the Sergeant.

'I've got me bleedin' orders, that I mustn't let you out of this room, and if you can't hang on, then open that bleedin' window, and piss out of it, but make sure no one's walking past and the wind is not blowing this way.'

We wondered what John would do. Would he call the Sergeant's bluff and pee out of the window, or had the Sergeant called his bluff and instinctively realised that this was a try-on by John? We did not have long to wait. With mutterings of 'unfair' and 'victimisation', John with a hurt expression on his face sank further into his seat.

Eventually it was my turn to face the Board.

'Sit down, Caffyn.'

'Yes, Sir.'

'Now, how have you found the last three days?'

Bloody hell! Does the silly old fool expect me to say they have been one of the most unpleasant and uncomfortable weekends I have ever spent in my life?

'I've found it most challenging, Sir. Some of the tasks certainly stretched me, and I believe that I have discovered in myself, strengths that I didn't know I had.'

There! That should please the old fool.

The Board questioned me about my background and education.

'I see you went to St Edward's School in Oxford. I have heard of the school, but don't know much about it. Does the School have a CCF, and were you in it?'

'Yes, Sir. It was compulsory. I took and passed both Cert 'A' parts I and II, and rose to the rank of Lance-Corporal.'

Oops! Perhaps that could be a mistake. They'll mark me down as junior NCO material, and I was aware out of the corner of my eye that Captain East Anglian was once again busily scribbling something down on his clipboard.

I felt I had to retrieve the situation. 'It was a very active CCF Sir, with an annual camp, which one year I attended at Brandon in Norfolk. We also had an annual inspection and at my last year at St Edward's the Inspecting Officer was Field-Marshal Montgomery.' There! That should impress them.

'Any famous old boys?'

'Well, Sir. What about Kenneth Grahame, Laurence Olivier, Douglas Bader and Guy Gibson.'

The last two names really caught the Board's attention, even though they had both been Royal Air Force. I felt that my chances of passing WOSB had suddenly improved.

The questioning moved on to my plans for the future, and then came the sixty-four thousand dollar question.

'Will you tell the Board why you believe that you are a suitable candidate to receive the Queen's Commission?'

'Well, Sir. I want to make the most of my two years National Service, and not spend the time doing as little as possible and counting the days to demob.

'I believe my time at boarding school has taught me to stand on my own feet, and as a prefect to accept responsibility and to use my initiative to make decisions when it was necessary. Being in the cricket, hockey and rugby sides has taught me to be a team player.

'My four years at Loughborough College of Technology, with half the curriculum being given over to practical instruction in the various College workshops, has given me a grounding in mechanical and engineering skills which should be useful in REME.

'I captained my House cricket team at St Edward's and I was captain of the successful Loughborough Colleges 2nd hockey XI, before playing for the first team. This has, even though it's sport, given me some experience of leadership.'

I hoped that was good enough to impress the Board.

'Humph!' This from Colonel Boss Man. 'Has your family had any military experience?'

Oh heck! I did not want to bring up my father's war record, in case the Board felt I was playing on it. But since they've asked, and maybe they have had sight of it, I'd better talk about it.

'Well. Yes, Sir. My father is Territorial Army. In September 1939, he was a major in the RAOC(E). After Dunkirk in 1940, he was posted as a Colonel to York commanding, I believe a RAOC workshop there. Then in 1942 he was posted to the War Office as one of the team that formed REME. From 1944 to 1945 he was DME 21st Army Group in North West Europe. He was demobbed with the honorary rank of Brigadier. Since then he has been, and still is Chairman of the Sussex Territorial Army Association and vice-Chairman of the National Association.'

I decided that was more than enough. I don't know whether the Board was impressed or not, but my interview seemed to have gone on for ages.

Colonel Boss Man looked to his colleagues, 'Any questions for Caffyn?'

Happily, there were none.

'Thank you, Caffyn. You're dismissed.'

A quick salute, and I was out of that room so fast that even a drill sergeant in the Light Infantry would have been impressed at the speed I could move when necessary. I was shaking like a leaf, and my shirt was sticking to my back with perspiration. I found the interview to be much more of an ordeal than the five-minute presentation.

~

The interview was our final ordeal. When all these had been completed, we were all herded into a room next to where the Board was debating and deciding whether we had passed or failed.

We all found the waiting a most unnerving experience. Whether we were from the infantry, artillery, armour, cavalry, or from one of the Corps, we had all been chosen as potential officers and had spent some three months working towards WOSB, which if we passed, we would attend Mons Officer Cadet School. Although I was concerned that I may have been marked down for my indifferent performance on the assault course and my boring presentation on the Trade Union Movement, I could not believe that these would be sufficient for me to fail WOSB. So I was mentally geared up for a pass, and I was certain that all the other candidates felt the same way. However, there were bound to be failures, and I prayed that I wasn't going to be one. It would have been a devastating blow to be rejected and one would not only have had to mentally adjust to returning to ones unit as a private soldier with immediate effect, but also face possible critical comments from ones family and friends. One would also have suffered a severe blow to ones confidence and self-respect. So, understandably the atmosphere in the room was very tense, with very little conversation, and if the others were feeling as I was, they were also probably mentally preparing themselves to the possibility of failure.

After nearly half an hour the door to the main lecture room opened, and our 'tie a knot in it' RAOC Sergeant appeared with a clipboard in hand.

'Right, listen in. I shall call out your names in turn and you will proceed past me into the next room, where the Board will tell you your fate. When they have finished, you will leave by the door at the far end of the room. Is that clear?'

'Yes, Sergeant.'

'Right. Adams you're first.'

Adams from the Shropshire Light Infantry stood up, and giving us a wan smile disappeared into the next room.

A few minutes later the door opened and the Sergeant called out for Hayward to come forward. We noticed, as more names were called out, that the time each candidate spent with the Board varied; some were quite short, whilst others were there for some time.

Robert, the Sapper mused: 'If you are in there for a short time, it must mean that the Board has told you you've failed and sent you on your way. If you've passed they're probably discussing how you performed, and what were your strengths and weaknesses.'

'Could be the other way round,' I suggested. 'If you've passed, they don't have much to say to you, whereas if you've failed they are probably telling you why.'

Before we could debate this any further, John, a Gunner, who had been standing by a window for some time called out, 'Come here and look at this.'

We trooped over to the window, and from there we could see each candidate leaving the building, some were walking jauntily with their heads held high, and others walked slowly away with their heads down. It didn't take a genius to work out who had passed and who had failed.

Eventually, it was my turn and with legs feeling like jelly and with sweaty palms, I entered the room, saluted and stood at attention in front of the Board.

'Right, Caffyn. Stand at ease', started Colonel Boss Man, 'we have been impressed with the way you tackled several of the tasks, where you showed enthusiasm, drive and a proper sense of urgency. Captain Anderson', the Colonel pointed to our chain smoking and pencil snapping East Anglian observer, 'felt that at times you had a little too much imagination, and some of your suggestions were somewhat impractical and possibly boarding on being facetious.'

My heart fell. I thought I had blown it at the imaginary river crossing initiative task. That was it then. I had failed.

Colonel Boss Man continued. 'However, we realise that this was probably down to enthusiasm, which however misplaced, is a quality we look for. Your talk, although not a subject I and my fellow officers know much about, and a word of advice here; in future you might be wise to chose a less serious subject and one that has a broader appeal. However, you nevertheless obviously knew your subject, which you delivered clearly and with confidence. Tell me, why did you choose the Trade Unions?'

'I had to prepare a thesis on the history of the Unions for my Finals at College, Sir.'

'Um. I see. Your assault course was rather weak and you obviously struggled with several of the obstacles, but you weren't the only one. However, you did have a go at all of them.

'Your interview highlighted your background and education, which are the sort of qualities we are looking for in officers, and although you did not have a great opportunity to show your leadership ability, you did enough to make us believe that it is there. So, in spite of the weaknesses we have pointed out; you have passed. Congratulations.'

In a state of shock, I managed to mumble, 'Thank you, Sir.'

'Now, this doesn't mean that you will automatically become an officer. You will be posted to Mons Officer Cadet School for four months of infantry training prior to being commissioned; but if at any time it is judged that your performance on the Course is below standard, you will be failed and returned to your unit. It is a tough Course, as the Army has only four months to turn you into officers and which normally takes two years at Sandhurst. Good luck.'

I saluted, walked out in a daze, but once outside, just as had the others, my head came up, and I walked away from the building with a definite spring in my step. I felt like throwing my beret in the air and shouting for the whole world to hear, 'I've passed, I've bloody well passed.' Which would have been behaviour definitely unbecoming for an officer.

~

I am sure that anyone who had taken and passed WOSB must have felt a sense of satisfaction and achievement. I know I did. Although probably not the hardest of selection boards in the Services, it was, nevertheless a challenge; especially as only some twelve weeks previously, we had all been civilians and National Service was regarded by the majority as a necessary evil from which, once one had passed the medical, there was no escape.

Some years later in conversation with the family and explaining the reason why I had not stayed in the Territorial Army, which from my very limited and parochial experience, I thought in the early 1960s to be rather amateurish, and after having being on active service in Malaya, I found part-time soldiering to be very unfulfilling. I felt that if I could not be a full-time soldier, then being a 'Saturday Night Soldier' was not for me. I reminded the family, during embarkation leave, of the pressure that I had been subjected to not to stay in the Army. Then, right out of the blue, I was told; 'Well, you know your father arranged for you to pass WOSB.'

I so couldn't believe what I had heard, that I had to have the statement repeated. I was devastated. Something, which I believed I had achieved through my own efforts, and with no influence from my father, had been completely blown away. I failed to understand why, many years after I had completed my National Service, this had suddenly come to light. Possibly it was felt I did not always appreciate that my father had my interests at heart, and had been trying to give me practical support. But the result had a totally negative effect on me. At a stroke my confidence and belief in myself had been completely demolished, leaving me totally demoralised.

I was so upset, that the following week I arranged to see a friend of mine, Dick Smart, who was at the time a half-colonel in the Ministry of Defence, to find out if there was any truth in what I had been told. Dick reassured me by emphasising that, my father as a TA officer who had been demobbed in 1945, would and could have had no influence whatsoever in the War Office, and efforts to manipulate a Selection Board's decisions, whose officers were drawn from all arms of the Army, would not for one second have been tolerated. I felt very relieved to hear what Dick had said. However, I have found it very difficult to forget what had been said, and there has always been that nagging question in the back of my mind; 'Did I really pass WOSB due to my own efforts and ability?'

Very many years later, I was relating the story to my old Brigadier, who was the Director of Electrical and Mechanical Engineering (DEME) in the Far East when I was posted to Malaya, and who had previously been my father's deputy in 21st Army Group. His reaction was such that his eyebrows shot upwards and nearly took off into space. He reassured me that it was totally impossible to arrange for someone to pass WOSB and quoted, as an example, the son of a senior general who had twice failed to pass the Selection Board.

Those of us who had passed were euphoric; however, this was tinged with sadness over those who had failed. They looked so dejected as they packed up their kit, and all we could do was to commiserate with them, offer them our sympathy and suggest that they could well be selected to attend another WOSB.

Barton Stacey Camp could not have been on anyone's social list for 'The Season', as the facilities to entertain or celebrate were obviously pretty low down on the Army's list of priorities. That evening, and it had to be admitted, after three days of adrenaline fed intense mental and physical effort, we were all somewhat exhausted and feeling rather 'flat'. So, we were not too disappointed that there were no facilities to celebrate, and we were quite content to lie on our beds chatting amongst ourselves, enjoying the lack of discipline and a moment of peace, and imagining that the worst was over and the months we were to spend at Mons OCS would be plain sailing. How naïve and innocent we were. We were sorry when the evening came to an end, as we were well aware, that once we had returned to our respective units, discipline in the shape of warrant officers and senior NCOs would be re-imposed with bedblocks, hut inspections, drill, PT and the assault course being the order of the day.

The following morning we said our farewells as we returned to our various units. However, we did expect to meet up again in a few weeks at Mons OCS.

~

Back at 2 Trg Bn we found that having passed WOSB, the atmosphere within 'D' Company changed. We were the senior platoon and were issued with the plastic white disks, which fitted behind our cap badges, boosted our morale and gave us a certain feeling of superiority and smugness. The more so when the platoon behind us kept trying to find out from us about the 'WASBEE'. We treated them in the same way as we had been treated by the platoon before us, by either playing down the various tasks, or indulging in the most outrageous 'line-shooting'.

It was sad though, to see a number of empty beds in our hut, as those who had failed were quickly posted out to other units. In the months we had spent at Honiton, our hut had bonded into a close-knit unit, sharing the good and the bad times, and we were all more than willing to help each other out when the going got tough. In spite of the discipline, the pressure and doing everything at the double, there were many occasions when we had good laughs, and we spent many enjoyable evenings in the camp NAAFI.

We found that our instructors, both senior and junior NCOs became more relaxed and especially so our two corporals, whom we had regarded as being right bastards, became positively human. They were obviously saving themselves for the incoming platoon that would start after we had left for Aldershot.

Obviously we had to be kept occupied and although the pressure was off, we were given lectures on sundry subjects; sent round the assault course every day and from the amount of time we spent in the gym, the PTIs were being kept busy as well. But, it was during the three weeks we had to wait before our posting came through, that Sergeant-Major Colquhoun spent a great deal of time with us on the Square, and taught us such intricate drill movements, that we came to appreciate and take a pride in our drill.

Eventually, our orders came through that we were to report to Mons OCS at Aldershot at the beginning of December 1958.

I was sorry to leave No 2 Trg Bn, whether it was because of its compact size or its location, but the Camp seemed to have a warm friendly atmosphere, compared to the seemingly cold and impersonal one at No 1 Trg Bn at Blandford. This may have been unfair on that Battalion, for as a raw recruit unaccustomed to service life, where everything was strange and somewhat frightening, I felt completely confused and disorientated by what I, and the other recruits were subjected to and by the size and complexity of the Camp. The weather may have played its part. For the time I was at Blandford, each day seemed to be dull, damp and rather misty; whilst my memories of Honiton, were of dry, warm and mainly sunny days; with the exception of the day of the Annual Administrative Inspection, which was more akin to the grey and dismal weather of Blandford.

Honiton was and still is a most attractive town, set in a lovely part of Devon, and when we were let loose on the unprepared burghers, we were always welcomed with friendliness, and I never heard of any trouble in the town from any of the companies, although in 'D' Company we were somewhat isolated.

One quickly got used to the swearing, abuse and bad language, realising that it was all part of the system and was used without malice, to help make soldiers out of us in the shortest possible time. The officers, warrant officers and NCOs were professional and ensured that our training was given in a sensible and intelligent manner; although in order to instil discipline and to make us obey orders without question, the instructors had, at times to be quite brutal in their approach; for as one sergeant pointed out:

'If you are in a battle and under enemy fire, you need to know that you can totally rely on those around you, and that you will obey orders without hesitation, for it is only by so doing that casualties can be kept down.' There was little doubt that the 'in your face' method, whether on the Square, or with barrack room and kit inspections did produce fear, and on many occasions the fear of punishment did ensure that we carried out, without question, orders from NCOs that seemed to us to make very little sense.

When we arrived at Honiton, we were still very raw recruits, and yet in the space of some ten weeks, we had been turned, however unwillingly and probably still resenting National Service, into some semblance of responsible soldiers. Having passed WOSB, and going on for officer cadet training, we had shown that we were determined to make the best of our National Service, and we were not prepared to sit on our backsides, and spend the two years with a totally negative and 'bolshie' attitude.

So, it was with a certain feeling of sadness that I left No 2 Trg Bn, and which many years later, I still look back on with a certain amount of nostalgia and affection.

Chapter Six

A Junior Officer Cadet at Mons OCS

One of the advantages of being an officer cadet, as I was now officially tagged, was the luxury of being able to use a car and not having to rely on public transport.

I drove into Aldershot, 'The Home of the British Army', on a grey, damp and foggy early December afternoon. My first impression was of a town whose economy appeared to be totally reliant upon the Army. There were very few signs of top quality stores, light industry or office blocks. Instead there appeared to be mile upon mile of gaunt barrack blocks, standard War Office designed married quarters and Nissen huts. Behind every unit guard room I drove past could be seen the inevitable parade ground, some empty and others occupied with troops being drilled.

The Army used to run two National Service Officer Cadet Schools, one at Eaton Hall in Cheshire, which was the family seat of the Dukes of Westminster, until the Army commandeered the place in the 1940s. The Hall was used to train officer cadets from infantry and cavalry regiments and most corps. After being commissioned the National Service subalterns were usually posted abroad to 'trouble spots' where they could fulfil the main objective of their job descriptions, which was to shoot at and be shot at by unfriendly forces. I was told at the time that Eaton Hall had a fearsome reputation. But, I subsequently learnt that Mons OCS, where Royal Artillery and Royal Engineer office cadets were trained was in fact a tougher place. However, when the Government announced that National Service would end in 1962, Eaton Hall was closed down and all NS officer cadet training was centralised at Mons OCS in Aldershot. I had never thought about it, but I had always presumed that the Royal Marines, although originally deployed as infantry on Royal Navy ships, were part of the British Army as their officers held the same ranks as the Army. Many years later on a short visit to Kosovo, where No 3 Royal Marine Commando was the lead unit in the Multi-National Brigade Centre (MNBC), I learnt that the Royal Marines were and are administered by the Royal Navy, even though they were and still are deployed overseas in a specialised infantry role on land based operations. So, I suppose it was logical for RM officer cadets to be trained at Mons OCS rather than at Royal Navy training establishments.

After driving around Aldershot for some time, trying to convince myself that I was carrying out a motorised reconnaissance of the town, whereas in reality I was lost, I eventually hit upon Queen's Parade, and I knew from my movement order that was where Mons OCS was situated.

Having taken the scenic route through and round Aldershot, my spirits were somewhat lifted as I drove down Queen's Parade, for though obviously being very Army, there was a plethora of playing fields either side of the road, which gave a feeling of 'openness' as opposed to the urban sprawl of the town. Shortly after I had passed 'The Officers' Club' on my port side, I came upon on my starboard side a fairly prominent sign advertising the fact that I had eventually arrived at Mons OCS. Turning to my right I drove up to the Guard Room, where the duty sergeant, having asked my name, perused his clipboard, raised his right arm and with pencil pointing the way, exclaimed:

'Over there, Sorr.'

'Sorr'? I wasn't one yet. Perhaps he had mistaken me for a real live officer, or perhaps he had been impressed by my 1948 Morris Minor, the early model with the headlights at low level and the split windscreen.

'You drives to those 'uts and you're in 'ut E4. You park behind the 'uts. Okay, Sorr?'

'Yes, thank you Sergeant.' What a nice man I thought, as I drove in the direction of his pencil; if all the WOs and NCOs were like him, Mons was going to be a pleasant place for officer training

I parked the car where directed, unloaded my kit and having located Hut E4, humped it into what was going to be my home, I hoped for the following four months.

~

'Who have we got here, then?' A stentorian voice greeted me. I turned and was confronted by a ferocious looking Warrant Officer from the Grenadier Guards. I quaked in my boots, as I looked up at him, in his immaculately pressed and tailored battledress, with his pace stick aimed straight at my heart, head thrust forward like an eagle and eyes like gimlets, which seemed to look right through me from under the peak of his hat and which was so angled that it appeared to rest on the bridge of his nose.

'And what is your name,' a pause, 'Sir?'

'Caffyn', no pause, 'Sir.'

'Right,' said he ticking my name off from a list on his clipboard, 'I am your Company Sergeant- Major. You will call me 'Sir', and I will call you 'Sir'. The only difference is that you will mean it, and I won't. Find yourself a bed and square away your kit. The evening meal is at 1800hrs. After that you're all on your own until reveille at 0630hrs tomorrow morning. Is that clear?' He lowered his pace stick aiming it in the direction of the others in the hut who had arrived before me.

'Yes, Sir.' We responded in what we trust was a bright and enthusiastic manner as the CSM, in true Guards style, marched smartly from the hut with head held high and pace stick delicately held at the point of balance and aligned perfectly parallel with the floor.

We spent that first evening getting to know each other. There were twelve in the hut, and we came from all branches of the Army, the Royal Tank Regiment, the Royal Marines, the Royal Signals, the Royal Engineers and from various Corps, such as the RAOC, the RASC and the REME (myself).

I had expected that the barrack blocks would be somewhat more upmarket than the ones I had already experienced at Blandford and Honiton, but I was disappointed to see that they were the same World War One design and construction. Fortunately, we quickly found out that the senior company had not as yet held their Passing-Out Parade, and until they had, we would be housed in the old barrack huts.

~

I wondered how we would be kept occupied during the fortnight we had to wait before starting our Course, and also wondered why we had been called to Mons so early. I need not have worried, for after four months in the Army, I should have learnt two basic lessons, never volunteer for anything and never appear to be idle. For the Army did not, and probably still does not believe in 'idleness', and it was a chargeable offence if one was caught being 'idle', especially on parade. Also every activity in the Army appeared to be urgent and had to be carried out 'at the double'.

Anyway, we were not going to be kept idle for that first fortnight. As officer cadets we were issued with further items of kit, as if we hadn't been issued with enough already. White belts, white rifle slings, white bayonet scabbard holder and white collar tabs, the latter had to be sewn, using the 'housewife' onto the lapels of our battledress blouses, and white lanyards were issued together with a tin of white blanco. We were also issued with a different type of bayonet and scabbard. This bayonet had a round short blade. The cleaning of kit was obviously going to feature as a fairly major Course activity. But we soon realised why we needed a fortnight to prepare for our Course. Mons OCS used a water based green blanco whilst REME and many other regiments and corps used a plastic based one. Therefore, before we could apply the new blanco, all our webbing had to have every trace of the plastic stuff removed, which entailed many hours of boiling in water to soften the blanco, followed by endless scraping and scrubbing, before the webbing was reduced to its original dirty pale khaki state and which met the approval of the CSM and the drill sergeant. All our white kit had to be cleaned as well, for if we had simply blancoed over that of previous cadets, then the build up of white blanco could have led to deep fissures appearing on the surfaces at most inopportune moments, especially on the Adjutant's or Passing-Out Parades.

~

It would appear that the Legal and Administrative staff in the War 'House', did not wish to be made redundant in a future government defence review, so justified their existence by constantly issuing new and modified Queen's Regulations, embracing every subject that man, or woman could dream up from how to park a main battle tank (MBT) in a multi-story car park, to the correct procedure for the use in hot climates of the khaki coloured Army issue fly swot. (Which I believe was originally demonstrated by Field-Marshal Montgomery in the desert in 1942.)

Obviously, all these new and amended Regulations had to be pasted into the Army 'Bible', and we spent many happy hours with Army issue cow gum so doing. At the same time I wondered, as these were the Queens' Regulations, whether Her Majesty had personally approved every new or modified Regulation, and I pictured her happily, or perhaps not, spending her tea break with her corgis at her feet conscientiously perusing each one. As I saw it, if she did not personally approve these; then any Tom, Dick or Harry in the War 'House' over their tea break, could have dreamed up and issued new Regulations in her name, of which she may have had no knowledge and which may not have best pleased her Majesty; especially as her subjects, we were bound by law to fight for 'Queen and Country'.

~

As well as the Company Sergeant-Major being from the Grenadier Guards, our platoon had a Drill Sergeant from the Irish Guards, Sergeant Fawcett, who was a great character, a fine drill instructor, a stern disciplinarian, and over the four months of our course grew a most impressive moustache, curling up at the ends.

Our Brigade of Guards instructors introduced us to 'proper' drill, of which Derek Colquhoun had given me a taste at Honiton. It was for all of us a rude awakening. After the first drill parade I, with others had come to the conclusion that there were two types of drill practised in the British Army. One, used by the majority, which was based on the Manual of Elementary Drill (All Arms) 1935, and the other as practised by the Brigade of Guards. The drill movements may have been similar, but the execution of these was of a much higher standard altogether, and we were left in no doubt whatsoever, which of the two systems we were going to be instructed in.

At least two Honiton sized drill squares could have fitted into the Mons parade ground, which gave the CSM and the various drill sergeants plenty of space to play around drilling individual platoons or the whole company. For the first drill parade, our platoon was on its own and we had the undivided attention of both the CSM and Sergeant Fawcett, who showed off their military skills by carrying out flanking movements, with the CSM to one side of the platoon and the Drill Sergeant to the other, which enabled them to spot any mistake, idleness or any other infringement of the Brigade of Guards 'Standard Operating Drill Procedures'.

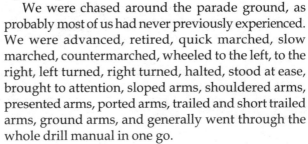

We were chased around the parade ground, as probably most of us had never previously experienced. We were advanced, retired, quick marched, slow marched, countermarched, wheeled to the left, to the right, left turned, right turned, halted, stood at ease, brought to attention, sloped arms, shouldered arms, presented arms, ported arms, trailed and short trailed arms, ground arms, and generally went through the whole drill manual in one go.

'You there in the middle rank, next to the tam-o'-shanter. You are being very idle, Sir. You will double round the Square, holding your rifle above your head until I tell you to stop, Sir.'

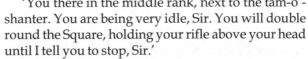

The Drill Sergeant

That punishment was a killer, the old .303 Lee Enfield rifle was not a light weapon, weighing in at some 9lbs, and after only one lap of the parade ground, ones pace had dropped to a slow jog, and arms were definitely tiring with the rifle almost resting upon ones head. But old 'eagle eyes' CSM could see out of the back of his head, and any slackening in the pace and failure in holding the rifle up, brought instant retribution by being given extra laps. By the time the CSM had relented, one was so knackered it was virtually impossible to continue to carry out drill correctly; with the result that one was dispatched once again around the parade ground.

There were many occasions when several of us had incurred the displeasure of both the CSM and the Drill Sergeant at the same time.

'You, you, and yes you three in the rear rank. Sirs, your drill is idle. Double over there and leave your rifles against that fence, then double round the Square until I tell you to stop. Now, Sirs. MOVE!!'

After a few laps, when we were at the furthest point from our rifles, the stentorian voice of the CSM would let rip:

'Right! Pick up your rifles, and fall in with the rest of the platoon. The last man back will be on a charge for being idle. Now, MOVE!!'

We would make a dash for our rifles, fighting amongst ourselves as we tried to check the numbers on the rifles, to ensure that each of us had picked up his own one. But, it only took us the once to realise that it was useless trying to do that, as the CSM would make us run round the parade ground again for being too slow to fall in. One just grabbed the first rifle that came to hand and sorted ownership out afterwards.

We were expected to execute every order instantly and without question. One cadet, not from our platoon, on being pulled up for some nefarious crime, was foolish enough to answer back

'Sergeant Fawcett,' roared the CSM, 'Take that cadet at the double to the Guard Room and charge him with insubordination and insolence.' To use an overworked Army expression, the cadet was removed at such a speed 'that his feet didn't touch the ground'. We never did find out what happened to him.

Although punishment was always swiftly and arbitrarily given for slackness and lack of effort, both the CSM and Drill Sergeant would go to considerable lengths to help cadets with genuine difficulties in executing certain drill movements. There was one member of our platoon who found it almost impossible to march swinging his left arm with the right leg and visa versa, but instead would march with either the left or right arms and legs swinging together. Sergeant Fawcett spent a considerable amount of time giving him individual coaching. Eventually his patience was rewarded when the problem was resolved, although marching never came naturally to the cadet in question.

Drill parades for the whole sixteen weeks of our training were always an ordeal, and I was thankful to come off the Square relatively unscathed. Although, we were cursed and shouted at, it was never done with the same degree of bad language and abuse that one suffered in basic training. It took quite a time though to get used to being cursed, with either the word 'Sir' added as a prefix or a suffix. If several of us were being collectively cursed, the prefix, or suffix changed to 'Gentlemen'.

~

Although, we were kept occupied, whilst we waited for our senior 'B' Company to return from Battle Camp, we did enjoy several days out of Camp. Our Company Commander, Major Langley was a Royal Marine, and he arranged for the Company to travel down to Portsmouth, and spend a day looking over HMS Victory, the Naval Base and the Dockyard.

It was unpleasant, cold, damp and a misty December day and not the weather that day-trippers would have chosen for their sightseeing; but the decision takers obviously thought that we were made of sterner stuff. We departed early morning in a convoy of Bedford RL 3 ton trucks, clasping our haversack rations, which by common agreement we were going to consume at the earliest moment, and save us the hassle of lugging them around for a good part of the day. One or two members of the platoon thought it would be a good idea if they were to eat their rations on the journey down to Portsmouth; but as the truck was not the steadiest platform for the consumption of food, we thought it was a bad idea and persuaded them not to do so, telling them they would have to be responsible for clearing up any mess.

At the gang plank to HMS Victory we were greeted by a venerable retired Chief Petty Officer (CPO), who proceeded to give us the full tour, obviously working on the principle that us 'Brown Jobs' were ignorant compared to the Senior Service.

'Now, lookie over there', as he pointed to the blunt end of the ship, 'That is where the Admiral had his quarters.' We were a little perplexed for, not being sailors we did not know to which admiral he was referring; but it did not take us too long to work out that as far as the CPO was concerned there was only one Admiral, and he himself looked old enough to have served under Nelson at Trafalgar.

'The dining room is still used today for official entertaining as HMS Victory is the Flagship of the Commander-in-Chief Home Fleet.'

We moved on.

'This 'ere is the Admiral's cot. To save space, all the officers' cots and the ratings 'ammocks were used as their coffins if they were killed. The sail maker would sew the bodies of the ratings, or what was left of them, into their 'ammocks, before they were committed to the deep over the side of the ship.'

We moved further into the bowels of Victory. 'This 'ere deck is the only one which still 'as its original timbers. All other decks 'ave 'ad to 'ave new decks laid.'

We eventually returned to what I believed to be the Quarter Deck, and viewed the spot where Nelson was shot. The CPO, thanked us for our attention, and it was obviously a surprise to him that us 'Pongos' (a slang term used by other services to describe soldiers) could actual pay attention for over an hour. However, we rather blotted our copybooks in the CPO's eyes, when we sat ourselves down on the Quarter Deck resting against the twelve-pounder cannons, and consumed our cheese and ham wads, crisps and apples. If he had his way, he would probably have had us sentenced to two dozen lashes of the 'cat o' nine tails' for daring to use his prized deck for, in his eyes, an anti-social purpose. Still, that would have made a change from running round the Mons parade ground with rifles held above our heads.

The afternoon was spent travelling around the Dockyard by boat, passing close by HMS Vanguard, the Royal Navy's last battleship. In the Government of the Day's 1957 Defence White Paper, which had also announced the ending of National Service, four battleships, with the exception of HMS Vanguard, were to be scrapped or sold off. Vanguard was commissioned too late for the Second World War, but did carry King George VI, Queen Elizabeth and the two Princesses to South Africa in 1947 for the Royal tour of that country.

HMS Vanguard's stay of execution was not to last long, for in 1960, the Government decided that she too was to be scrapped, leaving Great Britain for the first time in centuries without any big gun capital ships. Almost as an act of defiance against her fate, this very fine ship ran aground in Old Portsmouth Harbour as she was being towed to the 'knackers' yard.

It must have been hard, and probably still is for the Royal Navy, who over the centuries were responsible for putting in, and maintaining the word 'Great' into Great Britain to lose so much, as various governments have scrapped so many ships, that the Navy is but a shadow of its former self. Perhaps 'Little Britain' would now be more appropriate. Henry VIII must be turning in his grave. In 2001, I was fortunate to sail in the Type 42 Destroyer, HMS Edinburgh from Leith, Scotland to Portsmouth as the temporary, acting and unpaid godson to the ship's Communication Officer (SCO), and in spite of all the Defence Reviews, from the way I and others were treated by the ship's company, morale was good, in spite of the 'cut backs', and showed what a close-knit community a ship's company is.

Our education was not to finish with the Senior Service, for the Junior Service was our next port of call, in the shape of RAF Odiham; where we had fun climbing over and around Javelin fighters, much to the consternation of the ground crew, who were certain that we would depart from the authorised 'walk-ways' on the wings, and with our hob nailed boots crashing through the thin metal skin of the wings, immediately put out of action a significant part of Britain's air defences.

~

The 'powers that be' certainly tried to make the fortnight we had to wait for our senior company to return from battle camp and their Passing-Out Parade, as varied and interesting as possible. This included a visit to the Imperial War Museum. But the one activity, that I enjoyed most, was the day we were taken out to Long Valley, part of the Aldershot Training Area, and which over the sixteen weeks of our Course we would get to know pretty intimately as foot soldiers. On this first visit, we were introduced to the Centurion tank, which was arguably Britain's most successful tank design; for nearly four and a half thousand were produced, with some two and a half thousand being sold overseas. Its success had been due to the reputation it gained in Korea, with its very fine 105mm main armament, and I believe it was the first tank in the world to have had a stabilised gun platform.

The Royal Tank Regiment had generously provided a troop of three tanks for us to play with, which with our muddy boots we were allowed to clamber over, although the tank crews, much to our annoyance, were not keen for us to dirty the inside of their tanks. However, our disappointment was short lived, as the three tanks, with us festooned like Christmas trees decorations and clinging on for dear life, took off at what appeared to be their maximum speed across country, down the length of the rough terrain of Long Valley. Although exhilarating, it was also hair-raising, as it only needed one of us to lose our handgrip and disappear over the side of the tank, which could have been fairly terminal.

One tank commander asked me why they called the infantry 'grunts'. I replied that I had no idea. 'That's the noise they make when tanks run over them. Ha! Ha!' Before I had time to think of a suitable reply, he had disappeared into his turret, slamming the hatch behind him.

We were to make one further visit to Long Valley before our Course started, to see a demonstration of how to blow up objects, such as buildings, bridges, trains and anything else, which would help discourage unfriendly forces. A sergeant from the Royal Engineers, had already prepared primers, detonators, corded fuses and explosives, and explained with great enthusiasm how to inflict maximum damage on the enemy. We were allowed to light lengths of fuses, but our request to be allowed to attach these with detonators to a small quantity of plastic explosive was met with a firm 'No Way.'

Although these 'works' outings were enjoyable; we continued to be drilled, to scrub our webbing, to paste Queen's Regulations, and were kept fit in the gym under the tender ministrations of the Army Physical Training Instructors, who were not as abusive, and loud-mouthed as those I had previously experienced, and we generally finished the session with a game of basketball. But as with the CSM and the Drill Sergeant, it took us some time to get used to the PTIs ordering us to, 'get down and do twenty press-ups, **Sir** for being so bleedin' idle', or 'if you don't pull your finger out, **Sir**, I shall put you on a charge, **Sir**.'

~

The senior 'B' Company had returned from Battle Camp, and final preparations were being made for their Passing-Out Parade. I had been led to believe that this was one of the social events of the year and whether the Parade was held in June, December or any other month, woe betides anyone of note who failed to turn up. Passing-Out Parades, whether at Sandhurst or Mons were regarded as part of 'The Social Calendar'. Non-Military Sloane

Rangers were probably of the opinion that 'The Season' finished with 'Glorious Goodwood', but they were really missing some of the Country's most impressive events. No other Army in the world could and can match the sight and sound of a British Army Ceremonial Parade and especially so on an Officer Cadet Commissioning Parade, where the sight of serried ranks of immaculately turned-out cadets, the precision of marching feet and synchronisation of drill movements, have been so well orchestrated through the paternal tones of the RSM, CSMs and Drill Sergeants.

I could imagine retired Army officers probably struggling to fit themselves into their best uniforms, complaining that they had shrunk at the dry cleaners. Fathers would don their best suits trying to remove the bacon and egg stains from their old Regimental ties. Mothers would rescue hat boxes from lofts and attics, hoping against hope that their previous years Ascot designer outfits had not been subjected to frontal or flanking attacks by moths, and if so, praying that these would not be noticed at the post-Commissioning 'Bash'; which was where the mother of just-been-commissioned 'Little Johnny' could extol her son's military and social attributes to the Inspecting General's wife.

I imagined that the turn-out of senior officers was dependant upon which dignitary was taking the Salute, and was a function in army 'speak' of the 'inverse exponential growth factor', whereby royalty, however minor would guarantee a full house of top brass. The top senior officers from any of the three services would get a pretty impressive attendance; which was of importance to an ambitious junior officer who needed as a career enhancing move, to be in the right place at the right time and to be noticed and recognised by the Great and the Good. Government Ministers rated the lowest attendance, especially if the Government of the Day had recently introduced a Defence White Paper announcing a further cut back in the armed forces.

We wondered, with the OC of 'B' Company being a Royal Marine whether he had managed to 'bag' the Captain-General to take the Salute, but he was unsuccessful. However he did 'book' the Royal Marines Band (Portsmouth). The Inspecting Officer was one of the most senior Army generals, whose presence insured a pretty good turn out of VIPs, with both senior Army and Navy officers in attendance with the latter being in the minority. This may have been because the Navy had less ships for admirals to command, whereas the Army had more tanks for generals to play around with.

The day of the Parade dawned sunny but cold. As the junior 'B' Company we were not part of the Parade, but nevertheless we were smartly turned out, not only as spectators but also to help the guests find their seats.

I have never been able to decide the moment when I felt comfortable in a military environment, and although there was another four months of tough training as officer cadets before being commissioned, I think it was watching that 'B' Company Passing-Out Parade, which subconsciously awoke something inside me, and which made me begin to think that the Army might be what I was looking for in a career.

The Commissioning Parade at Mons may not have had the cachet of the Passing-Out Parade at Sandhurst, but it was nevertheless a pretty impressive ceremonial. The four companies of the School were drawn up in line across the length of the Parade Ground, with 'B' Company in the middle. The Royal Marine Band was stationed at the back. As at Sandhurst, the School Adjutant was mounted. Although the number of drill parades and punishment drills were going to cause us a considerable degree of hassle over the coming months; it was when one saw the finished and very polished performance of 'B' Company, both in its marching and drill movements, that one began to appreciate the very high standard set by the Brigade of Guards Company Sergeant-Major and his Drill Sergeants.

It has been written and said on many occasions, that the fearsome reputation of the Guards Regiments has been rightly earned on the battlefield, but it is to a large extent as a result of the obedience and discipline instilled on the Parade Ground. Obviously this is not the whole reason, as esprit de corps, Regimental honour, identity, loyalty and sheer bloody mindlessness all play their part. But there was no doubt that the epitome of drill was and still is to be found in Guards Regiments.

Drill was raised to a higher plane and it would not be wrong to describe it, as far as the Guards were concerned, as an art form. This was certainly reflected in 'B' Company's Passing-Out Parade. Their turnout was immaculate; their pristine white webbing, lanyards and lapel tabs hurt the eyes in the bright sun. As the Company presented arms, with left hands smacking against rifle slings on the second movement, clouds of dried white blanco rose from the ranks and slowly dispersed in the air on the slight breeze. The Companies quick and slow marched, advanced and retired, turned and wheeled to the left and to the right, all in perfect unison. The Royal Marines Band added another dimension to the Parade.

Military history has recorded that the many acts of bravery have been achieved with the support of a military band, and which can stir even the most faint hearted. I found on subsequent Passing-Out Parades, in which we also paraded that a band raised my morale and I marched with more 'zip' and pride.

Although I was aware of the reputation of the Royal Marines Bands, the 'B' Company Commissioning Parade was the first time I had actually seen and heard one of them performing. Their immaculate turnout goes without saying, but for me the music was all-important, and I believe that just as the Guards have raised drill to a higher level, the Royal Marines Bands have done the same with military band music. It was as a result of the 'B' Company Passing-Out Parade and although there are many very fine Regimental and Corps bands, those of the Royal Marines, to my mind stand out from all others.

Being new to Mons, and not having started our Course, the order of the Parade with its somewhat complex drill movements appeared confusing, but no doubt, when it was our turn all would be made clear. It was after 'B' Company had been inspected, had marched past the saluting base, and led by the Adjutant on horseback, had departed the Parade Ground from the steps to one side of the Saluting Base, that I was determined, come hell or high water, to be on the next 'B' Company Commissioning Parade.

~

The departure of our senior company from the Parade Ground was also a signal for the newly commissioned subalterns to depart the School, with almost indecent haste for their no doubt well-earned leave, prior to being posted to their units.

It did not take us long before we moved into what was going to be our permanent living quarters for the four months. The wooden huts appeared to be more modern than the ones we had been used to, and were altogether more comfortable. We would no longer have to battle with recalcitrant stoves, trying to generate some heat from them, for in our barrack huts we had the luxury of central heating. Neither, and this was an absolute blessing, would we have to make bedblocks every morning, nor leave our kit properly laid out for inspection. We also enjoyed the advantage of having an individual light above each bed. Furthermore, we were permitted a sensible number of personal belongings, and I brought from home, my radio, so that at Reveille, I could listen to the Test Match commentaries from Australia. These items of comfort, which may have seemed petty to many people, were very important to us and were a big morale booster following the weeks of privation we had suffered.

When we had settled in to our hut and stowed away our kit, we were summoned to the School lecture hall to be addressed by the Company Commander.

'Gentlemen.' That was a novelty. 'My name is Major Langley and I am your Company Commander, and as the old 'B' Company has departed, I now have the opportunity of introducing myself and your Platoon Commanders. You have already met the Company Sergeant-Major and your Drill Sergeants. Over the next few minutes I shall brief you on your Course, what is expected of you, and what you have to achieve before you are commissioned.

'You are here for a sixteen-week infantry course. You will be instructed in section and platoon tactics, culminating at Battle Camp in Wales; where all that you have learnt here will be put to practical use, right up to Company level using live ammunition. But before you get to Battle Camp, you will be subjected to a great deal of hard work. Becoming an officer is not a sinecure for a comfortable and easy life. By passing 'WASBEE', you have proved that you all have officer potential. What you now have to show and prove is that you have what it takes to be an officer, and that you have the necessary leadership qualities to command a body of men under all circumstances, including if necessary battle conditions. To be a good leader you must not ask your men to do anything that you are not prepared to do yourself.

'The aim of this Course is not only to instruct you in infantry tactics, but also to stretch you, both physically and mentally, so that you are fit to take on the responsibility of command. Some people confuse management and leadership. Let us be quite clear about this, leadership is about people, whereas management is about administration.

'You will undertake exercises, initially TEWTS, which for those of you who haven't heard of this acronym, is a Tactical Exercise Without Troops. Most of the section and platoon exercises will take place in the Long Valley Training Area, culminating in a three-day out of Camp Company exercise.

'You will attend lectures and after six weeks you will sit your first exam known as Military Knowledge One, or MK One for short. After fourteen weeks you will sit the MK Two exam. The minimum pass mark for both exams is fifty percent. Failure to reach the pass mark will mean that you have failed the Course; you will not be commissioned and you will be returned to your unit.

'I must emphasise that you will be under observation and your performance will be noted at all times, not just militarily, but also socially and how you get on with your fellow cadets.

'The standards we set here are high, as you have no doubt experienced from your drill parades. Drill is a most important part of your training, as it is by instilling obedience and discipline in you, that you, with confidence will be able to do the same with the men under you.

'Every month there is the Adjutant's Parade, where both the Adjutant and the RSM will inspect your personal turn out and your standard of drill, with the aim of ensuring that this will be up to the required high standard for your Passing-Out Parade. Therefore, these parades are important and believe me, are not to be taken lightly. Your turnout must be immaculate, as must your drill. Being 'named' for either bad turnout or bad drill, is a chargeable offence, where you will be paraded before the Adjutant and be punished accordingly.

'Fitness is obviously important, and as well as your normal PT sessions in the gym, you will, in order to build up stamina undertake four route marches. The initial one will be of four miles, then eight, twelve, and finally a sixteen-mile route march.

'Finally, the path you have chosen is not an easy one, as National Servicemen we only have sixteen-weeks to make officers of you, which takes two years at Sandhurst for those who are trying for Regular or Short Service Commissions. The Army needs a return on their investment, and this is the main reason why you will be under constant pressure and be stretched to meet the tight time schedule, so that the Army will get the most out of you in your two years service with the Colours. Thank you and good luck.'

We walked back to our huts in a rather sombre and sober mood. We knew that the Course was going to be tough, but perhaps we hadn't realised, or faced, just how tough it was going to be. I also wondered the reason why REME officer cadets had to undergo sixteen weeks of infantry training prior to being commissioned. I knew my eldest cousin who had done his National Service some four years before me, had spent only six weeks at Mons, and then spent ten weeks at what was to become the School of Electrical and Mechanical Engineering (SEME) at Bordon in Hampshire before being commissioned.

The Company Commander's words certainly gave us food for thought and it took us some time to assimilate all the implications of his briefing, and we had just come to terms with what lay in store for us, when to our surprise we were packed off on ten days Christmas leave. This was the first proper break, except for thirty-six and forty-eight hour passes I had had since I was called-up at the beginning of August, which now seemed a lifetime away. So, it was with more than a sense of pleasure that I packed my gear into my trusty Morris Minor and set off back to 'Silly' Sussex.

Chapter Seven

A Senior Officer Cadet at Mons OCS

The ten days Christmas leave passed all too quickly; but suitably rested and refreshed, on 27th December, I set off from home for the two-hour drive back to Aldershot. It was a relief that as officer cadets we no longer had to wear uniform out of Camp, but could be in 'mufti' and so long as one was 'smartly casual', with tie, jacket and, ideally cavalry twill trousers, one was not likely to be challenged by WOs and NCOs for being improperly turned-out. One piece of mandatory kit was the 'hat'. Except for church, indoors and in the Mess, one was expected, when in 'civvies' to be hatted, and this had to be approved by those in authority. Stetsons, deerstalkers, Australian bush hats and flat caps were definitely 'Non-U'. Trilby style hats, so long as they were not too ostentatious, were the preferred option and I chose a nice little number, almost alpine in style, with small feathers attached to the left side of the hatband.

Even though in mufti, we still had to observe military courtesy. In 1958/9, before the IRA terrorist outrages broke out both in Northern Ireland and mainland Britain, it was not unusual, especially near military camps and garrison towns to come across military personnel in uniform. This practice, for security reasons was stopped when the troubles in the Province really started, and all personnel off duty had to wear civilian clothes out of camp. However, during my time at Mons, it was commonplace to come across officers, WOs, NCOs and private soldiers. Obviously, in uniform one saluted and returned salutes at all times. This custom also had to be observed when one was in mufti.

'Right. Listen in.' This from the CSM. 'Today I am going to show you how to salute when you are in civilian clothes. I don't care what you do at home, but when you are in Aldershot, or near any other military establishment, you will pay respect to the Queen's Commission when you encounter an officer, just as you will also return a salute made to you. This doesn't only apply to you as officer cadets, but also, and God help us, after you have been commissioned. The procedure is this.' Whereupon, the CSM removed his Grenadier Guards SD hat, and whipped out of his pocket and onto his head all in one movement a very shabby and battered hat.

'Sir.' This from the comedian in the platoon. 'Did you buy that hat, or did your dog dig it up?'

Fortunately, for the 'comedian', the CSM appeared to be in a very good mood, and bar from glowering at the cadet, and muttering, almost under his breath, something concerning parentage, he proceeded with the lesson.

'Now, when you approach an officer, you raise your right arm, and with your right hand you take hold of the crown of the hat, and counting to yourself: on 'one' you smartly lift the hat off your head, at the same time you turn your head towards the officer or officers. After counting 'two, three', you smartly replace the hat on your head and smartly cut away your arm to the side and face the front. Don't forget, failing to salute an officer could result in you being put on a charge. Is that clear?'

'Yes, Sir.' We replied in unison.

The CSM continued, 'As officers you also do the same when you are saluted by a WO, NCO, or private soldier. Only this time you are responding to the respect that is being shown to the Queen's Commission.

There was one other item of civilian attire in which we had to be instructed, namely the correct method in holding and carrying an umbrella. We were left in no doubt that one's umbrella had to be perfectly folded, with the pleats all symmetrical and evenly spaced. I wondered how the charge of 'being in possession of an incorrectly folded umbrella' entered on one's annual confidential report would effect one's chances of reaching senior rank.

Again the Company Sergeant-Major carried out the instruction.

'Now, with the umbrella correctly folded, you hold it in your left hand like this,' and the CSM clasped the brolly just below the handle with the back of his left hand uppermost.

The CSM continued, 'When you are out walking with an umbrella,' - sounds to me like doggy walking I thought, 'You walk with a straight left arm with your umbrella as an extension to your arm. This is similar to marching with a drawn sword. Do I make myself clear?'

Again. 'Yes, Sir.'

~

Shortly after the official start of our Course, we were introduced on a drill parade and in an unexpected manner, to the School's Regimental Sergeant-Major. The first we knew was when this voice, with a broad Irish brogue boomed out as if from some quarter of a mile away.

'Company Sergeant-Major, dat cadet in de second rank of No 2 platoon is talking. Take his name. Yes, dat's de man.'

If we had been able, we would have looked round to see where the voice was coming from. But sheer blind fear kept our heads and eyes to the front. We did not have long to wait, for to our front there hove into view a majestic figure, over six feet in height, of ample proportions, who nevertheless carried himself with a ramrod straight back and with great dignity. He descended the steps onto the Square in a manner that one could only liken to a man-of-war in full sail, and on this occasion carrying a pace-stick, which acted like a bowsprit leading the way.

If there was one man at Mons who struck fear in all and sundry, it was the RSM. Officers were under the impression that they were in command of the School, but in reality they provided 'leadership', whereas, it was actually the RSM, CSMs and Drill Sergeants who really managed the show who, in my time were all from the Brigade of Guards. This was not a bad thing, as

The Regimental
Sergeant-Major

it insured, whatever the cost in extra drill and other punishments, we were trained by the best; and the very best was in the ample shape of Regimental Sergeant-Major Desmond Lynch, MBE. DCM, of the Irish Guards. To us he was known as 'Paddy' Lynch. He was a very brave man, wounded several times, taken prisoner in Italy, but who won a DCM in North Africa in early 1943, when as a sergeant he took charge of his company of Irish Guardsmen after all the officers had either been killed or wounded, and for three days held off continuous attacks by German infantry. Apparently, many were of the opinion that it was a good thing he was on our side.

Prior to being appointed as the RSM at Mons OCS, he had held the same position at Eaton Hall OCS. He was commissioned in 1961; retired in the rank of captain in 1973, but sadly died in 1996 aged 75. Although his reputation as a fighting soldier was second to none; apparently his greatest contribution to the Army was as the RSM at the two OCSs, where he instilled in his 'Young gentlemen' a sense of pride and respect for the standards and traditions of the British Army.

However, at the start of our Course most of us had not heard of, or even knew anything about RSM 'Paddy' Lynch. The reputation of the recently retired RSM Brittain, probably the most renowned RSM at Mons, had not faded. However, 'Paddy' Lynch very quickly stamped his personality and authority on 'B' Company, and although we were in fear of him, we respected him for his professionalism and for the high standards he set and which he instilled in us. I got to know him fairly well, for on a couple of occasions on the Adjutant's Parades, the RSM and I did not see eye to eye, and where I came off second best.

~

We had hardly time to settle in after Christmas, and get our brains into gear for the rigours of our Course, before we were let out to celebrate New Years Eve. I liked to believe that this was an act of kindness by the 'Brass', but in reality we were probably given leave out as an act of desperation; for no doubt both the Officers', WOs' and Sergeants' Messes were having separate 'knees-up'; which in the case of the officers, as there were several Scottish officers around, probably meant a riotously wild Hogmanay evening of Scottish dancing, embracing every known reel and no doubt accompanied by haggis, washed down with a hogs-head of whisky. The WOs and Sergeants' Mess 'do' was probably of a more dignified and mature nature as befits those from the Brigade of Guards.

If we had been confined to Camp, there would probably have to have been a Duty Officer, Sergeant and a Guard to ensure that we behaved ourselves, so somebody 'high-up' probably thought that the lesser of two evils was to let us out, so long as we reported back in time for first parade the following morning.

I suggested that it would be a good idea if we were to drive up to London, and see in the New Year from Trafalgar Square. So I filled the car with as many cadets as I could safely shoehorn in. This was before some bright spark in the Ministry of Transport had decided, by introducing seatbelts, to end the competition between students and officer cadets to determine how many bodies could be squeezed into an Austin A30 or Morris Minor. The competition was intensified in August 1959, when the British Motor Corporation launched the 'Mini', which introduced a further element to the game, and which spawned a whole generation of rather pathetic jokes, including the overworked elephant one.

However, rather erratically and with a distinct lack of power from the over-worked four cylinder side-valve engine, we set sail from Aldershot, hoping to reach Trafalgar Square before Big Ben struck midnight. Fortunately, we made it in time, and as this was long before traffic wardens, double yellow lines, traffic calming schemes and congestion charges, I was able to park within spitting distance of the Square. Although not the numbers as there were in later years, seeing and joining in the celebrations, as midnight sounded and linking arms to sing 'Auld Lang Syne' was a memorable experience.

As the night was still relatively young, I suggested that we should drive round to Eaton Square ('You do mean Eaton Square and not Eaton Hall, don't you?'), where the daughter of one of my father's ex-TA friends shared a flat. Fortunately we had on board someone whose knowledge of London was considerably better than mine, and in no time we had arrived in the 'up-market' Square. I have never been certain, whether the uninvited arrival at one o'clock in the morning of a group of rather exuberant officer cadets to a private party in the genteel surroundings of Eaton Square was entirely welcome. Charlotte did put a brave face on it, but I have always believed, in spite of my father's and step-mother's hopes, but not mine, that any furtherance in our relationship, cooled after that evening, and Charlotte went on to marry a London art dealer. Nevertheless, it was a fun evening, and helped us to put out of our minds, for at least a few hours, the expected rigours of the next four months.

~

New Years Day was not the best day of the year to get stuck into a highly stressed and pressurised Course. We certainly were not feeling at our best. The officers, who had obviously decided that 'discretion was the better part of valour', and that hangovers should better be suffered in solitude and in silence, had universally agreed to leave the 'field' clear to the WOs and Drill Sergeants, who obviously made of sterner stuff, appeared frighteningly 'bright eyed and bushy tailed'. They had obviously decided in order to shake the cobwebs and any slackness out of us, that a good dose of 'Guards' drill would do us no harm. We begged to differ. The session was a 'killer', and at one time there were more cadets running around the Parade Ground either with, or without rifles above their heads, than there were actually doing drill. Not an auspicious start to the Course.

It took us some time to realise that we would no longer be 'bugged' by the presence of very junior NCOs yapping at our heels like demented Jack Russells. As responsible officer cadets, it was expected that our peers would march us from one training session to another. This could be a rather stressful experience for the officer cadet in charge, as the rest of us were inclined to chat amongst ourselves as we were being marched from 'A' to 'B'. The long suffering C-in-C (Cadet-in-Charge) would be begging us to be quiet and to march in a smart and military manner, as it was not unknown for an officer, or more likely the CSM or Sergeant Fawcett, to set up an ambush behind the canteen or latrines, and spring this as we ambled past. The poor C-in-C would really get it in the neck, whilst the rest of us were given more rifle arm muscle strengthening exercises around the Square.

Just as at school or college, each session, lesson or lecture usually lasted one hour. Some of the lecturers often got carried away with enthusiasm for their particular subject; would overrun their allotted time, and would appear to have little idea of the pressure and panic he was subjecting us to; especially as this invariably seemed to happen when the following session was either drill or PT and involved a return to our hut, either to change or pick up our rifles. Neither the CSM nor APT Sergeants appreciated being kept waiting, and the excuse, 'but Sir, Captain Blobs kept us late,' didn't wash with them, and we would be subjected to a tougher drill or PT session than usual.

Later on in the Course, those cadets who demonstrated leadership qualities 'above and beyond the call of duty' were appointed platoon Junior Under Officers (JUOs); whilst the one JUO, normally from a senior and very good regiment who demonstrated General Staff qualities was appointed the Company Senior Under Officer (SUO). It certainly looked good on ones Army CV to have been a JUO or SUO at an OCS, but there was a downside by being in the limelight the whole time, when there were occasions that keeping a low profile was a better option. It was a reflection of the times that cadets from corps never seemed to be chosen for the SUO position. As one Quartermaster General (QMG) told a REME Brigadier, 'Technical people should be on tap. Never on top.' Although, it was ironic that in 2006, an ex-REME officer, Maj-Gen Tim Tyler, who was the son of one of my father's REME colleagues in WWII, assumed the office of QMG.

~

It seemed that we had not been at Mons for more than a few days, when we read in Company Orders that our first Adjutant's Parade was imminent. Each company was subjected to this monthly parade; which meant that we would have to face the ordeal four times. Fellow cadets had warned us that of all the activities we would face whilst at the School, the most feared was this parade taken by the Adjutant with the RSM in close attendance. The drill was not of major concern, for by now, some five months into our National Service, we were all fairly proficient in the 'noble' art. The main worry was 'The Inspection'. Being immaculately turned-out was not good enough, one had to be on a higher plane than immaculate.

The evening prior to the Parade, in all 'B' Company's huts there was a veritable scene of frenzied activity. Best battledresses were ironed, not once but twice, initially with the steam 'on' to put creases in the right places in both BD blouses and trousers, and then secondly through brown paper with the iron in a dry mode. Done properly, one ended up with razor sharp arm, trouser and box pleat creases. Although we all had our own irons, there was a shortage of power points, which was just as well, for had the whole Company been able to iron their BDs at the same time, the National Grid would no doubt have blown a fuse. Just as there were insufficient power points, there were not enough wooden tables for ironing, and we would go to extraordinary lengths to acquire some sort of flat surface on which an iron could be used. Of course, it was essential to check out what the surface had previously been used for; as one from the cookhouse could have harboured curry stains, which would only have shown under heat, and could have resulted in a variety of interesting and smelly stains appearing down the length of ones best and most treasured battledress. This would not have been appreciated by either the Adjutant or the RSM. Half-crown pieces were essential pieces of emergency kit, and were in constant demand.

Blancoing was one of my least favourite activities and which invariably resulted in my conducting a personal battle with my webbing, which for the Adjutant's Parade had to be our white kit. Applying the blanco too thinly would fail to cover over dirt or other marks, and too thickly could result in the blanco cracking at the most unfortunate moment. Practice was the only solution. But the problems with white webbing did not end with the blanco. There were those brass bits, whether buckles or straps which had to be polished using Brasso or Duraglit. But no traces of brass polish had to be left on either the white webbing or white blanco on the brasses. Not that easy to achieve. Our short round 'pig sticking' bayonets had to gleam like a mirror, and just as it was a chargeable offence to have rusty equipment, it was also an offence if one was caught using polish on ones bayonet. We were told that this was against the Geneva Convention, as rust or the residue of any metal polish could cause serious health problems to the opposition who had been bayoneted. We found that Solvol Autosol polish was the best for producing really gleaming metal. Bayonet hilts and scabbards were black and also had to polished. However, these items could prove something of a problem, for the black enamel could scratch, and it was very unfortunate if one had been issued with a bayonet and scabbard, which looked as though it had been in constant action since the Boer War. Painting over the scratch marks was an easy option, but great care had to be exercised in case brush marks were visible; or the black paint was of a different shade to that of the original, and an inspecting officer or warrant officer could easily see where an extra coat of paint had been applied to the scratch mark.

My best boots were not a problem, that is unless some idiot inadvertently trod on one of them leaving a nice pattern of stud marks; or I carelessly let the butt of my rifle fall onto a boot causing a deep scuff mark in the mirror surface of the boot. To remove such marks, including scratches was very time consuming, as the damaged surface had to be built up again with black boot polish, spit, a cloth and lots of elbow grease, with a final rub over with methylated spirits, which helped give such a deep shine to the boots.

From my experience of the first muster inspection at No 2 Trg Bn, Honiton, I was determined that my kit would be in perfect order, but I also suspected that the standard would be higher at Mons. By midnight, after I had been working on my kit for some five hours, I was getting thoroughly 'pissed-off', and was starting to develop a potentially damaging couldn't careless attitude. Some of my friends had this amazing ability to do the minimum amount of 'bulling', and yet they would sail through the inspection without any trouble, whereas I and other cadets hadn't the confidence to adopt such a cavalier approach, and we would conscientiously work on our kit until we believed it was perfect. However, on an inspection we would invariably still get pulled-up and have our names taken for some very minor infringement.

For our first Adjutant's Parade, we all got up earlier than usual at around 0530 hrs, grabbed a quick breakfast in the canteen, and then back to our hut, where there was just enough time to check our kit, and to carry out any final polishing, before it was time to prepare for the Parade. One of the great advantages of the Army's method of basic training, however unsubtle, was the speed at which 'bonding' took place. We would help each other out, with the stronger members of the hut helping out the weaker ones. Even though our platoon at Mons had only been together for a short period, we nevertheless, checked, re-checked and inspected each other to try and ensure that we would survive any inspection.

At the appointed time, very gingerly and one at a time, so as not to spoil the surface of our highly 'bulled' boots, we left our hut and fell-in outside with those from the other two huts which made up the platoon. Sergeant Fawcett hove into view looking, as was right and proper every inch the perfectly turned-out Irish Guardsman. He carried out a quick but thorough inspection, with a few sharp intakes of breath and clicking of his tongue when he saw something of which he did not approve, but by then it was too late to do anything about it.

The Drill Sergeant marched us to the Parade Ground, and there we waited standing at ease, together with the other 'B' Company platoons, whilst the right markers were correctly positioned. On the order to, 'get fell-in', each platoon marched smartly up to their right marker, and with 'eyes right' and left arms extended and with a great deal of shuffling of feet, each of the three sections in each platoon, with the tallest cadets at either end and the shortest in the centre, were gradually formed into perfectly straight lines to the satisfaction of the Company Sergeant-Major.

Then, standing at ease, we waited and waited and waited, until precisely at 1000hrs the Adjutant, who I believe was a Coldstream Guardsman, and a scion of a famous brewing family, appeared together with the RSM from the direction of the School's HQ. The Adjutant was a tall man but even he was dwarfed by the imposing figure of 'Paddy' Lynch.

The CSM quickly brought us to attention. We sloped arms, whilst the CSM saluted the Adjutant and informed him that 'B' Company was ready for his inspection. We were moved into 'open order' position, which gave both the Adjutant and the RSM, wielding his pace stick to the best effect, sufficient viewing space to carry out their inspection.

The Adjutant

Obviously as No 2 Platoon we were second in line, to be subjected to the eagle eyes of both the Adjutant and the RSM, and we were stood at ease whilst we waited our turn. This seemed to take an age as we stood there quaking in our boots, whilst from our right we could hear murmurs of 'take his name, that rifle sling is filthy', or 'his beret is not on straight', or 'you are a disgrace to your cap badge'.

Eventually, it was our turn, and our acting JUO brought us to attention, as the Adjutant started his inspection. Then disaster struck. The RSM, who I swear could have spotted a flicker of an eyelid at a hundred paces, suddenly raised his pace stick, pointed it in my direction and roared out in his broad Irish accent:

'C'ny Sgnt-Major, dat cadet in de middle of de back rank, he's moving his head. Take his name.' With a sinking feeling, I instinctively knew he was referring to me. This was confirmed a few moments later when a hand appeared from behind me and gripped my left shoulder. 'Yes, dat's de man.'

'Name, Sir?'

'Caffyn, Sir.'

'Right, Caffyn, you're on Adjutant's Orders tomorrow. Understand, Sir?'

'Yes, Sir.'

That was a bloody stupid thing to have done, and so unnecessary. I was convinced, and still am to this day, that my head did not move, but I had to admit my eyes did flick briefly to the left, which was instantly picked up by the RSM. But what was even more stupid, I went and did exactly the same at a later Adjutant's Parade and flicked my eyes towards the Adjutant as he was inspecting the JUO, which was instantly picked up by the RSM, and I had my name taken again. These very basic and very foolish mistakes were even more infuriating, as I was never picked up on the Adjutant's Parades for a dirty rifle, blanco on brasses, Brasso on webbing, or any other of the myriad bits of kit and equipment, which was attached to my person like a Christmas tree, and that an inspecting officer or RSM could find fault with, if they really tried hard enough, and had all the time in the world to look. Inspections were nerve racking. It was bad enough when being inspected from the front, as one had to keep ones eyes, and I'm a fine one to talk, rigidly fixed to the front, as the inspecting officer or WO would check the tightness of belts, rifle slings and any other accoutrement festooned around the body. This could prove highly dangerous to the individual, especially if he was very ticklish, and although I have never heard that it actually happened, there must be somewhere in Queen's Regs, a charge for 'Giggling and moving on Parade, due to extreme touch sensitivity.'

However for me, the worst part of any inspection, was when the inspecting officer, or WO came up from behind, and you only knew he was there because he suffered from halitosis. Again you had to stand rigidly to attention as pieces of your kit was pulled and pushed to ensure that everything had been correctly put together. It was a nerve-racking moment when you felt your bayonet being removed from its scabbard, and you hoped and preyed that whoever was inspecting it, didn't suddenly succumb to a sneezing fit or a bout of hiccups just as he was about to return the bayonet to its scabbard, missed and succeeded in puncturing ones left buttock!!

Bar from being on a charge, which was bad enough, the rest of the Parade passed without incident and we returned to our hut with a feeling of relief. It was of no comfort that I was not the only cadet who had had his name taken, as others were in the same boat for either dirty bits of kit, or some other minor misdemeanour. I had no idea whether moving ones head on Parade was a more heinous crime than leaving a speck of blanco on a brass buckle. I would find out the next day, but I must confess that I spent the rest of the day with a definite feeling of apprehension. At school if you had committed a fairly major crime like punching a school prefect; or failing to have a cold shower in the morning, when both the outdoors and indoors temperatures were below zero; or you told your housemaster what you really thought of him; you were paraded in either the Housemaster's or Prefect's Study and 'sent away'. This meant that the punishment was a canning, and you had to wait until the evening, when you were escorted up to a dormitory and bending over the end of a bed, you were given up to 'six of the best'.

I really did have the same feeling of having been a naughty schoolboy, who had been caught-out doing something stupid. At school one had an idea of what punishment one could expect, but I had no idea, being 'on a charge' for the first time on an Adjutant's Parade at an Officer Cadet School, what retribution I would be facing. In the bewitching hour before dawn when one is supposed to be at ones lowest ebb, I imagined that I could receive anything from a severe 'bollocking' to being RTUd. I had even heard stories of National Servicemen who had tried to get kicked out of the Army by committing sufficiently serious offences, to have been sent to the Army's Prison at Colchester; without realising that time spent in detention in 'The Glass House' was added onto the two years of National Service.

I, together with the other defaulters paraded for Adjutant's Orders outside his office at 0930hrs, where the CSM decided to put us through several dress–rehearsals to ensure that we didn't blot our copybooks, and be charged again for being idle in front of the Adjutant. This would have reflected badly on the CSM who, no doubt in such circumstances would have been on the receiving end of some friendly words of advice from the RSM.

The queue of defaulters quickly dwindled, as one after another we were marched in before the Adjutant, and just as quickly marched out again with rather glazed and set expressions. Eventually it came to my turn.

'Officer Cadet Caffyn.' The CSM stuck his head round the corner.

'Yes, Sir.'

'Right. Quick march.'

'Leftwheelepeyeepeyemarktime'altsalutatsorfstandtoattenshun.' All this without drawing breath.

'Officer Cadet Caffyn, Sir. Moving his head on Parade, Sir.'

The Adjutant looked me up and down with a facial expression, as if a nasty smell had wafted into his domain.

'Now, Caffyn. Although this might seem minor to you, I regard it as a serious offence.'

My heart fell. I could sense that he was going to come down on me like a ton of bricks.

'If you are to be commissioned you must learn to accept discipline and obey orders. As an officer you are expected to set an example to the other ranks, but how can you expect them to obey your orders, if you don't obey orders given to you. This shows a degree of irresponsibility on your part. Do you understand?'

'Yes, Sir.'

Perhaps this was the time to tell him that I disagreed with the charge, and that I had only moved my eyes. On second thoughts, not a good idea taking on the RSM, who had already proved that he was ferocious and fearless in battle, and could probably eat officer cadets for breakfast.

'Do you plead guilty and are you prepared to accept my award?'

The Adjutant was judge, jury and sentencing authority all rolled into one.

'Yes, Sir.'

'Right. Confined to camp for twenty-four hours, and I don't want to see you up in front of me again. This charge and award will be entered on your confidential record, and too many of these will see you being RTUd. Clear?'

'Yes, Sir.'

'Right. Dismiss.'

The CSM took over.

'Atsonsaluteaboutturnquickmarchepeyeepeyeswingthosearmsrightwheel mark time'altdismiss'

I breathed a sigh of relief. Irrespective of all the tough talking, I had been awarded the minimum punishment, which although not too onerous, was nevertheless a pain in the backside, as it meant I had to parade with the other defaulters behind the Guard Mounting Parade at 1800hrs, then again at 2200hrs, and finally again at 0600hrs, when the Guard was being dismounted.

As we did not usually get off duty until 1700hrs, and depending upon the days activities, which invariably included drill and probably some fieldwork; there was only an hour to re-blanco and re-Brasso webbing and brasses; clean and polish boots, before parading at 1800hrs. To meet the deadline, tea had to be skipped.

But it was the 2200hrs parade that caused the most concern. For this, one had to be in full battle order with helmet, ammunition pouches and small pack. This meant that an extra set of webbing and kit had to be cleaned and polished.

Although, as officer cadets we no longer had to undergo kit inspections, most of us continued the procedure that we had individually adopted at basic training, of fitting strips of cardboard into both our small and large packs, so that these could be more easily squared off correctly when positioned on top of our lockers.

On the 2200hrs defaulters parade, the small pack was meant to contain mess tins, mug, eating irons and all the other items detailed on the defaulter's parade list hanging on the door of each barrack room. If one 'went by the book' and filled the small pack with all the listed items, one ended up with a pack which had more protrusions than a mountain range, and yet even with all this kit, the small pack had to be perfectly 'squared off', after its straps had been clipped to the webbing cross braces, which were fitted to buckles both on the front and back of the belt. One usually first fixed the cross braces, pouches, bayonet and small pack onto the web belt, before putting on the whole assembly. This was really a two-man job, as assistance was needed to help hoist and hold the small pack in place on ones back, whilst one took a deep breath and tried to clip the male brass buckle of the belt into the female one without rupturing oneself.

As we were in the middle of winter, there was one further complication. Greatcoats had to be worn both by the Guard and by the defaulters. The coat was a fine piece of kit, guaranteed to keep one warm on the coldest of nights. However, the greatcoat had two disadvantages. Being thick, it meant that web belts had to be significantly let out to accommodate the extra bulk. Whoever designed the belt, should have been condemned to a lifetime of letting in and out belts after they had been blancoed and the brasses polished. It was not easy to slot the hooks of the brasses at either end of the belt, into the small top and bottom pockets, set at regular intervals on the inside of the belt. The belt had to be squeezed firmly together to carry out this manoeuvre, and which due to the robust construction of the belt, instantly cracked all the new blanco. Once the hooks had been forced into the correct pockets, the male and female brass buckles could be slid into their correct positions and 'locked' in place with the two brass slides. One had to experiment several times before arriving at the optimum position, by which time the fresh blanco had been ruined and it was not possible to re-blanco once all the accoutrements had been attached to the belt. Time only allowed for a certain amount of 'touching-up'. Asphyxia was a real danger if the belt was too tight; but a too loose belt, due to the weight of the kitted out small pack, caused the whole lot to ride up, resulting in near strangulation as the belt came to rest under ones chin. There was also a danger of being picked up on parade for standing 'like a sack of potatoes', as one tried to compensate for the shift in the centre of gravity, if ones webbing rode up too high.

The other problem with the greatcoat was that at the back there was a long slit which started at the hem and finished up near the waist. There were three small buttons, which were supposed to fasten the slit together, but invariably one or more of these buttons would come undone either before or on parade. Orderly officers had their own particular fetish with the inspection of cadets at Defaulters Parade. Captain Flood of the Royal Tank Regiment took a particular delight in checking the buttons at the back of the greatcoat, and I have always felt that, although it was probably unintentional; as the lighting was poor, he had to lift up the back of the coat to check, which was probably sufficient to 'pop' the odd button from its hole, resulting in the poor cadet being placed on a further charge.

We very quickly learnt that, if possible it was a wise precaution, to try and find out who was to be the Orderly Officer on the day when one was either on Guard Duty or on Defaulters Parade. Captain Fleming, Royal Cheshire Regiment and our platoon commander, together with Captain Flood were to be avoided. Not that they were bad officers, far from it; but they were inclined to do everything by the book, and if on the 2200hrs Defaulters Parade, the regulations laid down that small packs should be filled with the listed items of kit, then both captains would occasionally check that they contained the correct kit. If they were, your name would nevertheless be taken down to appear on Adjutant's Orders for not having a properly 'squared-off' pack; but if you had a properly 'squared-off pack, this could only have been at the expense of leaving out some of the listed items. So your name was still taken for Adjutant's Orders. From the Orderly Officer's perspective, this was certainly a case of 'heads I win and tails you lose.'

There was one other platoon commander, Captain John Stevenson, Royal Sussex Regiment. One always hoped that he would be the Orderly Officer for either Guard Mounting or Defaulters Parade. He was rather more laid back, and was never known to check greatcoat tail buttons, unless they were obviously undone, and he was more concerned at the 2200hrs Parade to ensure that small packs were properly 'squared-off', and did not appear overly concerned whether the listed items were included or not.

Peter Smith, a Royal Marine was with me on Defaulters' Parade, and after a great deal of thought and discussion, we decided to take a chance and not to fill our small packs, but to leave the strips of cardboard in place, and have perfectly 'squared-off' packs at the 2200hrs Parade. Fortunately, and to our great relief Captain Stevenson was the Orderly Officer that day, but for one heart stopping moment as he inspected us from behind, we thought he was going to order us to open up our packs. But, after what seemed an age he gave a grunt and moved to the front of us and I could swear there was a look in his eyes that said 'been there, seen that, done that'. But his only comment was: ' I must congratulate you both on the good state of your turn-out.' Peter and I gave a long sigh of relief, and we both came to the conclusion that, so long as one was immaculately turned-out and showed respect to ones superiors, it was possible to bluff ones way out of tricky situations.

Although being on defaulters was not very arduous, it was nevertheless a pain, for after the 2200hrs Parade, we had to dismantle our gear, including adjusting the web belt back to its original position. Then, it was re-blancoing and re-Brassoing our webbing and polishing our boots ready for the next mornings' Muster Parade. We all tried very hard to avoid having our names taken for Adjutant's Orders; for once on Defaulters' Parade there was more than an even chance of being pulled up and having ones name taken yet again.

Guard Duty was another hazard, for if one was picked up on the Guard Mounting Inspection; then, on the following day, one duly appeared before the Adjutant and ended up on Defaulters Parade. As with all Army camps, guard duty, however necessary, was a 'bind.

Fortunately with four companies, 'Alpha', 'Bravo', 'Charlie' and 'Delta', the duty usually only came round once during our time at Mons. Those that made the decisions must have thought that the School, being situated in the middle of Aldershot, was a far safer place than Honiton, for we only carried pick handles for Camp patrol, whereas at Honiton we had carried rifles. I am not certain that the inhabitants of that town would have been overly impressed to learn that the local Army commander thought they were so potentially dangerous, that we needed to carry rifles, howbeit without ammunition for guarding the Camp.

The night patrols did have one advantage over those at Honiton, in that there was a vending machine on one of the 'beats', and hot soup was always welcome in the middle of a cold winters night. It went without saying that there was tremendous competition to pick that particular patrol.

It did not take long for us to learn some of the 'tricks of the trade'. One of the senior companies had advised us that it was wise, if on Guard Duty, to clean and polish a second set of webbing prior to going on duty the next morning, so that one at least went on parade with clean kit and especially if that happened to be drill.

~

We certainly had opportunities to relax in the evenings, and the Officers' Club off Queen's Parade provided a haven, if one wanted to crash out and get some peace and quiet. The cinema provided an escape from the rigours of our Course, and it was whilst watching a film in an Aldershot cinema, where I experienced one of my more embarrassing moments, when with some of my friends, at a very poignant and quiet moment in the film we were watching, I dropped a nearly full box of Malteaser chocolates on the floor, which took off at ever increasing speed in a race to see which one could get to the front of the cinema first. It was a great shame that we were not watching a war film; at least then I could have pretended that the noise was machine gun fire.

More often than not, we stayed in our hut, either because we were too knackered after the days training, or we had to prepare our kit for the following morning, especially if it was the Adjutant's Parade. One evening when we were preparing for the next mornings parade, a bunch of officer cadets from Sandhurst wandered into our hut to visit Dick Pascoe, a friend of theirs. We spent a pleasant evening chatting over the differences between the Regulars Officer Cadets' Course at the RMA and our National Service one at Mons. They found it difficult to believe that we had to cover in sixteen weeks, what took them the best part of two years to complete. However, their curriculum embraced subjects that we did not touch, and they also had the opportunity to take part in sporting activities, which were certainly not included in our Course.

Although by 1958 Eaton Hall had closed, Keith Miller, the author of '730 Days until Demob' writing on the difference between the two Officer Cadet Schools:

'Eaton Hall near Chester was the Army's Training School for infantry and corps other than the Royal Artillery and the Royal Engineers, it was akin to a military boarding school with better quality rooms and baths, where 60-strong intakes were put through a 16-week course. As virtually all National Servicemen in the infantry would go abroad it was designed to create second lieutenants who would eventually command many of its platoons. Mons Barracks at Aldershot, for RA and RE training, was an altogether tougher place, based on the Sandhurst precepts.

181

'Overall the officer trainees hung the dread thought of being returned to units as failures. This fostered co-operation and comradeship, which was the key to success in tough, high intensity courses. As result the failure rate was very low.'

Irrespective to what many people may have thought at the time, those of us who went through Mons, were, and are probably still aware that we went through *'...tough high intensity courses'*, and can take pride that the majority successfully completed these and gained the Queen's Commission.

Our Course was not only about 'bull', drill and parades. The Army had in a very short time to turn all of us from whatever arm of the service we were in into officers, who had the ability to fight, command and lead troops into battle. National Service subalterns had to overcome one other hurdle. Many regular soldiers, who had been with the Colours for a number of years, and who had probably seen active service, were expected, in that situation to place their lives in the hands of a 'still wet behind the ears' National Service subaltern; who had in all reality, only been given a 'crash course' in leadership, command and tactical skills. There was a credibility gap, and we probably all found that it took time to win the confidence and respect of the troops under us.

~

Infantry tactics formed a significant part of the Course, and although at No 2 Trg Bn REME, I had received some very basic training in section and platoon tactics; we were about to embark upon a concentrated few weeks of instruction, both theoretical and practical on how to fight a section and a platoon. Our instructors, were in the main the platoon commanders, all captains from infantry regiments, with the exception of the aforementioned Captain Flood, who was from the Royal Tank Regiment, whose posting, no doubt, was to look after the interests of the RTR cadets, and to provide instruction in infantry/armour co-operation if necessary.

Our initial field training took place in the classroom and it was important to take notes, not only as an aide-mémoire for when we went into the field to put the theory into practice, but also for revision prior to the two Military Knowledge exams we were to take.

The platoon took their seats in one of the lecture rooms. We stood as Capt Fleming entered the room.

'Good morning, Gentlemen. Please be seated.' We sat.

'Before I start to talk to you about infantry tactics, it is essential that you understand the organisational structure of the Army. So this morning I am going to introduce you to the Army's organisation. As you have already found out on the drill square, everything is based on 'threes'. Starting at the bottom, three sections make up a platoon, each section commanded by a corporal with a lance-corporal as his 2IC. There are three platoons in a

182

company, with a subaltern as platoon commander and the sergeant as 2IC. There are three companies in a battalion, with a major being the company commander and a captain as his 2IC. There are three battalions to a brigade, with each battalion being commanded by a lieutenant-colonel, with a major as his 2IC. Three brigades make up a division, with a brigadier commanding a brigade. Three divisions make up a corps, each division being commanded by a major-general, and finally three corps make-up an army, with a lieutenant-general commanding each corps, and of course a full general commands an army.

'Other arms use different phraseology, although the basic structure is the same. For instance the Cavalry use the term 'troop' for a platoon and 'squadron' for a company, whilst the basic Royal Artillery unit is built around the battery.

'This is the basic structure, but for the sake of convenience, I have left out administrative and sub-units, which start at company level with a company HQ; a battalion which has a battalion HQ and so on. However, the Army has two manning levels, a war establishment one and a peacetime one. With the latter, units and formations are not at full strength; for instance brigades may only be made up of two battalions, and divisions of only two brigades and so on.

'As your Course proceeds, you will learn how other arms, such as the Royal Artillery, the Royal Engineers, the Royal Signals and the Armoured Regiments fit into the formation structures.'

The lecture continued. ' In the British Army, the term 'regiment' is either used to denote a front line formation such as the Royal Tank Regiment, or it represents a parent organisation for a number of infantry battalions, which have been raised and trained from the same geographical area, for instance the Cheshire Regiment.'

In subsequent lectures, we learnt the composition of infantry and armoured brigades, and how under certain battle scenarios, not only would brigade groups be formed for a specific operation, but also in the early part of the Second World War, ad hoc formations such as 'W' Force in Greece in 1941 were cobbled together. We asked about 'Battle Groups', and Capt Fleming explained that these were favoured by the American Army, and the make-up of such a group gave a much more flexible response to a specific threat in a fluid situation. He added that the British Army was now moving in the same direction, as the use of brigade groups was somewhat inflexible, did not necessarily give the right composition of units, and could be slow to respond to face a fast developing threat.

We had to be able to understand the difference between, the 'teeth' (fighting) arms, 'first' and 'second' echelons (forward and rear supply areas), and the responsibilities of the various supporting arms such as the

RASC (transport), the RAOC (spares), REME (electrical and mechanical) and the RMP (police).

As well as learning the organisation of the Army, we had to be able to interpret and memorise the symbols used on maps to identify the headquarters of armies, corps, divisions, and brigades; the symbols that were used to show infantry and armoured divisions, brigades, battalions and smaller units; and the hieroglyphics used to denote the boundaries between corps, divisions and brigades. There was a mass of information to assimilate, all of which we would be expected to know when we sat our first exam.

~

We were instructed in the British Roll of Regiments, and although it would have been virtually impossible to memorise the whole Roll, we were expected to know that the Royal Scots Regiment being the oldest regiment (1633) in the British Army, is the senior Infantry Regiment of the Line and takes precedence over all over infantry regiments; that the Life Guards (1660) is the senior Cavalry Regiment in the Army and the King's Troop, Royal Horse Artillery on parade with its guns, takes precedence over all the other regiments and has the honour of parading on the right of the Line.

The Army has always had a love of abbreviating the written word, which makes sense, for in the heat of battle, when confusion, noise and time are also enemies, orders need to be transmitted clearly, without ambiguity and extremely swiftly. We were therefore expected to learn the most common acronyms. We had already come across TEWT (Tactical Exercise without Troops), but AFV, APC, ARV, BC, BSM, CQMS, DF, DS, FOO, GP, GSO, HE, HESH, LAD, LZ, QM, R & R, RQMS and VHF were new to us and were just a fraction of the Army's vast dictionary of abbreviations.

We needed to know the difference between an 'officer commanding' (OC) as opposed to a 'commanding officer' (CO). We needed to realise that not all regiments used the same rank titles, as for instance a bombardier is a Royal Artillery corporal, and that in the Brigade of Guards a lance-corporal is the equivalent of a corporal in other regiments and units. Also as prospective officers, we also had to know the ranks and the sleeve insignia of all ranks in the Royal Navy, the Royal Air Force and of particular interest to us, the Wrens.

The amount of information that was being thrown at us would have done justice to a university course, without throwing in the parades, route marches and TEWTS.

~

We always looked forward to the instruction periods given by Capt Stevenson. He had a natural ability to present the subject that he was lecturing on in such a way, that we mentally hung onto his every word, and although the subjects were serious, he managed to deliver them with a touch of lightness and with humour.

'Today, I am going to attempt to instil in those woolly heads of yours, the art of section and platoon tactics. Now all of you, including those of you who have opted for quiet lives 'below the stairs' supplying those at the sharp end, who are doing all the dangerous work, must in your basic training, have been given some idea of infantry tactics.

'Now, the basic sub-unit is the section, which normally consists of ten men with a corporal as section leader and a lance-corporal as his 2IC. Each section will have a two-man Light Machine Gun (LMG) group, and as you have no doubt already fired it, the Army's LMG is the Bren. No 1 on the gun will normally be the lance-corporal, and No 2 will be any other member of the section stupid enough to volunteer, in army fashion, to carry most of the spare Bren magazines in addition to his own rifle ammunition. The rest of the section will be riflemen. In a platoon there will be a two-man 2-inch mortar team to give added firepower or smokescreen protection, whether in an offensive or defensive situation.

'We shall be practising section and platoon tactics in the field, but before we do that, there are some basic infantry rules you must follow. When you are in a 'advancing to contact' situation, if you are in file, place yourself between the lead and second sections. This way you can quickly respond to any threat and can communicate and issue orders quickly and clearly. You do not act like Dan Dare in 'The Eagle' comic and lead from the front. Nor, as a platoon commander do you bring up the rear, for if you do your men will, and rightly so, have neither confidence nor respect in your leadership qualities. Many of your platoon will probably be 'old sweats' who know every trick in the book, and they can make life hell for a young, baby faced and wet behind the ears subaltern. So, if you are unsure about anything consult your platoon sergeant. He will have several years experience behind him, and has a more than vested interest in not getting himself killed, through the gung-ho (that's an Americanism by the way) attitude of a raw second lieutenant. So listen to him, and take his advice. He will respect you the more as will the rest of the platoon, and he will pass on to you the skills that he has taken some years to acquire.'

Capt Stevenson picked up a piece of chalk and turning to a blackboard, began to illustrate his lecture.

'If you are advancing in file, and you come across a gap, shall we say in a hedgerow, don't cross it individually, as this will give an enemy, if he has the gap covered, the opportunity of taking out quite a number of you. Close up into groups and then rush the gap; by the time the enemy has woken up, most of the platoon will be across.

'When you are 'advancing to contact' across open ground, whether as a single section or as a platoon, advance in arrow head formation, and don't bunch up; keep well spread out, with about five yards between each man, so that you offer the minimum target area to the enemy. Do not as the platoon commander put yourself in the most obvious place at the head of the arrow. The enemy will be trying to identify the officer and take him out quickly, hoping that the rest of the platoon will act like headless chickens. In defence we would be doing the same. In the First World War we lost far too many officers, who would attack waving their useless service revolvers, which couldn't hit the proverbial barn door at thirty paces. It was therefore all too easy for the enemy to recognise and shoot officers right at the start of an attack. My preference is to be dressed like everybody else in the platoon, to carry a rifle and to place myself in such a position that I would not be too conspicuous, but at the same time I could still control the platoon. I would tie a short length of white tape to the back of my belt, so that the sections could identify me.

'Now, this is particularly important. When you are 'advancing to contact' and especially across open ground, you must always work out in your mind what action you are going to take at any moment, if you come under enemy fire. Although it is a natural instinct to go to ground, that is the worst thing you can do, as the enemy will either pick you off one-by-one; or they will bring supporting fire, such as mortars down onto your position. Depending upon where the fire is coming from, you must decide, whether it is the better option to double forward and attack the enemy, or to double back to the nearest cover. A well organised enemy who has situated his defences to give mutual protection, will not open fire until you have entered his 'killing zone', and which will inflict maximum casualties, but not close enough for you to attack without being totally annihilated. So, at every step of the way, decide what your options are if you come under fire and keep your platoon informed of your plans; such as; 'If we come under fire now, we will charge and attack.' There is nothing more terminal than, by not giving your men orders, they immediately go to ground, which is a natural reaction, leaving you to charge the enemy on your own and winning a posthumous VC.

'Let us presume that you are advancing in arrow formation across open ground from the cover of a hedgerow with No 1 section leading, No 2 on the left and No 3 to the right. You have positioned yourself as the right hand man of No 2 section, which gives you effective control over the platoon. Some two hundred yards ahead of you, and at two-o'clock is a copse of trees. To your left at about a hundred yards is another hedgerow.' The chalk, squealing horribly flashed across the board as Capt Stevenson drew a situation map.

'Right, you are half way across the field, when you come under heavy fire from the copse to your right front. As platoon commander, what do you do?'

We spent a few minutes considering the problem before coming up with our suggestions.

'Okay, that's enough,' interrupted Capt Stevenson. 'Now, there is never a correct answer. You must consider your options and decide what you believe is the best one, that will secure your objective quickly and with the minimum of casualties. In an 'advance to contact' situation, you are obviously expecting to run into the enemy. So, and this is probably the most important principle of infantry tactics: FIRE and MOVEMENT. You do not move unless you have a secure firebase to support you.

'I would suggest that as you prepared your plan from the cover of the hedge for your line of advance, you would have come to the conclusion that if there were any enemy ahead, they would probably be located in that copse. So I would leave my Bren and 2-inch mortar teams in the hedge, situated to give maximum covering fire if you were to take enemy fire whilst you were advancing across the field. Directly you came under fire, the Brens would provide covering fire whilst you withdrew back to the hedge, and the mortar would provide smoke. Having, hopefully all made it safely back to the hedge; you must make an appreciation, and from this form your plan. Then call together your sergeant 2IC and the section leaders for your 'O' (orders) Group, and explain your plan, so that each section commander is clear what his section's part will be in the attack. He will then brief his men. In this instance, there is really only one option, and as there is a hedgerow on the left, the attack must go in from the left flank. Remember 'FIRE and MOVEMENT'; so leave one section, the Bren teams and mortar to give covering fire and smoke as your attack goes in, in extended line from opposite the copse. You must synchronise watches and agree a start time and Start Line. You must also pick out some feature close to the copse, for the fire support teams to stop firing, otherwise you are liable to be mown down by your own covering fire. Also, you must remember that in any attack, you must continue through to the far end of the objective ensuring that it is clear of the enemy. Once you have secured the copse, and adopted all-round defence positions, then the fire support teams can move up to the copse, whilst the rest can give covering fire if required. Remember 'FIRE and MOVEMENT'. Any questions?'

We had none.

~

This lecture was the first of many, as we were instructed in further infantry advance and attack tactics. Then we learnt the principles of 'all round, in depth and mutually supporting' defence tactics. We learnt the importance of the correct positioning of section defences so that they had clear interlocking arcs of fire, and ideally channelling an enemy into a 'killing zone'.

Came the day when we were packed into Bedford 3 ton RLs, and driven off to Long Valley near Ash to put into practice, what we had hopefully learnt in the classroom. Each of us, in turn acted as platoon commander, and because of our numbers and the limited time available, the DS set scenario was a straightforward one, giving each of us the opportunity of putting in a short and quickly executed attack.

Eventually, my turn came.

'Right, Caffyn. Your axis of advance is up this track. Okay?'

'Yes, Sir'.

In my best leadership type voice and manner, I called my section leaders together. 'Right. Our axis of advance is up this track. No 1 Section will lead; then No 2, and No 3 will bring up the rear. I shall be between No 1 & 2 Sections. Each Bren team will be at the back of their section. Any questions?' There were none.

'Right, let's move out.' I had obviously seen too many John Wayne movies. We set off down the track with a hedge on either side. After about two hundred yards, the hedges finished and ahead lay an open field. The lead section commander raised his arm to signify a halt. I moved up to him.

'Any sign of enemy activity, John?'

'Not as yet.'

'Okay'.

I called the section commanders up for an 'O' Group.

'We've got to get across this field. We will advance in arrowhead formation with No 1 Section continuing to be the lead section with the Bren team on the right. No 2 Section on the left with the Bren on the left, and No 3 on the right with the Bren on the right flank. I, together with the platoon sergeant and the 2 inch mortar team (if we had one) will be in the middle behind No 1 Section. Remember, don't bunch, and make sure your sections keep the correct spacing. Any questions?'

We set off, with No 1 Section passing through the gap and quickly spreading out left and right into an arrowhead formation. I let No 2 Section pass through and they quickly shook themselves out to the left, as did No 3 Section on the right.

We continued our advance towards the next hedgerow, with the Sections keeping well spread out, whilst at the same time looking not only ahead, but also to the left and right to check for any signs of an enemy. Whilst making sure that we were keeping to our correct axis of advance and the sections were not bunching up, I was mentally working out the options open to me if we came under fire. ' If we are fired upon now, we will double back to the hedgerow we've just come through.' Some yards further on; 'If we come under fire now, I will order charge, and we will go straight into the attack.' Sure enough, we were about a hundred yards from the hedgerow to our front, when there was a crackle of rifle fire from our front, and from the flashes from the blank rounds being fired at us, I could make out the enemy's position in the hedgerow. I didn't hesitate.

'Charge', I yelled, and even in battle order with steel helmets, shouting and screaming, we must have made it to the enemy's position in record time. But, when we got there, the enemy had flown.

I spread the sections out along the line of the hedge, and then took stock. I was in somewhat of a quandary. Had I, by charging the enemy and putting in my attack finished my stint as the platoon commander, and it was now the turn of another cadet to take over? Or was I to continue and put in a properly prepared and organised attack on an, as yet undiscovered enemy position?

I did not have to wait long for an answer, for rifle fire broke out from a clump of trees to my front right. A LMG, in the form of a football rattle, also joined in. I realised that I was lucky; the situation I was faced with was the parallel of the one Capt Stevenson had lectured us on.

Still, I had to go through the right procedure, of carrying out a recce, preparing an Appreciation and then giving out my orders.

From my position in the hedge, and remembering to look through, and not over or round cover, I 'sussed' out the ground and prepared my plan. 'The ground is open and slopes away to the right of those trees. Difficult to put in an attack from there and will lead to us taking casualties. Ah! The left looks promising. We can follow this hedge round until it joins the next one at right angles, and we can advance up that one, until we are level with the trees. There looks as though there is a gap in the hedge opposite the trees, and the ground slopes down to the trees. We can use that as a Start Line and put in our attack across the short stretch of open ground'.

I crawled back to a dip in the ground behind the hedge and called the section commanders to me to give out my orders. I tried to remember how to draw up an Appreciation.

'Right. Listen in.

'Intention: To attack and dislodge the enemy from the clump of bushy top trees at two o'clock.

'Method: We will make a left flank attack. No 1 Section will give covering fire from this hedgerow. No 2 & 3 Sections will advance in single file to the left behind this hedgerow and then we will advance up behind the next hedge on the left. There is a gap halfway up, and we will cross that in groups. We will halt when we are opposite the trees. No 2 Section will be on the left, with No 3 Section on the right. I will be in the middle between both sections. Bill' (No 3 Section Commander), ' I want you to leave your

Bren team with No 1 Section to 'beef up' the covering fire. On my order, we will, at a walk, start to advance, awaiting my command to charge. Once we have reached the trees, keep going to the far side, to make sure we've flushed out the enemy. Jim' (No 2 Section Commander), 'when we've got through the trees, deploy your Bren Gun team and the rest of your section in defensive positions on the right of the trees, in case the enemy tries to put in a counter attack, before No 1 Section has joined up with us, and Bill make a sweep through the trees to make sure there are no hidden enemy and then deploy your section to the left of No 2 Section.'

I was certain that, by this time I had forgotten how to draw up and present an Appreciation correctly and I was probably omitting something. Anyway, I just ploughed on, hoping I wasn't leaving out anything important.

'Communication: If I had a Very pistol, I would fire a red light to start the attack followed by a green over white light to signal that we have secured the objective, and that No 1 Section should join us. But as I haven't we will have to use timings and hand signals. I reckon it will take us ten minutes to reach our Start Line. But, I will allow fifteen minutes. So we will synchronise watches. As we have no mortar bombs to put down smoke, Ian' (No 1 Section Commander), 'you will open rapid fire when you see us cross the Start Line, continuing as we charge into the attack, but shift your aim to the far side of the trees and cease firing when we reach the trees. When we have secured the objective, I shall from the edge of the trees give you the 'form up on me' hand signal, so bring your section up and deploy them facing in this direction to the left of Bill's and linking up on the right with Jim's section. This will give us all-round defence.

'Administration and Logistics: I don't believe in this attack, we will have any admin and logistic needs. Any questions?'

Fortunately for me, there were none.

'Right. Let's synchronise watches. In 30 seconds it will be 1131 hrs and 20 seconds. 10,9,8,7,6,5,4,3,2,1,zero. Okay. Brief your sections. We move off at 1136 hrs and 'H' hour will be 1151 hrs.'

I was trying to do everything by the book; for Capt Fleming our platoon commander, with his army issue clipboard and pencil, was monitoring my performance. Anyway it was too late for me to worry about it, as No 2 Section set off along the hedgerow. Although, I was somewhat concerned that I may have gone 'over the top' by bringing up Very pistols and mortars, when it was blatantly obvious we hadn't got either. But if we had, I was trying to show how I would have used them.

Anyway, everything went to plan. We crossed the Start Line at 1151 hrs, and I could hear the football rattles on my right as Ian's Bren gunners gave us rapid covering fire. By 1154 hrs, it was all over. We had captured about a dozen 'enemy' and secured our objective. After Ian's section had joined us and taken up defensive positions, I sank down with my back against a tree, and as I got my breath back, I wondered if I had forgotten anything. I had to admit to myself, that I had really enjoyed my stint as the platoon commander, and even though this was not for real, the adrenalin was really flowing, as I, and the others put in our attacks with verve and enthusiasm, shouting and screaming in the final charge.

As Capt Fleming busied himself writing notes, I pondered on whether there were two standards for judging the officer cadets on field exercises. One, with a higher standard for those who would be going into regiments which actually do the fighting, and the second with a lower standard for those who were to be commissioned into the support arms, and were not so likely to become involved in the nasty stuff at the 'sharp end'. But then I remembered something my father had once told me, that written into the Royal Warrant of May 1942, which was the official document approving the 'Formation of the Corps of Royal Electrical and Mechanical Engineers', there was a schedule which clearly stated that '*All officers and other ranks of the Royal Electrical and Mechanical Engineers shall be combatant in the fullest sense*', and were considered to be in the same category of those from the front line formations. So, my theory would not have held water, and anyway it would have been a very subjective judgement by the Directing Staff to determine whether Officer Cadet Joe Bloggs should have been assessed higher if he was being commissioned into the infantry, as compared to say, the Pioneer Corps.

After about ten minutes, Capt Fleming had finished his scribbling, and invited us to get off our backsides, and not be so idle.

'Right. Thank you, Caffyn,' he was giving nothing away. 'Thompson take over as platoon commander and Caffyn, you take over as No 1 on the Bren in No 2 Section. Right, the axis of advance is from the trees, up the valley towards the wood in the distance. Okay?'

The Bren was a fairy heavy weapon to carry round at the best of times, but when I had to do this after I had expended a fair amount of mental, nervous and physical energy as the platoon commander, and then perhaps have to put in two or three further attacks with the LMG was really going to test my stamina. Anyway, as James Thompson readied us for the move further up Long Valley, I made my way over to No 2 Section, and Bob, with a broad grin handed me the Bren and the football rattle as he relieved me of my rifle.

As there were thirty cadets in the platoon, and we could only carry out some six attacks a day, three in the morning and, after a wad and a mug of char from a NAAFI van, three in the afternoon, it took us the best part of a week for everyone to do their stint as the platoon commander under pseudo active service conditions. Our officers tried their best to vary the routine, but the Long Valley terrain was such, that it was only really possible to put in either frontal, or left or right flanking attacks. However, on a few occasions, we actually carried a two-inch mortar with a limited number of smoke bombs, enabling the fire support section to lay down smoke for an attack. This certainly added another, but rather hazardous dimension to our exercises. Although we had all undertaken training on firing the mortar, it was an inaccurate weapon in unskilled hands. Aiming was by judgement, and the only way to get the correct range for the target, was by manually holding the barrel at a higher or lower angle to increase or shorten the distance.

We had a sergeant from the Grenadier Guards to make sure that we didn't do anything stupid, such as not bedding the base plate firmly into the ground, otherwise the discharge of the bomb, could have sent the base plate shooting backwards, smashing into the knee or the private parts of the cadet who was acting as number one on the mortar; with the result that the mortar bomb would have shot off in a near horizontal trajectory at an unplanned and possibly dangerous direction. Although the mortar was intended to give protection to the attacking sections; it very rarely did, but provided a great deal of amusement, as the smoke was laid either too far away, or not far enough; or the wind was in the wrong direction, and the smoke would drift back and cover the fire support and mortar sections, so that they couldn't see when to give covering fire or when to stop; or it took so long to get the correct range, that the attack had successfully gone in and the action was over, before the smokescreen was laid. But having a mortar certainly added variety to what was becoming a rather monotonous set of field-craft exercises.

Being winter, it seemed to be very cold and miserable nearly every day we were out in Long Valley, and we all were kitted out in as many layers of clothes as we could get on without affecting our mobility too much. My standard gear was to wear pyjamas and No 2 battledress under my denims, and if I could get away with it, a commando woollen cap comforter on my head, which could be turned down to cover my ears. With all this extra clothing, we looked rather barrel shaped, and although one was kept warm when lying in any wet snow, we were definitely handicapped when we had to put in an uphill attack.

~

The Army Film Unit had produced many very effective training films during the Second World War, which were still being used and added to nearly fifteen years after the end of the war. We spent, which was most welcome during the very cold weather, many a happy hour in the centrally heated School Cinema, watching training films produced by the Army Kinema

Corporation, but I never learnt why it was spelt with a 'K'. Probably, because I never asked the question.

So, after we had finished our platoon attack exercises, it was time to move onto the next phase of our training, which was to be 'Patrols, and this is where the Army Training Films came into their own, as we probably learnt more about the three basic types of patrol: - fighting, recce and body snatching before we had even stepped outside the Cinema (or was it Kinema?).

Captain Stevenson, who was taking this instruction period, made the point very forcibly, that for a patrol to be successful, there had to be meticulous planning and that the purpose of the patrol had to be very clear.

'Now,' he began, 'let us imagine that an order for a unit to send out a night patrol, has originated from a higher HQ, where possibly a Brigadier has asked some bored Staff Officer having his elevenses, what lies in front of the defensive positions at map reference 257841. The GSO 1, 2 or 3, not having the foggiest idea, but not wishing to show his ignorance, informs the Brigadier that he will immediately get onto the relevant Battalion HQ, and ask for an update. However, before he can do that, he needs to find out from the Brigade's Intelligence Officer, where 257841 is and what unit is manning that part of the front. Having got the information, the unfortunate GSO is then left with another major decision; how best to contact the particular Battalion CO; whether by radio, land line, dispatch rider or by runner. As he does not know the Battalion's call sign, the codes for the day, and the time it will take to encipher a message; he probably will decide it is quicker and less hassle to pass the Brigadier's request on by using a dispatch rider, and although a secure land line will probably be the quickest and best option; the GSO, being a cautious but ambitious sort of chap, in order to cover his backside in case anything goes wrong, wants a written copy on file of his message to Battalion.

'The Order probably reaches Battalion HQ, by early afternoon, as the dispatch rider, probably not only loses his way, road signs having been removed, but also probably stops at a NAAFI van on his way from Brigade for a wad and a cuppa and to chat up the NAAFI girl.

'The CO no doubt explodes when he reads the Order; 'Bloody hell!! How do those buggers at Brigade expect me, before it gets dark to plan, carry out a recce and organise a fighting patrol to go out tonight, and the buggers also want us to capture and bring back alive an enemy prisoner?' To his adjutant, 'You better send for Lieutenant Hargreaves.'

'Poor Lieutenant Hargreaves. It is no good complaining that he had led a patrol out two nights previously. The Colonel explains that due to the short notice given by Brigade, he needs an officer with patrol experience, and he is very sorry but he, the Lieutenant has to go out again. No doubt Lieutenant Hargreaves will be successful. His CO will be pleased, as no doubt so will be the GSO back at Brigade; but will doubtless be shaken to the core as his Brigadier turns on him and gives him a verbal roasting:

'You bloody fool! What do you mean by ordering out a fighting patrol? All I wanted to know was the type and state of the ground at that map reference. Now the enemy has been alerted that we could be planning an attack.' The GSO 1, 2 or 3 is probably awarded extra duties, whilst Division is no doubt pleased at having a prisoner, and the Brigadier is no doubt pleased at being Mentioned in Dispatches.'

Captain Stevenson continued: 'Although this scenario is a rather light hearted one, I trust I have put over to you all the importance of clear orders; good, secure and a rapid means of communications; sufficient time for the planning, reconnaissance and proper preparation. However, do not fall into the trap and the temptation of taking the easy option, of using the same patrol leader and the same section to go out on patrol time and time again, purely for their experience and success rate. This could be counter-productive.

'The type of patrol will determine its composition, the weapons to be carried, and who will lead the patrol. It is vital for the man leading the patrol to carry out a reconnaissance as far forward as practical. Routes out and back must be planned, compass bearings taken, and distances estimated. In the eventuality of the patrol leader becoming a casualty, passwords need to be fixed and memorised by the whole patrol. Adjoining units must be briefed about a patrol going out with the likely timings, as the patrol could be returning, whether planned or not through another unit's lines. If the patrol is to be a fighting one, a decision has to be made whether a diversion, in the form of a short artillery or mortar barrage is necessary. Each man's task has to be allocated and explained. It is important at night that one person must be responsible for and adhere to the laid down compass bearings, whilst another may have to count paces to determine distances. It is important to realise that the length of a pace varies depending upon whether the patrol's route is on the level, uphill or downhill, but will probably be a combination of all three'.

Capt Stevenson finished his lecture by making the point:

'Whether you are the patrol leader or not, it is vital that the men going out on patrol are fully and clearly briefed, and if possible brought up to the forward observation point, so that they can see and appreciate the ground they will be moving over in the dark. All this should be done as early as possible, for it is vital for the men to get their heads down for a few hours kip, and to have a hot meal before they go out. As platoon commander or patrol leader, you must check that camouflage cream has been effectively applied to faces and hands, that any piece of equipment likely to make a noise or show up in moonlight is properly taped over, and you must also check that the patrol empties their pockets. Make each man jump and down to check for noise. Patrolling is a very important activity from which a great deal of information can be gathered, which should be of considerable use to the intelligence wallahs and on which operational decisions can be based. I hope that I have now emphasised in this short lecture, that for a patrol to be successful there must be detailed and meticulous planning.'

That was a very concentrated lecture and I had nearly filled a notebook recording all the points that Capt Stevenson had made.

~

It wasn't too long before we had the opportunity to put into practice all we had been taught about the art of patrolling. Half way through our Course the platoon was dispatched on a three-day exercise way out in the depths of Long Valley. The exercise rejoiced in some fancy name such 'Deep Dig' or 'Washed Out' or something equally meaningless. But before we set out, we were introduced to our new platoon commander, a captain from a Gurkha regiment, and like CSM Colquhoun at Honiton was softly spoken, with a great sense of humour, but very professional. We immediately took to him and, behind his back, nicknamed him 'Jungle Jim', as he had seen service in Malaya. I understood at the time, that it was somewhat unusual for there to be a change of platoon commander halfway through a Course. I believed Capt Fleming returned to his regiment.

We packed up the kit we would need for the three days we would be on exercise, and as it was still winter, we tried to cover all possible conditions from gales and pouring rain through to blizzards and freezing temperatures. However, as we were marching out to the exercise area, we were somewhat limited to how much we could practically carry.

Capt 'Jungle' Jim

After a couple of hours we climbed up onto a ridge with tall conifer trees, where we were ordered to halt, allocated our defensive position and ordered to dig in so as to give mutually supporting, all-round defence and should be prepared to occupy the position for up to three days.

Capt 'Jungle Jim' decided that Peter Smith of the Royal Marines and myself would make a good Bren team and detailed us to dig in just below the crest of the ridge, facing back towards the direction of our approach march. As we were going to be out in Long Valley for the three days, Peter and I decided that we would dig ourselves a really good LMG pit. Fortunately, the ground was not too hard, but it took us several hours to dig down some five feet, which would give us sufficient standing room, without having to crouch down too much, to man the Bren comfortably and effectively. Peter was a tower of strength, for when I felt I needed a 'breather' he would just continue digging. Must have been something to do with the air and training at Lympstone. The CSM wandered over at one stage, looked down at our excavation and with a broad smile; 'Bloody hell! What do you two think you're doing? This is only an exercise, you don't have to dig your own graves.' Eventually we pronounced ourselves satisfied with our weapon pit, and covered it with tree branches that were lying on the ground, before shovelling earth on top, and finishing off by replacing the turfs we had carefully cut and put to one side when we started. As we had been warned that the enemy might attack from any direction, we had left four gun slits for the LMG so that we could quickly and easily move it to give defensive covering fire when the attack came in from whatever direction. We had been warned that an attack would be put in within the following seventy-two hours.

Peter and I were pleased with our efforts, even though we had to put up with a fair amount of leg pulling from the rest of the platoon. However, we were the ones who were laughing, for when the rain came we were dry and warm in our bunker. We could also sleep in relative comfort as we had made our dugout large enough for one of us to lie down whilst the other kept watch. The rest of the platoon who had dug two-man slit trenches, were exposed to the elements. It was perhaps not surprising, but Peter and I found that our popularity had suddenly increased, for from the number of visitors we had, from the Company Commander down, it felt that our bunker was an 'open house' to everybody. I did suggest to Peter that as the bunker was big enough, we could make ourselves quite a tidy sum on the side by offering 'B & B' terms. A tempting but a rather impractical idea. Fortunately, for the rest of the platoon the rain that first evening did not last too long and it was dry but cold for the rest of the exercise. Some years previously when my cousin was on the same exercise, it rained so heavily for over two days that the exercise had to be called-off, as the slit trenches were fast filling up with water.

The first day had passed quickly, which was not surprising, bearing in mind all the digging that Peter and I did. I had hoped to get some rest in the afternoon before we were ordered to 'stand-to' for an hour at dusk. The Army, in their wisdom, always presumed, with historical justification that an attack was more likely to be made around dawn or at dusk, when the sun, whether in the east or the west, would be low in the sky and would be shining straight in the eyes of the defending force. In the half-light of dawn or dusk an attacking force would hold an advantage, picking out the defence positions, whilst the defenders would have difficulty in clearly making-out the attacking troops. Anyway, that was the theory, and whenever, or wherever I was on exercise, 'stand-to' was always observed at dawn and dusk. However, even when we were 'stood–down', Bren gun and rifle positions had to be manned, and feeding and attending to other personal needs were carried out on a rotational basis.

Fortunately, on this exercise we did not have to prepare and cook our own meals, as hot food was brought up from the School. It was a feature of all the exercises we were on at Mons, including Battle Camp in Wales, that hot food was brought out to whatever location we were at. This was much appreciated, welcomed and helped maintain morale, especially when after a long physical day, we were tired, cold, probably wet, and the effort of opening our 24hr ration packs, preparing and cooking our own meals may have been just too much, with some officer cadets possibly not bothering to eat.

After we had eaten our evening meal, the acting platoon JUO worked out a guard duty roster, which was somewhat complicated for our platoon, as earlier in the day orders had come 'down the line', from an unknown higher authority that we had to send out a recce patrol that night. As the prime objective for this was an intelligence gathering one, where stealth was a main requisite, the composition of the patrol was different to that of a fighting one. Nevertheless, I was chosen for the patrol, and at the appointed time, I left Peter in our LMG dugout and joined up with the other members of the patrol. However, due to various valid reasons, the patrol leader was unable to take us forward to give us a view of the ground we would be covering. So the briefing had to be given 'blind'.

'Okay, listen in,' Bob Humphries, from I believe the Durham Light Infantry (DLI), started nervously, 'At 2200hrs we shall set out from our positions and in single file go down the slope to our front, on a compass bearing of 205°. After about a hundred yards, we enter an area of gorse, brambles and low bushes. There is a path through this undergrowth. Our aim is to recce this path, see how far it goes, and when we come out into open ground, to establish what sort of terrain lies beyond the bushes, and whether it would be a possible approach for an enemy attack. We will blacken faces, hands and brasses. The upper and lower swing swivels on our rifles will be tied up with hessian, and other bright parts dulled. Make sure you have nothing on you or in your pockets that rattles. John, I want you to have the compass, making sure we march and stay on the 205° bearing and we shall be returning by the same route on a counter bearing of 25°. Bill, I want you to lead. John, you will be behind Bill, and then Harry who will be our pace counter. I shall be behind Harry. Anthony you will be 'tail-end Charlie'. Silence is vital. Are there any questions?'

'Bob,' I piped up, 'what happens if we come across an enemy patrol?'

Bob thought about that. 'We will go to ground and hope we aren't spotted. If we are then we shall have to fight our way out. One last point the password is 'Ascot'. Okay? Right, get some rest. We will assemble at 2130hrs.'

By 2200hrs we were all ready, with our faces and hands suitably blackened, and with caps comforters pulled well down on over our heads, we must have looked a right bunch of desperados; who even our mothers would have had difficulty recognising. From our defence positions, with Bill in the lead, we set off down the slope, with John peering anxiously at the luminous dial of the compass, and whispering to Bill, 'left a bit, too much, right a bit. Okay, keep going like that.' After about five minutes, we hit the rough stuff, and without too much trouble, Bill found the start of the path, and as quietly as possible we plunged into what turned out to be a very narrow track, with low branches, brambles and gorse smacking us in our faces as the path twisted and turned to the left and to the right. It was almost impossible to maintain silence, and as well as muffled expletives, I could hear from my position at the rear, Harry's stage whispers of '150, 151, 152' and so on.

Capt 'Jungle Jim' had decided to accompany us, and every now and then to liven up proceedings; he would from behind us, let off flares, which lit up the whole area in a garish white light. We had been told, in the event of being caught in the open when a flare went off, never to throw ourselves flat onto the ground, as an enemy would probably be able to pick up the movement. It was better to stand still, with eyes closed so as not to ruin ones night vision, and try to look like a tree. I never wanted to test this theory.

After, what seemed to be an eternity, we came to the end of the bushes and brambles and as the rain had passed, we were enjoying intermittent moonlight between the scudding clouds; so we could make out the type of ground that lay beyond the rough stuff.

Bob, having satisfied himself that we had fulfilled the objective of our patrol, signalled for us to re-form and make our way back. We were certainly more relaxed as we set off, when suddenly all hell broke loose. Blank rifle fire and exploding thunder-flashes were all around us. We had been 'bumped' by an enemy patrol. As Bob shouted, 'Run', a thunder-flash went off close to me, and Capt Jim tapped me on the shoulder and whispered that I had been hit. I quietly sank to the ground and lay there, as I heard the rest of the patrol disappearing into the distance like a herd of charging bull elephants. The enemy having ambushed us also faded away, but with considerably less noise. I quietly lay there, rather enjoying the peace, the chance of a rest, and making out between the scudding clouds the Pole Star and the Plough. But after some minutes, I began to worry that I might not be missed until well after the patrol had returned back to our defence position. Indeed, I might have been left out there all night, for I believed that Capt Jim had had to ask Bob whether, after the brief action, the patrol was complete. So Bob called a halt and carried out a head count.

'Bloody hell! Has anybody seen Caffyn.' Nobody had. So after another head count, just in case Bob had miscounted, or I had wandered off into the undergrowth to have a pee, he ordered the patrol to retrace its steps. Anyway, a few minutes later, I heard the noise of the patrol returning. Bob asked me what had happened.

'I've been hit in the legs by shrapnel,' I replied. To make a makeshift stretcher, two rifles were laid parallel on the ground with rifle slings strapped to them. I was hoisted unceremoniously onto this, and the rest of the patrol, took it in turns to carry me back to our FDLs (Forward Defence Localities). I would not recommend this form of transport. It was most uncomfortable and as we only had a limited number of slings to fix to the two rifles there were, inevitably gaps, with one of these being where my backside was. So, our return progress was accompanied by me cursing and swearing, as my bottom was struck by sharp bramble thorns and prickly gorse branches. Every now and then one or both of my 'stretcher bearers' stumbled, with the result that I was usually unceremoniously deposited into the nearest gorse bush.

I was so thankful when we came out into the open with the slope leading up to our ridge ahead of us. But I was somewhat bemused as we climbed the slope to see in the moonlight a very large mound sticking out like a sore thumb on the platoon's left flank. I wondered what it was, and then realised that it was the 'Peter and Anthony Folly'. It looked enormous, and I realised that although we had made ourselves a dry and comfortable LMG bunker, it could have been seen for what it was by an enemy and blasted out of existence before any attack was launched.

Fortunately, those of us who had been on the patrol were excused guard duties, and we were able to get a fairly good nights sleep, before 'stand-to' at dawn. After the night's activities, the next day was spent improving our positions, and we went forward to observe these from an attackers view point and make any necessary modifications to the layout, siting and camouflaging of both the slit and LMG trenches. Unfortunately, Peter and I could do nothing further to camouflage and disguise our carbuncle of a bunker. I did wonder if the enemy might take it for a Stone Age burial barrow, which we might have got away with on Salisbury Plain, but I felt that was too much to hope for at Aldershot. On active service, Peter and I would never have constructed such a bunker; we would have dug a slit trench and made do with that.

Following the lectures we had had on how to organise a FDL, we spent time ensuring that all the slit trenches were so sited that not only did they provide a full arc of fire, but were mutually supporting and interlocking. We had no idea from which direction the enemy was likely to attack, although we felt that, due to the narrowness of the track it was unlikely to come in from the direction where our patrol had 'recced' the previous night. So as to give 'all-round' defence the platoon was spread rather too thinly around the ridge. We tried to establish 'killing zones', where the enemy could be channelled into natural 'funnels' so that we could bring the maximum firepower onto those points.

~

Having spent some time on our defences, we were then left to own devices, and as we had now been warned that an attack would be put in sometime in the next twenty-four hours, we were able to maintain a partial 'stand-down' with only half the platoon on watch at any one time.

It was late afternoon, when in the distance came the sound of powerful engines and the familiar 'clanking' of tracked vehicles. As we thought the attack was about to come, we immediately manned our positions and checked that blank cartridges had been correctly loaded into rifle magazines, whilst Peter and I checked that our football rattle was in good working order. However, it was a false alarm, as out of the fading daylight a troop of three Centurion tanks churned their way up the slope to the ridge, with one tank turning off to the left and one to the right. As the middle one with the troop leader on board headed straight for our bunker, Peter and I were considering an urgent and sudden evacuation of our position, wondering whether we would indeed 'grunt' if run over; when the driver, or troop commander must have woken up and realised that we were not a Stone Age barrow, and at the last moment the tank veered off to the left and parked itself at the end of the ridge just inside the tree line. As it was not in a 'hull-down' position, the crew did their best to camouflage and break up the distinctive outline of the AFV (Armoured Fighting Vehicle) with branches and anything else they could lay their hands on. Peter and I were relieved that the tank had laagered next to us, not only for the extra firepower it brought, but its size was such, that it made our 'carbuncle' of a bunker look no bigger than that of a 'pimple'. The downside was that the enemy would try and take the tank out first, which would probably include Peter and myself as well.

After the dusk 'stand-to', the evening meal, and the allocation of guard duties, we settled down for the night. Another 'recce' patrol had been ordered to go out, and it was with a feeling of considerable relief that I was not chosen. I was still stiff, sore and with my backside not only black and blue, it also felt like a pincushion from being dumped in gorse bushes the previous night.

The tank crew alongside us battened themselves down into their steel monster for the night, leaving us with the problem of how to contact them in the event of a night attack. Obviously, if we were under mortar, artillery and small arms fire, we would be less than enthusiastic of leaping out of our nice, cosy, warm and secure haven, to cross over to the tank and talk to the crew on their external telephone. So, being REME, the suggestion was made that I should be able to provide a technical solution to this communication problem. After due consideration, I decided that we should tie one end of a length of thin wire to the right wrist of the tank commander, take the wire out through the tank's machine gun port and across the ground and through one of our LMG slits.

The night was fairly noisy with flares, thunder flashes and blank small arm fire in the distance, as the patrol was being subjected to the same treatment as we had received the previous night. Eventually, things quietened down, and we could get some sleep. It must have been around midnight, and it was my turn on watch, when there was a noise of heavy breathing from behind me, and the feared Captain Flood, 1 RTR had climbed down into our bunker.

'Right, when the enemy attack comes in. How are you going to contact the tank crew and warn them?'

I showed the Captain the wire, and explained that the other end was tied to one of the tank commander's wrists.

'Have you tried it out?'

'Yes, Sir. When we set it up.'

'Right. Give me that end,' ordered Capt Flood, and proceeded to give the wire a most tremendous 'yank', and then left our bunker to see what the result was. He did not have long to wait. There was a clang as the tank's turret hatch was flung open and the tank commander, in a top public school voice, furiously yelled down towards our bunker:

'Bugger you two!! What the fuck do you miserable grunts think you are playing at waking me up like that? You nearly cut my fucking wrist in two. I've a good mind to flatten your fucking bunker with you two buggers inside.'

Sudden silence.

'Oh, bloody hell!! Sorry, Sir, I didn't see you there.'

Captain Flood let fly with some very choice words of his own, which précised, demanded from the tank commander an answer why, instead of the crew being asleep, wasn't one of them on sentry duty outside the tank, and warning that it was a court-martial offence being asleep on duty, and suggested that the cadet tank commander would perhaps be better suited in the Pioneer Corps, digging latrines rather than being commissioned into the Royal Tank Regiment. I really felt sorry for the individual, for by the time the Captain had finished, he must have felt knee high to a grasshopper. Anyway the tank commander had the grace to apologise to Peter and myself for his remarks, offering by way of explanation that it was the sudden shock of being woken from such a deep sleep, and that his body had come into violent and extremely painful contact with several parts of the tank, which he hadn't come across before. I suggested he might like to change places and be sent out on a patrol, be wounded and be stretchered back between two rifles to know real discomfort. He declined my offer, so we wished him well and hoped he successfully completed the Course and was posted to his preferred regiment.

The rest of the night passed without any other excitement, until we were 'stood-to' at 0630hrs and 'stood-down' an hour later. As the attack hadn't come when we were expecting it, half the platoon was detailed off to carry out their ablutions and make use of the 'thunder boxes' before breakfast. All of a sudden, smoke bombs started coming in, onto and around our positions. Washing and shaving kit was sent flying, the hessian doors to the 'thunder boxes' were thrown open as cadets stumbled out into the open, hastily pulling up BD trousers and buttoning themselves up, with loo paper flying in every direction. It was not a simple operation to get out of the 'bogs' quickly. Braces were a necessary piece of kit, otherwise BD trousers would end up around ones ankles, a sight not appreciated by CSMs and Drill Sergeants. So when the call of nature came, it was either a question of removing ones BD blouse before slipping off ones braces, or leaving the BD blouse on and just unbuttoning the braces. Time could be saved by only unbuttoning the back of the braces, but time could then be lost with an arm up ones back trying to locate the errant end of the braces, which by this time had probably ended up around ones neck. So there was a fair degree of pandemonium when the smoke started coming in, as we dived headlong into our weapon pits. Orders were shouted out for sights to be set for two hundred yards, but how anybody could see at that moment whether the enemy was at one hundred, two hundred, or eight hundred yards, or were even putting in an attack was a mystery to me. In fact it could all have been a false alarm, and a ruse by the enemy to locate our rifle and Bren positions. Anyway, somebody who was possibly using a pine tree as a crow's nest, must have known what was going on, for the order was given:

'To your front. Rapid fire.'

Blank rifle ammunition was expended at an alarming rate, and Peter and I took it in turns to frantically wave our football rattle trying to convince the enemy, that we were maintaining the maximum cyclic rate of fire for a Bren gun of 500 rounds per minute.

We were certainly under attack, as thunder-flashes and small arms fire were inbound, and shortly after, the enemy in the shape of the Royal Inniskilling Fusiliers emerged from the smoke, grinning and muttering fairly loudly 'Bloody Sassenachs', to which we replied with equally good natured spirit 'Bloody Picts', and suggested they could do everybody a favour by retiring back beyond Hadrian's Wall.

In ten minutes it was all over. Our position had been overrun and the Royal Inniskillings had indeed disappeared in the direction of Hadrian's Wall via the A1. We emerged from our trenches. Then Capt Jim together with the CSM came round, and inspected rifles to make sure that all blank cartridges, whether fired or not, had been accounted for. Peter and I suggested that the CSM might like to check our rattle, but this was met with such a very stony look, that we thought we would be in trouble at the next drill parade.

Although Peter and I had felt smug with our bunker, and that we had remained warm, dry and had been able to sleep in comfort, the laugh eventually was on us, for we had to leave the site in the same condition as we found it. It did not take the others long to fill in and tamp down their slit trenches and then they wandered over to where Peter and I were manfully filling in our 'Folly'. They sat around offering us advice: 'Come on, you two idle lay-abouts, put some effort into it', and 'I could do better with a teaspoon', were two of the printable ones. Our suggestion that if they wanted to get back to Camp that evening, then some help would be appreciated, was greeted by; 'You dug the hole, you bloody well fill it in.'

Eventually, Peter and I had finished, and after we had spread some branches, pinecones and needles over the area, it was difficult to see any signs of where our bunker had been. As we relaxed leaning against tree trunks, Capt Jim carried out a post-mortem, and although he congratulated us on our efforts, enthusiasm and knowledge of the principles of defence and patrolling, he nevertheless pointed out mistakes, such as the unnecessary effort that Peter and I had put into what should have been a simple, short term LMG weapon pit, and how this would have given away our position to enemy observers. He noted that at the pre-patrol briefing, the patrol leader had not covered the action to be taken in the event of suffering casualties. Capt Jim emphasised the importance of head-counts, especially on patrol at night, when it was all too easy to 'lose' someone; and especially so after a fire-fight with the enemy, when it was even more important to check if any members of the unit, whether in our FDLs or on patrol, had been wounded or even killed.

Finally, in the early afternoon, somewhat wearily we marched back to

Camp, feeling rather pleased with ourselves, for we knew we had done well, but we were all really looking forward to being back in our own beds. But, before we could 'chill-out', there was the small problem of cleaning all our kit, pressing BDs, thoroughly cleaning rifles and all the other 'domestic chores' that had to be done, ready for the following mornings drill parade.

~

Exercises were a welcome break from the normal camp routine of drill, PT, assault course, lectures and route marches. Major Langley had warned us in his introductory briefing that we would be doing four route marches from four to sixteen miles. By the time we were half way through our Course, we had done the four and the eight-mile ones and we were getting to know the area around Aldershot; but by the time we had completed the final sixteen mile one, places such as North Town, Ash, Brookwood, Bisley and West End would become very familiar. Tracing the route of our marches from the map, I noticed that a short distance beyond West End was Donkey Town and I felt it would have been appropriate if we had included that place on our route march itinerary, as we felt like donkeys with all the battle kit we wore on these hikes.

~

We certainly never had a dull moment, and the pace quickened as we were forced fed with an increasing number of military subjects, which we were expected to permanently memorise and be able to recall at a drop of a military hat. I could understand the amazement showed by those officer cadets from Sandhurst over what we had to do in the sixteen weeks.

Not all the lectures were boring, and the ones we had on map reading were some of the lighter ones. It helped that Capt Stevenson was instructing us.

'Okay. Today I shall be instructing you in the joys of map reading. Not only does the Army place great store in their officers being competent in this, but also being able to read a map correctly has its place in the social world. Imagine that you are due to meet a girl, which you feel could develop into a promising relationship, but she has arranged to meet you at a certain spot, which you don't know and you need a map to find the place. However, if you cannot read a map and you miss the rendezvous, you might also miss the experience of a lifetime.

'It must be obvious to you all that you will never become competent soldiers unless you can map read, and not only read a map but interpret what is shown on it. Good maps such as the Ordnance Survey ones consist of a mass of detail. The large scale ones don't just show roads, and signs for churches, pubs and post offices; they also show the lie of the land, high ground, spurs, re-entrants with gradients, woods and marshy areas and so on.

'Now', and the captain picked up his chalk and turned to the blackboard,

'Faulty or ignorant map reading skills can lead to:

(a) Unnecessary loss of life, and

(b) Loss of valuable time.

To soldiers, maps can provide:

(i) Clear and accurate visualisation of the ground relief profiles.

(ii) Possible defence positions.

(iii) Patrol routes.

(iv) Possible attack approach routes.

(v) Estimating distances and time.

(vi) Picking possible fire positions.

'By mentally visualising the map in 3D, you can determine whether certain point are visible or not from other points.

'So a map is not just simply using it to quote six figure grid reference for whoever needs it. Every unit in the Army, whether they be 'teeth' or supporting ones, cannot function without the ability and training to read maps. I believe that in a battle situation the unit that can read, interpret and use a map better than the opposition has a distinct advantage. Now, open map OS247 and let's get some serious practice.'

I felt at the time, that we hadn't realised all the implications of map reading, for in a subsequent lecture, we were instructed on how to measure distances; how to take bearings; how to use a protractor; how to set and maintain direction by map and how to encode grid and slide references. All this led up to the use of the prismatic compass, which I have always felt, was one the Army's best pieces of equipment.

Again, Capt Stevenson was our instructor.

'Now, the Army's magnetic compass is made up of four components; the metal lid; the compass body; the eyepiece and the thumb ring. Being magnetic, compass readings will be effected by the presence of iron in the near vicinity, and the compass should not be used within forty yards of a field gun.

'Before using a compass it must be set. The first thing is to open it and lay it down flat. Okay? Now, loosen the clamp screw on the shoulder of the compass, and turn the verge ring until the bearing 115°, on which we wish to march is in the centre of the luminous Flash Patch, also called the Keystone, and in line with the 'lubber' line. Now rotate the compass until the North Point on the compass card coincides with the luminous direction mark. To follow the required bearing, all we have to do is to march in the direction on the hairline.

'There will be times when you will have to march on a magnetic bearing only, and with no other visual aids. Therefore it is essential that you all know how to measure distance by pacing. The usual estimation is one hundred and twenty paces to one hundred yards. However, each of you must carry out your own test, as the taller ones amongst you may take fewer paces for a hundred yards, whilst the shorter ones may take more. But remember, going uphill there is a tendency to take shorter steps; downhill longer ones.'

~

We were only a few days from our first military knowledge exam, and any spare time we had was spent revising. Memories of swotting for my 'Finals' at Loughborough came flooding back. I've always lacked confidence, and could never adopt a 'laid back' attitude to exams. To revise for my 'Finals' I would get up at six o'clock in the morning, study for two hours; sit the exam, and I was fortunate that all my exams were in the morning. After a lunch break, I would then revise for the exam the following day from two o'clock until six o'clock', then seven o'clock until nine o'clock and finally from half past nine until midnight. I only broke off for meals. Then I would be up at six o'clock again for a final revision, and so on for ten days. I got my Diploma, but after my 'Finals' and having spent eighteen years at boarding schools and at a residential college taking both term and annual exams, I never wanted to see an exam paper again. Now, I was faced with sitting not one, but two written exams. The only redeeming feature was that the military subjects were a darn sight more interesting than 'Metallurgy', Fuel Technology,' 'Work Study', 'Industrial Psychology', Statistical Methods' and others.

Anyway the day came for MK 1, and for three hours we worked our way through a whole host of questions, which comprehensively covered the Course syllabus. It was mind blowing how much information had been pumped into us and fairly astounding how much knowledge we had assimilated in just eight weeks. The fear of failure and being RTUd, and our determination and ambition (yes, ambition had now become one of my main reasons for wanting to become an officer), was enough incentive for all in our platoon to want to pass the exam. I had no idea how well or badly I had done, for we were not given our marks. It was just a tremendous relief and a weight off my shoulders when I was told that I had passed the exam. Now I really began to believe that I was going to make it to the Passing-Out Parade. There was even a subtle change in the attitude of our officers, the CSM and drill sergeants, as they too began to believe that we were not a company of 'losers'.

Nevertheless, we could not afford to relax. For, early on in our Course as one officer put it:

'Leading men into action, means that you are responsible for the lives of the men you command. It is not easy to make the right decisions when the shit hits the fan, and there are shells, mortars and grenades exploding around you; when machine gun and small arms fire is being directed at you; when you see men who you have served with being blown to pieces with flesh, bone, tissue and blood flying everywhere; and you are scared. Your men will look to you for leadership. Let them down, and they will lose their respect and trust in you. Make the wrong decisions and you will have to live with your conscience for the rest of your life.

'The Regular Army's Commissioning Course takes two years to prepare officer cadets to face such situations, but as the Company Commander told you in his opening address, we have only sixteen weeks to achieve the same result. So, take my advice. Listen and Learn. This does not only go for those of you who are being commissioned into infantry regiments, but also applies to those who are being commissioned into the supporting arms. In fact, it is possible that you may have an even greater responsibility, because the men under you will not have been thoroughly trained in infantry tactics, and in countries such as Aden, Cyprus and Malaya, where the Army is on active service, there are no front lines as there were in the Second World War or Korea. The enemy could attack from out of the blue and from any direction, and supporting units are just as likely to be in the front line as the infantry. So, whether you are Royal Signals, RAOC, RASC or REME you are just as likely to come under fire, and it will be up to you as their officer to compensate, through leadership, ability and knowledge, for any lack of infantry skills your men may have.

'We do not have the luxury of training you in the way and at a pace to suit you. It will be up to you all to prove to us that you have the intelligence, the guts, the determination, the ambition and the stamina to be fit to command men under battle conditions.'

~

After MK 1, the Company Senior Under Officer (SUO) and Platoon Junior Under Officers (JUOs) were confirmed in their appointments, with Peter Smith Royal Marines becoming our JUO.

We continued with more lectures, more drill and more Adjutant's Parades, and I once again went and committed the cardinal sin of, in the words of the RSM: 'Sorr, Orfficer Cadet Caffyn, did move his head on parade.' The Adjutant shook his head sadly, repeated the admonishment he had given me eight weeks previously and awarded me the same punishment. Once again I, and others debated about the 2200hrs defaulters parade and what to do with our small packs. I decided this time to fill the pack with the items it was meant to contain and try to 'square it off' as best I could. Again, luckily I had made the right decision, for the Orderly Officer that day was

Captain Flood, and my heart sank down into my boots as, from behind I felt the back of my great coat being lifted as he checked to ensure the buttons were properly done up. Then I felt him feeling my small pack, but fortunately, he assumed that I had filled it correctly, as his attention passed to the cadet next to me, who had such a perfectly 'squared off' pack that he must have left it empty except for the strips of cardboard in it. He certainly incurred Capt Flood's displeasure.

~

Although we received some instruction in wireless procedures, this was not in any great depth; possibly because the World War II sets that we were using at Mons were elderly, not very reliable and did not have a great range. Still, we learnt about nets, call signs, control, substations, the phonetic alphabet and the meanings of such words as 'Roger' and 'Wilco'. We knew that the call sign 'Sunray', referred to the commander of a unit or a sub-unit.

However, with the sets we had we were able to practice basic wireless procedure:
'Hello, Five. How do you hear me? Over.'
'Five. Loud and Clear. Over.
'One. Go to Golf Hotel X-ray 456248. Over.'
'Five. Golf Hotel X-ray 456248. Roger. Out.'

~

Before we went off to Battle Camp, we enjoyed one night exercise, and enjoyed was the operative word. The format was similar to the one at Honiton; but on this occasion there were some added refinements, such as flares being sent up at regular intervals, and the defenders, of which I was one, could improvise trip wires and booby traps. The plot was that the enemy 'Red' force had to infiltrate the friendly 'Blue' force defence lines without being discovered and capture our HQ.

In the afternoon we were taken out in two separate groups to a different part of Long Valley, which we hadn't been to before, where we were to recce the land and, for us in the 'Blue' defence force, to pick our defence positions and work out the enemy's likely approaches. Although Peter Smith and I had teamed up on a number of occasions, my closest friend was Bob Turner from the 'Devon and Dorsets', and whenever possible we tried to team up together, which we had managed for this night exercise.

From a slight rise, the ground sloped gently away for about a quarter of a mile to a clump of trees. The undergrowth in winter consisted mainly of bracken and heather with what I took to be well-defined animal tracks. I imagined in summer there were a lot of ferns, which probably gave good cover for adders. However, in February that was a hazard that should not bother us.

It was the weather that helped make this exercise so enjoyable. Although it was still winter, the night was overcast, warm, dry and with no wind. The position that Bob and I had been given was in a small depression and we were in the centre of the platoon's defence position, with other positions some twenty yards either side of us. There was an ill-defined path running through the depression. As Bob and I thought that this track could well be an approach route, we improvised some trip wires with string and empty cans we had brought with us; we also collected as many dry twigs as we could and laid them a short distance up the track under a thin layer of bracken.

At 2200hrs a green flare arched up into the sky to denote that the exercise was under way. It was very quiet as we waited, trying to pick up the first whisper of undergrowth being disturbed. Periodically, a flare would be sent up into the night sky and light up the immediate countryside, and as we had been trained, we peered, without success across 'no-man's land' to see if we could catch any sudden movement of an enemy dropping to the ground, or standing still trying to be a tree, but without success. Our training had been too good. The infiltrators had an advantage, in that they could shut their eyes when a flare went off, without destroying their night vision. Whereas, we had to keep ours open trying to spot them, thus ruining our night vision for several minutes. Bob and I decided, that when a flare went off, one of us would keep our eyes open, whilst the other would keep his tightly shut and preserve his night vision.

When the weather was kind, as it was on this particular night, I thoroughly enjoyed these night exercises; lying in wait in complete silence, trying to catch the first sound of a twig snapping, the soft rustle of undergrowth or seeing an outline of something darker than the sky, slowly appear to our front; generated a frisson of anticipation and excitement. The enemy would be moving very slowly, also listening for any slight noise that could give away our position. We had had no indication of where the enemy was, and we felt we had remained motionless for what seemed like hours, before Bob gently touched my arm and pointed to our left, where we could just make out a darker indistinct shape, hugging the ground and crawling so very slowly as he tried to infiltrate between our positions. The enemy was obviously cleverer than we had given him credit, as he had decided to ignore the animal track as being a too obvious approach that we would bound to have covered. We waited until he was level with us, and then we silently crawled over to him and 'nabbed' him. His part in the exercise was over, and Bob and I went back to our position and to watch and listen out for the next infiltrator. This went on for some three hours, and Bob and I had managed to capture one other infiltrator before a red flare burst overhead to denote the exercise was over. Although the exercise was not taken too seriously, we did learn some valuable lessons about night defence and infiltration tactics.

~

There were increasing signs that we were nearing the end of our Course, especially when Capt Stevenson gave us a lecture on the subject of 'The Behaviour of Officers'.

'Now, you don't need me to tell you, how as officers you should behave when you are with your regiments, battalions or corps. Holding the Queen's Commission is a privilege and, as you have been finding out these last few months has to be earned. Whether in uniform or in civilian clothes, you must always maintain the standards, which I hope we will have taught you here at Mons. You will salute and show respect to officers who are senior to you, as you will also show respect and return salutes to warrant officers, senior and junior NCOs and other ranks. Remember, they are saluting the rank, not you and if you are to gain and keep their respect, you must acknowledge this in the correct and proper manner. This applies just as much when you are out of uniform. You must learn, if you do not know already, to treat those who are under you fairly and justly. The men you will command are your family and you must look after them. Help and advise them when they need it. Listen to their worries and problems; for there will be situations, mainly in an overseas posting, where a soldier has no one else to turn to except his officer, and you can achieve a lot by just letting him unburden himself to you. You may feel helpless that you have not been able to offer any concrete help, but by just being there and listening, you may have achieved more than you think. Of course, there will be times when you will have to maintain discipline and put a soldier on report. When and if you believe that is necessary, don't hesitate to do it. You will earn nobody's respect if you are seen as being indecisive, and which will be taken as a sign of weakness. Don't try for popularity. As the company commander said, 'leadership is about people'. Don't ever forget that.'

The lecture continued in the same vein for some time, before Capt Stevenson moved on to the social behaviour of officers.

'As junior officers you will be expected to know the traditions and histories of the regiments or corps you will be joining, and this applies especially to Officers' Mess traditions. You must learn the difference between mess nights, dining-in nights and regimental guest nights. You must know the responsibilities of the PMC (President of the Mess Committee), and that of the Vice-President. You must learn whether your regiment stands or sits for the loyal toast, or whether it is a regiment that does not, as a matter of routine drink the loyal toast. In the 1st Battalion of my Regiment, the Royal Sussex, the toast is drunk seated; this stems from the time they served as marines; for in those days there was simply not enough headroom in 'men-of-war' ships to stand upright to drink the loyal toast; whereas the 2nd Battalion never served as marines and consequently stand for the toast. One other custom unique to the Royal Sussex is that it is the mess waiters who pass the port round the table and not, as is customary the officers.

'So traditions are very important, and you would be well advised to learn all about those of your regiment before you take your first step through the portals of the officers' mess. When on duty, you address officers senior to you as 'Sir'. However, in many messes where there is less formality, christian names may be used for officers up to and including majors. But never try that with the commanding officer, who should always be addressed as 'Colonel'. As subalterns you are addressed both on and off duty as 'Mr'.

'In most messes certain subjects are taboo, such as religion and talking 'shop', and the president can impose an arbitrary fine of 'drinks all round' on offenders. There are some cardinal sins that you must not commit. In the ante-room do not take the most comfortable armchairs around the fireplace, they will be for the colonel, the 2IC and other senior majors. To be safe when you first enter the mess ante-room choose the most uncomfortable chair in the furthest corner away from the fire. Do not at breakfast take from the ante-room table 'The Times', 'The Telegraph' or other quality newspapers; and especially if you are in a cavalry regiment, on pain of death, do you take the 'Sporting Life'. These are the prerogative of the senior officers of the regiment or the battalion. Breakfast, like a silent order of monks, is a non-talking meal. Officers find it difficult enough to concentrate on their food, as well as trying to balance and read their newspaper against a toast rack, without having to be engaged in some puerile

The senior living-in Member of the Mess

conversation from the 'sprog' subaltern of the regiment. For formal mess nights and especially for regimental guests nights, when dinner is announced, you do not, however hungry you are, leap up, shout 'whacko' and charge into the dining room ahead of everyone else. There is a strict order of precedence and you will be the last in. Behaviour like this, and also sitting in the colonel's, 2IC's or adjutant's place at table, will earn you so many extra orderly officers' duties that you will probably never have the chance to dine in the mess again before you finish your National Service; although you will be immensely popular with the other subalterns.

'One other word of warning. Mess and guest nights can be long affairs, and if you want to enjoy these in comfort, do not drink too many beers in the ante-room beforehand; stick to a glass of sherry, and go and have a 'pee' before dinner is served. Nobody leaves the dinner table until the colonel does, and if you have been appointed as 'Mr Vice', you do not leave until every other officer has left the table, however long that takes. So, if your bladder is bursting, you must cross your legs, tie a knot in it, pray and hope the band doesn't play Handel's 'Water Music'!

'In many officers' messes it is the custom for the most junior subaltern to be appointed the messing officer. This means that you have the responsibility, in conjunction with the mess sergeant of arranging menus that will meet with the approval of the officers, but ensuring that you do not exceed the mess food budgets. I can assure you that this is a thankless appointment. Officers expect to be fed as well as the Savoy Grill, but on a Lyons Tea House budget. Two tips. Always defer to the mess sergeant. He would not be in that position unless he was good at his job, and secondly try and please the adjutant. If he likes 'devils-on-horseback' as a savoury, then give him 'devils-on-horseback' at every mess, guest and dining-in night. It doesn't matter if the colonel doesn't like them. He will complain to the adjutant, who won't pass the complaint onto you. The adjutant will instead sort the colonel out.

'Now, another word of warning. National Service subalterns are not well paid and unless you are fortunate enough to have private means, you must watch your mess bills. You do not pay for your drinks at the time; you sign a bar chit, and your mess bill is presented to you weekly. Some regiments have expensive habits, so don't try and keep up with other officers. It is a real disgrace not being able to settle your mess bill.'

The lecture continued. I do not know how we managed to move onto the subject of how officers should behave at cocktail parties, but Capt Stevenson certainly brought the subject up. Although over the years, I have probably forgotten more than I ever learnt at Mons, his words on this subject have always remained with me.

'Now, I have a set procedure at cocktail parties. I always arrive half an hour late; stand by the door and pick out one or two attractive women, and I approach the first one and ask her outright if she will come to bed with me.'

We gasped, and could not believe what we had just heard. Then nervously, we started to laugh.

'Okay, you can all laugh, but you'd be surprised how many say 'yes'. They will certainly outweigh the number of slaps across the face you will get.'

I never knew whether he was just pulling our legs in order to keep our attention, or was telling the truth. At the time he was a bachelor. Captain John Stevenson certainly had the natural ability to put over a subject in such a way, that it was clear, made sense and which I would remember for many years, and this was especially true of his lecture on the 'Behaviour of Officers'. However, I never had the nerve or confidence to try his 'chat-up' approach at cocktail parties.

~

Before the time came for us to carry out the final part of our training at Battle Camp in the Brecon Beacons, the Army had decided that, as we would be firing live ammunition, we should have some experience and show some ability in firing platoon weapons; the Lee Enfield Mark 4 .303 inch calibre rifle; the Bren .303 inch LMG; the Sterling 9mm calibre sub-machine gun and the .38 inch calibre service revolver.

We were transported out to the Ash ranges and deposited, after a very bumpy truck ride across the rough tracks of the ranges, which did not do much for our high cholesterol bacon and egg breakfasts, to the 600 yard firing point on Ash Range No 1, where the platoon was divided up into two squads. I was in the squad detailed to act as the butt party, whilst the other squad shot their rifle classification test first. Before the 'shoot' could start we had to be transported to the butts. We looked round for the Bedford 3-Tonner to take us to the other end of the range, but the RASC driver obviously concerned about the state of the back of his truck after the bashing our stomachs had already suffered, had decided a further hair-raising drive across the rough ground to the butts was tempting fate and had made a tactical withdrawal.

This left us with no alternative but to plod manfully the 600 yards, vocally encouraged by the Sergeant i/c Butts to move 'your butts, Sirs', who was obviously pissed off as well at also having to 'do' the distance on his two feet.

We had been incredibly lucky with the weather during our Course and the two days we were to spend on the ranges, were no exception, and bar for a few light showers on the first day, our classification shoots were carried out in dry weather. There was nothing more depressing than lying on a firing point trying, through driving rain, to make out the target at 600 yards with water running off ones helmet into eyes, cheeks, neck and down the inside of ones BD blouse. Even the Army poncho, which was once described as a tent with a helmet stuck through the top, was not a great deal of use to ward off the rain in such situations; although it was long enough to cover ones backside, the lower regions were left exposed to the elements, and cold, soggy BD trousers and waterlogged boots did not lend themselves to accurate shooting.

We eventually filed down into the butts, to be confronted by a row of steel frames, targets, paper, pointer, flag, brushes and pots 'universal'.

'Okay', began the Butts Sergeant, 'Listen in and I'll explain the butts procedure. You, Sir,' and he pointed at Bob, ' will be the telephone orderly. Your position is by the field telephone there. The other end is connected to the Range Officer at the firing point. You will answer the phone when it rings and pass on all instructions. Clear?'

'Yes, Sergeant.'

'Right, now the rest of you. You will each man one of the target frames from No 1 to No 15. You will see that there is a front and back target frame; this allows for one target to be 'up', whilst the other one is 'down' and being 'pasted up'. Now the Army in its wisdom, and being cost conscious does not throw the targets away after each shoot; the holes get patched over, and you will see by each target a paste-pot and brush. After each shoot, you lower the frame and with either the sand coloured or black paper, you paste over the bullet hole, only using enough paper to cover over the hole. But, before you do so, you have to mark each shot, and signal this using the pointer.' The sergeant picked up a pointer with its diamond shaped head and proceeded to wave it up and down, from side to side and twisted it round to demonstrate whether the shot was a 'bull', an 'inner', a 'magpie', an 'outer'. For a 'miss' a flag was waved vigorously from side to side.

'As the first detail will be firing at six hundred yards we will be using the six-foot targets, which are those over there. Take two and fix them to the frames, one at front and one to the back. Now, I give the orders, so listen to me at all times. The cadet here will answer the phone and pass on to me the instructions from the firing point officer. Each detail will fire five rounds of single aimed shots, and then five rounds of rapid fire. The detail will then double down to five hundred yards, repeat the same firing procedure, and so on down to two hundred yards. But, after the five hundred yards shoot, we will change to the four-foot targets.

'However, the first shoot will be a five round sight zeroing one. Now, before we start, we will practice raising and lowering the targets. You, Sir; ring the firing point and tell the officer we are doing a practice.' Bob picked up the handset and cranked the handle of the field telephone. Squawking noises emitted from the handset, and Bob told the Sergeant it was okay to proceed.

'Right, on the words: 'Front targets…up', you pull as hard as you can on the chain on the right of the target frame, and get the target up as fast as you can. On the order: 'Targets…down', you again pull on the chain. Now I know these frames look old and somewhat battered and rusty. They are 1914/18 vintage, but they are properly maintained and work well, but you do need to put some effort to move the frames. Right, lets try it. Front targets…up.'

The butts shook as fifteen frames clanked, creaked and groaned as we hauled on the chains as hard as we could, and they moved skywards at various speeds of their own determination. The Sergeant had said the target frames were well maintained, but I felt that was a rather dubious claim. REME would have done a better job.

'Front targets…down'. I was surprised that it took as much effort to get them down as they did to get up, until I remembered that as we hauled the front targets down, the back ones rose. After a couple more practices of front and back targets 'up and down', the Sergeant professed himself satisfied that we were not going to get any better, and that too many 'ups and downs' could be counter productive.

The Sergeant himself spoke to the Firing Point Officer over the field 'phone and declared that we were ready. To save time, a signal system was cunningly devised; one ring for 'targets…up'; two rings for 'targets…down' and three rings for 'We need to talk.'

'Right, this is the zeroing practice. Watch for every shot and mark it correctly.'

We waited until the phone rang once.

'Front targets…up!'

We hauled on the chains as hard as we could. Then there was the sound of an almost instantaneous 'crack-whistle-thud' as the first bullet at supersonic speed tore through a target and buried itself in the sand trap at the back of the butts. This was followed a few moments later by the distant sound of the rifle being fired. Within a few seconds there was a barrage of 'whistle-crack-thuds' as all the rifles on the firing point opened up, to be followed by silence, as we feverish looked for the bullet hole in our targets and waved our pointers up and down and pointed out where each bullet had passed through. The zeroing practice shoot continued with the bullet holes gradually getting closer to the 'bull'.

The 'phone rang twice. 'Targets…down!' shouted the Sergeant, and once again we hauled on our chains. We then got onto the specialist business of pasting over the bullet holes. Most of the targets were sandy coloured, except for the bull which was divided horizontally into two segments, with one half being black; but we did not have to worry too much about these as only a very few bullet holes appeared in that half of the bull. We would assess the size of the bullet hole, tear a piece of paper to cover this, brush some of the Army's best cow gum paste on to the target and slap the piece of paper over the hole. The skill came in applying just the right quantity of cow gum. Too little and the piece of paper would not stick but, if it was windy it would take off into orbit; too much, and due to the inferior sticking quality of the Army's expensive adhesive, the piece of paper would slide gracefully down the length of the target. When it was pouring with rain with a force nine gale blowing, one needed a distinction grade in 'O' Level 'Target Patching' to get the patches to stick properly. Fortunately, the day we were in the butts a 'Pass' grade was sufficient to satisfactorily paste over the holes. There was nothing more infuriating, if one was on the firing point than to have the patches covering ones previous holes falling off, which for classification purposes caused confusion.

The next practice was the single aimed shot, with the object of getting the tightest possible group of five shots, ideally going through one hole. Once again we had to mark each bullet hole, but it was on this shoot, whether it was because I was too slow in marking, or whether the cadet on the firing point had seen too many Western films; but as I was moving my pointer up and down to signify a hit, there was a loud crack and the pointer was almost forcibly knocked out of my hands, as the cadet on the firing point had proceeded to put a bullet neatly through the centre of my diamond shaped pointer. I must give the Sergeant his due, he cranked the 'phone handle three times, and irrespective of the rank of the Officer at the other end of the line, gave him a piece of his mind and suggested that the cadet on firing point 'Twelve' should get himself up to the butts 'pronto', and stand in front of the target, holding up his pointer, and let the rest of the platoon blast this (the pointer, not the cadet) into extinction.

The last practice was the timed rapid fire. Those on the firing points had one minute, to fire five rounds as accurately and as rapidly as possible. This was before the introduction into general Army use of the FN Self Loading Rifle (SLR) with its single shot or automatic fire options. So, as we were still using my favourite, the bolt action .303 Lee Enfield rifle, it meant that after each shot, the bolt had to be worked to open the chamber, eject the spent cartridge and insert the next round 'up the spout' and close the bolt. It was quite a demanding task to get five aimed shots off in the one minute as due to lack of experience, coupled with the fear of running out of time, the tendency was to let rip with five badly aimed shots in well under the one minute. Then the detail had to lie there on the firing point feeling rather stupid, for what seemed an eternity before the targets disappeared from view.

In this practice we, in the butts, controlled the raising and lowering of the targets. When all was ready, the phone would give its one ring, the Sergeant would bellow, 'Front targets…up!' We would haul the bloody targets up once again as fast as we could, as the Sergeant started his stopwatch. Fusillades of .303 bullets would be tearing through our targets and burying themselves in the sand. Then, there would be silence; the Sergeant would have a great big grin on his face, as he watched the second hand on his stop watch fully complete 360°, before he ordered: 'Front targets…down!'

Once, the practice was finished, and with the targets raised, we pointed out the bullet holes on our targets. This was sometimes quite a complicated procedure, for there were instances when a cadet would have a pristine target with no bullet holes to spoil its well patched face, and it was either a question of the cadet had missed with all five shots, or that he had peppered the targets of his neighbours to the right and left of his firing point. The rule, in that instance was to deduct the lowest scoring bullet holes over five from the neighbouring targets.

We had soon got the hang of operating the target frames, even though our arms were stiff and hands sore. The firing practices down to two hundred yards went fairly quickly and relatively smoothly, and I even managed to finish with a bullet free spare pointer. I enjoyed my first time in the butts, even though there were periods of inactivity as the firing detail doubled from one distance to another, with periods of frantic actively as we raised, lowered and pasted-up the targets. Initially, I had also found the sound of .303 bullets 'cracking' over our heads and thudding into the sand rather disconcerting, and hoped that as the rounds were passing not too far over our heads, there were no ricochets. One got used to the sound quickly enough.

Once the two hundred yard shoot was over, it was time for us to leave the butts and move back to the six hundred yard firing point to start our classification shoot.

Although the .303 Lee Enfield rifle had quite a kick, it was my preferred weapon, and I found that on single aimed shots, I was able to achieve good results from six hundred yards on a six-foot target. I felt comfortable lying on the firing point, and being right handed, having my legs splayed out to the left with heels flat against the ground; with the loosened rifle sling wrapped round my left arm to give extra stability and with the rifle butt firmly pressed into my right shoulder to help minimise the kick back and prevent dislocation of the shoulder. I pressed my right cheek hard against the rifle butt so that with my left eye shut, I could with my right eye, accurately line up both the rear and fore sights with the centre of the bull of the target. With my right elbow firmly planted on the ground, this gave, in the words of a weapons training sergeant, 'a firmly based triangle, from your left arm across the shoulders and to the right arm.'

His other advice was, 'when you are comfortable in the prone position, and remember you cannot shoot straight if you are not comfortable; you take up the first pressure on the trigger, as the .303 rifles do not have 'hair' triggers, and slow down your breathing, breathe in, hold it, mentally count to 'three' and then gently squeeze the trigger. Do not snatch it. If you follow the right procedures, and so long as your rifle has been properly zeroed you will always shoot with accuracy.'

With the five aimed shots to zero the rifle, and the ten rounds we fired from each firing point from six hundred yards down to two hundred yards, by the time we had finished each of us had fired fifty-five rounds. Those of us who had stuffed a handkerchief or duster inside the right shoulder of our BD blouse to absorb the 'kick', suffered no more than a sore right shoulder, but those who hadn't taken that precaution ended up with badly bruised, black and blue shoulders. The worst effect was on our eardrums, which at the end of the classification shoot were ringing from the noise of hundreds of rounds being fired off.

Before we left Ash Range 1, we were introduced to the pleasure of firing the standard Webley .38 calibre Mark IV Service Revolver. This was a heavy beast, and even though it was meant to have a lightened trigger action, it still required quite an effort to pull the trigger whilst holding the barrel steady. At least the .38 model was apparently not as difficult to fire as the Great War .455 Webley, which was 11.25 inches long and weighed in at 2.4lbs, whereas the .38 model was 10.25 inches long and weighed 1.68lbs. Apparently the .455 revolver with its very stiff trigger action was very difficult to fire accurately, except at very close quarters, although the bullet was a proven and very effective 'man-stopper'.

We approached to within thirty yards of the butts, and the four-foot targets were raised. Before we did our 'Wild West' imitation, a Sergeant fully briefed us on the correct procedures to follow for firing the revolver.

'Now, you never try to fire the revolver like a western gunfighter.' (Bang, goes that idea) 'If you bring the revolver down from your shoulder to fire, the sudden reversal in the downward movement of the wrist due to the gun's recoil will probably break your wrist. You stand sideways on to the target, with the revolver pointing to the ground. Slowly and smoothly you raise your outstretched arm until it is shoulder high, then taking up the first pressure on the trigger, you hold your breath before squeezing the trigger to fire off a round. Remember to pull the trigger, once only. I don't want to see you lot emptying your revolvers in all directions. Clear?'

'Yes, Sergeant.'

Under strict supervision the detail, myself included, broke open our revolvers and loaded six rounds into the cylinders, before snapping them back into place. The Sergeant, from behind us, asked if we were ready. We said we were.

'Right, in your own time, one round only, carry on.'

I raised my outstretched right arm to shoulder height, and the weight of the revolver was such, that the barrel described several elliptical circles as I took aim on what appeared to be the very large target to my front, took up the first pressure on the trigger and holding my breath, fired. There was a loud bang, and my wrist jerked back. I waited for the others to fire off their one round, and then we waited expectantly for our shots to be marked. Except for one or two 'outers', most of the detail, myself included, was disappointed to have missed as red flags were waved at us. With the targets so close, I couldn't understand how, from thirty yards I could totally miss a four-foot target. Still, each of us had five more rounds to discharge.

By the end of the practice we had only marginally improved, and I felt pleased that I had hit the target three times, although all in the 'outer' ring – at three, seven and eleven o'clock. It was rather unnerving though being in the butts when live revolver firing was taking place. Bullets would 'zing' in from various directions with quite a few hitting the steel target frames and ricocheting off at all angles.

The Webley .38 revolver must have been my least favourite platoon weapons, and I certainly would not have liked to have 'gone over the top' in the First World War only armed with the heavy Webley .455 service revolver, knowing that the Germans would most likely take me out first. I would have preferred to have been armed with the Lee Enfield .303 rifle.

It had been a long day, and except for the life saving NAAFI van at lunchtime bringing us 'wads and char', we would probably have succumbed to malnutrition long before the day was over, and it was a relief to find there was transport waiting to take us back to camp.

The following morning, when once again, after a traditional breakfast, the 'Sugar and Treacle' driver did his bit to upset our natural digestive processes by careering across the Ash Ranges to No 6 range at breakneck speed. Fortunately we all managed to keep our breakfasts in their designated places.

The second day was to be live firing of the Bren LMG and the Sterling SMG. The former I had got to know well at Honiton and I was pleased to see that the base of our firing point was not concrete, so I stood a fair chance that I wouldn't end up this time with a red-hot cartridge lodged under my chin strap.

The range for this practice was one of the shorter ones, only about two hundred yards in length with no butts and no static targets. In their place were 'pop-up' figures operated by wire from a control hut, similar in principle to a railway signal box, where the signalman would pull and release levers to raise and lower the cable operated signals.

We all took turns to be No1 and No 2 on the Bren, and even with the 'pop-up' targets and the gun set to 'single', we all achieved a high proportion of hits, proving the accuracy of the Bren; which remained in service with the Army from 1937 right through to the Falklands Campaign in 1982. Our final practice with the gun set to 'auto' was to fire short bursts of, from two to three rounds, at the two hundred yard targets. We had been told that it was bad practice and frowned upon to empty the 29-round magazine in one burst, as the Bren had a tendency on automatic to run away from the firer.

I had not had a chance of firing the Sterling Sub-Machine gun, which we had been told, was the post-World War Two version of the Sten SMG, of which over four million in various guises had been produced. Apparently the Sten had two weaknesses, the feed lips of the magazine were easily distorted (the Sterling had the same weakness); although the magazine held thirty-two rounds, we were told to only load thirty 9mm rounds. The other weakness of the original Sten was that it did not have a safety catch, and if dropped it was liable to go off. However, the Sterlings did have safety catches, but it was still not advisable to drop them with a loaded magazine.

We fired from a hundred yards, as the gun was only accurate up to that distance, although that was debatable. We were told to fire only in short bursts of three to four rounds, otherwise with such a short barrel, firing off a whole magazine would 'hose' the area to the front with little or no accuracy. Although we were told to fire the gun from the shoulder, most of us managed to get a few rounds off from the hip, as the 'pop-up' targets would suddenly appear to our front, and equally suddenly disappear. I could understand, although a rather inaccurate weapon, the Sten SMG was nevertheless a very popular gun, which the Germans had attempted to copy towards the end of the Second World War.

~

So, after two enjoyable days, it was back to Camp; to clean and prepare our kit for our final Adjutant's Parade, which I 'sailed through' without having the RSM 'naming' me, and having to appear before the Adjutant a third time. We had to prepare and revise for our Military Knowledge Two exam, which was looming on the very near horizon. Although there were six weeks between the two examinations, we still had to assimilate a great deal of both theoretical and practical military knowledge, whilst at the same time not forgetting all the earlier stuff which had been pumped into us before MK I. With all our other activities, including the twelve-mile route march - which was a 'killer', it was difficult to find time to 'swot' up on everything we had been taught over the previous twelve weeks. But once again, we were fortunate with the questions and the whole platoon passed the exam, but as previously, we were not given our marks.

One afternoon, shortly before we went off to Battle Camp, a whole host of military tailors and outfitters arrived, and we were all measured for the uniforms and hats we would require after we were commissioned. Fortunately, and this is no reflection on REME, but the requirements for the

Corps' National Service subalterns were not as financially onerous as were those of the oldest and most respected infantry and cavalry regiments in the Army. However, by being measured for our uniforms we really felt that we were on the verge of successfully completing the Course; although there was still hazards ahead, and it was still possible to 'blow it all'; either at Battle Camp, by endangering the lives of the Camp Commandant, the Company Commander, the Adjutant and the RSM, by mistaking them for the enemy, and being a little too over-enthusiastic in laying down live supporting fire; or by interpreting Capt Stevenson's remarks about cocktail parties too literally, with complaints being made to the Adjutant that some officer cadets had been rather too forward in their suggestions and their behaviour was really unbecoming for future officers.

We had taken part in 'C' and 'D' Companies' Commissioning Parades, but we realised that when 'A' Company marched off the Square at the end of their Passing-Out Parade, we were now the senior company. But, before our Commissioning Parade, we had the little matter of the two weeks of Battle Camp and, on our return to Mons to undergo the sixteen-mile route march, and then being subjected to intensive drill rehearsals for our Commissioning Parade.

Chapter Eight

Battle Camp. Sennybridge

It was mid-March 1959, when 'B' Company prepared for deployment to Sennybridge in the Brecon Beacons, Wales for the two weeks of Battle Camp. Most of the considerable amount of kit and equipment we were taking was going by road in the School's transport of Bedford 3 ton RL trucks. Although there was permanent staff based at Sennybridge Camp, 'B' Coy had to be basically self-sufficient. So, one whole afternoon was given over to loading up the trucks ready for the convoy to leave early the following morning. Fortunately, those of us who had cars were permitted to use their own transport, and we tried to take as many of our fellow cadets as we could. Those, who hadn't got their own transport and could not get a lift, had to face a very uncomfortable ten-to-twelve hours in the back of the Bedfords. My Morris Minor was not a spacious car, and with personal kit, I could only take one passenger, – Bob Turner.

The following morning, we helped load the last minute items onto the trucks, waved 'cheerio' to those travelling down in them, and leisurely prepared to make our own departure. Bob was going to act as navigator, and had spent quite a considerable time the previous evening working out, what we hoped was the best route.

'Okay, Anthony, we need to take the A331 to Farnborough and Frimley. Then the A321 to Crowthorne and Wokingham, and the A329 to Reading, where we pick up the A4 all the way down to Marlborough.' I was already lost, but Bob was determined to work through the route. 'Then we take the A346 and A419 to Cirencester and the A417 to Gloucester, where we join the A40, which will take us all the way to Sennybridge, via Monmouth, Abergavenny and Brecon.'

'That's fine, Bob. But how far is it, and how long will it take us?'

'Well, I reckon from here to Sennybridge is about two hundred miles, and we should be able, stopping only for pees, to cover thirty-five miles in the hour. So, that should give us a drive time of six hours.'

'Okay.' I thought about this. 'We need to add on another hour for emergencies, such as a puncture, or wet weather and we're going to have to stop for petrol, and if I do all the driving, then I'm going to need a break. So, let's play safe and allow eight hours in all. Now the CSM said we should arrive no later than 1900hrs, otherwise we will get no food. So, I think we should leave here no later than 1100hrs. Do you agree?'

Fortunately, Bob did, and so promptly on the hour we drove out of 'B' Company's Lines for the long journey down to Wales. I had to admit that both Bob's map reading and timings were pretty accurate, for some eight hours and one hundred and ninety five miles later, after a straightforward drive with no hold ups, and as dusk was falling, we drove into the village of Sennybridge, nestling in the River Usk valley and surrounded by the imposing and rather daunting peaks of the Brecon Beacons.

The camp was beyond and to the north of the village, and was overlooked by an exceedingly high hill – Yr Allt – which at 1,156 ft must actually have been a small mountain. We were told that the record time for climbing Yr Allt from the camp was thirty minutes. Four of us tried it one Sunday morning and it took us considerably longer. I think the 'joker' who told us that definitely had a warped sense of humour and we vowed, given the chance, to extract vengeance on him. Still, once at the top, the views in all directions were breathtaking and the climb was well worth the pumping heart, the rasping breath and the aching legs.

I stopped at the Guard Room to ask the way to 'B' Coy Lines, and following directions, found that we were stuck at the back of the camp, with that very large hill completely overshadowing our huts. I parked, and Bob and I staggered out of the car, stiff and saddle sore after such a long drive. We found, and walked into the Company's admin hut. The trucks had arrived some time earlier, and we were one of the last to check-in.

~

'And who have we got here?' A well-known voice rang out from behind us. Bob and I slowly turned round to come face to face with the familiar figure of the CSM.

'What kept you then? Got tired of peddling?' The CSM was grinning from ear to ear.

Both Bob and I blinked twice. Was the figure standing in front of us, looking positively human and dressed in well-worn BDs and beret, our dearly beloved and respected Company Sergeant-Major? Where were the immaculately pressed BDs, sash, peaked hat, pace stick and mirror finished boots? Actually, thinking about it, we had never seen him off-duty.

'What are you two gawping at? Haven't you seen a real soldier before?

Now, go and get your kit out of the car, find yourselves a couple of beds. The evening meal will be in half an hour. After that, except for cleaning your kit,' so we hadn't escaped that chore then, 'your time is your own.'

Bob and I collected our gear and took ourselves over to the platoon's accommodation huts the CSM had pointed to, and found a couple of empty beds in one of the huts. The hut was old with a corrugated iron roof and held about ten beds. Through the door at the far end was a small clubroom, where we could relax, down a beer, play darts, chat and read. Some evenings we were so tired after a day chasing, or being chased up and down every mountain and hill within a ten mile radius of Sennybridge, that we could do no more than just collapse in the clubroom chairs.

So, after unpacking and quickly downing the evening meal, we explored the camp, which didn't take long and as the CSM had asked us so nicely, we thought we should clean our kit; for all we knew there might be a muster inspection parade in the morning where the CSM might well dish out some fiendish punishment for those with dirty kit.

By unspoken and universal agreement, we all turned in for an early night, as we felt that physically, we were going to be well and truly stretched for the two weeks.

~

The following morning, the Company assembled in the camp's lecture room, waiting to be briefed by Major Langley. After a few minutes, the SUO, who was standing by the door, shouted out:

'Attention.' We stood, fortunately without a repeat of the 'WASBEE' chairs episode, as the Company Commander walked in, followed by the platoon officers and the CSM.

'Please be seated.'

Again, another manoeuvre carried out without incident.

'Good morning, Gentlemen. I shall give you a brief outline of the programme for the next fortnight, but your platoon officers will brief you fully each morning.

' Now, over the last three months you have been instructed in the theory of infantry tactics and have had a limited opportunity to practice those tactics in Long Valley. Battle Camp is all about honing those skills, in a more realistic environment using live ammunition. I realise that many of you here are being commissioned into the Supporting Arms, but you never know if the skills you have been taught at Mons, may not be tested for real. For those of you who are being commissioned into infantry regiments, then you could well be applying these infantry tactical skills within weeks, especially if your regiment is deployed in Cyprus, Aden or Malaya.

'I believe that we are moving into an era where there will be more fairly localised armed conflicts anywhere in the world. Korea, although a very nasty war, was fortunately confined to the Korean Peninsula, and was triggered by the Communists in the north trying to seize, by force the democratic south. This could have escalated into a major conflict, if Russia had actively backed the North Koreans. It took a major effort by the United Nations to prevent that conflict escalating. Chinese communists have been trying for the last eleven years to take over Malaya. We have seen East Germany, Poland, Hungary, Rumania, and Czechoslovakia fall into the communism camp and become part of the Soviet Bloc. Yugoslavia under Tito is also a communist State, and towards the end of the Second World War the communists tried to take over Greece. I do not mean to scare you, but I believe that you should be aware that the world is still a dangerous place, and armed conflict, hopefully never again on a global scale could break out anywhere at anytime.

'Therefore, the two weeks of Battle Camp will be your last opportunity to practice infantry skills and to learn and correct any mistakes that you will undoubtedly make. The next time may be for real.

'You will be practicing section and platoon attack and defence tactics, culminating in a full strength company exercise, run by the Senior and Junior Under Officers. During the fortnight, you will also be taught and practice ambush tactics and house-to-house fighting skills. You will also have the opportunity to fire some of the infantry support weapons, such as the 2-inch mortar and the 3.5-inch anti-tank rocket launcher. You will see a demonstration of the 3-inch mortar and the 120 mm 'Wombat' anti-tank gun.

'Now, as you are all well aware, you will be firing live ammunition. At previous Battle Camps, we have found that this seems to worry some cadets. I can assure you all, that there is nothing to be concerned about. So long as you follow the safety regulations and obey what your officers and the Directing Staff tell you, there will be no accidents. We haven't lost an officer cadet yet, and I have no intention for 'B' Company to be the first. But do pay attention at all times to what you are being told. Are there any questions?' There were none.

'Right. JUOs, would you form up your platoons outside, and get ready to embus to be driven to your various training areas.'

Peter Smith lined us up outside, but before we climbed aboard the transport, we had to load live .303 ball ammunition boxes onto the trucks, which took up so much space that, whether there was a risk or not, we used the ammo boxes as makeshift seats.

The trucks turned right out of the camp, and began the long slow climb up a very long and steep hill towards Trecastle. Rumour had it, that some months before, a tank transporter loaded with a Centurion tank, lost its brakes coming the other way down the hill and was unable to take the bend at the bottom with disastrous results.

Eventually, we turned right off the main road, and bumped along unmade-up tracks to our training area. Dotted around the area at regular intervals were, not only numerous flagpoles, with red warning flags fluttering in the breeze, but also 'Danger. Keep Out. Live Firing' warning signs.

~

The next few days passed in a blur. We seemed to be either climbing up or charging down the sides of steep hills and crossing the many small streams that ran through the valleys. We would regularly come under 'fire', and go to ground in hedgerows, or in one of the many small woods in the training area, whilst an appreciation would be made, a plan worked out and the attack put in. The support section was the most popular place to be in during these attacks. We could rest up, whilst the other two sections worked their way round to either the left or right flank to launch their attack; which due to the rough terrain, invariably resulted in having to cross a stream, then climb a steep hill before they were ready to cross the Start Line. The support section would then, using live ammunition open rapid rifle and Bren gun fire at the enemy position. Safety precautions were very stringent, and the support section would only be given a narrow arc of fire, and would be ordered to 'cease fire', and have their weapons checked to ensure that there were no live rounds left 'up the spout', long before the attack went in.

The novelty of firing live ammunition at anything but static four or six foot targets, took some time to wear off. On the exercises at Mons, there was a certain satisfaction at firing rifles with blank ammunition, but the same could not be said of waving a football rattle to simulate live firing of the Bren LMGs. I believe there was an attachment which could be fitted to the end of the barrel of the Bren, which enabled most of the cordite gas from the blank cartridge to be diverted back through the gas port, so that the piston could be driven back to load and fire the next round. But at Mons we did not have the luxury of such Brens, and had to put up with our Drill Purpose (DP) LMGs and rattles.

There was a definite degree of pleasure in live firing. Within the arc of fire given by the DS, you could chose the spot you wanted to fire at, and if the distance was not too great, you could see the earth being 'kicked up' under the impact of the bullets. However, after a while, this became boring, and we would look round for more interesting, but inanimate targets to shoot at. On one occasion, when I was No 1 on the Bren in the support section, I noticed below us, and some two hundred yards distant a small stream, which had become blocked with a build up of twigs and other pieces of wood. Luckily, this fell within the arc of fire we had been given, and so I suggested to the rest of the section, that the dam should be our aiming point. When the order 'Rapid Fire' was given, we let loose with great enthusiasm, and with such a weight of shot that the blockage was blasted into extinction in a very few seconds. Although we had fun, it was seeing the impact of the bullets striking the water, and both the rifle and the Bren had a muzzle velocity in excess of 2,000ft/sec, that I began to appreciate the full force of the stopping power of the .303 round.

It was only later that I realised the feeling of power that holding and firing a weapon gave one. This was a dangerous and frightening thought and although we had only been firing at sticks damming a stream for a bit of fun; nevertheless, with a rifle or a Bren gun in our hands, we had the power to choose how we were going to use the fire power of our weapons to enforce or destroy what we had decided on.

I wondered what our reaction would have been, if we had been faced at having to fire on a live enemy. RAF pilots have spoken and written of their experiences during the Battle of Britain, that as they were usually unable to see the faces of the enemy pilots, they just felt they were shooting at another machine, and did not consider the human factor. Although the experience at Battle Camp of firing live rounds in a more realistic situation than at static range targets was invaluable; individually we would no doubt have had to face and cross a psychological barrier the first time we had to shoot to kill.

~

If one was in a position to enjoy its beauty, the scenery of the Brecon Beacons was pretty spectacular, with rocky tors sweeping up from valleys and then descending down to the many streams that ran along the floors of the valley. Woods broke up the broad expanse of the Beacons, and it was easy to see why the area made such an ideal infantry training ground. We lost track of the number of times, in full battle order we hauled ourselves up hills. Our shoulders ached and were black and blue as the webbing cross straps which supported our small packs and ammunition pouches bit into our shoulders. Our legs ached as we plodded along narrow tracks, which ran down into valleys, and from where the tracks would invariably end in us having to climb yet another hill.

'Advance to contact. Contact. Take cover. Attack.' Again and again we practiced the same drill, until we could have planned and put in a platoon attack blindfolded. Although firing the Bren was satisfying, nobody ever volunteered to be No 1 on the LMG, for lugging it around from one hilltop to another was certainly not for the faint hearted.

We were thankful that our Battle Camp was being held in the early spring. Grass was beginning to grow and buds and greenery were starting to show on trees and hedges. More importantly for us, the sun had some strength, and its heat on our backs was most welcome after four months of winter. Struggling up and charging down mountains in the rain, in mud, in a force eight gale and even in deep snow would not have been fun.

~

Although we were pretty fit, after several days of platoon attacks we had reached the stage when we felt we hadn't got the physical strength to do another day. Fortunately the DS must have realised this, for as we returned to camp late one afternoon, we were told that the following day we would be firing the 3.5inch anti-tank rocket launcher. This was a modern version of the World War II American Army 'Bazooka'. Like the other platoon support weapons, the rocket launcher required two men to operate it. No 1 held the launcher across his right shoulder, lining up the target through the sight, with right fore-finger curled round the trigger, whilst No 2 loaded the drum-finned and shaped charge projectile into the back of the rocket launcher, connected up the wires; made certain he wasn't directly behind the weapon, and tapped No 1 on the shoulder to indicate that the launcher was ready to be fired. Once he had lined up the enemy tank, No 1 depressed the trigger, which completed the electric circuit, and the rocket with flame spurting out of the back of the launcher, was on its way to the target.

We took it in turns to be No 1 and No 2 on the rocket launcher. We had been warned that as the rocket was fired, the weight of the projectile was such that, as it travelled down the length of the launcher, there was a weight transference from back to front, and unless one compensated for this, one was liable to have the projectile burying itself into the ground just feet in front of one's position. It was therefore necessary to aim high to allow for this, although too high an elevation could result in the rocket failing to clear the launch tube and sliding gently backwards, and could end up on the ground at the feet of No 2, and as the projectile was primed, the end result could have been messy. So, when it was my turn to be No 1, I was determined to make allowance for the weight transference, and I aimed for the top of the turret of the target tank about a hundred yards away, expecting the projectile to hit the tank tracks. No 2 tapped me on the shoulder; I took a deep breath, lined up on the turret and pressed the trigger. There was a slight delay whilst the electrical connection was made, followed by a hiss and a roar as the rocket accelerated down the launch tube, and despite all my best efforts, the front of the launcher dipped further and further until the projectile shot out of the tube and buried itself into a mole hill some thirty yards in front of me, and which probably gave the resident mole a bad headache. Unfortunately, we were not given the opportunity for a second shot, which probably came as a great relief to the said mole.

~

Although at Honiton, we had been instructed in the use of firing a grenade from the end of a rifle, we had happily not had to actually fire such a grenade. But at Battle Camp, we were going to do so. The same warning to firmly place and hold the rifle butt against the right hip, otherwise at worst the recoil of the rifle could have resulted in a broken hip, or at best being knocked backwards onto the ground with a very badly bruised one. The target was the same beaten-up and wrecked tank we had tried to hit with the 3.5-inch rocket launcher; and to have a better chance of hitting the brute, we were moved to within fifty yards of the target. Although the Army had withdrawn the No 68 anti-tank grenade in 1942 as being ineffective against armour; our instructors had decided that firing the anti-personnel Mills hand grenade at a tank would be good practice, at least for our hips. I enjoyed firing all the platoon infantry weapons that I used during my National Service, with the exception of firing the rifle grenade. I really could not see any advantage in firing, what was an obsolete weapon, especially as the Army was already phasing in the Fabrique Nationale Self Loading Rifle (FN SLR).

So it was with a certain amount of trepidation that I inserted the ballistite cartridge into the rifle chamber, applied the safety catch, and very carefully, even though it was only a DP one, withdrew the safety pin from the grenade and placed it in the cup shaped holder attached to the end of the rifle. I assumed the correct kneeling position and jammed the rifle butt hard against my right hip, and pointed the rifle in the general direction of the tank; released the safety catch, closed my eyes, said a quick prayer and pulled the trigger. I felt as if a mule had kicked me in the groin, and that I was being projected backwards further than the grenade was being projected forwards. I dared to open my eyes, and watched in sheer amazement, as the grenade described a somewhat lazy and erratic partial orbit, and landed with a 'clang' on the tank's engine compartment. The DS looked at me with amazement and newfound respect. For one dreadful moment, I thought that I was going to be detailed as the platoons' one man RPG (Rifle Propelled Grenade) section. My fear fortunately was groundless, as I was only congratulated on being able to hit something. My hip was sore for several days, and I was still of the same opinion as I was at Honiton, that the rifle grenade was definitely a 'dodgy' weapon, and it would have been safer, if the grenade could have been fired from a horizontal position and from behind cover.

There were obviously more dangerous weapons, and I can recall Desmond Hill, who was my form master at St Edward's School, and who was also a captain in the Combined Cadet Force (CCF), telling the squad one Field Day, of an anti-tank weapon produced in 1940, which had a very sticky bulbous glass warhead. The idea was that the operator would either throw the weapon, or preferably walk up to the tank and place it, where it was hoped the adhesive would hold long enough for the explosive to detonate. But the operator only had five seconds after letting go of the pistol grip, which activated the detonator to clear the area before the anti-tank bomb detonated. Desmond told us he had heard, apparently a true story, of an officer who was demonstrating the bomb to a group of high-ranking officers, and was warning them to be very careful when throwing it, and not wave the bomb over one's head, as it could get stuck to one's hair, and if this was to happen, one must not release the pistol grip, which would trigger the detonator. The officer, according to Desmond Hill, demonstrated and proved the danger when the bomb got stuck in his hair. He panicked and let go of the pistol grip, and Desmond, with a deadpan expression, reckoned that bits of him were found in the next county!

Before we had finished with anti-tank weapons, we were shown the Battalion anti-tank (BAT) 'Wombat' 120mm recoilless gun. The 'Wombat', which stood for 'Weapon of Magnesium/Battalion Anti-Tank' fired squash-headed armour-defeating shells with metal cartridges. After firing some of the gas from the cartridge was directed back through the breechblock and exhausted to the rear of the gun, which helped negate the recoil. The BATs looked like 'big boys' versions of the 3.5- inch rocket launcher, with their own carriage, wheels, sights and aiming rifle. It was a shame that we did not see it fired, and from what we had been told, the back blast of gases was impressive and there was possibly as much danger from behind the weapon as there was in front.

~

Charging up and down the Brecon Beacons putting in platoon attacks one after the other and digging in after each one, was usually enough to make us completely 'knackered' by the end of the day. Fortunately, we were not expected to do more than clean our boots, and remove any mud from our webbing and battledresses, which was just as well, for if we had had to blanco and Brasso our webbing, and press our BDs every evening, it would have been one task too many.

On those infrequent days, when we had not been so stressed, we left the camp in the evenings to explore the local 'night spots', which did not take long. Sennybridge had absolutely nothing except the odd pub, whilst the town of Brecon did not have much more to offer, although there was a cinema, but which only had one screening a day, with the performance usually starting before we had finished the days training. On the few occasions we did drive to Brecon, we ended up in the local café, which closed as far as we were concerned, far too early at ten o'clock. I became friendly with one of the girls who worked in the café, but any chance of a relationship was doomed before it started. It was a shame we were only at Sennybridge for a fortnight, for any spare time Rhoda had was on weekdays when we were working, and when we were free, she was working. It was a great pity, for as well as being attractive, she had a great sense of humour and we got on well.

As we were only temporary denizens of the camp, we were not expected to carry out any guard duties, and as we were on a five and a half day 'working' week we finished at midday on Saturday. After that the time was ours until we paraded on the Monday morning. The first Saturday, four of us drove down through the Brecon National Park, through Merthyr Tydfil and Pontypridd to Cardiff, and although the scenery was magnificent driving through the National Park, after the green of the South Downs and the Weald of Sussex, I found it somewhat depressing as we neared Cardiff passing coal mines, slag heaps and the dull grey granite houses. As we were still suffering from too many days of platoon attacks, we did not feel like exploring the sights of the City, and bar from hearing, as we drove past, an enormous roar from Cardiff Arms Park, where Wales must have been playing an international match, we drove through the City and then made our way back to Sennybridge.

On the second weekend, we decided to visit Swansea, but were disappointed when we got to the City to discover that Wales was 'dry' on Sundays, and bar from taking a short walk along 'The Mumbles', we drove straight back to camp. It was a shame that we did not have the time, and possibly the inclination to explore and enjoy the attractions of Cardiff, Swansea and the surrounding countryside.

I felt that all we wanted was to get Battle Camp out of the way as quickly as possible. After nearly four months at Mons, plus the time spent on basic training, we were all impatient for our Passing-Out Parade, to be commissioned and to be posted back to our regiments or battalions and to start doing some meaningful duties. We found that time hung heavily on our hands for the two weekends, and it was almost a relief on the Monday mornings to get back to battle training.

~

It was during the second week, that Captain Jim took us out one afternoon into a forest to be instructed in and to practice jungle ambush tactics. 'Jungle' Jim had served in Malaya when 'The Emergency' had been at its height, and was experienced both in laying ambushes, springing them and also being on the receiving end of being ambushed.

Capt Jim briefed us before we drove off into the forest.

'Right, many of you are probably unaware that we have been fighting a war since 1948 in Malaya. Communist Terrorists (CTs) under Chin Peng have been trying to take over the country. However, if the British Government had declared it a war, the British owned Rubber Estates and Tin Mines would have had difficulty with insurance cover, if they had been attacked by the CTs, and the Government would have had to pay compensation.

Therefore, by declaring the war an 'Emergency', the Government avoided paying out any compensation.

'I won't go into the history of 'The Emergency' and all the details now, but suffice it to say, that we, and by we, I mean the Commonwealth forces that are fighting in Malaya have virtually defeated the CTs, but the Country is not completely clear of them, and their tactics now are to ambush the security forces. In many places the jungle comes right down to the main roads, and the CTs lay their ambushes to take advantage of the cover that the jungle gives them, and where they can easily, quickly and silently disappear back into the jungle. The winding route up to Fraser's Hill was, and still is a favourite road for ambushes, and in 1951 the CTs ambushed and killed Sir Henry Gurney, the British High Commissioner on his way up to the hill station. But probably the most dangerous stretch of road for ambushes is the twenty-eight miles of bends around Slim River, north of the capital Kuala Lumpur. The road winds between jungle covered high banks, and it is impossible to police the whole twenty-eight miles, just as it is almost equally impossible to spot an ambush. The first anyone knows is when the ambush is sprung, firing beaks out and casualties are taken. This afternoon, I shall instruct you how to respond to being ambushed, for some of you may end up in Malaya, and as subalterns it will be your job and responsibility to fight your way out of an ambush with minimum casualties.'

Listening to the briefing, I was pleased that I was not in the infantry, and decided that no way would I volunteer for service in Malaya.

'Now,' continued Capt Jim, 'you will be driven along forest tracks, as if you were in Malaya, and you would expect to be ambushed. Therefore, you will remove the canopies and supports from the trucks. As these proceed down the forest tracks, each of you will be facing out, scanning the trees for any sign of an ambush. You will be issued with blank ammunition, but for safety reasons, do not put a round 'up the spout', and make sure that the safety catch is 'on'. Those on the Brens, make sure you do not lose your rattles. If and when you come under fire, debus immediately, by whatever means on the opposite side from the ambush; don't bunch up, as you will make an easy target, but spread out into an extended line and get into a firing position, and immediately open aimed fire onto the enemy's position. If it's possible the Bren team should move to either one end of the section or platoon, or onto higher ground if there is any. The objective of this 'immediate action' procedure, is to direct the maximum amount of aimed fire into the enemy and to start to win the firefight. Whilst this is going on, the platoon commander, or section leader will decide what to do. Speed is of the essence, but the options are limited; they are either a left or right flank attack or, if that is not possible, a direct frontal assault. As a platoon, the basic infantry tactic of two sections forward, and one back still hold good. The section, which has come under direct attack, should be the fire support one, with the addition of the Bren teams from the other two sections to 'beef' up the firepower.

'If the attack is to be a flanking one, then it is important for the platoon commander to get this moving very quickly. It is also important to go some distance into the 'jungle' before you turn in for your attack. Too shallow an attack will result in the enemy withdrawing before you reach them, and there is also a danger that you will run into the fire from your support section. By going deep into the 'jungle', you stand a very good chance of cutting off the enemy as they withdraw. How deep you go in is a matter of how thick the 'jungle' is, and the time it will take to reach a point to put in an attack. You've got to use your judgement and commonsense. Now, you probably are going to ask: how will the support section know when to stop firing? Again it is a matter of judgement, but when the section leader hears the noise of the other two sections charging like elephants, and fire coming in from the flank, he will know that it is time to cease firing.

'Now, the most difficult decision that the platoon commander may have to make is whether to order a direct frontal attack straight into the enemy's fire. If this is the only option, the attack must go in straight away, before either the enemy can 'pick-off' the platoon one-by-one, or before the platoon has time to realise the possible hopelessness of the position and adopts a defeatist attitude. The attack must go in with verve whilst the adrenaline is still high. Casualties may be taken but they will be far less than lying in a monsoon ditch and being shot one at a time. The frontal attack, carried out speedily, with maximum firepower, will not only dislodge the enemy, but may have disrupted any plans he had to move his position to a better one to bring more effective fire onto the platoon. Are there any questions?' There were none.

'One last point. In Malaya, the CTs have a nasty habit of laying booby traps on the debussing side of the ambush position. You have been warned. Right, JUO, get everybody outside, issue ten rounds of blank ammunition per cadet, and let's get going.'

We were soon on our way, and for the umpteenth time the trucks ground their way up the hill, which we were beginning to despise, but at least on this occasion, without canopies we could enjoy the view; well, we would have done, if we could have seen through the low cloud and damp mist.

After some six miles, at a place called 'Halfway', which was probably so-called as it was halfway between Sennybridge and Llandovery, we turned right off the A40 into a forested area which rejoiced in the name of 'Mynydd Bwlch-y-Groes. The Welch language must be the only one in the world, which is trying to eliminate the use of vowels! The signpost at the turn-off indicated that we were heading for a place called 'Babel', which I thought was most appropriate, as the dictionary definition of the word is: 'A scene of noise and confusion,' and I suspected that when we were ambushed, 'noise and confusion' would reign. Sure enough, after some ten minutes into the forest, on a straight stretch of track with a bank on our right and a ditch to our left, we came under sustained rifle fire from the 'jungle' on the right.

'Debus,' shouted Peter Smith. We didn't need a second invitation. We were out of the truck, into the ditch and returning fire before 'Jungle' Jim could say, 'Jump, get down and open fire.' Once again I was No 2 on the Bren, which meant I got to carry the rattle. Bob, as No 1 and I tried to work our way to the right as per instructions, which was not easy, as there was very little cover and we had to crawl not only along the ditch, but also over the recumbent bodies of the rest of the section, which resulted in a plethora of blasphemy being directed at Bob, as he inadvertently managed to ram the barrel and foresight of the Bren up some unmentionable places. Eventually, we made it to the right hand end, and whilst Bob lined up the LMG, I swung the rattle with great vigour. I felt this was one instance when the theory was wrong. In a real ambush with very little cover, as Bob and I tried to move, the enemy would have taken us out very quickly. We would have done better to stay where we were, and although perhaps not in the optimum position, we could still have provided some effective support fire, without probably being killed. However, whilst this was going on, Peter Smith, as our JUO, was putting into effect a left flanking attack and as we heard this going in, we ceased firing and rattling, and waited for the other two sections to appear with some captured 'enemy'. They shortly did appear, but with no prisoners; for the enemy had simply 'melted' away as the attack went in.

We were 'ambushed' twice more that afternoon, and on the second occasion, Capt Jim had said he wanted us put in a frontal attack. So, having come under fire, we debussed in a flash, shook ourselves out into extended line and we charged with Nos 1 and 2 Sections 'up', leaving No 3 'back' as support, across the track with great élan, shouting and firing our rifles and shaking our Bren rattles for all we were worth. Babel certainly lived up to its name. This time, as we swept through the 'jungle', we managed to take prisoners and surprise, surprise the 'enemy' were our old friends from Long Valley – the Royal Inniskilling Fusiliers. 'Got you this time, you Picts,' we cheerfully greeted them as we swept through.

'Aye, but it took you three bloody goes to do it, you Sassenachs,' came the reply.

There was no doubt that the ambush drills Capt Jim had put us through, would stand us in very good stead if we were to be posted to Malaya, but as far as I was concerned, I had no intention of volunteering for a posting where there was any likelihood of being shot at; although I realised that I would probably have no choice, but end up where the Army or REME decided I would best be out of the way. So although the ambush training was important, I probably did not take it quite as seriously as I should have done, if I was in an infantry regiment. Still, as far as I was concerned the afternoon was a welcome relief from the endless 'bog' standard section and platoon attacks.

~

The fortnight, except for the weekends passed very quickly, but before we reached the climax of the Company attack, we were driven deep into the Brecon Beacons to watch a live firing demonstration of the 3-inch mortar, but with dummy bombs to be given by our old friends the Royal Inniskilling Fusiliers. I felt we were getting so close to that Regiment, who rejoiced in the nicknames of either 'The Skins' or 'The Lumps' (which we felt were appropriate), that an affiliation should have been formed between them and 'Bravo' Company, Mons Officer Cadet School, (possibly nicknamed 'The Thickies' by the other Companies!!).

The 3-inch mortar had been introduced during the Great War, and with several modifications was still in Army use in 1959. It fired a 10lb bomb to a range of 2,750yards, and its weight in action was 126lbs. This meant that it usually had to be transported into action by, for instance the Bren Gun Carrier, as the three main sub-assemblies and three–bomb ammunition packs could only be man-handled for short distances. Unlike the 2-inch mortar, which used the 'FITA' (Finger in the Air) method for ranging, the 3-inch was a precision instrument, with spirit level, a sight and horizontal and vertical vernier calibrated scales to give accurate range adjustments. 'The Skins', or were they 'The Lumps' were determined to show off their prowess with the weapon, by marking out a small taped square as a target, and having once ranged the mortar, proceeded to place bomb after bomb into the square. They then demonstrated the high rate of accurate sustained fire that could be maintained, with three or four bombs in the air at one time. It must have been terrifying to an enemy to be under such a bombardment from a whole section of 3-inch mortars, with up to twelve bombs in the air at the same time.

We had been taught that it was basic infantry doctrine for an attacking force to have a 3:1 superiority over a dug-in defence at the point of attack. This ratio however, could be varied depending upon the degree of support that was available to the attackers, with artillery, mortars, tanks and air power. To use a modern military phrase, these are known as 'force multipliers', and in theory the greater weight of support multipliers an attacking force has, then the manpower superiority of 3:1 could be varied downwards, depending however upon the training, morale and professionalism of the attackers. The demonstration of the 3-inch mortar certainly proved the effectiveness of 'force multipliers'.

~

The day before the final Company exercise, we were driven once again deep into the hills to a derelict village and where we were going to be given training in house clearance tactics.

A staff sergeant from the permanent staff at Sennybridge gave the briefing.

'Right, Gents, today I shall teach you some basic drills that must be followed, if you are involved in house clearing.

'Before you and your men go charging headlong into a house, there are two vital principles that you must carry in your heads and never forget, and excuse the pun – on pain of death. The first one is, even if the enemy has withdrawn, you must assume that a building is still occupied by the enemy and secondly, even if they have withdrawn, you must expect and be prepared to deal with any calling-cards he has left behind like booby traps. The only limit to laying such devices depends upon the imagination and ingenuity of the individual.

'In the Second World War, the Germans were particularly skilled in setting booby traps. Some of their favourites using detonators, anti-personnel mines and grenades, were the loose floorboard which set off a mine when stepped on; the lavatory seat which when lifted or lowered set off a booby trap, as did pulling a lavatory chain; the crooked picture could conceal a grenade; turning a door handle and opening a door could be fatal. I could go on for a long time, but I just wanted to warn you of the dangers of house clearance. In one respect it is safer to flush out an enemy if he is still in the building, as this will probably mean that there has been no time to set booby traps. But don't bank on it. No, the greatest danger from booby traps is when the enemy has withdrawn some time previously. Chucking a grenade into a room first could be a good move, as the explosion and the shrapnel from the grenade could set off any such devices.

'Now, today, you will be split up into sections, with each section taking one house, and the section should be divided into two-man teams. But for safety we shall only have one team operating at a time. The fire and movement principle still applies; one member of the team stands watch and covers the other member, who in battle would throw a grenade into a room, shielding himself by a wall and then charging into the room directly the grenade has gone off, before any enemy, who are still alive have a chance to re-group. Once the room is cleared, the second team member will take over the lead and so on through every room until the house has been cleared. The same principle applies on stairs, one member of the team provides fire support from the bottom, whilst the other one moves up the stairs to a landing, and then the one at the bottom 'leapfrogs' the one on the landing and so on. Two other dangers, when you are clearing a room, keep close to the walls; the enemy both from above and below could fire either up or down through floors, and if they did, they would be more likely to fire into the centre of a room rather than at the sides. That is a point you should all remember if you are doing the shooting. The other danger is never show yourself at a window. There could be a sniper in another building and he will pick you off before you have a chance to blink. So always cross under a window on your hands and knees.

'Now, one section will advance up the street, and when you come to the first house, the first team will enter the building, clear it and rejoin the section; at the next house the second team will carry out the house clearing operation and so on, until the whole section has had a go. Incidentally, you will be using thunder-flashes. But one word of warning. Some of the buildings are occupied by the 'enemy'. You will come under fire, but for obvious safety reasons, the 'enemy' will have withdrawn, before you put in your attack. Any questions?'

'No, Staff.'

'Right, let's get going. No 1 Section over here.'

Although a subject we needed to take seriously, we nevertheless enjoyed the exercise. One section stayed back to provide covering fire if needed, whilst the other two sections, one either side of the street, slowly advanced in single file hugging the walls of the houses, with each of us watching out for movement from any of the houses on the other side of the street. Suddenly, we came under fire from a house on our right, which we returned with interest. The leading team rushed up to the front door of the house, one of them forced open the door, threw in a thunder-flash, shielded himself against the wall, and charged in through the door once the thunder-flash had gone off, and followed by the second member of the team. They cleared the house, and the Staff Sergeant was right, the 'enemy' had long gone.

We were all given an opportunity to be a member of a house clearing team, but although we came under small-arm fire we never saw the 'enemy'. Of course the 'enemy' were our unofficial affiliated friends from the Royal Inniskilling Fusiliers. One hoped that their briefing had been the same as ours and they hadn't decided to, unofficially inflict another Bannockburn on 'B' Company.

The day was great fun, but very noisy. As this was long before the days of 'Health and Safety in the Workplace' and the wearing of ear defenders; I am sure our ear drums were subjected to quite a hammering from the number of thunder-flashes, some let off in confined spaces, that were used that day. It was rather a pity that we could not have used Sterling sub-machine guns with live ammunition in room clearing, but I suppose it would have been too risky, especially from the danger of ricochets. But it would certainly have provided added realism.

~

After two weeks of running up and down numerous hills, or even mountains in the Army's training area, we had arrived at the final hurdle, the day long 'B' Company Exercise. Although the Company's officers would be observers, the exercise was to be run by the Senior Under Officer, acting as the Company Commander, with the Junior Under Officers acting as Platoon Commanders.

It was the worst day of the whole Battle Camp. Field Marshall Montgomery was reputed to have been a very good communicator and before every battle, all the units and troops under his command would have precisely known the objective, how it was to be achieved and their part in the plan. I wished that our SUO and JUOs had followed the same principle. It was a day when communication was virtually non-existent.

We 'yomped' from one location to another, and then we would put in an attack against what appeared to be a phantom enemy. We would then sit on our backsides for what seemed an age, without having the foggiest idea of what was supposed to be happening. Whoever said that soldering was ninety percent boredom with ten percent frenetic action was certainly proved right. For that was how the day went; and when we were called upon to move, it was only to climb another 'bloody' mountain, cross a stream, put in an attack, dig in and then sit on our backsides once again; whilst we waited for the next order to move, climb yet another mountain, cross another stream and put in yet another attack. As I was carrying a Bren gun for the whole of the exercise, I had never felt so tired, and ached so much from every joint and bone in my body. All this might have been bearable if us poor 'foot sloggers' had been properly and constantly briefed, so that we could understand and relate to what was going on. But no! We were just told that there was enemy ahead in some trees or in a hedge, and that one platoon would be the support one, whilst the other two put in either a left or right flanking attack. I suppose the SUO and JUOs benefited from running the Company, but for the rest of us, it seemed like a case of the 'blind leading the blind'.

We were only too relieved to get back to camp, remove our battle order equipment; get something to eat, and then 'crash out'. The next day we were to return to Aldershot, and after that final day, I didn't believe anyone was too sorry to leave Sennybridge. Well, except for a few of us who had managed to make friends with some of the local girls. I was sorry to say goodbye to Rhoda. She was a very nice girl.

The next morning, Saturday, we were up early to pack up all the equipment, other gear and personal kit into the Company transport. Those who were travelling back to Aldershot on the trucks, boarded up and the convoy set off on its long and tiring journey.

'Okay Bob. Are we going back the same way as we came?'

'Yes, Anthony.'

'Hope you can read the map upside down. Let's mount up and get going.'

Chapter Nine

Commissioned

Battle Camp was the final hurdle to be crossed before our Commissioning Parade, and it would have been an act of gross stupidity or incompetence to be RTUd at this late stage. Battle Camp had been very hard work, and at the end of it I had never been fitter, and probably would never again be so in the future. Since the beginning of the previous August I, together with all the others, had been subjected to eight months of drill, inspections, blanco, Brasso and boot polish. It was such a relief to have had a fortnight 'off' from such chores.

However, we knew that the pressure would be on again after our return to Mons.

At Battle Camp we had been treated with more respect and more as equals by the officers and the WOs who, as they had done so during the whole of our Course, helped, cajoled, instructed and guided us in the right direction; so that after sixteen weeks, we would be prepared, as far as the Army could make us, to be effective and professional subalterns. As officers, if any of us fell short of the high standards that had been instilled in us at Mons, it would have been be due to a flaw in our character and temperament, and could have resulted, when in a position to lead and command, to mistakes, possibly disastrous being made with a loss of respect and understanding from the troops who would be serving under us. The Army certainly did their best to ensure that those who were selected as 'potential officer material', were in fact fit to become officers, and there were enough 'checks' in the training to weed out those who would not, one way or another be competent officers.

I have long admired the Army's selection and training methods, and have always believed that British Industry was, in the 1950s and 1960s a long way behind in attaching the same importance to training as the three Services did. I have also always believed it was due to these selection and training methods that National Service subalterns proved to be efficient and effective officers.

~

The major problem on our return from Sennybridge, was the limited time, virtually overnight, we had to get our kit back to parade ground standard. The blanco room was a hive of frenetic activity, as all our webbing was scrubbed clean of mud, general grime, and dried before re-applying blanco. Although we had cleaned our second best boots every evening, a substantial amount of spit and polish was necessary to bring them back to an acceptable standard. Battledresses were certainly showing the worse for wear, and as we did not have the luxury of sending them to the dry cleaners, a great deal of brushing and rubbing with well dampened cloths helped to remove the dirt and mud. Again irons were in high demand. All this work had to be done on the Sunday after our return, ready for the Monday muster parade, when, for our last fortnight at Mons OCS, life would return to normal with drill parades, inspections and the final sixteen-mile route march. In fact the last two weeks would probably turn out to be the most stressful and hectic of the whole Course, as we prepared for our Commissioning Parade. It was in everyone's interest that this was of the highest standard, which if not, would reflect badly on the company commander, the officers, the CSM and the drill sergeants. Therefore, they were going to ensure that the officer cadets of 'B' Company would not let them down, with anything less than perfect turn out and drill. They needn't have worried though, as we had pride in what we had achieved and we wanted to show our families and friends that although National Servicemen, we were as good as the Regulars. So, there was an added incentive to the big Sunday kit clean up.

'Right, Sirs. Wakey! Wakey! Let's be having you. You've had it easy the last two weeks, but now you're going to know what real work is. So out of your pits and get moving.'

The CSM's stentorian voice blasted through into our sub-conscious, as we struggled into some sort of wakefulness. The CSM had switched on the barrack room lights, which were far too bright and as I came to, I wondered what the hell was going on. Normally dawn was breaking when the platoon JUO woke us in the morning, but to have the CSM do it when it was still dark outside, was harping right back to basic training. I opened one eye to see the CSM and Sergeant Fawcett, both once again immaculately turned out with razor sharp BD creases, gleaming brasses, mirror finished boots, scarlet sashes and peaked hats as they preceded from bed to bed, wielding their pace sticks like rapiers as they prodded each of us into some form of activity. I couldn't believe it. Where had the Battle Camp friendly and human faces of both the CSM and Drill Sergeant gone? They had returned to their martinet roles, stern, humourless and expecting instant obedience and discipline. As senior company, within a few days of being commissioned, we had hoped that we would be treated with a little more tolerance and even respect. Yet here we were, being turfed out of our beds as if we were raw recruits. It was really very demoralising.

'Right. Get a move on. You're on drill parade in an hour.' As they left the room, the CSM turned, winked, and with a broad grin on his face, 'See you later, Gents.'

We had been had! They had roused us an hour early. We decided if we got the chance, we would somehow get our own back. But we would probably be wise to wait until after our Commissioning Parade.

~

We had been back in Camp for a couple of days, and the aches and pains of Battle Camp were just beginning to wear off, when Company Orders detailed that on the following day, we would undertake the final physical task of the sixteen-mile route march. The Army, with the exception of the Light Infantry, expected that troops should be able to march up to four miles in an hour with a five-minute halt every hour. So, all being well, if we set out at 1000hrs, we should be back around 1430hrs. We would be marching in battle order with small pack, but thankfully wearing berets and not steel helmets.

I had developed a technique on route marches, that if I could mentally focus on a specific subject, idea or thought and examine this in depth; the march seemed to pass more quickly and especially so for the last few miles, as I wasn't so aware of the sore and blistered feet and twinges of cramp in my legs.

At Loughborough College, I had once walked eighteen miles in a night. Peter Fontes, a fellow student and I had driven, one Sunday up to Matlock in Derbyshire to see a couple of nurses we had befriended at a College 'hop' the previous Saturday. Peter had a 1932 Jowett Javelin saloon car, with its horizontally opposed two-cylinder engine. We had spent a very pleasant day with the nurses and had them back to the nurses' home by 10pm. This was at the top of the hill above the town. Anyway, Peter's car would not start and after freewheeling down the hill, the car still failed to start. We parked it by the police station and told the duty sergeant what had happened, and that as we had to get back to Loughborough, we would have to leave the car where we had parked it. He told us not to worry, and if we were to walk down to the bottom of the hill, and turn left into Matlock Bath, we would find the constable on duty there, who would stop a lorry and ask the driver to give us a lift back to Loughborough. It was a mystery where the constable was. We never saw him. We suspected that he was having an after-hours drink in a pub somewhere. By now, it was gone eleven o'clock, so Peter and I decided that as we were on the A6 main road to Derby, a lorry, if not a car would be bound to stop and give us a lift. Some six hours later and on the approaches to Derby, a lorry did eventually stop and took us to the outskirts of Loughborough. I've always felt certain that had we been in uniform, we would have got a lift without any trouble.

Fortunately, once again the weather was kind to us for our final route march. We smartly set off down Queen's Parade, but once round the corner, we relaxed and marched 'at ease' with our rifles slung over our shoulders. We were following the route of previous marches heading towards Ash, Worplesdon, Brookwood, West End and back to Aldershot. The first few miles, passed easily, but the initial interest in scenery, shops, people and vehicles soon passed. Then it was question of trying to put out of ones mind the feeling of legs beginning to ache; of feet getting hot and sore; of the beret feeling tighter and tighter; shoulders and back starting to feel the weight and strain of the small pack, the ammunition pouches and the rifle, as like an automaton one put one boot down in front of the other. 'Left, right, left, right', it seemed that the march would never end. Capt Jim and the CSM exhorted and encouraged us; but what I found the most demoralising was on rounding a bend after a long straight, hoping that it was the last one; only to be confronted by another long straight with another bend in the distance, and having gone round that, there was yet another straight ahead.

I was desperately trying to focus my mind on something and for no particular reason, the picture of the CSM and Sergeant Fawcett turfing us unnecessarily out of our beds, came into my mind. We were determined to get our own back and as we marched, I focused on how we might achieve that. Then, right out of the blue, a thought struck me. At St Edward's School, towards the end of the Easter Term, all the prefects would put on a satirical show, called 'The Rag Revue', where masters and other staff would be mimicked, characterised and generally ridiculed. The shows were invariably hilarious, which the masters thoroughly enjoyed, so long as the satire was not too pointed. I wondered if we could do something similar at Mons. We must in 'B' Company, have enough talent and ideas, to be able to put on a good satirical show. That way we could get our own back on the CSM and Drill Sergeant in a harmless and amusing way. I was really getting myself so worked up with this idea that I was woken up from my reverie by the voice of the CSM.

'Right everybody. We're just coming into Queens Parade. Smarten up, and lets finish in style, and show those Paras with their funny coloured berets, that we come second to nobody. Straighten up, swing those arms and keep in step.'

I couldn't believe that I had been so engrossed with the thought of putting on a revue, that I had forgotten about my sore aching feet and legs; my shoulders hurting from the cross straps supporting my small pack and ammunition pouches; and a headache caused not only from the band of my beret being a bit tight, but also from the shock waves which were sent up to my brain as each boot pounded the tarmac. After some eight months in the Army we had sufficient pride and self-respect that, even after four hours and sixteen miles, we marched down Queen's Parade in step and with heads held high. Even so, I couldn't wait to get my boots and socks off and 'crash out' on my bed.

'Right, chaps. Foot inspection in fifteen minutes. Dismiss.'

We saluted Capt Jim, took a few paces, broke off and staggered drunkenly back to our hut. Equipment was discarded without ceremony. Then with great difficulty, bending over to undo boot laces and very gently pull off boots, with feet that had swollen over the sixteen miles. The 'ouches and aarghs' coming from various beds showed there were a number of blistered feet and heels. The agonising sounds became louder as holed and bloodied socks were removed with extreme care. The smell of hot and sweaty feet hung in the air, as one by one we gently made our way to the ablutions and soaked our feet in cold water.

'Ah! What bliss. I could stay here for ever.'

'Come on, you lazy bastard. Let someone else in.'

Feet and toes carefully dried, and then:

'Room. Attenshun!'

'All right. At ease. Now lie on your beds, with your feet hanging over the end so that I can inspect them.'

'That's a nasty blister on your heel. How did that happen?'

'My sock got a hole in it from the back of my boot rubbing against it, Sir'

'How did you get that blister? Your boots too tight?'

'No, Sir. My sock worked its way down and made a ridge there.'

'I don't like the look of that. Better get yourself off to the MRS straight away.'

'Yes, Sir.'

'That's disgusting. Don't you ever cut your toe nails?'

The cadet in question looked suitably embarrassed.

'Now, I don't like the look of that. Does it hurt? I think you've got foot rot. The foot certainly smells. Get it seen to immediately.'

'Yes, Sir.'

Capt Jim continued making a close and thorough inspection of every body's feet. He certainly did not shirk, what must have been one of the less enjoyable duties for an officer. The care that he took showed his commitment to those under his command. He must have been a very popular and well-respected Gurkha officer.

~

As we lay on our beds recovering from the route march, I mentioned to Bob Turner my idea of holding a 'B' Company satirical 'end of term' show lampooning our officers, warrant officers, NCOs and anybody else who had been involved in our Course. I told Bob about the St Edward's 'Rag Revue', and said I did not want the revue to be malicious, but that it should be light-hearted and hopefully funny. Bob thought it was a great idea, and when we mentioned it to the rest of our hut, they were also enthusiastic. Bob and I went round to the other platoon huts, where again we were met with the same enthusiasm. One cadet, and I didn't want to know how, said he could get his hands on some Alan Melville scripts. Another said he could get some material from the Cambridge University Footlights Revue. Before we knew it we had a show, and so as to get some order into it, Bob and I appointed ourselves as Director and Producer respectively.

I went to see Major Langley to explain what we wanted to do, and to ask his permission. He also thought it to be a great idea, and said we could use The Officers' Club. He also offered, within reason any help that we needed. Bob and I suddenly got cold feet. What had we started? The show was generating a momentum of its own, and unless we applied the brakes, it would all get out of hand. We had plenty of volunteers ready to perform, and plenty to work behind the scenes. But, what proved to be our greatest asset, was a cadet from another platoon, and I've often wished I had remembered his name, who turned out to have a natural talent for writing the most hilariously funny situation sketches. So, and he didn't need a second invitation, we set him the task of writing scripts 'taking-off' the RSM, CSM and the drill sergeants.

However, before we really got stuck into organising and rehearsing the show, we were sent off for ten days Easter leave, which worked to our advantage, for on our return to Mons, Bob and I were handed various scripts and other material suitable for our revue

It was fortunate that after sitting the MK II exam we had finished with lectures and other activities; so the two weeks after Battle Camp were only filled with drill, PT and rehearsals for our Commissioning Parade, and this gave Bob and I time to properly organise our show. The Officers' Club did not boast a stage, so a great deal of ingenuity and improvisation went into designing and building one, together with adequate lighting. Those cadets, who had volunteered for back-stage roles were absolutely brilliant. No official initiative test could have been more difficult. The support team 'scroungers', somehow by hook and by crook begged, borrowed and acquired whatever was needed. Credit also had to go to our officers, warrant officers and NCOs, who willingly lent spare uniforms, kit and other 'props'.

~

There was certainly a different atmosphere after we returned from Battle

Commissioned

Camp. We were the senior company, and looked upon with a certain amount of awe and respect by the other companies. The junior 'B' Company had arrived, and were no doubt busy pasting up Queen's Regulations, and having a days outing to HMS Victory. It was all rather similar to school, where a new boy would not dare to speak, let alone look at a senior boy, unless first spoken to by the latter.

Drill, which was always a major Course activity, became even more so, as we rehearsed our Commissioning Parade. The RSM would regularly put in an appearance, and from the steps leading down to the parade ground and with his eagle eye, would not hesitate in his broad Irish brogue to offer his 'advice', which only a fool would ignore. If we had learnt nothing else, and which especially applied to me, it was never to put a foot wrong on drill parades, incur 'Paddy' Lynch's displeasure and end up on Adjutant's orders. We continued to rehearse all the drill movements that had been 'drilled' into us over the previous four months, until we could have carried them out in our sleep. This time though, we had the added incentive that this was our Commissioning Parade, and we had been told that Major Langley had arranged for the Royal Marine Band (Portsmouth) to be on the Parade. We even practised, in the unlikely event of wet weather, the indoor Parade, but we had been told that there hadn't been one since RSM Brittain had been 'The Sergeant-Major'; who must have been the most renowned RSM in the Army, and after his retirement, successfully enjoyed a short show business career. He was followed by RSM J.C.Lord, who according to military legend was fond of introducing himself to a new intake of officer cadets as; 'I am Regimental Sergeant-Major J.C.Lord. The JC does not stand for Jesus Christ. He may be the Lord up there,' with an arm pointing skywards, 'But I am the lord down here. So don't forget that.

The military tailors put in a second appearance, but on this occasion, instead of taking measurements, they brought our uniforms, including the No 1 Blues and the formal mess kit. SD hats were tried on, and I was determined that mine needed styling, as it looked too much like a pork pie on my head. Sam Brown belts were also tried on and adjusted. Any doubts we harboured about successfully completing the Course were completely dispelled with the delivery of our officers' kit, and we proudly, but rather surreptitiously, looked at the single officers' pip on each shoulder of our uniforms.

~

A few days before the Parade, the platoon officers gave each member of his platoon their final interview and assessment. I wondered, when my turn came how Capt 'Jungle' Jim, was going to carry out a full Course review, as he had only been our platoon officer for half the Course. But, his predecessor had obviously left copious notes, as Jim reviewed my performance from week one. Although I had not been made a Junior Under Officer, a position I have always believed, was filled by either an infantry, cavalry or Royal Marines cadet and not by one from a supporting arm; I was nevertheless very pleased when Capt Jim told me that I had been assessed as being 'above average', which I found particularly gratifying as I was being commissioned into a support corps, when there were so many cadets from the 'teeth' arms. This certainly boosted my confidence and morale and helped me mentally, when I was told, some years later and totally erroneously, that my father had arranged for me to pass WOSB.

Just as the rehearsals for our Commissioning Parade gathered pace, so did those for our show. Bob and I had decided to call it, with great originality, 'The 'B' Company Rag Revue', and we had even managed to produce a programme and persuaded the Company Office to Roneo it. The amount of talent we found in the Company was quite amazing, and it became very difficult to turn someone down, but we tried our best to give all those who volunteered some involvement, however small. As our evenings were mainly 'free', at least after the necessary blancoing, Brassoing and boot polishing, we managed to fit in quite a few rehearsals. As director and producer, Bob and I had given ourselves one of the longer Alan Melville sketches to perform, and we needed every available moment to learn our lines and to rehearse.

The day of the performance arrived; the dress rehearsal had passed without too many cock-ups. The back stage people had done a splendid job. They had rigged up a curtain (manually operated) and even managed to provide spot and flood lights, although I felt that the lighting outside some of the Guard Rooms was not as effective as it should have been.

Invitations had been issued to all the 'B' Company officers, warrant officers and NCOs. We expected a hundred percent turnout, but we had underestimated the interest being shown in the sole performance of 'The 'B' Company Rag Revue', for as Bob and I peered through a gap in the curtains, we noticed the Adjutant and the RSM amongst others. Before the curtain went up there was even a rumour that the School Commandant was in the audience, but as we didn't know him and so couldn't recognise him, we were unable to confirm the rumour. We were certainly going to perform to a packed house. Bob and I were definitely suffering from butterflies, for if the evening did not go down well, we as the organisers would be in the firing line, and I was thinking that there was probably still time for our assessments to be downgraded. We wondered whether the RSM had a sense of humour, for as we were not expecting him in the audience, we were lampooning him, howbeit in a gentle and non-malicious way in some of the sketches and songs.

We need not have worried. The evening was a great success, with the exception that Bob and I forgot our lines in our sketch and had to ad-lib furiously, which the audience thought was hilarious, as they had realised what was happening. Those we 'took-off', such as the RSM, CSM and drill sergeants, seemed to enjoy our 'mickey taking', and in fact 'Paddy' Lynch laughed louder than anyone else. (Well, he would wouldn't he as the RSM!)

Afterwards the VIPs came up and congratulated us; said how much they had enjoyed the show, and as far as they knew, it had never been done before, and as the National Service Mons OCS Courses finished some months later; Bob and I probably had the distinction of being the only officer cadets ever to organise and put on a satirical end of Course 'Rag Revue'.

In spite of the challenges we had faced in putting on the show, Bob and I thoroughly enjoyed our one evening of theatrical production, even if we had forgotten our lines. Afterwards as we found it difficult to come down to earth, with adrenaline still at record levels; all of us involved in the show stayed behind in the Club, downed a few beers and released all our tensions, which had built up over the previous four months, singing with great enthusiasm but little harmony, all the rugby and other dubious songs we could remember. It was a memorable evening and a great way to end our Course, for in less than forty-eight hours we would have passed-out of Mons OCS, have become history and been entered in the National Service 'ledger' as just another statistic.

~

Our penultimate day was spent on the dress rehearsal for our Commissioning Parade. It was a lovely sunny day, which was just as well, for 'B' Coy and the other companies together with the band spent some three hours, marching in both quick and slow time, advancing and retiring, being inspected, and marching past the saluting stand in review order. The rehearsal was carried out under the watchful eye of the Adjutant, who was backed-up by the non-stop vocal output from the RSM, CSMs and drill sergeants, constantly exhorting, criticising and 'taking the names' of cadets from other companies, who were found to have been 'idle or extremely idle' on parade. Eventually, the Adjutant, possibly either through boredom or the sun had 'reached the yardarm', professed himself satisfied with the standard of the drill, and we rehearsed the final drill movement of the Company leaving the Parade Ground, by marching up the steps behind the Adjutant on his horse, and figuratively speaking 'into the sunset'. On the actual parade, marching up the steps was a very symbolic act, for at that moment, we ceased being officer cadets and became subalterns.

The British Army has always been second to none in ceremonial, and even though the Mons Commissioning Parade could in no way be compared with the splendour and ceremony of Trooping the Colour or Beating Retreat on Horse Guards Parade, our Parade was very personal to those of us who were being commissioned. We knew that on the Day, we would feel a considerable sense of pride and achievement as the Company with 'eyes right' marched past the Inspecting Officer, the School Commandant and other VIPs on the saluting base, as families and other guests rose to their feet as a mark of respect as we paraded past.

Although a tremendous amount of work, effort and 'aggro' been put into preparing for the Parade, we knew it was going to be well worth it; not only from the relief that we had successfully completed the Course, but after some nine months in the Army we had finally received the Queen's Commission.

After the rehearsal, the rest of the day was spent in preparing our personal kit and packing; for after the parade we would be leaving Mons for the last time. Best BDs were pressed with the creases razor sharp and in the right places; boots were highly 'bulled' with mirror finish toecaps; belts, gaiters and rifle slings were immaculately white blancoed, and brasses and bayonets were polished until they gleamed. After some nine months in the Army, we found it difficult to realise that we were probably cleaning our kit for the last time, and in the future we would probably be privileged to share the services of a batman. As we sat on our beds cleaning and polishing, we reminisced about the Course; the good and bad days; the pressure; the 'bull'; the drill; the parades; the exercises; the exams, and Battle Camp. We had bonded as a platoon and I was going to particularly miss the camaraderie of our hut.

We had been very fortunate that it had not been a bad winter, and except for a few days, we had had very few spells of cold, wet and windy weather. Otherwise our Course would have been a lot harder and considerably more unpleasant than it actually was. As it had been such a fine day for the Commissioning Parade dress rehearsal, we were looking forward to another fine day for the actual Parade and to march off the Parade Ground with style.

But our luck had finally run out. The day of our Commissioning Parade dawned very wet and windy, as a depression with its associated cold fronts passed over Aldershot. We could not believe it. One of the most important days of our lives was going to be spoilt by the vagaries of the British climate. The decision was made to cancel the ceremonial parade, but the Company would nevertheless parade and be inspected in one of the School's vehicle sheds. Neither the other companies, nor the band would be on parade. We were on our own.

We assembled outside the company lines, with ponchos draped over our BDs trying to keep our highly 'bulled' kit in good order, which was going to be very difficult, with rain running down our faces and necks; our carefully blancoed white rifle slings, belts and bayonet scabbards were getting wetter and wetter; and the muddy puddles were not doing much for our highly polished boots as we marched to the vehicle park. Once under cover, we did our best to clean ourselves up.

Even the CSM and drill sergeants were looking equally fed up. All the hard work they had put in to prepare us for our Commissioning Parade was to a large extent wasted. When we had made ourselves as smart as possible, we were ordered to 'Get on Parade', followed by 'Right Dress' and then 'Open Order, - March.' We were stood easy, whilst families and friends filed in from the rain and were shepherded into guest pens at either end of the vehicle shed. The SUO paraded in the front of the Company, with the JUOs in front of their platoons. The CSM and the drill sergeants took post at the back of the Company. The SUO took over the parade and called us to attention as the Inspecting Officer and his entourage of the School Commandant, Adjutant, RSM, Company Commander and the Platoon Officers appeared from around the corner. We sloped arms; we presented arms; we were inspected; we closed ranks; we sloped arms; we turned right; we quick marched; we executed a smart 'eyes right'; we left wheeled; we marched out into the rain; we were halted and dismissed. And that was it. We were commissioned. But thanks to the weather instead of the occasion being one of ceremony and celebration, it all ended with great disappointment as a very damp squib with no photographic record of the occasion.

Cadets met up with those families who had attended the parade. For the rest of us, we returned to our hut for the last time; went over to the QM stores and handed in our rifles, bayonets and other kit, changed into our 'civvies'; made our farewells; climbed into our cars, and in the rain we drove away from Mons OCS to our various Regiments and Units to start life as very junior subalterns.

All I was left with was Army Form B. 108J: '23578036 O/CDT (PTE) Caffyn. Discharged having been appointed to a commission. Queens Regulations, 1955 Para 503 (xvii). Effective date of Discharge 17 Apr 1959.' From that date I became 460546 2Lt Caffyn REME.

~

My next posting was to No 6 Vehicle Training Battalion at Bordon, Hampshire, a unit within the REME Training Centre, which in 1961, together with No 4 Armt Training Battalion was to become the School of Electrical and Mechanical Engineering (SEME). I had been given a weeks leave, which I spent at home, and for the first time since the previous August, there was time to relax, reflect on the previous nine months, and to speculate on how ideally I would like to spend the rest of my National Service, but which would probably bear no relation to how I would actually spend it.

Thinking back to the train journey down to Bournemouth and how 'anti' National Service I had been; how I was going to hate every minute of the two years, which seemed at the time that it was going to be an eternity; how I had thought of ways and means, without actually doing anything about it, of trying to fail my medical. Yet, to my surprise, some nine months later I was enjoying army life, even though I, with all the other National Servicemen who had been selected for officer training, had gone through a much longer and harder training regimen than those who had stayed in the ranks. I still believed in the reasons why I wanted to become an officer; but what I couldn't quite decide, even in the self-imposed bad times of being on adjutant's orders, or the tough times at Battle Camp, whether I had either been 'brain washed' into accepting military life, or I had actually found a lifestyle that I could identify with, enjoy and could possibly make a career out of. Even those dreadful first ten days at Blandford had become a distant memory. My only problem was that I was expected after National Service to join the family business, and my father would probably have gone ballistic if I didn't do so. Anyway, I needed more time to reach a decision; but even having survived the worst part of the two years National Service, I was starting to positively think about, if not becoming a Regular, at least going for a Short Service Commission, which would have meant a further three years in the Army.

I wondered whether ten years of boarding school life had inured me to the rigours of discipline; to having my life totally organised for nearly every minute of every school term; to being used to accepting orders without question, and being used to the lack of privacy which a boarding public school gave, and 'public' was the right word in this context, with thirty bed dormitories, communal bathrooms, and dayrooms. Only prefects had studies. My subconscious had probably been programmed to accept all these things; allied with one of the weaknesses of boarding school in the 1950s that one did not really have, outside academic studies, to think for oneself. Therefore, for all these reasons, army life was not too great a culture shock, and I was beginning to appreciate the comradeship, and the sense of belonging to a family which military life engendered.

The British, by and large have a respect for their armed forces, and I found this to be especially true in the late 1950s and early 1960s. When, on leave I would be asked what I was doing, and I replied that I was doing my National Service in the Army, a look of respect and interest would come into peoples' eyes. From personal experience, it was always easier to 'thumb a lift' if one was in uniform. Yes, there was definitely a cachet in being a member of Her Majesty's Armed Forces, which I appreciated, enjoyed and felt part of.

The standard of training, whether it was with 'D' Company at No 2 Trg

Bn REME or at Mons OCS, was very professional. I have more memories of the warrant officers and senior NCOs; from CSM Derek Colquhoun at Honiton to RSM 'Paddy' Lynch, the CSM and Drill Sergeant Fawcett at Mons OCS, than I do of the officers, with the exception of Captains 'Jungle' Jim and John Stevenson. The officers were always supportive and were constantly monitoring our progress. It was just that on a day-to-day basis, we had far more contact with the former, which was only right and proper, for it would have been wrong for officers to interfere with the skills of the senior NCOs, who were in a much better position to turn reluctant National Servicemen into effective and professional soldiers. I must admit that when I arrived at Mons OCS, and learnt that a major part of our training was to be given by Brigade of Guards warrant officers and drill sergeants, and which due to their reputation, made me feel definitely apprehensive. This fear was misplaced. Yes, they were strict but fair; and their standards and professionalism was of the highest order. They taught me unquestioning discipline and instant obedience. In conjunction with our officers, they taught me to accept and issue orders, and to use my initiative and to make decisions. But above all, it was the Brigade of Guards warrant officers and drill sergeants, and I must include CSM (subsequently Major) Derek Colquhoun REME, who instilled in me a set of personal standards and behaviour, which has lasted and stood me in good stead all my life. If I gained nothing else from my National Service, I shall always be grateful to all my instructors for giving me confidence, self-discipline and self-respect.

My leave passed all too quickly; but it did seem strange to change for the very first time into BDs sporting the single subaltern's pip on each shoulder epaulette, webbing belt, brown shoes, swagger stick and officers SD hat. On 24th April 1959 I said my farewells and embarked on the next stage of my National Service career as a REME subaltern.

Chapter Ten

Technical Training. SEME Bordon

It was a fine, sunny and warm day as I drove into Bordon, which lies halfway between Petersfield and Farnham on the A325, and appeared from the formation signs to be completely inhabited by REME units. I had no idea what to expect or where to go, but fortunately, the Camp was well sign posted, and I very soon saw one for 'The Officers' Mess. 6 Veh Trg Bn'. Very many years later, during the IRA troubles, I stopped off at Bordon to visit Col Jim Allen who had been my second boss at the REME LAD 13/18th Royal Hussars in Malaya. I was interested to see that all the direction and unit signs in the Camp had been removed, and Colonel Jim, who was the Deputy Commandant of SEME at the time, explained that due to mainland IRA terrorist attacks; the MoD had ordered that all direction and unit signs at army bases were to be removed.

After a left and right turn, the tree lined drive led to what, I was later to learn, was the standard 1930s style Officers' Mess, built when Hoare Belisha (of beacon fame) was the War Minister; but my first thought was that 'this will do very nicely, thank you.' Some years later it became the WOs and Sergeants Mess. I parked the car under an oak tree as far from the main entrance as I could, to avoid taking a senior officer's parking space. As I climbed out of the car, I self-consciously put on my hat, checked to see it was straight, and with my cane tucked under my right arm, with as much confidence and dignity as I could muster, strode towards the front door of the Mess. I didn't know what to expect. I removed my hat as I entered the entrance hall, and except for the echo of my footsteps on the highly polished floor, I was greeted by absolute silence. There wasn't a soul around. My first impression was of the smell of furniture polish, which was obviously used in liberal quantities, for although the smell was not unpleasant it was nevertheless somewhat overpowering. I looked round; to my right was the ante-room, spacious and elegant, with very comfortable leather chairs and newspapers and periodicals neatly arranged on various tables; whilst on my left was the dining room, with its long and highly polished table, with silverware displayed both on the dining table and sideboards. Cutlery with crisp white places mats were also laid out with military precision. It all looked impressive and very civilised, and I began to appreciate the benefits of being an officer. I was wondering what to do next, when from behind me a quiet voice spoke:

'Good morning, Sir. Just arrived?'

I jumped out of my skin. I hadn't heard any footsteps. I turned round to see a Mess Orderly.

'Yes,' I replied.

'I'll just fetch the Mess Sergeant, and he'll book you in and show you to your room, Sir.'

The sudden change from one day being an officer cadet, where one could even be ordered about by the most junior of lance-corporals, to the next day when they would have to salute you, call you 'Sir' and take orders from you, took quite a bit of getting used to. No doubt their feelings were somewhat different.

The white-coated Mess Sergeant appeared.

'Morning, Sir. Can I have your name please?'

'Second Lieutenant Caffyn, Sergeant.' That was a bloody silly thing to say. He could see I had one pip up. Just 'Caffyn' would have done.

'Right, Sir. I'm afraid that as we have a large number of living-in officers in the Mess, and as you will be only with us for a few weeks, you will be quartered in the Mess annex. If you would come this way, Sir.'

He turned and led me through a door at the back of the hall, along a short passage, and out of another door, where there was, and I couldn't believe it, a row of wooden huts. I had hoped I had seen the end of them at Mons.

The Sergeant went up to one hut, opened the door, entered and said: 'Here you are, Sir. This is your room. The bathroom is at the end of the passage. Lunch will be at 1230hrs, and dinner this evening will be at 1930hrs. If you have any further questions, don't hesitate to ask me, or one of the Mess Orderlies. Alright, Sir.'

'Yes thank you, Sergeant.'

I was disappointed not to have a room in the main Mess, but nevertheless the room had all the basics, and it was nice to have privacy after nine months. I unpacked and then prior to lunch, wandered into the ante-room to be greeted by shouts of welcome from Roger Macdonald-Smith, Peter Sykes, Colin Blaney and Pete Smith, who had also been in 'B' Company at Mons, howbeit in different platoons. We had all started at Blandford on the same day, before being posted to 'D' Coy at Honiton.

THE REME WAR OFFICE TEAM 1942

Photo: Collection of the author

1. Sitting: The DME, Maj Gen 'Bertie' Rowcroft with the DDMEs
Standing l to r: Brigadiers Caffyn, Storer, and Bloor,
responsible for the formation of REME October 1942

THE BEDBLOCK

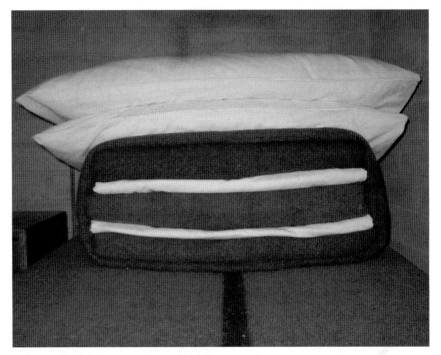

Photo: Lt F. Chitty. Sussex Army Cadet Force

2. The infamous bedblock

NO 1 TRG BN REME, BLANDFORD

Photo: REME Museum

3. Passing Out Parade. No 1 Trg Bn REME, Blandford

ANNUAL ADMIN INSPECTIONS

Photo: Lt Col (retd) R.P.Rust. Late REME & RAEME

4. Final 'D' Company Inspection, before closure of No 2 Trg Bn REME,
Honiton by Maj-Gen L.N.Tyler DEME. 17th February 1959

Photo: REME Museum

5. Annual Admin Inspection. No 6 (Veh) Trg Bn REME

NO 6 VEH TRG BN REME

Photo: the author

6. Recovery Training

Photo: the author

7. Austin K9 Recovery Vehicle

Photo: REME Museum

8. World War II gun testing equipment

Photo: REME Museum

9. World War II gun testing equipment

10. 5.5-inch Gun-Howitzer

Photo: the author

11. 5.5-inch Gun-Howitzer
Breech Block

Photo: the author

12. 5.5-inch Gun-Howitzer
Elevation Quadrant

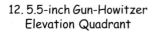
Photo: the author

NO 2 TRG BN REME, HONITON

Photo: REME Museum

13. Entrance and Guard Room. No 2 Trg Bn REME, Honiton

TRAINING CENTRE, ARBORFIELD

Photo: REME Museum

14. The Poperinghe Barracks Guard Room, Arborfield

DME, DEME, DDME, AND EMELET

Photo: Collection of the author

15. The DME, Brig E.R.Caffyn &
the DDME, Col D.V.Henchley
21st Army Group
Hamburg. 1945

16. The DEME, Brig D.V.Henchley
OBE, MA, C Eng
Far East Land Forces (FARELF)
Malaya -Singapore. 1958-1961

Photo: Brig D.V.Henchley

17. The 'Baby' EME (EMELET),
2 Lt Anthony Caffyn 10 Inf Wksp REME & LAD
13th/18th Royal Hussars Malaya. 1959-1960

Photo: the author

Photo: Lt Col (retd) R.P.Rust. Late REME & RAEME

18. Brig D.V.Henchley. DEME. FARELF, and Maj Rust. REME
(ex-OC 'D' Coy 2 Trg Bn REME, Honiton).
Malaya 1960

MALAYA 1959

19. Entrance to Johore
Bahru, Malaya. 1959

Photo: the author

20. Evening,
Fishing Kampong
Officers' Mess,
10 Inf Wksp

Photo: the author

21. Open Day,
10 Inf Wksp.
OC's Office first floor
on right.

Photo: the author

Photo: the author

22. The Ferry at Temerloh

Photo: the author

23. 'Where the Hell's the Echelon?'

24. Beserah Beach

Photo: the author

25. My camouflaged Land Rover, Beserah Beach

Photo: the author

26. Setting up Ground Wireless Station Beserah Beach

Photo: the author

10 INFANTRY WORKSHOP REME, ANNUAL EXERCISE

27. The latest beach wear modelled by the Officers 10 Inf Wksp Beserah Beach

Photo: the author

28. S/Sgt Davis with supporters Land Rover Flotation Exercise Kuantan

Photo: the author

29. Return journey from Beserah to 10 Inf Wksp Pandan. Laterite Track Temerloh to Bahau.

Photo: the author

30. Annual SMG Classification, Majedee Barracks, Johore Bahru

Photo: the author

31. Checking scores

Photo: the author

32. Young python killed in the Workshop

Photo: the author

BOGGED DOWN SCAMMELLS.
10 INFANTRY WORKSHOPS REME

33. 'What the hell do I do next?'
Petrol Scammell and 1RAR
Bedford RL truck bogged down
on Rubber Estate, after the
Australians had been let loose
from the Jungle Warfare School
Tebrau, Johore 1959

Photo: the author

34. 6x6 Petrol Scammell
still bogged down after
the 1RAR Bedford RL has
been recovered. Tebrau,
Johore 1959

Photo: the author

35. 6x4 Diesel Scammell
bogged down on way to
recover Petrol Scammell.
Rubber Estate Tebrau,
Johore 1959

Photo: the author

13TH/18TH ROYAL HUSSARS (QUEEN MARY'S OWN)

36. Railway Station, Ipoh

Photo: the author

37. Officers' Mess 13/18H, Ipoh

Photo: the author

38. REME LAD 13/18H Vehicle Park, Ipoh

Photo: the author

13TH/18TH ROYAL HUSSARS (QUEEN MARY'S OWN)

39. 13/18H Camp Lines,
Ipoh

Photo: the author

40. 2 Recce Flight
Army Air Corps,
Ipoh Aerodrome

Photo: the author

41. RAF Sycamore
Helicopter,
Ipoh Aerodrome

Photo: the author

FERRET SCOUT CAR RECOVERY.
13TH/18TH ROYAL HUSSARS (QMO)

Photo: the author

42. 'There's a Ferret Scout Car down there somewhere'.
Grik-Kroh Road, North Malaya

Photo: Courtesy Mrs Sylvia Wright

43. The EME, Capt Hugh Wright claims salvage rights.
Grik-Kroh Road, North Malaya 1960

FERRET SCOUT CAR RECOVERY.
13TH/18TH ROYAL HUSSARS (QMO)

44. ASM John Woodfield checks the recovery gear layout.
Grik-Kroh Road

Photo:
Courtesy Mrs Sylvia Wright

45. The ASM takes a well-earned breather.
Grik-Kroh Road

Photo: Courtesy
Mrs Sylvia Wright

46. The 'Malay Kampong Handyman's Course'.
Grik-Kroh Road

Photo: Courtesy
Mrs Sylvia Wright

'A' SQUADRON'S AIR PORTABILITY EXERCISE
13TH/18TH ROYAL HUSSARS (QMO)

47. 5th Troop 'A' Sqn approaching 'The Gap'

Photo: the author

48. Soggy lunch break, 'The Gap'

Photo: the author

49. Crossing the Kuantan Ferry

Photo: the author

'A' SQUADRON'S AIR PORTABILITY EXERCISE
13TH/18TH ROYAL HUSSARS (QMO)

50. Father Jones celebrating Mass, Beserah Beach

Photo: the author

51. Ferret Scout Car Bandar Paka, East Coast

Photo: the author

52. 'The Assault Section' L/Cpl Pawley REME (front right) Sungei Trengganu Ferry

Photo: the author

'A' SQUADRON'S RETURN TO IPOH
13TH/18TH ROYAL HUSSARS (QMO)

53. Loggers playing Mah Jongg at Maran between Temerloh and Kuantan

Photo: the author

54. 'Ambushed!' The Assault Section waiting to be called forward

Photo: the author

55. Daimler Armoured Cars on patrol near Ipoh, and well spaced out for safety reasons

Photo: the author

56. Capt Hugh Wright and Sgt Manston preparing ammunition for LAD Annual Classification shoot

Photo: the author

57. Hugh Wright over ambitious, Port Dixon

Photo: the author

58. Watching a film. Officers' Mess 'C' Sqn. Gapis Estate

Photo: the author

13TH/18TH ROYAL HUSSARS (QMO)

59. Combined Bands 13th/18th Royal Hussars, 1st/3rd Royal East Anglian, and 1st/7th Gurkha Rifles. Polo Tournament. Ipoh. April 1960

Photo: the author

60. Polo Tournament Ipoh. April 1960

Photo: the author

61. The wife of Shah Aly Khan presenting Polo Cup to Gen Sir Rodney Moore. The CO Lt Col D.Coker on right

Photo: the author

REME YOUNG OFFICERS LAND ROVER
FLOTATION TRAINING

62. Packaging Land Rover,
Chenor, Perak

Photo: the author

63. Launching Land Rover,
Chenor, Perak

Photo: the author

64. 'Hurrah!' It floats.
Land Rover Flotation,
Chenor, Perak

Photo: the author

IPOH GLIDING CLUB

Photo: the author

65. Preparing for take off

Photo: the author

66. Fast tow take off

IPOH FLYING CLUB

67. Tiger Moth taking off

Photo: the author

68. Ipoh from the air

Photo: the author

69. The Kinta Valley
open-cast tin mines

Photo: the author

REST AND RECREATION

70. Aborigine Headman's House, Kinta Valley, Ipoh

Photo: the author

71. Temiar Aborigine Headman, Kinta Valley, Ipoh

Photo: the author

72. Interior Aborigine Headman's House. (L to R) Mike Butler, Gillie Turl, Headman, and Johnny Hok. Kinta Valley, Ipoh

Photo: the author

REST AND RECREATION

73. Tin Mine at Tambrun, South of Ipoh

Photo: the author

74. Panning for Tin

Photo: the author

75. Peter Waddy 'Jungle Bashing'

Photo: the author

REST AND RECREATION

76. The Commonwealth War Memorial, Singapore, commemorates 30,000 men and women who died in the Japanese attack on Singapore

'They Died for all Free Men'

Photo: the author

77. The Ban Po Shu Pagoda, Kek Lok Si Monastery, Penang

Photo: the author

78. Vipers. Snake Temple, Sungei Kluang, Penang

Photo: the author

HOMEWARD BOUND

79. Although I had flown from the UK to the Far East in a RAF Transport Command Comet (Not BOAC)...

Photo: the author

80. And had flown internally in Malayan Airways DC3s...

Photo: the author

81. I returned to the UK in a Britannia of British United Airways

Photo: the author

Captain Stevenson in his lecture at Mons, had warned us that in every Officers' Mess, there were 'living-in' senior officers and especially those who were confirmed bachelors, who had probably developed some rather peculiar and eccentric habits. Woe betide any junior officer and especially a 'sprog' subaltern who had committed the cardinal sin of parking his car in the wrong place, had occupied a favourite chair in the ante-room, or had taken the wrong seat at the dinner table. So I made absolutely certain that, by parking the car under the oak tree at the extreme edge of the car parking area, I was not taking the parking space of an elderly, gouty and irascible major.

The irascible, elderly single Major

However, even then I got it wrong. For just prior to lunch, a loud voice emanated from the entrance hall:

'What blithering idiot,' and an elderly major appeared in the doorway of the ante-room, 'has parked his tin pot Morris Minor under my oak tree?'

I couldn't believe it. I had parked well away from the main entrance to the Mess, as I couldn't believe a senior officer would park his car that far away.

I replied: 'Er I did, Sir.'

'You new here?'

'Yes, Sir.'

'Well, move your car. That's my space. Anyway, what's your name?'

'Caffyn, Sir.'

'Any relation to Ted Caffyn?'

'Yes, Sir. My father.'

'Humph.' The major picked up a copy of the 'Mechanical Engineer' and sat down in what was obviously his chair by the fireplace.

I didn't think he was impressed, and maybe my father and he had crossed swords sometime in the past. Anyway, I made haste to move my car and parked it near a row of rubbish bins, thinking that must be safe, until the Mess Sergeant came up and quietly had a word in my ear that the bins couldn't be cleared.

What a start to my commissioned life! When I returned to the ante-room, a captain came up to me and said:

'Don't worry too much about the major. He only likes to park there, so he can pee against the tree when he's had a good evening out.'

Although lunch in the Mess was an informal affair with officers, depending upon their duties, drifting in and out at various times, I realised that officers enjoyed a degree of gracious living, and I appreciated sitting at a large, well laid dining table and being waited on by the Mess Waiters. I also realised that this life style only existed in camp. On exercise or on active service, officers 'roughed it' along with all the other ranks of a unit. Still, it was nice to enjoy the comforts when one could.

~

That first afternoon we were left alone to our own devices, but we had orders to assemble in the ante-room at 0830hrs the following morning.

Promptly at the appointed time, a captain strode into the room.

'Right, Gentlemen. I am the Training Officer and it will be my responsibility to ensure that you follow and successfully complete your technical training. You will spend eight weeks here at No 6 Veh

'...parked his tin pot Morris Minor under my oak tree?'

Trg Bn and then two weeks across the road at No 4 Armt Trg Bn. After that you will spend two weeks at Arborfield on a Young Officers Course, before you are posted to your units.'

I then embarked upon ten weeks of one of the most enjoyable parts of my National Service. It was as if I was back at college again, but studying far more interesting subjects. We would get up and breakfast at a civilised hour, before walking down the road to where the main vehicle workshops and lecture rooms were situated.

No 6 Veh Trg Bn occupied a large area, and the first time we walked down the road from the Mess, I was struck by both the variety and age of the buildings, some of which I understood went back to Victorian days. As the Army had embarked on a major update of their equipment, plans had been approved in 1959 for a major reconstruction of Bordon at a cost of some three million pounds. We were not to benefit from these modernisation plans; but the two large vehicle workshops with their attached classrooms, where we were to spend at least half of each day in theoretical instruction, were probably adequate for the depth of technical knowledge we required. Our instructors were in the main staff sergeants, whose knowledge and lecturing skills could not be bettered, but were based on school classroom techniques. Desks, blackboard, chalk and exercise books were so reminiscent of school days, and we even had weekly written tests to ensure that we had been paying attention, and not been asleep or daydreaming during the instruction periods. If anybody was marked at less than fifty percent, he was given extra tuition, which was not popular with the instructors. The unfortunate subaltern also had to use his spare time swotting up the subject, using the text pamphlets with which we had been issued, together with notes made in our exercise books. It only needed detention to be given as a punishment and we would really have been back in a school regimen. Failure in any of these tests could result in a posting as a regimental officer to one of the REME training battalions which, as we had experienced at Nos 1 and 2 Trg Bns was regarded as a fate worse than death.

However, unlike school, the subjects we studied were all interesting, and especially those that covered 'A' vehicles, which in Army 'speak' referred to armoured fighting vehicles (AFVs), whilst soft skinned ones were classified as 'B' vehicles. But our course was not all theory, and we did have the opportunity to climb over and drive some of the vehicles. Unfortunately, as the Army was being re-equipped with new AFVs; 6 Trg Bn had to make do with obsolete vehicles for training and there was a distinct lack of 'A' vehicles, with the notable exception of a Centurion Armoured Recovery Vehicle (ARV), which was REME kit anyway. I presumed that eventually the new Saladin Armoured Car and the Saracen Armoured Personnel Carrier (APC) would be made available for technical training purposes; but we had to make do with classroom instruction on the Bren Gun Infantry Carrier, which had been introduced into the Army in 1938, and the Daimler Armoured Car (DAC) of World War Two vintage.

Tanks have always interested me, and I was disappointed that due to my partial colour blindness, I was prevented at my medical from nominating the Royal Tank Regiment as my second choice. So my only experience with armour, was the time we rode on the backs of Centurion tanks along Long Valley in Aldershot. Although, very many years later, I was able to sit in the commander's seat of a Challenger II MBT(Main Battle Tank) and operate the turret and sights. But at 6 Veh Trg Bn, we had to make do with classroom technical instruction on the Centurion with its Meteor engine, a de-rated version of the Rolls-Royce Merlin Spitfire engine; its Horstmann type suspension system and the Merritt-Brown gearbox. If the Army were unable, or unwilling to let No 6 Trg Bn have a Centurion tank for technical training, there was even less likelihood that they would let us have a Conqueror MBT to play with, especially as only one hundred and eighty were ever produced. This tank was heavy in every respect with, at the time, its massive 120mm main armament and weighed in at 65 tons, compared to the 105mm main gun of the 51 ton Centurion tank. Even the current Challenger II MBT at 57 tons weighs less than the Conqueror did. Our instructors were very good, and did their best to make our lectures as interesting as possible, using whatever aids they had. In the workshops, we were able to see actual components and sub-assemblies, such as engines, gearboxes and suspension units. Nevertheless, although important, it would have been more instructive and interesting, not to mention fun, if Armoured Fighting Vehicles had been available for our technical training.

~

After we had covered the AFVs, we moved on to 'B' soft skinned vehicles, such as the Bedford R.L. 3 ton and the Morris 30 cwt trucks; the Austin K9 Gantry truck; the Land Rover and the FV1801 Austin Champ. The latter was the British Motor Corporation's (BMC) answer to the American Jeep, but was most unpopular with REME mechanics, as it was a complex vehicle, a beast to work on and unreliable. As these soft skinned vehicles were on the strength of every Army unit, we were able to put the theory into practical use.

Although we were disappointed that we were unable to get our hands on any armoured vehicles, we nevertheless very much enjoyed and gained valuable practical experience with the REME recovery vehicles. These ranged from the Centurion Armoured Recovery Vehicle (ARV), to the two versions of the very practical and hard working Scammell recovery vehicles; the Pioneer 6 x 4 diesel engine model and the more powerful Explorer 6 x 6 petrol engine one. The Pioneer SV/2S diesel recovery vehicle was first introduced in 1936, and production continued until 1945.

On some of the recovery tasks we carried out, we found that, due to the heavier and more modern equipment the Army had been equipped with from 1940 onwards, the Pioneer was underpowered. The 6 x 4 diesel Scammell did not have the benefit of a power-operated winch, and in order to prevent the front end 'rearing up', if recovering or towing a too heavy load, short concrete beams were carried in slots attached to the front of the vehicle. It also suffered the disadvantage of neither having front wheel drive nor front brakes; but with a top speed of less than 25mph, this was not too great a disadvantage.

The 6 x 6 Explorer FV11301 was my favourite recovery vehicle. The model, which had first been introduced in 1951, was extremely robust with good cross-country capability, front wheel drive and braking provided on all six wheels. It was a thirsty beast, with petrol consumption of three miles to the gallon, and needed a seventy-gallon petrol tank. It could lift three tons with the jib in the inner position and two tons extended. Standard recovery equipment, which I was to be very thankful for in Malaya, consisted of snatch blocks; ground anchors; gun planks; tow rope; a steel towing bar; a distance frame for suspended tows; a Hollobone drawbar for recovering or towing AFVs and 450 feet of steel winch cable. After studying the Owner's

Handbook, for which one needed a doctorate in electro-mechanical engineering, we were permitted to drive the Explorer around the more open, wider and less inhabited parts of the workshop area; for with its 20inch 4-spoke steering wheel; eight lever controls which, according to the Handbook operated the main gear change, handbrake, Neate brake, transmission brake, winch brake, front-wheel drive engagement, power winch take-off and winch engagement; it was not a vehicle to take out for a quick Sunday afternoon spin!

We spent a week on recovery training on Bordon Heath at the back of the Camp. Here were a variety of derelict soft skinned vehicles, upside down or on their sides in ditches, small ravines, waterlogged craters or stuck up banks. The more they were used for recovery training, the more derelict they became. Anyway, one Monday morning, we climbed aboard 6x4 and 6x6 Scammells. Staff sergeants drove us onto the Heath, parked by one of the wrecks and told us to recover the vehicle. We had spent the previous week on the theory of recovery, which was much more of specialist subject than I had realised. A FITA (finger in the air) approach would have been disastrous.

On any recovery task, the first but obvious decision that had to be made was how to recover the vehicle. A general, but simple rule of thumb was 'what goes in should come out the same way', and therefore the recovery pull should be made from the direction the vehicle got bogged down, turned over or whatever. That decision having been taken, calculations had to be made which took into consideration, the weight of the vehicle to be recovered, whether it was upright, on its side or upside down, the condition of the vehicle, which may have been involved in an accident, and the state of the ground it was on or in. The winching and lifting capacity of the recovery vehicles needed to be part of the equation, for example on the 6x6 Scammell, the winch tension-limit device was set to cut the engine at 15 tons, but with the use of snatch and change direction blocks, the ratio of a 1:1 pull could be doubled or quadrupled up to give a 2:1 or 4:1 pull, which gave an increased recovery capability. Once these calculations had been finalised, the number of ground anchors needed to secure the recovery equipment could be worked out. Ground anchors, vital for recovery, could be a pain, as each anchor plate needed up to ten anchor pins to be fully driven into the ground, in order to prevent snatch and change direction blocks moving during the actual recovery pull. Failure to secure these properly could result not only in equipment damage, but possibly personal injury as well. In a large and difficult recovery, several ground anchors would be needed, and getting the pins out of the ground, once the job was finished, especially on hard ground, could be a long and physically exhausting operation; but, as our instructors were constantly emphasising, safety was of prime importance.

Incorrect calculations, could result in accidents and serious injuries, and as one staff sergeant put it:

'Recovery is dangerous, and although the equipment we use is more than adequate for the job, like all equipment there can be breakdowns, and if a steel rope was to snap, especially under tension, it will whip back with possibly lethal results, especially if a hundredweight snatch block is attached to the end of it. So when a recovery operation actually starts, make sure that everybody is out of the way, and that nobody is standing directly behind the recovery.'

However, the first task we were given was a simple one of recovering a truck from a ditch, requiring no more than a straight 1:1 pull. As the week progressed, the recovery tasks became more difficult and complex, requiring a degree in mathematics, which was always my weakest subject at school. The final task was to right and recover a Bedford 3 ton truck lying on its side in a water filled crater, and for which the instructors said we had to use both Scammells. We used the steel winch rope from the 4x4 diesel one to hold the truck steady, so that it wouldn't slide sideways, and we used the winch rope from the petrol Scammell to right the vehicle, before hooking it up for a straight 1:1 winch out. Although it was not strictly necessary to use both Scammells on this task, the instructors wanted to give us experience in using two recovery vehicles together at the same time.

The surprise, at least to us, of the week was when a Centurion ARV was driven onto the Heath. This was a Centurion tank chassis with its turret removed, but with a power operated winch installed. The ARV came into service in 1956/7, so as far as we were concerned, having been used to WWII equipment, this was a very modern piece of kit. The winch had a 70,000lb capacity, which could be increased with snatch blocks up to a capacity of 202,500lbs, and as all the derelict vehicles on the Heath were soft skinned ones, the recovery of these posed no problem to the ARV. We just shackled them up to the winch rope, put the Centurion in gear and dragged the derelicts out of wherever they had been dumped. However, a further surprise was that we were all going to be given the chance of driving the ARV. The driver's compartment was on the right of the hull, and the driving position was nearly a prone one, and from the driver's hatch, gave rather restricted vision. We must have given our instructors heart attacks as each of us, in turn, tried to control the beast and keep it in a straight line; but however hard we tried, the ARV progressed across the Heath crabwise, but fortunately not at its maximum road speed of 35 mph. Gear changing was tricky, and the Centurion ARV, with a mind of its own, would either drift off to the left or the right, and had to be brought back to the correct direction of travel, by either applying the right hand brake to stop the track on that side to turn right and visa versa. The poor ARV was very tolerant, as were our instructors, who from their positions in the superstructure and commander's cupola must have suffered severe bruising and nausea from some of the manoeuvres, which we inadvertently put the Centurion through. Nevertheless our driving proved the robustness of the Vickers designed recovery vehicle. However, although we all enjoyed driving the ARV, we did not unfortunately learn a great deal of the principles of armoured vehicle recovery.

Nevertheless, I was sorry when the week's recovery course was over. I would certainly have welcomed more recovery training; and had I known it at the time, extra practical experience would have stood me in very good stead in Malaya.

~

We hadn't been long at Bordon, before each of us was handed a form, which we had to complete, and to state a preference for where we would like to be posted to, after we had completed our training. I hadn't given this any thought, but I found it hard to believe, as we would only have a year to serve after our training, that REME had enough vacant postings to satisfy all our preferences. But, a choice had to be made, and as I thought that I could visit Germany or Cyprus at any time; I opted for a distant posting, which I would probably normally never visit, and so much the better if I could do it at the taxpayers' expense. So, conveniently forgetting my resolution, after our anti-ambush drill at Battle Camp, of not volunteering for service in Malaya, I put my name down for the Far East; hoping for Hong Kong or Singapore. It was a standing joke amongst National Service subalterns that one ended up in precisely the opposite direction to their stated preference. So I felt I stood a good chance of probably ending up at Catterick.

After some nine months of intensive regimental military training at Honiton and Mons, our technical training at Bordon was very unmilitary. The only visible signs being that we were in uniform, and saluted senior offices and returned salutes from other ranks. There were no parades, and if there were any formal Dinner or Regimental Guest Nights in the Mess, we were not included. This, I felt was a shame, as traditions are such an important part of Army life, and I believed that, even though REME being a young Corps, which had only been formed seventeen years previously in 1942, needed every opportunity to build up tradition; a Guest Night with the officers in Mess kit (bum freezers) would nevertheless have given us 'sprog' subalterns experience of a formal Mess social event. We would have learnt about the duties of the President of the Mess Committee (PMC) and of Mr Vice, an honour usually afforded to a junior subaltern; who was responsible for proposing the loyal toast; and the correct response to the PMC's; 'Mr Vice – The Queen', being 'Gentlemen - the Queen,' and not

'God help Her'. We would have learnt that at a Guest Night, no officer leaves the dinner table before the Colonel and his principal guest, and that the PMC should not leave until all the guests have left the dining room. But Mr Vice must not leave until all the diners have left the room, which could result in a long wait, if two officers were in deep conversation re-living old campaigns. This could leave Mr Vice isolated at the other end of the table with nobody to talk to. He could also be in immediate danger of suffering serious injury from an exploding bladder, if he, in his ignorance as a newly commissioned subaltern, had downed too many beers in the ante-room prior to the dinner.

However, many of us would no doubt end up being posted to a Light Aid Detachment (LAD) attached to an infantry, artillery or cavalry regiment, and it was important that as a junior subaltern one knew the history, traditions and habits of the parent unit.

The orderly officer at weekends was a captain, presumably because there was likely to be more trouble from soldiers, who had been out of Camp either on a Saturday evening out, although there wasn't much on offer in Bordon, or were returning from weekend passes. Subalterns were the weekday orderly officers. In order to gain experience of the duties, one of us 'shadowed' the weekend duty captain, and we would then have one stint as orderly officer on a weekday. It was not an onerous duty, lasted twenty-four hours, and there was not a great deal to do prior to guard mounting at 1800hrs. Whether one called the guard out or not during the night, was left to the orderly officer to decide, and bar for dismounting the guard at 0600hrs in the morning, that was really it. This did not mean that there was any slackness in guard duties. The same procedures were carried out as at Honiton. Two hours 'on' and four hours 'off', with two-man patrols following set routes around the Camp to cover all the important areas. As opposed to the two basic training battalions at Blandford and Honiton, which were, to use a modern expression, 'people intensive', the technical training battalions were 'equipment intensive' and although there was a constant stream of trainees passing through Bordon, these were in much smaller numbers than at Nos 1 and 2 Trg Bns, and during the time I spent at both Nos 4 and 6 Trg Bns, I never heard of any troubles.

~

The summer of 1959 was a hot one, to such an extent that the tar on some of the side roads around Bordon melted in the heat. It was during this period of hot weather that I drove up to Loughborough to attend the wedding of one of my closest friends at College. I decided to wear my No 1 uniform with my father's Sam Browne belt, which looked as though it had seen better days, and probably deserved its own World War Two campaign medal.

Both John and I celebrated our twenty-first birthdays at Loughborough, but his was a month before mine. It was a tradition that a twenty-first birthday should be celebrated with ones friends, but John who was courting at the time, and it was his wedding I was driving up for, had decided to celebrate his birthday with his fiancée, which we felt was definitely 'unsociable'. We therefore organised a lunchtime party for John at a local pub near the college airfield on the Derby Road, where the aeronautical and automobile faculties were situated. We managed to pour two pints of beer and eight whiskies into him before our lunch break finished. But we lost John at tea-break time, and it was some minutes before someone rushed into the canteen and said there was a pair of feet sticking out from under the door of one of the 'bogs'. We panicked, fearing the worst, and wondering what we could tell his fiancée. Fortunately, he had felt tired, and so had laid down in the 'bog' and gone to sleep. I believe though that he suffered a monumental headache that evening.

For some unknown reason, I had decided to try and out-drink John on my twenty-first birthday, and had arranged to take over the back room of the Volunteer Pub in the centre of Loughborough. Apparently, during the course of the evening, I was seen sitting by myself at a table, looking rather miserable with three pints of beer and nine whiskies lined up in front of me. I drank the lot, including a gin and orange, which someone had put down on the table. It was a great twenty-first party, but I was very ill that night, and felt so dreadful the next day that I vowed I was never going to get that drunk again. A vow I have managed to keep, with one exception, when I deliberately allowed myself to be 'nobbled' by the Sergeants' Mess at 10 Infantry Workshop in South Malaya, where I was having a great time and was posted four hundred miles further north, against my wishes to the LAD REME 13/18th Royal Hussars.

~

The Army, or it might have been the top 'Brass' in REME, had decided in their wisdom, that we should take and pass our motorcycle test. After my efforts, they probably wished they hadn't adopted such a policy. I don't know whether it was because I had always driven four-wheel vehicles, starting at the age of fourteen on a Ferguson tractor, but I had an instinctive dislike and fear of two-wheeled vehicles. I had once tried a friend's Vespa motor scooter, but had managed to fall off within ten yards.

So, I had a distinctly sinking feeling in the pit of my stomach, when the announcement was made that we were to spend a week on motorcycles before taking our test in Alton. A number of subalterns on the Course already held m/c driving licences, whilst the others, with me being the only exception, were used to riding motorcycles. The Army's standard motorcycles for learners appeared to be rather elderly 250cc BSAs, all of which had seen better days. For the first two days, our instructors had us riding round and round a workshop compound, which to those who had experience with 'bikes, must have found utterly boring; but it was very necessary for me to learn how to control a machine with only two wheels, and with which I had little or no confidence. I felt far more comfortable driving a Centurion ARV. I was fairly competent riding in a straight line, but it was the turns that let me down, and after I had, with a definite lack of dignity fallen off several times, the staff sergeant diagnosed the problem and suggested that; 'I should change out of first gear and apply a bit more welly, Sir!'

Eventually, after two days they either judged that I was competent enough to be let loose on a public highway, or as the Course was in danger of running behind schedule, the only way to get me up to speed was the kill or cure, figuratively speaking, experience of the open road. I felt sorry for the others, as I was obviously holding them back, and as one of the instructors pointed out; 'We can only go as fast as the slowest member of the group.' Which did wonders for my morale. I wished though I had a Ferguson tractor under me, as I am sure that I could have out-performed all of them on it. Our usual route was north from Bordon on the A325 towards Farnham before turning off on a 'B' class road towards Alton, which had the advantage of not having a great deal of traffic on it. The convoy of a dozen of us would be led by one instructor at the front, with the other one at the back to 'chivvy' along the slow-coaches, which meant me. The instructor could also stop and pick up any pieces, which may have fallen off my bike.

After a couple of days being 'tail-end Charlie', the instructors had worked out a cunning plan, and instead of putting me at the back of the convoy; they inserted me into the middle, which meant I dared not let a gap open up with those in front; otherwise I would be under vocal and physical pressure from those behind. The policy worked, although initially we only travelled at a safe and steady speed of 30mph, but as I became more proficient our speed was gradually increased until we reached, what I thought to be a far too dangerous speed of 45 mph. I felt fairly secure so long as the road ahead was reasonably straight and the surface dry, but put me round some bends on a wet road, and I became totally paranoid that I was going to fall off, which I invariably did. I believe it was somewhere between Liphook and Grayshott on a minor road, where there was a very sharp blind left hand bend, which almost doubled back on itself before dropping down a steep 1 in 10 hill. This seemed to be a favourite route of the two staff sergeants. It used to terrify me as I turned to the left, with the road dropping away very sharply in front of me, and I would be frantically braking to slow the 'bike down, even using my booted feet as brakes on the road, and I never knew, even to this day why I didn't end up flying over the handlebars. Fortunately for me, we never did try that stretch of road in the rain; otherwise I was certain that I would have really come unstuck.

The instructors, no doubt had to take us out on all types of road, but I've often wondered whether it wasn't cafés that governed the routes we took. The staff sergeants had obviously carried out reconnaissance in depth over a period of time, for they certainly knew the best ones; although I was never certain whether their judgement was based on the quality of the coffee, or the attractive waitresses. However, we weren't too bothered. These stops made a pleasant break from the monotony of riding round and round the same routes at very dignified speeds.

After a week we were deemed competent enough to take our motorcycle test, and on the appointed morning we donned our crash helmets and set off in convoy for the town of Alton, where we were to be tested. I did wonder how this was to be done, as the 'bikes weren't equipped to carry a pillion passenger on the back. But when we got to the Test Office in Alton, the tester explained that we were to follow a circular route around the centre of the town, and he would be moving around to observe and note our performance. At the end, he called us all together, and announced that we had all passed. I didn't know who was the more surprised and shocked, the staff sergeants or myself. Nevertheless, it was with a feeling of achievement that I took off the 'L' plates and stored them in one of the pannier bags, before we set off back to Bordon. We had had several showers that morning and in places the road was quite wet. Going round a left hand bend, the rider in front of me developed a fairly major wobble on a wet patch of road, so I started a wobble as well, but over compensated and ended up lying on the road, with the 'bike on top of me, much to the alarm of the occupants of a car passing in the opposite direction, and which probably gave them more than a few grey hairs. Fortunately, except for my pride I was not hurt; but I added a few more dents and a broken head light glass to the poor old motorcycle, which, probably like the occupants of the passing car, had aged in the week under my tender care.

I had hoped that once the test was over, we would say 'goodbye' to the motorbikes. But that was too much to hope for. We next had to experience cross country riding, and just north of Bordon was the ideal 'trials' area; open sandy heath land, with masses of gorse, bracken and small hillocks, all bisected with innumerable tracks, which had obviously been used many times for motorbike scrambling. I hoped that this heath land was War Office property; otherwise, if it was common land I could imagine a clash of interests with the local populace out walking their precious pets or offspring. However, upon reflection the locals were probably all service families anyway.

If I had had problems riding a motorcycle on the open road, these were nothing compared to those I was going to experience trying to control a 'bike and myself over rough ground. I honestly tried my best, but the lack of confidence I had in my ability to ride a motorbike, meant that I was more of a hindrance to the rest of the group. Our instructors having held an emergency 'O' group, decided to put me at the back and let me proceed at my own pace. Through bitter and painful experience, I, at very close quarters became intimately acquainted with the local flora and fauna, and I very quickly learnt the right way of approaching obstacles and the right line to take when negotiating them. Even though it was summer, I at least managed to finish each day's training before darkness fell, and being allowed to proceed at my own pace, I was able at the end of the course to hand back to the Army a serviceable 'bike, which did not require major attention from an accident repair shop, and hopefully still had a good few years of use left in it from other nervous subalterns.

Although I had passed my motorcycle-driving test, and I still hold a current licence; I have never ridden a motorbike from those days at Bordon to the present day. I felt and still do, more comfortable and confident on four wheels; but I never had any self-confidence when it came to two wheels. I suppose the only talent I had with a motorcycle, was the ability to lay it on its side on any surface, in all weather and at any speed.

~

May gave way to June, and the weather got better and better. Day after day of clear blue skies and hot sun, and bar from the one orderly officers' duty, we were able to enjoy the fine weather to the full. We usually finished work by 1700hrs, and after that the evenings were our own. We had soon discovered on the western edge of Bordon, set amongst pine trees a very good officers' sports club. It had tennis and squash courts, and was also the home of the Bordon Garrison's Cricket Club. After an evening meal in the Mess, we would drive over to the club, play tennis and if we were still feeling energetic, squash; before retiring to the bar, and as the evenings were very warm, we would sit on the veranda with our beers and put the world to rights. We spent many an enjoyable evening there. It really was an idyllic existence, and memories were fast fading of the harsh regime we had been subjected to at basic training and the tough one at OCS.

As well as the REME units, there was also a Royal Army Service Corps (RASC) transport company based at Bordon. John, an RASC captain and his wife Prudence 'adopted' us, and wherever possible saw that we were not left out of unofficial social events. 'Pru' was a great character, and was responsible for organising weekly Scottish Dancing in the officers' sports club. This was great fun, but had the distinct disadvantage of a shortage of women; it wasn't really the same dancing eight-some reels, the Gay

Gordons or the Dashing White Sergeant with a fellow officer. However, the
Scottish Dance evenings became very popular and were so well attended,
that as the officers' club was fairly small, there was a danger of personal
injuries, with an over enthusiastic eight-some reel set, colliding with others
at a fair rate of knots. 'Pru' and John had their work cut out, not only in
teaching us the reels, but also trying to control these, when we were in full
flow like whirling dervishes. John would bring proceedings to an abrupt
halt by stopping the record, if things were getting too frantic and in danger
of getting out of control. With the very hot weather, I don't believe we ever
drank the bar dry during a Scottish Dance evening, but it must have been a
pretty close run thing.

There was no let-up in the hot weather, and we would drive over to
Frensham and park at the far end of a track by the Frensham little pond,
change into our bathing costumes and cool off in the rather murky waters
of the pond. Afterwards we would retire to the local hotel, where in the
lounge bar above the counter hung a glass 'yard of ale'. The owner would
challenge us to drink the 'yard of ale', and taunted us when none of us
would take up the challenge; saying it obviously didn't bother us that the
wife of an army officer had accepted his challenge and had successfully
downed the whole 'yard'. Knowing her zest for life, we had a funny feeling
that this must have been 'Pru'. It was, and at that time she was the only
woman to have done so at the Frensham Ponds Hotel. She and her husband
John not only helped to fill our spare time, but their kindness made me
realise what a close knit 'family' the Army was and probably still is.

The Services have often been accused of being cliquish, but when
politicians send them into hostile environments, sometimes on dubious
grounds, with the risk of being wounded or killed, and where they carry
out their duties without question; it is no wonder that the success of the
British Armed Forces, has always been achieved through the trust, loyalty
and close comradeship that a Regiment, a Ship's Company or an Air Force
Squadron generates.

~

Roger Macdonald-Smith, a fellow officer and I had become friends. Roger
whose home was in Pulborough, West Sussex owned a 1932 chain driven
G.N. Frazer Nash, which he liked to enter in two-lap speed trials at
Brands Hatch. Roger would come and stay over with me at weekends,
so that we only had a short drive up to the circuit. Although I knew
precious little about Frazer Nash cars, I nevertheless acted as Roger's
mechanic; but fortunately I was never called upon to exercise what little
mechanical skills I had, and I believed that even changing a chain would
have been beyond me.

These speed trials were fun, with great camaraderie and enthusiasm between the drivers. Roger would be in a class by himself, and it was always an impressive sight to see him wrestling with the steering wheel, as he hurled the large car round the bends trying to stay on the tarmac track. One didn't need to know when Roger was doing his two-laps; for over the distinctive low roar of the large cylindered engine, one could hear from anywhere in the circuit, the 'clunks' of the chains as Roger changed gear. With no competition, Roger always won his class. It would have been difficult to improve on those weekends at Brands Hatch. The sun blazed down from a cloudless sky, and lying on the grass, in the middle of the circuit, with eyes closed and listening to the sound of Roger's Frazer Nash speeding around the circuit, reminded me of Dornford Yates' books where Major Berry Pleydell and Captain Jonathon Mansel would, in their Rolls-Royces sweep through the poplar tree lined French roads on lovely summer days with only the sound of the cars' engines and the tyres whispering across the road surface.

~

Our classroom work continued. We had covered 'A' vehicle engines, gearboxes and suspension assemblies. We had had a brief look at the training pamphlets of the new Saladin Armoured Car and Saracen Armoured Personnel Carrier. We had worked our way through 'B' soft skinned vehicles, and as the temperature rose outside, so it did in the lecture rooms, which made staying awake extremely difficult, especially for the first session after lunch. It was a relief to get outside for some practical work.

We were nearing the end of our eight-week course at No 6 (Vehicle) Training Battalion, but before we left to cross the road to No 4 (Armament) Training Battalion, we were introduced to the intricacies of the Electrical and Mechanical Engineering Regulations, abbreviated to EMERS. Basically, these were glorified workshop manuals for every type of Army equipment and for which REME had the responsibility of servicing, repairing and maintaining in battle fit condition; whether they were vehicles, guns, electrical, or instruments. But they were not just repair manuals; EMERs also laid down standards of repair and, as I was to find out later, they were the Corps bible, and like Queen's Regulations had to be constantly kept up to date.

~

No 4 (Armament) Training Battalion was situated across the road from the Officers' Mess, and was the smaller of the two Battalions at Bordon. Our Course was only to last a fortnight, and the prime objective was for us to learn about gun design and maintenance. We were to be shown the faults, mechanical problems and breakdowns that could and did occur with the Army's two main field artillery pieces, namely the 25-pounder and the

5.5inch medium howitzer. We were also to learn a little of artillery theory, types of ammunition, and the difference between supercharge, full charge and reduced charge ammo.

The Course was held in Camp and it was a disappointment that we were not taken to the ranges to see demonstrations of both guns being fired. The best we could expect was to watch training films. The Battalion also had a comprehensive 'Black Museum' of horrors, showing what could happen to barrels, breechblocks, and other gun parts when serious faults occurred.

The heat wave had still not broken, and as we filed into the lecture room on the Monday morning, we were obviously going to suffer as the day wore on. The walls were lined with diagrams and pictures of gun components and assemblies, and displayed on tables were a selection of these components and assemblies, together with associated testing equipment. To our ignorant eyes, they all looked complicated, and we wondered how we were going to learn about gun technology in only two weeks.

A staff sergeant came into the room.

'Right, Gentlemen,' he began in a very brisk and businesslike voice; 'Please be seated. I am Staff Sergeant Mackenzie, and over the next fortnight I shall be instructing you in how artillery pieces work, and the faults that can develop with them. As you know REME is responsible for the repair of every type of Army equipment, and this includes guns and small arms. We are also responsible for gun instrumentation, including sights, fire control, predictors and height and range finder instruments. But before we can discuss these, you must know how guns work, and we shall be using the Army's two field guns, the 25-pounder (pdr) and the 5.5inch medium gun howitzer for our study. I should also warn you that you will have a written test at the end of each week. So you need to take notes.'

I had thought that when I had finished at Loughborough, the days of sitting exams and tests were finally over. I had been certainly been doing them from when I was eight years old, and here I was at the age of twenty-three still having to sit written tests. As I sat at the desk looking out of the window, whilst Staff Mackenzie rabbited on about something, I realised I had been taking tests or exams for fifteen out of my twenty-three years, and that was, as I tried to mentally work out, somewhere in the region of sixty-five per cent of my life had been spent taking bloody exams or tests. That was a depressing thought, and no wonder I had had enough of them, and here we were, faced by having to sit another two.

'......is made up of several major components.'

'Oh shit,' I thought, 'what have I missed?'

Staff Mackenzie walked over to a large exploded diagram of a gun on a wall, and holding a pointer:

'First of all there is the barrel, which the shell travels up after it has been fired. At the rear end of the barrel is the chamber, which holds either the cartridge case or a bag charge. Smaller calibre guns such as the 25 pdr use brass cartridges, whilst the 5.5inch gun uses bag charges. The next component is the breech-block, which allows for the opening and closing of the rear end of the chamber for breech loading and unloading. The component that supports the barrel and carries the recoil mechanism is the cradle. The whole gun assembly is mounted on the gun carriage, and the back of this, that extends from the axle to the ground is known as the trail, and generally ends in a spade, which is a blade under the gun trail, that digs into the ground and prevents too much rearward movement of the gun on recoil. All clear so far?'

No response. 'Okay, let's proceed.'

We had been busily making notes, trying to keep up with Staff Mackenzie's rapid explanation of a gun's major components, and at the same as writing, we had to watch his pointer flash from one part to another on the diagram. But worse was to follow. For hardly stopping to draw breath, the Staff Sergeant continued:

'Now, as you can imagine, gun barrels over a period become worn out and have to be replaced. This operation in an active service environment can be dangerous, is time consuming, requires heavy lifting equipment, and is expensive if the whole barrel assembly has to be changed. The better option is for a barrel to be made up of tubes. The innermost one, known as the 'A' tube is the actual barrel, with the rifling and chamber formed on the inside. Other tubes, logically called 'B', 'C, 'D' and so on, are shrunk on top of one another. The gun is then known as a 'built up' one. This means, and this applies to the 25 pdr, that a worn 'A' tube can be removed and a new one inserted relatively easily, without having to heat and expand the outer tubes.

'There are two types of barrel wear, abrasive and erosive. Abrasive wear, which is relatively small, is caused through the friction generated by the shell as it passes up the barrel. Erosive wear is far more serious, and is caused by the hot gases generated by the firing of the cartridge. These blow past the shell's driving band in the first few milli-seconds of firing, before the driving band is fully engaged with the rifling; and as the explosion temperature is higher than the melting point of most steels, the gases and the high temperature starts to 'eat in' to the surface of the bore where the rifling starts. Once erosive wear has started, it will continue to 'eat in' to the surface at an ever-faster rate, as more and more gases are forced past the driving band.

'Eventually, the erosive wear is so bad that there is a loss of accuracy, range and velocity. We measure the amount of erosive wear in the chamber, and will condemn a barrel, if this is over the limit as laid down in EMERs. Any questions?'

'Yes, Staff. What is the chamber, the shell driving band, and why is there rifling?'

'Okay,' continued Staff Mackenzie, as we sat there, pencils poised above our notebooks.

'The chamber is that part of the barrel where the charge or cartridge is inserted, and where the firing explosion takes place. The driving band is a soft metal band, which is pressed into the body of the shell, and as it passes up the barrel, the band engages with the rifling and the shell starts spinning. Rifling, which can either be 'uniform' or 'gain twist', gives a spin to the shell, which gives it gyroscopic stability and keeps it going in the right direction. Now, I know you are going to ask about the two types of rifling, and we are in danger here of going into too much detail, and which is not part of your Course. However, to satisfy your curiosity, 'uniform' rifling are grooves cut into the barrel in a regular pattern, whereas 'twist gain' is rifling which is small at the bore end of the barrel and becomes steeper towards the muzzle end, and this gives increased forward thrust to the shell, before it starts spinning and is meant to help accuracy and trajectory. 'Twist gain' rifling is generally used on larger calibre guns, as bigger shells need greater spinning, although too much spinning or twist will effect stabilisation. Clear?'

Staff Sergeant Mackenzie certainly knew and was enthusiastic about artillery; but there was so much detail in the content of his lecture that we felt we were getting mentally punch drunk, and we all breathed a figurative sigh of relief when we broke off for a lunch break.

All too soon we were back in the lecture room, with Staff Sergeant Mackenzie looking far too bright and breezy, whilst we were still suffering from the effects of the mental concentration of the three-hour morning session. I knew it was going to be a long afternoon, and I felt a post-prandial nap would be most welcome, especially as the forecast was that the heat wave was about to break with violent thunderstorms, and although all the windows were wide open, the air was heavy and humid.

'Right, let's get started,' Staff Mackenzie began in his crisp business-like manner; 'This afternoon we shall deal with breeches. Now, the breech-block is situated at the rear end of the barrel assembly and contains the breech mechanism, which allows for the opening and closing of the rear end of the gun for the loading and unloading of the shell. There are two main types of breech mechanism. The sliding block is the mechanism used on the 25 pdr, and consists of a block of steel with ribs on the side, and engages with grooves on the side of the breech ring, which is a heavy piece of steel fixed to the end of the barrel and carries the breech mechanism.

When the block is slid open either to one side or down, the breech is exposed and the shell, cartridge or bag charge can be loaded into the breech chamber. For closing, the breechblock is slid back and it also moves slightly forward to press against the charge, or cartridge case and locks the mechanism in place. The other type of breech mechanism, which is what the 5.5inch gun has, is the interrupted screw type. The block is cylindrical with segmented threads cut into its outer surface, and when the block is swung shut, it fits into the internal segmented threads in the breech of the gun, and the mechanism is turned through ninety degrees and locked in place.

'There are also two types of firing mechanism. For the sliding block, in guns, which use cartridge cases, and where the primer is in the base of the case, there is a spring-loaded striker pin in the breechblock, which is released by a firing lever or lanyard. For the screw type on guns that are designed to take bag charges, a primer similar to a blank cartridge is fitted into the firing mechanism of the cylindrical breechblock, and is fired electrically or mechanically by firing pin. The flame from the primer passes down the vent, which is a hole drilled through the breech-block, and ignites the bag charge. All clear?'

With the oppressive heat and humidity, it was really getting extremely difficult to concentrate on the Staff Sergeant's words, and my mind began to drift towards the coming evening, where Roger and I were taking two girls, we had met at Scottish dancing to the cinema in Haslemere, and I hoped that I would not fall asleep during the performance.

Fortunately, Staff Mackenzie, who was I believe also feeling the heat, decided to dismiss us when he had finished with breech-blocks and breech mechanisms. It was such a relief to return to our rooms, shower, crash out onto our beds before changing into 'civvies' and going to pick the girls up.

~

Thunder clouds had been building up during the afternoon, and shortly after Roger, the girls and I had left Bordon, the heavens opened and we were lashed with torrential rain, making it very difficult to see where I was driving, as the single speed windscreen wipers tried, unsuccessfully to cope with the volume of rain and hail hitting the windscreen. Within two miles from Camp, flash floods were building up and I carefully and slowly drove through these in low gear, keeping the engine revs up. But, as we went through these with no trouble, my confidence rose and I felt that even half an hour's torrential rain could not cause major flooding. But, I was shortly to be taught a very salutary lesson for my cockiness, for as we neared Haslemere, we drove down a short and rather steep hill into a hollow, before the road climbed up to a 'Tee' junction. As we approached this, we could see that that there was a flood in the hollow.

'Do you think we can get through that?' Asked one of the girls.

'This doesn't seem to be any worse than what we've driven through already,' I replied.

'Are you are sure?' Asked Roger.

'Yes,' I replied, feeling slightly less confident. 'I'll drop down to first gear and keep revving the engine.'

As we approached the water, I slowed down, changed down to first gear, revved the engine, let the clutch out and gently accelerated and drove into the flood. And then we stalled, and as we sat there in the middle of the hollow, whilst I tried to restart the engine, water started to pour into the car through the bottom of the doors. The foot wells soon filled up, and the poor girls in the back, with their feet resting on the back of the front seats did their best to stay dry. For Roger and myself, there was nothing for it, but to remove shoes, socks and roll up our trouser legs and see if there was anything we could do. But as we stood in the murky and muddy floodwater, we realised that we were well and truly stuck. We had a hill both behind and in front for us. Fortunately it had stopped raining, so all we could was to wait for the floodwater to subside, and then hope that the water had not got into the car's electrics.

But lady luck was on our side that evening, as a driver passing the 'Tee' junction saw our predicament, luckily carried a tow-rope, and very soon had pulled us up to the top of the hill. Unbelievably, the engine fired and very slowly, testing the brakes as I drove, which was a bit difficult as the foot wells were still full of water, we made it to the Haslemere Hotel; and although the Hotel staff were somewhat nonplussed when Roger and I walked into Reception, barefooted and with trousers rolled up above our knees, they were nevertheless very helpful, lending us towels and the use of a bathroom to get cleaned up, for which we were very grateful. Needless to say, we didn't get to the cinema that evening. But even though we emptied the water out of the car directly we got back to Camp, the smell from the muddy floodwater hung around for weeks.

~

The next morning, bright eyed and bushy tailed after the previous evenings extra-mural activities, we waited pencils and notebooks to hand for a day of sheer concentration as Staff Sergeant Mackenzie led us through the complexity of gun design and construction. At least the storm had cleared the air. We were taken through the recoil mechanism, recuperator, articulation, extractor, equilibrator, obturation and all the other parts that go to make up a gun.

'You should now have a better idea of how a gun works,' Staff Mackenzie continued, 'and I now want to take you through some of the problems that can occur and which involves REME. I shall leave out instruments such as sights; for in many instances with the use of calibration testing equipment, faults can easily be detected. No; what I want to talk to you about are the major faults that can occur. Yesterday, I told you how barrels could and still can easily be changed on 'built up' guns. But we still have to know what the likely life of a barrel will be. This is decided by the term 'Effective Full Charges', abbreviated to EFC. This measure refers to the probable life of a barrel, if it was to fire nothing but full charges. But most firings are at reduced charge, so it is important to refer to tables to establish the number of reduced charges that can be fired, to equate with the maximum number of full charges before a barrel becomes worn out. In the case of the 25 pdr this could be as many as five thousand reduced charge firings, but in a high velocity gun the EFC could be considerably less and measured only in hundreds of firings. It is necessary to understand EFCs before we move onto problems. Everybody happy with EFCs?'

'Yes Staff.'

'Right. There are three major problems that can happen in the firing of a gun. The first one is 'hang fire'. This is where there is either an ignition failure of the cartridge primer in the interrupted screw breechblock, or in the primer of the metal cartridge case. The correct procedure is for the gun crew to wait in case there is delayed ignition, before opening up the breech and unloading. The second problem is a misfire, where there is a total failure to fire. This could be caused by either an ammunition or mechanical fault; such as a weak striker spring; a worn firing pin tip; or the breech-block, through wear, not pressing firmly against the base of the cartridge; and in the case of bag charges, the vent passage could be fouled and blocked. Again the crew must wait some time to ensure there isn't going to be late ignition.

'The last problem is the most serious one, as it could cause loss of life and injury; and this is the premature explosion and detonation of the shell. If this occurs inside the barrel it is known as 'bore premature'. There are a number of causes for this, ammo and faulty ammo assembly failure, or the faulty setting of fuses, and degradation through storage at high temperature of the explosive filling. There could also be mechanical defects in the gun, such as the steel choke becoming displaced, which partially constricts the bore and reduces the calibre of the 'A' tube. There could be excessive barrel wear that impedes the progress of the shell down the barrel, or there could be movement in the chamber liner. The result, invariably, is the gun is blown to pieces and as I have had already said there could be loss of life and limb.

'We will now move onto the Army's two basic artillery pieces. The 25 pdr, which was first introduced in 1940, is the basic field piece, and as I have already described, the barrel has a removable tube liner, so it can be changed in the field. The firing platform is in the shape of a wheel, and is capable of all-round fire. The gun can be readied for firing in one minute, has a vertical sliding block breech mechanism, and can fire armour piercing, high explosive and smoke projectile quick firing ammunition, over a range of twelve thousand five hundred yards with a standard charge, and thirteen thousand four hundred yards with supercharge. The normal rate of fire is four rounds per minute. The 25 pdr has proved to be a most effective and reliable field gun.

'The 5.5inch gun-howitzer was first introduced in 1941, is classified as a medium size artillery piece and is deployed as corps artillery, whilst the 25-pounder is deployed as divisional artillery. The 5.5inch has an interrupted screw breech mechanism, fires a hundred pound breech loading shell to a maximum range of sixteen thousand yards. The normal rate of fire is two rounds per minute. The 5.5inch gun is easily recognisable as it has two distinctive vertical 'pillars' either side of the barrel, which act as spring balancing presses that counter the weight of the barrel.

'Before we finish for the day, a quick word on ammunition. I've already told you that both guns fire HE shells, but there are different types of high explosive projectiles, which are colour banded to denote the shell filling. For instance, a Lyddite shell is yellow; a TNT one is a yellow shell with a green shoulder band and 'TNT' stencilled in black on the band; Pentolite is a yellow shell also with a green shoulder band, but with a thin black line superimposed on the green band. And if that isn't complicated enough, an Amatol 80/20 shell is also yellow with the green band; but if the mixture of ammonium nitrate and TNT is other than 80/20, the fraction is stencilled in black below the green band. Smoke or phosphorus shells are green, whilst AP shot, shrapnel and star shells are black with different colour bands or tips. You won't be tested on ammunition, but I thought you should be aware of the many different types of shells.'

In spite of the volume of information that Staff Sergeant Mackenzie was feeding us, I enjoyed his lectures, which were helped by the number of gun assemblies and components that were available for practical demonstration, and which made it easier to absorb the information and certainly made the subject more interesting.

~

We were getting near the end of our time at Bordon, and as I walked into the Mess one lunchtime, I noticed an official War Office envelope in my pigeonhole. My posting had come through. With a feeling of dread and with butterflies in my stomach, I tore open the envelope and fully expected to see either the word 'Catterick' or 'Blandford'. To my amazement I read the words, 'Posted to FARELF, Singapore'. I just couldn't believe it. I had only put the Far East down as a reason for not staying in the UK. I knew absolutely nothing about Singapore or Malaya, bar from the fact that, as

Capt 'Jungle' Jim had explained at Mons, there was a nasty shooting war going on out there. I hoped that I would be based either in Singapore or Hong Kong. I had really been hoisted with my own petard.

In the ten weeks we had been 'living-in' Officers in the Mess, we had made friends with many of the permanent staff majors, captains and their families, who had made us most welcome. One captain, the father of one of the girls from the abortive trip to the cinema at Haslemere (who was still talking to me, - the girl not the father), told me that Singapore and Hong Kong were two of the best postings in the Army. The captain who was coming up to complete twenty-two years service in the Army, and as he did not expect to be posted outside Europe again, very kindly handed on to me what tropical kit he had, including two Australian Army bush shirts, which were considerably more comfortable than the British Army ones, and as we were the same size, his white tropical mess kit jacket. I was really most grateful, and especially for the advice he passed on:

'The humidity is very high in Singapore and Malaya, and fungus forms very quickly on clothes, and your houseboy will know this, but don't leave clothes in a wardrobe or in an enclosed space for more than two days. They must be hung out in the open air to dry. If you have a camera, either send your films homes, or seal them in a glass vacuum container, as fungus can ruin films or transparencies very quickly. Prickly heat around the waist can be very nasty, so make sure you take tins of baby powder with you, which is most effective in easing the rash. If you're 'up country' in Malaya, and leeches attack, never pull them off you, as you will leave part of the leech impaled on your body, which will probably turn septic. Burn them off with a lighted end of a cigarette. You must take a daily anti-malarial tablet, and it is a court-martial offence if one goes down with malaria, and it can be proved that you haven't been taking your daily tablet. So don't forget to take it.'

I was very grateful not only for the kit he let me have, but also for the advice he gave me, which was to come in very useful. Although for all my bravado in volunteering for the Far East, I was, however beginning to wonder what I had let myself in for.

~

We only had two more days to go, before our final test and the end of the Course. So as Staff Sergeant Mackenzie entered the room, in his usual bright and breezy way, we wondered what else could he possibly teach us about artillery. At No 6 Veh Trg Bn we had only spent a week on each of the subjects we were instructed in; but here at No 4 Armt Trg Bn we had spent a fortnight just on guns, and at times we had wondered amongst ourselves whether we were in REME, or whether without anybody telling us we had been transferred to the Royal Artillery. We could certainly hold our own in any discussion group with RA officers. Anyway, Staff Mackenzie was not about to disappoint us on our last instruction day. In fact, we were going to have more technical artillery 'speak' thrown at us that day, then the previous nine days. (We still didn't work at weekends).

'Right, Gents, today I shall be instructing you in the procedure for the sighting, aiming and firing of an artillery piece. I shall be using a lot of technical terms, so you better pay attention, concentrate and make certain that you make comprehensive notes of all these terms. So, let's get started.

'Now, some of you may have heard of a German 17inch First World War gun that answered to the name of 'Big Bertha'. Now before 'Bertha' could be laid. And what are you sniggering at, Sirs? Various procedures had to be followed to ensure that a shell from 'Big Bertha' hit the target. These procedures still apply. So, aligning the gun with the target is known in artillery terms as 'Laying', either in direct or indirect fire. Direct fire is when the target is in view of the gun, and sighting is straight forward using a low-powered telescope with cross wires, and the sight can be brought in alignment with the target by using the elevating and traversing mechanisms. Laying a gun for indirect fire is more complicated and to align the gun correctly, it is necessary to establish an arbitrary aiming point; which can be a church, a chimney of a large building. But whatever is chosen, it must be a fixed structure, and the angle between this and the target is measured. This angle is set on the gun's panoramic sight, and by moving the gun, so that the sight is pointing at the aiming point, then the barrel of the gun will be aligned on the target. To set the gun, it will be necessary to adjust both the elevating and traversing gear as detailed in the Firing Tables, which tabulate the range and time of flight for any elevation of the gun using a specific charge and type of shell. However, there are other factors that must be taken into consideration. A shell, once fired can drift, which is the sideways movement of the shell and is caused by its rotation due to the rifling. Accuracy can be affected by the droop of the barrel, which is the vertical curvature of a barrel due to gravity and possible manufacturing faults. Heat from the sun on one side of a barrel can also cause a 'bend' in the barrel. The lateral deviation of a shell is known as azimuth, but by firing ranging rounds, corrections can be made by using the gun's traversing gear. The 5.5inch gun has quick loading gear, which is a mechanism that allows the barrel to be quickly brought back to the horizontal plane, by disconnecting it from the elevating gear, loading and re-connecting without disturbing the set-up of the gun.

'Now, and I hope you are following me; there are few more definitions that you must know, and these are mainly angles. For instance, the Angle of Departure is the angle between the horizontal plane and the axis of the gun bore; the Angle of Descent is that angle between the horizontal plane and the line of arrival of the shell as it hits the target; the Angle of Incidence is the angle between the surface of the target and the line of arrival of the shell; if this is at a right angle it is known as the zero angle. The Angle of Projection is the angle between the line of sight and the axis of the bore when the gun is fired; and finally the Angle of Sight is that angle between the horizontal plane and a sight line connecting the gun to the target. Have you got all that?'

I hoped I had. But I was beginning to panic about how, with only a day to revise before our final test, I was going to memorise this as well as the other 'stuff' we had been lectured on since our first exam the previous week.

Staff Mackenzie ploughed on relentlessly:

'There is also Target Elevation, which is the angle between the line of sight from gun to target and the axis of the bore when the gun is laid. The angle of elevation of a gun barrel is measured by using a Clinometer, which has an inbuilt spirit level; and when the desired elevation of the barrel is set on the clinometer's scale, and the barrel is elevated until the spirit level bubble is level, then the barrel will be at the correct elevation. It is important to know about Calibration, which is the process of determining the muzzle velocity of a gun; which is the speed of a shell as it leaves the muzzle and is measured in feet per second and is also a measure of the power of a gun. Muzzle Energy is the amount of kinetic energy contained in a shell the instant it leaves the muzzle and is measured in foot-tons.

Now, there are only two more definitions you need to know; the first is Trajectory, which is the path of a shell through the air. In a vacuum this would be a perfect parabola, but with air resistance and gravity it becomes a compound curve, steeper at the target end than at the gun end; and finally Vertex, which is the highest point reached by a shell in its trajectory. Squaring a shell's time of flight to the target in seconds, and quadrupling the result can give an approximation of the height in feet.

'Well, Gentlemen. I would ask for questions, but we are out of time. That is the end of the Course. I hoped you've enjoyed it and found it interesting. I have enjoyed taking you, and I wish you all the best for the rest of your National Service.'

We were rather dumbstruck at the speed he wound up the Course, but as he picked up his papers and made for the door; he paused before he reached it and with a wide grin:

'Oh! By the way. Today's lecture was not part of the Course and you will not be tested on anything I have told you today. But, I felt that in order to understand guns, and what can go wrong with them, it is advantageous to know how they are laid, and the procedures to be followed prior to firing. I hope you've found it all interesting and trust that the copious notes you have made today will come in useful one day. Goodbye and good luck, Sirs.'

Staff Sergeant Mackenzie was out of the door so fast, that we didn't have a chance to throw our notebooks at his retreating backside for leading us on, and putting us under such pressure, worrying how we were going to remember all the technical terms he had thrown at us without a pause. However, in spite of his practical joke, Staff MacKenzie was a very good lecturer, was enthusiastic about his specialist subject, and knew how to put this over in such a way that we never got bored and lost interest.

~

So, we came to the end of our technical training. We had learnt a great deal, and all the instruction had been given in a most professional way; mostly by staff sergeants who knew their particular subjects, and were able to put these over in a very clear, understandable and user friendly manner. After the strict disciplinarian regime of Blandford, Honiton and Mons OCS, which was obviously necessary to make soldiers of us, it was such a welcome change to be in an academic military atmosphere, which played down regimental activities, such as drill and parades. This did not affect our behaviour. Discipline and obeying orders had been fully instilled in us, and as new subalterns we were well aware of our responsibilities, and at all times we behaved in a proper military manner. But, without the pressures of regimental duties, we learnt in a more relaxed and effective environment. With the good weather, and we certainly took advantage of the heat wave, we had made full use of the Camp's sports and social facilities, and I drove away from Bordon with a feeling of sadness. It had been a very happy, instructive and satisfying ten weeks. I wondered whether the same would apply on the final fortnight of my training at the REME Training Centre, Arborfield.

Chapter Eleven

Junior Officers' Course. REME Training Centre

As I drove over to Arborfield from Bordon, I thought it somewhat ironic that the Garrison, situated south of Reading had originally been, prior to the Second World War the home of the Army Remount Depot, where horses were given their military equine basic training, but due to the demise of horse power, and its supersession by mechanical horse power, the depot should be taken over by REME, the Corps formed in 1942 to maintain the Army's electrical and mechanical equipment.

Those of us who had survived from the start of our training at Blandford, were now to face our final two weeks training at the REME Officers School, before taking up our postings. I checked in at the Hazebrouck Officers' Mess, to be directed to the National Service subalterns' standard hutted annex quarters.

The following morning we assembled in another standard wooden hutted lecture room, which was to be our home for the next fortnight. We stood as two captains entered the room.

The taller one opened the batting.

'Good morning, Gentlemen. I am Captain Courtney and this is Captain Townsend. We shall be your instructors over the next two weeks.'

We decided, using correct military wireless procedure, to identify them amongst ourselves with the call signs 'Sunray Charlie' and 'Sunray Tango'. 'Sunray' being the call sign for the boss man.

'You will learn about the Corps, its history, its organisation, and its responsibilities. We shall also be spending a day out of camp for a map reading and wireless exercise. A number of you who are being posted overseas, will probably need inoculations and vaccinations and these will be given next week. Now before we start, you will be issued with name badges, and which are on the table behind you. You will wear these at all times. There are many courses going on here, and it is policy that everybody, whether officers, warrant officers, senior or junior NCOs and other ranks wear name badges.'

Having a cynical mind, I wondered if the real reason wasn't for senior officers to be able to identify anyone of a lower rank who failed to salute, or to show them the proper respect.

'Right, Captain Townsend will now brief you on the history and organisation of the Corps. I will see you later, Gentlemen.'

I had been thinking for some time that we had been in the Army for some eleven months, and we had never been given any information about REME. I felt that this was something that should have been covered much earlier when we were in 'D' Coy at Honiton. I was aware that my father had been a REME TA Officer, but bar from knowing that he had been in the War Office in 1942 as a member of the team that formed REME, and that he had been Director of Mechanical Engineering (DME) 21st Army Group in North West Europe from 1944 to 1945; I knew very little about his service life, and especially about his part in the setting-up of the Corps. I believe that shortly after REME was formed, my father was sent out to the Middle East, to carry out a tour of inspection of vehicle repair facilities in North Africa. About the only comment he had ever made to me, was that in early 1942 when Major General Rowcroft was looking around for officers to join his team in the War Office; he had heard of this young TA RAOC(E) Colonel in York, who had a reputation of getting things done, and so the General had brought my father down to London. I knew that many ex-servicemen, who for very good reasons have never talked about their war experiences, but I always felt that my father could have told me a great deal about REME, especially when he knew that I was going into the Corps for my National Service.

Captain Townsend came in to bat first wicket down.

'Okay, Gentlemen, I am Captain Townsend, and I shall today be taking you through the origin of the Corps, its organisation and its responsibilities.'

The Captain turned his back on us and wrote on the blackboard:

REME. HISTORY AND ORGANISATION

'You must take yourself back to the 1930s, when the Army, by and large was not mechanised, and there were many officers in cavalry regiments who believed that the horse would be, for the foreseeable future the main form of transport in their regiments. I have always felt it an interesting fact that even in the mid-1930s, the Army only had just over three hundred tanks of Great War and post-Great War vintage, so perhaps one can understand the views of the cavalry. After the end of the First World War, the government of the day introduced a ten-year defence plan, working on the assumption that there would not be a major war for at least that period. This policy was changed in 1932, when the government decided that the Army should be mechanised and brought up to a war footing. The responsibility for the maintenance of what electrical and mechanical equipment the Army had at the time, had been an absolute 'buggers muddle'.

'The Royal Army Service Corps and Royal Engineers had their own workshops; and the Royal Armoured Corps, the Royal Tank Regiment, Royal Artillery and the Royal Signals also had their own unit fitter tradesmen. It was decided in the 1920s as an economy method, that a high proportion of the First World War equipment should be 'mothballed' and stored in Ordnance Depots. So it was logical that the RAOC should take over the repair and maintenance of the Army's mechanical equipment, although specialist electrical equipment was still left in the hands of their respective Corps.

'So the RAOC, not only continued with its main function of stocking and supplying the Army's equipment and spares; but was faced with setting up a separate mechanical engineering division, staffed with officers, NCOs and technicians with mechanical experience and technical qualifications. The RAOC(E) Division set up front line Light Aid Detachments (LADs), mobile and static workshops. But with the increased mechanisation of the Army prior to the start of the Second World War, the RAOC(E) had to significantly expand in a very short time, in order to maintain and repair the vast amount of new and increasingly complex equipment that was being rushed into service.

'It is a fact that in the winter of 1939/40, some forty percent of the British Expeditionary Force's equipment was in workshops, and the BEF was virtually immobile. The workload placed on the RAOC, especially with their other responsibilities, only confirmed what had long been realised, that it was vital all engineering and technical services should be centralised into a new organisation, which would have complete responsibility for the maintenance and repair of all the Army's mechanical and electrical equipment. I have over simplified what in reality was a far more complicated situation, but that is how the decision was taken by Government to set up a new specialist Corps, which was to be named the Corps of Royal Electrical and Mechanical Engineers. I suggest we take a break now. So, be back here in half an hour. Okay?'

We were wandering around the lawns outside the Officers' Mess, when a captain came up to me, looked at my name badge and asked:

'Do you come from Eastbourne?'

'Yes, Sir,' I replied.

'I'm Doug Holman, and I'm here on a weeks course for TA officers. I'm the OC of the LAD attached to 258 LAA ('P' Battery) Royal Artillery in Eastbourne.'

'Pleased to meet you, Sir. But what does LAA stand for?'

'258 is a Light Anti-Aircraft Regiment. It was a heavy anti-aircraft one until 1950 when it converted to its present role. The Regimental HQ is in Brighton, with Batteries in Hastings and Bexhill as well as Eastbourne.'

We had a chat, and as I was due for three weeks embarkation leave before flying out to the Far East, I asked Doug if he would like me to help him with the LAD on their twice-weekly Drill Nights. An offer he was only too pleased to accept.

Although there were other TA units in Sussex, Doug said that the majority were Royal Artillery TA units.

I asked him why, but he didn't know the answer.

Some years later, I came across a copy of the Territorial and Auxiliary Forces of Sussex Official Handbook 1950, which confirmed that the majority of the Territorial Units in Sussex at that time, were indeed Royal Artillery ones, for the reason that:

'Modern artillery was born in East Sussex. In the year 1543, "Ralph Hogge and his man John, they did cast their first cannon," at Buxted. In the sixteenth century Sussex was the Black Country of England, iron was dug and forged all over the county, but the majority of the forges were here in East Sussex. From the time of Ralph Hogge iron cannons were made in this district until the forges were closed down. It was customary in those days for men from where the cannons were made to be "learned in the art and mysterie of Artillerie," so Sussex men from these parts served their guns against the Grand Armada in 1588. There the Sussex guns proved their superiority – the brass cannon of the Spanish over-heating quicker than the Sussex iron.'

There are still many examples of the iron smelting industry in East Sussex from the name 'Clappers Wood' on my late father's land, to 'Gun Hill', a half mile from my home, where cast cannon were proved and where 'The Gun Inn' now stands.

After my chat with Doug Holman, I had to rush back to our lecture room as I had the impression that the Captains 'Charlie & Tango' were rather regimentally minded, and would not tolerate a 'sprog' subaltern being late for one of their lectures. Fortunately, I was just in time.

'Right, let's continue,' as Capt 'Tango' walked into the room and at the same time pointing to the blackboard:

REME. HISTORY AND ORGANISATION

'So, in early 1942, Major-General Bertram Rowcroft, who was commissioned into the RASC, was appointed as the first Director of Mechanical Engineering and tasked with setting up the new Corps. The formation of the Corps was authorised by Royal Warrant in May 1942, and King George VI decreed that the name of the new corps would, from the outset be preceded by the word 'Royal', and so REME came into being on the 1st October 1942.

'Our present badge is made up of a lightning flash, which symbolises electrical engineering, and the horse forms part of the crest of the Institute of Mechanical Engineering, to show our close links with civilian engineering. The globe is to show our world wide engineering responsibilities, and is chained to the horse as a symbol of power under control. Incidentally, we are the only Corps or Regiment, to have the Corps name directly under the royal crown. All the others have their names at the bottom of their badges. The Corps motto is 'Arte Et Marte', which translated means 'by Skill and by Fighting'. We have our own Patron Saint, St Eligius, who was born near Limoges in France in the year 588. He was apprenticed as a metalworker and a goldsmith, and it was because of his artisan origins, his craft skills and piety that he was adopted as the Patron Saint of the Corps.

'To staff the new Corps, there was a general transfer of Ordnance Mechanical Engineers (OME) officers and senior NCOs out of the RAOC (E), the RASC and into REME.

'The system of providing various repair levels was initially set up by the engineering branch of the RAOC between the wars, and although there were LADs in front line formations, the repair policy was generally to back-load equipment to field or static workshops; whereas REME policy, as laid down by General Rowcroft was, and still is, to carry out repairs as speedily as possible and as far forward as practical, so as to get equipment back into action with the minimum of delay. REME is responsible for the repair and maintenance of every item of Army equipment, with the exception of 'tentage, saddlery and harness'.

'So, the first line of repair is the Light Aid Detachment, usually commanded by a captain, and its duty is to recover damaged equipment, carry out light repairs or replacements in the field using its own vehicles, and to get the equipment back into action. If the damage is too extensive, and the main criteria is time, for a LAD has to be mobile as it moves with its parent unit; then it is back loaded to a second line workshop, and each brigade has a REME workshop attached to it. The composition and equipment of the brigade workshop, which is usually commanded by a major, depends upon the type of brigade, whether an armoured or an infantry one. The second line workshop is, however a front line unit, has to be fully combatant and must also be mobile to move when its brigade moves; and for this reason there are time constraints on the repairs that are carried out at this level.

'The next echelon is the third line repair workshop, usually commanded by a lieutenant colonel, which acts as an overflow for the brigade workshop, and also carries out repairs which does not require the use of extensive and elaborate testing equipment. These workshops must also be sufficiently mobile to keep up with the formation they are attached to.

'The final echelon is the fourth line of repair, Base and Advanced Base Workshops, Command Workshops and Central Workshops. These workshops under the command of a colonel are static units and are equipped with heavy plant and machinery, so that they can carry out major repairs, rebuilds and overhauls beyond the capability of the front line workshops. Base Workshops, and especially overseas ones, usually have a manufacturing function where it can be difficult to obtain replacement spares quickly enough. I haven't mentioned the REME Inspectorate, but in every fourth line workshop there is a section of the Inspectorate to check the quality of repaired equipment and to ensure that it meets the right standard.

'It is very difficult in the limited time I have, to cover the whole breadth of REME's activities and responsibilities, but before finishing I must mention the training battalions. These are concentrated into a Training Brigade and a Training Centre. The Training Brigade with its HQ at Blandford is made up of seven battalions, which cover basic military training at Nos 1 and 2 Bns; with driving and basic trades training at Nos 7,8,9,10 and 11 Bns.

'The REME Training Centre which comprises Nos 3,4,5 and 6 Trg Bns is based here at Arborfield and is responsible for all higher grade trade training including telecommunications, radar, armaments and vehicles. As you know Nos 4 and 6 Bns are based at Bordon. The Training Centre also carries out officer and artificer training. Also, at Arborfield is the REME HQ Officers' Mess at West Court.

'I have already mentioned the REME Inspectorate, which was set up in 1948, and is responsible directly to the head of REME, a major-general who is the Director of Electrical and Mechanical Engineering (DEME). The Inspectorate is responsible for the setting and the maintenance of all repair and equipment quality standards throughout the Army.

'One final point. Although we are a technical Corps, we are all soldiers first and foremost, and that means that if we are ordered to fight in battle we do so without question.

'Now, I would like to take questions, but I'm afraid we have run out of time. If you have any, you can catch me at any time during the course.'

Whew! This was turning out to be another high-powered Course. Not only with the content but, being held at the HQ REME Training Centre, where many courses were being run simultaneously, there was a plethora of senior officers and by senior officers, I mean any officer senior to us from lieutenants upwards, all of whom required to be saluted; just as we were duty bound to return the salute from anybody junior to us. Our right arms were well exercised.

~

The Capts 'Sunrays Charlie and Tango' were very professional, which was absolutely right; and they kept us on our toes, didn't tolerate any slackness, and were quite prepared to give a stern verbal dressing-down if and when necessary. This moment came, when we were to be let loose around the local countryside on a daylong combined map reading and wireless signals exercise. However, before that day came, we were to spend a few hours on Warren Heath with the man pack Wireless Sets No 38 to practice our signals procedure. The No 38 set had been developed in 1942 for short-range infantry communication, with a range of up to one mile using a 12 ft whip aerial. With its limited range it was going to be ideal for us as we roamed round the Heath, transmitting and receiving as many ridiculous messages as we could get away with, before 'Sunrays Charlie and Tango' stopped us.

The afternoon was not a total success as we found that reception was badly effected by dips, hollows, tall trees and electricity pylons. The set did not take kindly to being dropped, and the valves were particularly vulnerable to shock treatment. So, as the afternoon progressed, the number of working sets decreased, as we used up the best part of a years supply of spare valves in just a few hours; with the probable result that the RAOC had to re-adjust their maximum/minimum valve stock levels for an obsolete WWII wireless set.

Although a not too serious exercise, we had nevertheless learned and improved our wireless procedure, and were better prepared for the combined map reading and signals exercise.

The Capts 'Charlie and Tango' spent a day briefing us.

'Right, tomorrow you will be going out in teams of three in Land Rovers on a one day map and wireless procedure exercise. Recovery is one of REME's main responsibilities, and there could be many occasions, when as the officer in charge of a LAD or Workshop Recovery Section, you are called out to recover a damaged vehicle, and all you have to go on is a map reference, which being in hostile territory has been encoded. So the aim of tomorrows' exercise is to instruct you all, not only in map reading, but also in your ability to encode and decode grid references, and to transpose such grid references correctly on to map overlays. You will also be receiving and transmitting encoded messages and acting upon them. You will use correct wireless procedure at all times.

'We shall give each team an encoded grid reference, as you must presume you are in a hostile environment and which must be transposed into a clear grid reference before you leave.'

I wasn't certain who was supposed to be hostile around Arborfield Cross, and as far as I knew, our old friends from Mons OCS, 'The Lumps' had long since disappeared up the Great North Road in the direction of Hadrian's Wall.

The morning was spent being instructed in transposing encoded grid references onto overlays and then with chinograph coloured pencils marking these up on the perspex covers protecting the maps on our map cases. Most of us had never had the opportunity to 'mark-up' maps; so even though this was only a practice drill, preparing us for the main event the following day, we were able to exercise our artistic ability to the full. By the time we had finished, most of the perspex map covers looked more like those of a four star general commanding an army group, with a multiplicity of different coloured unit and sub-unit signs, numbers and letters all somehow connected to squiggly and seemingly disjointed lines. It was just as well this was a practice exercise and not for real. If it had been, I very much doubt that we would have even reached the Guard Room before we had got lost.

However, it was most unfortunate that during the course of the briefing, at a rather important moment, there was a sudden, unexpected and very violent hailstorm. The hailstones were nearly the size of golf balls, and within moments the view from the windows of our lecture room was of a completely white world. The noise from the hailstones hitting the corrugated roof of our hut was quite ear shattering, making it difficult to clearly hear the briefing, and I've always believed that some of the errors that crept into the encoding and transposing of the grid references during the exercise were as a result of the hailstorm.

'Now,' Capt 'Charlie' continued, 'You will be in Land Rovers, a team of three to each vehicle with a man pack wireless. Captain Townsend and I will also be in a Land Rover with a wireless and acting as the base station. We will assemble here at 0900hrs tomorrow morning, where you will be given your call sign, the frequency you will set your wireless to, the numeric transposition code and your first encoded grid reference. When you have transposed your specific map reference, you will work out the shortest and quickest route to that point, without I must emphasise exceeding the speed limits. Your drivers have been instructed to adhere to these at all times, and even if you did persuade one of the drivers to exceed the limit, and you were stopped by the police; you personally will be responsible for settling any fines. Understand?'

'Yes, Sir.' We chorused.

'Right. To continue. When you have arrived at your first grid reference, you are to radio in and tell us what you have found there. We shall then give you another encoded map reference and you will go through the same procedure again. It must be pretty obvious to you all that our call sign will be 'Sunray'. Right. Any questions?'

We spent the afternoon learning how to operate the standard WWII Army wireless sets we were going to use. This may well have been the No HF 19 set, although I was never certain, as the Army appeared to have had a multiplicity of sets in their inventory, with Wireless Set No 1 introduced in 1933 through to Wireless Set No 88 in 1947. If we were using No 19 sets, they were fairly elderly, having been developed in 1941 for 'A' vehicle use, but were later modified as general purpose sets for either mobile truck or ground station operation, with a range of up to 15 miles.

~

The following morning, we were all seated in our lecture room well before 0900hrs, waiting for Capts 'Sunrays Charlie and Tango' to appear, brief us and get us started on what we believed was going to be a fun day out. When they appeared, they split us into two groups with each 'Sunray' taking one group. Roger MacDonald-Smith, Colin Blaney and myself made up one team; were given the call-sign 'Echo Mike' and a encoded map reference of 'Yankee Two Zulu Four' which we interpreted as grid reference 76485398. As instructed we tuned our wireless to a frequency of 7.8MHz and tested that the base control station was receiving us. Then we set off.

Our first reporting point was a short distance down the A327 from the Garrison between Farley Hill and the REME HQ Officer's Mess at West Court. We stopped, looked round and wondered what we had to find of interest at that map reference, so we could radio in, report what we had found and get our next encoded grid reference.

I asked Roger, 'I don't want to query your decoding and map reading skills, but we are in the right place, aren't we?'

Roger gave me a dirty look, but nevertheless checked his figures, which Colin re-checked and agreed that we were where we were meant to be. We looked around again, but could see nothing of significance. In case that was the right answer, I decided to radio in and report our position.

'Sunray. Echo Mike. How do you read me? Over.'

Nothing; except a high level of static. I tried again. Again, nothing but static.

'What shall we do?' I asked the others. They looked equally puzzled. At that moment there was a polite cough from our driver, who seemed to be in some sort of a daydream as he stared up at the sky. We couldn't begin to fathom out why he found something in the sky so riveting. Colin looked up.

'Got it,' he exclaimed, 'Look we're almost under four rows of pylons, and weren't we warned that power lines generate an electromagnetic field under and close to them, so that they very effectively mask the transmission and receiving of any radio signals?'

Colin was right. We were standing almost at the centre of where pylons from the four points of the compass met very close to the main road.

By this time our driver had decided that looking up at pylons was a boring occupation, and had switched his attention to something at ground level, which he obviously felt was more interesting.

We suggested he might like to move a hundred yards down the road. This time we had more success; contacted control, and told them we had found the pylons. 'Sunray' appeared pleasantly surprised; but nevertheless gave us another encoded grid reference, which Roger and Colin transposed into 'English', before passing the map reference over to me to work out the shortest and quickest route to our next reporting point.

The exercise was beginning to hot up, for it was becoming clear that due to the previous days hailstorm, two or three of the teams had misheard some of the instructions from 'Sunrays Charlie and Tango', as we began to pick up some very plaintive wireless messages.

'Sunray. Golf Hotel. How do read me? Over.'

'Golf Hotel. Signal strength one. What is your location? Over.'

'Sunray. We're stuck in a sand and gravel pit, and sinking into the sand. What shall we do? Over.'

'Golf Hotel. You're meant to be officers. Use your initiative. Over and out.' Later.

'Sunray. Charlie Delta. We have a problem. Over.'

'Charlie Delta. Use correct procedure. I read you signal strength six. What is your problem? Over.'

'Sunray. We think we've made a mistake. We're at 75905975, but we're in the middle of a police college. They think we're disguised infiltrators, and I believe we're going to be arrested. We need help. Over.'

'Charlie Delta. You were briefed that you would be in a hostile environment. You're on your own. Over and out.'

We managed to keep going without losing ourselves, and were able to decode, locate and radio in our positions without causing any national or international incidents; although in one or two locations we nearly came to grief; the worst one being when I decoded a grid reference incorrectly, and we ended up in the middle of an unmanned level crossing, and were about to radio in our position when we heard a train approaching. We moved out very quickly, and I had to eat humble pie when I discovered I had transposed one digit incorrectly, which fortunately for me turned out not to be a too serious mistake.

Over the radio we picked up messages that some of the teams were still experiencing problems.

'Juliet Kilo. This is Sunray. Do you read me? Over.'

'Sunray. We read you strength four. Over.'

'Juliet Kilo. We've had a message from the Adjutant at RMA Sandhurst. You should not be there. Report to the main gate Guard Room. Understood? Over.'

'Sunray. Roger. Out.'

But our favourite message was from the team who were obviously lost, whether deliberately or accidentally, and ended up on the Square of the Woman's Royal Army Corps College at Bagshot. The team was given a warm welcome by the women officer cadets, who apparently were all for hijacking them into their college; a move actively discouraged by the authorities, who with ruthless efficiency sent our team packing. This was followed up with a complaint to the Arborfield Garrison Adjutant; who by this time was getting fed up with all the telephone calls he was receiving, and the Capts 'Charlie & Tango' were ordered to curtail the exercise and reel us in.

'Sunrays Charlie and Tango' were not amused, and once we had assembled back into the lecture room, they made their feelings abundantly clear, stating in an unambiguous manner that we were immature, irresponsible and totally unfit to be officers, certainly in REME, and they felt that even the Pioneer Corps would have difficulty in accepting us. I harboured a nasty suspicion that if they had had sufficient seniority, they would have had our postings cancelled, and had us transferred back to No 1 Trg Bn at Blandford on regimental duties, with enough extra orderly officers duties to last us for the rest of our National Service.

~

Fortunately, we were coming to the end of our fortnight at Arborfield, and the one redeeming feature about our Young Officers Course was that we did not have to sit a test at the end of it. That was a definite relief.

I think that 'Sunrays Charlie and Tango' had forgiven us for our poor showing on the map reading and signals exercise, for a few days before we were to disperse and go our separate ways, we were taken round the REME HQ Officers' Mess at West Court, a large 18th century manor house, with the oldest parts dating back to the 16th century. We were told that the site on which West Court was built goes back to Roman Days, and the House is actually built across where the Roman road ran from London to Bath, and which, according to the map appeared to rejoice in the unfortunate name of 'The Devil's Highway. The Corps is very fortunate to have such an imposing HQ Officers' Mess surrounded by some 16 acres of lovely grounds and gardens.

I was to learn at a later date, that there was the Barrow Hills Officers' Mess at Chertsey, which stood in grounds owned by the Fighting Vehicles Research and Development Establishment (FVDRE), and where REME officers had been so closely involved in the development of maintenance techniques, that many REME officers regarded Barrow Hills as their Mess, which they believed was more imposing than West Court.

I was perhaps slightly premature in thinking our two captains had forgiven us; for they had arranged the visit to West Court immediately after those of us, who were being posted to the far-flung present or past outposts of the British Empire, had been inoculated against smallpox, cholera, yellow fever and whatever else the medics thought necessary to protect us from all the 'nasties' that might attack us in those foreign parts. Anyway, those of us who had been used as pincushions were feeling rather sore and sorry for ourselves, and we could not really enjoy West Court or its facilities to the full.

~

So, rather like a damp squid, our Course at Arborfield came quietly to an end. There was 'no end of term' party, which in retrospect was a shame. We had been together for twelve months and had survived everything that had been thrown at us, from the first bad days at Blandford; through better times at Honiton and Mons OCS; through the technical and rather academic training at Bordon, until finally we had reached the climax of our training on the Young Officers' Course at the HQ REME Training Centre, Arborfield.

We quietly said our thanks and farewells to the Captains Courtney and Townsend, and apologised if we had let them down on the map reading and signals exercise. It certainly had not been our intention to do so; for 'Sunrays Charlie and Tango' were very professional and taught us a great deal not only about the Corps, but also on how we must behave as young National Service REME subalterns, and what duties and responsibilities we could expect in our various postings. I just wished they had loosened up slightly and showed some humour. Perhaps we were irresponsible, and needed a stern and serious schoolmasterly approach, to make us realise that we held the Queen's commission, and that in a very few weeks some of us could be in command of REME soldiers in an active service environment.

As I drove away from Arborfield at the start of my three weeks of embarkation leave, I had time to look back over the previous year, and review what I had gone through to reach the position I was now at.

Although I had nothing against the Armed Forces, but except for belonging to the Combined Cadet Force (CCF) at School and passing Certificates Part I and II, I had never bothered to form an opinion about the Services. It was only when the threat of National Service loomed on the horizon, was I forced to consider that, unless I was declared medical unfit,

I was going to have to spend two years of my life in the Army, which I was opposed to, and believed that this would take two years out of my life at an important stage of my career.

The Army, to give that organisation credit, had in the space of the two years to turn hundreds of thousands of young men, who by and large were probably anti-National Service, from civilians into soldiers, and to get a return on the investment in the time and effort spent on training them. I can only write about my experiences; and I have to admit that the first few days at Blandford, even with my time at boarding school was a significant culture shock. I could understand why, with the limited time the Army had available, the necessity for the training measures that had to be taken to knock individuality and independence out of us; to mould us into soldiers used to military discipline and obeying orders without question; to accept punishment for failing to obey orders, or failing to reach the necessary standards of personal performance. From initial basic training at Blandford, through to being commissioned from Mons OCS, although the training we were given, mainly by warrant officers and NCOs was tough, I never witnessed any bullying, or the picking on individuals by junior NCOs. All the instructors were professional. The Army policy appeared to work in that we were turned into effective, but possibly unwilling soldiers, whether commissioned or not in the shortest practical time.

I have never had any doubt in my mind, that National Service did me a power of good. The Army gave me confidence, self-respect, self-discipline and a sense of pride in what I had achieved. I recall my father once telling me, when he was Chairman of a Magistrates Bench, that the Bench used to have a number of young men who regularly appeared in front of the 'Beaks' for petty offences. The young men would disappear for their two years of National Service and, according to my father, the vast majority of the young men never appeared before the Bench again. There must be a moral there. There are valid reasons why it would not be practical for National Service to be re-introduced into the armed forces, but with the growth of unsocial behaviour, binge drinking and drug taking by young people, surely it would be possible to introduce a form of National Service, not necessarily in the military, but in other services such as police forces. This would possibly have to be selective as the majority of young people are responsible and self-disciplined; as witnessed for example, by the very many thousands of teenagers who have either joined one of the County Army Cadet Forces or the Royal Navy and Royal Air Force equivalents.

I was surprised though, the time it took to be trained ready for a posting to a REME unit. Cavalry and infantry subalterns were I believe posted to their regiments or battalions straight from being commissioned; whereas I had spent another ten weeks on technical and young officers training courses before I served with an unit. In fact with the infantry training I underwent both at 'D' Coy, Honiton and Mons OCS, I felt I was a better-trained infantry subaltern than a technical one. Presumably the Army believed that this was the right policy; but after nearly twelve months of training, and three weeks of embarkation leave, REME only had eleven months of practical and effective use from me before my two years' service was completed.

However, I hoped the Army and REME were going to be satisfied with the return they were expecting from the investment they had put into my training.

The Army, on the whole, disliked National Service, and were pleased when the Government declared that it would finish in 1963. The Army had to divert too many of their most experienced and senior Warrant Officers and senior NCOs, not to mention officers and other ranks to the training and administration of National Servicemen; who once trained would only have a limited time to serve before they returned to 'civvy' street. The Army wanted a wholly volunteer and professional force. However, the Army's many commitments including Korea, Malaya, Aden, Kenya, Cyprus, Egypt, Germany and other bases around the world, could not have been fulfilled without National Servicemen who served with distinction and bravery as witnessed by the three hundred and ninety five who lost their lives post-1945.

The one thing, of which I was certain, was that having started as being anti-National Service, I was now comfortable with and enjoying military life. I hoped the second part of my National Service in the Far East would be even more rewarding.

(End of Part 1)

Part Two

Arte et Marte

"REME has stood up to every stress and strain and has done its stuff in a manner that is beyond all praise."

Letter from Field Marshall. B.L. Montgomery to Brigadier E.R.Caffyn. July 1945.

Chapter Twelve

The Far East

I had three weeks embarkation leave before reporting back to Arborfield. I told my father that as I was enjoying and was comfortable with army life, I was considering signing on for a short service commission. As Chairman of the Sussex Territorial Army Association, and a founder member of REME, I had presumed that he would have been pleased that I wanted to extend my service. But, I was taken aback by his reaction. He was totally opposed to this, arguing that, although he did not put it this way, it was my duty to join the family business. He said that one of my cousins had already joined the Company, and his younger brother would also be doing so, when he had qualified as a chartered accountant. My father pointed out that as my brother had gone into farming, I was the only one left from our side of the family to run the after-sales and building maintenance side of the business. My father said, as he was getting on a bit, he wanted to take life easier. I pointed out that I wasn't planning to sign on as a regular, but only to do another three years on top of the two years of National Service. Even that did not go down well with him, and as a consequence for the three weeks of my embarkation leave, I was subjected to intense pressure from dawn to dusk.

I kept my word with Doug Holman and gave him a hand in the LAD REME 257 LAA Regt based in Eastbourne. I was aware that the Regular Army was going through a significant equipment upgrade, and that, as the poor relation the Territorial Army was being handed down the Army's obsolete and worn out WWII equipment. The LAD had very little equipment, bar from a few General Service (GS) trucks; two of which were kitted out for either workshop or electrical repairs, but were nevertheless kept in good order, thanks to the enthusiasm and commitment of Sergeant Hurd, the MT Sergeant. I offered to run a weekend map reading exercise, which Doug gladly accepted, and when I asked him about transport, he replied that we would have to use our own private cars and claim mileage allowance. I found it rather depressing after what I had been used to; but I couldn't fault the commitment and enthusiasm of the members of the LAD, who were prepared to give up their spare time, two evenings a week, two weekends a month and for two weeks annual camp to be part of the country's volunteer reserve forces. Although, I only helped Doug Holman for three weeks, I was impressed with the high turn out, not only for drill nights but also for the one weekend I was with the LAD. This was due, in no small measure to the respect, popularity, commitment and enthusiasm of Doug, who could not do enough for the welfare of all the members of the LAD. In only three weeks I learnt how a good officer, through his commitment and personnel leadership skills, earned the respect and trust of the troops he commanded.

The three weeks embarkation leave passed all too quickly. One major problem, I was faced with, was working out the kit I needed to take with me. I had received plenty of advice of what I would require, if I were posted to Singapore or Malaya, where I would only need tropical kit all the year round. However, I could well be posted to Hong Kong, which has seasons; and in the cool winter months, battledress would definitely be the order of the day. As my reporting documents had detailed that I would be flying out to Singapore, there was a weight limit to how much could be taken. Those of us who were being posted to the Far East had been issued with basic jungle green kit at Arborfield; which would enable us to start off wearing the correct gear, and not have to resort to wearing the thick serge BD trousers and short sleeve order in the hot sticky tropical climate. We really would have looked and stood out like new boys at their first school. However, we did anyway in our jungle greens, for until we had been posted to a unit we had no unit or formation shoulder flashes.

~

Before my leave was up, there was the outstanding major problem to be resolved of whether I was going to sign on for a short service commission or not. I was still under intense pressure from the family not to do so. In the 1950s prospective farmers were exempt from National Service, so long as they spent two years working on the land, an exemption that was subsequently removed. Mic, my elder brother, although he had studied at Cirencester Agriculture College had apparently faced similar pressure four years previously, but after spending two years working on a neighbour's farm, became a farmer.

Whether it was the pressure, or whether it was as a result of the three weeks I spent helping Doug Holman with the LAD, but I caved in and told my father I would not sign on for a short service commission but would join the family business, but if I did not stay on in the Army I would join the

TA instead. This I did. It was a decision I have always regretted. After full time soldering, and especial serving in Malaya towards the end of the Emergency, I realised that part-time soldering was not for me; and after my initial interest during embarkation leave, I resigned only after a few years. I felt at the time that the Territorial Army was living up to its reputation of being 'The Saturday Night Soldiers'. This was probably unfair of me, as subsequently the TA became very professional part time soldiers; deployed on active service and peacekeeping duties on an increasing number of occasions, by Government having to compensate for their policy of constantly reducing the defence budget and strength of the Regular Army.

At the end of my leave, my father drove me up to Arborfield, which I believed was the first time he had been back there since he was 'demobbed' in 1945. The Army, like any organisation had its fair share of 'office politics', and there was apparently, a certain amount of resentment when my father was appointed Director of Mechanical Engineering (DME) in the 21st Army Group (21AG); which was probably regarded as the 'plum' REME job at the time. A small number of officers believed that the appointment should have gone to a regular officer, and that as a TA officer my father had effectively blocked the promotion of a regular REME officer. But what wasn't appreciated at the time, was that General Rowcroft realised that by 1944, the majority of REME officers in 21AG were TA and 'Hostilities Only' officers, and he believed that they would accept a TA DME, rather more readily than a regular one. With the run down of the armed forces, which included the Territorial Army, at the end of the war; my father who as Chairman of the Sussex Territorial Army Association, and also as Vice-Chairman of the National Association under the late Duke of Norfolk became so involved, as did other County Chairmen, fighting battles with Government to preserve the Volunteer Reserve Forces, that he rather broke his links with REME; which did not go down too well with those who had resented his appointment as DME 21AG.

~

There were four of us from No 1 Trg Bn, Blandford who had been posted to the Far East; but unfortunately I had had to say goodbye to Roger Macdonald-Smith, Colin Blaney, Peter Sykes and Pete Smith who had all got postings either to Germany, Cyprus or staying in the UK. I was sorry that none of them had got a Far East posting, for although I was friends with the others, those four were close friends and we had shared both good and bad times over the previous twelve months.

We had a thirty-six hour wait at Arborfield before we were due to fly off to Singapore. Today it seems unbelievable, but my flight to Singapore, at the ripe old age of twenty-three would be the first time I had flown. Any trips abroad had either been by cross channel ferry, train or car to Paris with my mother, or to Switzerland with my father and stepmother, and once to Austria with friends from Loughborough. Although I was looking forward to the flight, I was beginning to get butterflies in my stomach, and wondered why I had put in for an overseas posting that was going to involve me in flying half way round the world. I was beginning to wish that the Army hadn't introduced air trooping, but were continuing to use troopships like the SS Nevasa to move troops around the globe, and where I could have enjoyed, hopefully, a relatively lazy six weeks cruise to Singapore.

Before the advent of package holidays, flying was still a novelty and to many people there was probably a fear factor; especially when memories of the Comet crashes at the time were still in peoples' minds. I had no idea what transport aircraft the RAF was flying, but I felt relatively certain that they were probably some fairly elderly and safe four-engine propeller driven ones, and certainly not one of the modern jet engine ones, with a less than proven safety track record, and which I was fairly sure that RAF Transport Command hadn't as yet got in their inventory.

~

There was great interest in the national newspapers over the breakfast table on my last morning in the UK, as the headlines proclaimed 'Issigonis's new baby, – The Mini.' There were pictures of the new car in all newspapers, whether broadsheet or tabloid, proclaiming that the Mini at a retail price of under £600 would bring car ownership to the masses. It would be another twelve months before I saw the car. For shortly after breakfast, we were driven to Reading railway station to catch a train down to Swindon, where a coach met us and drove us out to the large RAF Transport Command Base at Lyneham. We were led into a reception centre, where all the necessary documentation was completed, before we were ushered into a large waiting room, where some fifty to sixty other Army and Air Force personnel of all ranks were already seated. After waiting for several minutes a Flight Lieutenant entered the room, walked to the dais at the front and pulled down a large map of the world, and marked up to show all the places to where the RAF flew.

'Good morning, everybody,' he began, 'I am here to brief you on our flight plan for today's flight to Singapore. The aircraft will be a Comet and the entire flight including refuelling stops will be twenty-four hours.'

There was a stir in the room when the word 'Comet' was mentioned, and I must admit I was surprised, for I didn't know the RAF were using those aircraft.

'The first refuelling stop will be Nicosia in Cyprus, the second will be at Karachi, Pakistan and the last one at the RAF Katunayake Base in Ceylon (Sri Lanka).'

The Flight Lieutenant then went through the safety procedures; where the emergency exits were, how to put on life jackets and how to inflate them if we had to ditch in the sea; where the oxygen masks were and the correct position to adopt if we were to crash land either on land or in the sea. Nowadays with air travel so much an accepted part of life, these instructions are so commonplace that I doubt if the majority of air travellers listen to them, but to me, who had never flown before, these safety instructions rather put the fear of God into me.

The Flight Lieutenant ended his briefing by reassuring us that:

'The RAF has flown more than a million servicemen around the world, and we have never lost one yet, and we don't intend to do so now. However, due to technical reasons there will be a four-hour delay before we take off. There is food available in the canteen, but I would ask you not to leave this reception area, as the flight could be called earlier. Okay, any questions?'

After the briefing, as the Flight Lieutenant hadn't as yet left the room, I got into conversation with him and asked him about the aircraft.

'Aren't Comet IIs only strengthened versions of the original Comets that crashed?'

Yes,' he agreed, 'They have rounded cabin windows instead of the square ones, where metal fatigue caused cracks to appear in the corners of the windows. When BOAC sold us these aircraft, they warned us not to fly above a ceiling of 24,000ft, and to give each aircraft a thorough visual inspection after every twenty-four hours flying time, but we don't pay too much attention to that.'

That's very encouraging I thought, so I asked him what the reason was for the delay.

'Oh, there's a problem with the emergency braking system.'

I suppose it was the, probably misplaced reputation that RAF fighter pilots had during the Second World War of having a 'devil may care' attitude that I wondered whether this also applied to Transport Command. But I felt reassured that if they were concerned about the emergency braking system, they must have a more responsible attitude. My reaction was probably typically that of an ignorant 'brown job'.

~

Many years later I was on a flight out of Aberdeen airport to over-fly the North Sea Brent oil field. The aircraft was an elderly four-engine turbo-prop one and as we approached the oil field, I asked if I could go up to the flight deck to film our approach. The captain agreed, and I was amazed at the size of the so-called flight deck. It was so small, with just room for the pilot and his co-pilot. The windscreen had self-adhesive, but cracked coloured plastic sheets stuck over the windows to cut down on the glare. The grey haired pilot seemed to be fighting the controls, so I asked him why he wasn't flying on 'George'. He managed to lift one hand off the 'joy' stick just long enough to point a finger at a lever marked 'Auto Pilot' with a label stuck across it, stating in large letters 'U/S'. I then noticed the compass also had a 'U/S' label stuck across the dial, just as there were on several others. I asked the pilot what he had done before his present job. He explained that he had been a RAF fighter pilot. On our return leg via the Shetlands, where we over-flew the oil terminal at Sollum Voe, he demonstrated his flying skills round the coastlines of both the Shetland and Orkneys Isles, at times flying below cliff height, and almost standing the aircraft on one wing as he threw it into tight turns. It was exhilarating and most of which I captured on film.

~

We managed to get some food in the canteen, but whilst we waited for the flight, there was very little to do except chat amongst ourselves, read some magazines or try and get some sleep. Eventually at around 1800hrs we were told the aircraft was ready, and we were bussed out to the Comet in its RAF livery, gleaming in the evening sunlight. I boarded the aircraft and found myself a seat at the rear of the cabin. I didn't know what to expect, and I was pleasantly surprised as to how well appointed and comfortable the interior was. The aircraft was not full, and as the pilot obviously wanted to make up for the delayed take off, the burly flight sergeant who was going to be our flight attendant, wasted no time in once again going through the safety procedures and checking that we had firmly belted ourselves up.

It was a lovely summer evening. The aircraft climbed rapidly and smoothly, banking to the South, and from my window the whole panorama of the English countryside was spread out below me like a patchwork quilt, and looking absolutely beautiful in the evening sunlight. The fields were a vibrant green, but where the harvest had not as yet been gathered they were of pale gold, but where it had been, smoke could be seen rising from burning stubble. Trees and hedgerows stood out in a darker green with villages nestling in the Somerset and Wiltshire valleys. In the distance I could see the sprawling mass of the city of Bristol and even further in the distance as the aircraft climbed ever higher, the waters of the Bristol Channel shimmering in the evening sunlight. This being my first flight, and thus the first time I had seen the English countryside from the air, the beauty and peacefulness of rural England really struck home to me, and even before we had crossed the coast I was beginning to feel a little homesick.

We were soon over the English Channel and as the sun gradually sank in the west, the coastline of France was bathed in the last rays of the sun as it gradually sank below the western horizon. France quickly became a dark mass, and to those on the ground, we must have appeared as a fast moving evening star, with the sun's rays reflected from the polished surface of the aircraft.

We had been in the air for almost half an hour, when the two flight sergeants passed down the cabin handing out cardboard boxes. This was our three course evening meal. Although there were no facilities on the Comet to serve hot food, or alcoholic drinks, the RAF nevertheless did us proud on the quantity and quality of the cold meals they provided on every leg of the flight. The burly flight sergeants, who could not have begun to compete with attractive air stewardesses, did their best to ensure that we had an enjoyable flight. However, this being long before the introduction of in-flight entertainment, there was nothing really to pass the time except read and try to get some sleep. On each leg of the flight, the aircraft captain kept us fully informed of our progress, by passing round an information sheet, which gave details of height, speed over the ground, estimated time of landing, weather details and other information, which he felt we would find of interest.

About five hours into our flight, we began our descent to Nicosia airport, where we landed at 0100hrs local time and as we descended the steps from the aircraft, the warm scented Mediterranean night air greeted us. The transit lounge where we waited whilst the aircraft was refuelled was deserted, dingy and rather depressing. The small bar was open, where a rather surly Cypriot, who obviously was not best pleased at having to stay open at that ungodly hour, got his own back by having the nerve to charge 4/6d (23p) for a small bottle of local beer. In my imagination, I did wonder whether he could possibly be an EOKA agent, who not only passed information back to his superiors on the arrival and departure of British troops, but also the monies he made for grossly overcharging for the bottles of beer. We impoverished National Service subalterns, unanimously decided to boycott the bar and refused to buy any beer, although the other ranks, who appeared to be on a better pay scale than we were, were quite happy to fork out the 4/6d for their beer. We were not sorry, when after ninety minutes we were called forward for boarding and the next leg of our flight down to Karachi.

Once in the air again, the flight sergeants handed out further boxes of cold chicken and salad, and as we hadn't filled ourselves up with beer at Nicosia, this was most welcome. After about an hour I managed to get off to sleep, which was not too difficult, the Comet being such a quiet aircraft and the flight was, up to this point a smooth one.

It seemed that I had hardly shut my eyes, before I was woken by the rays of the morning sun flooding into the cabin and right into my eyes. I had had about three hours sleep, and it was only a short time later at around 0700hrs local time that we began our descent to Karachi International Airport. We ran into a fairly serious tropical storm, which caused the aircraft to 'bounce' up and down for several hundred feet at a time as we continued our turbulent descent. The lower we got, the hotter the cabin became. I have subsequently flown many times, but I have never experienced such a roller coaster descent. Sweating like a pig, I never knew how I managed to hang on and not have to reach for the brown paper bag. I was very thankful when we touched down and taxied in to what appeared to be a rather depressing airport. Even though it was raining, as we stepped onto the tarmac, the oppressive heat hit us, making it difficult to breathe, until we became used to the hot and sticky atmosphere. Everything seemed to be composed of grey tones. A grey sky, grey tarmac, grey earth and grey airport terminal buildings. The Pakistani Immigration officials were very thorough, and closely inspected our International Smallpox and Cholera cards. We had heard that Karachi was not the healthiest of places and disease was fairly widespread. We had certainly been warned not to drink the water, as 'gippy' tummies were very common. As we walked through the airport entrance hall, stallholders selling all sorts of knick-knacks and souvenirs pressed in on us from every side. We were glad when we had run the gauntlet and moved out into the open air. 'Open Air!' That was a laugh, - hot, sticky and smelly. What a depressing place. Emaciated beggars clad only in loin-cloths, assailed us from all sides and holding out their hands begged for alms for the sake of 'Allah'. What an introduction to what, I supposed could be called 'The Mysterious East'.

We were bussed through the outskirts of the city to the BOAC Rest Hotel, where, in comfortable surroundings, we enjoyed a full, but somewhat greasy, traditional English breakfast. This was a very pleasant surprise as I had envisaged that we would be confined to the airport transit lounge, with stalls only selling local Pakistani food, but which would, nevertheless have made a welcome change from cold chicken salad. From what I could see from the bus that ferried us to and from the Hotel, the outskirts of Karachi looked very dreary and grey in the cloudy, wet conditions. There were rows of decrepit hovels, pot holed main roads with few cars, but many single-deck buses, vying for precedence on the road with the multitude of oxen carts led by skinny loin-clothed Pakistanis. Even the palm trees looked tatty. I was certain that there must have been more attractive parts of Karachi, but we were unfortunate to have driven through, what was at the time, possibly one of the least salubrious areas.

It is always unwise to make a judgement on first impressions, and the wet conditions and grey skies did not help, but from what I saw on our short stopover, I felt that there was a fair degree of poverty, and I also felt sad that there was a gulf between the western world and what I supposed could have been described, at that time, as possibly a third world country; but which certainly no longer holds true. I was however glad when the refuelling and the servicing of the aircraft was finished; and although I appreciated the breakfast, I was thankful when we had boarded the Comet with a new crew, taken off and left Karachi behind. It was a relief when we broke through the storm clouds into brilliant sunshine, leaving the turbulence behind as the captain set course for our five-hour flight down to Ceylon (Sri Lanka). The aircraft was beginning to feel like home.

We had been up in the air for about two hours, when the flight sergeants passed down the cabin once again handing out cardboard boxes containing the standard RAF cold chicken salad. Whilst we ate, I had time to muse on what I would find when we landed in Singapore. Except for knowing from a map where Singapore and Malaya was, I had absolutely no knowledge of the country or its people. I was aware that Sir Stamford Raffles had something to do with Singapore's past, just as I was aware that the Japanese had invaded and occupied both Malaya and Singapore in 1942. I had read somewhere that we had built a large Naval Base on the Island, and also that large calibre guns had been installed facing south, as it was expected that if Singapore were ever going to be attacked, any invasion would come from that direction, but certainly not from the north. Rumour had it that the guns could not be traversed through 180 degrees to face mainland Malaya; although I was sure I had also read that this was not true. The real reason apparently, was that the ammunition for the guns was armour piercing for firing against ships, whereas to counter an attack from the mainland, high explosive shells were needed, of which there were none.

It seems ridiculous now, but in August 1959 I had no idea how civilised Singapore was. Was there mains electricity? What were the buildings and roads like? Was the Island as poor as Karachi had appeared? Were there many private cars? Was it still a British Colony or had Singapore been granted independence? If so, what sort of government was in power? These and many other questions passed through my mind, and I wished whilst on embarkation leave I had done my homework and learnt more about the Island. My knowledge of Malaya was even worse. I knew, from the ambush training we did with Captain 'Jungle' Jim at Battle Camp, that there was a kind of war, called 'The Emergency' going on in the country. I had heard of the Malacca Straights, an island called Penang and a town called Kuala Lumpur, and that was about the sum total of my knowledge, which I realised as I stared out of a port side window of the aircraft, was woefully inadequate.

As I looked out of the window I could make out the west coast of India far below us. I understood that as a military aircraft with military personnel in uniform on board, we were not permitted to over-fly India, but instead we had to take the long route to Singapore via Ceylon. We seemed to be flying at a great height and whilst I was thinking about this, the Captain's information bulletin was passed over to me, and what caught my attention immediately under the heading 'Altitude' was the figure of '42,000ft'.

'Bloody hell,' I thought, 'what did that flight lieutenant say back at the briefing at Lyneham?' That BOAC had stipulated that Comet IIs should not be flown above a ceiling height of 24,000ft; yet here we were with the Indian Ocean some eight miles below us. Perhaps the aircraft captain had misread his instructions about a ceiling of 24,000ft and thought they had stipulated a maximum height of 42,000ft.

As a first time flyer, I was beginning to feel rather nervous and worried, for as I looked back out of my side window, I could see the horizontal tail fin constantly flexing up and down. As I had studied metallurgy at College, the words 'metal fatigue' flashed into my mind.

At the precise moment I was studying the tail fin, an alarm bell sounded in the cockpit, which could easily be heard throughout the length of the cabin as there was no door to the cockpit, only a curtain which had been drawn back to leave a clear view into the flight deck. Immediately the 'No Smoking' and 'Fasten Seat Belts' sign came on, and one of the flight sergeants came pounding down the length of the cabin and disappeared towards the rear of the aircraft. After a short time he reappeared and went forward to the cockpit, only to reappear once again with a torch in his hand. When he was opposite me, he knelt down, and the thought did flash through my mind that perhaps he was going to pray; but no, he lifted a hatch up from the floor and disappeared from view, torch in hand. After a few minutes he reappeared, fixed the floor hatch back in place, before returning to the cockpit. The 'No Smoking' and 'Fasten Seat Belt' signs were switched off, and the flap appeared to be over. The Flight Sergeant, sweating and breathing rather heavily came back down the cabin and sat down in an unoccupied seat on the opposite side of the aisle from me.

'What was that all about?' I asked. 'It sounded rather serious.'

'Not really, Sir,' the Flight Sergeant replied. 'For some unknown reason, which we have never been able to discover, on almost all the flights with this particular aircraft the same fuse blows. It's not serious, but we have to check it out, and go through the proper safety drill, which does make our passengers a bit apprehensive.'

He could say that again, and I was not too sorry, when in the late afternoon, the pitch of the engines changed as the captain throttled back and we began our forty-five minute descent to the RAF base in Ceylon. Although I had no previous flying experience, the Comet seemed to be a marvellous aircraft in which to fly. The engines at cruising height were very quiet, and except for the descent into Karachi Airport, the ride was very smooth.

We were only a few thousand feet up, gradually losing height with the noise from the engines barely above that of a whisper as we flew over the Gulf of Mannar, crossed the coast and shortly after we touched down at

RAF Katunayake and taxied into the terminal building. What a difference from Karachi. We stepped down onto the tarmac to a lovely warm and sunny tropical evening. Everywhere there were palm trees and lush green vegetation. In the distance I could make out jungle-covered mountains, with the highest, which I later learnt was Mt Pidurutalagala rising to a height of 8,200ft. We were taken by bus through the RAF Base, along palm tree lined tarmac surfaced avenues, with the many wooden constructed buildings that went to make up a military base, neatly spaced out, with tropical shrubs and plants such as hibiscus and bougainvillea in full flower. The officers were dropped off at the Officers' Mess; set amongst palm and other trees with a large well-maintained lawn in front. It was really a most delightful spot, and we sat on the veranda thoroughly enjoying our evening meal of steak and chips; and even though we were many thousands of miles from home, the chips in particular were most welcome. I, for one was very sorry when the bus returned to take us back to our aircraft. The RAF looked after us so well, and even after only ninety minutes, I wished our refuelling stop could have lasted longer; for from what little I saw, Ceylon looked a delightful country. But in the gathering dusk, we boarded our Comet for the last time and took off to the east into the night sky for the final four-hour leg to Singapore.

As darkness fell, I tried to settle down for some sleep. The effect of a good meal and only three hours sleep in the previous thirty-six hours, from the time I woke up at Arborfield, and which now seemed such an age away was beginning to catch up on me. I must have gone off, for the next thing I remember was being shaken by one of the flight sergeants, who said as we were starting our approach into Singapore, it was time to fasten seat belts. I looked out of the window and could see pinpricks of lights as we flew down the Straights of Malacca, and then quite suddenly as we banked to port, there on our left in a blaze of light was the city of Singapore – The Lion City. We flew parallel to the waterfront, losing height the whole time. We left the lights of the city behind; the aircraft banked starboard out into the South China Sea and then turned through 180degrees, as the captain lined up the Comet for our final approach into the RAF Transport Command Base at Changi on the eastern tip of Singapore Island. With a final adjustment to the flaps and the throttling back of the engines, there was a gentle 'bump' as the pilot put the aircraft down as if he was landing on glass. The flight lieutenant back at Lyneham was right; the flight including stops took almost precisely twenty-four hours. We stepped down onto the tarmac and even though it was midnight local time, it was still hot and humid with the sultry and scented air of the tropics.

Although the flight, with the exception of the blown fuse incident had been near perfect, I felt somewhat sad as I turned to look back at the Comet, bathed in floodlights as our kit was unloaded, and which had been our temporary home for the past twenty-four hours; but it was still a relief to be on terra firma again, knowing that this was not a refuelling stop.

For a first flight, I could not have been looked after any better, and although I took many commercial flights in the years ahead, there were occasions that I wished I was flying with RAF Transport Command.

~

After documentation, and having gathered up our kit, we hung around the entrance hall wondering whether we were going to be collected, or whether we would have to wait until morning for transport. We were told that the REME Officers' Mess had been informed of our arrival. So I presumed, as we had been delayed for four hours some poor duty driver had to be turfed out of his bed at midnight to come and collect the four of us.

Eventually after nearly an hour and a half, a REME cap badged soldier appeared. Our driver had arrived with a Land Rover and trailer for our kit; and at two o'clock in the morning, we really were on the last leg of our journey to take up our postings for which we had trained for almost a year.

Although excited at finally having arrived in Singapore; as the REME Base facilities were situated on the western side of the Island, at 0200hrs we were so tired that the drive seemed to take an age. Although the driver was prepared to be chatty, I was afraid that we were not in the mood to join in; although we did ask him about one building, lit only by street lights that looked forbidding and rather threatening.

'Oh that's the infamous Changi Jail, where many British POWs were incarcerated by the Japanese Army in 1942.'

With my knowledge of Singapore being so very abysmal, I was surprised not only by the size of the city, but also in the wee small hours of the morning, how much traffic and how many people there were around. One area was particularly smelly as we drove through it. 'This is the Rochore Canal Road, it's always very busy, but you don't want to ask what gets thrown into the canal. The Singapore to Johore Bahru express bus service starts from here.' I was to get to know the bus service well.

On the few occasions that I had been in London after dark, the neon advertising lights in Piccadilly Circus had always impressed me, but I wasn't prepared for the multiplicity of illuminated advertising signs in the centre of Singapore. I felt they rather put Piccadilly Circus to shame. However, we soon put these behind us, and our driver sensing our impatience, told us we hadn't got much further to go; and eventually some forty-five minutes after we left Changi, we entered the main REME Base and drove up through Rowcroft Lines, until the driver stopped outside a low building.

310

'Right, Sirs. We've arrived. This is the Officers' Mess.'

We thanked him, took our kit out of the trailer and walked into the entrance hall of the Mess, where the Mess Sergeant greeted us.

'Good morning, Sirs. We had just about given up on you. Anyway let me show you to your rooms. If you want breakfast in the morning, this is served up to 0830 hrs, with lunch at 1300hrs. But see how you feel.'

We gathered up our gear and the Sergeant took us down a path, and we could see from the camp lights that the Officers' accommodation consisted of a number of wooden huts down from the Mess, which appeared to have been built on the top of a low hill.

The Sergeant pointed out my room, and with a feeling of relief, I opened the door, switched on the light, and got the shock of my life as I saw small lizards darting across the walls and the ceiling. I was certainly not expecting to have lizards, however small they were in my room, and I wondered what other 'nasties' there might have been lurking around. I also wondered how I was going to get any sleep, as the room was very hot and humid. I noticed there was a fan, which I quickly switched onto maximum, and as it gathered momentum, I wondered how I was going to put up with the squeaking from its dry bearings, which appeared to need a very good lubrication service. However I was impressed by the spaciousness of the room, which was furnished with standard W↑D furniture of bed; wardrobe; chest of drawers; easy chair; bedside table with a light; a desk; a rug and something I had only read about in Somerset Maughan's books or seen in films, - a mosquito net.

As it was very hot, I couldn't get out of my battledress fast enough and which now seemed so incongruous in the tropics; quickly stripped down to my underpants and lifting the mosquito net, climbed into bed to find that the bedclothes consisted of a single sheet, which I quickly kicked off. I lay there perspiring freely, trying to get to sleep with the noise of the fan whirling and squeaking above my head; not really cooling the humid hot air but simply circulating it. The mosquito net was probably very effective keeping out mosquitoes; but it seemed to act as a barrier to whatever air was being circulated, and I wondered if I dared lift up the sides of the net to try and get some air movement over me. I decided against it, as it would be most embarrassing to have gone down with malaria within hours of landing in the Far East; and as we hadn't been issued with any Paludrine anti-malarial tablets, there was a danger that I could have been charged for failing to take the daily pill.

Eventually in spite of the noise of the fan, the chirping of crickets, cicadas and other assorted insects, the tension of the last twenty-four hours drained away and the relief that I had arrived safely, took effect and I drifted off into a deep sleep.

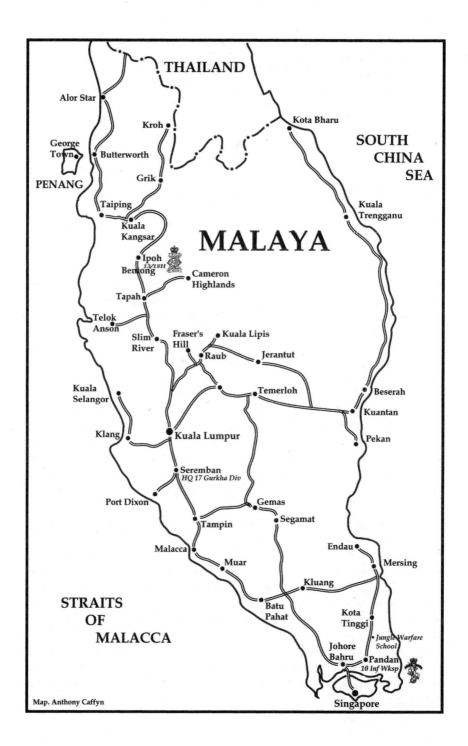

THAILAND

Alor Star

Kroh

George
Town
PENANG

Butterworth

Grik

Taiping

Kuala
Kangsar

Ipoh
13/18H
Bemong

Tapah

Telok
Anson

Slim
River

Kuala
Selangor

Klang

Kota Bharu

SOUTH
CHINA
SEA

Kuala
Trengganu

MALAYA

Cameron
Highlands

Fraser's   Kuala Lipis
Hill
          Raub   Jerantut

Temerloh   Beserah

Kuantan

Kuala Lumpur   Pekan

Seremban
HQ 17 Gurkha Div

Port Dixon   Gemas
                         Segamat

Tampin

Malacca
        Muar   Endau
                         Mersing

STRAITS
OF
MALACCA

Kluang

Batu
Pahat   Kota
             Tinggi

Jungle Warfare
School

Johore
Bahru   Pandan
        10 Inf Wksp

Map. Anthony Caffyn

Singapore

Chapter Thirteen

Up The Sharp End. Well Nearly

Never in my wildest dreams, did I think that I would spend my first day, in one of the most exciting parts of the world fast asleep; but sleep I did. My batman, actually a Malayan houseboy, woke me with the traditional early morning mug of tea and the cheerful greeting *'Tabek, Tuan!'* ('Greetings, Sir!'). I've always preferred coffee, but any thoughts I might have had of becoming a tea drinker, disappeared with that early morning mug of tea. The NAAFI tea was strong enough to put hairs on ones chest, with tea leaves like miniature tree trunks floating on the surface. As there was no fresh milk, the condensed milk together with a liberal amount of sugar made it not only rather sickly, but the relative density of the tea was such, that a teaspoon held upright in the mug, would take some five seconds for the handle to reach the side. For very many years afterwards I couldn't face tea, although later in North Malaya with the 13th/18th Royal Hussars, I did occasionally drink tea with a slice of lime, which I must admit I found quite refreshing.

As the houseboy had woken me up, but nevertheless feeling like death warmed up, I decided to get up and make my way up to the Mess not only for breakfast, but also to check whether there were any orders to report to someone, somewhere, at sometime. But no one seemed to want to take any interest in the four of us, and being a Saturday the Mess was almost deserted. So after a bacon and egg breakfast, I staggered down the slope to my room, already perspiring freely in the unaccustomed humid and hot tropical climate, turned up the fan to maximum, collapsed onto the bed and 'crashed out'. I believe it was Winston Churchill who, when travelling long distances, worked on 'tummy time' and not local time. Subconsciously, I must have been following the same principle, for when I next woke, my tummy told me it was lunchtime, and so feeling hungry I made my way up to the Mess once again; had lunch, retired to my room and went to sleep again. Again 'tummy time' did its stuff, and I woke thinking it must be time for the next meal, and made my way up to the nearly deserted Mess for dinner.

It was obvious that except for subalterns and a few unmarried captains, most of the REME officers were married and lived out of camp. So being a Saturday evening the four of us had the dining room to ourselves. Afterwards, we sat in the ante-room chatting and wondering where we would end up; reading various out-of-date English magazines and getting up to date with the local news in the English language newspaper 'The Straits Times'. There was a very good radiogram in the ante-room, and we had fun playing some of the 78rpm and 33rpm long playing records.

As it was a very hot and humid evening, the windows and doors had been opened, and the lights of the Mess naturally attracted a wide range of insects. There were a number of the small lizards moving at great speed across the walls and ceiling with their tongues flicking in and out and gobbling up small insects. Some of the lizards appeared to have lost they tails. I asked the Mess Sergeant about them.

Chichaks at work and play

'They're house lizards called chichaks and they are very useful for keeping down insects. As you can see they stalk their prey and when they are in striking distance, their tongues flick out and 'bang', one dead and consumed insect.'

'Why have some of them not got any tails?' I asked.

'Well, Sir. If you try and catch a chichak by its tail, it will shed it. Also each chichak has its own territory, and if another one moves into this, it will see the intruder off, and the intruder may lose its tail to the chitchak defending its territory.'

Still suffering from jet lag, we all went off to bed early, and I went to sleep very quickly.

I find jet lag totally unpredictable. This first flight to Singapore, I had no trouble in catching up on sleep; yet on my next trip to Singapore some fifteen years later, I was unable to get to sleep the first night, and went without sleep for some forty-seven hours, which didn't do my golf much good at the Royal Singapore Golf Club; and the third time I flew to Singapore, I suffered no jet lag at all.

So my first day ended very quietly; and I hoped that the following day I would be more with it, and could start taking in my surroundings.

The jet lag had disappeared by the Sunday morning, and I was feeling 'bright eyed and bushy tailed' when I went into the Mess for breakfast; the other three were already there, and I went over to join them, greeting them with a bright and breezy 'Good Morning'. They looked up and mouthed a reply, and I wondered what was going on. I looked around and there were a number of other officers having breakfast in complete silence; most of whom were looking the worse for wear. With so many attractions in Singapore, it was evident that no sensible red-blooded single officer would spend Saturday evening in the Mess. Breakfast on the Sunday was obviously a time of silent reflection and contemplation over the previous evenings social activities.

The mess sergeant had warned us that there was a 'happy hour' before lunch, when the Mess would be full of officers popping in for a drink before they all disappeared to wherever they were having lunch. The influx, like an English rugby scrum in full flow, was led by a large ginger haired officer, who I learnt was Colonel Kinchin, the commanding officer of 40 Base Wksp; one of the two Base Workshops in Singapore, the other one being 41 Base Wksp. As 'new boys' and not knowing anybody, the four of us, just stood in one corner, holding our 'stengahs' (whisky, ice and soda) and listened to the conversation. It was obvious that amongst the REME officers there was a very close 'family' feeling, which civilians, who have not experienced service life, would probably find difficult to understand and accept.

The conversation was full of names of places, which obviously meant nothing to me.

'Well yes, we're off to the Singapore Swimming Club. Their curry lunches are really first class…'

'Personally old boy, the wife and I prefer the Tanglin Club. It's far smaller, more intimate and most of the REME Directorate officers are members…..'

Oops! That sounded like a put down.

'Won't be staying long, as we thought we would take the kids to Mersing this afternoon…'

Where the hell was Mersing? I found out some years later. It was a delightful small fishing town on the East Coast of Malaya, where one could hire a boat out to one of the lovely islands off the coast; one with twin peaks – Pulau (Island) Tioman, which rejoiced in the nickname of 'Big Titty' and where, so it was rumoured part of the film 'South Pacific' was shot.

'Tracey says that our amah is simply dreadful. She feels she can't leave the children with her…'

'Met up with this lovely Eurasian bird wearing a tightly fitting cheongsam at the Cockpit Hotel. She was terrific and we had a great evening…'

'You had more luck than I did. John and I started at the Satay Club and then went on to the 'Happy World', where I tried to chat up what I thought was a lovely bit of Chinese fluff, but John nudged me and whispered 'transvestite'. 'She' looked gorgeous but you can always tell the difference by the size of the neck, men have thicker ones than girls. ..'

'I thought you only found transvestites in Bugis Street...'

I was getting a quick insight into the pleasures of Singapore nightlife.

'Can't remember where I ended up last night, but I remember I downed a great number of Tiger beers. The bloody place didn't sell Anchor beer. I was sick as a pig...'

'We had a quiet evening, ate at Raffles and had a few of their 'gin slings'....'

And then, finally:

'Hello. Just arrived. Tell me is Desmond Lynch still the RSM at Eaton Hall?'

I told him that Eaton Hall had closed down, but assured him that 'Paddy' Lynch was now the RSM at Mons OCS.

'Great guy. Should have won a VC in North Africa, or was it Italy. Mind you he had an eye like a hawk. Could spot a raised eyebrow from yards away. Had me on Adjutant's Parade once for twitching my nose. I wanted to sneeze.'

I explained that he had got me twice.

'That's good, you won't be a proper officer unless you've had your name taken on an Adjutant's Parade by the RSM.'

I felt chuffed about that, as I watched a chikchat, catch and swallow an insect, which did not do much for my appetite. I turned as a voice from behind me:

'You must be new here.'

'Well yes, Sir.' Play safe, I thought, as I didn't know his rank. 'Is it that obvious?'

'Well yes, it is by the way you're watching the chikchats. You see the Navy and the Air Force only do a two year tour of duty out here; but the Army posting is for three years, and there is a saying that for the first year you watch the chichaks, the second year you ignore them, and the third year you go up the wall with them.'

'How long have you been out here, Sir?'

'This is my third year, and I can't wait to get home in six months time.'

He drifted off to talk to another officer, as another one came up to me.

'Have you been posted to a unit yet?'

'No, Sir.'

'Drop the 'Sir'. I'm Peter James and I'm only a subaltern as well. Where are you hoping to get posted to?'

'I don't really know. I'd like to stay in Singapore.'

'Tell you what. I'm the MT Officer at District Workshop. If you're clear tomorrow, walk over the road and ask for Lieutenant James. Okay?'

Just as suddenly as the Mess had filled, so it emptied; and only a few of us sat down to lunch. I very quickly learnt, that the traditional Officers' Mess Sunday lunch was curry, which seemed to me to be a rather odd dish to have in a very hot and sticky climate; whilst back in Britain, on a cold summers day many people would probably have a salad lunch. Some years later in Singapore, I was introduced to a dessert that rejoiced in the name 'Gula Malacca', which was a cold sago pudding served with coconut milk and a thin black treacle sauce, and which at first I thought sounded disgusting; but in fact it was delicious and the perfect antidotal sweet to a hot Malay curry.

~

In the afternoon I decided to go for a walk and explore the area. As I walked down the hill and left Rowcroft Lines named after REME's first Director General, Sir Bertram Rowcroft. I walked along Ayer Rajah Road and was impressed at the vast complex of Army camps; barracks, workshops, vehicle parks, officers' and sergeants' messes, married quarters and bashas for the single soldiers. Pasir Panjang looked as though it was Singapore's equivalent to Aldershot. I was amused to read from the road signs how little pieces of England had been brought here. I noticed Kensington Road, Portsdown Road, Stockport Road and there were many others. I turned into South Buona Vista Road and strolled across Kent Ridge with a stone plaque on which was inscribed: 'By Gracious Consent of Her Majesty Queen Elizabeth II this ridge was named Kent Ridge', following a visit by their Royal Highnesses the Duke and Duchess of Kent. I wandered on to Marina Hill. From there the ground to the west fell away down to the sea. Except for palm trees near the coast, the open ground below me consisted of bushes and rough scrub, and had obviously been cleared of jungle in the not too distant past. To my left between trees I could just make out the tops of one or two pagodas, which I later learnt was the Haw-Par Villa, also known as the Tiger Balm Gardens; full of tableaux depicting scenes, mostly of grisly battle scenes from Chinese mythology, interspersed with grotesque figures, trees and dragons.

Out to sea, I could make out various islands, including Pulau Bukum, with its oil storage tanks, which a few years later the 'Bukum Bombers' tried to blow up. Further to my left across from Keppel Harbour I could just make out the island of Blakang Mati, which was the island fortress guarding the sea approaches to Singapore. Some years later its name was changed to Sentosa, and it became a holiday resort. A war museum is housed on the island, which includes a dioramic tableau of Admiral Lord Mountbatten taking the Japanese surrender in Singapore in 1945.

The area around Pasir Panjang village had once been a rubber estate, but had been decimated in the fierce fighting that had taken place in February 1942, between the 44th Indian Brigade and the advancing Japanese XXV Army in the final defence of Singapore; and this explained the lack of trees around Kent Ridge and Marina Hill.

I tried to visualise what it must have been like in those dreadful days of 1942, and to imagine that the ground over which I was walking was once the scene of bloody battles.

Clouds started to build up; the air seemed to become heavier and more humid, and as I thought that there must be a storm brewing, I hurried back to the Mess before it broke. Walking was not the pleasure that it was back in England, and even after only two days, I found the atmosphere was so oppressive and debilitating that I was perspiring even before I had taken a step. I hoped that this was only a case of acclimatisation and that in a week or two, I would be used to the tropical climate.

A film was usually shown in the Mess after dinner on a Sunday evening; and it was on that first Sunday, in the middle of the screening of a comedy that the storm which had been threatening from late afternoon finally broke, and we were witness to the most dramatic electric storm I had ever experienced; with the City being vividly illuminated by the most brilliant display of almost non-stop sheet lightning. The rain thundered down onto the roof of the Mess to such an extent that the noise completely drowned out the film's soundtrack, and the screening was stopped until the storm had abated. It was certainly an impressive introduction as to what a tropical storm could be like.

~

The four of us had expected to be summoned to the REME FARELF Directorate on the Monday to learn of our postings, but once again it was not to be; and I felt as if we were outcasts, and had become the band of forgotten subalterns who nobody wanted. The only excitement after breakfast and swallowing my daily Paludrine tablet, was to return to my room and to find that my houseboy had moved all my clothes, boots and shoes outside into the open. I asked him what he was up to, and he explained that unless this was done every two to three days, fungus would start to grow on everything. I remembered the advice I was given at Bordon that the same would happen with films, transparencies and camera lenses, and that I must either keep these in a vacuum-sealed container, or to post the films back to the UK at the earliest opportunity.

I decided to take up Peter James' kind invitation to show me around District Workshop; so after an early lunch, I left Rowcroft Lines and crossed over the road, walking past the signposted entrance to 40 Base Wksp, until I came to a smaller one which proclaimed I was now at the entrance to

District Workshop. I went into the Guard Room and asked for Lieutenant James. The duty sergeant directed me towards the MT Park and said I would find him there.

I was very taken with the Workshop, and although I had not visited 40 Base Wksp, I could see it was a very large major unit spread over a wide area; whereas District Workshop was much more compact, and being smaller seemed to have an intimacy and friendliness that was probably missing in its neighbour. I was introduced to the commanding officer, who could not have been nicer, and asked if I would like to come and work for him and I said I would very much like to.

I was however, somewhat confused over the different types of REME workshops. There were Base and Advanced Base Workshops, Command Workshops, Central and District Workshops. Peter James, who was considering signing on for a regular commission, had obviously done his homework on the Corps organisation and history, and did his best to explain the differences:

'Base, Advanced, Command and Central Workshops are basically 4th line static units, whereas a District Workshop, which is also basically a static unit, is a 3rd line unit. Here in Singapore, 40 and 41 Base Workshops carry out heavy repairs and have manufacturing capabilities. They also employ many civilians. We here at District Workshops carry out repairs for the units in the 'District', and anything which is beyond us, is back loaded to either 40 or 41 Base Workshop.'

'Where' I asked, 'is 41 Base Workshop and why are there two such major units in Singapore?'

'41 is situated on the Bukit Timah Road, which is the main highway between Singapore and Malaya; and was set up to ease the pressures on 40 Base Workshop due to the work-load coming from 'up country', as a result of the expanded number of Army units involved in fighting the terrorists in Malaya.'

Peter continued: 'The initial plan for a REME workshop to be set up in Singapore, was to be at the Ford Factory also on the Bukit Timah Road, which the Japanese used as their main repair workshop. But I always thought that was a lousy idea.'

'Why was that?'

'It was in the boardroom of the factory that the surrender document was signed by General Percival, GOC Malaya and by General Yamashita, the so-called 'Tiger of Malaya' of the Japanese XXV Army on the 15th February 1942. I thought it would be very demeaning for a REME workshop to be set up at the place where we surrendered after being so ignominiously defeated. Luckily the plan came to nothing, as Ford wanted their factory back. So Pasir Panjang was chosen as the site for the main REME Base on the island.

319

District Workshop was going to be built elsewhere in Pasir Panjang, but due to various factors it was decided to build it next door to 40 Base Workshop; the only trouble was that this area was very swampy, which first had to be drained and I read, that with the help of Japanese POWs, some ten thousand piles had to be sunk into the ground to support the foundations.'

I was fascinated by Lieutenant James' explanation, and was determined that if I had any input in my choice of posting, I was going to ask for District Workshop, as I felt 40 Base Workshop being so large was probably very impersonal, whilst District seemed to me to be an ideal posting. I had no idea of what was happening 'up country' with the 'Emergency', but I thought it would be wiser and safer to remain on Singapore Island.

I thanked Peter James for his time and set off back to Rowcroft Lines and the Officers' Mess.

~

Tuesday morning dawned and with it the summons for the four of us to present ourselves to the REME Directorate (FARELF), GHQ Tanglin at 1000hrs. Promptly at 0930 hrs a highly 'bulled' Land Rover pulled up outside the Mess, and an immaculately turned out soldier leapt out and threw us a parade ground salute; the likes of which I hadn't seen since Mons OCS. Obviously, I thought GHQ must be very regimental; probably with a surfeit of sergeant-majors and full of 'bull'. We drove down Alexandra Road, passing the British Military Hospital (BMH), and then down Tanglin Road. I noted that roundabouts were known as 'circuses' and I was intrigued by the depth of the monsoon drains running alongside the roads. Obviously not something to fall into on a dark night. We turned left into Middlesex Road and entered into the GHQ (FARELF) complex. This covered a large area; the grounds were immaculately maintained with neatly mown grass, at least what passes for grass in the tropics; flowering hibiscus; bougainvillea; frangipani trees with their

The height of sartorial elegance

attractive scented flowers as well as many other shrubs. As we turned into Richie Road, I noticed many military personnel, immaculately turned out, marching smartly up and down paths from one building to another. They all looked very businesslike; for most of them carried folders under their left arms, which allowed them the freedom of the right arm to salute anybody they passed. 'Oh lord,' I said to myself, 'I'd thought we had left all this bullshit back in the UK.' It brought back memories of all the regimental training we had gone through at Mons, and I realised that it was over four months since I had been on a drill parade. We drove up to a low wooden building, with a sign that proclaimed that this was the REME Directorate (FARELF). I followed the others out of the Land Rover, feeling extremely conspicuous in my new 1944 Pattern jungle green uniform. The dhobi wallah back at the Base believed in the benefits of using plenty of starch in the laundry. My shirt, which had started out with immaculately pressed creases in the sleeves, was fast becoming a shapeless jungle green sweaty mess. My short trousers, which had been starched to such a degree that I could have stood them on the ground and jumped into them, were standing up better to the heat. I always felt stupid wearing the short trousers; they came down to just above my knees, were baggy and with the heavy use of starch they stuck out in front of the rest of my body when I was standing; and they pointed skywards when seated, probably showing more of one's private bits than a kilt. At least the dhobi wallah didn't put starch in my knee length socks.

Well-starched shorts

We entered the Directorate, and were issued with numerous forms to fill in, which virtually amounted to having to write ones' life history yet again on various AF pieces of paper, which looked very similar to the ones we had filled in at our medicals, at Blandford, Honiton, Mons, Bordon and Arborfield. I would have thought that a copy of these would have found their way out to the Far East. On the other hand, I suppose it kept clerks fully and gainfully employed, but it did appear that this was possibly a case of what was to be known as Parkinson's Law: 'Work expands to fill the time available for its completion.'

After we had completed the paperwork, we were shown to seats, where we tried, with the overhead fans doing no more than circulating hot air around the office, to look comfortable and composed as we waited to be interviewed by the DEME himself, Brigadier Henchley. Eventually, it was my turn and I marched smartly, at least I hoped it was smartly into his office and threw him my best Honiton taught salute. He invited me to sit down, and after asking after my father and stepmother, he got straight down to business. I expressed my desire to be posted to District Workshops, but the Brigadier smiled, shook his head and explained that he wanted me to get as much experience with REME units as I could in the eleven months before my National Service finished; and as he didn't believe I would get that experience in Singapore, he was therefore posting me to 10 Infantry Workshop (10 Inf Wksp) in South Malaya. I was disappointed, but all I could do was to thank him, salute and leave his office. In the orderly room a sergeant clerk handed me some papers; from which I read that transport would arrive at the REME Mess at 1400hrs to take me that very same afternoon across the Causeway into Malaya and to 10 Inf Wksp.

~

Although I wasn't aware of it at the time, I later found out that Brigadier Henchley, as a colonel had been DDME to my father in 21st Army Group in North West Europe in 1944, and they had remained friends after my father was demobbed in 1945. I subsequently got to know Douglas Henchley well, and my friendship with Douglas now in his 90s has continued into the 21st century. Some years after he retired from the Army, he became Bursar at the Henley Management College, and I met up with him when I was on a course there. I used to call in and see him and his wife, Persis at their home near Henley on my way home from business trips to Cowley. It was at one of my visits that Douglas talked about his concerns over the future quality of REME officers. He felt that as the Army was being reduced in size; a bright, intelligent and ambitious REME major in his mid-thirties, would look to the REME peacetime establishment and see that, although there were a fair number of lieutenant-colonels in the Corps; there were fewer full colonel appointments; far fewer promotions to brigadier and only one major-general. Douglas was worried that the best officers, and this not only applied to REME, were leaving the Army whilst they were still young enough, and where there were better opportunities, to carve out for themselves and their families, a successful and profitable civilian career; leaving behind those officers who had less ambition and drive. A theory propounded in a book I read many years ago, 'On the Theory of Military Incompetence', by Dr Norman Dixon, who was an ex-British Army Royal Engineer officer.

It is a sad reflection that it has taken over sixty years since the formation of REME for one of their officers to become a three star general (lieutenant-general). The remark by that Quarter-Master General that 'Technical people should be on tap and never on top' has been indicative, I believe, of the long held view displayed by the top brass in the War Office, and subsequently by the MoD, that only officers from the infantry or armoured regiments are capable of filling the top posts in the Army. Officers from all the technical corps in the Army are highly trained, very professional, hold university degrees and they should be in the mainstream of command opportunities. I know of one TA subaltern, who before being commissioned was a skilled vehicle technician, but as she did not have a technical qualification, either an engineering degree or diploma, she could no longer serve in REME. As advanced technology takes over the battlefield, it is even more vital that officers with the right technical qualifications fill the highest positions in the Army.

~

I was really disappointed that I hadn't got a Singapore posting. Although I had only been on the Island for five days, and had not been into the City; I already felt an affinity with Singapore; a feeling that was to grow even stronger on two subsequent visits in later years. I was certain that an appointment to District Workshop would have been a happy one for me, and I was also equally certain that there were many attractions in Singapore that would have appealed to me.

However, there was nothing I could do about it. Back at the Mess I packed up my kit, and went for an early lunch. After an initial awkwardness as a 'new boy', I found my fellow officers to be friendly and approachable.

I felt it most unfair, when some months later an infantry officer told me that officers from infantry and cavalry regiments visiting the REME Officers' Mess, believed that they had inadvertently entered the WOs' and Sergeants' Mess, and that it was only the subalterns who raised the tone. This was, I felt, an example of Army snobbishness, and those officers who made such derogatory remarks did not do credit to their own cap badge. When REME was formed in October 1942, it was necessary to transfer a significant number of officers and senior NCOs out of the RAOC(E); but due to the demands of the Second World War REME had to expand at a very fast rate. To cope with this very rapid expansion, many senior artificer warrant officers with practical workshop knowledge were commissioned to provide a strong experienced cadre for the training of the influx of new recruits. By May 1945, REME numbered 8,000 officers, 160,000 soldiers and 100,000 civilians, compared to the year 2005 total REME strength of just 8,000, in an Army numbering under 100,000.

The remarks concerning the REME Officers' Mess may, on the face of it, have had some validity; but bearing in mind that the major REME units in Singapore were static base workshops, where many senior officers had come up through the ranks in the Second World War, and were commissioned for their technical and mechanical knowledge, and their ability to successfully manage both large numbers of REME craftsmen and local civilian employees. They were professionals and had the ability to ensure that the Corps' major units, in the words of Field Marshall Montgomery, who was apparently a great supporter of REME, '....kept the punch in the Army's fist', which was of such prime importance with the on-going 'Emergency' against the Communist Terrorists. I cannot deny that in Malaya, on an active service deployment, those REME regular officers

I met, who were mainly with 1st and 2nd Line units were younger and had been commissioned from Sandhurst.

~

Although before I flew out to Singapore, I was wondering what the infrastructure was like on the Island and I had been very pleasantly surprised by what I had found; I now asked myself whether Malaya was like Singapore, or whether its infrastructure was more backward. I didn't have long to wait to find out; for promptly at 1400hrs a Land Rover drew up outside the Mess displaying both the Brigade and REME unit signs. I loaded my kit into the back and climbed into the front passenger seat. I asked the driver his name and also about 10 Inf Wksp. John was a National Serviceman, was longing to get home and back into 'civvy' street. With the difference in rank, he was somewhat guarded in his remarks and replied:

'It's not too bad, Sir. It's a bit primitive compared to the workshops down here on the Island. You've got a brand new Officers' Mess though. And at least we can get into Singapore easily.'

'How do you do that?'

'There's a half-hourly bus service from Johore Bahru to the Rochore Canal bus terminal in Singapore. It only takes about half-an-hour, although the buses are bone shakers and have seen better days.'

Conversation lapsed as I was more interested in looking at the scenery. We drove along North Buona Vista and Holland Roads, passing between low undulating hills dotted with palm trees; rough scrub; patches of secondary or primary jungle; a few small rubber plantations and several pineapple farms. We swung left into Bukit Timah (Silver Mountain) village with the island's highest hill at 581 feet. A short distance further on at the 8½ mile post we passed the Ford Factory, and I tried to imagine the drama that took place there on the evening of 15th February 1942. We sped through kampongs (villages) with their open fronted shops, with Malays, Chinese and Indians and their children, and there always seemed to be lots of children, standing and sitting around. I learnt later, that a Malayan husband and wife regarded it as a very bad omen for their marriage if they had no children. The average number of children was six per family.

We drove through Mandai village, round a bend, passing the Woodlands Petrol Storage Depot and then as we rounded a left hand bend, the three-quarters of a mile long Causeway, like an umbilical cord, linking Singapore and mainland Malaya came into view. The road, railway and water pipeline ran side by side across the Straits of Johore. As we neared the Malayan side I could still see signs of the repairs made to the Causeway, after naval depth charges blew a seventy-foot gap in it, as our retreating forces withdrew into 'Fortress Singapore' at the end of January 1942. Later a fellow officer pointed out that the gap was blown at the Johore end, and it did not create too great a barrier to the advancing Japanese troops, especially as the breach was only four feet deep at low tide.

As we drove across the Causeway, I asked John what the large building was sticking up like a sore thumb from a hill overlooking Johore Bahru (JB):

'Those are government offices, Sir. It is known locally as the Kremlin.'

The tower of the building stood out to such an extent that it must have given the Japanese commanders a first class look-out and artillery observation point over to the Straits, prior to their landing on Singapore Island on 8th February 1942. I made a mental note to find out more about the disastrous Malayan Campaign.

'What's the building below the 'Kremlin' between the trees?'

'That's the Sultan of Johore's Palace. It's known as the Istana, which I think is Malay for Palace. He also owns a small zoo up there, next to where you can see the Mosque.'

We drove off the Causeway and into Malaya. I didn't know what to expect, but what I hadn't bargained for was Customs. It hadn't occurred to me that, as Singapore and Malaya were two separate states, there would be border formalities on the Malayan side. As Singapore was a 'free' port, I presumed Malaya needed to control imports being brought into the country. I was at a later date, nearly charged import duty on a slide projector I had bought in Singapore. I got away with it when the Customs official decided that the projector could be used for educational purposes. I tried the same argument at Stansted on my return to the UK, but the British Customs official was not as broad minded as the Malayan one.

Generally military vehicles were waved through without stopping, and John quickly drove through the centre of JB. My initial impression was that it was a bustling town, full of cars, trishaws, bicycles and stalls. The smell of cooking from the food stalls wafted into the Land Rover, and made me realise that I was hungry. John expertly threaded the Land Rover between the various hazards, as we took the road northeast out of JB to Kota Tinggi and Mersing. Some four miles out of town, having driven through rubber estates, we passed Majedee Barracks, the home of a Gurkha Regiment. Another four miles and we entered the village of Pandan, crossed the modern bridge over the Sungei (River) Tebrau and immediately John turned right through the gates of 10 Infantry Workshop. I had arrived at what I hoped was going to be my home for the rest of my National Service.

Chapter Fourteen

10 Infantry Workshop REME

I must admit that my first impression of the workshop was not a favourable one. The buildings were of wood with corrugated iron roofs, many of which had been painted white at some stage in the past, judging from the amount of peeling paint and had obviously seen better days, and which bore no comparison with the relatively modern buildings of the Singapore District Workshop. I was beginning to feel depressed and bemoaning the fact that if Brigadier Henchley had not served with my father, and thought he was doing him a favour by giving me as much experience as was practical in the remaining time left of my National Service, I would probably have ended up in Singapore.

I had to agree with John's comments that it all looked rather primitive. He dropped me off outside the Guard Room and went off to deliver my kit to the Officers' Mess. I 'checked-in', and the duty corporal directed me to a two-storey square building standing a short distance in from the Workshop entrance. This turned out to be the admin block; the ground floor was plaster rendered, although the first floor was of wood but painted in a strong blue colour. It was here that the OC, 2IC and the orderly room were located.

I climbed the external stairs up to the orderly room, a large open plan office with some ten clerks busily typing and carrying out other admin duties. The chief clerk, a WO II got up from his desk and came over to me.

'Good afternoon, Sir. You must be Mr Caffyn. We've been expecting you. I'll take you in to meet Major Rowlerson, the 2IC.'

He led me to an office to the right of the orderly room, knocked on the door and announced:

'Mr Caffyn, Sir.'

Major Rowlerson, a middle aged officer, rose from his chair with a welcoming smile, and after I had saluted him, shook my hand and said how pleased he was that I was joining the Workshop.

'Come and meet the OC.' He knocked on the door to his right, and without waiting for a 'come in', opened the door, 'Mr Caffyn, Sir.'

Major Denys Wood, the officer commanding appeared to be in his late thirties, and as he rose to greet me, I could see that he was a tall slim man. Again I was given a warm welcome, and I was beginning to recover from my disappointment over being posted away from Singapore. The OC and the 2IC questioned me about my training and then Denys Wood announced:

'Now, you will be taking over as the MTO, with responsibility for all the unit's vehicles. Sergeant Ellis is the MT Sergeant, very experienced and I should listen and take his advice.

'Your predecessor is returning home in the next few days, as he has completed his National Service. He will show you the ropes. Now we are not a large unit, and consequently the Officers' Mess is small. The advantage is that it has only just been built and is the one modern building in the Workshop. This site used to be a pineapple-canning factory, but after the end of the Korean War, when the Malayan Emergency was at its worst, 10 Infantry Workshop was transferred here as the workshop to 99 Infantry Brigade. Incidentally, you will need Brigade formation badges. These you can get from the QM, and your houseboy will sew them onto the sleeves of your shirts. I am afraid that you will be the only living-in officer in the Mess, as our establishment is for only one subaltern. I hope you won't find it too lonely.

'Now, as the only subaltern you will not be expected to be the orderly officer every day. The duty is shared out with the Warrant Officers and senior NCOs as well. I think that is all for the moment. Get settled into your room, and I'll bring the other officers over for you to meet at 1700hrs. Okay.'

'Yes, Sir'. I saluted and left his office. Major Rowlerson arranged for one of the clerks to take me over to the Mess. I had a good look round as we walked through the workshop, which was a hive of industry as repairs were carried out on Bedford 3 ton RLs, Austin 1 ton GS trucks, Land Rovers and sundry other soft skinned vehicles that comprised the vehicle establishment of an Infantry Brigade.

My guide led me through a security gate, which marked the rear perimeter of the workshop. Ahead, standing by itself on an area of recently cleared land, was a small, single story building, with the low pitched tiled roof carried over at the front to provide a sheltered open terrace area. Behind was a similarly designed small annex to the Mess. This was the Mess kitchen. Behind this was a six-foot chain link fence, which carried on beyond the end of the Mess down to the river's edge. The jungle appeared to come right down to the fence. The Mess fronted the Sungei (River) Tebrau, which at this spot was some fifty yards wide. To the left of the Mess the river swung to the right, where amongst a grove of palm trees was a small kampong, with fishing boats pulled up on the bank. A Malay, dressed in a shirt and a sarong was wading through the water casting a fishing net. The opposite bank was a dark and dank mangrove swamp, which looked somewhat threatening. I had no idea whether there were any crocodiles in Malaya, but I was not fully reassured, when one of the Workshop staff sergeants in answer to my question replied:

'I don't know, Sir. But we've never seen one.'

I hoped he was right, for there was nothing to prevent a crocodile, or a communist terrorist (CT) walking, if a 'croc' does walk, straight into the Mess from the river. In spite of my fears, the location of the Mess could not have been bettered; for in the late afternoon the rays of the sun picked out the river, making the swamp look less forbidding, and highlighting the palm trees and the kampong. It was a rather beautiful and peaceful scene.

There were two bedrooms, one bath/shower room with a separate loo. The ante-room and dining room were combined. In spite of the heat and humidity, the Mess with the new and squeak free fans at full speed, and with the windows and doors wide open remained relatively cool. The dining table at one end of the room could seat twelve, whilst the ante-room end was furnished with low tables, comfortable chairs and rugs scattered around on the highly polished parquet floor. I felt I was very lucky to be in such a modern and pleasant Mess, although I was somewhat worried about being the only living-in officer. I could imagine evenings and weekends being very lonely.

Shortly after 1700hrs, all the officers came over to the Mess and I was introduced to them. I had obviously met the OC and the 2IC; but Major Rowlerson was due to return back to the UK in a few weeks. His replacement, when he arrived was Major 'Jock' Roberts, a charming and very approachable Scotsman. With the exception of the two majors, the others officers were captains. Peter Berkshire, with an eye patch was stocky and of medium height; Gerry Marsh, tall but with only one arm. The story was, that he was driving down a road in Egypt, with his right arm resting on the open window of the car, when a vehicle came the other way at great speed, and before Gerry could withdraw his arm, the side of the other vehicle smashed into it. George Clarke, tall and with a rather stern expression, but who had a very good sense of humour, and finally John Maskell, who was the RAOC officer responsible for the Workshop's spares requirements.

They made me welcome and I quickly realised that despite my initial impression of the Workshop, the unit was a well run, efficient and happy one, and I felt that I would settle in very easily.

The officers soon left to return to their families, and I was left to my own devices, as Bob, who I was taking over from, was busy packing and filling MFO boxes with his belongings for transportation back to the UK by sea.

~

I was relieved that Bob would not be leaving for some days, for as the 'new boy' to Malaya I felt, for the first few nights, I would have been distinctly uneasy and nervous being on my own; especially when at 2200hrs the rear security perimeter gates were closed and locked, cutting the Officers' Mess off from the Workshop. The only means of communication was an internal telephone link to the Guard Room.

During the 'Emergency', areas of Malaya were designated either 'Black' or 'White'. The former denoted that those areas were not clear of CTs, whilst the latter denoted those that had been cleared of known terrorists. The State of Johore had been declared 'White' the previous January, and I hoped that the authorities were right, for it would have been only too easy for a rogue and unknown CT unit to attack the Mess. Bob and I would have been very 'soft' targets, as our service revolvers were locked away in the armoury. However, despite my fears, I was going to be on my own that first night, as Bob announced he was spending the night in Singapore, and so I sat down to a lonely evening meal, served by the Malay cook/houseboy, who departed as soon as he could, leaving me to my own devices. I read for a short time, but found it difficult to concentrate; so I took to watching the chichaks chasing insects up the walls and the ceiling, with their tongues flicking in and out as they caught and devoured them with great relish. I felt the comment made to me that after two years, one figuratively goes up the wall with them was right; but I also had a feeling being the only living-in officer in the Mess, that this was going to happen to me long before I had even seen one years' service.

The one thing that surprised me was that there was no mosquito net over the bed. I would have thought that this would have been essential, being so close to the river and the mangrove swamp. Mosquitoes and other insects could have easily flown in through the open slotted vents above the door and windows at ceiling height. In fact I never did use a mosquito net at 10 Inf Wksp, although I did resort to burning joss sticks and anti-mosquito smoke coils. Paludrine tablets must have been effective, although I did wonder whether they were more of an anti-malarial suppressant; for over twenty years after I returned home from the Far East, I used to suffer every other year, just for a couple of days with a fever and shakes, but which mysteriously never reappeared after I had been on a safari in Kenya and had taken two different types of anti-malarial tablets.

~

The orderly sergeant unlocked the gate at 0600hrs, to allow the cook/ houseboy through to wake me up with the inevitable strong and thick brew of NAAFI tea, whereupon he retired to the kitchen to prepare a full English breakfast for one.

With Bob not returned from Singapore, I had no idea what time the workshop opened up, and whether there was such a thing as morning muster parade. So I decided to play safe and be in the MT Section by 0800hrs. This was a wise move, as I found that, in order to avoid the hottest part of the day, work started early, and the place was fairly buzzing when I arrived. Thanks to the overhead signs, I found my way to the MT Section without any trouble. As I walked into the 'office', a large shirtless fair-haired man, without a beret, rose to his feet and came to attention. I couldn't blame him for his state of undress, for even at this early hour it was already hot and sticky. I noted from his wrist strap that he was a sergeant.

'Good morning, Sir. You must be Mr Caffyn, our new MT Officer. I am Sergeant Ellis, your MT Sergeant.'

No wonder he was perspiring freely; I thought that he really needed to take some weight off.

'Good morning, Sergeant. You better brief me on what our responsibilities are, and as I know virtually nothing about running a MT Section, I shall have to rely upon you to help and advise me. So let's get started.'

'Well, Sir. We look after all our own vehicles. These are the Bedford RLs, the Austin fifteen-hundred weight trucks and the Land Rovers. Oh, we do have a couple of Austin Champs, which nobody likes, as they are sods to work on. Then there are the recovery vehicles. We have two 6x6 petrol and one 6x4 diesel Scammells, and a very old Austin K9 Gantry, which isn't much use except for lifting purposes when we are on exercise. Finally, being a mobile workshop, we have the specialist vehicles, such as the machinery, the instrument, the wireless, the welding and the electrical ones, as well as the spare parts trucks. I suppose in all we have about forty vehicles on our strength. The Bedfords, the fifteen-hundred weights, the Land Rovers and the recovery vehicles are in regular use, but the specialist workshop ones are only used when we are on exercise; but they have to be maintained in full working order, and have to be ready to move out at a moments notice.

'Now, each vehicle has its own logbook, which records its full history of usage, maintenance and repairs.' The sergeant learnt over his desk and pulled out a long green folder. 'Now this is the logbook for the OC's Land Rover, and you can see that everything is recorded here. Every time one of vehicles is out on a job, the driver has to fill in a worksheet, listing the journey and timings. You've probably noticed we have our own POL (Petrol, Oil, Lubricants) point, and no driver can draw fuel without written authorisation. We virtually run a shuttle service with 221 BVD (Base Vehicle Depot) RAOC up the road at Tebrau, either collecting spares or returning items that have been written off as BLR (Beyond Local Repair). Annually we have the REME CIV inspection on all our equipment and vehicles. This is something we dread, and requires a lot of spit and polish for weeks before hand. If we get a bad report, this reflects on the OC, who obviously passes his displeasure down the line. Fortunately it's not due for another nine months.'

I mentally worked out that the next one would be due in May and, bugger it; I would still be at 10 Inf Wksp for it. I well remember the panic that had set in at No 2 Trg Bn Honiton, when their annual inspection was due.

Sergeant Ellis continued for some time explaining the intricacies of running a MT Section. He made it sound horribly complicated, but upon reflection I felt that he was 'talking–up' his job, as I would probably have done if I was in a similar position. But he did rather play down one other responsibility the Section had, and which in reality turned out to be the most difficult, and this was to provide transport and drivers for the OC, the officers and other personnel. I was always surprised by the number of valid journeys that had to be made each day; and it required the skill of a juggler to have the right number and type of vehicles in the right place at the right time with the right drivers, and to ensure that these returned to the Workshop at their designated times, ready for the next assignment. There were times, when I was so stretched that I had to make use of the OC's Land Rover and driver, and just pray that a message wouldn't come down from the Orderly Room informing me that the OC wanted his Land Rover and driver ready at such-and-such a time to visit REME Directorate in Singapore or Brigade HQ at Kluang. I had some very narrow squeaks, and if the OC's driver had been delayed returning from some legitimate errand I had sent him on; I would no doubt have been in the proverbial mire, and the sergeants would probably have been toasting me in Tiger beer for getting them off the orderly officers' duties for a week or two.

After Sgt Ellis had finished his briefing, he took me on a walk-about around the workshop, and I was impressed by the standard of our own vehicles. They were all clean, with the paintwork in good condition, as were the REME unit and brigade signs on the front wings and the backs of each vehicle. The wheel nuts, and various electrical accessory and towing attachments were clearly painted in white, red, yellow or black depending upon their function. The vehicles were obviously being maintained in good order, which helped reduce the hassle when preparing for the annual CIV Inspection.

~

I noticed that all the officers, including Bob were sporting a purple and green medal ribbon. I asked him about it.

'Oh. It's the General Service Campaign Medal, and it's awarded to everyone who has, and is still serving in Malaya whilst the 'Emergency' is still on, as it is regarded as an active service posting. Yours will come through in time. Actually, there's quite a bit of hassle about the medal. There are many of us who have spent a considerable amount of our service time in Malaya, fighting to defeat the CTs, and I believe we fully deserve the award of the GSM. But it makes me feel sick to see senior officers, who are only on flying visits to Singapore, flock across the Causeway, to spend twenty-four hours in Malaya, just to qualify for a GSM. Anyway I'm going into Singapore this evening. Do you want to come? There's a family, the Chaplins I want to visit, who have been very kind to me, and have treated me like one of their family. Actually, I've been going out with Angela their eldest daughter. Her father is a Royal Navy lieutenant at the Navy Base. I'm sure they won't mind me bringing you along, and I can explain I'm showing you the 'fleshpots' of the city before I return to the UK."

I readily agreed to his suggestion.

Bob arranged for a taxi to take us into JB, where we caught the Johore Bahru – Singapore express bus into the city. 'Express' was the right description. The driver stopped for neither 'man nor beast'. The horn was definitely the most overworked piece of equipment, and probably needed replacement on a weekly basis. However, replacing the vehicle's road springs and shock absorbers was obviously of very low priority. The bus, and I travelled on many of them in the coming months, was an absolute boneshaker. Although they ran every half an hour, they were invariably packed with every race imaginable, - Chinese, Indian, Malay, Tamil and usually one European, - me. The smell was fairly overpowering, which I eventually got used to and also to crushing cockroaches underfoot. There was simultaneous non-stop chatter going on in several tongues, invariably conducted at high volume.

I always enjoyed the bus journeys, and the locals did not appear to be at all fazed by having an Englishman in their midst. The only thing I could not get used to was the spitting, even though there were signs posted throughout the bus stating 'Spitting is Forbidden'.

The Singapore bus terminal was in Rochore Canal Road, which was a bustling centre for Chinese stallholders and shopkeepers. The smell from the canal was overpowering, and I was always glad to get away from the area and walk towards the centre of the city.

Bob decided to get a taxi from the terminal to River Valley Road where his friends, the Chaplins rented a flat. They were absolutely charming, made me very welcome, and insisted that I should visit them when I came into Singapore. I was soon to take them up on their kind offer.

It did not take me long to be fully conversant with the duties of the MTO.

It was not a very arduous job, and the OC was right; Sergeant Ellis had everything under control. I was always prepared, without pulling rank to run any errands, such as visiting the Hong Kong and Shanghai Bank in JB. I had an ulterior motive for this, as my office was, without doubt the worst in the Workshop. It backed directly onto the river and being tidal, at low tide on a hot steamy afternoon, the dank and miasmatic smell from the mangrove swamp, together with whatever garbage and debris was floating downstream, and which permeated into my office, was enough to drive a man to drink. How Sergeant Ellis put up with it, I do not know. After two years, he probably was inured to it.

The bank run was the one I particularly enjoyed. I was accompanied by one of the Workshop staff carrying a Sterling sub-machine gun, whilst I had a loaded revolver in my holster. The bank itself was well guarded, as there were at least two Sikh armed guards on duty at any one time, caressing their twelve-bore shotguns and no doubt hoping for trouble.

~

One afternoon, when I hadn't been long at 10 Inf Wksp, John Maskell, our RAOC officer asked whether I might like to accompany him, as he had business to conduct at 221 Base Vehicle Depot (BVD), Tebrau, a few miles north of Pandan. The depot was a very big one and was the main vehicle storage base, certainly for all the units in Singapore District, 99 Gurkha Infantry Brigade Group and possibly 28 Commonwealth Infantry Brigade Group up north as well. There were rows of not only the 'B' echelon soft skinned vehicles, but also the AFVs (armoured fighting vehicles), such as the WWII Daimler Armoured Car (DAC), the Ferret Scout Car, the Saracen Armoured Personnel Carrier (APC), and the Saladin Armoured Car, which was just coming into service to replace the DAC.

When John had finished whatever business he had to conduct, we retired for a drink at the RAOC Officers' Mess. This was situated near the top of a hill, and we sat outside on the terrace with our stengahs in hand, watching the sun slowly sink in the western sky, which I hoped would give us one of those lovely and colourful tropical sunsets. John was joined by one of his RAOC friends, who appeared to be in a rather philosophical mood, and apropos nothing in particular, suddenly broke into our conversation.

'You know the 'Emergency' is coming to an end. The CTs are on the run, and most of their top people have been killed, captured or driven across the border into Thailand. Those that are left are being hounded from their bases deep in the jungle. They have been cut off from their food supplies and are getting no support from the local people. Of course Chin Peng is still at large.'

I was very interested in what I was hearing. I still knew very little about the background to the 'Emergency', and I felt that here was a chance to learn all about it, and the measures that had been taken to defeat the Chinese Terrorists.

'Who is Chin Peng?' I asked. 'I've just arrived out here and I know very little about the 'Emergency'.'

David, for that was his name, looked towards the setting sun with a distant look in his eyes. After a moment or two, he cleared his throat and in the style of a university lecturer, he began:

'The basis of the 'Emergency' really goes back to the Second World War when the Japanese invaded and occupied Malaya. A group of British Officers stayed behind in the jungle to harass and attack the Japanese wherever possible. This was the nucleus of Force 136 and they recruited Chinese communists, who hated the Japanese for invading China in the 1930s into helping them. The Chinese formed themselves into 'The Malayan Peoples' Anti-Japanese Army'. We armed them and trained them in jungle warfare; but those who were 'in the know' realised that after the war, the Chinese communists would probably turn their guns against us, and attempt to turn Malaya into a Communist State.

'And that is precisely what happened; for after the end of the war 'The Malayan Peoples' Anti-Japanese Army' was re-named 'The Malayan Peoples' Anti-British Army'. Chin Peng is the leader of the Malayan Communist Party. He believes in the Mao Tse-Tung theory of rural revolution; that to win control of a country, it is essential to win control of the rural areas first; then the urban areas would become isolated and implode. I believe it's Robert Thompson, an Englishman in the Malay Civil Service who has developed the 'Domino Theory' which is, if one country falls to Communism, the next one to do so will be its neighbour and so on. We've seen what happened to the French in Indio-China, and if the Communists were to take over Malaya, then it could be Thailand, Laos, Cambodia, Vietnam and probably Singapore and then Indonesia. That is why it has been so important to defeat the CTs in Malaya.'

'Are there only Chinese in 'The Malayan Peoples' Anti-British Army'?' I asked.

'Basically, yes. As I've already said 'The Malayan Peoples Anti-British Army' grew out of 'The Malayan Peoples' Anti-Japanese Army', who were mainly Chinese.'

'But why the Chinese, when there are several other races in Malaya?'

'I believe it is due to the Chinese character. However many years or generations they have lived in Malaya, Singapore or any other country; they still regard China as being their 'home', and if they have seen that 'home' become a Communist State; then it must be right for other countries, through revolution to overthrow their elected governments and become communist as well. However, Chin Peng did change the name to the Malayan Races' Liberation Army, to try and attract Malays and Indians to join his terrorist organisation but with very little success. Am I boring you?'

'Not at all,' I replied.

'By June 1948 Chin Peng was ready to start his revolution to forcibly remove the British from Malaya, many of whom ran the tin mines, the rubber estates, the police and the Civil Service. They and their families would be murdered and those local people who worked for the British would be terrorised, also possibly killed, and who the CTs contemptuously referred to as 'Running Dogs'.

'The first shootings took place on rubber estates at Sungei Siput, north of Ipoh, where the estate manager, Arthur Walker was shot. Police stations, tin mines and rubber estates were attacked, and the CTs would then disappear back into the jungle. Fanatical hard core CTs were particularly strong and active here in Johore. Their leader was Goh Peng Tun, who was a particularly nasty piece of work. He would fill a sandbag with iron spikes fixed to a trip wire, and when the leading soldier in a jungle patrol activated the trip wire, the sandbag would swing down and impale the second soldier. He would also set up an ambush and fix hidden pointed stakes right in the place where he knew soldiers would debus from their vehicle. It was at Kluang some miles north from here, that Goh had taken a man who he knew had helped the police, pegged him out under the blistering hot sun to be eaten by ants, and brought his wife to the man, and sliced open his wife's pregnant stomach in front of him. It was atrocities like this that forced civilians, through fear to help the CTs with food and information. It was only earlier this year that this part of Johore was declared safe and designated a 'White Area'.

' What happened to Goh, and how many CTs are there?' I asked.

'Goh was killed in a massive RAF bombing raid on his camp. When the 'Emergency' started there were about fifteen hundred hard core terrorists, which was the same number as there were in 'The Malayan Peoples' Anti-Japanese Army'. But there were also thousands of Malayan Chinese Communists known as the 'Min Yuen', who were not active, but lived and worked at every level of Malayan life. They supported the CTs by providing food and information, usually through the many hundreds of thousands of Malayan Chinese who used to live in squatter camps on the fringes of the jungle, and who also either supported the CTs, or were terrorised into passing on the food and information about the security forces.

'Although the Army's strength was rapidly built up, including the Gurkhas, the SAS and units from Australia, Fiji and New Zealand; a very important decision was taken early on, namely that the armed forces were to act only in support of the civil power, as the Government realised the importance of winning the 'hearts and minds' of the local population. Although the Army has played a major part in the campaign against the terrorists, the Police Force and the Special Branch have borne the brunt of the fight against the CTs. As you travel through Malaya you will see lots of new villages, where four hundred

thousand Chinese squatters have been relocated with proper facilities and security. This has resulted in the CTs having had their food and information supply cut off.

'In 1951, they actually ambushed and killed Sir Henry Gurney, who was the British High Commissioner on his way up to Frasers Hill, a hill resort north of Kuala Lumpur.

'We got much better in jungle warfare, and brought in Iban Dyaks, head hunters who are skilled in jungle tracking. We have also won the 'hearts and minds' of the aborigines, who live in the deep jungle in the mountains running down the spine of the Country. 1952 was the year in which the fighting peaked. One of the more unpleasant tasks was that every dead CT had to be brought out of the jungle, usually slung between two poles, to be identified by the police. You can guess what condition the dead CTs must have been like in our hot, steamy and humid climate, after a patrol had spent several days coming out of the jungle. The Ibans had a much more practical solution; although I don't believe that they were allowed to practice it; and that was to only bring the head of a dead CT, wrapped up in a sack, to the nearest police station.

'Also a scale of payments was introduced to those who provided information which directly led to the capture or killing of CTs. Payments were also made to terrorists who voluntarily came out of the jungle and gave themselves up. This became more and more effective as the CTs were driven further and further into the jungle. With little food their morale, except for the fanatical hard core, sank lower and lower, as they came to realise that Chin Peng's revolution was doomed to failure; with an ever increasing number of CTs walking out of the jungle and surrendering.

'Lieutenant-General Sir Harold Briggs and General Sir Gerald Templer were probably the two men who achieved the most in the fight against the CTs; the former as Director of Operations and the latter as High Commissioner, they implemented the policies that have been so successful in defeating them. In fact General Templer was given the nickname of 'The Tiger of Malaya'.' (This I thought was unfortunate as the Japanese General Yamashita was given the same nickname after allied forces were driven out of Malaya in 1942). *'However, as well as keeping the military pressure up on the CTs, he strongly believed in winning the hearts and minds of the local population and especially delivering what the government promised; so that the CTs, the Min Yuen and the Chinese squatters realised that democracy worked. When Templer left in 1954, the worst of the' Emergency' was almost over.*

'But, it was granting Malaya full Independence in 1957, which was probably the final straw for the CTs, as they could no longer claim they were fighting to get rid of the European Colonial Power; for we are leaving, not under pressure, but of our own free will and in our own time. Having given the Malays their independence; at the request of the Malayan Government the

Commonwealth Forces are still operational in order to finish the job of completely defeating the CTs once and for all.

'I'm sorry if I've gone on too much, but there's a lot to tell and it's been a long war spread over twelve years, with many civilians, security and armed forces, killed and wounded. And whatever you may hear to the contrary, it's been a war. Most of the rubber estates and tin mines are British owned and their insurance cover, placed through the London insurance market, is for loss of stocks and equipment caused through riot and civil commotion, but would not have been covered in a civil war. If the 'Emergency' had been officially called a war, then the insurance policies would have been declared null and void, and the many compensation claims against the Government could possibly have ruined the Malayan economy'.

I realised that David had only been able to give a brief outline of the 'Emergency', but he had whetted my appetite to learn more about it. John Maskell was in a hurry to drop me off at the Workshop on the way to his home and family; for as happens very quickly in the tropics, darkness had already fallen, and the mosquitoes and other insects attracted by the lights, were starting to become very active.

~

The briefing I had received from David could not have come at a more appropriate time, for very shortly afterwards, in early September we started to prepare for the Workshop's annual exercise, which would take us out of our static location.

As a 2nd Line Brigade Workshop, we were expected to be fully mobile and combatant to support 99 Infantry Brigade, wherever it moved to; and although it was very unlikely to be relocated in Malaya, there was always a possibility, as the 'Emergency' appeared to be winding down, for the Brigade to be moved elsewhere in the Far East or even to the Middle East. So an exercise to test the Workshop in its mobility role made perfect sense, and for several days prior to our departure, a great deal of work was carried out by all sections of the Workshop. The MT Section ensured that all the transport we were taking was serviceable and fully operational. I did not want to see any vehicle breaking down within just a few miles of Pandan.

I asked Major Rowlerson where we were going to, and he showed me on the map a place called Beserah, a few miles north of Kuantan on the East Coast, which was halfway up the Peninsula. I asked him how we were going to get there.

'It's going to be a long haul. Unfortunately, on the East Coast the Kota Tinggi road finishes at Mersing, and from there through Endau up to Pekan, south of Kuantan; some one hundred miles, there is only a laterite track. There are seven rivers to cross and no proper ferries. So, we've got to take the long way round, travelling up the main west coast road to Seremban, which is the headquarters of 17 Gurkha Division, and then on up to KL (Kuala Lumpur), before turning east through Bentong and Temerloh and eventually to Kuantan. Beserah is about eight miles north of Kuantan. You will find it's a good trip. I wish I was coming with you.'

'You're not coming, Sir?'

'No. Someone has to stay behind to mind the shop, and I'm due to leave for the UK within the month. Major Roberts will be coming though.'

I looked the route up on my map and estimated the distance was over four hundred miles. Although the main roads were good, I doubted with the number of vehicles in the convoy that we could average more than twenty miles in the hour, so we would be travelling, if we didn't break up the journey for nearly twenty-four hours.

The day before we left was one of frantic activity loading up all the trucks, not only with personal kit, but ensuring that the specialist workshop vehicles carried all the equipment that might be needed by a workshop on the move, but which at the same time, at any location still had to function as a fully operational repair workshop.

~

We set off at first light, which was about 0630hrs. We were a convoy of some thirty vehicles, and as it was an Army standing order that vehicles should not travel head to tail, and cause traffic chaos, sufficient gaps had to be left between each vehicle to enable civilian cars, buses and lorries to pass in safety and with the minimum inconvenience. Consequently our convoy stretched over several miles as we proceeded north at a maximum speed of 40mph.

I was interested to see that the exhaust pipes of civilian lorries did not come out low down at the back of the vehicle, but were taken up behind the cab; which was just as well for the health of those travelling behind, for from the amount of black smoke and exhaust fumes that were emitted, most of the overloaded trucks were obviously badly serviced and maintained. I was also fascinated to see that there was invariably a man in the back of a lorry perched just behind the cab, who seemed to be armed with a jemmy or similar instrument, which he would use to bang on the roof of the driver's cab to warn him of an overtaking vehicle. I was told this practice started during the Japanese occupation, and was used to warn drivers of approaching Japanese Army vehicles.

The road north to Seremban wound its way through endless rubber plantations; most of which appeared to belong to the Dunlop Rubber Company, and as we drove past these estates, we could see Tamil speaking Indian tappers at work, either cutting new 'v' grooves in the bark of the rubber trees, or else collecting the latex from small cups attached to the trees. The British were responsible for starting the Malayan rubber industry, with seeds smuggled out of Brazil, germinated at Kew Gardens, exported and planted in Malaya. The drive north, at our slow speed was rather boring and I felt that when I had seen one rubber estate, I had seen the lot. Occasionally, the immaculate serried ranks of rubber trees were broken up by padi fields, usually near kampongs (villages), with their wooden houses and shops set back from the road. Between the buildings there would often be a row of drooping dragons-blood trees, with their overhanging branches nearly touching the ground. Occasionally, as we drove through a kampong, a very nasty smell would waft into the cab of my Land Rover.

'Phew!! What's the hell's that stench?' I asked my driver the first time.

'That's the smell from the durian fruit, Sir. It's meant to be very good for you, but I've never tried it. The smell puts me off.'

The smell of the durian fruit was only matched, by the revolting smell of sheets of latex lying out in the open to dry.

Driving through kampongs broke up the monotony of rubber estates; the children would stop whatever they were doing and cheerfully wave at us, and if we had to stop for some reason, would race up to the trucks begging for money, chocolates or sweets. Some begged for cigarettes, knowing that British servicemen received a free tin of fifty cigarettes every week. Lord Nuffield apparently started this custom in WW II for soldiers who were on active service, and was continued after the war, at least up to the end of the 'Emergency' in Malaya. I used to give my tin away, as I couldn't get on with full strength Capstan cigarettes in the hot humid climate, but instead smoked menthal filtered Consulates, which I found much cooler.

In all the kampongs, there would invariably be skinny looking chickens pecking away for food; that is if they were allowed to and were not being chased by equally skinny looking 'pye' dogs. At one end of most kampongs would be the police station, usually the most impressive looking building in the village. To one side an odd shaped Heath Robinson type armour plated vehicle would be parked, with slits for the driver and vehicle commander. These were APCs (armoured personnel carriers) extensively used by the police during the Emergency.

As we drove north, we passed through New Villages, where Malay Chinese squatters had been relocated. The Malayan Government had provided the timber for the villages, and laid on electricity and decent sanitation. A high double row wire fence surrounded each New Village, with watchtowers at intervals along the perimeter fence. Entrance gates would be closed at dusk. The relocated squatters were responsible for their own security, and the penalties were high if they continued to actively support the CTs. However, these New Villages succeeded not only in cutting off the food supply to the terrorists, but equally as important, prevented them getting into the Kampongs and terrorising the villagers. The facilities in these New Villages were better than the Malay Chinese squatters had been used to in their hovels, and proved to them that the Government delivered on their promises. The relocation programme was an important step in winning the hearts and minds of the rural population.

I had hoped that I could have taken my turn driving, just to break the monotony. But I was given to understand there was a standing order forbidding officers to drive military vehicles and rumour had it that it was a court martial offence if an officer crashed a vehicle whilst at the wheel.

Eventually, after a long tiring day, we camped some miles south of KL, ready for an early start the following morning, as the OC wanted to be through the City before the rush hour started. As a consequence my first visit to the Capital of Malaya was made in darkness, and I was unable to see in the breaking dawn anything of the centre of KL. We took the Bentong road out of the City, and very soon we had left the coastal plain and, after passing the Batu Caves, a tourist attraction, we started to climb up into the mountains, which run down the spine of the Country.

In some twenty miles we were to climb from the coastal plain up to nearly three thousand feet at Bukit Tinggi. The road zigzagged for several miles, with the dense, dark and threatening jungle pressing right down to the road. I was relieved that this area had been declared a 'White Area', for at the height of the 'Emergency' the miles of double bends must have been a natural for CT ambushes. Our poor heavily laden workshop vehicles, in the lowest gears with over revving engines and in serious danger of overheating, groaned, creaked, and complained as they were coaxed by their perspiring drivers up to the pass at the top between Gunung (Mountain) Sempah on our right at 3,952ft and Gunung Ulu Kali on our left at 5,820ft. This was not the highest mountain in Malaya; Gunung Tocken in Pehang State, at 7,186 was the highest. Legend has it that this mountain is made of diamonds and is guarded by devils; a story believed to have originated due to the quartz crystals, which could be seen gleaming through gaps in the jungle. But maybe it was the gold shining in the sunlight, as gold is mined in Pahang State. At last, after what seemed an eternity, with the sun well up in the sky, and the heat and humidity building fast, we started on the downhill run to Bentong. I was not looking forward to the return trip through the mountains.

We made a stop at Bentong, which gave me a chance to wander through the main street. It was a busy and bustling place. The shops were gaudily painted with their neon name signs in Malay, Chinese, Indian or English. Most of them seemed to be run by Chinese, and even in Bentong, which could not, by any stretch of the imagination be described as the centre of the universe, there were shops selling the latest wirelesses; record players; still and ciné cameras; wristwatches and jewellery, which to the younger generation were regarded as status symbols. Every shop seemed to have a wireless playing at maximum volume. Chinese shopkeepers played Chinese music; Indians played their music and the Malays theirs. It all added up to a total ear-piercing cacophony of discordant music. There were many stallholders selling fruit and groceries; whilst others were Malayan, Indian or Chinese food stalls. The smell was appetising and I felt very hungry, especially as the previous evening's meal and our breakfast in the morning had come from our 24hr composite (compo) rations. Children, skinny 'pye' dogs, cats and chickens roamed freely. However I was rather put off not only by the sight of cockroaches scurrying freely between the stalls, but also by wizened old men with brown betal stained teeth and chins chewing the betal nuts, which they then spat out onto the pavements, or wherever was convenient. Some of the street vendors, attracted custom by knocking and rubbing two pieces of bamboo together, which surprisingly produced a most attractive and melodious 'clacking' sound. I stood watching one street vendor, absolutely fascinated by the tune he was producing with his two pieces of bamboo, which he then passed to me and invited me to have a go. All I could produce was a very flat and tuneless noise, which nevertheless had the street vendor and others near-by in fits of laughter.

All too soon it was time to 'mount up' and set off on the next part of our journey to Temerloh. Having once got through the mountains, we made good progress the forty-six miles through Karak to Temerloh, which we reached late morning. We drove into the town, round and down a left hand bend and there before us was the Sungei Pahang, at 260 miles the longest river in the country. In 1959, there was no bridge, although preparatory foundation work was in hand to build one. Some eighteen months later, I read in an English newspaper that the bridge foundations had been washed away when the river was in flood following very heavy rains. The only means across the Sungei Pahang was by ferry and the river at this point, some hundred miles up stream from its mouth, was still fairly wide. There should have been two ferries, propelled by a motorboat lashed to one side of each ferry; but one was unserviceable. Each ferry could take a maximum of two lorries, two cars and numerous cyclists at one time. However, as there was a lot of civilian traffic, it was going to take some considerable time for all our vehicles to be ferried across.

About a mile outside the town on the far side of the river, was a straight stretch of a recently built road, and after we had crossed the ferry, we parked along this stretch until all our vehicles were across. The sun was almost directly overhead, and I have never experienced such suffocating heat. For about a hundred yards on either side of the road, the jungle had been cut back and the only shade was underneath our vehicles; but this afforded very little relief, as the road surface itself was almost hot enough to fry an egg. For over two hours we had to wait there until the last vehicle had crossed the ferry; and if we had the supplies, we could have set up a nice little business frying and selling eggs on the bonnets of the workshop vehicles. That is, if any of the locals were foolish enough to venture out 'in the midday sun'! Although the noonday temperature was probably not much over 100° Fahrenheit, the humidity was very high, and with no wind, the air we breathed was hot and stifling. It seemed to be so much hotter than back in Pandan.

It was one of the longest two to three hours I have ever experienced, sweat poured off me and by the time we moved on, my shirt was wringing wet. The relief on our faces was palpable for all to see, as the last vehicles joined us, and we could continue once again on our journey to Kuantan. However, there was one further torture to endure, and especially so for the drivers. The vehicle cabs were like ovens, with the seats almost too hot to sit on; but the steering wheels were blisteringly hot, and our poor drivers suffered for several minutes once we had started moving, before they cooled down.

We still had some ninety miles to cover to Beserah, and fortunately for most of the first thirty miles to the town of Maran, the road had been rebuilt, with gradual gradients and gentle bends, which we were able, as the traffic was light, to reach, at our convoy speed of 40mph within the hour. But all too soon we were back on the old narrow road, which wound its way tortuously around the jungle-covered foothills of the eastern side of the central mountain range. As we left the West Coast and climbed over the mountain range, we had also left behind the rubber plantations, but were now in an area where forestry was the main industry, and we passed several timber mills on the road through to Kuantan. There were some four hundred sawmills in 1959, with most of the felled timber being for internal use; but there was apparently a flourishing, if small export market. I was horrified, when I returned to Malaya in the mid-1970s, to see vast tracts of forest had been cleared of timber, which must have had some effect on the ecological balance of the environment and the wild life. Malaya is such a beautiful country, that it made me sad to see man destroying so much of its natural beauty purely for financial gain.

After we left Bentong, we had entered a 'Black Area', and had been issued with live ammunition. Those who had been in Malaya for some time were definitely blasé over carrying ammunition; whereas I, as the 'new boy' to the country was somewhat apprehensive about the need in certain areas to be armed; especially as the 'old sweats' took pleasure in regaling me with stories of some of the more horrid acts of terrorism carried out by the CTs during the height of the 'Emergency'. So after we had left behind the modern road at Maran, being in the back of my Land Rover, I kept a sharp lookout to both the left and right of the road, as it wound its way up and down jungle covered hills and round sharp left and right bends. I was trying to remember what Captain 'Jungle' Jim had taught us about anti-ambush techniques back at Battle Camp, but which seemed to be so long ago as to be in a different century. I worried about what my reaction would be if we were ambushed, and I had to open fire with the specific aim of shooting to kill another human being, even if he was doing his best to kill me.

The reality was the CTs had been so decimated, that in 1959 there were very few active ones still left, and these had become totally disillusioned and demoralised, as they were forced deeper and deeper into the jungle, without food and medical supplies. They were hardly in a position to mount an attack anywhere; but with my lack of experience, I found it difficult to accept this and felt there was always an exception to the rule.

In the year I spent in Malaya, there were very few reports about CT sightings, but one I do recall was a report in 'The Straits Times', that an army major on leave at a friend's rubber estate, was out shooting game one day, armed with his 12-bore shot gun, and came across a CT amongst the rubber, and promptly captured him; when all the CT wanted to do was to surrender!

Before we reached the East Coast we had to cross the Sungei Kuantan, a few miles short of Kuantan itself. This could only be done by ferry, and I had visions that the crossing would be a repeat of the one at Temerloh, and it would take a further two to three hours to get the Workshop vehicles across. Fortunately, although still hot and humid, the excessive heat that we had experienced at Temerloh had decreased, and so the ferry crossing might not be so bad; although I was sure that it was still going to take a long time. However, as the ferry closed down at dusk and as the OC did not want to split the Workshop on either side of the river, he decided that we should harbour for the night before we reached the ferry, and so we made camp on the edge of the Kuantan airstrip.

For these overnight stops, we did not bother to set up officers' and sergeants' messes, and as we had all been issued with 24hr compo rations, we were responsible for preparing our own meals. The compo packs varied, and it was always interesting to open up one's pack, and see whether you had cornflakes or porridge, Irish stew or steak and kidney pie, or beef curry with rice, and chocolate or boiled sweets. A certain amount of swapping took place. As the name suggests, we had to make our compo rations last the twenty-four hours, and plan accordingly for breakfast, lunch and the evening meal. The main courses were in self-heating tins, so one was always guaranteed a hot meal, so long as the self-heating system worked. Bearing

344

in mind the limitations of the packs, I found they did the job they were designed for, and I personally thoroughly enjoyed the Irish stew.

It had been a long day, and once darkness had fallen by 2000hrs, there was very little to do, except sit around and chat. But we were tired and all we wanted to do was to roll into our camp beds or bed rolls and get a good night sleep. The officers and senior NCOs had to take a stint as the duty officer, and as junior 'sprog', I was allocated the 0300-0400 hrs slot, which I felt was the worst one; for it meant that having just managed to get off to sleep again, reveille was being called at 0530hrs. For the second night running, I struggled to assemble the camp bed I had drawn from the quartermaster's stores in the back of my Land Rover. We had brought mosquito nets with us, and I managed to string this up from the canopy roof cross-bars. It was quite snug and I managed to sleep fairly well until shaken awake shortly before 0300hrs.

The OC wanted to get going early the next morning, for although the ferry didn't open until daybreak, if we left it too late we would be caught up with civilian traffic, which would delay our crossing. So, although we arrived at the ferry before it had opened, Denys Wood ordered all the drivers to pull into the side of the road nose to tail, in the hope that at least we should be first on when the ferry opened.

It was a grey, miserable and wet dawn, and as we stood by the ramp leading down to the ferry, the rain fell steadily, making a soft hissing sound as it struck the water. The ferry opened for business, and we then encountered the first problem of the day. Normally two ferries operated, a heavy vehicle one, and a lighter one. It was just our luck that the heavy one was non-operational, and every vehicle whether heavy or light would have to take the one ferry, together with cars, bicycles and pedestrians.

However, before the ferry opened, lorries carrying strips of rubber, pineapples, coconuts, bananas and other fruit were forming a second queue in parallel to our one. Agreement was reached with the ferry operator that the operational ferry would take on each crossing one civilian lorry and one military vehicle. We inched forward at a snail's pace, and being at the back of our convoy, I could see the civilian queue getting longer and longer as the morning wore on. This was made even worse by large timber lorries, which being so heavy had to make the crossing with no other vehicle on the ferry.

In the warm rain, I wandered to the front of the queue. On either bank of the river, steel-sheet ramps led down to the ferries, which like the Temerloh ones were built of wood. But instead of a boat attached to one side propelling the ferry, the Kuantan ones was pulled across the river by wire ropes connected to winches, which were driven by slow revving diesel engines. A very slow process.

It took some six hours before my Land Rover crossed the Sungei Kuantan. It was an extremely boring morning and our patience was taxed to the limit; but one thing I was quickly learning, the locals were not to be hurried; life was conducted at their own pace, and we would have to conform to this. Unlike Temerloh, where we waited until the whole workshop was across, the various workshop sections were sent on ahead once they had crossed the river. So, as I was 'tail-end Charlie', I only had one Bedford RL truck with me, when eventually we cleared Kuantan and turning north, we took the main East Coast road, which followed the coast right up to Kota Bharu, the most northerly East Coast town in Malaya before the Thai border. After nearly eight miles we drove through Beserah, a wooden hutted kampong, and just beyond, between the trees I had my first glimpse of the South China Sea.

The rain had stopped by this time, although it was still a grey, overcast and humid afternoon. The road ran parallel and close to the shore for a couple of miles, and even with no sun, it nevertheless looked a most inviting and attractive beach, with rows of palm trees giving onto white sands; although the sea was a dirty muddy colour and rather angry with waves breaking some distance out from the beach. After another mile or two, although the road continued in a straight-line north, the coast curved away, so that there was a hundred yard grass strip between the two. Ahead, one of my MT soldiers waved us down, and directed us right onto the grassed area, which was to be the Workshop's field base for the duration of the exercise. Vehicles were parked under trees around the perimeter. My driver was directed to park the Land Rover in a small clump of saplings and bushes. Everyone was busy. Camouflage nets were being unrolled and draped over the workshop vehicles.

This activity was often accompanied by shouts of:

'Watch it, Bill; there's a bloody snake here,' or 'You can fuckin' climb up here with the camo net; you've just fuckin' knocked off the whole fuckin' tree snake population of Malaya when you reversed in under this tree. The canopy is crawling with them, so you can come up here and fuckin' sort them out.'

Although I wasn't prepared to test them, the pretty rainbow coloured trees snakes were meant to be harmless, and we certainly dislodged a fair number, as the taller Workshop vehicles brushed against the underside of branches as they were reversed into their parking bays. Fortunately, my driver and I didn't have that problem, and by the time, we had draped the camouflage net over the Land Rover and in-filled any gaps with pieces of shrub, it was difficult to spot the vehicle at more than a few yards. As we were on a tactical exercise, we had to dig two man slit trenches, so sited to give the best all-round defensive field of fire. With tree roots spreading in

346

all directions, it was not going to be an easy task to dig the 6ft by 2ft by 4ft deep two man weapon pits, unless we took axes and saws to some of the roots. This probably would not have been popular with the locals, and may have resulted in the Army having to pay compensation to the Sultan of the State of Pahang for causing environmental damage, which would not have looked good on the OC's confidential report. So we just dug eighteen-inch shell scrapes, which did minimum damage to the ground and could easily be filled-in and the surface made good; but tactically would have given us very little protection against a CT attack.

Whilst the others were finishing off their shallow slit trenches, I took the opportunity to explore the area. I never found out who chose this spot for a camp, but it could hardly have been bettered. The grassed area led, through a row of coniferous, palm and other trees down to the soft white sands of the wide gently sloping beach. I could see from the beach that we were in a long sweeping bay with the headland of Tg Galang to the north and to the south Tg Tembeling. There was no doubt that when the sun came out, our camp was sited in a beautiful holiday picture postcard spot. As we were going to remain at Beserah for several days, the officers' and sergeants' messes were set up, and we chose for the officers' one, a spot at the north end of the camp set under trees which, hopefully would provide some shade and be slightly cooler.

I was wondering what to do next, when the order was given to 'Stand-to', and we all burrowed down into our two man shell scrapes, trying to look as inconspicuous as possible with our personal weapons at the ready; but as were no longer in a 'Black Area', all our ammunition had been locked away in the Armourer's truck. After half-an-hour, when darkness had set in, the order to 'Stand-down' was given, and I scrambled to my feet rather stiff and sore and holstered my revolver. At least standing in a slit trench, it is possible to move about to a degree and ease stiffening muscles and joints, but in a shell scrape, wiggling your backside was about as far as one could go, and even that had to be done with caution, otherwise in an hostile location, the enemy could regard the wriggling bottom as a too tempting target!

The workshop cooks had managed to rustle up a decent evening meal, and afterwards we sat around chatting and downing a couple of bottles of Anchor beer, which was the maximum daily allowance when on an operational deployment, and although we were only on exercise, the OC decreed that tactically we should regard ourselves as if we were in an operational situation, and therefore the two bottles per man per day rule was in force.

It was a very pleasant evening, for the clouds rolled away exposing a near full moon, which brightly lit up our surroundings; with the outlines of the palm trees silhouetted against the night sky, and the waves breaking onto the shore were split into a myriad of phosphorescent particles.

Guard duties had been allocated, and each officer had to do his stint as duty officer for an hour. As the junior officer, I was detailed for the 0500hrs to 0600hrs watch, which once again was the worst possible time, as it was going to be difficult to get back to sleep again, as 'Stand-to' was at 0700hrs, just as dawn was breaking.

I decided I needed to sort out my sleeping arrangements. Assembling and dissembling the camp bed I felt was an unnecessary chore; for having slotted it on the floor between the back seats, it was nearly impossible to climb in from the back of the Land Rover without the bed tipping up and depositing both me and itself on the ground. The only way was to clamber onto one of the front bench seats and from there, try and fix the khaki coloured mosquito net to the roof cross-bars of the vehicle and around the camp bed, without it collapsing on top of me in the middle of the night. Then lying down on the bench front seat, I would slide over the backrest and try to get onto the bed. Having done so, I found that I would be lying with my head hanging over the end of the tailgate, and I certainly wasn't very keen in having any local predators, reptiles or inquisitive scorpions carrying out a detailed examination of my head. Therefore, I would have to slide over the back of the front seats feet first and end up with my toes protruding over the tailgate of the Land Rover, which no doubt would be too much of a temptation for a Malayan carnivore to ignore. So somehow having shoe-horned myself onto my camp bed, I would then have reach over to close the tailgate; with the risk that the camp bed's centre of gravity would shift towards the back of the vehicle, resulting in the camp bed tipping up and depositing me unceremoniously on the ground. All this had to be carried out in total darkness, without the luxury of possessing a torch. But having once got myself comfortable, there was the problem of untangling myself for my duty officer stint, and then going through the whole procedure once again when I had finished the hour.

After a great deal of thought, I decided to do away with the camp bed, and instead use the squabs from the bench back seats as a mattress in the foot well of the Land Rover. I tried sleeping with the tailboard up, but couldn't stretch my feet out. I tried tying down the rear end of the canvas hood, but found that it made it too stuffy to sleep, just as did the mosquito net. For the exercise, we had changed out of our starched short trousers and brown shoes into long trousers and jungle boots. So I slept fully dressed with my trousers tucked into my socks, my shirt buttoned up to my neck and with the cuffs of the sleeves fastened around my wrists, exposing the minimum amount of flesh to marauding mosquitoes, and putting my faith in the effectiveness of the daily anti-malarial tablet.

Eventually, having sorted out my sleeping arrangements I went off into a deep sleep; only to be shaken at what seemed a moment later for my duty officer stint. I was sure the ASM (artificer sergeant-major), who was just finishing his duty had picked the wrong officer. But no! I had slept so soundly that it was 0450 hrs and time for me to go on duty. It was pitch dark, and although the ASM had handed over the Workshop torch, I didn't want to use it too much and exhaust the batteries before we returned to Pandan. One of the advantages of being in a hot tropical country with no real change of seasons, and although prevailing north and northeast winds blow from October to April and southwest winds from May to September, we did not have to contend with bitterly cold snow, ice, and gales. So except for regular torrential rainstorms, it was no hardship to sleep out in the open. I decided as duty officer, I should check on the various sentry posts, and hoped I wouldn't find anybody asleep on duty. However, all I succeeded in doing was either tripping over sleeping bodies and being soundly cursed, or bumping into well-camouflaged vehicles. The sentries were all awake and alert, and they all correctly challenged me for the password, whilst shining a torch in my face. This resulted in me temporarily losing my night vision and as I blundered around the camp, I became even more unpopular by tripping over even more sleeping bodies. I even surprised myself by finding a sentry where I didn't think there was one. I was not certain whether he was meant to be there or not. Anyway he gave me quite a shock when he challenged me. However, my hour soon passed, and I took a certain pleasure in waking up the next duty NCO.

I climbed into the back of the Land Rover and tried to get another hours sleep before reveille and 'stand-to' at 0700hrs. I was just drifting off to sleep again, as the first flush of dawn could be seen on the horizon of the South China Sea, when there was a soft 'thump' as something alive landed on the canvas hood of the vehicle. Petrified, I sat up, wondering what was up there as I heard it move towards the back of the Land Rover. I looked round for a weapon, and as I had handed over the torch to my successor, all I had was my .38 service revolver but with no ammunition. I picked this up, and anxiously waited for whatever it was to show itself, which I imagined was going to be a venomous snake. A small pointed head, silhouetted against the dawn, peered down at me from the roof of the vehicle. I lunged at it, waving my revolver and shouted 'Bang, Bang'. Whatever it was promptly disappeared and was probably just as frightened as I was. The next day I watched some tree rats, similar to our grey squirrels, playing around in the trees above my Land Rover, so I reckoned that one of these had been my unknown and unwelcome visitor.

~

I have a fear, but also a morbid fascination of snakes, and having read that there are a hundred and thirty varieties of snakes in Malaya, with the King and Black Cobras being the most dangerous. I had visions that snakes would either be constantly slithering across the ground towards me, or that I would be tripping over them. In fact bar from a snake charmer in the grounds of St Andrew's Cathedral, Singapore and another one with a python wound round his neck outside the Tiger Balm Gardens also in Singapore, the only other ones I saw were in the Snake Temple in Penang. There were times when walking along tracks in secondary jungle and across rough ground, there were rustling noises in the undergrowth, as some form of wildlife slithered away. Some years later, at a Red Indian Reservation in Florida, I witnessed a demonstration given by an Indian on how to handle snakes. He maintained that snakes are just as frightened of humans, as humans are of snakes and given the chance will get out of the way.

However, they will fight if they are cornered and feel threatened. To prove his point he gently picked up a snake, which just wound itself around one of his arms. But when he suddenly snatched up another one and obviously scared it, it reacted by sinking its fangs into one arm. He also maintained that it was possible to tell the difference between a swimming poisonous snake and a non-poisonous one by the position of the head, poisonous ones, with venom in their fangs swim with their heads only just visible above the water, whereas non-poisonous ones hold their heads much higher out of the water. Fortunately I never had to put this to the test in Malaya.

As I was watching the tree rats playing, one of the sergeants came over holding a rainbow snake, which had got entangled in the camouflage netting on his truck. It was about three foot long and beautifully marked and coloured. The sergeant assured me that it was completely harmless, but I wasn't prepared to put it to the test as the poor creature was obviously terrified, and was hissing and spitting at each of us. The sergeant eventually took it some distance away from the camp and let it go.

~

After we had been 'stood-down' the OC announced that being Sunday, there would be no military duties, and we were free to spend the day as we pleased.

The day, in contrast to the previous one dawned cloudless, and it was obvious from the start that it was going to be an absolute scorcher. But in the early morning light, the beauty of Berserah and its coastline was fully revealed; with the green of the grass, the various hues of the palms and other trees; the white gold of the sands, already warming up underfoot from the heat of the early morning sun, and the blue of the South China Sea, with the crests of the waves sparkling in the sunlight as they broke some distance from the shore. But above all, was the feeling of total peace and tranquillity. There was little traffic noise from the road, and no aircraft flew overhead. With the exception of the odd Malay child who came to stare at us, we had the beach to ourselves. This was my idea of what a tropical paradise should be, although the facilities were not quite up to those of a five star hotel with waiter bar service.

The acting cook sergeant announced that our breakfast was ready, and with the exception of the OC, the rest of us settled down, to what we thought would be a breakfast of fruit with toast and marmalade. But the cook sergeant had excelled himself, for from somewhere he had managed to lay his hands on some hen's eggs. We didn't dare ask him where and how he had got them, and what bartering took place for payment. Anyway, we were very grateful to him as we enjoyed our ration of two boiled eggs each.

After we had finished, we sat around chatting, waiting for the OC to appear for his breakfast. It was generally agreed by all the officers, that in Denys Wood we had a very good commanding officer. He was fair, approachable, ran a professional and efficient workshop where moral was high, and with a happy atmosphere. The other officers, who had known him for far longer than I had, were all agreed that Denys should go far in the Corps; which in fact he did, retiring with the rank of major-general.

In the five months that I knew Denys, he gave me the impression of being a rather serious person, with perhaps not the broadest sense of humour, which was possibly more sophisticated than the rest of the Officers' Mess, as our humour was probably more at bar room level.

Anyway, the OC duly appeared for breakfast and attacked his first boiled egg with gusto, and having finished this:

'I say these eggs are jolly good.' Whereupon he brought his spoon down on the top of the second one with great force, but which unfortunately was only very lightly boiled. The force that Denys used to crack open the egg had the same effect as a grenade exploding, as a combination of egg white, yolk and shell flew in every direction, but with the greater part landing on the OC's face and immaculately starched and pressed bush shirt. We had the greatest difficulty in containing ourselves from breaking out into spontaneous and involuntary laughter at the sheer unexpectedness of the incident, as we offered our sympathy and helped clean him up. The cook sergeant was absolutely mortified and was full of apologies. I have always believed that this was nothing more than an unfortunate accident. Denys was too well liked and respected, for anyone to play a trick like that on him. However as he disappeared to change, I was ashamed that we could not contain our pent up laughter any longer. I hoped that the OC did not hear this.

~

The officers' 'thunderbox' was the only object, which although suitably camouflaged, stood out like the proverbial sore thumb and rather spoilt the idyllic surroundings. Still, although somewhat primitive, it was more of a convenience to use, than having to disappear and 'bog' down in the bushes armed with a shovel and sheets of loo paper.

Before it became too hot to walk along the beach bare footed, and having to cover up shoulders and heads against the strength of the sun, as it was possible to get severely sunburnt only in minutes; I wandered along the waters edge, watching tiny crabs scurrying sideways along the wet sand, and disappearing in a flash into the sand as they sensed danger. There was a multitude of seashells on the beach, and their varied shapes and colours of delicate pink, blue, orange, peach and other shades of the colours of the rainbow were incredibly lovely. I managed to scrounge an empty box from the cooks, and spent a happy hour collecting and starting off my collection of seashells to which I later added coral.

The Sunday passed all too quickly. Most of the workshop, myself included spent the greater part of the day swimming. The water was beautifully warm, and as the previous days' storm had moved away, the sea was calm with waves breaking some distance out, where the shallow water started. I wondered about jellyfish and sea snakes, but if there were any around that day, they kept well clear of us. Maybe they had a rest on Sunday! I asked Gerry Marsh about the danger of sea snakes.

'I don't believe there are any here on the East Coast; but it is inadvisable to swim in the sea off Singapore, Penang and particularly off the West Coast of Malaya, where there are many mangrove swamps, which is a natural habitat for snakes and reptiles.'

That's encouraging, I thought. What about the mangrove swamp opposite the Officers' Mess at Pandan?

'There is an Army standing order', continued Gerry, 'that if you do go swimming and are bitten by a sea snake, you must catch it. There are many types of such snakes, all poisonous, and you've got about an hour to get to hospital or a medical centre, so that the snake can be identified and the correct serum injected. To be honest, unless you're near civilisation, there's very little chance of getting the antidote in time.'

I wondered how one went about catching a sea snake after it had bitten you, and if you did manage to catch the snake, how did you know it was the one that had sunk its fangs into you. Sea snakes were obviously a danger, as I often read in the Singapore and Malayan newspapers of people, and especially children who had died from sea snake bites.

Later, I was standing on the edge of the water, looking out to sea when Jock Roberts came up to join me.

'It's beautiful isn't it?'

I agreed with him.

'I find it very difficult to imagine what this was like in December 1941, when the Japanese invaded Malaya. They actually landed up the coast at Kota Bharu on the 8th December. The battleship 'Prince of Wales' and the battle cruiser 'Repulse', called 'Force Z' sailed from Singapore Naval Base to try and intercept the Japanese invasion fleet, but without success. However, unfortunately, enemy aircraft had spotted them. The ships were returning to Singapore, when there was a report of a Japanese landing right here along this stretch of beach between that headland,' Jock pointed to the north, 'and that one there,' as he pointed to the one south at Kuantan. 'It was a false alarm but 'Force Z' under Admiral Phillips decided to investigate, and of course they found nothing; but the Japanese Air Force found the ships, and both the 'Prince of Wales' and the 'Repulse' were sunk out there with the loss of 840 men,' Jock pointed out to sea from where we were standing, 'The ships were sunk in less than two hundred feet of water, and apparently their outlines can still be seen from the air.'

I agreed with him that it was very difficult to imagine what hell the sailors on board the ships went through under the intense Japanese air attack. We stood silently for a minute or two, as if we were paying our respects to those who had perished.

'You know,' Jock continued, 'our credibility, respect and reputation as a colonial power vanished with our defeat by the Japanese in Malaya and Singapore, and it will never return. You've seen what happened to the French in Indo China, and although the CTs are now on the run here in Malaya, in the early days of the 'Emergency', when the security forces were not properly organised, the CTs nearly succeeded in taking over the country. Giving both Malaya and Singapore their independence has helped defeat the communist threat. But what we're seeing, is the demise of the supposed superiority of western culture, and it all goes back to our defeat in 1942.'

That Sunday evening and night was breathtakingly beautiful. The very warm tropical air, the slight breeze rustling the tops of the trees, and the waves breaking on the shore were the only noises. We sat on the beach, enjoying the peace and tranquillity, and watching in the moonlight the phosphorescence on the waves. Words could not describe the beauty and atmosphere of that place.

But reality soon took over. We 'stood-to', guards were posted and the rota for the duty officer stint was decided. Fortunately, I was given a better time of from midnight to 0100hrs, which meant I could get back to sleep when I had finished my hour.

~

Monday morning and we were back to military duties. 99 Infantry Brigade had organised a vehicle flotation exercise to take place on the banks of the river at Kuantan. Half the Workshop was to observe this, whilst the other half prepared the Workshop to receive other units' vehicles and components for repairs.

The object of the exercise was to show that it was a practical proposition to float a Land Rover vehicle across a stretch of water with the minimum of equipment. As we arrived, preparations were well in hand for the demonstration. An infantry platoon had laid out, on a gentle slope down to the river, the canopy from a Bedford RL truck. A Land Rover, with its hood and supports removed, and the windscreen folded flat, was carefully and slowly driven onto the centre of the canopy, which was held taut by a six-man team. The canopy was then wrapped round the sides and the ends of the vehicle, and securely tied down across the top with the canopy ropes. The effect was as if the vehicle had been parcelled up. It was of course most important that there were no holes or tears in the tarpaulin, otherwise water would have poured in and the Land Rover would have ignominiously sunk, which would have been an interesting recovery job. The most difficult part of the operation was pushing the 'packaged' Land Rover into the water, and it took several men to do this. Staff Sergeant Davis, who was my recovery sergeant, was licking his lips over the prospect of having to bring in one of our Scammells to recover one sunken and packaged Land Rover. Much to our surprise and the disappointment of Staff Davis, the Land Rover rode high in the water, and it was an easy operation for three or four men to swim across the river, pushing the vehicle ahead of them.

The biggest problem was getting the Land Rover back on dry land again. The landing spot had to be carefully chosen; shallow water with a gently sloping but firm riverbank. The vehicle had to be pushed well into shallow water, before the canopy was unwrapped, so that water did not flood the engine and electrics. It would have been difficult to drive the Land Rover off the canopy and up the bank, if the river bottom was of soft mud; as the wheels would fail to get a good purchase, and unless the men held the sides of the canopy very tightly indeed, the spinning wheels would wrench this from their hands, and it would end up becoming wrapped round the wheels. The secret was to engage the clutch very gently, with only a light application on the accelerator. The whole operation went very smoothly, and the Land Rover was soon back on dry land again, no worse for its packaged swim.

The word of what the 'mad English' were up to, very quickly spread, and before the exercise had properly started, it seemed that all the local children and half the adult population of Kuantan had come out on every type of transport to witness our exploits. There was almost a carnival atmosphere as the crowd let out 'Umms' and 'Aaghs' in various languages as the operation proceeded.

The demonstration was a success, which was going to stand me in good stead some months later. Not to be outdone, the Australian Army tried to go one stage further than their British counterparts; for I later read an article, where an Australian Army major had come up with this idea of anchoring two wire ropes to one bank of a river; then swim them across to the other bank, hoping there were no crocodiles, where the ropes would be firmly anchored, pulled very taut and parallel with each other, and at the same width as the track of a jeep type vehicle. The wheels would then be removed, and some brave soul would then drive the jeep along the ropes on its brake drums. The article did not record whether this was successful, or whether the Australian Army suffered a sudden and unexpected shortage in its stock of jeeps, as the vehicles and their drivers ended up with the fishes and crocodiles. However, it must have been a fairly spectacular sight if it had worked.

The only other incident of note before we set out on our return journey to Pandan, was a visit by Col Ken Briant, the Commander Royal Electrical and Mechanical Engineers (CREME) at 17 Gurkha Division, Overseas Commonwealth Land Forces (OCLF) HQ at Seremban. Rumour had it that the Colonel had 'gone native' and we had half expected to be sent out foraging for snakes, scorpions, cuttlefish, tripe and chicken intestines, spleens, kidneys and pancreases. Our fears were groundless and Col Briant was quite happy to join us for a meat stew with mashed potato, although we didn't like to ask the cook sergeant what had gone into the stew.

~

All too soon, it was time for us to pack up the workshop, load up the vehicles and clean up the site to ensure that we left this absolutely spotless. The OC decided to send a Land Rover detachment down the East Coast from Kuantan down to Pekan, where the metalled road ended at the ferry across the Sungei Pahang. From there the map showed a laterite road down to Nenasi; but for the next forty miles to Endau, the map only showed a cart track with five rivers to cross, and no indication whether there were any ferries at these river points. I asked the OC if I could join the detachment, which he refused, as he was possibly worried that there would have been insufficient officers left to carry out the night duty, and he might have had to a duty stint himself. So, with the rest of us wishing him 'Good Luck', Peter Berkshire with a couple of Land Rovers set off on his exploratory trip down the East Coast, which in 1959 had very rarely been tried. We had visions, that he would be forced to return; or even worse would get stuck somewhere along the route, neither being able to go forward or backwards, and we would receive a wireless message asking for assistance. As the track followed the coastline, any rescue operation would probably have had to be made from the sea involving the Navy; that is pre-supposing they had any ships left in the Naval Base, which if they had, and they successfully carried out a rescue, would no doubt have given great satisfaction to the Senior Service, at the expense and embarrassment of us 'Pongos'. A signal would no doubt have been flashed to the Fleet proclaiming, 'The Navy: 'One'. The Army: 'Nil'. Still, we would have eventually got our own back, when in 2005, the bicentenary of Trafalgar, 7 Bn REME won the RN Field Gun Competition, the first time the Army had won this since 1907.

Denys Wood had decided on a different route back to Pandan; but first we had to cross the Kuantan and Temerloh ferries once again, which fortunately was carried out smoothly and with the minimum of delay. Shortly after we left Temerloh, we swung left off the main road, onto a smaller metalled road, which gave onto a laterite track and headed south through the small towns of Mengkarak, Triang, Mengkuang and Ayer Hitam, before joining the main west coast road at Bahau. After about half an hour we stopped and pulled to one side of the track for a late lunch break. We were surrounded by thick primary jungle. It was stifling hot, as the jungle pressed in on us from both sides, and seemed to act as a cauldron, which contained the heat in the cleared track area. I did not feel very hungry, and as we had been issued with 24hr ration packs, I decided I wanted to keep the steak and kidney pie for my evening meal, and so I heated up the packet of rice with the curry powder. The result was disgusting, and I had to throw away my culinary efforts. No doubt the monkeys, which we could hear chattering and screaming at each other in the jungle, enjoyed a meal of cold army soggy curried rice after we had moved out.

According to the map the OC was using, the metalled road ended at Triang; but the map also showed there was a track down to Bahau some forty miles further south, which Denys believed, was suitable for trucks. Before we set off, as we were shortly going to enter a 'Black Area', we were issued with ammunition. Although there was very little chance of coming across any CTs, I wished I carried a Sterling Machine Gun; for I felt that if I ever did have to fire my .38 service revolver, the noise of this being fired would probably have been more frightening to any CT, rather than a bullet which could have travelled anywhere in a 180° arc both vertically and horizontally.

The OC was right. After we passed through Triang, the metalled road finished and we took to the laterite track, which was wide enough for the workshop trucks, but was fairly uneven and bumpy, and there was no way we were going to maintain our maximum speed of 40mph. The scenery on either side was most impressive, with multi-hued evergreen trees growing to well over two hundred feet, but with their branches of vibrant green leaves, only growing from half way up their trunks as they competed with each other to catch the sun's rays. Many of the trees had intertwining creepers and vines growing up their trunks, and often these would be hanging down from the trees, and brushing the tops of our trucks as we drove past them. The jungle under this green panoply was dark, dank, smelly, unwelcoming and somewhat menacing. But it was the noise that made the most impression on me. Monkeys were constantly chattering and screaming at each other. Looking up at the trees, I caught the odd movement of monkeys or gibbons swinging from tree to tree, and on one occasion actually caught sight of flying foxes flying from one tree to another. I wondered whether we would see any elephants, tigers, honey bears, civit cats or deer, and hopefully the barking deer with its doglike yelp. But if there were any, they were probably in the deep jungle and would have been put off by the noise of our engines.

Driving through a 'Black Area', I decided to keep a good lookout, although the chance of being on the receiving end of a CT ambush was virtually negligible; but, as in the previous Black Area, in order to relieve the boredom, I mentally worked out the action I would take if we ran into an ambush, and there were plenty of ideal ambush places along the track. After some three hours we came to a more open area, and the OC decided to make camp for the night. On our right there was a mountain range running from north to south, with Gunung Palong some five miles south of us at 2,116 being the highest. After our evening meal, and I did enjoy my steak and kidney pie, as we were still in the 'Black Area', extra security precautions were taken and the sentries were doubled. As dusk fell, the mosquitoes woke up and descended upon us like a hoard of locusts. Even though I had buttoned up my bush jacket, the mosquitoes were ferocious enough to bite through clothing. Although it was a pain to put up, and was stifling to sleep under, just to try and get some protection and some sleep, I resorted to my mosquito net, which proved no deterrent to the mosquitoes. I was detailed to do the officer's guard duty at 0200hrs, which was one of my least favourite hours to be on watch. As well as doubling the sentries, the OC had ordered that no lights were to be shown, noise must be kept down to an absolute minimum, and that weapon magazines were to be checked, to ensure that ammunition had been correctly loaded, but without one 'up the spout' and that safety catches were on. It was all too easy when filling a magazine for the rims of the cartridge to be incorrectly seated, resulting in the weapon jamming, which could have had serious consequences in a fire-fight.

Little did I know how little sleep we were all going to get that night, for at around 2100hrs, it sounded as though World War III had broken out. Unbeknown to us, about a mile away was a battery of the Malayan Federation Army Artillery Regiment. As there was a suspected CT camp some five miles ahead of us in one of the gunungs (mountains), the gunners fired off a salvo of suppressive fire with their 25 pdrs guns at fifteen-minute intervals throughout the night. I don't whether they frightened any CTs, but they certainly scared the living daylights out of us, when that first salvo was fired and we heard the sound of the shells whistling overhead. However, the mosquitoes seemed impervious to the noise of artillery fire, and continued to attack with unabated enthusiasm and vigour. Any meaningful sleep was going to be out of the question.

Even between salvos, the jungle noises were enough to keep me awake. As well as being attacked by the biggest and most vicious mosquitoes I had ever come across; the chirping, whirring and croaking of crickets; grasshoppers cicadas and tree frogs was loud enough to put the world's best symphony orchestra to shame. But in spite of the noise, I must have drifted off to sleep, for the next thing I knew I was being shaken awake for my one hour of duty. As I moved off to check the various sentry posts making sure that they were all alert and awake, I had the shock of my life, and for one moment of sheer panic, I thought the enemy was creeping up on us, as I saw small lights flitting through the jungle. I was about to shout out, 'We're about to be attacked', when one of the small lights flew past the end of my nose, and I realised that they were fireflies. I breathed a great sigh of relief, and realised what I fool I would have been if I had panicked and woken everybody up. Having calmed down, I enjoyed watching them as they zoomed hither and thither in their own choreographed aerial ballet. I managed, in the dark to check on all the sentries, who were alert and in a whisper, challenged me every time. I doubt with the 25 pdrs booming away, that any of the sentries could be anything but fully alert. However, there was some relief from the noises, as the jungle insects and creatures had obviously decided that 0200hrs was past their bedtime, and except for the guns, all was quiet out there in the jungle. At least I hoped it was past their bedtime, and the silence was not due to human presence, as CTs crept unheard up to our position.

With my lack of experience, coupled to a certain extent by fear, the dark had played tricks on my imagination, and I was very glad when, as dawn broke, we 'stood-to' and the days' normal activities started. At least with daybreak, the guns stopped firing which was such a relief. As the OC wanted to make it back to Pandan before dusk, we had a quick breakfast, and ensuring we had left no sign of our presence, we were 'on the road' by 0800hrs. The laterite track continued through the jungle, with monkeys and gibbons warning others of our presence. The track passed very close to the Gunung, which the Malayan artillery had been targetting. We had soon passed through Kampong Ayer Hitam, leaving the Gunings behind us, and shortly before joining the main road at Bahau, we were back again in the main rubber plantation area of Malaya. Once we had driven through Bahau, our speed increased, and with little traffic on the road, we managed the thirty miles down to Gemas, the site of a major railway junction in very short time. Although we still had another 140 miles to travel before reaching Pandan, we stopped and whilst the men prepared and consumed their midday meal, we went to the Government Rest House at Gemas and had lunch there. Many of the larger towns throughout the Federation boasted Rest Houses, which offered clean and simple accommodation. Standards varied, and although the one in Malacca was good; the Gemas Rest House looked tacky and rather tired. Still it was pleasant to enjoy a change of menu.

Although the midday stop turned out to be quite a long one, we still managed to arrive back at the workshop shortly after dusk, to find the East Coast detachment had arrived back a few hours ahead of us. They had had a comparatively easy trip; but as there were no vehicle ferries they needed to use their initiative in crossing some of the smaller rivers, where they had to construct rafts out of whatever material was to hand, but which were strong enough to take the weight of a Land Rover and trailer.

We left the unpacking of the trucks to the following morning, and after ensuring that the men had had a hot meal, the officers disappeared to their homes whilst I walked over to the Officers' Mess, carrying my evening meal with me from the cookhouse, as my houseboy had finished for the day. The guard sergeant locked the gate behind me, and I settled down to eat my supper in solitary isolation. Afterwards I retired to my room, showered, listened to the radio, which my predecessor had sold me, and as we had been out of circulation for ten days, caught up with the news on either Radio Malaya or Radio Singapore, before I lit my anti-mosquito joss sticks and retired to the comfort of a proper bed.

At Tebrau, as well as the RAOC Base Vehicle Depot, the BBC had a World Service station and transmitter situated there, so I could pick up their broadcasts and programmes very clearly, and which somehow made me feel closer to home. The evenings were lonely, and I found, after the early novelty factor, that eating alone evening after evening in the Mess was depressing. Even listening to the radio palled after a while. My only companions were the mosquitoes, chichaks and other flying insects. There was one particularly large bug, the name of which I didn't know, but which I took an instant dislike to, for attracted by my room light, it would fly in through one of the high level slats, and collide with the fan and emit the most ear piercing scream. The nights were never quiet; with the constant chirping of the crickets, cicadas and other vocal nocturnal insects.

In spite of what I had been told, I was always worried that I would open my door in the morning, to find a large and hungry crocodile lying outside and basking in the early morning sun. Fortunately, it never happened. However, I was very shaken, shortly after I had arrived at 10 Inf Wksp, when early one evening, I glanced out of the window at the back of my room and there, waddling past a few yards away was what, in my initial shock, I took to be a small dragon with its forked tongue flicking out, as its grey scaly head and keen eyes constantly moved from side to side, as it searched for food. I was told that behind the Mess there was a family of iguanas. The adults were about four foot in length, grey and scaly with long tails, and to which I became quite attached. But that first sighting, being so unexpected did frighten me.

~

The next few days were spent cleaning, carrying out repairs and servicing our vehicles, and ensuring that logbooks were fully and correctly filled in. Fortunately, we had had very few breakdowns, and those we did have, were quickly put right by the roadside and did not hold us up. Although I initially felt that the Army's vehicle maintenance policy seemed rigid and unnecessarily fussy; it worked, and if the exercise failed to achieve anything else, it did prove that 10 Inf Wksp could effectively carry out its prime function of being the brigade's operational second line workshop, both in a static or mobile deployment.

With Sergeant Ellis's support, I ensured that the MT section vehicles, and especially the Scammell recovery vehicles were quickly back in good working order, and ready for any demands that the OC might demand of the section. S/Sgt Davis looked after the Scammells with loving care, and unless I was involved in other duties, I would accompany him on road test, and I was interested to see that he often drove with his left hand on the gear lever, and I asked why he was doing that rather than keeping both hands on the steering wheel.

He explained; 'I can learn a lot about whether a vehicle has a fault in the gearbox or clutch, by holding my hand like a manual stethoscope on the gear lever and sensing any irregularities; just as I can sense possible faults in other parts of the vehicle through my driving seat. Of course listening to the engine is important, and that is usually the first indication that there is a fault. But I can tell a lot from using a stethoscope, and I can pick up early signs of bearing failure or excessive tappet noise, and even piston 'slap'.'

Staff Davis taught me a great deal about identifying potential vehicle faults using only basic skills, without having to rely upon sophisticated diagnostic equipment. I've often felt that such modern equipment has replaced the traditional methods of vehicle diagnosis, and that today's vehicle technicians, relying upon such equipment, do not have the skills of a previous generation.

~

News that I was a hockey player had reached REME FARELF, and I was called down to the REME Base at Pasir Panjang for a Corps trials match. Although I wasn't given my old college position of left back, nor my Honiton position of centre forward, I was given the right back position, which was okay with me. I must have done well enough in the trial to be chosen to play for the REME team representing Malaya and Singapore. I found hockey a totally different game in the Far East. Back in Britain, being a winter sport, I was used to playing hockey on muddy pitches, in the cold with driving rain, fog and gales; but in Singapore I was playing on hard and dry pitches, which gave a much faster and more enjoyable game. I found the Asians, whether Chinese, Indians or Malays were extremely proficient hockey players with very good stick control. Playing against them certainly improved my game, but when I returned to the UK, the game was never the same, as once again I played in the cold with rain, sleet or snow. The only downside of playing in Singapore and Malaya, was the oppressive heat, and as a result games were played late afternoon, when it was supposed to be a touch cooler. But I felt that this was often an illusion.

~

Shortly after our return from the annual exercise, the OC called me into his office and announced, that for the very first time we were to have two subalterns on the Workshop strength and that Second Lieutenant David Rose would shortly be joining us.

I was pleased with this news, not least because it would be company for me, but for another reason, there would be one more person on the orderly officer duty roster. If it were only the officers who carried out this duty, it would have come round every five days. Fortunately, with the WOs and senior NCOs also on the roster list, my orderly officer duty only came round about once a month. It was not an arduous duty, and with the workshop being so compact and confined, it was not difficult to guard, except perhaps from an attack by my imaginary crocodiles from the mangrove swamps opposite to the officers' mess or by snakes. With Johore Bahru some eight miles away, and taxis not expensive, I used to expect some trouble from soldiers returning from JB the worse for drink, but I never did have any problems on my watch. The only excitement that I experienced was when Peter Berkshire drove into the workshop one evening, and decided to test the fire drill. He and I started a small fire in a safe place and which would not get out of hand. We raised the alarm and then stood back to watch the result. This was somewhat chaotic, with men rushing around like headless chickens, shouting at each other and generally panicking. It was a very good thing that it was not a real fire, as the workshop with all its vehicles, equipment and paperwork could have gone up in smoke. As a result fire drills were carried out at regular intervals over the following few weeks.

One evening, whilst I was sitting reading an out-of-date English magazine, I heard a commotion from the workshop, and being the only officer in Camp, I felt I should go and investigate. A python had been spotted slithering under one of the vehicles. The Sergeants' Mess quickly emptied and the ORs (other ranks) streamed out of their bashas (huts). We armed ourselves with spades, pick handles and any other weapon that came to hand. The poor creature did not stand a chance, it slithered from vehicle to vehicle, until it was cornered with no escape and it turned and faced us, terrified with its head moving from side to side, spitting at us as its tongue darted in and out of its mouth, until it was quickly dispatched. It was a young python, only about six-foot long, and although I don't like snakes, I couldn't but feel sorry for the poor creature as we hounded it from vehicle to vehicle.

I felt relieved that we had killed the snake, as it could have caused quite a few problems if it had been left to freely roam through the workshop complex. However, a few years later I would have held a different view, as the python would have been an asset in keeping down the rodent population in the workshop.

~

Although the Workshop was professionally, efficiently and expeditiously carrying out its primary task of keeping the Brigade's vehicles fully operational, life was really not too onerous. There were times when emergencies arose and the Workshop operated under pressure, but more often than not, there was little stress and tension. Being an operational support unit, regimental duties, such as parades played a very minor role in the activities of the Workshop. Although, I felt that the Workshop had a 'laid back' air about it, I believed that this was a sign of just how good 10 Inf Wksp was in doing its job and how well it was run.

My normal routine, was to read the 'Straits Times' over breakfast, then stroll over to my office; check the vehicle status reports and discuss with Sgt Ellis the servicing and maintenance programme, and find out if there were any particular problems. If there were, my MT Sergeant was so efficient that he had usually resolved these before I needed to be involved. The allocation of the MT vehicles to carry out the daily duty runs, seemed to take the most time, and I would try and do one of these myself. Being the MTO, I, on occasions, unfairly pulled rank and took those which involved driving into Singapore to collect spares or other necessary items.

The officers would foregather in the Mess for a drink, usually 'Jungle Juice' (iced lemonade) before lunch. After lunch, it was back to the MT section to see if any problems had arisen. If there were, they were generally to do with either drivers arriving back late from the mornings' duty runs; or having had 'run-ins' with local car or van drivers, who steadfastly believed that any minor 'shunt' was the fault of the Army drivers, and who in their opinion should not be on the road, as obviously they had not been properly trained. The reality was invariably the other way round. Whatever the reasons, the afternoon schedules usually became totally unscheduled. Some army units, in the hottest part of the day would close down for a two hour siesta after lunch, and then start work again, or play sport when it had cooled down somewhat. However, we continued straight through to 1700 hrs before we finished for the day, and I would return to the Mess, have tea and lie on my bed reading or snoozing for a couple of hours, before taking a shower, changing and eating my solitary dinner. This did not happen every evening, as the family whom Bob had introduced me to before he returned to the UK, kindly took me under their wing, and I would frequently take the Singapore–Johore Bahru express bus service into Singapore to spend the evening with them.

Over drinks one Sunday lunchtime in the Mess, I was listening to Gerry Marsh and Peter Berkshire talking about a Gurkha Religious Festival they had witnessed at the Gurkha Majedee Barracks down the road, and I asked them about this.

Peter started; 'This was the Gurkha Festival of Dashera, which is probably their most important one, but Gerry, you know more about its background than I do.'

Gerry continued; 'The legend of Dashera goes back into the mists of time. A king, Dasarath ruled over the kingdom of Ayodhya. His favourite wife persuaded the king, against his better judgement, as he wanted his eldest son Ram Chandra to succeed him on the throne, to agree that her own son would succeed him. The king's wife even managed to have Ram and his wife, Sita Devi banished for fourteen years into the jungles of Chitra Kut. Rawan, the then king of Ceylon, had failed in courting Sita Devi, who had married Ram instead; so the king kidnapped her whilst Ram was away hunting. Ram pursued Rawan for many years, and fought a great number of battles against him, but without defeating the king and winning back his wife. Eventually Ram turned for help from Danga, the Goddess of War, and promised to fast for eight days if she would give him victory over Rawan. He fasted for the eight days, and the following day he defeated Rawan and was reunited with his wife. That's the legend.'

Peter took up the story; 'The festival lasts two days. The first day is given over to dancing and eating. The 'women' dancers in their long flowing robes move so sinuously and with such grace, that it comes as a shock to find out that the dancers are actually Gurkha soldiers, as women are forbidden to take part in the dances. The second day, and this is the one that is widely known, is the main part of the Festival and commemorates the victory of Ram Chandra over King Rawan. The Gurkhas re-enact the victory by chopping off the heads of ducks, chickens and goats and which symbolises the killing of Rawan's soldiers. The finale, which represents the death of King Rawan, is when an ox is beheaded with one stroke of the kukri, the Gurkhas' knife. It is considered bad luck if the man carrying out the decapitation of the ox does not achieve this in one clean stroke. One of our previous officers actually took a photograph where the ox, still standing, has been decapitated, but the head had not reached the ground.'

After hearing the story I was glad that the Festival of Dashera had taken place a week before I arrived at 10 Inf Wksp, as I felt I would have been far too squeamish to have watched it.

Some weeks later, Peter and I took a detail down to the range at Majedee Barracks for their annual classification on the Sterling SMG. As we drove over an area of open land, Peter pointed out the spot where the ox had been decapitated, and where there were still signs of dried blood on the ground. Whilst I supervised the detail, Peter stood at one end, and to my surprise, produced a German Luger pistol, which took the same ammunition as the SMG. He loaded the magazine, and using an empty cigarette tin as a target, he hit the can eight times out of ten shots from a distance of thirty yards. After the detail had finished their classification, Peter invited me to have a go with the Luger. I had never fired the pistol before, but without any practice, I hit the cigarette tin five times with the other five shots kicking up the sand close around it. I mentally awarded myself a six-inch group. The Luger seemed to be a well-designed and balanced pistol, and to achieve a fifty per cent hit rate with no prior training, proved to me how easy it was to shoot with great accuracy, whereas with the British Army .38 Service Revolver, I had the greatest difficulty in hitting the proverbial barn door at thirty paces. However, the .38 Revolver having a simpler cocking and firing mechanism was possibly more reliable than the Luger.

~

My brother officers were very kind, and the Berkshires and Marshes would often invite me over to their homes in JB for dinner, which made me realise and appreciate what a close knit community the Army was and still is; how they look after each other and even if there is good natured banter between units, such as the infantry being referred to as 'grunts', the RAMC as 'Linseed Lancers', the Royal Engineers as 'The Mud Larks' and the RASC as 'Ally Slopers Cavalry'; when the chips are down they all close ranks.

I was also included in their family weekend outings. One Sunday Peter Berkshire took me with his family up the East Coast just south of Mersing to swim, collect shells and enjoy a picnic lunch. Unfortunately, it was a miserable grey day with light rain, which lasted on and off all day. Peter turned off the main road shortly before we reached Mersing, and bumped down a rough track to the beach. He parked amongst some bushes, where we managed to change into our bathing costumes, with his children leading the way across the rather muddy sand to the sea, which was looking as grey as the sky. Fortunately, the sea was warm; indeed it felt warmer in the water than out, for with no sun and a steady drizzle it was one of Malaya's colder days. The only trouble we had was drying off in the rain and changing back into our clothes after our swim. In spite of the weather it was still a most enjoyable day, and it was kind of Peter Berkshire to include me with his family.

On another Sunday, Gerry Marsh invited me to join his family for the day. We started off at the RAF Officers' Club at Changi. This was a most beautiful place. The Club was situated near Changi Point, on the eastern tip of Singapore Island, which was a favourite spot for the locals. The Club boasted a very large swimming pool, the water of which was so warm that it was a real pleasure to swim in, and I wondered why I ever bothered to swim in the cold sea back home. We sat under sun umbrellas, watching children happily and noisily swimming from the long sandy beach; the yachts of the RAF Club sailing around Changi Point in a competitive regatta, and motorboats making trips to the nearby islands of Pulau Ubin and Pulau Teking Besar. Gerry, even with his one arm was an extremely strong swimmer, and could completely outrace me with my two arms.

After lunch we returned to Singapore City via Punggol Point on the north east of the island, from where we looked across the Straits to mainland Malaya. The kampongs were set amongst palm trees, with many of the single storey 'attap' houses built on stilts, where the 'Kon seletar' (Men of Seletar) lived. They were some of the original inhabitants of Singapore, and known as the 'Orang Laut' (the Sea Men). The whole area around Punggol Point was given over to fishing or crabbing. Fishing gelongs, stood out from the shore. The attap huts were supported on stilts and were reached along a narrow plank supported by nibong palm poles. The floors of the huts were made of netting, which could be lowered or raised. The fishermen lowered nets into the shallow water, and the fish, drifting with the tide came up against the nibong poles, and apparently would not swim through the poles, which were about two feet apart and instead would swim along the length of the poles, until they were trapped in the nets under the huts. We watched for some time, fisherman preparing their nets and hanging them from rows of wooden traps. Fishing was invariably carried out at night and strong lanterns were hung in the huts to attract the fish.

Back in the city, we stopped at Raffles Hotel for a drink, where Gerry was rather concerned as to how his young son should address the barman. It was general practice for waiters and barmen to be addressed as 'Boy' by adults, but Gerry felt, and I agreed with him that it was not right for a ten year old to do so. Unfortunately, we couldn't think of a suitable alternative except, 'waiter'.

Gerry decided that we would finish off the day by visiting the Botanic Gardens, and on the drive there, he pointed out places of interest, such as C.K.Tang in Orchard Road, the Chinese Emporium, with its pagoda shaped roof and eaves, and the two stone lions outside the entrance. Gerry said it was the place in Singapore to buy ivory figurines, woodcarvings and all types of oriental curios. I mentally made a note to do that before returning home.

We left Orchard Road, rounded Tanglin Circus, into the Tanglin District, where GHQ FARELF was situated, and at the end of which we entered the Botanic Gardens, which were founded in the nineteenth century by the then local Agri-Horticultural Society. The Malayan rubber industry started in the Botanic Gardens, as the rubber seedlings, which were bought over from Kew Gardens were planted there, and seedlings from those trees were used to plant out the rubber plantations in Malaya. The Gardens were well laid out, with casuarinas, bamboo and frangipangi trees planted in groups throughout the gardens. The frangipangi were my favourite with their scented white and yellow or pink centred flowers. Each tree was labelled, and the Rain Tree particularly fascinated me, for although it hadn't rained for a few days, water was constantly dripping from its foliage. The lake with its lilies and lotus blossom was a peaceful place; which was in contrast to another part of the garden, which was optimistically labelled 'virgin jungle'. Here a small colony of long-tailed monkeys lived, and although wild, they had no fear of humans, and demanded to be fed with peanuts bought from kiosks. Failure to do this would result in them throwing tantrums and in monkey 'speak', they would launch into such a diatribe of invective language, that one felt compelled to buy a bag of nuts just to keep the peace. I believe that some years later, the monkeys became such a nuisance and menace, especially to young children, that they had to be moved, presumably to Singapore Zoo. At the far end of the gardens was the Orchid House, with every imaginable type and colour of orchid. My interest and love for these plants started in Singapore.

It was a most enjoyable day, but I was sorry that I never did have the opportunity of visiting the RAF Club again. I couldn't thank Gerry and his wife enough for giving me such a memorable day.

Without doubt the social event of my time at 10 Inf Wksp was being invited by the DEME, Brigadier Henchley, one Saturday evening to join a party of young officers that he and his wife were hosting at the Tanglin Club. This was a formal affair. Fortunately, I had been advised shortly after I had arrived in Singapore to get myself a white sharkskin dinner jacket. I was given the name of an Indian tailor at the Naval Base, who not only made my DJ, but within twenty-four hours, had run up a lightweight suit for me as well. As I left the REME Officer's Mess at Pasir Panjang, I hoped that there were girls in the party, for I was big headed or naïve enough to feel that they would find me irresistible in my white tuxedo. I was soon brought down to earth with a bang, as the other subalterns in the party were also wearing white dinner jackets, and being based in Singapore obviously knew the girls, and I felt rather an outsider.

However, it was a most enjoyable evening as we dined and danced into the early hours of the morning. Later that morning I was invited, together with the other officers back to the Tanglin Club to swim and have lunch. The Club was small, exclusive, and being close to GHQ FARELF, its membership was largely made up by senior officers from GHQ, which resulted in there being a rather formal atmosphere.

~

After about two months David Rowe, the other NS subaltern arrived. David had actually been commissioned before me; I took to him immediately, and we got on very well together, which was so important with only two living-in officers in the Mess. As Denys Wood had mentioned, it was the first time that the Workshop had had two subalterns, but no one seemed to know whether this was going to be a permanent appointment, or whether David was posted in to the unit prior to his return to the UK; for it seemed unlikely that I would be posted elsewhere. The OC may have known, but if he did, he wasn't letting on. In the very unlikely event that I was transferred to another unit, I hoped I was replaced at 10 Inf Wksp, otherwise I'm sure David would have found it very lonely living in the Mess by himself.

David hadn't been with us very long, when Denys Wood casually announced at lunch one day that in a couple of days, we would be taking part in a series of young officers' tests at Nee Soon Garrison on Singapore Island, and we had better do some 'swotting up'. Neither David nor I had any idea about these tests, and as none of our fellow officers could enlighten us, we were completely in the dark about what subjects we had to study. So we decided to follow the adage that 'Ignorance is Bliss'.

I never knew who was running these tests, but the Directing Staff (DS) were mainly officers from front line units. If David and I had been given guidance on what the tests were about and what we needed to swot up on, we could have done well. But working on the 'ignorance was bliss' theory, was in this instance a disastrous assumption; for not only did we come bottom of the 'class', but I was never certain whether we actually scored any marks. As an example, I was on one test stand overlooking Blakang Mati Island, which was manned by a captain from the 1st/3rd East Anglian Regiment, and who in a rather superior tone asked me:

'What do you know about 'The Yellow Peril'?'

'Well, Sir,' I replied, 'it's a very nasty disease, and causes the skin and the whites of eyes to turn yellow. It can be caused by hepatitis, and I believe it has something to do with too much bile pigment in the blood. Anyone who has jaundice should stay off alcohol for several months.'

I thought the Captain was about to do himself a mischief. He turned red and his eyes stood out as if on stalks.

'You blithering idiot! I wasn't asking about jaundice. I wanted to find out what you know about the Chinese Peoples' Army. You obviously know nothing about it. Now bugger off.'

'Yes, Sir,' I mumbled. I saluted and took myself off to the next test stand feeling thoroughly dispirited, and aware that I had not only let myself down, but also the Corps. I could just imagine the conversation in the 1st/3rd Officers' Mess that evening; 'Do you know, I had this absolute idiot of a REME Second Lieutenant in front of me this afternoon, and I asked him about the 'Yellow Peril'. He was so ignorant that he thought I was asking him about jaundice, and not about the Chinese Army. Typical Corps subaltern! Mind you I know a lot more about jaundice now.'

I could imagine this story would have been greeted by waves of laughter.

The tests were spread over two days, at various locations around Singapore including Palau Blakang Mati, which we reached courtesy of the RASC ('The Old Wagon Train') boat service, which operated LCMs (Landing Craft Men) from Keppel Harbour over to the island.

My performance was not a total disaster, for on the platoon weapons test, where I was asked to give a talk on how to strip and reassemble a Bren gun, I was in my element as this would have been my 'chosen subject'. I mentally thanked the training I had had in the CCF at school, where we were made to strip and reassemble the Bren blindfolded and which I had not forgotten. I also picked up some bonus 'brownie' points, when asked by a DS officer the lethal range of a hand grenade, and replied that it depended on whether the grenade had landed on hard or soft ground, and if the former, the cap could travel up to two hundred yards. The DS officer seemed suitably impressed that a supporting arms subaltern would know the difference.

The final session was given over to live firing of the recently introduced FN Self Loading Rifle, which was replacing the .303 Lee Enfield rifle. Although it was the first and only time I fired the FN, I did not like it as much as the old Lee Enfield; but appreciated with its larger magazine and auto or single shot capability, that it was probably a more effective infantry weapon, especially against the 'Yellow Peril'!

Whilst David and I waited at Nee Soon Garrison for my Land Rover to come and pick us up, I read with interest prominently displayed notices, warning soldiers about the danger of being tattooed. There were many

Chinese secret societies (Tongs), each of which had its own distinguishing mark. There was, and probably still is, intensive rivalry between each society, and it was not unusual for gangland killings and fights to take place between the Tongs. A soldier, in all innocence may have had himself tattooed with the mark of a Chinese Tong, and could have ended up very dead in the Rochore Canal, killed by a member of a rival Tong.

Shortly after the end of the young officer's test, the OC called David and I up to his office, and gave us a thorough dressing down for the poor showing we had made on the tests. We had not only let ourselves down, but also the Workshop and the Corps. He finished by saying that failing these tests would be recorded on our annual confidential reports, and could affect our future military careers. This last remark made me see red, and if it hadn't been for Peter Berkshire, who seeing I was about to let loose, shook his head and put one finger up to his mouth to indicate silence. I was going to tell the OC that as a National Service officer, I didn't care a stuff about my confidential report, and further more, if he had taken the trouble to brief David and I properly, and given us sufficient time to prepare for the tests, then we would not have let anybody down. What made me even angrier was that these tests were held on a regular basis for young officers, and therefore Denys Wood or 'Jock'Roberts as the 2IC had, to my mind, no excuse in their failure to ensure that we were properly prepared. Still, I was grateful to Peter Berkshire, for I hated to think what the consequence would have been if I had 'blown my top'.

~

David and I weren't in the doghouse for too long, for the OC included both of us in a visit he and 'Jock' Roberts were making to HQ 17 Gurkha Division (OCLF). I had no idea what the purpose was for the visit, but as the round trip distance from JB to Seremban was some three hundred and eighty miles, it was obviously going to be a very long day.

Once we had arrived at the town, David and I were left to our own devices for a couple of hours, whilst the OC and 'Jock' Roberts did what they had to do at Division. David and I wandered about the town, which I thought was delightful, with spacious padangs, on one of which was a full sized replica of a Malay long house, standing on stilts and built of a dark wood. But I felt the most beautiful part of the town were the Lake Gardens, which were on two levels, separated by a wooden bridge. Trees grew right to the edge of the banks of the lakes, and at the time David and I were there, the air was so still, that it was difficult to differentiate between the actual trees and their reflections in the waters of the lakes. To one side was a flower garden with colourful displays of hibiscus, orchids and other plants.

As the others had finished their meeting in good time, we had lunch and spent the early afternoon at the Sungei Ujong Club. This was a truly delightful place, situated on a hill, and with views of the jungle covered gunungs to the south of Seremban. Although the clouds were bubbling up as they invariably did in the afternoons, there was still plenty of sun and it was very hot and humid. With all the windows open and the fans going full blast the clubhouse was spacious and cool. The pool with its clear blue water shimmering in the sunlight looked cool and so inviting. We were joined by three REME officers from Division, Noel Harrison, Bob Perkin and an old friend of mine; actually he wasn't an old friend, but soon became one, for Ronnie Rust was the OC of 'D' Coy at Honiton, and was looked upon as 'God' by us recruits in 'D' Coy. Still it was a very pleasant interlude to our normal days activities, and it was thoughtful and kind of Denys Wood to include David and myself.

~

One evening David and I were in the Mess, when there was a message from the Guard Room to say that a friend of Bob, my predecessor had come to see him. I went over to the Guard Room and the visitor introduced himself. His name was Douglas, a manager of a local rubber plantation, and he and Bob had become friends. He was surprised when I told him that Bob had returned to the UK. I invited him over to the Mess, and after a couple of drinks, as Douglas knew the best places to go to in Johore Bahru, the three of us piled into his car and set off for the town. Douglas certainly knew the best restaurant for authentic Chinese food, and later we ended up at 'Amy's Bar' where, having had at least one too many whiskys, which at that time was my preferred drink, I was somewhat rude to the local European police inspector, who fortunately for me had a good sense of humour. He suggested to Bob that he and David had better take me back to the Workshop. By this time, I had lost interest in the inspector, and was eyeing a very attractive Chinese girl sitting at the next table. She came over and sat down at our table, smiled at me and said it would cost me thirty Malayan dollars. I was tipsy enough to seriously consider the offer, for she was very lovely, sitting there in a tight fitting cheongsam, slit very nearly up to her waist, and showing far too much of a very shapely leg. Fortunately for me, David and Douglas dissuaded me from making a fool of myself, put me in the car and drove back to Pandan. I would have liked to have got to know the girl, but only if she hadn't been 'on the game'. I never knew whether it was the company or my behaviour, but I never saw Douglas again.

~

As I was commuting frequently into Singapore, especially at weekends, I decided that a car would be an advantage and would give me greater flexibility, as I was spending a small fortune on bus and taxi fares. Further more the Chaplins, whom Bob had introduced me to before he left for the UK, had very kindly asked me to join them on Sundays, which they spent at the Singapore Swimming Club, and as a consequence I was seeing more of Angela, their eldest daughter. I felt I was taking too great an advantage of their hospitality, as they would drive out of their way either to drop me at the Rochore Canal bus station, or take me right over to the west side of the Island to the REME Officers' Mess at Pasir Panjang. I had heard of a RAOC captain at 221 BVD, who was advertising his American 1949 Ford Custom for sale. I met up with him in JB one evening, and after giving the car the once over, he invited me to try it out. It was a big car, with a very large V8 engine, an absolute gas-guzzler, but when I put the steering wheel mounted gearshift into first gear and put my foot hard down on the accelerator, the car took off like a scalded cat. I thought it would make a good 'passion wagon'. Anyway, although I was advised against buying the car, as the owner had a reputation for sharp dealing and was not to be trusted, after a certain amount of haggling, I went ahead and brought the car for six hundred Malayan dollars (seventy-five English pounds). For the first few days I had no trouble with the car, but on the first Sunday, as Angela's father was Duty Officer at the Navy Base, I had driven the rest of the family down to the Singapore Swimming Club, but when we wanted to return to their flat, the car absolutely refused to start, and I was covered with embarrassment as I had to order a taxi to take us back to Killiney Road.

On the Monday I arranged for a local garage to collect the car. Their report was that the carburettor was worn out and needed replacing; but the cost of a new one was almost more than I had paid for the car. Not wanting to spend that amount of money, I asked if they could do a temporary repair, which they did, but without giving any guarantee. This was a wise decision on their part, for I was never certain whether the car would start or not; and it let me down on two further occasions, when Angela and I had been to the cinema. So after keeping it for six weeks, as I was becoming increasingly worried about the state of the tyres, the 'play' in the steering wheel and the deteriorating brake performance, I decided to sell the car. The problem was how to get the best possible price for it. In 1959 there weren't that many American cars around.

I hawked my Ford Custom round various back street Chinese car dealers, finally ending up in Rochore Canal Road, which was known as the 'Thieves Market'. The best offer I could get was three hundred and fifty Malayan dollars (forty-four English pounds), which I accepted; deciding to cut my losses, as I was certain that the car was going to cost me a great deal of money in repairs in the very near future. So, it was back to public transport, which in fact was not that expensive. The cost of a taxi from Johore Bahru to the workshop at Pandan was only two dollars (five shillings).

The first time I went into the centre of Singapore, I had been surprised by just how many cars there were in the City, and I was pleased to see, that except for Mercedes Benz diesel engine taxis, the vast majority of cars were British; either British Motor Corporation's Morris, Austin, MG, Riley, Wolseley, or Roots Group's Hillman, Humber and Singer. There were no Japanese cars, as memories of the Japanese occupation were still too fresh in many people's minds. By 1980, the last time I visited Singapore, the position had been reversed.

It intrigued me to see that at road junctions traffic lights had no 'amber'. They went directly from 'red' to 'green' and visa versa.

'It's for safety,' was the explanation, 'There used to be 'amber' lights, but the locals regarded them as the signal either to put their feet hard down on their accelerators before the 'green', or to continue at speed before the 'red', and at junctions traffic would move from all four directions simultaneously, with the inevitable results. So the 'ambers' were done away with; which in theory has made it safer at traffic lights, and the 'Accident and Emergency' Departments of the local hospitals are apparently less busy.'

Except that is, when I'm sitting in the back of a Land Rover, for as we crossed the major Dhoby Ghaut junction on the 'green', I was totally and unexpectedly catapulted into the foot well of the vehicle, as a car, which had obviously 'jumped' the lights hit us amidships. Fortunately, the Land Rover was barely marked, whereas the car was looking decidedly the worse for wear, which served the driver right; even though he screamed at us, in what I took to be his best Cantonese that it was my driver's fault. Driving in Singapore was invariably exciting. Local drivers only believed in one speed, flat out with horns blaring. How pedestrians, cyclists, trishaw drivers and animals survived was a mystery. I once saw a dog run out from the side of a road in front of a car, fully expecting it to be run over, but it emerged unscathed from the other side as it ran between the front and the rear wheels of the car.

~

Unless one of my fellow officers had invited me to join him and his family, I invariably spent Sundays at the Singapore Swimming Club. It was a great advantage that I could always find a bed at the REME Officers' Mess at Pasir Panjang, as this meant I could travel into Singapore after duties finished at midday on Saturdays, and spend the weekend there. After a couple of months Angela and I had become quite friendly, and we would often meet up for a Chinese meal, or to go to see a film. A visit to the cinema was always an attraction, as the Cathy and the Lido cinemas were air conditioned, and it was such a relief to have a break from the hot and humid conditions. It was in Singapore that we saw 'South Pacific', the first film I had seen in Cinerama, with the three projectors projecting the film onto the three screens, with the join between each screen and projected picture barely noticeable. The system certainly gave an added dimension to the film, and was more impressive than CinemaScope.

One of the first things I did when I arrived in Singapore was to get myself a camera. At that time I was completely ignorant of photography, but which later was to become a very serious and rewarding hobby. One of the officers in the Pasir Panjang Mess advised me to look for a camera in Change Alley, which was world famous for its unique atmosphere and multi-race shops selling a wide range of products. I was told not to tamely accept the asking price, as it was expected of one to haggle, which was all part of the Eastern tradition, but if you didn't do so, you lost all respect in the eyes of the shopkeeper. I have always found that haggling is totally alien to my nature; so having changed some money with one of the money changers at the entrance, I walked along this thriving, exciting and colourful alley, until I found a camera shop. With the advice of the shopkeeper, I chose a range-finder camera, a copy of a Leitz model with two extra lenses, - a medium telephoto and a wide angle one. I was asked sixty Singapore dollars (eight English pounds) for this, which was such an unbelievably cheap price that I couldn't bring myself to haggle, and just tamely accepted the asking price. No doubt the shopkeeper regarded me as a complete 'round eye' idiot, but I felt that I had made a good buy; which I certainly proved in the year ahead, and bar for one film, which I hadn't wound onto the 'take-up' spool correctly; I took over six hundred colour slides and black and white photographs in Malaya and Singapore.

~

A few miles north of 10 Inf Wksp, on the Kota Tinngi road was the FARELF Jungle Warfare School (JWS), which had a very high reputation, mainly due to the professionalism of the instructors, the majority of whom were Australian Army, and who were very experienced in operating in jungle conditions.

The initial part of the Jungle Warfare Course was spent 'in house', before the trainees were allowed out to carry out further training on a neighbouring rubber estate.

One day one of our sergeants, and I didn't know how he got his information, told us that the Australians, who were going through the Course at the JWS were being let out into the rubber plantation the following day. This didn't mean anything to me, but everyone else looked somewhat worried.

I was not kept in the dark for long, for early the next morning my telephone rang. I picked it up.

'Second Lieutenant Caffyn, the MTO here.'

'This is the Jungle Warfare School. I'm Captain Howard. The 1st Battalion the Royal Australian Regiment (1 RAR) are out on exercise, and they have bogged down a 3-ton Bedford truck and a Ferret Scout Car. Can you recover them, please? The locations are…'

I got hold of Staff Sergeant Davis in charge of the recovery section. We consulted the map and located the rubber estate the RAR were using.

'It looks,' said Staff Davis, 'as if there are two ways into the plantation from the main road. A smaller one here,' Staff Davis pointed to a thin line on the map, 'and a wider one here,' pointing to a thicker line. 'This one looks a better track for the Scammell, even though it's further from the workshop. I'll take one of the petrol ones as it's got a power winch.'

I left him to get on with getting all the recovery vehicles with associated equipment and kit ready, and told my fellow officers what was going on. They smiled and reckoned that the two hours it took before the Australians called for help was a record even for them.

To help the recovery crew, I decided to carry out a 'recce' myself and make sure that we had the right recovery kit. The map we had been issued with was not a large scale one, but between David Rowe, who had decided to come long as well, my driver and myself, we managed to find the wider entrance to the rubber plantation and set off down a narrow laterite track, which had been built up above the level of the surrounding ground. I was beginning to see why this estate was used for jungle warfare training, the topography varied from the usual serried ranks of rubber trees, to mangrove swamps and secondary jungle. After some two miles, we drove round a left hand bend, and there before us, was the abandoned Bedford RL truck, at an angle with its nearside sunk into marshy ground, with the offside still on, but partially blocking the track. It was not the best location for recovery, for the ground was very swampy on either side of the track, and immediately beyond the truck was a stream, crossed by a narrow wooden bridge. After the bridge the track swung sharp left up a fairly steep slope. The driver of the Bedford had probably come down the track too fast and had slid on the, possibly wet wooden planks of the bridge and slid gracefully into the swamp. I felt that we were going to have problems with this recovery. Whilst I was working out how I would undertake the task, Staff Davis arrived with the 6 x 6 Scammell. We decided to ignore one of the basic rules of recovery; namely to pull the vehicle out the way it went in. So as the Scammell was facing the front of the Bedford, we would pull it out in the direction it was facing. The 6 x 6 was reversed and the winch rope was unwound, and passed through pulleys along the side to the front of the vehicle and connected to the truck. Staff Davis gave the 'go ahead' to start slowly winching in. The Bedford just tilted further on its side and sank even further into the swamp.

We decided that the principle 'what goes in must come out the same way' was going to be the right one. However, this gave us only one other option. We would have to recover it from the back. But this raised another snag, the rubber plantation track was in the shape of a 'U', and the distance between the two entrances from the main road was over ten miles. For this 'in and out the same way' recovery, we only needed to move the Scammell some fifty yards, but with the track partially blocked by the Bedford RL, I didn't feel that there was enough room left for the 6 x 6 to 'squeeze' past; but to get into position for this 'pull' would entail a journey of over twenty miles in total. The Scammell would have to reverse for some distance before it could be turned, and although we knew there was no problem getting back to the main road and to the next estate entrance, we had no idea what condition the rest of the track was like, and how difficult it was going to be to get the 6 x 6 into position up the track from the stream and the bridge. Staff Davis estimated that this could take up to three hours. It really was most annoying, as we only needed to move the Scammell such a short distance.

Anyway, there was nothing for it; I told Staff Davis to get going, whilst David Rowe and I went to look for the Ferret Scout Car. This was some five miles further on, and like the Bedford had gone off the track with its nearside in the swamp. This was going to be a simple recovery job, as the track, although narrow ran straight for some distance in both directions from the Ferret; but it was a mystery how the Scout Car had left the track without a bend in sight. Having seen all I wanted to, we decided to return to the site of the bogged down Bedford and wait for Staff Davis to appear after his twenty-mile trip. We drove down the slope and turned right to cross the bridge over the stream, and we couldn't believe what we saw. The Scammell, was still on the other side of the bridge, but with its nearside in the swamp. Staff Davis had decided that, if he was very careful and driving very slowly, there was just sufficient room for him to squeeze past the truck, which would not only save the twenty-plus mile journey round to the back end of the Bedford, but also save two or three hours. However, the edge of the track collapsed under the weight of the 6 x 6, throwing the near side of the vehicle down into the swamp. I was horrified. The recovery team were frantically knocking in ground anchors, so that a snatch block could be laid out and the winch rope passed round this and back to the Scammell, so that, hopefully it would winch itself out. After an hour we gave up, and I told Staff Davis I was returning to the workshop to get the 6 x 4 Scammell.

This arrived on site early afternoon, and it was obvious that we needed to recover the Bedford first, so as to give ourselves enough room to winch the 6 x 6 Scammell out. However, we could use the jib of the 6 x 6 to hold the truck steady, whilst the 6 x 4 Scammell winched the Bedford out of the swamp and back onto the track. A simple, copybook recovery, which should have been completed within an hour, but due to bogging down the 6 x 6 took us over five hours. We were now faced with the more difficult problem of recovering the Scammell. Using ground anchors, snatch blocks and the winch from the 6 x 4, we tried everything to pull the 6 x 6 out backwards. But nothing worked, and we only succeeded in breaking up more of the track and pushing the Scammell further down into the swamp. There was no alternative. To move the diesel 6 x 4 fifty yards, it would have to make the twenty-plus mile trip round to the other side of the bridge, so that we could try a forward 'pull'. By now it was late afternoon, and darkness would have fallen by the time this Scammell had re-joined the 6 x 6 one. It set off straight away. All I could do was to drive back to Pandan, and organise hot food and blankets to be taken out by my driver to the recovery site. I also arranged with the cook sergeant for my driver to take up breakfast in the morning. At least I had the satisfaction of knowing that both Scammells and their crews would be together, and the men would have had a hot meal, and with the blankets should have been relatively comfortable for the night. Having organised all this, I decided there was nothing else I could do; so I retired to the Mess and joined David Rowe for, I felt a well-deserved drink, whilst our houseboy prepared our supper.

Next morning, I had just started breakfast, when my driver appeared at the Mess. He had taken breakfast up to the recovery crews, and was very surprised to find that the 6 x 4 diesel Scammell hadn't turned up the previous evening, and Staff Davis and the rest of the 6 x 6 crew had no idea where it was. I felt that potentially, we could have a serious situation. Something had obviously happened that had prevented the 6 x 4 crew joining up with the others. Had they been involved in an accident? If so, were there any injuries? Or had they just broken down? They couldn't have lost their way, for the track had no turn-offs. Although Johore had been declared a 'White Area', the thought went through my mind that some deep rooted CTs had come out of the jungle looking for food; had come across the 6 x 4 with only a two man crew and no weapons, and following their usual practise of only attacking the security forces when they, the CTs had numerical superiority, had ambushed the vehicle. I cursed myself for not going with my driver the previous evening, and after delivering the food and the blankets to the petrol 6 x 6 Scammell crew, driving on to check that the diesel 6 x 4 Scammell was still on its way. If anything had happened to them, I knew I would never forgive myself. I also cursed whoever was responsible for the decision not to equip recovery vehicles with wirelesses, which was probably based on cost by the 'bean counters' and not on operational necessity!

Forgetting breakfast, we set off immediately, and I told my driver to take the first turning into the rubber estate. About four miles in, I saw something green ahead, which quickly materialised into a Scammell tilting over at a fairly steep angle. The crew looked very cold, very tired and very hungry. The corporal explained that they had been driving along on headlights, which were never terribly effective on the 6 x 4 diesel, and the driver had failed to spot a large pile of stone chippings to one side of the track, which the Scammell had run onto, and then slid off so that the offside wheels had ended up in a ditch.

This was turning into a nightmare. The previous day, thanks to the Australians, I just had a Bedford RL and a Ferret Scout Car to recover; but after twenty-four hours I had only succeeded in recovering the Bedford; but to achieve this, I now had two bogged down Scammells, as well as the original ditched Ferret Scout Car. We might have been cursing the 1 RAR for initially causing all the problems; but if they knew what was going on, I felt they were having a good laugh at us incompetent 'limeys'. Whether it was to save embarrassment either to them or to us, but fortunately no Australian 'digger' (soldier) put in an appearance during the two days of the recovery.

I stayed with the crew, whilst I sent my driver on to the 6 x 6 Scammell to bring all the food and water that he could. When he returned, I sent him back to the workshop to tell Sergeant Ellis to send up our last operational recovery vehicle. As our other 6 x 6 petrol Scammell was 'off the road' for repairs, all that was left was the very elderly WW II Austin K9 Gantry vehicle. This was a tall vehicle, with a high centre of gravity and with a gantry protruding from high up at the back. It could not tackle heavy work, as its main function was to give suspended tows to soft skinned vehicles.

Fortunately, we managed with care, to use the Austin K9 to pull the Ferret out of the swamp, and having attached a rigid bar, I sent the Austin and the Scout Car back to the workshops. The two man crew of the 6 x 4 Scammell, having got some rather cold congealed breakfast inside them, worked like Trojans hammering in ground anchors (with a little ineffective help from me), which was not the easiest of jobs on hard ground, and connected up a snatch block and with the winch rope they managed to get the Scammell to winch itself back on the track again. Due to the hard ground, it took a considerable effort and time, which we could ill afford to extract the ground anchors.

As my driver had decided to remain at the workshop, I squeezed into the cab of the 6 x 4, and we set off for the six miles to the site of the remaining bogged down 6 x 6 Scammell, and which we all knew was going to pose quite a problem.

We managed to reverse the 6 x 4 Scammell down the slope, but due to the sharp bend leading directly to the wooden bridge over the stream, we had to park the vehicle at right angles to the bogged down one. We passed the winch rope round a tree, which saved knocking in ground anchors, and using a change direction block connected it to the ditched vehicle. We started winching-in, and the 6 x 4 Scammell shuddered and shook as it took up the strain of its bigger and heavier brother; but the only result was that more of the bank collapsed and the 6 x 6 Scammell sank further into the swamp.

Staff Davis and I held further discussions and decided that because of the angle the vehicle was now at, we had lost the option of recovering it from the direction it had gone into the swamp. It would have to come out forwards, but there was only some six to eight feet from the front wheels of the 6 x 6 to the wooden bridge, and in that distance we somehow had to get both front wheels onto the track, without the back wheels sliding further into the swamp, and causing the back of the vehicle to swing round at an even bigger angle to the track. If the back of the Scammell had swung round and ended up at right angles to the track, recovery would have become extremely difficult, and we would have needed our second 6 x 6 Scammell, even if not fully repaired, with its superior performance to that of the 6 x 4. However, the first job would be to rebuild and reinforce the bank of the track, which then needed to be chamfered off to enable the nearside wheels to ride up onto the track more easily. We would then have to pack the bank with gun planks from both Scammells, and hoping these would be strong enough to bear the weight of the vehicle as it was being winched out. The 6 x 6 Scammell had guide rollers located on the nearside, which would enable us to run the winch rope from the back, along the side of the vehicle, through the rollers at the front, around the tree trunk with the end secured to ground anchors firmly embedded in the ground. As the rope was winched-in, not only would we have a forward pull, but also the rope passing down the side of the vehicle would, we hoped act as a restraint to the Scammell sliding further into the mire. However, we obviously needed further support on the side of the vehicle to prevent the back-end sliding sideways into the swamp as it was winched forward. We would have to use the 6 x 4 Scammell for this; but it was in the wrong position. We didn't want it up the slope and around the bend from the 6 x 6. There was no alternative; it would have to be sent round the twenty miles of track so we could use the vehicle as an anchor from behind the ditched one.

Whilst we waited for the 6 x 4 to turn up, Staff Davis and I ran through our recovery arrangements, checking that we hadn't overlooked anything. I asked him if we needed to lay out a snatch block and run out more cable to do a 2:1 or even a 4:1 pull. He thought, with the diesel Scammell providing a sideways anchor, the 6 x 6 should be able to winch itself out on a straight 1:1 pull. Eventually after some two hours, the 6 x 4 Scammell arrived. Ideally, this should have been placed at right angles to the ditched one, but we hadn't the space to do this, so the 6 x 4 was parked down the track, with its winch rope passed round a change direction block, securely anchored to the ground and the rope attached to the tow bar at the back of the 6 x 6.

Staff Davis briefed the crews,

'Okay, if we get it right, this should be an easy operation. But if we don't, we're going to be in an even worse mess. Corporal Jones I want you to be in charge of the 6 x 6; but take the winching-in of the rope slowly and very gently, and only use the drive to help you out. Don't worry about the back-end. I will be directing Craftsman Potter in the 6 x 4 from the track. Mr Caffyn will be ahead of you; follow his signals, and if he gestures with both arms across his body like this, then stop everything immediately. Clear?'

Cpl Jones nodded.

'Okay. Now Potter, I want you to take in the winch rope, until it is taut, but you must keep it taut the whole time; so when the 6 x 6 starts to move, you must let the winch rope out a little at a time. Craftsman Evans, you will stand in front of the 6 x 4 and you will pass my signals on to Potter. Too much rope let out too quickly and the back of the 6 x 6 will slide into the swamp. But watch me and I'll give you the necessary hand signals. Any questions?'

There were none.

'Right, let's take our places. Briggs I want you on the offside of the 6 x 4 so you can see the bank by the 6 x 6. Now once the 'pull' starts, if you see the bank collapsing shout out, and we'll have to stop.'

We took up our positions, with Staff Davis in the most dangerous position between the two Scammells; for if a winch rope should snap, or ground anchors gave way and a snatch block, under tension took flight, he would not stand much chance of escaping serious injury. But, in order to see and direct the recovery he had to stand in that position. Both Scammell engines were started up, and once Staff Davis was satisfied that the winch rope between the two Scammells was taut, he signalled me to tell Cpl Jones to start winching-in. This he did very slowly, and I had such a feeling of relief as the 6 x 6 started to move forward, and the nearside front wheel came onto the track. The back was swaying about somewhat, but Craftsman Potter did a first class job in holding his winch rope taut as the fourteen-ton petrol Scammell slowly but inexorably dragged itself along and up the gun planks onto the track and onto the bridge. Staff Davis gave the signal to switch everything off. There was silence for a moment then, spontaneously we all started cheering with relief. We spent some time making good the damage to the bank, as the Army were only allowed to use the track with the agreement of the estate manager, and any damage could have led to a large compensation claim. With proper planning and preparation the recovery had, in the end been straightforward. However, we only had ourselves to blame for making it more difficult. Although Staff Sergeant

Davis had made a mistake in believing he could 'squeeze' the 6 x 6 Scammell past the Bedford RL, he had more than redeemed himself with the professionalism he had shown in recovering the Scammell from such a potentially 'dodgy' position.

My fellow officers were amused by and tolerant of our recovery efforts, but held the opinion that it was useful experience in an operational environment. The most important lesson I learnt was to ensure that all was well with the men under me, and not just expect that there would be no problems, however simple the task was. I should have gone out that evening and made sure that the crew of the 6 x 4 Scammell had joined up with their colleagues; and as they hadn't, I would have laid on a hot meal and blankets to be taken to them in the evening and breakfast the following morning. We all hoped that 1 RAR would not continue to test the aquatic capabilities of both their soft skinned vehicles and our recovery vehicles; although we had our doubts, and for several days we waited a call from the JWS asking for our help in recovering ditched vehicles. Fortunately, this never came. The Australians had either moved out, or were afraid of what we might do to their vehicles if they had called us out for a second time.

~

Christmas was approaching, and I found it difficult to come to terms with the climate, as in Mainland Malaya there are no clearly defined seasons. The only variation being the two monsoons, the northeast one, which blows in from the South China Sea from October to March, and the southwest one from June to September with lighter winds and less rain. However, in April and May and again in October and November, which are known as the 'Doldrums', there are frequent heavy thunderstorms. Also there are frequent rain-squalls during the southwest monsoon, and these are known as 'Sumatras', as they usually blow in from Sumatra, along the coast from Malacca down to Singapore.

Mornings are usually cloudless, but hot and humid. Clouds would build up late morning or early afternoon and a storm would break late afternoon or early evening. The rain would be torrential; up to one inch in an hour, and it is not unknown for fifteen inches to fall in one day, and the deep monsoon drains are unable to handle this volume of water. On one occasion a storm broke when I was driving into JB, and the rain was so bad that I couldn't see the road, and had to draw off to one side and wait for it to stop.

I soon became fed up with every day being hot and humid and I began to long for British weather, to feel cold rain and the force of a gale on my face, and to wrap up in warm and waterproof clothing. Even those cold and frosty days we spent out in Long Valley at Mons appeared attractive. So, I found it difficult to get into the Christmas spirit, even when we held a cocktail party in the Mess. Gerry March had organised a Satay man, who when he walked in through the Guard Room gates, in his loin cloth, wide banana leaf hat, balancing the long pole across one shoulder, with all his cooking implements balanced in woks at either end, caused a certain amount of concern and amusement to the Guard Commander; but who was determined not to let the Satay man out of his sight, and personally escorted him to the Mess. I was rather surprised that the Sergeant didn't make one of us sign for him. Anyway, the Satay man squatted down on his haunches on the narrow terrace outside the Mess and produced the most appetising and mouth watering chicken, beef and mutton satay, all accompanied by the traditional peanut and chilly sauces. It was the first time I had tasted

this traditional Malay dish, and I enjoyed it so much that I made rather a pig of myself. I was so sorry when he finished, packed up his gear, was paid and left, once again closely escorted by the Guard Commander. Although, I wasn't aware of it at the time, Indonesia, Singapore and Malaya all have their own variations of satay; but it was that first experience at 10 Inf Wksp, which set the bench mark, as far as I was concerned on what a good satay

The Satay Man

should taste like. I have had the dish many times subsequently, but nothing can compare with that produced by the Pandan Satay man.

The cocktail party was a great success, with guests not only from other units, but also local dignitaries. David and I felt somewhat out of it, as most of the guests knew each other, but it was a good start, if it could be called that, to the Christmas Festivities.

David and I had tossed a coin, as to who was going to be duty officer on Christmas Day. I lost, which meant David would do the Boxing Day duty. As expected Christmas Day dawned hot and sticky. Church Parades seemed a thing of the past, and bar from opening Christmas cards from home, and glancing through the latest batch of Eastbourne newspapers that my mother regularly sent me, the morning passed quietly. I went round to the Sergeants' Mess, the Corporals' Club and the other ranks' bashas to wish all and sundry a Happy Christmas. The sergeants invited me in for a drink, which, being on duty I had to decline. Late morning my fellow officers arrived at the Mess, ready to carry out the long established Army tradition of the officers serving Christmas dinner to all the men; although it didn't seem right to have roast turkey with all the trimmings, followed by Christmas pudding in such a hot humid climate. The cooks had done a splendid job in producing such a memorable meal, which together with the two bottles of Anchor beer was much appreciated by everybody.

After the men had eaten, my fellow officers took themselves back to their homes for their Christmas lunches. I was pleased that David had been invited by one of the officers to spend the day with his family. Many of the warrant officers and sergeants also had homes to go to, and as most of the men went into Singapore in the afternoon, the workshop was very quiet, and with the exception of those of us on duty, deserted. I sat in the Mess eating my solitary alcohol free lunch, reading the Eastbourne newspapers and feeling lonely and rather homesick. Later, only dressed in shorts and flip-flops, I sat at my desk, with perspiration pouring off me as I wrote a long letter home. I realised that I mustn't feel too sorry for myself, as there were units of the British Army serving

The Orderly Officer's solitary Christmas lunch

in many parts of the World, who were in the same boat. But Christmas should be a family day, and it is sad when one couldn't be with them.

However, Boxing Day was a much happier day as the Chaplins had invited me to the Singapore Swimming Club, where Christmas was celebrated in traditional style. Having always been used, back at home, for the whole country to close down for at least two days, I was surprised to find that the city was as frenetically busy as if it was a normal weekday. It made me realise that Singapore was indeed a very cosmopolitan city, with a polyglot of languages and religions; but bar from very isolated instances, each race respected the traditions of the others.

As part of the Christmas and New Year celebrations, the Workshop held an 'Open Day'. The various workshop departments had been busy designing and building a train, swings, roundabouts, a coconut shy, a ducking stool and all the other attractions one normally associates with an English village fête. This was a great success, and it was heart warming to hear the laughter and happy screams of the local children, who had flocked to the Workshop and had such a memorable time.

Except for the loneliness on Christmas Day, I was pleased and happy that I had been posted to 10 Inf Wksp, which although relatively small, was one, which Denys Wood had welded into an effective and professional unit. I had an English girl friend in Singapore, which I could quickly travel into; and I had become very fond of the city, which I found so vibrant and exciting. I was very fortunate that the second year of my National Service was passing in such agreeable surroundings, and as we went into 1960, I was looking forward to the final seven months of my National Service at 10 Inf Wksp before 'demob'.

But my nice cosy world was about to be shattered.

~

One morning, early in the New Year, the OC called me into his office. When I had climbed the stairs and arrived at his office, Denys was looking stern and I wondered what I had done wrong.

'I've received a message from HQ REME FARELF,' he announced, ' I'm sorry but you will be leaving us.'

I was completely stunned. This had come completely out of the blue.

'Where am I going to, Sir?'

'You're being posted as 2IC to the LAD (Light Aid Detachment) the 13th/18th Royal Hussars stationed in Ipoh. The Regiment is an armoured car one, and I'm sure that you'll learn a lot by being in an LAD at the 'sharp end'. I shall be sorry to lose you.'

My comfortable cosy world was collapsing around me. Ipoh was some four hundred miles north of Johore Bahru, and from what I had heard, there could be a greater danger from active CTs, who hadn't been killed or surrendered to the security forces.

I failed to understand why I was to be posted, and I went to great lengths to try and get this cancelled, even writing direct to the DEME, Brigadier Henchley, asking if I could stay at 10 Inf Wksp. He kindly replied that he wanted me to have as much experience as possible, and having served with an infantry workshop, he believed that I would gain valuable experience working in an LAD attached to a cavalry regiment. I didn't realise at the time how close my father and Douglas Henchley were, and I now believe that Douglas was hoping I would take a regular commission. Very many years later, he paid me a very big compliment, by saying that: 'You had real potential, and your father didn't do you any favours when he forced you into the family business.'

There was nothing more I could do. I just had to accept the posting with as much grace as I could muster. Denys Wood and his wife were very kind and invited me to their home for a farewell dinner. It was a most pleasant evening, but I rather put my feet in the mire, by reminding Denys of the boiled egg episode at Beserah.

'Oh yes,' he replied with a straight face, 'most droll.' End of conversation.

I was due to catch the overnight 'Bamboo Express' train to Ipoh, and on my last day I was invited by the Sergeants to their Mess at lunchtime to have a farewell drink. Sergeants usually took pleasure in seeing if they could get an officer drunk. They had an easy target with me. I was so fed up with leaving, that I was quite prepared to be 'nobbled'. I lost count of how many whiskys I downed. The party overran the lunchtime break; so the doors of the Sergeants' Mess were closed, and we continued quietly to drink, hoping that the OC wouldn't have cause to walk in. The senior NCOs were a great bunch and I was going to miss them. Around 1500hrs, I staggered back to my room, collapsed onto the bed, and after the room had finished spinning, I fell into a deep sleep.

Some two hours later, I woke with a bad hangover and feeling like death warmed-up. Still, I had no one to blame but myself. I wanted to get drunk. A cold shower helped sober me up, as I got down to doing my packing. As I was travelling by train, I didn't want to burden myself with too much luggage and so sold my radio to David Rowe. I've often wondered what happened to it. It had done valiant service, being passed on from one subaltern to another. Hopefully, when the workshop moved to Borneo, and then Singapore in the mid-1960s, the radio went as well.

I had already said my farewell to Angela and her family the previous Sunday, and thanked them for their kindness and hospitality; saying that as I had leave due to me, I would try and take some of this in Singapore, although I did want to visit the island of Penang.

John, who had been my driver for the five months, drove me into JB for the last time, dropping my luggage and me at the hotel by the railway station. I thanked him for what he had done for me and we shook hands, saluted and wished each other all the best for the future.

Unexpectedly, my fellow officers turned up to say their farewells, but before doing so, they treated me to dinner at the hotel. All too soon, it was time to board the train, and it was a real wrench to say 'goodbye' to them. When I first arrived they had been so kind and supportive, and over the months I had made good friends with them. Sadly, I never did meet up with them again.

~

I made my way to my reserved so called air-conditioned first class sleeping compartment. 'Air conditioned?' That was a laugh! An electric fan fixed right behind my head on the bunk, and which not only was likely to give me a stiff neck from the draught, but also keep me awake from the noise of the fan's motor. The bed itself was not the most comfortable, with a thin Dunlopillo mattress, which had seen better days. I tried to get to sleep, but the fan was too noisy, so I switched it off, and within moments the compartment was too stuffy and I was perspiring freely. I decided to leave the fan on, and hoped that the rhythm of the wheels on the track would lull me to sleep. But before I dropped off, I thought back to my time at 10 Inf Wksp and how much I had enjoyed the posting. I also thought, when everything was so new, of the days I had spent exploring the town of Johore Bahru, which I had found so attractive and interesting. The Sultan of Johore's Palace (Istana) with its immaculately laid out and maintained grounds. The beautiful mosque, perched on the top of a low hill, with its four tall white painted domed minarets, interspersed with bands of the palest of greens. Against a deep blue sky and in bright sunlight it looked like a picture on a chocolate box. Inside the mosque the white and green theme was continued, with the floor of beautiful Italian marble, a monumentally large Persian carpet and, hanging from the high roof, two very large ornate chandeliers, purported to have come from Czechoslovakia. Of all the mosques I visited in Singapore and Malaya, the one at JB was my favourite. Across the road from the mosque was the Sultan of Johore's zoo. This I found rather sad, as I felt the elephants, tigers, crocodiles, monkeys, snakes and birds were all kept in far too small enclosures.

On another day I decided to visit the 'Kremlin', the large rather forbidding government building. Fortunately, the viewing gallery at the top of the tower was open to the public, and from here there were magnificent views in every direction. When the Japanese had driven the Commonwealth Forces out of mainland Malaya, and before they invaded Singapore Island, they had used the tower as an artillery observation post; but the Australian General Bennett, refused to let our artillery open fire on the Japanese position, on the grounds that 'unnecessary shelling of Johore Bahru should be avoided', and had apparently given an undertaking to the Sultan of Johore, that he would do all he could to ensure that the Sultan's Istana was not damaged by bombing or shelling, once allied forces had withdrawn across the Causeway. I looked south across the Causeway to Woodlands and the oil storage tanks, and through trees I could just make out the War Memorial, in memory of those Commonwealth troops who had died defending Malaya and Singapore. I looked down on the Causeway and could distinctly see the signs of where this had breached by naval depth charges on 31st January 1942. I had been told that the Causeway had been blown nearer the Malayan end than the Singapore one, and together with the shallowness of the water, the gap had not proved too great a barrier to the invading Japanese.

By 1959 it was so different. From the view I had from the tower, I could make out at the Malayan end of the Causeway, four enormous elephants' tusks made of wire and covered with stiff paper mâché in a form of an arch surmounted by a large crown. This was to celebrate the Installation of

Sultan Ismail on 10th February 1960 as the new Sultan of Johore; as the previous Sultan had died in May 1959 at the age of eighty-five.

In spite of the draught and the noise from the fan, I realised that mentally looking back at my time at 10 Inf Wksp, was helping me to relax, and although I was being posted much further north, I was thankful that the 'Emergency' was all but over; for at its height, the overnight trains in both directions were frequently attacked by the CTs as they passed through miles of rubber plantations, rice padi and secondary jungle. A pilot locomotive and wagon with armed police on board would travel just ahead of the main train, and the police would fire their Bren guns into suspected CT ambush positions. There were usually troops in transit travelling on the overnight trains and they were briefed to be ready to defend the train against an ambush. An officer would be detailed as the Officer-in-Charge of the troops on the train, and would be responsible for organising the defence in the event of a CT attack. Fortunately by 1960 it was no longer necessary to take such precautions, as I had no wish to be the O-in-C train. Surprisingly, in spite of the distraction of the fan, my depressed mental state about leaving 10 Inf Wksp, and being worried about how I would find life attached to a cavalry regiment, I managed to get several hours sleep. After some twelve hours, the train drew into Ipoh railway station, and as I stepped off the train, I was as ready as I ever would be to make the best of a posting I didn't look for and didn't want.

Chapter Fifteen

13th/18th Royal Hussars (QMO)

As I stepped off the train, my first impression was of the heat. I thought Temerloh was hot, but Ipoh seemed even hotter. I wondered how I was going to stand it. The sun, almost overhead blazed down from a near cloudless sky, with its heat reflected from the white platforms and station buildings. Having got over the shock of the heat, I looked round and a tall Englishman dressed in slacks and an open necked shirt stepped forward and introduced himself as Captain Hugh Wright, who would be my boss at the LAD. We quickly loaded my gear into the back of his car, and set off from the rather ornate and impressive colonial style railway station and through the town, which at first impression looked larger, well laid out with plenty of open spaces and cleaner than Johore Bahru. Hugh took me to his house and introduced me to his wife, Sylvia and his two sons Michael and Ian.

Over lunch, Hugh took the opportunity of briefing me:

'You will probably find regimental life rather different to what you have been used to at 10 Inf Wksp. The Regiment is like a self-contained family, and you will find that it will possibly be more regimental than you have been used to. What you may have heard about the cavalry is probably based on hearsay, and has very little bearing on today's cavalry regiments. They are very professional. Yes, they like their horses, and the Regiment has its own stables and takes part in polo tournaments. The 13th/18th Hussars is a very good regiment, but fortunately for you as a National Service subaltern, it is not one of the wealthiest ones, where officers preferably need a private income. You will find that every regiment in the British Army has its own history and traditions, and this Regiment is no exception. Don't forget that REME only has eighteen years of history, whereas both the 13th and the 18th Hussars, before they were amalgamated in the early 1920s, go back over two hundred years.

'There is a Regimental H.Q. with a Headquarters and three Sabre Squadrons. The LAD and the Royal Signals detachment are part of H.Q. Squadron. You may be surprised that the Camp seems fairly empty. This is because one of the Squadrons is on Internal Security (IS) duties in Singapore, and another one is on operational duties near Kuala Kangsar, some forty miles north of Ipoh. Both R.H.Q. and H.Q. Squadron are based here at Ipoh, together with the third Sabre Squadron.

'You will be meeting the officers this evening, and one word of advice. You are probably used, in REME Officers' Messes, to calling senior officers 'Sir', but in the Mess here you address the CO as 'Colonel' both inside and outside the Mess, and everybody else by their Christian names. But outside the Mess, it's back to 'Sir'. The Commanding Officer is Lt-Col Douglas Coker and the Adjutant Captain Angus Anderson. You will be in HQ Squadron where your Squadron Leader will be Major Bill Denney who won the Military Cross in North West Europe in 1945.

'The LAD has an establishment of fifty, but you won't see them all here, as each Squadron has its own fitter section. You will find our WOI, ASM Woodfield a tower of strength, very experienced and together with many of the LAD has served with the Regiment for many years. I'll take you round to the LAD after lunch. Do you have any questions?'

'Yes, Sir. Why is there a Squadron in Singapore? I didn't think there were any CT problems there.'

'Drop the 'Sir', it's Hugh off duty. About four to five years ago, there were serious riots in Singapore, and it was necessary for the Army to be involved to support the police and enforce the curfew. I don't know how the troubles started but they acquired the name of the Chinese Schools Riots.'

The more I saw of Ipoh, the more I liked what I saw. As we drove up Ashby Road we passed imposing Colonial style houses, each set in large gardens with frangipani trees in full bloom and hibiscus bushes in full flower. We turned into Ramillies Camp, which, on first impression seemed to have grown 'like topsy' with little cohesive planning. To be fair though, the 13th/18th Hussars were not the only unit stationed in the Camp; in reality it was more of a small Garrison. 3 Coy RASC were based next to the Regiment, and also within the Garrison were the 1st Loyals Regiment in Colombo Camp, the 2nd/6th Queen Elizabeth's Own Gurkha Rifles in Surla Lines and the command post of Headquarters 28 Commonwealth Brigade; with the Brigade's main Headquarters at Taiping some fifty miles to the north. Being in a different Brigade, I had to arrange for the camp tailor to change my 99 Infantry Brigade shoulder flashes to those of 28 Commonwealth Brigade.

Hugh took me straight to the LAD and introduced me to the ASM and the other senior NCOs who were 'in Camp' and not with the detached Squadrons. The LAD was laid out either side of a hard standing area, with the 'open plan' workshop buildings on one side and the LAD offices and stores section on the other side. Beyond the LAD were the Guard Room, the vehicle park and parade ground (I hoped I had seen the last of those at Mons OCS), and beyond these were the two Nissen huts housing Regimental Headquarters (RHQ). Spread out in a haphazard fashion around the side of a low hill were a hotchpotch of buildings, which comprised the Squadrons' Lines, the cookhouse, the Quartermaster's (QM) Stores, the WOs and Sergeants' Mess', the Corporals' and WVS Clubs and the ORs' bashas. The Officers' Mess occupied a large wooden Colonial style house on the highest part of the Camp. To one side and below were the officers' quarters, built of wood with attap roofs. These were perfectly adequate, but I had been rather spoilt by the modern Officers' Mess at 10 Inf Wksp. The more senior unmarried officers occupied the better quality huts nearest to the Mess, whilst the subalterns were in those both further away and at a lower level. Rank does have its privileges! The men's bashas were of various ages, but had recently been 'upgraded' with the installation of fans; improvements had also been made to the cookhouse and the NAAFI canteen and a new sewage system installed, which in a hot and humid climate was very necessary.

Hugh showed me the office I would be working from, and told me that my first task would be to get the EMERs up to date, as my predecessor who had left a few weeks previously, hadn't had time to do so. As it was approaching 1600hrs, Hugh said that the officers should be stirring as it was teatime, and took me up to the Mess to introduce me to those officers who were there. I was a little perplexed about the use of the word 'stirring', as I was sure that it had nothing to do with tea. I very soon found out that the Regiment, whilst in Camp, followed a very civilised routine. Work started at 0700 hrs and continued until 1300 hrs. After lunch in the Mess, and during the hottest part of the day, unless there were specific duties to be carried out, it was siesta time until 1600hrs. The Regiment was very sports orientated and worked on the theory that it was somewhat cooler in the late afternoon, which was really an illusion, the time between tea and dressing for dinner was given over to sport.

As Hugh had warned me, there were not many fellow officers around, but the ones I was introduced gave me a warm welcome; and it was a very pleasant surprise to see Johnny Hok, who had been at St Edward's School at the same time as I had, although a year behind and in a different House. It was fortunate, as far as I was concerned that there was not a formal dining-in night in the Mess my first evening, as it gave me an opportunity to settle in, and try to learn some of the Regiment's traditions. I was interested to see a large portrait of Lord Baden-Powell hanging from one wall of the dining room. I was told that he had been Colonel of the Regiment for many years. Capt Angus Anderson, the Adjutant, whom the other subalterns appeared to treat with the greatest respect, warned me that I was to report to RHQ at 0800hrs the following morning for an interview with the Commanding Officer.

~

Whereas at 10 Inf Wksp, the officers had been dressed in jungle green shorts with long socks, I was pleased to see that the Regimental standard form of dress was long trousers with bush jackets, which I thought far more suitable for grown men. So I felt rather stupid and very conspicuous as I made my way to RI IQ in my highly starched shorts, knee length socks and Australian jungle green shirt. As I entered the Nissen hut, I literally bumped into the RSM, WOI Eric Garbutt, who looked me up and down with a disapproving eye.

'Good morning, Sir. Just joined us I see. You'll find the Camp tailor by the WVS basha.' Hint taken.

The Adjutant also looked at me with disapproval, but the CO could not have been nicer and welcomed me with great warmth.

'Good morning, Mr Caffyn. Welcome to the Regiment. I'm pleased that you have joined us. Brigadier Henchley is an old friend of ours. Now even though you wear a different cap badge, as far as I am concerned you are a member of the Regiment.'

After further pleasantries, I saluted and left his office. The warm welcome I had received made me realise, even after only one day, that I had been accepted as a member of the Regiment; and even though I hadn't wanted to leave 10 Inf Wksp, I felt that I was going to enjoy my time with the 13/18H. Before I left RHQ, the Adjutant showed me into his office and invited me to sit down.

'Now,' he began, 'the Colonel has no doubt told you that we regard you as a member of the Regiment. As such you will, as a member of HQ Squadron participate in all parades including my monthly Adjutant's ones. The only exception being, when the Regiment parades in remembrance of a Battle Honour, such as Waterloo or Balaklava. As a member of the Regiment you will be subject to all the subalterns' duties and disciplines. You will carry out orderly officer duties. I must warn you though that being a subaltern in the Regiment is not a sinecure for an easy life, for being on the lowest step of commissioned rank, training and discipline need to be instilled, so that the high standards the Regiment expects from its officers is maintained. Put a foot wrong, and you will be given extra orderly officer duties, and I warn you that once you are on the slippery slope of doing 'extras', it is very difficult to get off them. With only two Squadrons in Camp, the orderly officer duties come round often, and your fellow subalterns welcome those of their colleagues who have been given 'extras', as it means their turn for orderly officer does not come round so often. The senior subaltern can also award 'extras'. So, be warned, even though your have a different cap badge, you are regarded as a member of the Regiment, and your behaviour and performance will be judged as such. Any questions?' A short pause. 'Good. Welcome to the Regiment. We have a high opinion of Captain Wright, and I am sure you will learn a lot from serving under him. Now get yourself round to HQ Squadron Offices, the Squadron Leader is waiting for you. Good morning.'

I was summarily dismissed. I had left the CO's office with a warm feeling, and the Adjutant, in the space of a few moments, had managed to put the fear of God into me, and left me wishing I was back with 10 Inf Wksp.

I made my way up to HQ Squadron lines, and was warmly greeted by Major Bill Denney M.C. the Squadron Leader and Squadron Sergeant-Major (SSM) Harris. Major Bill was a great character, very likeable and a most able Squadron Leader. I was told that he had won his Military Cross in Holland in January 1945, when his Troop was supporting the infantry on an attack to clear a village prior to the crossing of the Rhine; and despite a series of savage counter attacks spread over several hours, which Bill's Troop managed to repulse and where he displayed outstanding leadership.

After I left SHQ, I debated whether to go to the Camp tailor first, or report to Hugh Wright at the LAD. I decided on the latter. Hugh introduced me to the other senior NCOs, the AQMSs Buchan and Whiting and Staff Sergeant Wagstaff, who were in charge of the Squadrons' fitters sections. I also met Armament Sergeant Beavon responsible for the repair of the Regiment's weapons, and Sergeant Morton who was the senior NCO vehicle specialist.

I felt that Hugh Wright was somewhat in a quandary as to how best to use me. Most 'Baby EMEs' (the nickname the Regiment gave the 2IC of the LAD), including the NS subalterns would spend at least a year with their unit, and could be trained for certain duties and responsibilities. But as I had less than six months to serve before returning to the UK, it was hardly worth training me for any specific duties, and as a consequence I ended up as a general dogs-body. As Hugh had already mentioned, he took the opportunity to give me the responsibility of updating the EMERs. There were thirty of these comprehensive workshop manuals covering all the equipment and vehicles in the Regiment's inventory. The EMERs were constantly being altered and updated as modifications were introduced and specifications changed. The LAD had received all of these and they had all been read and, where necessary acted upon. But due to a shortage of staff, these had just been allowed to accumulate in a large pile, with very little effort to sort them into vehicle or equipment categories. My first priority was to sort this mountain of 'bumpf' into various sections and then place them in the correct sequence in their binders and discard the superseded sheets. As an aid, I drew up a large progress sheet, which I fixed to one wall, listing all the EMERs together with their sub-sections, which I ticked off as I completed each section. This enabled Hugh, the ASM and myself to check progress.

There were times when I felt like chucking in the job, for on more than one occasion, I would have completed a section, only for a new batch of technical sheets to arrive, and I would have to start all over again to re-sort that particular section. It was a very boring task, but I realised that it was an important one, for a specification change or modification could be safety related and if not carried out, could result in serious consequences. It was also important that the ASM and other heads of departments were made aware of any vehicle or equipment changes. The job was of such magnitude that even after six months I hadn't completed it before I left the Regiment. However there were extenuating circumstances, as I was involved in other duties and was unable to make, thank goodness, the EMERs update a full time task.

~

At 10 Inf Wksp, being a Brigade Infantry Workshop, the vehicles we were servicing and repairing were soft skinned 'B' Echelon ones. The more modern vehicles, such as the Saracen Armoured Personnel Carrier (APC), being new in theatre, were allocated to those units in the north of the country, who were still operational in hunting down the CTs. As well as the normal Bedford RLs, Land Rovers, and other soft skinned vehicles, we also carried out first line repairs to the six wheeled Saracen APCs, Daimler Armoured Cars and Ferret Scout Cars. The Alvis Saracen, which had recently been introduced into the Army, was powered by a Rolls Royce B80 petrol engine, capable of developing 160 BHP, carried ten men and its sole armament was a turret mounted 7.62mm Browning machine gun. The Daimler Armoured Car (DAC), based on the Daimler 'Dingo' Scout Car was introduced into the Army in 1942, had a three-man crew, and was fitted with the Tetrach Light Tank turret with a 2-pounder gun and a co-axial 0.303 machine gun. It was powered by a 6-cylinder 106 BHP engine, and saw action in North Africa and Europe. Although elderly, the DAC gave valuable service in Malaya. The Alvis Saladin was the DAC replacement, also with the B80 Rolls-Royce petrol engine, and was introduced into the Army in 1959; but in 1960 had not as yet been deployed to Malaya. The Daimler Ferret Scout Car was introduced in 1952, and was so successful that over 4,400 of the rear-engined 4x4 two-man Scout Cars were produced before production ceased in 1971. The Rolls-Royce B60 engine gave it a top speed of nearly 60 mph, forward as well as in reverse! The Ferret saw service in every internal security campaign from Malaya, through Cyprus and Aden to Northern Ireland, and was also in service with 36 other countries.

~

I very soon found that I was accepted into the Regiment in the fullest sense, when somehow I was conned into becoming the Assistant Messing Officer. Officers' Messes have mess committees under the chairmanship of a Mess President, who are responsible for the smooth and efficient running of the Mess. One of the more important members of the committee is the Messing Officer. Although the Regiment's officers, were not too bothered about the standard of food when they were on operations or on exercise; it was a different story when it came to the food served in the Mess. As Capt Stevenson had lectured us at Mons; they became very 'picky' and expected Savoy Hotel Grill Room quality on a Lyons Corner House budget. Lieutenant Martin Whitaker was the Messing Officer when I arrived at Ipoh; but after I had been appointed his assistant, it was strange how suddenly he was either detailed for training courses, or was on an exercise (HQ Squadron did not generally 'do' exercises), or had discovered that he had leave due to him. The result was that, in a very short space of time, having been shown the basic duties of a Messing Officer, I became the official Messing Officer, which at the time, I took to be a great honour for an attached subaltern, but subsequently learnt it was an appointment given to the junior subaltern in the Regiment.

Every morning, after breakfast I would hold a meeting in the Mess with the Mess Sergeant and the Officers' Mess Head Cook, who happened to be a very talented Chinaman. The Sergeant would inform me what rations were available, and we would supplement these, depending how much money we had in the 'kitty' from the Local Overseas Allowance (LOA), which was an extra payment made by the Army for overseas service. After we had fixed the menu for the day, the Head Cook would go into town to barter and buy local produce at the lowest possible price.

~

I had learnt very quickly when I started my National Service, that they were two types of 'enemy' as far as the Army was concerned. The obvious one being the 'official' one and for which the Army trains to fight. But the other one was an 'internal' enemy. As a raw recruit everybody with one stripe and above was the 'enemy' as they tried to boss one into becoming an effective and co-operative soldier. Trying to rebel against the 'system' brought instant retribution in the form of fatigues, extra parades and other punishments. As one moved up the Army 'pecking' order, the 'enemy' changed. As an officer cadet, one had to keep on the right side of the senior

NCOs and especially the drill sergeants, the sergeant-majors and especially, as I found out to my cost, the regimental sergeant-major. I had presumed, once I had been commissioned, that the internal 'enemy' would have become a thing of the past. But no! I felt that 'The Adjutant' could be the subaltern's 'enemy'. The Commanding Officer of a Regiment, could possibly be regarded as a minor 'enemy' and if he was married, as could his wife, if she felt that the subalterns did not match up to her exacting standards. (In the 13/18H, Margaret Coker, the CO's wife was an absolute dear, a great horsewoman and very supportive of the subalterns). In the 1950s, it was apparently an advantage for commanding officers to be married, if they wanted to progress up the Army's chain of command. The senior subaltern, who only got his position by age and length of service, could also be regarded as a minor 'enemy', as he had the power to hand out extra orderly officer duties to junior subalterns, primarily for social 'gaffes'.

I had determined at a very early stage of my posting to the 13/18H, not to fall foul of the Adjutant, who I liked and we got on well. But Angus was, quite rightly a most efficient adjutant and ensured that the subalterns maintained the highest standards. So it was quite a challenge to try and complete my six months without incurring 'extras'. To minimise the risk I decided to take every opportunity to be out of Camp, whether on an exercise, on other duties or on leave. I achieved the dubious distinction of serving six months without being awarded 'extras', but I felt at times it was a close run thing.

But what increased the risk of my incurring the Adjutant's displeasure, was my appointment as the Messing Officer. Capt Stevenson had warned us that a Messing Officer should keep on the right side of the Adjutant. Angus had his favourite dishes, and I very quickly learnt that at Dining-In and Guests Nights, if I put 'Chicken à la King' followed by the savoury 'Angels on Horseback' (or perhaps it was 'Devils on Horseback') on the menu, then the Adjutant was perfectly happy, even if every other officer in the Mess was heartily sick of these two dishes. This also included the Colonel, who generally communicated through the Adjutant, and if the Colonel disapproved of the menu I had arranged, but the Adjutant did not; then the Colonel's comments would have got lost somewhere in the pile of paperwork on the Adjutant's desk; who was probably too busy anyway writing up the daily Regimental Orders to pass the Commanding Officer's disapproval on to me. He was also astute enough to realise that I was bound to act on being made aware of the CO's displeasure and to change his favourite dishes. So, both Angus and I were on the same side when it came to Mess dinners, and so long as I kept him happy with his favourite dishes, I was reasonably safe from being awarded 'extras'; but if he let the Colonel get at me, and force a change of menu for dishes he didn't enjoy, then not only did he, Angus suffer, but I would probably have been given extra orderly officer duties for letting Mess standards fall. The Adjutant was known to have, on occasions, an unfortunate habit over dinner, of reminiscing how he had given 'extras' to previous Messing Officers for letting the catering standards of the Officers' Mess slip. Although, I never experienced this during my tenure.

It was just my bad luck that Angus was a living-in officer. As each Tuesday and Thursday were 'Dining-In' Nights for the living-in officers, and as these were formal evenings, we would be formally attired in mess kit. 'Chicken à la King' followed by 'Angels on Horseback' twice a week was rather more than the members of the Mess could stomach, and it took all the ingenuity of the Mess Sergeant and myself to come up with a choice of menu which was acceptable to the Officers and at the same time did not incur the Adjutant's displeasure.

~

In theory a Regimental Guest Night would be held monthly when it was mandatory for all the officers, both those living-in and living-out of Camp to attend. Although I had been commissioned for some nine months, my very first formal regimental dinner was to be with the 13th/18th Royal Hussars. However, just prior to the dinner, I thought back to Mons OCS and the lecture that Capt Stevenson had given us about Regimental Guest Nights. He had emphasised that the members of the Mess were meant to foregather in the ante-room at least fifteen minutes before the guests arrived. For the living-in officers this did not present a problem, but there were apparently occasions when a living-out member would arrive after the guests, and who would then have to resort to a variety of subterfuges so as not to be spotted by the Mess President. Returning from the 'loo' being the most common one. The senior officers had invariably invited the guests, and once they had all arrived, the junior officers would discreetly move to the far end of the ante-room and give the senior officers a clear field to entertain their guests. Capt Stevenson warned that this manoeuvre did not always meet with the approval of the senior officers who, led by the Colonel and accompanied by their guests would descend upon the junior officers, both from the front and from one flank to ensure that they did not escape, and were forced to engage in social small chat, which apparently could be quite daunting. At my first Guest Night I found that our guests believed, that as we were a cavalry regiment, all the members of the Mess would be very knowledgeable about all matters equine; and I was at a definite disadvantage as I could only discourse on a different type of horsepower.

We had been warned by John Stevenson of the risk, especially when serving in a hot climate, where pre-dinner drinks, especially amongst the newer and younger members, usually consisted of downing a fair quantity of chilled beers. But this was fraught with danger, as it was important to know precisely when the Mess Sergeant would announce that 'Dinner is served'. There was even a possibility that a Mess Sergeant could have had a nice little earner on the side, by tipping the wink for a small consideration, to those who needed to 'ease springs' five minutes before the announcement of dinner being served. A Colonel with a wicked sense of humour could, without hesitation lead his guests in a headlong gallop into the dining room; whilst at the other end of the ante-room there would be a mad scramble in the opposite direction by those who had consumed too much beer, to get to the 'gents' before they had left it too late to do so; and were condemned to sit through the dinner and speeches with a rapidly expanding and painful bladder. Timing was vital, as it was nearly a court-martial offence to arrive at the table after grace had been said and everyone was seated. If the Officers' Mess was sited in a garden and the 'gents' was not a large one, many of the shrubs outside the Mess would enjoy an unexpectedly warm watering! It was also an unspeakable crime for an officer to leave the table for whatever reason before the dinner was over and the Colonel had escorted his guests from the room. Although I was never certain what the procedure was if a guest needed to leave the table and powder his nose before the end of the dinner. If that had happened, there would no doubt have been a general exodus by many officers offering to escort the guest to the loo, who would probably have been elbowed out of the way in the rush, and had to wait his turn at the back of the queue.

However, I found my first Regimental Guest Night to be a memorable affair. All the 13th/18th officers splendidly attired in their mess kit and spurs rather showed up the plainness of the REME mess kit. Even though we were not in the UK, the table nevertheless was heavy with the Regimental silver, although I was assured that the majority of which had been left back at the Regiment's Home HQ in Yorkshire. From his portrait, Lord Baden Powell looked down on the assembled company with benign approval, as the Regimental Band played suitable music from the ante-room; neither the Dining Room being large enough nor boasting a balcony to accommodate the band. I could not enjoy the dinner, as I was on tender hooks, praying that my choice of menu would meet with the Adjutant's approval. I only began to relax, when from my lowly position below the salt, I saw Angus's head nod with approval as the mess waiter served him 'Chicken à la King', and I knew I was home and dry.

There were many aspects of Regimental life that made me realise that a Regiment is really a family, and the Guest Night reminded me of the traditions and histories of the two original Regiments; the 13th Hussars formed in 1715 and the 18th Hussars formed in 1759 and which in 1922 became the 13th/18th Royal Hussars (Queen Mary's Own), with the nickname 'The Lilywhites'. The 13th Hussars also enjoyed other nicknames, 'The Evergreens', 'The Geraniums' and the 'Ragged Brigade'. The 18th Hussars for some reason never acquired a nickname. Although I was only with the Regiment for a short time, it was with a feeling of sadness, when I learnt that in 1992 'The Lilywhites' were condemned to history, and were amalgamated with the 15th/19th The King's Royal Hussars to become 'The Light Dragoons'. Governments never appear to understand that the reputation of the British Army over many centuries has been built on the regimental system.

The Regimental Guest Night was an impressive affair; however with two Sabre Squadrons out of Camp on deployment, it probably could not compare to a full Regimental Guest Night back in the UK, or in BAOR when the Regiment was together as a complete unit, but which I, unfortunately never experienced.

~

Many years later I experienced a memorable Guest Night when I was fortunate to be a guest at the National Army Cadets Colonel Commandants' Dinner at the Royal Artillery Mess at Woolwich, which arguably must be one of the finest Officers' Mess in the British Army, with its impressive and famous Silver Room. I was quite speechless as I entered the magnificent beautifully proportioned Dining Room, maintained very much as it was in Georgian Days; with its six great chandeliers, the royal portraits on the walls and the Georgian mirrors, which made such a perfect setting for the four large mahogany dining tables, three of which ran lengthwise down the room, with the top table, which I was fortunate to be on, placed across the room at one end. The tables were decorated with many of the silver pieces from the Silver Room and some hundred candles in their silver candelabras lit the room.

We filed in to take our places at table to the sound of the band playing 'The Roast Beef of Old England.' At the end we witnessed the removal of the thirty-six foot long tablecloth runners by mess staff, who twisted them at each end to form a coiled spring, and at a signal from a mess steward, the waiters at one end of the four tables, gave a pull and the long runners slid down and over the ends of the tables in one smooth and swift movement. After the tables had been cleared, the port circulated and the loyal toast drunk, the 'Post Horn Gallop' was played by two expert musicians on the long coach horns, (apparently never bandsmen in the Royal Artillery) from diagonally opposite ends of the dining room, and which was followed by a rendition of 'John Peel' on the shorter post horns. It was an experience I shall never forget.

To return to my first Regimental Guest Night. As the dinner progressed there was a distinct difference in the volume of noise from the table. From the top table, the Mess President, the Colonel, other senior officers and guests would no doubt be discussing in calm, measured and dignified tones weighty worldly matters (although 'shop' was never discussed in the Mess); whilst below the salt the subalterns were engaged in discussing far more light hearted matters at a higher decibel level. After the loyal toast had been drunk sitting down, an honour bestowed on the 18th Hussars when Queen Mary was the Colonel-in-Chief (although, traditionally the Regiment did not usually drink the loyal toast), the port circulated and cigars lit; the noise level increased to such an extent that it was no longer possible to hear the band play the Regimental March, as a hint that the dinner was over and they wanted to 'go home'. However, Bandmaster Kershaw could not leave until the Colonel called him in to the dining room for his glass of port, and to offer him and the band our thanks for the music they had played during the dinner.

Eventually, the Colonel rose from the table and led the guests and senior officers into the ante-room at a stately and slow dignified pace, leaving Mr President and Mr Vice at the table (the latter being the very last to leave), while those of us with fully extended bladders took every possible short cut to get to the 'loo' or to the bushes outside in the shortest time. Shortly before I arrived at Ipoh, the practice, by subalterns of jumping out of the first floor dining room windows in their urgency to get to the bushes was banned. This had developed into a Mess game, resulting in a number of injuries and with the two detached Squadrons; HQ Squadron and the one remaining Sabre Squadron were in serious danger of running short of fit able-bodied subalterns.

Those guests and senior officers of a more serious disposition, retired to a quiet corner of the ante-room to carry on with their conversations, or to indulge in a rubber or two of bridge. Apparently, it was not advisable for a new subaltern when he joined a Regiment to declare that he was a bridge player, as he would probably have been called on to make up a four at Guest Nights. I cannot imagine that it would have been a good career move, if the new second lieutenant was partnering a very senior and distinguished officer, but who however was a bad player and was responsible for them constantly losing rubbers (if that is the right expression), and advised his senior and distinguished partner that he should take up playing 'Patience'.

Once the guests had departed, it was time for the serious part of the evening to start. There were many Mess games, some fairly placid and quiet, but others were boisterous and very noisy. It was a good job that the 13/18H Officers' Mess stood in its own grounds, otherwise the local civilian neighbourhood, which included the Prime Minister of the State of Perak, would have had real cause to complain; which would not have led to maintaining good Anglo-Malay relations, and could have thrown into jeopardy the official policy of 'winning the hearts and minds' of the local populace by depriving them of their sleep.

My favourite game was a variation of snooker, but played without cues. Each player would be allocated a ball and would have to dispatch it as hard as he could across the table into an opposite pocket, but missing the pocket, meant that the player had to fight his way round the table to retrieve his ball, before another officer claimed it. The game was further complicated by it being a simultaneous multi-player one, with balls colliding with each other and shooting off the table to all points of the compass at great speed and force. This game was a natural for cavalry officers, as the winner was generally the officer, who not only managed to pot his ball the greatest number of times, but also used his spurs to best effect when he had to reclaim his ball after a 'miss'. Sadly to say being without spurs, I was at a distinct disadvantage and generally finished with the lowest score, but with the greatest number of cuts and bruises than any other officer. Not at every Guest Night, but the conclusion to the evening was sometimes signified when an officer who had upset his peers would be dunked, fully dressed in a bath of cold water. It did not happen when I was with the Regiment, although there were times when I felt I might be in line for a dunking through my fellow subalterns being heartedly sick of 'Chicken à la King' and 'Angels on Horseback'.

~

With two Squadrons on detached duties, the orderly officer duty came round with monotonous regularity. Including Mike Butler, who was the Assistant Adjutant at RHQ, there were only ten other subalterns in Camp, and unless any of my fellow subalterns were on 'extras', and there was invariably someone, then the orderly officer duty came round every ten days. I must admit I was apprehensive the first time it was my turn. Before I reported to the Adjutant, I ensured that my houseboy had properly polished my brown shoes, my Sam Browne belt and the strap on my SD hat, and that my trousers and bush jacket were clean and pressed. As a National Service subaltern whose Army pay, including Local Overseas Allowance, was rather a pittance, and having got myself kitted out at 10 Inf Wksp; it was an added expense to have to get myself further kitted out with long trousers, bush jackets, a No1 white jacket for guard mounting duties, 13ᵗʰ/18ᵗʰ Hussars lapel badges, and to change all my 99 Infantry Brigade shoulder flashes to 28ᵗʰ Commonwealth Brigade ones. With only six months service with the Regiment, this extra expense put an unnecessary strain on my finances.

I could feel Angus eyeing me up and down as I entered his office to start my duties as the orderly officer. Fortunately, I must have passed his visual inspection, for all he did was to hand me 'The Bag'. This contained counters with numbers stamped on them. Drawing a stamped one, showed the time you had to call the guard out, even if it was at the most unsociable hour of 0300hrs. There was also one counter which was blank, and which everyone tried to pick, for it meant that the guard did not need to be turned out during the night. I never worked out whether this was a trick or not, and that one was expected to show keenness and devotion to duty by calling out the guard anyway. I was lucky enough to pick the blank counter on two occasions, and neither being over ambitious nor being a Regular, I decided not to call the guard out on those two nights. Angus also handed over the Orderly Officer's check-list and the report sheet, commenting that he hoped that there would be nothing out of the ordinary to note down on the report sheet. The check-list was comprehensive, and as well as covering the usual items, also included carrying out a random check of the stock inventory of the Tech Stores, and ensuring there were no problems at the W.V.S. Centre.

It was always a pleasure to visit the Centre, which was run with great efficiency, but with kindness and understanding by 'Midge' Divett, who had been the Regiment's W.V.S. worker for a number of years. The Centre provided Games, Writing and Sitting Rooms, with the record player being the most popular and used item. 'Midge' would run a weekly Whist Drive, Tombola evening and an inter-unit Darts Match. She would also organise Social Telegrams and send off 'Say it with Flowers' orders. In the days before mobile phones and e-mails, the work of the unit's W.V.S. Centre was important in both helping to keep up moral and maintain links with families back in the UK. In 1960 there were still many National Servicemen in the Regiment and for the vast majority, the posting to Malaya was their first experience of being away from the UK, and the work of the W.V.S. was vital but also much appreciated.

Fortunately, I very rarely had any problems with either the quality or quantity of the food when I inspected the Cookhouse, and the men had very few complaints. I followed the same procedure as I and others had been subjected to at 2 Trg Bn REME, and carried out random mug inspections, but without resorting to the heavy handed tactics of the orderly officers at Honiton of putting those with dirty mugs on a charge. Instead if I found a trooper with a dirty mug, I would warn him that if I found the same the next time I was orderly officer, I would have to place him on a charge. Hygiene was always important, and I felt that there was an added risk of germs in a hot and humid environment.

Guard Mounting was held at 1800hrs. For this I would be in No 1 Dress uniform with the Regimental Silver Message Cross-Strap. The Guard would be paraded on the Square. I would stand to one side and wait until the Guard Commander, a Sergeant would march over, salute and report that the Guard was present and ready for inspection. Having inspected the Guard, I would issue the order to 'Close order march', followed by 'Left turn' and give the Sergeant the order to march the Guard off the Square and to the Guard Room. Although, thanks to the training I had undergone at Honiton and Mons OCS, I was confident of my standard of drill; I was nevertheless nervous, when I could see out of the corner of my eye, the Adjutant leave his office, and watch the Guard Mounting Parade; and I always expected to be called to his office and told that the Guard Mounting was a shambles, and I would be awarded several 'extras' to ensure that I would get the Mounting up to the required standard in the future. Although Angus watched me on several occasions, he must have been satisfied with my performance, as I was never admonished.

The Orderly Officer's duties were not onerous, and having carried out all the checks; mounted the Guard, inspected the defaulters, called out the Guard and dismounted them the following morning; the main disadvantage was being confined to camp for the 24 hours of the duty, and also having to stay awake to call out the Guard in the early hours of the morning. Those subalterns, who had been 'awarded' seven days 'extras', were virtually confined to camp for a fortnight, as they needed to catch up on sleep on the alternate nights they were not doing their extras orderly officer duties.

Angus, as was natural, preferred at the end of an orderly officer's duty, to be handed an almost blank report, as this meant that he would not have to be involved in, or initiate action as a result of an incident during the orderly officer's stint. I was happy to oblige on all occasions, except for my final orderly officer duty.

Immediately following Guard Mounting, defaulters had to report to the Guard Room, and on this last occasion, a trooper who was under open arrest, failed to turn up for the defaulters' parade. The Duty Sergeant and I eventually found him lying on another trooper's bed, dressed only in shorts, and he obviously had no intention of turning up for 'defaulters'. I had no idea what he was up to, but decided that he possibly felt that as I was only an attached Corps officer, I would take no action. If this was what he believed, he was sadly mistaken; for if I had tamely told him to get the correct kit on and get down to the Guard Room, I would have lost any respect not only from the trooper and his mates, but also from the NCOs. So, to show that I wasn't a soft touch, I placed him under close arrest, and had him marched down to the Guard Room and locked up in one of the cells.

All was peaceful for some three hours, until I received a telephone call in the Mess from the Guard Commander reporting that the trooper's wife had burst into the Guard Room and was in hysterics. The background noise coming over the telephone certainly sounded as though another World War was breaking out. I went down, and even some distance from the Guard Room, I could hear the screams from the wife as she launched into another fearsome tantrum. She managed to break the hold of the Duty

Corporal and rushed through to the cells and clung to the bars of her husband's cell, alternatively screaming at us in sheer rage, or begging us to release him, as she maintained that in a foreign country she was frightened to be left alone at night, and couldn't manage without her husband. I couldn't quite work out her reasoning, as there must have been many nights when her husband was either on guard duty or was on an exercise, and she was on her own at night. I stood there, feeling absolutely helpless and wondering how I was going to get rid of her. I even played with the idea of locking her up as well until she had quietened down.

Fortunately, the decision was taken out of my hands, as the bush telegraph must have been working overtime over the 'incident' that was being played out in the Guard Room, for a corporal turned up, who obviously knew her and her husband and offered to take her home. We arranged a taxi, and she left accompanied by the corporal as 'quiet as a lamb', and looking as though 'butter wouldn't melt in her mouth'. She certainly threw a bravado performance, but I never did find out whether it was genuine or not. I was rather cross with the Guard Commander letting her in to the Guard Room in the first instance, but I was also rather pleased with myself that I had not succumbed to the easy option of releasing the trooper, which would have been detrimental to maintaining good discipline. When I later learnt of the trooper's record, I realised that I had made the right decision in placing him under close arrest.

I think Angus Anderson that evening, must have regretted that he was a living-in officer in the Mess, as I felt it necessary to disturb him on two or three occasions to keep him informed on what was going on. In actual fact, as I had never faced such a situation before, I was looking for guidance that I was following the right procedures. But Angus, quite rightly didn't interfere and let me make my own decisions on the best way to handle the incident. Nevertheless, my report the following morning, was rather lengthy. I never found out what action was taken against the trooper. I suspected, as I was not called upon to give any evidence that the charge was heard and justice dispensed at Squadron level. I was nevertheless relieved that I was leaving a few days later, as I had a nagging feeling, probably completely unjustified, that somehow and quite anonymously retribution might have been taken.

~

The working day started at 0700hrs when it was still relatively cool and I would often take the HQ Squadron morning muster parade. Most of the morning was spent in the LAD, unless there were other duties, such as being on the feared monthly Adjutant's Parades, which gave Angus Anderson and RSM Garbutt the opportunity of ensuring the drill standard of the two home based Squadrons was up to 'scratch'. This was only right and proper, but it was still unnerving, for if the Adjutant or the RSM spotted a drill mistake made by a subaltern, retribution would have been swift. The standard of the Regimental drill was excellent, and after the 1959 Annual Administrative Inspection, the GOC 17 Gurkha Division was heard to comment to several senior infantry officers that, 'The best drill parade I have seen in the Far East has been from a cavalry regiment.' I felt sorry for those infantry regiments, who were no doubt put through intensive drill parades to ensure that they were never bested by a cavalry regiment again.

On several occasions I took the weekly HQ Squadron Pay Parade, which always worried me. I would sit on the pay desk with Pay Sergeant Hudson on my left, and two witnesses standing behind, who probably had no idea of what they were supposed to do, and wondered why they had been 'volunteered' for the job. The Squadron troopers, craftsmen and other attached personnel would be paraded in front of the pay desk, and would be called forward one at a time. After the requisite number of salutes had

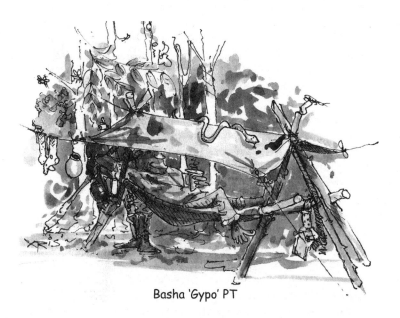

Basha 'Gypo' PT

been exchanged, the Pay Sergeant would state the amount of the pay, less any stoppages for items such as breakages or barrack room damages. I would write the amount in the soldiers AB 64 Pt 1 Service and Pay Book. I would sign this and hand it to the soldier who would confirm that his pay was correct, and he would hand his Pay Book back to me. After receiving his monies, he would salute and march smartly (?) away, and then we would call the next man. The Pay Parade could take some time, and the worrying moment came at the end, for if there was a deficiency, the subaltern taking the Parade would have to make this up out of his own pocket; however, if there was a surplus it didn't work the other way. Fortunately, I never suffered either a surplus or a deficit, and as far as I knew neither did any other subaltern. This was due to the very efficient and professionally run Pay Office by the Regimental Paymaster, Major Peter Bridgeland, ably assisted by Sergeant Hudson and their staff of four, all from the Royal Army Pay Corps (RAPC).

We would work through until 1300hrs, when the officers would retire to the Mess for a glass or two of 'jungle juice' prior to lunch; and then, in the hottest part of the day it was accepted practice to retire to one's bed and stripped down to underpants, enjoy a two-hour siesta. I fell into this life style very quickly, and it took me quite some time to kick the habit after I had returned home.

Tea was served at 1600hrs, after which all officers were expected to participate in, or support Regimental sports or other activities, such as horse riding. After a couple of months of this routine, Mark Barty-King, the senior subaltern, who had won a Military Cross in Aden 1959 when attacking a rebel fort, decided that the two hours of 'kip' in the afternoon was being abused, and issued orders that all subalterns would be involved in recreational activities after 1600hrs, and any subaltern found to be 'skiving' would be awarded 'extras'. To reinforce the point, Mark set off the fire alarm one afternoon, and stood back as we all ran around, captains included, like headless chickens in various directions, not knowing where our assembly points were. Eventually, some semblance of order was restored and a headcount showed that a number of subalterns were missing. A search of their rooms resulted, I believe in a record number of 'extras' being awarded to those who had slept through the fire alarm.

It was fortunate that I played hockey, for I was never caught out practising 'gyppo PT' in the afternoons, as I would usually be involved in either practice games, or matches against other Army units or other teams in the Ipoh and District Civilian League. Still, with only half the Regiment's hockey players available, we did well in reaching the final of the Divisional Cup, where we were beaten 3 –1 by the 2nd /2nd Gurkha Rifles.

It was during one match, on a particularly hot afternoon, when as centre half, my legs suddenly stopped working and I was hardly able to move, and felt that I had completely run out of energy, although my mind was crystal clear. All I could do was to stand still in the middle of the pitch and use my hockey stick like a scythe targeting the legs of the opposing team. After the match, I was quickly taken back to the Mess and made to swallow several salt tablets. Dehydration was a frightening and unnerving experience.

~

Work to a large extent still mainly revolved around the updating of the EMERs and helping out in the Spares Department; for as a LAD, we did not have the luxury of a RAOC sub-unit handling our parts requirements, and there was non-stop form filling, in triplicate, to explain losses in the G 1098 inventory, and why components were being returned as being BLR (Beyond Local Repair).

After the Federation was granted Independence in 1957, preparations were put in hand to build up a new Maintenance Corps for the fledgling Malayan Federation Army, and certain REME units were transferred over, minus their British elements, but which left these new Malayan maintenance units somewhat short of expertise and equipment. 2 Inf Wksp based at Taiping, some fifty miles north of Ipoh was our second line workshop, after the Ipoh workshop premises was handed over to the Federation EME Workshop. This unit and the LAD helped each other as much as possible. One day, as Hugh had some business to discuss with the OC of the Federation Workshop, he took me along to meet the major, an Englishman, an exuberant and very enthusiastic character, who took great pleasure in showing me an official looking medical card with the words '*Major Smith* (not his real name) *is considered to be mentally unbalanced, and if found must be returned to Kampong Rambutan Mental Asylum* (not its actual name). *He is not considered to be dangerous'*. He had great charm, and had somehow persuaded the matron of that institution, not only to give him the card, but to sign it as well.

~

At the beginning of February 1960, 'C' Sqn took over the operational role in the north of the country from 'B' Sqn in support of the anti-terrorist campaign. The Squadron was based in the Gapis rubber estate, which they shared with a Federation police platoon near Kuala Kangsar (a town with an attractive mosque) some forty miles north of Ipoh. Several of my fellow officers, myself included, went up to visit 'C' Sqn late one afternoon, and were warmly welcomed by Major Phil Tillard, the recently appointed Squadron Leader, who gave us a conducted tour of the camp, which did not take long.

The Squadron appeared to be comfortably ensconced in their 'Gurkharised' tents, but with electricity supplied by a generator, a shower facility and an adequate cookhouse. The squadron offices, stores, officers' and sergeants' messes were located in a run down and dilapidated two-storey house. There was very little entertainment, bar from a film show three times a week, with a rather ancient film projector and a screen, which looked as though it had seen better days as a sheet. Apparently there was very little time for relaxation as the 'B' Sqn' post-operational report stated; 'Work increased, and overnight we found a requirement for six troops every day of the week. From November 1959 until February 1960 every Sabre troop, and a composite troop from Sqn HQ was on duty every day. We did manage to get time off for Christmas day with the Regiment.'

Operation 'Java' which was to run for several months was planned to clear the last few known CTs out of Northern Perak, which for 'C' Sqn turned out to be a rather boring and fruitless exercise. By early 1960, most of the CTs had fled into Thailand, with only a small hardcore of six terrorists left in the depth of the Bubu Forest, with orders not to tangle with the security forces, but to wait the time, when they could emerge from the ulu (jungle), reform and become an effective Communist fighting force.

'C' Sqn's work load was primarily escorting food convoys; although there were occasions when the Squadron had to 'hoof it' it into the jungle on foot patrols for up to five days at a time. From the 'C' Sqn report; 'Each troop has been doing a foot patrol or ambush every day of the week, and has been in ambush (not funny – the first night ten men were forced to report sick, as they had blown up like balloons from bites), or on guard or on road patrol, four nights out of every six.'

~

I hadn't long been with the Regiment, when in the Mess one day I was intrigued when 2nd Lieutenant 'Gillie' Turl announced that he would be away for a month, as he had been appointed as the 'Hussar Admiral'. I asked him what was this about.

'There are sixteen boats powered by outboard motors based at Grik, which not only patrol the Perak and Temengor rivers north and west of Grik, but as roads and tracks are non-existent, the boats re-supply and bring in reinforcements to the units carrying out anti-CTs sweeps in the deep jungle near the Thai border. The officer in charge of the boats is unofficially known as 'The Admiral', and apparently I will have the responsibility of not only carrying out the river operations, but ensuring that the boats are in good working order the whole time. I'm really looking forward to the deployment, as it sounds I shall be my own boss.'

I envied 'Gillie' and wondered if a REME NS subaltern had ever been appointed as 'The Admiral'. Sadly I never had the opportunity of finding out, and had to leave Malaya with the title only of 'Officer i/c Land Rover Flotation'.

~

One of the anti-terrorist measures adopted by the security forces during the 'Emergency', was that every ounce of food being transported in Northern Perak had to travel in military escorted convoys. This measure had been successful in preventing food being surreptitiously dropped off at kampongs for onward transmission to the CTs. The Regiment was heavily involved in escorting these convoys, which were due to cease at the end of

March 1960, but were still in full operation in February. Both Daimler Armoured Cars and Ferret Scout Cars were used, not only as the lead and rear vehicles in a food convoy, but also interspersed throughout the convoy. There were two main road routes into Thailand from Malaya; the East Coast one from Kota Bharu, and the West Coast one north from Alor Star. However, there was another route into Thailand in the centre of the country, which led north from Kuala Kangsar on a fairly good metalled road for seventy miles to Grik; but the next thirty-four miles up to Kroh on the Malaya-Thai border was on a single width laterite track. This road was one of the Japanese invasion routes into Malaya in December 1941. It was also the route that the Regiment was operationally involved in escorting the food convoys, and for 'B' and subsequentually 'C' Squadron, this meant a tiring day return trip of some two hundred miles.

It was on a return journey from Kroh down to Grik that there was to occur what Hugh Wright was to call 'The Recovery Highlight of the Season', when halfway between the two towns, a 'C' Sqn Ferret Scout Car, coming round a bend, had skidded, left the laterite road and plunged down a thirty foot near vertical bank, ending upside down in the Sungei Rui. At the completion of the recovery, I was tasked to write a report for record purposes of the operation, which I did under the title:

'Operation Snatch Block'
It was at 2100hrs on Fri 5 Feb 60 when the telephone in the Mess rang, and I was told that the EME, Captain Hugh Wright, wanted to speak to me. Subject: Recovery. A Ferret Scout Car belonging to 'C' Sqn had gone over a 30ft bank and landed in a river. Location: The 112½ milestone north of Ipoh. Twenty miles from the Thai border and right in the middle of 'bandit' country.

The 'C' Sqn Scammell had left Gapis estate for Grik, fourteen miles short of the scene of the accident. From Grik it was reported that the road was unsuitable for such large recovery vehicles. If this were so, we would have to make use of Trewella hand winches, which would have meant it was going to be a long job. The EME asked me to prepare the 'B' Sqn Scammell and to load a Trewella winch with its associated kit. I was also to warn the crew to be ready to leave the Camp at 0400hrs the following morning. Capt Wright, ASM Woodfield and myself would leave by Land Rover at 0430hrs. Confirmation would come through later.

It was necessary to check the authenticity of the report. On the Regiment's previous tour in Malaya in 1950/52, one squadron had been sent out on an anti-terrorist sweep, and not long after they had departed, an outside 'phone call was received by RHQ, with a report that some of the squadron's vehicles had been involved in an accident at a certain kampong. The LAD's recovery section was readied and was on the point of leaving, when someone realised that the named kampong was some two hours drive away, but the squadron had only left an hour previously, and they could not possibly have reached that village. The recovery section was stopped, and then there was a tense time waiting to see if another telephone call would be made. There wasn't, and the conclusion was that if the recovery section had set off, they would have driven into an ambush with fatal results.

By 2230hrs the 'B'Sqn's Scammell and Land Rover had been fuelled and kitted up, even though we came across one minor problem, when we discovered the LAD storeman was out of camp and had the stores key with him. A minor case of breaking and entering occurred.

At 2245hrs Capt Wright appeared. We were going. But the three of us in the Land Rover were to leave even earlier at 0345hrs, so that we could get to the scene of the crash by first light, carry out a recce, make a plan, and then return to Grik to load up the necessary Trewella winch equipment we would need from 'C' Sqn's Scammell.

I arranged an early call at 0315hrs and as we were going into 'bandit' country I wanted the Duty Armoury storeman to have the Arms Store open at 0330hrs. There was nothing more to be done, so we all settled down to get whatever sleep we could.

There was a violent hammering on the door. I groaned and opened my eyes, only to tightly shut them as the guard shone a torch in my face.

'0315hrs, Sir, and Capt Wright says will you put the spare wheel on the Land Rover?'

Taking advantage of what camp lighting there was, I staggered down to the LAD vehicle park. Found our Land Rover, and then went on a spare wheel hunt (the Land Rover had only been re-sprayed two days previously). Eventually I 'borrowed one'.

I drew out three revolvers with thirty-six rounds of ammunition and also .303 rifle ammo for the crew of the 'B' Sqn Scammell. The armoury storeman issued me with strict instructions that the boxes of ammunition were not to be opened, as they were G 1098 kit. I couldn't really work out the logic behind that, especially as we would be working close to the Thai border and a known CT infiltration route into Malaya.

I collected Hugh Wright and ASM Woodfield from their houses, and as we believed the recovery would be completed within the day, we did not bother to take any personal kit. Taking the wheel in turns and fortified from a thermos of black unsweetened coffee, we covered the 112 miles to the scene of the crash by 0730hrs. The last six miles had been very slow, as the road was no better than a track. To our amazement, we found that the 'C' Sqn 6 x 4 Scammell had managed to reach the scene, although it had crossed two wooden bridges with only a couple of inches to spare.

Dawn had broken, and our first view, through the bushes and undergrowth, *was of the Ferret belly up in the middle of the river. The bank, at this point was some 30ft high and nearly vertical, and the road, if it could be called that, was 10ft wide with a 6ft high bank on the other side.*

The ASM, without a moment's hesitation fought his way between the bushes and undergrowth and leapt into the river. We expected to see him disappear from view, as we had no idea of the depth of the river, and the Ferret could have finished up on a sandbar. John Woodfield decided to first remove its wheels before righting the vehicle. First problem. No wheel brace. So Hugh Wright and I drove back to Grik to borrow one from another of 'C' Sqn's Ferrets parked at the police station there. Whilst at Grik, a police sergeant told us that there had been another accident to a military vehicle twenty miles down the road towards Kuala Kangsar. He had no further details. 'B' Sqn's 6 x 6 Scammell had arrived some time before, and so we gave Cfn Hassell the wheel brace and told him to take the Scammell and join up with the other one. The EME and I set off in the other direction to check out the police report. We met the Austin K9 Gantry, which we had asked to be sent out from 2 Inf Wksp at Taiping. The crew reported that it was not a serious accident, and that a Morris 1ton vehicle had rammed the bank of the road it was travelling on, and that they would recover it on their return journey to Taiping.

We returned to Grik and called on my old friends from the Jungle Warfare School, the 1st Bn the Royal Australian Regiment, who were one of the infantry regiments on Operation 'Java', and I hoped that they had stopped driving Bedford RLs and Ferret Scout Cars into swamps. They had a tactical Ops HQ at Grik. Whilst Hugh and I waited for a 'phone call from 'C' Sqn at Gapis, we had the opportunity of watching 1RAR at work, and whilst we were there, a patrol brought in a Temiar aboriginal who had information about CT movements. An interpreter was on hand to question the 'abo', with the result that the Tac Ops HQ radioed their base camp for troops to be air lifted into the suspect location.

There are some twenty different aboriginal tribes in Malaya; the biggest group being the Senoi with a population of over twenty thousand, but who are split into two sub-groups, the Semai and the Temiar, and it is the latter who dwell in the deep jungles of North Malaya, whilst the former live in jungles further south.

A telephone message came through with the news that there was a Sterling Sub-Machine Gun missing. This meant that we could not leave the scene until the weapon had been found, as it was standard operating procedure never to let any arms or ammunition fall into the hands of the CTs. We also learnt that Sergeant Davies, the vehicle commander, had broken both legs and several other bones as well, but had managed to grab and hang onto a branch of a tree over the river, as he was thrown out of the turret of the Ferret. The driver, Trooper Beasley, had been trapped in the vehicle when all the hatches banged shut as it careered down the bank. He was extremely lucky in finishing upside down in the river with his head in an air pocket under the wireless. Both Sgt Davies and Tpr Beasley were also extremely fortunate that they had with them on the Ferret, a Junior Chinese Liaison Officer (JCLO), Sim Choon, who was thrown clear, lay stunned for a few moments and when he came to, heard Tpr Beasley's shouts, and showing great bravery dived into the river and rescued him from the upturned vehicle. Many JCLOs might have just disappeared from the scene of the accident.

For this act, Sim Choon was to receive the Commander-in-Chief's Commendation. Sgt Davies was helicoptered back to Taiping, and then flown back to the UK, where he was expected to make a full recovery.

Hugh and I thanked the Australians for their assistance and returned to the recovery site. Whilst we had been away, the ASM and his team had cleared the bank of all undergrowth and righted the Ferret, which was now facing the bank.

John Woodfield decided to use a 2:1 indirect pull. So in the blistering midday heat, stripped to the waist, sweating profusively, we knocked twenty-four ground anchor pins into the hard laterite surface of the road. The snatch block and winch rope was laid out to the 6 x 4 diesel Scammell, which was anchored at right angles thirty yards down the road. Everything was ready and the ASM gave the order to winch–in. The Ferret came up the bank very easily and smoothly, but shortly before it reached the top of the bank, the winch override came into operation and the recovery pull came to a halt. There was nothing for it but to alter the layout for a 4:1 pull and to disconnect the override on the Scammell's winch. We tried again, and this time succeeded in raising the scout car to within a few feet of the top, when there was a very nasty cracking sound, and the 6 x 4 Scammell shook as the pull came to an abrupt stop. The rope had jumped out of the anchored down snatch block and was jammed between the pulley and the block. The rope could not be moved either way, so we had to run out a 'check' layout from the 6 x 6 petrol Scammell, which was parked beyond the diesel one, to hold the Ferret whilst the trapped rope was freed. The snatch block was badly damaged; so another one was laid down and secured with ground anchors to the track, and the 4:1 indirect pull layout prepared. The engine of the 6 x 4 was started again and the winching began. Another foot or two gained, and as the gradient of the bank was steeper at the top, the nose of the scout car simply dug into the bank, and it obviously wasn't going any further. The winch was reversed, the rope played out and the Ferret slid back into the river.

The edge of the road was cut away to lessen the angle at the top of the bank; but this had to be done with care, as we were in danger of reducing the width of the road, which would not have pleased the locals, as the road, at that point would probably have been too narrow for lorries and single-deck buses to pass. We also laid gun planks horizontally from the road extending to about 4ft

*down the bank, hoping that the front wheels of the Ferret would ride up onto
these and up onto the road.*

*We tried once again and succeeded in reaching the same place as the previous
pull, when the rope jumped out of the snatch block again. The 'check' tackle
was laid out once again from the 6 x 6 Scammell, whilst the jammed snatch
block was freed, fortunately undamaged, otherwise we would have been running
extremely short of snatch blocks.*

*Whilst all this was going on, Hugh Wright decided as the time was after
1700hrs, that we must look for and locate the missing Sterling SMG in the
river before dusk. On the other side of the river, right opposite to where we were
working was a path, which we could clearly see through the trees and bushes,
and which was reputed to be used by CTs entering and leaving Malaya. So
gathering an enthusiastic band of 'volunteers', myself included, who were not
needed on the actual recovery, and setting a good example, Hugh leapt into the
muddy, dank and smelly waters of **the** river, whilst the rest of us followed him
with somewhat less enthusiasm. The water felt so cool after all our exertions
that we forgot about the health hazards we could face, especially contracting
leptospirosis from the rat urine infested water. We formed a line abreast across
the river, and slowly worked our way up stream; sometimes sinking up to our
necks in mud, and other times tripping over sunken tree trunks and ending up
on with our faces under the water. After about half an hour of fruitless searching,
Cfn Scoote, who was shivering badly with cold, was ordered out of the water,
and whilst he was climbing the bank, tripped over a hard object in the
undergrowth and uncovered the Sterling. We were so relieved; otherwise we
would have had to stay at the scene until the SMG had been found.*

*Whilst we were doing our water babies act, the ASM and his hard working
body of men (Cfns Hassell, Carter, Millward, Slater and Rowbottom) had carried
out further clearing of the bank and laid down more gun planks.*

*Hugh rightly decided, as most of us hadn't eaten all day, that before starting
on another pull we needed some hot food. So, from our 24hour compo packs we
heated up and consumed scotch mutton stew, followed by chocolates, sweets
and mugs of tea. Refreshed, at least to a certain extent, we returned to the fray.*

*Although we were in a 'bandit' Black Area, we could not spare the manpower
to put out sentries in defence positions to protect against the unlikely possibility
of a CT attack. Instead we locked our weapons away in the cab of one of the
Scammells, and to hell with the risk!! A few years previously at the height of
the 'Emergency', we would probably have needed infantry support to set up all
round defence positions against probable attack by the terrorists; especially if they
believed that they had both numerical and fire power superiority. A recovery
job in a rather isolated position would have been a far too tempting target.*

*The locals from the nearby kampong had turned up early in the morning
and decided that they were in for a most entertaining and enjoyable day.*

However, we had disrupted the bus service between Grik and Kroh, but after some negotiation, which also involved bringing into the settlement some of the tins of free cigarettes we had with us, we managed to persuade the bus drivers to stop the buses just short of our position, and the passengers would transfer from one bus to the other, and the buses would turn round and return to where they has started from.

After we had eaten, and checked the layout, we decided there was just enough daylight left for one more pull before darkness fell. As the light was fading, the locals were moving in closer and closer to watch the action. I was standing slightly to the left of the recovery pull, with my back to the bank on the other side of the track. Three local young men, dressed in bright shirts, sarongs, sankoks but barefooted, squeezed past me and stood on my right shoulder, in a direct line with the Ferret.

The ASM gave the signal to start winching. Whether it was my recovery training from 6 Veh Trg Bn, Bordon, when we were instructed never to stand in a direct line with a pull, or a sudden premonition, but without standing on ceremony, I ordered the three young men to move to my other side, which they did with some reluctance, giving me dirty looks as they passed me. But I wasn't in the mood to be messed about, and gave them a good push as an incentive to move quicker, as the scout car, once again was winched up the bank.

Suddenly, there was an almighty 'crack' and under extreme tension, the wire rope parted company with the Ferret and together with the snatch block whipped back and buried itself in the bank, where the three Malays had been standing only a few seconds before. If I hadn't moved them, the weight, size and the velocity of the snatch block and wire rope would have smashed them to pulp. Not only did the Malays look shaken, but I was trembling as well, for I was standing only a couple of feet from where the snatch block buried itself into the bank, and the end of the rope could have cut me in two as it whipped past me. Although the Malays could not speak English, and my knowledge of their language was not much more than the common courtesies and ordering a beer or a coke; they gathered round me, grinning from ear to ear with relief, grabbing both my hands and shaking them with such vigour, that I felt I would end up with two dislocated shoulders. Fortunately, I managed to disentangle myself, and giving them a final pat on the shoulder, walked away to join the others to check on the damage.

I have mentally relived that moment many times and have tried to determine, whether it was my training that had made me move those young Malays, or whether I had a premonition that something was going to go seriously wrong. I never came up with a clear-cut answer, but whatever the reason was, I was so relieved that I had become officious, moved them and probably saved their lives.

In the immediate aftermath, we were all rooted to the spot, paralysed with the shock and horror of what had occurred, and what could have occurred, as in the gathering gloom, we watched the Ferret under its own accelerating momentum hurtle backwards down the bank and disappear from view as it entered the river at speed, throwing spray up in every direction. End of the day, and we had very little to show for our hard work except, on the positive side, finding the Sterling Sub-Machine Gun; whilst on the negative side, we had a badly damaged snatch block, a fractured shackle pin, a suspect winch rope and a Ferret Scout Car once more back in the river where it had been some twelve hours previously.

We left four men on guard, who were to be rotated every four hours, and the rest of us drove back to the 1RAR Tac Ops HQ at Grik to phone 'C' Sqn at Gapis, and ask them to send up 24 hour compo packs and blankets. But the Australians wouldn't hear of us asking for support from 'C' Sqn. They were unbelievably generous and helpful. We had descended upon them, totally out of the blue, with only rations enough for one day, and with neither washing kits nor bedding. Typically unprepared 'Poms'! Yet they not only willingly fed us, but also lent us camp beds and let us use their razors. I knew we would have done the same for them, even though I had a low opinion of 1RAR after my previous experience with them at 10 Inf Wksp, and the vehicles they had bogged down, when they had been let out from the Jungle Warfare School, and which had caused me such aggro. However, the way they helped us made me realise that I had seriously misjudged them. They were very professional, efficient and appeared not to be too hidebound by laid down operational procedures, which possibly gave them more flexibility and initiative than we operated under.

From that time, I have had the greatest respect for the Australian Army. There were very close links with their Army, for during my time with the Regiment, we had the Lieutenants Peter Bourke and John McEnerny from the Royal Australian Armoured Corps (RAAC) on a nine months attachment and they were great assets, not only to the Regiment but to the Officers' Mess as well.

We had returned to the scene of the accident by 0800hrs the next morning. The ASM had decided to change his plan, and to 'leapfrog' the petrol 6 x 6 Scammell over the 6 x 4 diesel one up the road from the Ferret. His idea was that the 6 x 4 would winch the scout car up to the embedded gun planks, hold it steady, then tackle which had already been laid out from the 6 x 6 would actually pull the Ferret onto the road.

Whilst all the groundwork was being carried out, as Hugh Wright and I had appointed ourselves as the cooks and 'char wallahs', we set off to the kampong about a mile up the road to buy tea, condensed milk, sugar, and any other food items we could use. The locals were delighted to see us, and in the village store and café insisted that we joined them for a cup of their locally brewed tea, which tasted more like eau de cologne. They had so little to offer,

413

but their hospitality and friendliness could not have been bettered; and I found myself in the rather embarrassing position of being regarded as the local hero by saving the three Malays from serious injury the previous evening.

Although I had done a week of recovery training at Bordon, I felt that it would be presumptuous to offer advice to Hugh Wright and John Woodfield, who had vastly more knowledge and experience than I had. I wasn't much help with the physical work either. The Scammells' crews knew the best way to lay out snatch and change direction blocks for whatever ratios of direct or indirect pulls were needed. I could, however, help to knock in ground anchors using a 7lb sledgehammer. But I wasn't very successful with that, either completely missing the anchor pin and nearly ruining my manhood, as the sledgehammer disappeared between my legs, or only hitting the pin a glancing blow. At least I was usefully employed directing civilian traffic, brewing tea and preparing food.

A report of the LAD's activities in the May 1960 REME 'Craftsman' magazine stated that: 'Mr Caffyn, our new 2Lt, being voted the best Char Wallah east of Suez – he has since been recommended for a 'Malay Kampong Handyman's Course' for which he appears to have a natural aptitude.'

By midday, and after several further unsuccessful attempts, it became obvious that we needed to shorten the tackle attached to the Ferret; for at 6ft from the top of the bank, the snatch block fixed at the front of the scout car fouled the one anchored on the track, so that we could not raise the nose of the scout car sufficiently to get the front brake drums onto the gun planks, and which would then enable us to change tackle to that from the 6 x 6 Scammell. So, yet again the Ferret was returned to the river, whilst a rope in the form of an 'A' was wound in and around the vehicle. But this pull was no more successful than the previous ones, as on winching-in, the nose of the Ferret dug further into the bank before it had even reached the gun planks.

A new approach was needed. After some thought the ASM decided to use a dead tree, some thirty yards back in the jungle as an anchor. So we all went 'jungle bashing' wielding our parangs as we cleared two paths. One, from the 6 x 4 Scammell to the tree, and the other from the tree to the top of the bank above the track. Gun planks were placed around the tree, and a snatch block fixed to it, with another snatch block fixed to the front of the scout car. The plan was that by utilising the tree, we had given ourselves extra height for the snatch block on the front of the Ferret not to dig into the top of the bank, but it would to continue to rise as it passed over the road to the other bank, with the scout car still attached.

Whilst all the preparation work was been undertaken, I cooked a meal using up the last of our rations. The locals were still out in force, and without doubt our recovery operation would be their main talking point for many months if not years to come. We also had visitors from 1 RAR to see how we were getting on, and once again to offer any back-up help we might need. They really were a great bunch.

By 1900hrs all was ready. Dusk was falling. It was a race against time whether we could complete the pull before it was too dark to do so. The ASM was stationed at the top of the bank overlooking the Ferret. Cfn Carter was stationed at the tree, and Cfn Rowbothom was positioned by the door of the 6 x 4 Scammell. Everybody else was ordered to stand well clear; an order the local Malays obeyed with alacrity. It was getting very dark, and to add to the heightened feeling of tension, the nocturnal jungle noises seemed to have started early and were louder than usual. The ASM gave the order to start the engine on the Scammell, and to slowly start the winching-in. The wire ropes quivered under the tension as the strain was taken up, and the Ferret started, once again to rise up from the river and mount the bank. As it neared the top, there was a shout from Cfn Carter at the tree. The tree had moved.

'Carry on,' shouted the ASM.

The winching continued. The front of the Ferret reached the gun planks, and with the extra height of the snatch block fixed to the tree, mounted them and slowly approached the top of the bank. Suddenly there was an ominous crack. The winch rope had once again jumped out of the pulley of the snatch block.

'Don't stop. Carry on as fast as you can.' Shouted the ASM to Cfn Hassell, the Scammell driver. With sparks flying from the jammed rope in the snatch block as it, under protest and making expensive noises, continued to winch in the scout car, until it reached the point of balance, hung there for a moment and then fell forward onto the road. Everybody was shouting and cheering. It had taken thirty-six hours, and a great deal of hard sweaty work. But everybody had weighed in, even including the 'best Char Wallah east of Suez', and we pulled together as only a good, well-trained team could do.

It was completely dark by this time. Hugh Wright set off to Grik to fetch water and beer, and also check to see whether the Australians were prepared to give Cfns Carter, Hassell, Millward and myself accommodation for a second night. By the light of the head and jib lights of the Scammells, we collected all the tackle and other gear and loaded these onto the two recovery vehicles. We also dragged the Ferret to one side of the road. Cfns Slater and Rowbotham, as they had slept in the Australian camp the previous night, were left to spend the night with the Scammells. Capt Wright, ASM Woodfield and Cfn Scoote returned to Ipoh, arriving back at the Camp at 0400hrs the next morning. The rest of us, through the kindness and generous hospitality of the Australians slept in camp beds back at their Tac Ops HQ at Grik.

After the unfortunate introduction I had to 1RAR, I could not fault the willingness they had displayed in helping us, and although I was probably never going to be able to return their hospitality and friendliness, I was not going to forget them. After the Aussies had given us breakfast, one of their *captains very kindly drove us up to the recovery site. It was with sadness that I said goodbye, and thanked the captain for all 1RAR had done for us, and wished them all the best in the future.*

In the daylight we were able to do a better job of clearing up and making good the damage to the bank and to the road. However hard we tried there was still going to be signs of the recovery operation, but at least the bus service between Grik and Kroh restarted. We put the wheels back on the Ferret and connected it up to the diesel 6 x 4 Scammell for a suspended tow back to Gapis estate. We had a last brew up of tea; said cheerio to those locals who had turned up, and who I felt were going to miss the excitement of the recovery, and finally at 1145hrs the two Scammells, in convoy set off for the 112 mile journey back to Ipoh, at a maximum speed of 20mph. We stopped briefly at the Police Station at Grik to say that the road to Kroh had been cleared, and after an uneventful drive reached the 'C' Sqn camp in Gapis Estate at 1630hrs. There we left the diesel 6 x 4 Scammell and the Ferret Scout Car, as both vehicles belonged to 'C' Sqn. The petrol 6 x 6 Scammell had a higher top speed than the 6 x 4 diesel one, and as the main road from Kuala Kangsar to Ipoh was a good one, we made good progress, driving into the Regiment's Lines at 1830hrs. 112 miles at an average of 16miles in the hour was not too bad. But after a cold bath, clean clothes, a good meal it was a relief to get to bed early for a good nights sleep.

Hugh Wright was correct, it was the recovery job of the season, and I was so pleased to have been part of the recovery team. It was an education to see how well the members of the LAD worked together under the direction of the ASM, who was a tower of strength. The more so as the 'C'Sqn recovery crew had only the previous day finished a 24 hour recovery job. John Woodfield admitted that he had made one bad mistake, in first removing the wheels from the Ferret, which although helped in righting the vehicle, but had been a definite hindrance when trying to winch the vehicle over the top of the bank onto the track. He believed that with the wheels left on, the front of the vehicle would not have dug into the bank as it neared the top. I wasn't so sure, as the track was only ten feet wide, and the two snatch blocks being used would still have fouled before the Ferret had been fully pulled onto the track. Leaving the wheels on, and using the dead tree earlier would probably have resulted in the recovery being successfully completed in one day; but that was presuming that we were not going to suffer equipment failure with jammed snatch blocks, bent ground anchor pins and a fractured shackle pin.

This was the end of the report I wrote a few days after we returned to Ipoh. The Ferret Scout Car was recovered back to 40 Base Wksp in Singapore, and after four and a half months of major work was returned to the Regiment in full working order.

~

It was a relief, even for two days to be away from the influence of RHQ, and this feeling wasn't just a figment of my imagination, for when 'B' Sqn settled in at Gapis Estate, they reported; 'Here, remote as we possibly could be from RHQ, we settled down to enjoy our last few months of operations.' Any regimental headquarters was vital to the smooth running of a regiment, but it was synonymous with correct military conduct and discipline. Although it was the commanding officer who would be judged on the efficiency, professionalism and performance of his regiment, it was the adjutant and the RSM who were responsible to see that these and other standards were implemented and maintained. I guessed with the 13th/ 18th Hussars there was a love/hate relationship between the squadrons and RHQ.

I was enjoying my attachment to the Regiment; but as part of HQ Squadron, whose responsibility was to ensure the smooth running of the Regiment, and to answer the time honoured call; 'where the hell is the echelon?' I found, as did many others, that the presence of RHQ was rather like having 'Big Brother' watching over ones shoulder the whole time. Although I was determined not to be awarded 'extras'; this was not a question of being regarded as a 'goody two shoes', but rather, as I had so little time left to see as much of the country as possible, I did not want to lose precious days being confined to Camp, especially as I had ten days leave due to me and I wanted to visit the island of Penang.

HQ Squadron had occasionally, after a full refresher course in map reading, been known to venture out on exercise, and in late 1959 had taken themselves off to the East Coast at Kuantan. I felt that it would do RHQ a power of good, if it followed HQ Sqn's example and took themselves off for a 'jolly' for a week or so, and left HQ Sqn personnel to run the Regiment, which I am sure we would have done with great efficiency and panache.

~

The 17th Gurkha Divisional Boxing Finals were being held at Seremban over the last weekend of February 1960, and as we had three members of the LAD representing the Regiment, Hugh Wright decided that the rest of the LAD should support the team. But instead of driving the three hundred and sixty mile round journey in one day, Hugh thought that the LAD could do with a break, and arranged that we should spend the weekend at Port Dixon on the West Coast some twenty miles south of Seremban. As my birthday fell at the end of February, the trip would be a happy way of celebrating the day, and would certainly make a change over my previous sixteen birthdays, which were spent either at boarding school, college or Mons OCS. Upon reflection, I realised that I hadn't spent a birthday at home since I was eight years old

I travelled with Hugh in his car, which gave me the opportunity of seeing more of the countryside. Ipoh, the largest town and capital of Perak State, lies in the middle of the Kinta Valley, which is the centre of the country's tin mining industry. In 1960 Malaya was the world's largest producer of tin, and for over two thousand years Malayan tin has found its way to the Middle East. As we drove south we passed many open cast tin mines with their dredges, which were such blots on the landscape, and as we left the valley, the mines gave way to rubber plantations, interspersed with acres of rice padi. On our left, in the distance was the mountainous central spine of the Country, and as we passed through the town of Tapah, we passed the turning off to the Cameron Highlands, the popular hill station. Although I had no opportunity to visit the Highlands whilst I was based at Ipoh, as it was still mandatory to travel in a military escorted convoy, I did spend a short time there some years later. The road wound round many bends for thirty-eight miles, as it climbed from near sea level at Tapah to six and a half thousand feet at the Cameron Highlands. There were many tea plantations near Tanah Rata, a short distance from the hill station. Here was Fosters Smoke House, - a hotel, bar and restaurant with a delightful old-fashioned atmosphere. There was a nine-hole golf course and many bungalows, several being corporate ones. The air was so fresh after the heat of the lowlands, that in the evening, it was cold enough at 50° Fahrenheit for open log fires to be lit, although the nocturnal noises appeared to be more vocal and louder than anywhere else I visited in Malaya. The Cameron Highlands was, and must surely still be a beautiful hill station, with its spectacular views, its three waterfalls, its beautiful butterflies, such as the Rajah Brooke, the Birdwing and the Malayan Owl, to name but three of the eight hundred species of butterflies found in Malaya.

But that was in the future. Back to 1960. There was not a great deal of traffic on the road south to Kuala Lumpur (KL). What lorries we came up behind, swiftly moved over, when the driver was warned by the banging on the cab roof by the 'guard' travelling in the back. There seemed to be a lot of pigs being taken to market or wherever, and I felt sorry for the little porkers as each one was packed, lying down in a small cylindrical rattan basket, with no room to stand up, and there were usually several rows of these piled one on top of the other in the backs of the lorries we passed. I hated to imagine what condition they were in when they arrived at their destination.

Some miles south of the town of Bidor, we started driving through the twenty-seven miles of endless bends, with the jungle pressing down on both sides of the road, from Slim River through Slim Village and down to Tanjong Malin, a rubber-tapping town with a population of twenty thousand that had been a hot bed of CT activity, and where by the end of 1952, some fifty-two members of the security forces and local civil administration officials had been either killed in ambushes or murdered. General Templer using a carrot and stick approach, however won the 'hearts and minds' battle in Tanjong Malin, and for the remaining eight years of the 'Emergency' the town became one of the most peaceful areas in the country. The road south had so many bends with little opportunity to drive fast, that it was easy to see why it had such a bad reputation for CT ambushes.

In early January 1942, Slim River was the location of a major battle with the advancing Japanese Army, that saw the destruction of the 11th Indian Division, and which had such a catastrophic effect on the defence of southern Malaya.

Seven miles north of KL, Hugh took a short detour to the Batu Caves, a network of caves running deep into the limestone hills, but unfortunately we did not have time to visit these, and after a quick snack lunch at the cafeteria, we were back on the road again, reaching Port Dixon late afternoon. Hugh drove down to the waterfront, with the sea looking an amazing deep blue in the late afternoon sun, and then we continued south for another eight miles, when Hugh turned off the road on to an expanse of open ground, which led down to the sea. This was a Malay Territorial Army site. The rest of the LAD had arrived before us and had already set up camp; the 24-hour compo ration packs had been opened and a meal prepared which we ate around an open fire, watching the sun go down in a ball of fire with darkness, as it does in the tropics falling very quickly. The nocturnal insects started their nightly chorus as we sat around the fire drinking Anchor beer and talking to a very late hour.

The Malay TA Camp was in a beautiful location. It gave on to sandy beaches with the sea looking very inviting. To the north the coast curved away towards Port Dixon, whilst to the south there was a bay, known as the Blue Lagoon for the coral, which could be seen just below the surface at low tide, but due to the sharpness of the coral and the danger of infection if cut, the lagoon was not the best place for swimming. Hugh and I walked through the shallow waters of the bay towards Cape Rachado, the headland at the end of the Blue Lagoon. We followed a small path to the top of the headland, where stood a lighthouse. From here there were magnificent views of the coastline, with tree-lined bays and small headlands running south towards Malacca. In the distance a range of jungle covered hills topped with a ring of clouds rose up into the sky. Out in the Straits of Malacca two dark painted junks made their leisurely way northwards.

Later in the morning, Hugh took the LAD back towards Port Dixon, but a few miles short of the town, we turned off the main road and drove down a narrow track which led to the Si-Rusa Club. Here amongst palm trees was a water sports centre and cafeteria. I was such a failure at water skiing, that at Hugh's suggestion, I tried aquaplaning on one board. This was more successful, and I was happily towed round the bay for over ten minutes, until my arms ached so much that I had to let go. Most of the members of the LAD had never tried water skiing or aquaplaning before, and we all had great fun, making so much noise with our laughter and splashing from falling off skis into the water, that we probably frightened away any sea snakes that were in the vicinity. We all appreciated getting away from our normal days activities (and RHQ), and it was typical of Hugh's leadership style that he always put the well-being and welfare of the members of the LAD as a high priority, which certainly helped to maintain the morale of the unit.

Late afternoon Hugh and I changed into Mess Kit, and leaving the rest of the LAD to the tender mercies of the ASM, we drove to the St. Paul's Institute in Seremban, where the Divisional Boxing Finals were being held. We took our seats, greeting the other officers from the Regiment as the bell sounded for the first round of the opening bout. We turned, faced the ring to watch the fight, and to our amazement one of the boxers, spread eagled and unconscious on the canvas was being counted 'out' within thirty seconds of the bell. Fortunately, it was the 1st Foresters man who was out 'cold', and Corporal Baillie REME, who for a bantamweight boxer packed a powerful punch, had put him there. He was subsequently the runner up to the Malayan Bantam Weight champion and also to the FARELF Flyweight Champion. Unfortunately, the two other LAD personnel representing the Regiment did not fare so well. The first string welterweight Sergeant Mullinger, although being ahead on points, sustained a cut eye and the referee had to stop the fight, and Craftsman Riding, our second string welterweight met a better boxer. With two squadrons away on detachment, it was always difficult for the Regiment to field, whatever the sport, its best teams and as a consequence, regrettably we lost the Finals seven bouts to four.

~

The next day saw our weekend break come to an end, and after packing up and cleaning the site, we departed on the long journey back to Camp. I liked Ipoh. It was modern, clean, well laid out with wide roads bordered by the flame of the forest and the scented frangipani trees, bougainvillæa, hibiscus and orchids. The houses on the outskirts of the town were spacious with large well-maintained gardens, and were evidence of the wealth of the town, its economy being based on the tin mining industry in the Kinta Valley. Although hot, I used to enjoy walking along the path running alongside the banks of the Sungei Kinta to the Meh Prasit Sumaki Siamese Temple, which housed the 75ft reclining figure of the Lord Buddha, the largest in Malaya, and where devout Buddhists donated gold leaf to cover the statue. On the outskirts of Ipoh were numerous caves, which used to be hiding places for robbers; but subsequently became hiding places for CTs on the run, and it was in one of these caves that Siu Mah, commander of the 11ᵗʰ Regiment in Pahang, who led the ambush that killed Sir Henry Gurney, the High Commissioner on the road up to Fraser's Hill in October 1951, was betrayed by fellow terrorists and killed by the security forces in March 1959.

The CTs had operated a most efficient courier network. Chin Peng had appointed a young and pretty Chinese girl - Lee Meng, to set up and run the CT communication system, which she did with ruthless efficiency, under the cover of being a casual labourer in the local tin mine around Ipoh. It took Special Branch some considerable time before they discovered that she worked in, and controlled the whole Malayan CT communication and courier network from Ipoh.

The town bordered on the northern, eastern and western sides by jungle covered mountains, with the highest being on the east with Gunung Karbu rising to over seven thousand feet, and being in a bowl, Ipoh seemed to be hotter than other towns in Malaya.

There was not a great deal to do in the evening. There were two air-conditioned cinemas, showing the latest British and American films, and I used to go to these fairly regularly, irrespective of what was showing, just to feel cool. There were several bars and restaurants, but these were a poor substitute for the entertainment that was available in Singapore. There were a couple of Turkish baths and massage parlours in town, and there were invariably stories circulating about the services offered by the Chinese masseuses. However, these stories were always second hand, and we never knew whether they were true or not. One of our fellow subalterns surprised us one day by saying that he was going to try out one of these Turkish baths and dared us to accompany him. But we were cowards. On the chosen evening, we all sat at a nearby bar, making sure that he actually went into one. Some time later, he emerged looking somewhat thoughtful, but assured us that he only had a Turkish bath, although he was quieter than usual for some days after.

~

In March 1960, 'A' Squadron, which had been on a six month Internal Security deployment in Singapore returned to Ipoh, and I had the opportunity of meeting the Squadron Officers, 'Jock' Bell, the Squadron leader and Captain (later Major) Peter Waddy, who was the Squadron Second-in-Command. Peter was a keen photographer, and had set up a darkroom in his bathroom. He was instrumental in promoting my interest in black and white photography, and I spent many happy evenings helping him develop and print the films he had taken. He taught me so much about dark room technique that what started out for me being a happy 'snapper', developed over the years into a very serious hobby, becoming semi-professional at one time. I have always believed, that without the added dimension of colour, more skill was needed in producing exhibition class black and white prints, where composition and the juxtaposition of light and shade were all important.

I would spend hours in my darkroom, for I believed it was only through darkroom technique and creativity that an ordinary black and white negative was made into a prize-winning print. It was thanks to Peter starting me off, and I kept in touch with him for many years, that I gained my Licentiate of the Royal Photographic Society (LRPS) in 1983. Sadly my dark room is no more, and I have succumbed to the temptations of digital photography and computer manipulation; although I must admit the scope for creativity that computer software offers has to a certain extent, satisfactorily replaced the darkroom, and it's considerably cleaner and cheaper.

Peter was also a record collector and owned the first stereo gramophone I had seen and heard, for in early 1960 such equipment was relatively new to the market, and stereo records had only recently reached the record shops.

~

It was in March that the LAD received a shock, when we learnt that we were losing our EME, Hugh Wright, who was taking up the position of Adjutant at HQ, 17 Gurkha Division at Seremban. We were all very sorry to see him leave. I knew that we all had respect, confidence in and could trust Hugh. He ran the LAD very efficiently, but with humour and a human touch. I felt I was losing a very good friend, and as he left I wished him and his family, who had been so kind to me, all the best for the future. Very sadly, at the early age of 45, Hugh died suddenly in 1974, shortly after his promotion to full Colonel.

We waited with a certain amount of trepidation for his replacement. One advantage of serving in a Regiment is that when a vacancy occurs, appointments are made from within the unit. One of the disadvantages of a Corps such as REME, is that promotions and appointments are usually made from other units, where the individual is not known to the unit he is joining, and visa versa. This was the case with our LAD, but as it turned out, we had nothing to worry about. Captain Jim Allen, our new EME, was a worthy successor to Hugh Wright, and soon settled into both LAD and Regimental life, and exhibited the same qualities in running the unit as Hugh.

Many years later I was to catch up with Jim who, as a full colonel was Deputy Commandant at the School of Electrical and Mechanical Engineering (SEME) at Bordon, (No 4 Armt and No 6 Trg Bns appeared to have disappeared) and subsequently when he was serving at HQ Land at Wilton.

It was probably my imagination, and I possibly did the Corps a great disservice; but from my limited experience, I felt at the time that those REME officers who were stationed in static workshops in Singapore, and whose responsibilities were more akin to managing large engineering factories, employing a significant number of civilian staff as well as REME personnel, and where the risk of being involved in combat situations were minimal, needed qualities that were different to those REME officers stationed in front line units in Malaya. In 17th Gurkha Division, the responsibilities of the LADs and 2nd Line Workshops in a mobile and operationally fluid role, were to provide the technical back-up for those 'teeth' units fighting the CTs, but whose officers could well have, at the height of the 'Emergency', been involved in a combat role fighting off CT attacks and ambushes. REME needed officers for LADs and 2nd Line mobile workshops, who being nearer 'the sharp end' were not only technically competent, but were also fully trained fighting soldiers. As the Schedule of the Royal Warrant on the formation of REME laid down, *'All officers and other ranks of the Royal Electrical and Mechanical Engineers shall be combatant in the fullest sense'*. To prove the point, REME suffered between 1,400 and 1,500 battle casualties in North West Europe in 1944/5.

There was one other reason that was put to me at the time, and which could be interpreted as being snobbish. Regiments, such as the 13th/18th Hussars were, and still are 'families', and each Regiment is a close-knit community. This is particularly true of the Officers' Mess, and it is vital, especially under active service conditions that there is complete trust, confidence and understanding between all the officers. This is also true for promotions within the Regiment, where the strengths and weaknesses of every officer are known, and there is little risk of someone being promoted 'beyond the level of his competence'. A large Corps like REME, which in the 1950s and 60s had worldwide commitments, was unable to achieve the close 'bonding' that a Regiment, whether a single or two battalion one could do. It was therefore important that any attached officers, like the EME of a Regimental LAD, was of such a calibre that he fitted seamlessly into the Regiment, and it was surely right for a Regiment to expect such an appointment to have been made with that factor taken into consideration.

~

The Army, certainly when I did my National Service, was almost obsessive that unit standards were maintained, and I counted myself very lucky moving from Pandan to Ipoh that I escaped the annual Administrative and Technical Vehicles Inspections, and also the annual physical fitness tests both at 10 Inf Wksp and at the 13th/18th Hussars. A great deal of very hard work was put in by all and sundry prior to the two Inspections, as no Commanding Officer or Officer Commanding would tolerate anything less than an 'Excellent' grading, and which was entered onto his Service Record.

However, I managed to keep my hand in with both the Sterling Sub-Machine Gun and the Lee Enfield .303 rifle on the Surla Ranges at Ipoh, when Annual Classification Tests were under way. The ranges could only be reached by passing through the Camp of the 2nd/6th Queen Elizabeth's Own Gurkha Rifles. Both the Camp and the ranges were overlooked by a high jungle covered gunung; and a story going the rounds at the time, was that the Gurkha Battalion then in Camp was on parade, when a group of CTs, hidden in the gunung, let loose with both rifle and Bren LMG fire onto the parade, resulting in possibly the fastest exodus from a parade ground in the history of the British Army.

By 1960, the CTs had been flushed out of the gunong and the ranges could be used in complete safety. However these lay in a bowl with gunungs on three sides, and seemed to be the hottest spot in and around Ipoh; but it was with relief, whilst the afternoon classification tests were being carried out, to sit on the bank of the stream that ran alongside the ranges, and cool one's feet in the water. However, it was advisable to have a tin or packet of cigarettes to hand, to burn off the leeches that quickly gathered and latched themselves onto ones legs.

I was somewhat concerned, when after two months in Ipoh, my hands started to bother me. The Medical Officer referred me to the skin specialist at 28th Commonwealth Brigade HQ, who diagnosed that I was suffering from Dermatitis, which was probably caused by the heat, and he did not feel, that even with medication, it would clear up completely until I was back in a cooler climate; which it did eventually when I returned to the UK.

~

In the close-knit Regimental community there were always incidents, whether true or not, but which brought a smile to everyone's faces. At Ipoh airport there was a Gliding Club, and I said that I was interested in learning gliding. The answer was a shake of a head.

'That's not possible, the Club only has one two-seater glider, and that was written off last month, when coming in to land it collided with Sergeant Beavan's head.'

I asked what had happened to the Sergeant.

'Oh! He just had a headache'.

I never did find out why a glider and Sergeant Beavan's head should be on the same glide path at the same time.

There was never a satisfactorily explanation how one troop managed to get a Saracen APC across a stream, but managed to leave the bridge at the bottom of the stream, or how another troop managed to turn a Daimler

Armoured Car upside down in the sea off Port Dixon. The story that I most enjoyed, which was apparently true, was that of the ambitious and immaculately turned out sergeant, who walking past RHQ one day, noticed that the rest of his Squadrons' Sergeants were parading outside the RSM's office. Thinking he was missing something important, he joined the end of the line, but was less than pleased when the RSM marched out of his office, and gave each of the assembled sergeants two extra duties for scruffy turnout. The RSM had no sympathy for the sergeant who complained that he wasn't meant to be there, and told him that he would have to do the extra duties for not minding his own business.

'A' Sqn, which was on Internal Security (IS) duties in Singapore in the latter half of 1959, took part in a joint IS exercise with the police. The Squadron acted as 'rioters', and were in the unique position of being able to provoke the police with impunity. The police, apparently entered into the spirit of things with such gusto, that one constable became so aggressive with the 'rioters', that he had to be calmed down with a gentle tap on the head with a sandbag. The Squadron decided to make the exercise more realistic, and laid six inch nail imbedded planks across a road and 'bagged' one police vehicle, a Chinese lorry and two cyclists, before they were persuaded that perhaps they were taking the exercise too enthusiastically, and that it was important as 'rioters' that they kept the police and local populace on their side!!

~

It was in April 1960, that the decision was made to send half of 'A' Squadron across Malaya and up the east coast to Kota Bharu, near the Thai border; a distance of over five hundred miles. The exercise was meant to be an air-portability one, but as the RAF had neither got the aircraft nor the budget to fly 'A' Squadron with their Ferret Scout Cars and Land Rovers with their trailers up to Kota Bharu, it was decided that the exercise would be one to determine how quickly the half Squadron, in an emergency could get up to the Thai border on the East Coast.

When I heard about the proposed exercise, and having spent a week at Beserah on the East Coast with 10 Inf Wksp, which had whetted my appetite to see more of that side of the country, I was determined to somehow get on the exercise. It would also mean I would be away from the influence of RHQ. I badgered Jock Bell, the Squadron Leader, that as I not only knew the East Coast, but also knew an ideal spot for a base camp a few miles north of Kuantan. I was certainly economical with the truth; knowing only eight out of a two hundred and thirty mile coastline from Kuantan to Kota Bharu, could hardly be construed as an intimate knowledge of the East Coast. Jock Bell eventually agreed to take me, and Jim Allen was also prepared to release me. However, to satisfy RHQ, there needed to be a valid reason for me to be on attachment to 'A' Sqn. So it was decided that four members of the LAD would accompany me, who as well as providing emergency mechanical cover, would also act as the Assault Section in case we were needed in an infantry role.

The original intention was that the half Squadron would only take Ferrets, Land Rovers and trailers; but as the RAF were unable, or perhaps unwilling to participate in a joint duo-Service air-portability exercise, it was decided to take two Bedford RL trucks to act as the 'B' Echelon and carry essential supplies. Having loaded up and hitched our quarter ton trailer to the Land Rover, we left camp as dawn was breaking, turned south, and by lunchtime we had made such good time, that we had passed through Tanjong Malin, and some miles further on we turned east onto the Fraser's Hill and Raub road. The day had started with sunshine, but as we drove up into the central mountain range and to the junction known as 'The Gap', where the road to Fraser's Hill, the principle hill resort turned off to the left, the weather had

The Assault Section

really closed in and we were subjected to severe tropical rain. Jock Bell called a halt, and the Squadron drove off the road, parked along the verges as we all tried unsuccessfully to prepare a meal in the rain.

As we waited the order to move off, I looked at the junction with the narrow road leading off to Fraser' Hill, and tried to imagine what it must have been like for Sir Henry Gurney, his wife and his secretary that Saturday morning in early October 1951, as they drove up to the hill station to spend the weekend there, to round a bend and suddenly, and quite unexpectedly to come under sustained and ferocious Bren gun fire from the CT ambush. Sir Henry, trying to protect his wife was killed instantly, but his wife and his secretary survived by lying on the floor of the High Commissioner's Rolls Royce. It was ironic that the CTs under Siu Mah, were really waiting to ambush a military convoy that they had learnt from their intelligence was expected on that road, as they badly needed to capture the weapons from the convoy. But after lying in their ambush positions in vain for two days and nights, the CTs decided, in frustration to attack the next vehicle that came into view. It was tragic that it happened to be the High Commissioner, and apparently Siu Mah had no idea who was in the car. The shooting of Sir Henry Gurney had repercussions throughout Malaya; as many people felt that if the High Commissioner could be killed in broad daylight, what chance was there for the Government and security forces being able to defeat the terrorists and prevent a communist take-over of the country. The new High Commissioner, appointed by Churchill was General Sir Gerald Templer, who enthusiastically embraced the 'Briggs Plan' and provided the necessary drive and commitment that ensured the final defeat of the communist terrorists, which earned him the nickname of 'The Tiger of Malaya'. Lt-Gen Sir Harold Briggs was responsible for masterminding the largest social revolution then known in Asia, the resettlement of 600,000 squatters into New Villages, which did so much to isolate the CTs from their supplies and intelligence.

After a short break, we continued our journey. Although the five of us comprising the Infantry Assault Section were warm and dry in our Land Rover, I felt sorry for those in the Ferret Scout Cars, as both the drivers and the vehicle commanders had to have their turret hatches open and the crews got very wet. The conditions were so bad that as we descended from 'The Gap' down to the town of Bentong on a straight stretch of road, the Ferret in front of me suddenly veered off the road and disappeared into a ditch. The driver had been completely blinded by the rain. Fortunately the vehicle sustained no damage, and was fairly easily recovered back onto the road. As we left the mountains behind, we also lost the rain, and we soon drove into Bentong and joined the main road from Kuala Lumpur to Temerloh, which 10 Inf Wksp had travelled along the previous September. The traffic was light and as both ferries were this time operational, we managed to get the Squadron across the river in what must have been record time. Jock Bell was keen to press on, and wanted to get across the ferry at Kuantan by nightfall. We didn't quite make this, and were forced to make camp on the same airstrip as 10 Inf Wksp used the previous autumn. After the evening meal, we sat round the fire and chatted whilst Jock consulted his map, trying to work out where north of Kuantan we could establish our base camp, and where 'B' Echelon under Peter Waddy, the Squadron 2IC would be left, whilst the Sabre Troops drove on to Kota Bharu.

I committed what is regarded in the Army as a cardinal sin. I volunteered for something. I told Jock of this lovely stretch of beach at Beserah some miles north of Kuantan. I must have been very poetic in my description, for he did not hesitate, and detailed me to lead the Squadron to the location early the next morning. As Jock wanted to be at the site in time for breakfast, he ordered me to leave at 0530hrs, with the rest of the Squadron following on half-an-hour later. I began to regret my enthusiasm in mentioning the beach at Beserah. It had been broad daylight when 10 Inf Wksp had arrived at the site, but on this occasion I was going to have to find it in the dark before dawn broke. I could imagine nothing worse than having to stand in the middle of the road, wave Jock down and admit, 'Please Sir, I can't find it.' Jock would probably have had my guts for garters, and made some rude comments about Corps personnel and their lack of map reading ability. Still, there was nothing for it; I was committed, but I wished I had kept my big mouth shut.

At 0530hrs the next morning, I set off with my intrepid assault section, with Lance Corporal Pawley as my driver, who was one of the most cheerful characters in the LAD and always with a grin on his face. I expressed my fears to him, and he immediately made me feel better when he replied; 'Don't worry, Sir. We'll find it.' I wished I had his confidence. The Kuantan ferry opened early and we were one of the first vehicles across, but it was still pitch dark as we drove north from Kuantan. I knew the Squadron was only thirty minutes behind me, and driving fast to catch us up, as I had to keep stopping to check if I had found the right place. All I could remember was that the entrance to the site was marked by a gap in the scrub that bordered the road. After about eight miles, I thought I recognised the spot. I told Corporal Pawley to stop. But it was not the right place. I told him to continue up the road very slowly, whilst I went along the foreshore, as I felt I had a better chance of recognising the 10 Inf Wksp camp site from that side. In a panic and an absolute sweat, I stumbled along the beach, but nothing looked familiar.

However, after about a mile, just as I was about to admit defeat and as dawn was breaking, the surroundings began to take shape, and I thought I recognised a line of trees at the back of the beach. To my utter relief, I had found the right spot. I ran through to the road, where I could see the headlights of the Land Rover about a couple of hundred yards away. But what really frightened me was that about a quarter of a mile behind the Land Rover, I could see the lights of the Squadron's vehicles coming up fast. I urged Corporal Pawley to get a move on and to drive into the site; and then, with great aplomb, I stood in the middle of the road and directed the Squadron through the gap in the scrub, as if I had been waiting for them for some time. Little did they ever know what a close run thing it was, and how much of a blue funk I had been in. I hate to think what the outcome would have been if the Squadron had driven past before I had found the beach, and left me having to catch up with them and admit I was lost. However, it did not take long for the base camp to be set up, and as the sun rose over the South China Sea, Jock Bell and the others thanked me for directing them to such a beautiful spot.

It was great being back at Beserah, and I was impressed at the speed at which the Squadron made themselves 'at home'. They had obviously done this many times before. We set up the Officers' Mess in the front half of a large tent, with the back being our sleeping quarters. However we did not have any 'thunderboxes', and once again it was a shovel job and bogging down in the bushes.

Although there was a certain logic in the small detachment from the LAD being on the exercise; not only for our mechanical skills, but also for the ability to act as infantry if we were ever needed in that role and to fulfil the Royal Warrant of 1942 that, 'All officers and other ranks of the Royal Electrical and Mechanical Engineers shall be combatant in the fullest sense'. However, I was not certain how effective we would have been in that role, as we had not been issued with any ammo. Perhaps the presence of Father Jones, the Ipoh Garrison Roman Catholic Padre also being on the exercise may have been of some comfort, as someone in RHQ, with an odd sense of humour, obviously thought that as we had no doctor with us, we would be more in need of spiritual rather than medical help. Father Jones was a delightful man, very human with a great sense of humour, and he certainly added to our enjoyment at Beserah. Being C of E, I nevertheless found it a rather moving service, as I observed Father Jones celebrating Mass on the beach on the Sunday morning.

After two days of R & R (Rest and Relaxation), and leaving the 'B' Echelon behind, the rest of us in Ferrets and Land Rovers, set off for the two-day dash up to Kota Bharu. The distance was not great, some two hundred and thirty miles, but we would have to cross eight ferries, and each one could take two to three hours to get the Squadron across.

We left before dawn, with the road following the coastline, and after thirty miles reached the ferry at Chukai as dawn was breaking. The ferry operator obviously worked union hours, and it was some half-an-hour before he deigned to open up. This and the next two ferries were rope operated and as a consequence very slow. In fact the head of the Squadron had crossed the second ferry five miles up the road before the tail had crossed the first. A further thirty miles and we crossed the ferry at Kuala Kerteh, a fishing kampong with the wooden fishing huts built on stilts, but their corrugated roofs looked rather out of character. The next ferry was at Banda Panka, which was a far more charming and attractive fishing kampong, with the attap roofed wooden huts tightly clustered close to the beach, with tall palm trees behind and which gave a feeling of peace and serenity.

Our progress north was rather like a royal procession, as most of the locals were Malays, and they would drop whatever they were doing and come to the roadside to wave and cheer as we drove past. The Malays we came across were, and presumably still are, a very friendly, natural, dignified race, but with charm and are rather easy going. So long as they were able to grow rice padi, have access to the many fruit trees and spices that grew in profusion in every kampong, and were able to trap fish in the rivers, they were perfectly happy, and didn't really need a great deal of money; but if they did, selling a few strips of latex from rubber trees would provide sufficient for their simple needs. In every kampong we drove through, life seemed to revolve around the local store, which invariably, even in the most remote kampong displayed Coca or Pepsi Cola signs outside the store, and as it was unwise to drink the local water, being able to buy a bottle of chilled coke from the generator-operated refrigerator was always welcome.

We crossed the next ferry at Kuala Dungun having covered some eighty miles, and crossed five ferries in six hours, which wasn't bad going. Jock Bell decided to stop for a lunch break, and we supplemented our Army rations with fruit bought at the local store. One of my fellow officers had discovered the communal kampong bath tucked behind some bushes, and I never knew how he did it, but he managed to persuade a Malay woman to scrub his back whilst he took a bath.

That afternoon, we covered another fifty miles, but only had to cross one further ferry at Maran, before we decided to harbour for the night just south of Kuala Trengganu. This was another beautiful spot. We parked our vehicles in the shade of the palm trees that grew at the back of the sandy beach. The road north hugged the coast from Beserah to Kuala Trengganu, and it was a feature of the East Coast that there were so many lovely places, which were completely unspoilt and undeveloped. I was certain that one day in the future, when a road had been built between Endau and Kuantan and all the rivers had been bridged, with the ferries committed to history, that there would be large-scale tourist development on the East Coast. I hoped its beauty and charm would not be spoilt, and that the simple and happy lives of the Malays in their kampongs would not be adversely affected.

The Sungei Trenggani was a wide river, and the ferry was propelled in a similar way as the one at Temerloh, and could take four Ferret Scout Cars on each crossing. Unfortunately, there was quite a bit of civilian traffic, and it took several hours for the Squadron to cross the ferry. These delays were most frustrating, especially as my Assault Section was invariably 'tail-end Charlie', and we always had the longest wait before crossing a river. The result was that we had to go 'like a bat out of hell' in order to catch up with the rest of the Squadron. Although, at the time it was still frowned on for an officer to drive an Army vehicle; in order to give the others a break, I did take over the wheel on a number of occasions, and it was on one of these 'catch-up' jobs that I nearly came seriously unstuck. We crossed many streams and although the road surface was tarmac, the bridges were invariably built of wood, with planks laid at right angles to the road, but with two other planks laid on top, parallel with the road and spaced apart at the same width as a vehicle's wheels. I had driven over many of these bridges without any trouble, as it was only necessary to line up the Land Rover before the bridge to make sure that the wheels ran along the parallel planks. But on this one occasion, it had been raining and the road and bridge surface was wet.

Although, our speed was limited towing a trailer, I was nevertheless driving fairly fast to catch up with the others, and as I drove over the bridge the trailer slid sideways on the wet surface of the wood with the rear wheels of the Land Rover following suit. Fortunately the road was straight and there was no oncoming traffic, as the Land Rover and trailer 'shimmied' from side to side for several hundred yards, before I managed to regain full control of the vehicle. Needless to say after this scare, I retired from driving.

Bar from one further small ferry at Jertat between Kota Bahru and Kuala Trengganu, we covered the last ninety miles in good time, but we still did not reach our destination until evening and just as darkness was falling. My Land Rover was still 'tail-end Charlie', but we had managed to catch up with the rest of the Squadron just as we reached Kota Bharu. This was just as well, for Jock Bell had decided we would make camp down on the beach beyond the town, which we drove straight through down to 'The Beach of Passionate Love'. If we hadn't caught up, and without a wireless, and not knowing Jock's intention we would have become hopelessly lost.

Having ensured that my assault section was settled in, I went to join the other officers, who were all standing around in a group, and discussing whether we should rough it on the beach for the night, or hire for the Officers' Mess, one of the holiday chalets that were situated at the back of the beach. We decided upon the chalet, and led from the front by the Squadron Leader, we all trooped into the bar-restaurant. An Indian, who appeared from the back and seemed to be the manager greeted us:

'Good evening, Sirs. How can I help you?'

'We want to hire a chalet for the night,' replied Jock.

The Indian's eyebrows took off vertically upwards, as he looked at each of us in turn; and doubtless his mind was in overdrive, as he wondered why five grown men wanted to hire one chalet. However, he was obviously not one to lose the opportunity of making a quick 'buck'.

'Most certainly, Sirs', he continued, and it was a good job we had left Father Jones back at Beserah; 'and may I have the honour of laying on the women for you?'

It was our turn for eyebrows to shoot upwards, and I thought that 'The Beach of Passionate Love' was obviously going to live up to its name. However, we turned down his kind offer, which probably made him wonder further about us, and he was obviously disappointed that his vision of having a very profitable booking was fast disappearing. He did badly by us, as the chalet letting rates were for two people, which we paid him and then, as there were only two beds, we brought our camp beds into the chalet. However, to add insult to injury, we then decided to join the rest of the lads outside for our evening meal. This was probably a wise decision, for if the food in the restaurant was to the same standard as the condition of the chalet, we may well have ended up with gippy tummies.

The rooms were dirty and smelt of stale sex, with cockroaches and other insects having a free run. As one of my fellow officers remarked:

'It's obvious that these chalets are used for one night stands, and I now know how 'The Beach of Passionate Love' got its name.'

In reality, the name was due to the turtles that came ashore and laid their eggs. There were apparently several beaches on the East Coast favoured by the turtles, but the beach at Kota Bharu was probably the most well-known one. It was a shame that as it was not the egg-laying season, I was never to see the turtles.

Any visitor to our chalet could have been excused for wondering what was going on. The two beds were so dirty and smelly, that we all decided to sleep on our camp beds, which we put down anywhere we could find a space, after we had done our best to eliminate the chalet's cockroach population. If one of us had wanted the loo in the middle of the night, it would have been similar to being on an obstacle course, having to climb over bodies and camp beds in the dark. It would probably have been easier, quicker and certainly quieter to have opened a window and peed from there.

Still not trusting the food in the restaurant, we joined the rest of the Squadron for breakfast on a grey, cold, damp and windy morning. The sea was rough and it was obvious that there was a storm out in the South China Sea. At the north end of the beach was a small fishing kampong. Drawn up on the rather steeply sloping beach were gaily-painted fishing boats, with the Malay fishermen in the brightest coloured sarongs I had yet seen in Malaya, waiting for the sea to moderate. They were all staring out to sea, and as I followed their gaze, I saw that their interest was centered on another fishing boat, a hundred yards out to sea, that was beating up and down the shore, obviously not able to beach in the high seas.

We were all disappointed in the 'The Beach of Passionate Love', and felt our beach at Beserah was more attractive; and although we had planned to spend the day at Kota Bharu, Jock Bell decided and we fully agreed with him, that we would be better off if we rejoined the 'B' Echelon a day early.

Kelantan State, which means 'The Land of Lightning' and of which Kota Bharu is the capital is famous for its fine filigree silver work, which has been described 'as beautiful in form, original in design, and almost as perfect in workmanship as anything of a similar kind to be found in the East'. The silver work was carried out in individual homes to original designs, and before we left Kota Bharu, I bought myself a miniature silver Malayan Kris (dagger), with a tortoiseshell blade and the most delicate filigree worked scabbard. It was probably the weather and the route we took back through the town to rejoin the main road south, but I found Kota Bharu a rather depressing place with dreary wooden shacks lining the streets. There were no signs of the famous Malayan brightly coloured and elaborately designed 'Batik' sarongs, which was one of Kota Bharu's main industries.

We were all looking forward to getting back to Beserah, and were frustrated not only by the delays we encountered at the ferries, but also as we couldn't do the journey in one day, we had to harbour up for one night south of Trengganu.

We passed two further glorious days at Beserah. The storm in the South China Sea had soon passed, and we spent the time swimming and just lazing around. We spent the evenings, sitting round a large fire chatting, with a nearly full moon shining out of a cloudless night sky, which only further highlighted the phosphorescence of the waves. An English speaking Malay wandering along the beach, stopped and told us that he had heard there was a beach some miles further north, where turtles, out of season, were nevertheless coming ashore to lay their eggs. Three or four of my fellow officers were keen enough to set off in the middle of the night on the chance they might catch a glimpse of this rare annual event. They returned the next morning, black eyed and disappointed.

All too soon the two days of rest and recreation had passed, and sadly we packed up camp and set off for our return journey to Ipoh. The weather was overcast but excessively hot and humid, so halfway between Kuantan and Temerloh we stopped at a loggers camp, with its own café and quickly downed quantities of either Pepsi Colas or the local bottled fruit drinks. At one table, I stood and watched four Chinese loggers playing the traditional game of Mah-Jongg, which has been played in China from the days of Confucius. I have my Grandfather's Mah-Jongg ivory and bamboo set, and although an indifferent player, I knew enough of the game to follow the moves of the four Chinese, and I was interested to see that although they were playing with the traditional three suit, 'bamboo' (tiao), 'rings' (tung) and 'characters (wan), they were not using the 'Seasons' and 'Flowers' tiles, which I believe is a fairly recent western innovation. I envied the speed at which they played and wished I was as competent as they were. The Chinese have marvellous descriptive terms, which they have used for the names of some of the winning Mah-Jongg hands; 'The Thirteen Grades of Imperial Treasure'; 'Four Blessings Hovering o'er the Door'; To Catch the Moon from the Bottom of the Sea', and 'To Gather Plum Blossom from the Roof'. At the other extreme, one of the penalty hands rejoices in the name of 'Letting off a Cannon', which I have always felt has an unfortunate connotation.

We made good progress that day, were not held up for too long at the Temerloh Ferry, and managed to reach Bentong on the edge of the central mountain range before we decided to harbour for the night.

The following morning we swung north and started the long climb up into the mountains. The road wound steadily upwards, a thin grey strip cut, like a scar through the green of the jungle-covered sides of the mountains. The weather on our return trip was infinitely better than on the outward journey, and the view from 'The Gap' was truly spectacular, especially to the east, where some twenty miles away we could see the mass of gunungs of the Krau Game Reserve rising to nearly six thousand feet. To the west the mountains fell away to the coastal plain of Selangor State and beyond this to the Straits of Malacca.

Some forty miles south of Ipoh in the town of Tapah, at the road junction to the Cameron Highlands, there was another minor road that headed north. I was somewhat surprised when the Squadron turned off the main road and onto this minor road, which was narrow and meandered up a valley surrounded on both sides by the foothills to the central mountain range. I felt that there must have been a reason why we had taken this route, and I was not kept in doubt for long. Coming round a bend I saw the Squadron had stopped. Word came back that we had run into an ambush, and the Assault Section was needed to flush out the terrorists. After a moment of panic wondering how we were going to do this without any ammunition, I realised that the reason for the detour onto this minor road, was to justify my inclusion on the exercise, which had been 'cushy' so far and to test my section in an infantry anti-ambush role.

I left the rest of the section with the Land Rover, whilst I went forward to find out what was going on. At the head of the column the Squadron Leader, Jock Bell pointed out the location of the 'enemy' in a group of rubber trees some two hundred yards ahead. I carried out a quick 'recce'. On my right was a bank; I climbed up this to see whether I could put in a right flanking attack, but the ground was open and we would have been exposed to hostile fire for too long before we reached the trees. I thought about using smoke, but realised that the Ferrets were unable, due to the narrowness of the road, to manoeuvre into the correct position to fire off smoke bombs, which they hadn't got anyway. To the left the ground dropped sharply away and was covered with secondary jungle. Although I could not see the bottom of the bank, I suspected that there was a stream there, and as far as I could see we would have cover right up to the 'enemy's' position. I told Jock my plan, and tongue in cheek, asked that when I blew my whistle, (that is if I had one,) would he give me covering fire from the machine guns of however many Ferrets that could be brought up into a supporting fire position and also put down smoke. Jock looked at me in a rather old fashioned way, but decided to go along with the 'charade' of providing supporting fire and smoke without having any of either.

I was really getting into my stride of acting in an infantry officer mode, and was determined to show the cavalry that, even as a Corps officer, I was no slouch when it came to putting into practice my Mons OCS infantry training.

I returned to the back of the column and started to brief the Assault Section:

'Situation… Intention… Method…' Oh! To hell with that.

'Look a fake ambush has been set up in a group of rubber trees some two hundred yards ahead of the leading Ferret. We can't go right, as the ground is too open. So we're going down this bank on the left. I suspect there is a stream at the bottom, and we will wade through this, until I think we're opposite the 'enemy', and we'll climb up the bank and put in our attack from the left flank. Okay. Any questions?'

There were none.

'Right let's go.' And without any more ado, I set off crashing through the secondary jungle, making such a noise that any snakes, enjoying a siesta would have taken fright long before we reached them. My guess

'O' Group briefing

was right; there was a stream at the bottom and I leapt into the knee high water with great enthusiasm, but followed with somewhat less enthusiasm by the rest of the section. With myself leading and brandishing my service revolver in a threatening manner, with the rest of the section behind me, following my example with their Sterling Sub-Machine Guns in the 'high port' position. We rounded a bend in the stream and were totally gobsmacked as we nearly ran down a Malay who, with his sarong hitched up around his waist, was squatting in the stream where he was happily and peacefully communing with nature. His facial expression changed from quiet concentration, to amazement, to sheer

Charge with elan!

terror in an instant, as he looked up and saw, what to him must have seemed like the whole of the British Army, bearing down on him at great speed, in a very threatening manner, with their weapons in a 'ready to shoot' position. In reality we were trying to protect our weapons from getting wet as we charged along the stream. The poor Malay, and I hoped he did not suffer any long-term mental or physical effects, as he would have deserved a place in the 'Guinness Book of Records', for establishing the

"...what seemed like the whole British Army bearing down..."

world record in a Sarong Fixing Competition, as he beat a very rapid strategic retreat into the 'ulu'. This all happened so quickly, that we did not falter in our headlong rush along the stream.

After about a quarter of a mile, I reckoned we must be opposite the 'enemy', so I climbed halfway up the bank, where I could hear voices and made out some jungle green uniformed figures milling about above me. I collected my section; we quietly climbed up the bank, and then emerging from the scrub, we charged brandishing our weapons, maniacally shouting and screaming to scare the shit out of the 'enemy'.

I was rather pleased with myself, for I had executed what, in my mind was a model Mons OCS infantry section attack. Those we charged were also most impressed; the only trouble being that I hadn't attacked the 'enemy', but had eliminated the 'umpires'. The 'enemy' led by Lieutenant 'Ned Kelly' McEnerny, RAAC was still a hundred yards away. Sheepishly and feeling very stupid, we climbed the opposite bank and put in a half hearted right flank attack across the open ground with neither covering smoke nor supporting fire. It would have been simpler if I had gone that way in the first instance, and I would probably have saved that poor Malay from possibly being a candidate for a future heart attack. Not a good example of 'winning the hearts and minds' of the local populace.

All too soon we arrived back at Ipoh, and it was good to jump into a cold bath, wash off ten days of accumulated dirt and dried salty sea water, change into clean clothes, have a decent meal and collapse onto a proper bed. The next day I was given some funny looks, as the story went round the Mess of my failure in not being able to differentiate, although dressed alike, between 'umpires' and 'enemy', and how I had 'wiped' out the Squadron Leader, the 2IC and other 'A' Sqn officers in an effective and well executed infantry attack. Even the adjutant was amused, although I wondered if he was weighing up whether I could be given 'extras', for significantly 'reducing' the officer strength of a sabre squadron. It was said of RSM Demond Lynch in 1943, that it was a good job he was on our side, but I was worried, after my abortive attack, that someone might express doubt whether it would be wise to have me on our side!!

~

A number of the 13/18H officers rode, and in 1960 the Regiment owned twelve horses, which were ridden at both race meetings and polo tournaments. The major tournament that was held when I was with the Hussars was the April Polo Meeting, which the Regiment organised and acted as hosts. It was at this tournament that I nearly had a major fall out with the C-in-C FARELF, General Sir Richard Hull. He had come up to Ipoh to act as a mounted umpire for the matches. I was detailed to act as a 'longstop' behind one of the gaols, with the duty of verifying that a goal had been scored, and of retrieving the ball, if that is what it is called, and returning it to the umpire. During one chukker, the C-in-C obviously thought that I was being too slow at returning the ball to the field of play, and shouted at me to 'get a bloody move on'. I took exception to his remarks, but realised that answering him back wouldn't have got me anywhere; so when I returned the ball to him, I ensured that I held it in such a way that I had two fingers on the ball giving him a reversed Churchill salute. A petty gesture but I felt better for it.

I had never watched polo before, and I was impressed at the speed and vigour of the game. I felt that the poor mouths of the polo ponies must have suffered as a result of the force that their riders exerted on the reins to pull the ponies up and to instantly change direction. I learnt many years later, that professional polo ponies have a short career and when they are finished with, are not much use for anything else.

Lieutenant General Sir Rodney Moore, who was the Director of Operations, was a firm favourite with the spectators; many of whom were local Chinese, obviously great supporters of equestrian events, and no doubt a fair amount of 'on course' betting took place. The General played polo at only one speed, - flat out. He was not a small man. However, totally dwarfing his pony, he would charge across the field, come to an abrupt stop, turn on a sixpence, and immediately take off at full gallop in the opposite direction, wielding his polo stick like a lance in a jousting tournament. The crowd loved it, and he was always loudly cheered when he either rode onto or left the field.

The Regiment obviously regarded the Ipoh Polo Tournament as being one of the major events of the social calendar, with tented stands and music provided by the combined bands of the 13th/18th Hussars, the 1st/3rd East Anglian and the 1st/7th Gurkha Rifles Regiments. It was a lovely setting, so long as one ignored the large Chinese cemetery with its many stone monuments of various shapes and sizes next to the polo ground.

It was a shame, but a number of social activities had to be cancelled at this time, as the country was in official mourning following the death of His Majesty, the Yang di-Pertuan Agong, the Paramount Ruler of the Federation of Malaya. The Paramount Ruler is a constitutional ruler and is elected for a period of five years from among the nine State Constitutional Rulers.

~

'A 'Sqn was not left in peace for long and was soon on the road again, when in May 1960 the Squadron had to make a fast dash down to Singapore as part of an Internal Security (IS) exercise. It said a great deal for the Squadron Fitter Section that the thousand-mile round trip was completed without a single mechanical breakdown. Later, when I was on leave in Singapore a fellow REME officer, who had flown out to Singapore with me, told me that he had been attached to 'A' Sqn on the IS exercise, which he hadn't been looking forward to. Not having worked with the cavalry before, he was still under the traditional but erroneous impression that cavalry officers would all be a toffee-nosed and horsy bunch, who only did 'soldering as a hobby'. But as he said to me; 'I was not at all pleased when I heard that I would be working with your lot, but I was surprised as to how professional, competent and efficient they were.'

Although my experience was very limited, I found it difficult to accept that in 1960 there was a single regiment in the British Army that did 'soldering as a hobby'. In fact the professionalism of the 13th/18th Hussars was proved in 1966, when based in Germany, they represented Great Britain in the annual NATO tank gunnery competition for the Canadian Army Trophy, which they won with, at that time the highest score against teams from Belgium, Canada, Germany, the Netherlands and the United States. A record that could still stand, as I have heard that we no longer enter a team for this competition, if in fact it is still held.

~

My 730 days of National Service was coming to a close, and I was seriously regretting that I had given my word to my father, that I would not sign-on for a Short Service Commission, but leave the Army when my two years were up.

However, before I left the Regiment I had one more duty to perform.

One morning, Jim Allen came up to me, and told me that there was to be a REME Divisional Young Officers Exercise to be held shortly for officers of the rank of captain and below. I had a dreadful feeling for one moment that I was being detailed to take part in this exercise, but I breathed a great sigh of relief when Jim said that I was apparently the only officer in 17 Gurkha Division who knew how to float a Land Rover across a stretch of water, and which was going to be one of the initiative tests for the young officers. As no doubt they wanted to come out top in the exercise, I was therefore detailed to instruct REME officers in the 28th Commonwealth Brigade in vehicle flotation. If it was true that I was the only officer in Malaya who knew this technique, I felt I should also have instructed the REME officers in 99 Infantry Brigade as well, so all would start from the same 'level playing field'.

My first objective was to find a suitable stretch of water, and whilst I had initially thought of the Perak River north of Ipoh; I could not find a suitable spot with easy access and a gently sloping bank. Eventually, knowing that there were a number of man-made lakes left over from defunct tin mines, I found the ideal spot at Chemor ten miles north of Ipoh. One scorching hot morning I met up with my 'class' of five captains. Lance-Corporal Pawley had driven me up to the lake in my Land Rover, which we were going to use for the exercise, and I could see from the grin on his face, that he was going to enjoy the sight of seeing the five captains being taught how to 'swim' a Land Rover. L/Cpl Pawley obviously had more confidence than I had, but he always was the eternal optimist. I had only seen this done once before at Kuantan the previous September, and I hoped that I could remember everything; as the last thing I needed was to be responsible for sinking and losing a Land Rover. I also wondered how the 28th Commonwealth Brigade REME officers had learnt that I had experience of vehicle flotation when I was in 99 Infantry Brigade. Sometimes the Army surprised me. There were times when there was a lack of communication between units on important matters; and yet on something which was relatively unimportant, such as being a hockey player, or supposedly knowing how to float a Land Rover, inter-unit communication had been very good.

We all stripped off and donned our swimming costumes. I first instructed the captains on dry land how to 'parcel-up' the Land Rover, then I got them to lay out the Bedford RL canopy we had brought with us on the edge of the water. L/Cpl Pawley was all for helping them, but I forbade him to do so, for on the actual test the captains would be on their own. I must admit that as a junior NS subaltern, I was enjoying myself bossing regular captains. Very many years later I had to give a lecture to the biennial Army Cadets County Commandants' Conference in the ballroom of the Royal Artillery Officers' Mess at Woolwich, and I had sitting in front of me and, hopefully listening to my every word, one four-star general, two three-star generals, one two-star general, fourteen brigadiers, fifty-three full colonels, twenty-eight half colonels and several majors, captains and lieutenants. As a retired National Service subaltern, I enjoyed that moment as well.

Anyway, the captains wrapped up the Land Rover for the second time, and I held my breath and crossed my fingers, hoping that the canopy hadn't any holes in it, as the vehicle was pushed into the lake. I was so relieved when the Land Rover, having initially dipped down into the water, bobbed up, found its natural buoyancy and rode high in the water. I also breathed a sigh of relief that I wouldn't have the embarrassment of contacting the LAD, to admit I had lost one of our vehicles in the deep water of a man-made lake, and could I please have a recovery team and divers to pull my Land Rover out of the water. At least the recovery of the Ferret Scout Car on the Grik-Kroh road would have given us some experience in water recovery.

It was so hot, that both L/Cpl Pawley and I joined the others in the stone coloured water of the lake; irrespective of what health hazards there were and we spent some considerable time swimming the Land Rover round and round, until eventually we tired of the game, recovered it back to the bank and unpacked the vehicle. I was happy that the instruction and practice had gone so well, but I must admit it was with a feeling of relief that, with the very wet Bedford RL canopy on board, we drove back to Ipoh with one intact and dry Land Rover.

Unfortunately, I had left Malaya before the Young Officers' Tests took place, so I never did find out whether my team of REME captains from 28 Commonwealth Brigade had come out 'on top'.

~

That was the last military task I performed with the 13th/18th Royal Hussars and indeed in the Army. The time had come to take down the pictures from the walls of my room, and together with the Chinese and Malay ivory and jade items I had bought in C.K.Tang's Emporium in Singapore, pack them and my other belongings in a tea chest for the sea journey back to the UK. Until my movement order arrived for me to travel by train down to Singapore, I filled in the last few days, which felt rather 'flat' by still trying to bring the EMERs up to date.

Even though I was still officially the Messing Officer, for the last few days I began to change the dinner menu away from 'Chicken à la King' and 'Angels on Horseback', knowing that Angus couldn't give me 'extras' as I wouldn't be around to do them. Although I wanted to get back home, I was sad to leave not only the Regiment, which I had become firmly attached to and had joined their Association, but also Malaya, a country I had come to love, and which I felt must be one of the most beautiful places on earth.

So, whilst I waited for my movement order, I would lie on my bed at 'Gyppo PT' time, recalling all that had happened during the previous six months, not only Regimental life, but also the off-duty activities I had shared with my fellow officers, and the two leave periods I had taken in Singapore and Penang, and which I supposed came under the heading of R & R (Rest and Recreation).

Chapter Sixteen

Rest and Recreation

Weekends never dragged when I was stationed at 10 Inf Wksp, which was not only thanks to the hospitality of my fellow officers, but also the proximity of Singapore meant there was plenty of recreational activities to help pass the time. At Ipoh, the situation was different, and Sundays could be a very long and boring day; even lunch in the Mess was a routine affair, although the married officers with their wives normally put in an appearance for their stengahs or gin and tonics before the traditional curry lunch. As the Messing Officer I tried one Sunday to vary the menu, but nearly got lynched and would probably have incurred 'extra' orderly officer duties if the Adjutant hadn't fortunately been out for lunch that particular Sunday. So fixing the menu for Sunday lunch was the easiest of the week, and although I got fed up with the curry lunches and resorted to omelettes, my fellow officers seemed happy to maintain the curry tradition. Many years later, I was involved, as an employer in a number of Territorial Army weekend exercises, and invariably at the end of an exercise the Sunday lunch was curry.

Ipoh boasted an airport where the gliding club was based. Before he left the LAD, Hugh Wright had introduced me to the club members, but I was sorry that I was unable to learn to fly gliders after that unfortunate coming together between Sergeant Beavon's head and the club's only twin seat training glider, which resulted in the glider coming off second best and having to be 'written off'.

However, I could help launch the single seat gliders, which was rather a hair raising experience, as the tow would be from the back of a Dodge truck, which had had the body, doors and windscreen removed. Hugh would drive the truck down the runway at speeds of up to 80mph, whilst I, clinging onto any handhold I could find, would check that the wire towrope was running smoothly. I felt that Ipoh vied with Temerloh as one of the hottest places in Malaya, and as the airport was surrounded by gunungs, there were always good thermals. It didn't take long for a glider pilot, once the tow had been dropped, to find one and we would watch him spiralling upwards and moving from thermal to another. I must admit I was green with envy. Storms clouds invariably built up in the afternoons, and on one Sunday, as these drifted in from the mountains, a young Chinaman was in the air, and Hugh was becoming increasingly concerned as the glider rose higher and higher in a good thermal as the dark storm clouds rolled-in. Hugh explained the danger:

'It's going to get extremely rough if he gets into those clouds. But not only that, as there are no instruments in the cockpit, he won't know his height or even if he is flying upside down or not.'

As the wind increased in strength, the glider was blown further to the west, and we leapt into Hugh's car and did our best to follow the glider, as it flew in and out of the cloud base. Eventually, before the storm hit Ipoh, the Chinese pilot managed to land the glider in the playing field of one of the local schools, which presented quite a problem on how to get it back to the airport.

There was also a flying club at Ipoh Airport. If I couldn't get up in a glider, then I was determined to be taken up in one of their Tiger Moths, as I felt that an aerial view of Ipoh, the Kinta Valley, the open cast tin mines and the jungle covered gunungs would be stunning. I talked to the club secretary, who agreed that I could be a passenger in one of their elderly biplanes, and which made the flight of Army Air Corps Auster aircraft parked nearby look positively modern.

So the following Sunday, I turned up armed with my camera and spare rolls of film to be presented with an official form that I had to sign stating that; 'The Ipoh Flying Club will in no way be held responsible for the death of or injury to Anthony Caffyn.' I stood around waiting for my European pilot to turn up. A few minutes later I felt a tap on my arm, looked round but couldn't see anyone; another tap and I looked down to see a diminutive Chinaman, who only looked about sixteen years old, peering up at me with a great big smile on his face. This was my pilot. He didn't look old enough to pilot a bicycle let alone a Tiger Moth. I had a moment of regret that I had asked for this flight, and had also 'signed my life away'. However, I need not have worried. He was a very good pilot, even if he did have a propensity of wanting to fly either upside down, 'looping the loop' or going into spins; but which I wasn't too keen on in an open cockpit, with only a lap strap holding me in. I knew he thought I was 'chicken' only wanting to fly straight and level, but I was more interested in taking good photographs rather than indulging in aerobatics.

Rest and Recreation

The view from 4,000ft was spectacular. Below, the Kinta Valley was laid out like a map. To the north and east the jungle covered central mountain range rose up from the coastal plain to a height higher than we were flying at. Odd shaped individual gunungs stood out from the valley floor, which seemed to indicate that many thousands of years previously, the Kinta Valley was below sea level. To the west and south there were views of the many open cast tin mines that spread like carbuncles over the surface of the Valley, with mile upon mile of soil deposits, man-made lakes and the rickety wooden constructed dredges. I realised that a country to survive economically, to be prosperous and to provide a better life for its people, needed a strong natural resources base, but from the air it did seem such a shame that so much of the landscape of the Kinta Valley had been given over to open cast tin mining. Ipoh, from the air, looked as well laid out as it did on the ground, a neat and clean town and I could make out the attractive railway station, the colonial style government buildings, its racecourse and the green of its parks and open spaces.

After about an hour, there was a whistling sound from near my right hip, I looked down to see what was amiss, and realised that the sound was coming from a voice pipe. I picked it up and whistled back. My pilot asked if I had seen enough. It was surprising the difference in temperature at 4,000ft. I was only dressed in a short sleeve shirt and casual slacks, and after an hour I was feeling quite cold. So I replied that I was ready to land. He banked the aircraft, and the masts of the Radio Malaya relay station built on the top of a gunung passed under one wing; and the steady beat of the engine changed pitch as the throttle was pushed back, and the sound of the wind whistling through the wing struts and wire stays and against the canvas of the wings gradually decreased. My pilot made a perfect three-point landing. I thanked him for a really memorable flight, and although I had disappointed him in not wanting any aerobatics, I did nevertheless get the photographs I wanted.

I stopped going to the airfield on Sundays after Hugh Wright had moved on, for after his departure, the gliding club had a problem finding a replacement driver for the Dodge with the necessary experience to ensure that the gliders were safely launched.

~

Peter Waddy's great interest was in photography, and after he had returned with 'A'Sqn to Ipoh in early March 1960, I would join him, and only armed with cameras, we would spend Sundays exploring the area round Ipoh. One Sunday, as well as dropping in to see 'C' Sqn at Gapis Estate, we decided to visit the Mosque at Kuala Kangsar, close to 'C'Sqn's camp. On the road north we drove through rubber estates, where strips of rubber formed from the latex would be laid out to dry by the side of the

445

road, and the smell from these was so revolting, that unless we closed the car windows, the smell would stay in our nostrils and linger in the car for hours afterwards.

On the way we crossed the new Iskandar Bridge over the Sungei Perak, and looked down on a Malay houseboat, built from long lengths of bamboo, with a small ratton shack perched on top drifting, with no visible sign of propulsion, slowly down the river. We had passed the Mosque several times on our regular visits to 'C' Sqn, but had never bothered to stop before. Although this was an imposing building, we found the interior disappointing. However, it was possible to climb up one of the minarets, and from the balcony at the top there were fine views of rubber estates, jungle, distant mountains, but more spectacularly the view, about a mile away of the Sultan of Perak's Istana (Palace) with its gold leaf domes, which could be seen shining in the sunlight from many miles away.

On another Sunday, Peter and I were driving on the Tanjong Rambutan road out of Ipoh and passed the entrance to a large deserted sand pit. Peter thought that this looked interesting and reversed back into it. In one corner we noticed, partially hidden by trees and lallang grass, bamboo steps leading to a cleft some fifty feet up between the near vertical sides of two gunungs. Peter and I climbed up the steps, with what looked like spots of dried blood on some of the rungs. At the top, a path led through a deep gorge and even though the sun was almost directly overhead, the near vertical sides of the gunungs prevented any sunlight penetrating to the path. All around us were bushes; trees with their foliage growing from high up on the trunks trying to catch the sunlight; ferns and damp creepers were clinging to and hanging down from the rocky surfaces of the gunungs. It was dark and rather creepy, and we had no idea where the overgrown track led. After a few minutes Peter and I felt that common sense should take over and we should retrace our steps, for although the area around Ipoh had been declared a White Area, this did not guarantee that there were no CTs in the jungle; especially as the few who had not been killed, captured or had surrendered, were constantly being harassed by the security forces and forced to keep on the move. Although further west of Ipoh, it was known that there were a group of six hard-core terrorists living in the Bubu Forest, who could well have decided to move east to escape the attention of the security forces.

However, just as were about to turn back, we noticed a bright light ahead of us and we decided to investigate. In a few minutes we emerged into a different world. A world of sunlight and vibrant greens as the gunungs opened out and we emerged into a large natural bowl surrounded by the mountains and in this bowl grew every imaginable tropical plant and shrub. But what caught my eye were gigantic rhubarb type plants, whose stems must have been five feet in length and with broad three-foot leaves. This sunlit bowl was such a contrast from the dark track we had been following. Peter and I would like to have gone further, but the belukar (secondary jungle) was too thick, and as we hadn't brought parangs (jungle knives) with us, we had to retrace our steps. Peter pointed out some more dried bloodstains on rocks, and as we returned back to the car we speculated as to where they could have come from. The path looked little used, but it could have been one of the routes set up by Lee Meng the ex-schoolteacher, who ran the CT communication network with such great efficiency and ruthlessness from Ipoh, until she was arrested in July 1952. CT Couriers travelled long distances by various means and routes between message pick-up and drop-off points. Maybe the bamboo ladder and track we had discovered had been such a CT route.

~

Peter and I were building up quite a reputation in the Mess for our photographic expeditions, and there was soon a queue of subalterns wanting to join us on our Sunday trips. During the week we would pour over a large-scale map of Ipoh and its surroundings, and decide where we would head for the following Sunday.

This did lead us into some unexpected encounters. One Sunday afternoon, whilst walking down a narrow track, we came across a group of Chinese youths, who had caught a scorpion and was taunting it, by setting fire to a ring of twigs, which they had laid around it. The poor scorpion, completely surrounded by flames, dashed hither and thither trying to escape, its tail with its powerful poisonous sting raised in a menacing manner over its back. The youths were laughing and prodding the scorpion with a stick. We were rather sickened by their behaviour and did not stay to see whether the scorpion stung itself to death; but no doubt it eventually turned up as scorpion soup on someone's table.

On another trip, on our way to explore a tin mine, Peter noticed some bamboo steps (for which he appeared to have a natural aptitude in discovering), leading up to a cave in the side of a gunung. We climbed these, but it wasn't until we got to the top did we discover the purpose of the steps, when the stench of acrid bat guano hit us. We had found a bat cave, and the steps were obviously used by the local Malays to collect the guano, which was used as a fertiliser. We took a few steps into the cave, but immediately beat a hasty retreat, as our presence had obviously disturbed the bats, which took off in their hundreds and flew past us. We hoped their radar was switched on and functioning properly, as they were so close we could feel the beat of their wings and the rush of air on our faces as they flew past and around our heads. The noise was quite deafening and frightening, and we were glad to get to the bottom of the steps again.

Peter had heard of a tin mine worth visiting at Sungei Siput some twenty miles south of Ipoh. Mike Butler, a fellow subaltern who was also the assistant adjutant joined Peter Waddy and I for this expedition. We arranged with the Mess kitchen to provide us with haversack rations, and as no doubt it was going to be a very hot day, bottles of Pepsi Cola.

It was when we left the main road onto minor ones and laterite tracks, that the unusual configuration of some of the gunungs could be seen. These appeared to be of sandstone, and the bases were invariably eroded and bare of vegetation, which probably proved that many centuries ago, this particular stretch of the Kinta Valley was under water. We passed one tall rock covered in vegetation (or it originally might have been a gunung), some 150 to 200 feet high, standing as thin and straight as a pencil, as if on sentry duty between two other gunungs. Its shape must have been formed over many centuries through wind and weather erosion.

With Mike map reading, we successfully found the track, which led to the tin mine. This soon became unsuitable for vehicles, and so having parked Peter's car in the shade of some trees, we set off on foot, not knowing how far ahead the tin mine was. The track wound along the side of a gunung, with the trees on the other side of the track preventing us seeing what was ahead. It was stiflingly hot and we had only walked a short distance, but already our shirts were stuck to our backs. I was carrying our lunch in a small pack slung over my shoulder, and with every step it seemed to get heavier and heavier. After about half a mile, the track widened and the trees thinned out, as we entered a narrow valley with a stretch of yellowy-green water in front of us, which was crossed by what looked to be a very rickety long bamboo bridge. But before we reached the bridge, we came across a group of four Chinese women dressed all in black, and protected from the sun by their large brimmed rattan hats, squatting by the side of a shallow pool of water, and using wooden bowls, were sifting through the silt looking for particles of tin. This must have been a slow, laborious and frustrating job. A short distance further on we came upon what appeared to be the miners Rest Hut, outside of which sat two of the local Chinese 'lovelies'. Wearing their working clothes and with scarves tied around their heads, they were not looking their best, and it might have been for this reason that they turned their backs on Peter and I as we tried to photograph them; but it was more likely it was the superstition, believed by many Chinese women, that a camera lens was regarded as an 'evil eye' and would bring bad luck.

We walked across the bridge, which with no handrail was as rickety and fragile as it looked. One slip and it was a thirty-foot drop into the dark murky water below us. The path continued on the other side of the bridge along a narrow ledge between the side of a gunung and the water on our right. Eventually, the tin mine came into view. It looked most impressive and was obviously one of the larger ones in the area.

Even though it was Sunday the mine was being fully worked. Powerful water cannons, which drew water from the lake behind us, blasted into the sandstone subsoil, which had already been excavated to a depth of about fifty feet. The resultant mix of water and sand slurry was pumped up a long pipe mounted on a steeply ramped bamboo trestle bridge, which at the top was attached to a long gently descending filter bed, split into sections with crosspieces. The water and sand slurry flowed out of the pipe onto the filter bed and as the water ran down, the sediment and silt was trapped between the crosspieces. At the end the water was returned to the man-made lake. Although we didn't actually see the operation, presumably all the slurry in the filter bed was subsequently panned for tin.

Peter, Mike and I stood watching the whole operation for some time with interest and a certain fascination at what seemed to be a simple 'Heath Robinson' layout, but was obviously an effective method of open cast tin mining.

Although it was their country and they were used to the climate, I felt sorry for the workforce who had to work for long hours in such heat. By 1300hrs, we had seen enough, and we looked round for a cool, shady spot where we could eat our packed lunch. I suggested that there seemed to be some shade at the base of a nearby gunung. We walked down to the spot, only to find, from their droppings that water buffalo had had the same idea. Eventually, we found a certain amount of shade by a stream, and it was such a relief to cool our overheated and sweaty feet in the water, and not really caring if the leeches found us. The bottles of 'Coke' that I had been carrying all morning were, in danger of exploding through expansion of the liquid caused by the heat. Fortunately we never had to put to the test the rate of expansion of Pepsi confined in a glass bottle at high temperatures. To try and cool the bottles, we plunged them into the stream, but we were so dehydrated that we couldn't wait for them to cool down, and pulled them out straight away.

'Okay,' I said, 'Who's got the bottle opener?'

Peter looked at Mike, who shook his head. Mike looked across at me. I shook my head. I looked at Peter, who shook his head. We started to argue as to whose fault it was in not bringing one, but we soon realised that arguing amongst ourselves wasn't going to solve the problem. We were in desperate need of liquid and although back in England, in similar circumstances, we might have risked drinking water from a country stream; no way did we dare risk drinking possibly rat urine infested water in Malaya. There was nothing for it, we had to use small rocks to try and break off the bottle tops, which we eventually succeeded in doing, howbeit with a certain amount of broken glass. We brushed the glass particles away, and not really caring whether we had missed some, we downed the very warm 'coke' in record time. Whilst we sat by the stream, Peter, who also appeared to have the same natural ability as finding bamboo ladders, pointed out some dry bloodstains on one of the rocks, and we speculated how they got there.

We should have learnt our lesson that in future photographic expeditions, we needed to check with each other that not only had we got drinks, but also a bottle opener. But we didn't, and there were times when Peter and I were so thirsty, that we had to beg from 'fringe' aborigines, small pieces of sugar cane that we would suck and then chew to extract all the liquid to prevent becoming dehydrated.

~

Not all our trips were successful. We had heard of some waterfalls in the jungle near Kampar, a town twenty-four miles south of Ipoh. With Mike Butler joining us again, the three of us set off one Sunday afternoon, and having parked the car, we started to climb into the foothills. To reach the falls, we had to walk through a very squalid area on the outskirts of Kampar. The homes were small wooden hovels, around which Malay children played, mixing with pye dogs, pigs and chicken, and amongst the animal and bird droppings. The smell and general filth were beyond imagination, and we couldn't get to the open ground beyond fast enough. I was perplexed by the state of this place. It was no better than one would find in a very third world 'shanty' town. Yet in 1960, Malaya had the highest standard of living in South-East Asia, and there should have been no need for this poverty. Malays are very family orientated and proud of their homes; and Chinese 'Squatters' had, under the Gurney/Briggs plan been re-housed in New Villages.

The waterfalls were most disappointing. We had hoped that these would have been spectacular, but instead, all we found was water tumbling down between rocks. The one redeeming feature of the afternoon was the butterflies, such as the dark 'Blue Jungle Glory', the 'Rajah Brooke' and a number of 'Milkweeds'. They were every imaginable colour of the spectrum, deep reds, purples, gold, blue and many others. We watched fascinated not only by their sheer number, but also by the myriad of the colours as they flew in what appeared to be a set circle, and then landed on the rocks. After a few minutes, as if by a given signal, they took off and disappeared into the jungle.

~

Probably our most interesting expedition was the Sunday we decided to take ourselves into the jungle to try and find an Aborigine camp. The three main Aborigine groups being the Negritos, a race of Negroid pygmies in the north of the country; the Proto-Malays in the south; and in the centre the Senoi, split into two sub-groups, - the Temiar in the north and the Semai in the south. The Senoi inhabited the central mountain range, with the Temiar being the more secretive and inaccessible of the two groups, living in the high mountain moss forests of the watershed that divides the States of Perak and Kelantan. We were hoping to find a settlement of Temiar Abos, who it was known were living on the fringe of the jungle.

The CTs had made extensive use of the Abos in the deep jungle, forcing them to grow food and act as couriers, guides and spies. The Malayan Government had moved several thousands out of the jungle and tried to resettle them closer to urban areas, with the aim of depriving the CTs of their 'eyes and ears'; but the experiment had proved a failure, largely due to the difficulty the Abos had in coming to terms with a different culture, and also not being immune to the deseases and viruses common in the more civilised and populated areas, and so they were returned to their jungle habitat. However, a few of the Temiar, known as 'Fringe Abos' remained near to towns, and it was such a group that we were going to try and find.

Peter, Mike Butler and I were also joined by two other subalterns, Johnny Hok and Gillie Turle, the latter having returned from his months' stint as the 'Hussar Admiral' of the Grik Fleet. We drove east out of Ipoh and left the car at the Kinta Valley Water Intake Works, and then walked for some two miles up a track alongside the main water pipe until we reached a small hut, where we stopped for a rest and wondered how we were going to find an Abo. Near the hut was a large banana tree, and as we sat there, we helped ourselves to some of the fruit, carefully peeling back the skin, as it had been known for very small snakes to be found inside bananas. We were on the point of wondering whether to continue up the path, or to admit defeat and return to the car, when, as if by magic, a grim looking Aborigine was standing before us, holding what appeared to be a 12-bore shotgun. We were so surprised and not a little concerned as to whether the Abo had any plans to use the gun. The Temiar Abos at the Kinta Valley Water Intake were reputed to have been 'ex-hostile' ones, who had co-operated fully with the CTs, and were armed by them with shotguns and Sub-Machine Guns. They lived near the CT Camps and were tasked with the subversion and domination of neighbouring Aborigine settlements. These particular Abos had 'self-renewed' (a euphemism for surrendered), and had been re-settled. We hoped that their 'self-renewel' was genuine and permanent. We learnt later that the Protector of Aborigines at Ipoh, Richard Corfield had had to reprimand these particular Abos, who instead of using water from the Sungei Kinta, found it more convenient to tap into the main Ipoh water pipe.

Mike Butler was fairly proficient in Malay and asked the Aborigine if he would take us to his ladang (settlement). Before agreeing, he indicated that he wanted some cigarettes. Although we still hadn't learnt our lesson about carrying water bottles on our trips, we had nevertheless realised the bargaining power of carrying the free issue tins of cigarettes with us. We handed over half a dozen cigarettes, but the Abo showed his disapproval of this offer by raising his shotgun, and we had to increase our offer to ten, which was accepted.

He indicated that we should follow him, and we retraced our steps for about a quarter of a mile, when the Abo suddenly veered off left onto a path which was hardly discernable and one that we would have been very fortunate to spot. Our barefooted Aborigine set a very fast pace along the path with the belukar (secondary jungle) pressing on us from both sides. After some ten minutes of a stiff climb up the side of a hill, we came upon a clearing in the jungle. Here stood the headman's house built, in the shape of a cross, on stilts, out of bamboo, rattan and attap.

The Temiars, unlike the Negrito Aborigines do not live off the jungle. They are basically farmers. The whole settlement clears the ladang of trees and scrub. Then the main crops of tapioca, hill rice, millet and maize are planted and are shared by all. Individual families grow sugar cane, vegetables, fruit and medicinal herbs. To avoid moving every year, many Temiar settlements simply clear another patch of jungle and plant up a new ladang alongside the existing one.

As we stood in the clearing, taking in the scene, an attractive bare breasted young woman appeared at one of the window openings of the house. The influence of the West had obviously reached the fringe Abos, for as Peter and I reached for our cameras to photograph the woman, she ducked down so only her head and shoulders showed in the window, and she would only allow herself to be photographed in that position. On a subsequent Abo hunt expedition, Peter and I found another Temiar fringe Aborigine ladang, where the women in the settlement all wore bras.

The headman had, by this time thawed, and was smiling and laughing. His wife, also smiling, dressed in a blouse and sarong came down the steps from their house and joined her husband, who by this time had discarded his shirt and was dressed only in his loincloth; but the illusion of primitive life was rather spoilt by the large wristwatch he was wearing on his left wrist. He disappeared for a few moments, but returned carrying a very long blowpipe, which must have been some seven feet long. We were obviously being given the 'full tourist tour'. He loaded a dart through the mouthpiece of the blowpipe, which we hoped hadn't been dipped in the deadly poison sap of the Ipoh tree, and with legs askew, leaning slightly forward and holding the blowpipe close to his mouth, he fired the dart at one of his chickens; obviously with no intention of hitting it, but his aim was so accurate that the dart ruffled the comb of the bird before imbedding itself in a log.

We were then invited into their kongsi (house), which we felt was an honour. We sat on bamboo mats, in the communal central area; with each wing of the house partitioned off, and where we presumed each family lived. The wife offered us slices of sugar cane, which we eagerly sucked and the sweet liquid was very welcome and most refreshing. There could not have been a more original way to 'take tea' on a Sunday afternoon, and as we were quite overcome with the friendliness and hospitality we had been shown by the headman and his wife, before we left, we gave the headman the rest of the tin of cigarettes. He was delighted.

Although we had thoroughly enjoyed ourselves, I couldn't help but think that our western culture had reached the fringe Abos, and that although the headman was prepared to show us round his ladang and to invite us into his kongsi, we had to pay the 'entrance fee' of cigarettes and consequently felt rather like tourists. The headman must have been watching us for some time to judge whether we were suitable tourist material, and having decided that we were, and having also probably realised that we were military and therefore would have cigarettes with us, he decided to show himself.

On our way back to the car we came across three young Abo women, laughing and chattering amongst themselves; but when we appeared, made it plain by sign language that they were hoping we would give them some cigarettes. I had a few Consulates in my pocket, so I handed them one each, but from the way they held the cigarettes we could see that they weren't really smokers.

We did one more Aborigine hunt, which entailed a long walk along a jungle track and crossing over an Abo constructed bamboo suspension bridge across a small river, before we reached the aborigine encampment. I was fascinated by the construction of the bridge. The bamboo floor and the hand rails were lashed together with rattan, and from trees on either bank creeping vine had been used to anchor and support the bridge. The Abos were obviously well aware of the principles of suspension bridge construction. The settlement was a poor one, and the Abos were not very friendly; but in return for some cigarettes we were handed, rather unwillingly a few slices of dry sugar cane. On the return journey, as we crossed the bridge, we noticed a Temiar fisherman, with his wife and daughter working their way down stream. We scrambled down the bank, and waited for them to come up to us. They were rather depressed, for due to the lack of rain, the water level in the river was low, and they hadn't caught a fish all day.

Our expeditions helped to pass what would generally have been rather boring and quiet Sundays. There was no television in the camp, and bar from reading, listening to the radio, eating a curry lunch and sleeping, there was very little else to occupy ones self with. I envied those officers who had horses and could spend the day out riding and hacking. Nevertheless, our trips enabled us to see more of the countryside around Ipoh, the tin mining operations, and to meet up with the Temiar aborigines.

~

I had not taken any leave since I had arrived in the Far East, and I felt that I should take my entitlement; for at the time I believed that I would not likely return to Singapore or Malaya again. So as I had two weeks due to me, I had to decide where I was going to take my leave. It was possible to take indulgence flights with the RAF, but these depended upon there being flights to the right place at the right time, and although it was probable that I would have reached my chosen destination; there could have been problems with the return flight, either being cancelled, or being 'bumped' off the aircraft with senior officers from any of the three services being given priority. In spite of these potential difficulties, I toyed with the idea of trying to get to Hong Kong, where many servicemen spent their leave. However, I quickly dismissed the idea. I loved Singapore and I've never had an urge to visit Hong Kong, which I felt, probably unjustly, was just another overcrowded and noisy city. I would have liked to have spent some of my leave in Australia, and although it was possible to fly there on an indulgence flight with either the RAF or the RAAF, there was a risk of not getting a return flight in time to report back to the Regiment. As I had fallen in love with Malaya, I wanted to see as much of that country as I could before leaving, and decided to spend half my leave in Singapore and the other half visiting Penang Island.

In 1960, Malayan Airways on their internal flights were using Dakota DC3 aircraft, which although noisy, I thoroughly enjoyed flying in. However, I was rather nervous on my first flight from Ipoh. The afternoon storm had built up, and as we taxied to the end of the runway, this broke with a vengeance, with thunder, lightning and torrential rain. I assumed that the pilot would delay the take-off until the storm had abated, but being an Australian, he was made of sterner stuff and wasn't going to let a little local storm spoil his schedule. I watched out of the window as the Dakota lumbered down the runway, with the wing on my side of the aircraft swaying up and down so much in the cross wind that at one stage, I thought the wing tip would scrap along the tarmac. But the pilot obviously knew his aircraft, and after what seemed an eternity we levitated into the air. I was always grateful for the boiled sweets that the delightful and charming Malay

454

and Chinese air hostesses would hand round prior to any take-off and landing, and no more so than on this particular flight.

We had soon passed through the storm, and reached our cruising height of around 4,000 feet. It was not until sometime later that I noticed the passenger one row in front and across the aisle from me was Tunku Abdul Rahman, the first Prime Minister of the Independent State of Malaya. I was tempted to have gone across to him and to tell him how much I was enjoying my year in his beautiful Country. However, he was busy studying papers, and I hadn't the nerve to disturb him. In retrospect I wish I had, for he apparently had a great sense of humour and enjoyed following the horses. He had studied law in England, but it had taken him twelve years to pass his final bar exams, for he admitted that 'I spent too much time at the races.' He guided Malaya through the first years of Independence and negotiated with Singapore, North Borneo and Sarawak for the creation of Malaysia in 1963, although Singapore withdrew in 1965. The Tunku retired in 1970 and is regarded as Malaysia's founding father.

I enjoyed flying at the relatively low level of 4,000 feet rather than at 30,000 feet, as there was so much to see from the aircraft window of the topography of the country as we flew south to Kuala Lumpur. The cloud formations were amazing, with banks of both cumulus and cumulonimbus clouds rising to many thousand of feet, with dark and threatening undersides, but shining white in the sunlight like magnificent cathedrals. The pilot threaded the Dakota between the cloud banks as if we were flying down a valley to try and miss the storms, but at times these could not be avoided and with our seat belts fastened we would fly through these as if on a roller coaster ride.

The plane landed at KL, where the Prime Minister left the aircraft, and my opportunity of speaking to him had gone. In these days of high security and bodyguards, I was struck by the casual way Tunku Abdul Rahman walked across the tarmac and was greeted by an aide. There was no sign of any police protection. The same seemed to apply in Britain certainly up to the mid-sixties. My late uncle, who was Senior Pro-Vice Chancellor of Sussex University was receiving, as were others, an Honorary Degree. One of the others recipients, was the then Prime Minister, Sir Harold Macmillan. Towards the end of the official lunch, the Prime Minister asked for a taxi to take him to Brighton Railway Station, as he had to return to the House of Commons. My uncle offered to give him a lift to the station, which the PM accepted, and without any ceremony, security or police protection drove him to the station where Sir Harold simply caught his train to London.

We landed at Singapore's Paya Lebar International Airport early evening, and I took a taxi to the REME Officers' Mess at Pasir Panjang. Although, I never regretted that I had been posted up country, I was nevertheless very pleased to be back in Singapore again. I loved the city, the people and the bustle and excitement of the thriving and economically prosperous Island State. When I had first arrived in Singapore in August 1959, there were still many election posters stuck on walls and other places extolling the people to vote for the Peoples' Action Party (PAP) under Mr Lee Kuan Yew; whose party had won the first election following independence from Britain in June 1959.

I loved exploring the City on foot, however enervating it was in the heat and humidity. Taxi drivers invariably followed me and kept calling out:

'You want ride, Johnny?' The name used by taxi and trishaw drivers for servicemen. They obviously believed that I was quite out of my mind, which I probably was, pounding the hot pavements of the City; but I ensured that I didn't miss seeing any of the sights; from the sampans (rowing boats), tongkangs (lighters) and twakows (small cargo-boats) off Collyer Quay or moored in Singapore River, to the snake charmer in the grounds of St Andrew's Cathedral, and taking tea in the Pavilion of the Singapore Cricket Club overlooking the Padang (sports ground). Behind this the Supreme Court and City Hall where, in the Conference Chamber, the Japanese surrender was signed on the 13th September 1945.

But it was the bustle of Chinatown that I found most exciting. The enticing smells of food being cooked and sold from the street stalls, the shrill cries of the street vendors selling every imaginable and strange type of merchandise. The chatter and laughter of children, and down narrow streets off New Bridge Road, colourful washing hung out to dry on long poles from the first and second floor windows of the houses. The Death Houses of Sago Lane where the dying lay waiting for their passing to the other side. The Street of the Undertakers and the infamous Bugis Street, where the only way to tell the difference between the women and the transvestite men was by the thickness of their necks, – the men having the thicker ones. But I found Chinatown took on a special atmosphere at night; with the confusing din of various Chinese dialects, the discordant noise of Chinese music with gongs, cymbals and the clicking of wooden bamboo sticks, together with the myriad of other sounds and sights that made up the frenetic activity of night time Chinatown.

~

I had written to Angela and told her that I was coming down on leave to Singapore, and that I hoped to see her. She replied that she was unable to take any time off from her job, working in the craft and curio shop at the Seaview Hotel, but we should be able to spend the evenings and the weekend together.

Angela's Malay colleague in the shop had kindly invited both of us, as her guests to a relation's wedding. We arrived at the bride's parent's house early in the afternoon to the over-amplified sound of a Malay band, which must have been heard over a wide area of the City. The bride was out of sight in the house, awaiting the arrival of the groom. He eventually arrived with his father, who was dressed in a full-length dark blue robe. Two men holding bamboo poles, with sprigs of red, orange and blue paper tied to the ends, escorted the bridegroom and his father as they slowly walked towards the bride's house; the groom with downcast eyes holding a small posy of flowers in front of him. All his friends and guests laughed and shouted jokes at him; but the bridegroom did not smile, for if he did, it would have been taken as a bad omen and a sign that the marriage would be a childless and unhappy one. Outside the entrance to the house a dais with two chairs had been set up, decorated with bunting, paper flowers and coloured lights, on which the bride and groom sat, dressed in their respective families' ancestral crimson and gold motif robes. The bride wore on her head a circlet of pearls from which was fixed a white lace head dress. The bridegroom wore on his head a tall headpiece of the same crimson and gold design as his robes. The bride and groom sat unsmiling, with their hands resting in their laps with fingers stained with a brown dye, which would not fade for a long time, and showed to the outside world, that they had recently been married.

After the presentation of the couple, we all sat down to a wedding breakfast, where I tried to eat the hottest chicken curry I had ever experienced, even though, by the time we were served the food it was actually cold.

One evening as Angela and I were returning to her parent's flat in Killiney Road, where there were a number of open fronted shops, and where one could watch skilled woodworkers carving intricate patterns on camphor wood chests, a little old Chinese woman passed us, walking with tiny steps, and I noticed that she had the most incredibly small feet. Angela told me that the binding of Chinese girls' ankles when very young was an old custom, but that, quite rightly the practice had been made illegal.

Before my leave was up, Angela's parents took both of us for dinner on the roof restaurant of the Ocean Park Hotel, some six miles east of the city centre. This was a memorable evening. The heat of the day had gone to be replaced with the warm scented night air. From the roof one could see across the bay not only to the bright lights of Singapore waterfront, but also to those reflected off the sea from the many ships and cruise liners moored outside the south mole. Further to the right were the garish and colourful neon advertisements, many mounted on scaffolding from the tops of buildings in the Chinatown quarter of Singapore. Nearer to the hotel the hurricane lamps of the fishing geylongs sparkled on the water. It was a cloudless night and the stars shone brightly out of the clear sky, and I was thrilled to see in the night sky to the south of Singapore and low on the horizon the Southern Cross. There was no doubt that dining out in the open, on a warm and scented tropical night in an exciting part of the world, brought its own special magic.

~

Before I left Singapore and whilst I still had the opportunity, I knew that I must visit one very special place; the Kranji War Memorial built on a small hill overlooking the Straits of Johore. From the entrance, wide steps lead up between cypress trees to the Memorial, with its tall centre section with wings on either side. Inscribed on the wings are the names of the 30,000 men and women who died defending Singapore against the Japanese invasion in 1942. 13,494 from India and Pakistan; 11,414 from Great Britain; 2,770 from Australia; 1,301 from Malaya as well as others from Canada, South Africa, New Zealand and the Netherlands.

It is a beautiful monument built by the Imperial War Graves Commission. At the base of the memorial, inscribed in six languages, are the words 'They died for all free men'. In front of the Memorial stands a simple tall stone cross, and as I stood before this with the Straits of Johore in the background, I tried to imagine what it must have been like for the troops that night of 8/9th February 1942, when the Japanese crossed the Straits and landed on Singapore Island; but within the space of seven days on the 15th February, Lieutenant- General Percival had surrendered the Island to the Japanese General Yamashita at the Ford Factory at Bukit Timah, with over 50,000 Commonwealth troops marched off to captivity; although the Australian Major-General Gordon Bennett had made an unauthorised 'midnight flit' from the Island, which tarnished the reputation of the Australian units, for although they only comprised 14 per cent of the British and Commonwealth forces in the defence of Malaya and Singapore, they incurred over 70 per cent battle fatalities.

The Kranji War Memorial, according to one army general is symbolic 'of a wider vision which should be taken in the future, which would make for lasting peace, and it should serve as a stern memorial to all people of the grim realities of war'.

~

All too soon my leave was over, and as I checked into the Malayan Desk at Paya Lebar International Airport for my return flight to Ipoh, I realised that except for possibly a few hours waiting for my flight back to the UK, I had virtually said 'goodbye' to Singapore; a city I had come to love and was sorry to leave, but I felt I had seen and explored most of its sights. I had also thanked and said goodbye to Angela and her family. They had been so kind and made me feel part of their family on their Sundays at the Singapore Swimming Club, when I was stationed at 10 Inf Wksp.

As the Dakota climbed away from Paya Lebar, I felt a sadness, as I looked out of my side window at the rows of bungalows at Kallang, the Merdeka (Freedom) Bridge, Raffles Hotel, Singapore River, the harbour with its many ships and the business and commercial centre of the city. As the aircraft swung north, I could make out the MacRichie, Peirce and Seletar Reservoirs in the centre of the Island, and was one of the reasons for the surrender in February 1942; for much of Singapore's water came via the pipeline across the Causeway from Mainland Malaya, and once this had been 'blown', there would not have been enough water in the reservoirs to sustain the infrastructure of the City for any length of time.

We crossed the Straits of Johore, passing over the Causeway and the Naval Base. The countryside below was not the neat chequerboard pattern of England, but was mainly dark green rubber estates with nearer the coast, the lighter greens of the rice padi fields. As we flew further north, the jungle foothills of the central mountain range came into view, with smoke rising from the many logging campfires. Ahead the cumulus clouds were building up over the mountains.

All too soon, after a short stop at Kuala Lumpur, we descended and landed back at Ipoh, fortunately not in the middle of a tropical storm. I was quickly back into a military 'mode' and carrying out my day-to-day duties. I was however, looking forward to my second weeks' leave in Penang, and which I managed to fit in only a few weeks before I left the Regiment in mid-July 1960.

~

As the Malayan Airways Dakota from Ipoh, banked and lined up its approach low over the sea to Bayan Lepas airport, the Island of Penang reminded me of a turtle with outstretched legs. As I left the aircraft, I was looking forward to my leave on the Island that has been called 'The Paradise of the East'.

Penang was one of the Straits Settlements, but with Malacca became one of the eleven states of the newly independent Federation of Malaya in 1957. It was Britain's oldest colony in Malaya and was founded in 1786 by Lieutenant Commander Francis Light RN, who decided that the sheltered waters between Penang and Province Wellesley on the mainland, would make an ideal anchorage for British frigates and sloops, so that they could defend the trading ships, which had sailed from the East Coast of India, from attack by French frigates in the Bay of Bengal. On August 11th 1786, Francis Light landed on the Island, hoisted the Union Jack and took formal possession of Penang in the name of 'His Brittanic Majesty George III'; and as this was on the same day as the birthday of the then Prince of Wales (later George IV), he named the township George Town.

The Island had originally been called Pulau Pinang – 'The Isle of Betel Nuts', so named by the Chulias (South Indian Tamils) who had come to the Island to trade for the betel nut.

A taxi took me to the Officers' Runnymede Hotel in the City of George Town, which was the first town in the Federation of Malaya, prior to Independence, to be granted the status of a City in December 1956 by Queen Elizabeth II.

I hired a car, and took in the sights as a good tourist should; the lovely sandy beaches along Gurney Drive; the Botanic Gardens, where a monkey did its best to join me in the car, and showed his displeasure that I did not have any nuts for him; Penang Hill, reached by the elderly funicular railway, with its cooler temperatures, lovely walks and marvellous views across to the mainland; a ferry trip to Butterworth on the mainland, where there was a RAF Base, and where also the railway to Penang Island terminated at the Prai Railway Station. Passengers completed their journey by ferry to the railway terminus at George Town, where no train has ever arrived at or departed from.

Touring by car, I found the West Coast of the Island to be very scenic and picturesque; driving through a patchwork of dark green palm trees with the lighter greens of rice padi fields, with Chinese coolies, all dressed in black with their wide brimmed hats working the fields, as were water buffalo busily foraging for food. Driving down side roads and set amongst palm trees, I came across the most attractive individual wooden houses, built on stilts, surrounded with hibiscus and other flowering shrubs; all immaculately maintained.

But by far the most imposing and exciting attraction on the Island was that of the world famous Kek Lok Si, – the 'Monastery of the Western Paradise of the Pure Land Sect of Buddhism'; conceived by the Buddhist abbot, the Venerable Beow Lean in 1885. It was a very hot day when I went round the Monastery, which is built on several tiers, with various halls and temples on each level, such as the 'Hall of the Great', or to give it its local name of 'Leong Kong Cheng' (Dragon Strikes Bell), so called from the head of a dragon which from its mouth, water constantly drips; the 'Hall of the Heavenly Kings' and the 'Hall of the Eighteen Lohans'. But to get to the top tier of the Ban Po Shu (Ten Thousand Buddhas Pagoda), I felt I needed the agility and stamina of a mountain goat, as I climbed the many steps to the top level with sweat pouring off me. But once there, the panoramic views of the surrounding countryside made the climb well worth it. A short distance away from Kek Lok Si is the Burmese style Rama V Pagoda, named after a king of Burma.

The visit to the Monastery was well worth the effort, but I was very pleased to get down to ground level, where there was a food market selling not only the normal produce, but also livestock ranging from turtles to flying foxes. Being a Sunday, there were many visitors of all races, resulting in an absolute bedlam of noise, with high-pitched Chinese voices being the most prominent. The smell from the various food stalls was quite overpowering, especially from those stalls selling durian fruit, with its rich, sickly and unpleasant odour. Although I was offered 'blanchan' (shrimp paste); 'laksa' (a rich dish), which is eaten either sweet or sour and mixed with plenty of chillies; 'harkoes' and durian cakes, all I wanted was to sit in the shade somewhere downing two or three ice cold 'cokes'.

It was at the café that, checking my camera, I discovered the film had torn, and I taken twenty or so pictures on one frame. This had happened to me once before in Singapore on their National Day, when the Malays whatever their race, paraded in their colourful national costumes in the grounds of the Istana Negara Singapura, the official residence of the Head of State, the Yang di Pertuan Negara. I had taken a thirty-six-exposure film, only to find that the film in the camera had not wound on, and I ended up with one very over-exposed frame and thirty-five blank ones. I thought I had learnt my lesson after that experience, but at Kek Lok Si, it had happened again. Fortunately, I was able to do something about it, as I found the darkest spot I could to open the back of the camera and wound the film past the torn slots.

Although, my legs ached, and my shirt was soaking wet, I went round the Monastery again, passing the fish and turtle ponds, which have a special significance for, on the 15th day of the Chinese Fourth Moon, during the Wesak celebrations, Buddhists bring many captive turtles, fish and birds to the Monastery to liberate them; for the turtle, just as is the crane, a symbol of longevity, which is what I needed as I dragged myself around Kek Lok Si for the second time, cursing myself for my stupidity in not checking that the take up spool on the camera rotated as I advanced the film. As I had run out of flash bulbs, I had to do the best I could in the various halls and temples, by resting the camera on anything solid to keep it still, whilst I took time exposures. I was very glad to return to my hotel and collapse on my bed.

~

I had not seen many snakes in Malaya, except for those of the snake charmer in the grounds of St Andrew's Cathedral in Singapore. But, there was one attraction, which however unwilling, I felt I should visit. I have never liked snakes, but nevertheless I have a morbid fascination for them. So I drove down to the Snake Temple at Sungei Kluang, south of George Town. The snakes – vipers, were supposed to be the disciples of the Chinese Deity Char Soo Kang. As I entered the Temple, the heat, smoke and smell from the many smouldering joss sticks, lit to drug the vipers, hit me, and my eyes watered from the fumes. Many of those who saw service in Malaya have their favourite snake stories, and I was no exception. As I wandered around the smoke filled and badly lit Temple, I was very careful where I stepped or what I touched; for there was no guarantee that the vipers, who were certainly very sleepy, and only came to life at night after the joss sticks had been extinguished, would not rear up and bite a hand or another part of one's anatomy if suddenly disturbed. It was so hot that I felt I had to rest against something. There was a ladder leaning against one wall, and with a feeling of relief I put a hand out to one of the rungs, and have a 'breather'. Just as I was about to touch the ladder, I glanced at it, and to my horror I saw that I was about to grasp a viper, which had wrapped itself around the rung I was reaching for, and which in response may have reared up and bitten my hand. I beat a hasty retreat out of the Temple. Even though I had barely recovered from the shock of almost grasping that viper, my morbid curiosity took me round the corner to where, in a fenced-in pit was the biggest snake I had ever seen. I was told it was some twenty-five feet long. Its' coils seemed to be endless. It was apparently fed on live terrified chicken, which were dropped into the pit, where the python would bite them to death, crush them in its coils and finally eat them head first. Not a sight I wished to witness.

~

There were an abundance of snake stories. One of 'B' Sqn's troops was carrying out a pre-dawn patrol whilst on Operation Java, and came across a twenty-foot python lying stretched out in the road. The troop sergeant went to its head to see if it was alive, whilst the troop leader inspected and lifted its tail. The python woke up at this indignity, and immediately took evasive action by slithering off into the jungle in one direction, whilst the sergeant disappeared into the jungle in the opposite direction, and was not seen again for several hours. On another occasion as a Ferret Scout Car drove under a tree, the wireless aerial knocked a snake out of a tree, which fell through the hatch of the open turret and took up residence in the interior of the Ferret, with its occupants baling out of the vehicle in record time. Apparently a determined counter-attack with wireless aerials restored the status quo. Although the majority of the species of snakes in Malaya were not venomous, the unexpected could suddenly occur and which happened to another 'B' Sqn troop. They were peacefully, if somewhat slowly motoring along a jungle track, and the driver of the leading Ferret Scout Car suddenly found himself in eyeball-to-eyeball contact with a King Cobra, which had unexpectedly reared up level with the driver's hatch. The snake was apparently the more surprised to be confronted by a goggled face, and took off in fright before the driver had time to react.

My week was soon over, and although I had enjoyed visiting and exploring the Island, which I wouldn't have missed; I did find it lonely being on my own, and it was a relief to fly back to Ipoh and to return to the companionship of my fellow officers.

Chapter Seventeen

The 730 Days Are Over

Shortly before I left the Regiment, a touring showbiz company, who were doing a lightning three-week tour of military bases in Malaya and Singapore, put on a show for the Garrison. Although they looked hot and very tired, it was a most amusing and enjoyable performance, which was much appreciated, and it was a good morale booster for those serving in Malaya to realise that they had not been forgotten back at home.

By July 10th, I was packed and waiting for my movement order and travel warrant. I was beginning to get a bit 'twitchy', as I had visions that I would still be in Malaya after my 'demob' day of August 6th. There was a rumour going round that the last National Service intakes in November 1960 were going to have to serve for thirty months and not the twenty-four months. This was more than a rumour. It was fact.

I had visions that some bright 'spark' in the War Office, would wake up to the fact that it would be cheaper and give a better return to extend by six months from 30th June 1960, the service of all those who were currently doing their National Service and who were fully trained, rather than call-up and train new intakes.

Although I was looking forward to returning home; I was nevertheless feeling sad that not only was I leaving a country which I had come to love, but also saying 'goodbye' to all the good friends I had made at 10 Inf Wksp, the 13th/18th Royal Hussars and the other REME officers I had met in the REME Officers' Mess in Singapore.

~

I needn't have worried, for on 14th July my movement order arrived. I made my farewells to the members of the LAD, HQ Squadron, RHQ and my fellow officers. I was relieved that I had got through the six months without being awarded 'extras', as I believed most of the other subalterns who were in Ipoh at the time, had been awarded extra orderly officer duties. I was sure that the Adjutant, Angus Anderson was never aware of my determination not to incur his displeasure. I liked Angus. He was a very efficient Adjutant and quite rightly he saw his brief as ensuring that the younger and junior officers in the Regiment were trained in, and maintained the high standards and the professionalism that the Regiment was known for.

Jim Allen, the EME took me to Ipoh railway station to catch the day express from Penang to Kuala Lumpur, which left Ipoh shortly after midday. There was a lump in my throat as I leaned out of the window of my reserved compartment and waved 'goodbye' to Jim, as the 'Golden Arrow' express from Penang to KL pulled slowly out of Ipoh station for the one hundred and forty mile journey to K.L., which it was due to reach shortly after five o'clock in the evening; and if my mathematics was correct, we would be travelling at the average express speed of thirty miles an hour. However, it didn't really bother me at what speed the train travelled; for as I had now left the LAD and the 13th/18th Hussars behind, I just wanted the journey back to the UK to go smoothly. I had very mixed feelings. After two years it felt strange that I was shortly to become a civilian again, and I couldn't decide whether I was doing the right thing by so doing, or whether, as I had enjoyed my two years with the Colours, I would do better by signing on for another three years.

Although I had driven through Kuala Lumpur on a number of occasions, I had never had an opportunity to visit the Capital, and after the train pulled into the uniquely ornate but graceful Moorish architecture of the railway station, I had about two hours before darkness fell to see something of K.L. and to have a meal, as the overnight 'Southern Cross' express to Singapore did not depart until 2200hrs. I didn't really have the time to see more than the multi-minarets of the Sultan Suleiman Mosque, and the imposing Moorish-style Government buildings with the large padang opposite; where a fortnight later the victory parade would be held to celebrate the ending, after twelve years of the war which was called, for political reasons 'The Emergency'. 'A' Sqn of the 13th/18th Royal Hussars under Jock Bell would be the lead contingent in the mounted Commonwealth section of the parade.

After a meal in the Station Hotel, I retired to the Coliseum Bar in the station, and waited to board the 'Southern Cross' overnight sleeper to Singapore. The train left on time for the two hundred and fifty mile journey, where it was due to arrive at 0800hrs the following morning. A leisurely journey, if one was comfortable enough to enjoy it, but the fan behind my head on the top bunk of my sleeping compartment whirred noisily away, making it difficult to get off to sleep. I tried the bottom bunk, but without the dubious benefit of the fan, was soon bathed in perspiration from the heat and humidity of the small compartment. Thank goodness I wasn't sharing with another officer.

~

Although at the time of my call-up in 1958, I was angry and disappointed that I hadn't done my National Service straight from school in 1954, I was relieved that I had been deferred for four years; otherwise, if my service career had followed the same path from 1954 to 1956, I could well have been in Malaya when the CTs were far more active and aggressive. However, by 1959 the number of CT attacks and ambushes had all but ceased, as the security forces had gained the upper hand over the terrorists and the policy of winning 'the hearts and minds' of the local people had been so successful. Chin Peng had by 1951 realised, that his previous tactics were counter-productive and had antagonised the local population. In October of that year, he had issued a new directive, laying down that civilian trains were no longer to be ambushed; although attacks on military ones should continue, as should the indiscriminate killing of the police and security forces. So, if I had been in Malaya four years earlier, I could well have found myself as Officer i/c Train.

Some years ago, a fellow REME National Service subaltern told me this story, which he swore was true. In 1953, he was travelling on a military train from Singapore to Taiping, where he had been posted to 2 Inf Wksp, and that he had been appointed Officer-in-Charge of the train. This he thought was rather unfair for a NS subaltern aged twenty, not from a front-line unit, with virtually no anti-terrorist or anti-ambush training. In those days, the train carriages had no glass windows, only wooden slats covering the openings. The train was ambushed, and the man standing next to the REME subaltern was shot. The subaltern immediately went through to the carriage, where there was a Gurkha Company to order them to get into firing positions and shoot back at the CTs. He was horrified to find that the Gurkha soldiers, who were accompanied by their wives, were fast asleep with their heads resting on the laps of their wives. As it was so hot, the Gurkhas had removed their boots and socks, and were lying across the seats with their bare feet hanging out of the train between the wooden slats of the windows. Whether it was the sight of some one hundred and fifty pairs of bare feet, or whether the CTs were suspicious that the security forces had a new secret weapon; but the attack was not pressed home and the CTs disappeared back into the jungle.

~

Eventually, I got off to sleep, and only woke up as the train was approaching the Singapore railway terminus; which meant I had missed breakfast. A driver met and drove me to the REME Officers' Mess at Pasir Panjang, where I was told that the flight back to the UK, would be delayed for at least two days, as the aircraft, a Britannia, was stuck at Istanbul awaiting for a new engine to be flown out from England. I greeted this news with mixed feelings; for once I had started my journey home, I wanted to get back without any delay. But if there was to be a hold-up for a day or two, there were far worse places to spend them than in Singapore. I phoned Angela, who was very surprised to hear from me, as she thought I was well on my way home. We managed to fit in a couple of films and Chinese meals, before, once again I said goodbye to her and the family; and on 19th July, I with others were 'bused' to Singapore International Airport at Paya Lebar.

We took off in the evening sunshine, and as the aircraft gradually gained height, Singapore disappeared in the dusk below us as we first swung south out to sea, before turning north to fly up the Malacca Straits, and across the Bay of Bengal to our first re-fuelling stop at Dum Dum International Airport at Calcutta. Also on the aircraft were the show business people who had finished their tour of the service bases in Malaya and Singapore. I got chatting to them, and they said they were absolutely shattered. They had flown out from England three weeks previously, and without any chance to acclimatise to the hot sticky climate, had been thrown into the deep end, giving two performances a day. They were real 'troopers'.

After five hours we came into land at Calcutta, and there must have been a strong cross-wind, for as we touched down, the aircraft bounced into the air again, and we proceeded down the runway, fortunately at diminishing speed in what seemed to be a series of decreasing 'bunny hops'. Whilst the aircraft was being refuelled and serviced, we were entertained in the transit lounge with a series of short films, extolling the virtues of India in general and Calcutta in particular.

The second leg of our flight to Istanbul was a long twelve hours one, and as this was before the days of in-flight entertainment, there was very little to do, except chat, read and sleep. Although we were only flying at a height of 20,000 ft, it felt very cold in the cabin, for not only was I wearing lightweight tropical clothes, but also after nearly a year in the Far East, my blood had probably thinned. It was a long night with very little sleep as we over-flew India and Pakistan. Dawn broke somewhere over Afghanistan or Iran, and the terrain below looked mountainous with little sign of civilisation and very inhospitable.

~

During the night I reflected on my two years National Service. Before I was called up, I had been totally 'anti'; and my initial introduction to army life at Blandford, even with my boarding school experience, had been a severe cultural shock. Nevertheless, as I became used to and accepted the life style, I had not been long into my National Service, before I realised that I enjoyed military life and that I could possibly make a career in the Army. It has always been one of my regrets in life that I did not go against my father's wishes, and sign on for at least a Short Service Commission. Whether having been at boarding school from the age of eight until eighteen, was used to school discipline and the regimen, which had prepared me for my ready acceptance of Army life, with its discipline and regulated life style is debatable. But I should have signed on for a further three years.

There was no doubt that I had enjoyed my two years, and I was certainly fortunate with my deployment to the Far East and especially in being posted to Malaya. I was also extremely fortunate in serving with two first class units, both of which were so different, but where I learnt a great deal and gained valuable experience. The Services look after their own, and even with its many Regiments and Corps there is a comradeship, which is not replicated in civilian life. As my experience with the 13th/18th Royal Hussars had shown, a Regiment is like a family, and I have always believed that the success of the British Army over many centuries and many campaigns has been built upon the Regiment. Woe betide any government with their Defence Reviews, that seem to come around with increasing regularity, which tries to abolish the Regimental System; although amalgamations of infantry regiments, as proposed by the Committee chaired by General Sir Lashmer 'Bolo' Whistler in 1957, which resulted in the formation of 'Large Regiments' do seemed to have worked.

Regiments used to be known as 'County' ones, for recruitment was from close geographical areas; but with recruitment for the 'Large Regiments' spread over a wider geographical area, I have often wondered whether the close family County Regimental ties could have been weakened. Just as there is no longer the 13th/18th Royal Hussars, I have always felt sad that my county of Sussex no longer has its own Regiment, especially as the Royal Sussex Regiment was General Sir 'Bolo' Whistler's own Regiment

Although there were many National Service men who did not enjoy their two years with the Colours, there was no doubt that until the government of the day abandoned its 'East of Suez' policy, the Services with their many global commitments, could not have fulfilled these without National Service. I was lucky in that, although officially on active service in Malaya, the chance of seeing action was negligible; but I felt for those National Servicemen who saw action in Malaya, Korea, Cyprus, Kenya, Aden and Oman, which resulted in the deaths of 395 National Servicemen who were killed in action between 1947 and 1963.

On a personal basis, I felt that the Army had instilled in me a standard of self-discipline, self-respect and also given me maturity and a sense of responsibility that has never left me. I am also proud of the fact that, at the end of the day, I had done my bit for 'Crown and Country', but which nowadays, in our permissive and politically correct society, may be a rather old-fashioned view.

~

As the sun rose, and the cabin warmed up, I could enjoy the flight more; although as I looked down on the inhospitable terrain below, I was hoping that the aircraft would not develop a nasty technical fault, which would entail us having to put down somewhere in the wilds of Iran or Turkey. I need not have worried, for in the late morning, we touched down at Istanbul's Atatürk International Airport for our second refuelling stop. I stood outside the transit lounge watching the Britannia being serviced, but an airport worker warned me to beware of the strength of the sun, as at noon the temperature was approaching 120° Fahrenheit. I found this hard to believe, as for the first time in a year there was no humidity, and it felt quite cool in the dry heat. The aircraft looked smart in its new British United livery, as the previous company, which had the air-trooping contract had been taken over only a week before.

The last leg of the flight, which seemed endless, was over Italy, Switzerland and France, and so it was late afternoon before we touched down at Stanstead Airport. Having cleared Passport Control, the Customs official then charged me, in 1960 values, over £30 in duty on the goods I had bought in the Far East. I was rather upset that I had to pay duty on my slide projector, for when I took it into Malaya from Singapore, the Malayan Customs Official said that as the projector had an educational use, duty did not apply. I knew I was home when the British Customs Official was not of the same opinion, and was obviously not impressed by the 'Crown and Country' bit.

I walked out of the Terminal building, fully expecting that there would be transport laid on to drive me and other REME personnel back to Arborfield. But there was nothing, and neither were there any written orders at the airport; so I took a train to Liverpool Street Station, crossed over London to Victoria Station and phoned home to say that I was catching the next train to Haywards Heath, and could I be picked-up from the station. I was too tired to be good company that evening.

After a good nights' sleep, I tried to find out to where I should report. But nobody in REME wanted to know. It was as if I no longer existed. As a wise retired colonel said to me, 'That's the Army for you!'

The only communication I ever received from the Ministry of Defence in September 1969, was a letter which announced that under the Army Reserve Act, 1969, *'your liability to recall as an officer is extended under the conditions of the new Act until 1974 or until you reach the age of 45, whichever is the earlier.'*

My National Service had started with a 'bang' on the 7th August 1958, but had ended in a 'whimper' on the 20th July 1960.

Postscript

The Volunteer Reserve Forces

Britain's worldwide military commitments in the 1950s were such, that a conscripted Army could only have met these. But with the ending of National Service in 1963 and the Government of the Day abandoning their East of Suez policy, resulted in a significant reduction in Britain's worldwide commitments, and which could be met with a smaller fully professional Regular Army; although its main task, being part of NATO, and being based in West Germany was to face the Warsaw Pact Forces. If the unimaginable ever happened, the Territorial Army was tasked with the defence of the UK.

Even though the Cold War is no more, Britain has become involved in an increasingly number of local global conflicts, such as Iraq and Afghanistan, which an under strength and over stretched Regular Army can barely cover, without the Government having to mobilise and deploy the Volunteer Reserve Forces, in a role for which they were not originally trained for. I feel, as a Postscript to my book, I must express my opinions over the Government's policy on the use of our Volunteer Reserve Forces.

In 1986, the Government set up the National Employers Liaison Committee (NELC), subsequently re-named SaBRE (Supporting Britain's Reservists and Employers). The Committee was made up of employers, business organisations and the TUC, with the aim of promoting employer support for the Volunteer Reserve Forces (VRFs). Regional Reserve Forces' and Cadets' Associations (RFCA) were, and still are responsible for promoting the SaBRE policy of gaining 'Employer Support'

As an employer and a member of the South East Reserve Forces and Cadet Association Employers Liaison Committee, my involvement over the last few years has been with the Territorial Army (TA). During the Cold War, the role of the TA, if the unimaginable happened, was to defend the

Country after the UK based Regular Forces had been deployed to mainland Europe. Therefore, with the end of the Cold War, it was necessary to redefine the role of the TA. Government policy following their Strategic Defence Review (SDR) 1988, was that it was unlikely there would be a major conflict for at least ten years. However, the Government, on the face of it, did not consider the probability of there being an increase in localised minor, but nasty conflicts. Since the end of the Cold War our armed forces have been involved in the Balkans, Iraq (twice), Afghanistan, Sierra Leone and Northern Ireland.

Major and minor conflicts throughout history have shown that, despite the use of advanced weaponry, it is only the infantry, or to use the expression made to me by that tank commander at Mons OCS, - 'grunts', that can capture and hold ground so that military objectives are achieved. It does not seem sensible for a Government, with the increasing number of military commitments, to reduce the number of the Army's infantry regiments and battalions at a time when they are most needed. The Government has reduced the Defence Budget, from £34.6 billion in 1999-2000 to £31 billion in 2004-5, whilst at the same time authorising the Ministry of Defence to continue with very expensive equipment projects; such as the Eurofighter, the Astute hunter submarines, the Type 45 destroyers and the Nimrod MRA4 patrol aircraft; all conceived during the Cold War, and I do wonder on which poor 'third world' country these very expensive and sophisticated weapons systems are going to be unleashed.

Lewis Page in his excellent book; 'Lions, Donkeys and Dinosaurs' highlighting 'Waste and Blundering in the Armed Forces', argues that the 'bills' for all this new expensive weaponry peaked at the same time, which the MoD could not fully fund, and so was under pressure by the Treasury to make savings. One of the easiest options to free up some 'cash' to overcome the deficit was to disband some infantry regiments; which was more politically acceptable if those regiments were based in parliamentary constituencies where the Government had no sitting MPs. This was preferable to cancelling equipment contracts in Government held constituencies, which could have resulted in factory closures, loss of jobs and votes with the possible loss of parliamentary seats.

As a new role was needed for the Volunteer Reserve Forces (VRFs), it was only logical for Government to reach the conclusion that the Volunteer Reservists, and especially the Territorial Army, should be used to reinforce the Regular Forces where necessary. I am pleased that an important and meaningful role has been found for the TA. However, I am concerned about the effect on Reservists, who are only part-time soldiers, if they are mobilised on too may occasions.

The Reserve Forces Act (RFA) 1996 defines the 'call-out' (mobilisation) powers for Reservists. This can be from the Queen if she believes that there is a threat to national security; also from the Secretary of State for Defence, if he believes that military conflicts are probable. He can also order mobilisation for the VRFs to be deployed globally for peacekeeping, humanitarian and disaster relief operations.

RFA 96 lays down clearly defined procedures for the 'call-out' of the VRFs. The mobilisation period can be for nine months, but is more likely to be up to twelve months with pre-deployment training, actual deployment, post-deployment briefing and leave. Volunteer Reservists can only be 'called-out' once every three years, but the MoD is trying to extend this, wherever possible to one year in five.

The role of employers is also laid down in RFA 96. Employers employing Reservists must release them under a compulsory mobilisation order (although there is an appeal procedure for exemption or deferral). However, an employer can withhold his, or her permission if a Reservist employee wishes to volunteer for voluntary mobilisation. So long as correct procedures are followed, employers are legally bound to reinstate Reservists after deployment to their former jobs without loss of pay, or to an alternative but similar level of employment. The MoD pays financial compensation to employers, but which is not all embracing.

My concern is that although support by employers for their TA employees who have been deployed has been very positive, will that employer support continue in the future, unless there is a perceived direct threat to the UK? National Service finished over forty years ago, and it is probable that the majority of employers in the UK now have no military experience, and therefore may find it increasingly difficult to release skilled, experienced and well-paid staff for overseas deployment, when employers' major concerns are 'bottom-line' profits and increasing shareholder value.

The Government's strategy document; 'Future Use of the UK's Reserve Forces', states that the VRFs would be an important component of the Country's defences, as they would be liable for deployment worldwide. They would be used to provide additional capability to the Regular Forces in any large-scale operation, such as the invasion of Iraq in 2003. They would be used to reinforce Regular forces for on-going peacekeeping and humanitarian operations, such as in the Balkans, Iraq, and Afghanistan, and they would be used to provide specialist cover, where there was a shortfall in the Regular Forces.

It is Government and MoD policy to integrate the TA into the Regular Army, with Reservists enjoying the same rates of pay only whilst on deployment, which is obviously a cheaper option for the Government rather than paying a larger number of deployed Regulars. However, Government defence cuts has resulted in the Army in 2006, being some 10,000 under strength, with retention being a major issue, as experienced officers and senior NCOs resign, thus creating a shortage of skilled and experienced training personnel. So, the MoD has had to increasingly rely on the VRFs. But in the Strategic Defence Review 1988, the Government cut the strength of the TA by 18,000. However, since the Iraq invasion in 2003, nearly 16,000 Reservists have resigned from the TA (which the situation in Afghanistan could exacerbate), and although there is usually a high turnover, the current strength of the TA in 2006 at 32,000 is 7,000 below its full strength. As with the Regular Army, there is, apparently a high exodus of officers and senior NCOs from the TA, which could result in recruits receiving inadequate training for operational deployment. The MoD maintains that those who have resigned from the TA are only the 'part time' soldiers, and those who are left are those who are prepared for perhaps, fairly regular overseas deployment. So long as employers are in agreement.

I am worried there is a danger that 'over-use' of the TA could be counter-productive. However willing Reservists are to be deployed, research has shown that following deployment to Iraq, TA soldiers were 'more likely to suffer from psychological difficulties' than their Regular colleagues. Also those Reservists were more likely to suffer from mental stress, worrying about their families and job prospects, especially the latter, for since April 2004 employers are now informed, through the MoD of employees who have signed–up or have re-engaged for the Reserve Forces. Although there is as yet no proof, there is a concern that employers may discriminate against employing Reservists; a worry that has also been aired in America, where a report in the New York Times in April 2003 stated that '….some employers may be tempted to avoid hiring Reservists for fear they will disappear for months or even years at a time.'

It is right that the Reserve Forces have an important part to play in the UK's defences. This Country has been well served by our VRFs in two world wars, but without National Service, it will fall upon the VRFs to provide the extra capability for the Regular Forces to meet their increasing commitments. I have the impression that the Government uses the VRFs as 'Temps', as it is cheaper for them to do this, rather than fund a full strength Regular Army, capable of meeting all their operational commitments; and which only has a strength of 101,000. As a matter of interest the Navy's strength is less than 36,000, and the Air Force 48,000; a total of 185,000, which is probably below that of the combined military and civilian strength of the Ministry of Defence.

The Reserve Forces Act 1996, together with the excellent efforts of SaBRE to promote our Volunteer Reserve Forces and to expand the 'supportive employer' campaigns, shows the importance of the Reserve Forces to this Country's defences; but it would be unforgivable, if through taking advantage of both the volunteer reservists and employers, the Government was responsible for the demise of, in particular the Territorial Army. Something that the Labour Government tried to do in the early 1960s, but in the face of fierce opposition, singularly failed to do so.

Bibliography

Books and publications consulted:

Barber, Noel. *The War of the Running Dogs. The Malayan Emergency 1948-1960*. Collins 1971

Dickenson. R. J. *Officers' Mess. Life and Customs in the Regiments*. Midas Books 1977

Fellows, Roy. *The Jungle Beat*. Travellers Eye Ltd 1999

Holman, Dennis. *Noone of the Ulu*. Heinemann 1958

Hogg, Ian. V. *The Illustrated Encyclopaedia of Artillery*. Quarto Publishing plc 1987

Hunt, Eric. *History of the 13th/18th Royal Hussars (Queen Mary' Own) 1947 to 1992*. The Light Dragoons Charitable Trust 1996

Jewell, Brian. *British Battledress 1937–61*. Osprey Publishing Ltd 1981

Kennett. B. B. & Tatman. J. A. *Craftsmen of the Army. Vol 1*. Leo Cooper Ltd 1970

Khaw. K. H. *Penang - Paradise of the East*. K. H. Khaw 1959

Miller, Keith. *730 Days until Demob*. National Army Museum

Page, Lewis. *Lions, Donkeys and Dinosaurs*. William Heinemann 2006

Bibliography

Papineau. A. J. G. *Guide to Singapore & Spotlight on Malaya.* Papineau
  Studios 1959

Scurr, John. *Jungle Campaign.* The Book Guild Ltd 1998

Sustainer. *Reveille & Retribution.* Bulldog Publishing Ltd 1998

Sustainer. *Spit & Polish.* Sustainer Publications Ltd 1999

Sustainer. *Friend & Foe.* Sustainer Publications Ltd 2001

Smyth, Sir John. *The Life of General Sir Lashmer Whistler.* Frederick Muller
  Ltd 1967

Thompson, Peter *The Battle for Singapore.* Piatkus Books Ltd 2005

Thorne, Tony. *Brasso, Blanco & Bull.* Rogerson Press 1998

Warren, Alan. *Singapore. Britain's Greatest Defeat.* Hambledon and
London 2002

~

The Royal Electrical and Mechanical Engineers. Tenth Edition 1998/99
Method Publishing Co. Ltd 1998

A Short History of R.E.M.E.

'The Craftsman' Magazine. May 1960

The Journal of the 13th/18th Royal Hussars (Q.M.O.) Malaya 1960

Classical Military Vehicles. March 2003